U.S. PRESIDENTS AS ORATORS

U.S. PRESIDENTS AS ORATORS

A Bio-Critical Sourcebook

EDITED BY HALFORD RYAN

Greenwood Press
Westport, Connecticut • London

Library of Congress Cataloging-in-Publication Data

U.S. presidents as orators : a bio-critical sourcebook / edited by
  Halford Ryan.
     p.   cm.
  Includes bibliographical references and index.
  ISBN 0–313–29059–8 (alk. paper)
   1. Political oratory—United States. 2. Presidents—United
States—Language. 3. Rhetoric—Political aspects—United States.
I. Ryan, Halford Ross. II. Title: US presidents as orators.
PN4055.U53P648   1995
808.5'1'0883512—dc20   94–43039

British Library Cataloguing in Publication Data is available.

Library of Congress Catalog Card Number: 94–43039
ISBN: 0–313–29059–8

First published in 1995

Greenwood Press, 88 Post Road West, Westport, CT 06881
An imprint of Greenwood Publishing Group, Inc.

Printed in the United States of America

The paper used in this book complies with the
Permanent Paper Standard issued by the National
Information Standards Organization (Z39.48–1984).

10 9 8 7 6 5 4 3 2 1

Contents

Acknowledgments

I want to thank the contributors to this book. Without their careful scholarship and tight writing, which I trust fulfills Aristotle's dictum that style must be clear and appropriate to be good, the volume would not exist.

I also want to thank Mildred Vasan of Greenwood Publishing Group, for she initiated this project and shepherded it to completion. In fact, students and scholars of the history and criticism of American public address, which includes presidential rhetoric, owe a particular gratitude to Greenwood's commitment to the discipline of speech. Greenwood is sensitive to the democratic needs of an informed citizenry to scrutinize, with the help of rhetorical criticisms in book-length forms, the persuasions of their public figures and presidents.

An Introduction to Presidential Oratory

This book is about the nexus of oratory and politics that was practiced by certain men who attained the presidency of the United States of America. Accordingly, section one treats rhetoric in history and politics, and section two discusses presidents as public speakers. At the end of the introduction is a bibliography that lists specific sources cited, as well as general works that consider together oratory and the presidency.

I. PRESIDENTIAL ORATORY

The oldest academic textbook in the Western world is about public speaking. Corax of Sicily composed *Techne*, sometime after 467 B.C., in order to instruct citizens in the practice of public speaking in the courtroom, which was later carried over to the assembly. Historically linked to a democratic government, speech was an integral part of Athenian democracy. Greek citizens participated in the daily government of Athens, pleaded their own cases before juries of peers, and the better orators amongst the citizenery delivered ceremonial addresses on festive occasions. The Greek rhetorical tradition, refined by the Romans, passed on by the trivium of grammar, rhetoric, and dialectic in medieval and renaissance universities, and studied in the liberal arts curriculum in the twentieth century, is inextricably linked, as it was in Athens and is now in the United States, to the practice of free speech in an open and democratic society.

Inherent in the art of oratory is the basis for its criticism. At first, the "do's" and "don'ts" predominated, but over the centuries commentators and practitioners progressed to the point where systematic appraisals could be mounted and ethical judgments could be assessed about the means and ends of public persuasion.

In 1943, William Norwood Brigance, professor of speech at Wabash College, my alma mater, edited two volumes entitled *A History and Criticism of American Public Address*. Unlike previous anthologies of speech texts that contained headnotes of basically biographical, historical, and political information, *A History and Criticism of American Public Address* was the first book to offer monographs that criticized the speeches and effects of American orators. Thus, space, which was heretofore allocated to speech texts that were usually available in a number of places, was devoted exclusively to an exegesis of the effects of public address. Eventually, a trilogy of volumes was published, the third being edited in 1955 by Marie Hochmuth (Nichols), a professor of speech at the University of Illinois, who was my dissertation adviser. Although fifty years have elapsed since these archetypal works, and the discipline of speech has moved forward, some constants, first pioneered in *A History and Criticism of American Public Address*, remain in this book.

Each essay grounds the president in his milieu. Presidents shape, as much as they are shaped by, political situations. Each essay makes clear the exigencies the president addressed, finessed, or dodged. But this book achieves more than merely situating a president in biography and history.

Each essay focuses on the criticism of the president's rhetoric. Criticism implies both positive and negative assessments. The authors are as quick to excoriate rhetorical deceptions as they are to praise oratorical eloquence. A corollary of speech criticism is to revise how the president might have better persuaded. When an author discusses deficiencies in presidential speeches, he or she suggests a plausible verbal strategy, which arguably had at least as good a chance, if not a better one, than the president's actual choice.

The methodologies used in these essays do not stray far from traditional, classical criticism. The authors are not engrossed in fitting speeches to theories and theories to speeches. They are intent on expounding presidential addresses on criteria that are as serviceable today as they were two thousand years ago.

Since the time of the *Rhetorica ad Herennium*, whose authorship around 90–80 B.C. was originally attributed to Cicero but now is acknowledged as unknown, the five classical canons of oratory have informed the theory, practice, and criticism of public address. One may expect the essayists to treat the rhetorical canons without belaboring the Latin terms or being slavish to the system.

Inventio, or invention, was concerned with how the speech came into being, what language, chosen from among logical, emotional, and ethical appeals, the speaker selected. Whenever possible, the essays appraise the arguments that the presidents employed or rejected in their speeches. The authors based their findings on drafts and manuscripts that were researched in archival materials.

Dispositio indicated how the speech was arranged for persuasive effect. At the minimum, the ancients advised that a speech have an introduction to gain the attention and good will of the audience; a body that presented the major arguments for or against the issue at hand; and a conclusion, or peroration, that appealed for action or a change of attitudes and beliefs. As the essays demonstrate, some presidents were fastidious about arranging their speeches, often editing them up to the time of delivery, whereas others were satisfied with a first draft or minimal revisions thereof.

Elocutio was the canon for style, word choice, diction. The presidents herein preferred a style of language that ran from the banal to the burnished. In Cicero's time, this was known as the Asian-Attic controversy, whether an orator should speak in a florid, Asian style, or in a simple, Attic diction. Thus, Franklin Roosevelt and John Kennedy could be conceived as Asian orators, presidents who preferred polished prose, whereas Harry Truman and Dwight Eisenhower might be termed Attic orators, presidents who communicated in plain and simple language. Of the five classical canons, *elocutio* has often taken the harshest beating, often berated for encouraging the purple patches of prose: alliteration, anaphora, epistrophe, apophasis, asyndeton, hortatory subjunctive, and rhetorical question. John Kennedy's chiasmas and hortatory subjunctive from his Inaugural Address, "Let us never negotiate out of fear, but let us never fear to negotiate," is surely purple, yet that Asian *elocutio* has indelibly linked Kennedy's elegant oratory with his presidency.

Memoria was the canon for memory, as the ancients memorized their speeches for maximal effect on their listeners. Freed from the constraints of a manuscript or cumbersome notes, the orator concentrated on delivering the speech with good eye contact, energetic gestures, and a forceful, cadenced voice. On the whole, U.S. presidents have not been robust practitioners of the canon of memory. Even acknowledged great presidential orators, such as George Washington, Abraham Lincoln, FDR, and JFK, read their addresses from a manuscript. Since the advent of television, the teleprompter enabled a Dwight Eisenhower, a Ronald Reagan, or a Bill Clinton to have good eye contact with the audience. However, this twentieth-century technology, although it tries to disguise the fact that presidents read their televised addresses, still validates the ancient's advice for the speaker to have penetrating eye contact with the audience.

Actio was delivery, which entailed gestures, eye contact, vocal pacing, and platform presence. *Actio* is perhaps the cardinal canon in terms of effect, as one has only to compare a Franklin Roosevelt with a Herbert Hoover, a Jimmy Carter with a Ronald Reagan, a George Bush with a Bill Clinton. Whereas invention, arrangement, style, and memory are readily amenable to critical explication, delivery, fleeting by its very nature, is extremely difficult to sound. Mr. Justice David J. Brewer, appointed to the Supreme Court of the United States in 1889 by President Benjamin Harrison, expressed the ineffable effect of *actio*:

This marvelous power is incapable of complete preservation on the printed page. The presence, the eye, the voice, the magnetic touch, are beyond record. The phonograph and kinetoscope may some day seize and perpetuate all save the magnetic touch, but that weird, illusive, indefinable yet wonderfully real power by which the orator subdues may never be caught by science or preserved for the cruel dissecting knife of the critic. It is the marvelous light flashing out in the intellectual heavens which no Franklin has yet or may ever draw and tie to earth by string of kite. (ix–x)

As Brewer presciently predicted in his classical periodic sentences, this book has not found a "Benjamin Franklin" among the contributors who could capture the essence of a president's delivery. But they have tried, often making the most of scant sources for the early presidents. As for media presidents, authors have indicated sources in presidential libraries that would help the researcher to obtain audio-visual materials of a president's *actio*.

While on canons, it is efficacious to indicate the criteria used to construct the canon of significant presidential persuasions. This listing, located at the end of each essay, catalogs chronologically important speeches and gives references for locating authoritative speech texts. Although the State of the Union Address is the only constitutionally mandated presidential oratory, by custom and necessity other kinds of speeches figure prominently in presidential persuasions.

Inaugural addresses, often perceived narrowly or dismissed merely as ceremonial rhetoric, assume their rightful stature in this book, as they are the first and sometimes the foremost speech in which the chief executive focuses the next four years. As FDR's First Inaugural Address announced the New Deal and Harry Truman's solidified the Cold War, so did Richard Nixon's Second Inaugural Address presage the bitterness of his second term, and Jimmy Carter's was a harbinger of his tenure, which was perceived as weak and vacillating.

War rhetoric has always been problematical. Ranging from formal requests for war, to communications that announce the bombs are falling while the president speaks, to *ex post facto* rationalizations, war messages have been prone to deceit. Excepting an armed attack on the United States, as at Pearl Harbor in 1941, it is not intuitively and indubitably obvious that Americans should offer their lives on foreign shores. So, presidents have resorted to truths, half-truths, and lies in order to motivate the American people and their Congress to declare wars, police actions, and operations.

For a country whose eagle's head is turned toward the olive branch in the right claw in the Great Seal, the United States seems often at war, in fact brandishing the arrows in the eagle's left claw. From James Madison's prototypical war message in 1812 to Woodrow Wilson's in 1917 and Franklin Roosevelt's in 1941, U.S. presidents carefully communicated why the freedom and safety of the American people were at stake. But from Truman's Korean "police action," to Johnson's and Nixon's Vietnam War, to Reagan's attacks on easy pickings, to Bush's "Operation Desert Storm," the justificatory rhetoric has necessarily devolved to melodrama, character testing, Manichaean dualities, and political NewSpeak: "War is peace, and peace is war."

But until World War II, presidents of the United States focused almost exclusive rhetorical attention on domestic issues (except for the War of 1812, the Mexican War, the Spanish-American War, World War I, and assorted imbroglios in Central and South America, which were not America's finest hours). Hence, the contributors have explicated those questions that preoccupied different presidential administrations: federalism, states' rights, the tariff question, nullification, union versus disunion, progressivism versus conservatism, imperialism, laissez-faire versus planned economy, and civil rights. Beginning especially with FDR's New Deal down to the present, the debate still rages as to the proper role of a strong, centralized federal government in ensuring life, liberty, and the pursuit of happiness for the American people.

After World War II, chief executives increasingly focused their attentions, and hence the public's urgency, on foreign affairs. Beginning with Truman, and the other star players were Eisenhower, Kennedy, Johnson, Nixon, Ford, Carter, Reagan, and Bush, the American people, with the connivance of Congress, were persuaded to spend billions and billions of dollars on containing Communists around the globe, and when the apparent need arose, to shed American blood in foreign countries. Even Bill Clinton continues to deploy American forces as the world's policeman, but is interestingly constrained from offering the all-too-easy rationalization of fighting Communists, and Americans continue to give their lives in the line of duty. A bitter after-taste lingers in some of the essays on the post–World War II presidents with regard to presidential crisis rhetoric, for unsavory wars surely affected Truman's popularity, Johnson's decision to step down, Nixon's divisive rhetoric, and Bush's inability to capitalize on a war, although successful, whose aims were oversold and underrealized.

The other kinds of presidential rhetoric, the acceptance speech, the campaign address, the occasional speech, the commencement address, the dedicatory speech, the State of the Union address, and the farewell address, have been included with respect to the appropriate president. Generally, the essays give press conferences short shrift, as this format is not defined as public address. Occasionally, a press conference was so important that an author prudently discusses it.

Nor are the essayists remiss in not treating televised campaign debates. Many critics carp that the original Lincoln-Douglas debates in 1858, which serve as the archetype, have been so debauched by the interests of journalists and commentators and sponsors and participants that contemporary televised debates are little more than glorified press conferences. Yet supporters retort that face-to-face encounters manifest the candidates under fire, allow them to attack and defend, and force them to discuss issues they might otherwise ignore, which is exactly what happened in the seven debates between Stephen Douglas and Abraham Lincoln. However, it is a commentary on contemporary candidates and audiences that *neither* seems to be able to sustain the Lincoln-Douglas format of a one-hour opening speech, an hour-and-a-half reply, and then an half-hour rebuttal. Whatever the case, televised campaign debates have played an important persuasive role in presidential elections, arguably enabling John Kennedy, Jimmy Carter, Ronald Reagan, and Bill Clinton to prevail over their opponents. These confrontations are treated from Kennedy forward, except for Richard Nixon, who managed to get himself elected in 1968 and 1972 without debates, having learned well his lesson in 1960.

II. ORATORICAL PRESIDENTS

"Oratory," opined Justice David Brewer, "is the masterful art. . . . The orator dominates those who hear him, convinces their reason, controls their judgment, compels their action. For the time being he is master." This book treats twenty-one of the forty-two U.S. presidents as orators, as men who wielded "the masterful art" over the American people. Inevitably, someone will question why twenty-one are selected, or even more pointedly, why X president is included and why Y president is excluded. In order to address that vexing editorial problem, which probably cannot be resolved to everyone's satisfaction, the reader needs to understand the various definitions of an orator that are implicit in this book.

The English word "orator" derives from the Latin *orator*, which meant an envoy, ambassador, or spokesman, and generally meant a public speaker or advocate at the bar. If one were to apply that definition, then all forty-two American presidents would be included, for almost all delivered an inaugural address and an occasional speech.

But for various reasons one hesitates to designate all U.S. presidents as orators. Cicero conceived speakers in his *De Oratore* and *Orator*, written in 55 and 46 B.C., as cultivating and practicing the art of polished public persuasion. Nor would all American presidents fulfill Quintilian's conception, outlined in his *Institutio Oratoria*, c. A.D. 96, of the ideal speaker, *Vir bonus dicendi peritus*, the good person skilled in speaking.

In point of fact, oratorical prowess has never been a necessary or sufficient condition for the presidency, as Andrew Johnson and Calvin Coolidge bear witness, and as James G. Blaine, Thomas Dewey, and Adlai Stevenson ruefully realized. Moreover, twentieth-century tastes no longer appreciate spread-eagled orations of an earlier era, or bloviation, which was Warren G. Harding's term for his ability to say little in ringing phrases.

Some presidents, particularly at the beginning and end of the nineteenth century, presided over lackluster administrations. In fact, during what is generally accepted as America's "Golden Age of Oratory" from the 1830s to the Civil War, one remembers for their oratory Senators Daniel Webster, Henry Clay, Thomas Hart Benton, and John C. Calhoun, but no U.S. president, save John Quincy Adams, Andrew Jackson, and Abraham Lincoln, comes to mind for oratorical prominence. In the late nineteenth century, silver-tongued orators, such as George William Curtis, Robert Green Ingersoll, Henry Ward Beecher, and William Jennings Bryan, whose unsuccessful three-time candidacy for the presidency warrants the claim that not all great orators can attain the Oval Office, plied their persuasions without any chief executive's being their peer in oratorical eminence. Even into the twentieth century, which is generally marked as the beginning of the rhetorical presidency, some presidents, such as William Howard Taft, who delivered numerous speeches, and Coolidge, paradoxically given the appellation of "Silent Cal," were not orators. Hence, by the cultivated

Roman standard, a Woodrow Wilson or a Franklin Roosevelt, but not a Harry Truman or a Jimmy Carter, was an "orator."

At the other end of the definitional continuum is the Greek word "rhetor," which meant a speaker, particularly one skilled in the art of persuasion. Rhetoric, which in contemporary political parlance runs the gamut from bloviation to baloney in the minds of many, had a positive connotation to the ancient Greeks, except Plato, who held in the *Gorgias,* c. 387 B.C., that rhetoric could make truth appear the untruth, and untruth appear the truth, a charge against rhetorical practices that is as legitimate in the late twentieth century as it was in the fourth century B.C. But Plato's was not the only ancient conception of public speaking.

Aristotle held in his *Rhetoric,* c. 330 B.C., that the art of rhetoric consisted of seeing the available means of persuasion. Aristotle believed that persuasion was produced by three means: logical appeals, emotional appeals, and ethical appeals, by which Aristotle meant a speaker's good will, good sense, and good moral character. He also thought a speaker's style of language should be clear and appropriate.

Other ancient Greek theorists and practitioners, such as Thrasymachus of Chalcedonia in the fifth century B.C., Isocrates in the fifth–fourth centuries B.C., and Demosthenes in the fourth century B.C., held that delivery played an important role in making the speaker persuasive. The Greeks also invented the role of logographer, or speech writer. Logographers, such as Antiphon and Lysias, who composed speeches for clients in the fifth century B.C., were the precursors of the presidential speech writer, who has openly or covertly assisted presidents beginning with George Washington. Thus, Greek theorists, taken as a whole, defined a rhetor as one who had mastered the art or technique of public discourse, which encompassed how to move an audience with an emphasis on argument, language, and delivery.

Merely a handful of presidents could be conceived as rhetors, as speakers who understood and practiced the theory, or any theory for that matter, of public persuasion. Only three presidents in the modern era, Woodrow Wilson, Franklin Roosevelt, and Richard Nixon, received formal training and substantial practice in rhetoric as collegiate speakers and debaters. Certainly John and Quincy Adams, Thomas Jefferson, and James Madison read and applied classical rhetorical works. Yet Madison and Jefferson were constrained by weak voices that marred their presentations.

Conversely, one could not characterize most other twentieth-century presidents, such as Herbert Hoover, Harry Truman, Dwight Eisenhower, John Kennedy, Lyndon Johnson, Gerald Ford, Jimmy Carter, George Bush, and Bill Clinton as classical rhetors, for they were essentially without formal instruction in the art. In truth, these presidents were exemplars of Plato's conception of rhetoric as a habitude. Plato belittled speakers, such as those presidents who did not master rhetoric from a theoretical perspective, but who picked it up along the way as a kind of knack in speaking to the American people.

Ronald Reagan presents a unique case. Trained in acting, which is an artistic counterpart of persuasion, Reagan was given the sobriquet of the "Great Communicator," which is inexplicably more (or is it less?) than the sum of orator and rhetor.

Although the art of public speaking was born and bred in ancient Greece and Rome, and was carried over to and practiced in the American republic to the present day, classical definitions approximate but cannot encompass the parameters of an orator for this book.

Surprisingly, a noted nineteenth-century critic captured something of the essence of an orator. Chauncey Goodrich, a professor of rhetoric at Yale College in the early nineteenth century, lectured on rhetoric and compiled an anthology of British speeches, which was entitled *Select British Eloquence*. Goodrich's theory of public speaking is not so remote as one might imagine:

The end of public speaking is *not* to be eloquent. I say this because an error on this subject has had great influence in corrupting eloquence. . . . It has produced a tendency to speak for the sake of delivery, of attracting the attention of constituents, of establishing a reputation for eloquence. But this attitude always defeats its object. . . . The true end is to address just and pertinent remarks on the subject under contemplation. To this, genius is not indispensable—sound sense and thorough knowledge, with good style and clear arrangement, are sufficient. But one more quality is necessary—a certain degree of *vivacity* without which men will not listen. (viii)

As for vivacity, Americans listened to "Give'em Hell, Harry" in 1948 and liked what they heard; contrarily, Herbert Hoover, who carefully crafted a speech as an engineer might construct a bridge, succeeded only in boring audiences with his droning voice.

Goodrich's conception ran closer to the ground: An orator delivered an address to an audience for some desired effect. Goodrich also assumed, and here he was firmly grounded in the Greek and Roman traditions, that the good speaker supported claims with evidence and reasoning. Thus, if one accommodates Greek and Roman connotations of an orator as a speaker eloquent with Goodrich's conception of a speaker successful, then one comes much closer to understanding a Gerald Ford, a Jimmy Carter, and yes, even a Herbert Hoover, as a presidential orator.

And as speakers, the presidents have practiced the rhetorical presidency. As it was originally conceived by James Ceaser et al., the rhetorical presidency is more plebian than patrician: "Popular or mass rhetoric, which presidents once employed only rarely, now serves as one of their principal tools in attempting to govern the nation" (159). The rise of the rhetorical presidency is due to three factors: a modern doctrine of presidential leadership, the mass media, and modern presidential campaigns. Implicit in the doctrine is the tenet that the president persuades the people to move the Congress when it is intransigent. Thus, Woodrow Wilson excercised the rhetorical presidency in his 1919 speaking tour to actuate the people to move the U.S. Senate to ratify the League of Nations treaty, and so did Franklin Roosevelt in his 1937 campaign to "pack" the Supreme Court. These examples also illustrate a caveat with regard to the rhetorical presidency, for it is a mistake to equate presidential speaking with presidential governing, as success is not guaranteed: Wilson and Roosevelt lost.

The modern rhetorical presidency is apparently a creature of the twentieth century. With the advent of the railroad and the airplane, the telegraph, the radio, motion picture newsreels, and eventually television, presidents naturally and increasingly availed themselves of emerging technologies to reach beyond the immediate listener to the mass audience.

But this book revises the compass of the rhetorical presidency. Granted, pre-twentieth-century presidents' ability to function as "modern" rhetorical presidents were hampered by the technology of their times, and it is true that early presidents did not unseemly seek the office, for it supposedly sought them. But in fact, the rhetorical presidency, without the adjective "modern," was practiced by earlier presidents, as the essayists demonstrate, beginning with George Washington, and including the two Adams, Jefferson, Jackson, and Lincoln. Moreover, presidents from Washington forward used newspapers to reach larger audiences than actually heard them speak. Indeed, William Jennings Bryan believed in 1906 that "The age of oratory has not passed; nor will it pass. The press, instead of displacing the orator, has given him a larger audience and enabled him to do a more extended work" (x). And the persuasive goals of many of these early presidents were remarkably similar to their twentieth-century counterparts: They delivered speeches to gain support from the people and to move the Congress.

"As long as there are human rights to be defended," wrote Bryan, "as long as there are great interests to be guarded; as long as the welfare of nations is a matter for discussion, so long will public speaking have its place" (x). In fine, the essayists in this book have selected presidential oratory that has usually innervated the people, often enervated the Congress, and occasionally eviscerated the Constitution. They have propounded whether the presidents' oratory preserved, protected, and defended the Constitution of the United States or preserved, protected, and defended their own tenures in office, the two ends not necessarily being the same or salutary. And they have validated Abraham Lincoln's famous, ethical maxim, spoken in Clinton, Illinois in 1858, that "You can fool all of the people some of the time, and some of the people all of the time, but you cannot fool all of the people all of the time." Considering the state of the Union, the persuasive effect of presidential oratory is that presidents are of late gaining ground in Lincoln's first two clauses at the expense of the third clause. Plato would have said "I told you so."

BIBLIOGRAPHICAL SOURCES

Andrews, James R. *The Practice of Rhetorical Criticism.* New York: Macmillan, 1983.
Andrews, James, and David Zarefsky. *American Voices: Significant Speeches in American History, 1640–1945.* New York: Longman, 1989.

Brewer, David J., ed. *The World's Best Orations*. 10 vols. St. Louis: Ferdinand P. Kaiser, 1900.

Brigance, William Norwood, ed. *A History and Criticism of American Public Address*. Vol. I and II, New York: McGraw-Hill, 1943. Vol. III edited by Marie Hochmuth. New York: Longmans, Green and Co., 1955.

Bryan, William Jennings. *The World's Famous Orations*. 10 vols. New York: Funk and Wagnalls, 1906. See especially vols. 8–10 for American speeches.

Ceaser, James, Glen E. Thurow, Jeffrey Tulis, and Joseph Bessette. "The Rise of the Rhetorical Presidency." *Presidential Studies Quarterly* 11 (1981): 158–71.

Cohen, Herman. *The History of Speech Communication: The Emergence of a Discipline, 1914–1945*. Annandale, VA: Speech Communication Association, 1994.

Filler, Louis, ed. *The President in the Twentieth Century*. Englewood, NJ: Jerome Ozer, 1983.

Friedenberg, Robert V., ed. *Rhetorical Studies of National Political Debates*. 2d ed. Westport, CT: Praeger, 1994.

Germino, Dante. *The Inaugural Addresses of American Presidents: The Public Philosophy and Rhetoric*. Preface and foreword by Kenneth W. Thompson. Lanham, MD: University Press of America, 1984.

Goodrich, Chauncey A. *Select British Eloquence*. Introduction by Bower Aly. Indianapolis: Bobbs-Merrill, 1963. *Select British Eloquence* was originally published in 1852.

Inaugural Addresses of the Presidents of the United States from George Washington 1789 to George Bush 1989. Washington, DC: U.S. Government Printing Office, 1989.

Martel, Myles. *Political Campaign Debates: Images, Strategies, and Tactics*. New York: Longman, 1983.

Oliver, Robert T. *History of Public Speaking in America*. Boston: Allyn and Bacon, 1965.

Podell, Janet, and Steven Anzovin, eds. *Speeches of the American Presidents*. New York: H. Wilson, 1988.

Reid, Ronald F., ed. *Three Centuries of American Rhetorical Discourse: An Anthology and a Review*. Prospect Heights, IL: Waveland Press, 1988.

Ryan, Halford R. *Franklin D. Roosevelt's Rhetorical Presidency*. Westport, CT: Greenwood Press, 1988.

———, ed. *American Rhetoric from Roosevelt to Reagan*. Prospect Heights, IL: Waveland Press, 1983.

———, ed. *The Inaugural Addresses of Twentieth-Century American Presidents*. Westport, CT: Praeger, 1993.

Tulis, Jeffery K. *The Rhetorical Presidency*. Princeton: Princeton University Press, 1987.

Wallace, Karl R., ed. *History of Speech Education in America*. New York: Appleton-Century-Crofts, 1954.

Windt, Theodore, ed. *Presidential Rhetoric (1961–to the Present)*. 3d ed. Dubuque, IA: Kendall/Hunt, 1983.

U.S. PRESIDENTS AS ORATORS

Stephen E. Lucas and Susan Zaeske

George Washington
(1732–1799)

> The preservation of the sacred fire of liberty and the destiny of the republican model of government are justly considered as deeply, perhaps as finally, staked on the experiment entrusted to the hands of the American people.

George Washington was neither a gifted writer nor a captivating orator. Possessing a meager formal education and always diffident about his abilities as a speaker, he made his reputation as a man of action rather than as a man of words. Yet throughout his public career he produced a steady stream of letters, addresses, messages, and speeches designed to express his views and to persuade other people to them. Like most eighteenth-century gentlemen, he was acutely aware of his public persona, and he took care to write and speak so as to create a favorable impression of his motives, character, and achievements. Always mindful of the importance of uttering the right words at the right moment, he chose both his words and his moments for public utterance with great care.

Washington's career as commander-in-chief of the American army during the Revolutionary War was punctuated by a series of rhetorical triumphs that enhanced the heroic stature he achieved by his military victories. His first act as commander-in-chief was to present a speech to the Continental Congress accepting his appointment. This address, in which Washington renounced any pecuniary compensation beyond expenses, forged the first link in his reputation as a disinterested patriot who placed the good of his country above personal reward. His most famous wartime speech was delivered to the potentially mutinous officers at Newburgh, New York, in March 1783. Rejecting all overtures that he lead the army against the civil authority, Washington "prevented this revolution," in Thomas Jefferson's words, "from being closed, as most others

have been, by a subversion of that liberty it was intended to establish.'' Nine
months later, in a speech romanticized in John Trumbull's painting *The Resignation of General Washington*, he returned his commission to the Continental
Congress and took leave of public life. The simple eloquence of his words,
punctuated by the physical surrender of his commission, drew tears from members of Congress and secured his fame on both sides of the Atlantic as a modern
Cincinnatus.

Returning to Mount Vernon, Washington believed his days in public life were
over. Like many other leaders of the Revolution, however, he became increasingly concerned about the strength and stability of the new nation. When a
constitutional convention was called to meet at Philadelphia in May 1787, Washington was elected as its presiding officer. Although he did not become openly
involved in the ensuing public debate over ratification of the Constitution, he
exerted considerable influence behind the scenes by a vigorous campaign of
letter writing. Once the ratification process was complete, all eyes turned to
Washington to head the new government. On February 4, 1789, he was chosen
as first President of the United States by unanimous vote of the electoral college.
He proved to be not only one of the country's greatest chief executives, but also
one of its most skillful practitioners of the art of presidential rhetoric.

WASHINGTON'S PRESIDENTIAL RHETORIC

Inaugural Addresses

Presented to both houses of Congress in New York City's Federal Hall on
April 30, 1789, Washington's First Inaugural Address is a neglected masterpiece
that deserves to be ranked with the First Inaugurals of Thomas Jefferson, Abraham Lincoln, and Franklin Roosevelt for its impact on the course of American
history. Designed to get the new government off to a smooth start, it succeeded
so brilliantly that today we forget how unsettled the political situation was when
Washington took office. The battle over ratification of the Constitution had produced deep divisions among Americans. At the time of Washington's inauguration, two states, Rhode Island and North Carolina, had yet to adopt the new
frame of government, and many Antifederalists in the other eleven states were
far from reconciled to it. Some were still hopeful of calling a second constitutional convention to rectify the handiwork of the first. Fully aware that many
Americans shared the Antifederalists' reservations about the Constitution, especially since it lacked a bill of rights, Washington knew his inaugural address
would be of pivotal importance in generating good will, trust, and confidence
in the new government.

Most of the process by which the address was composed remains shrouded
in mystery. Rejecting a seventy-three-page draft prepared by David Humphreys
sometime before early January 1789, Washington appears to have called on
James Madison, a fellow Virginian and the major architect of the Constitution,

for assistance in preparing a briefer, more suitable address. There are, however, no surviving drafts by Washington or Madison. Nor do either man's private papers reveal how the final version was written. If Madison was responsible for much of the prose, and there is no way to know for sure, the speech as a whole unquestionably reflected Washington's thinking and expressed ideas that had appeared time and again in his public discourse or personal correspondence.

Washington began with an almost penitent explanation of his decision to accept political office. Dwelling upon his personal desire to remain in retirement at Mount Vernon, his "inferior endowments from nature," his lack of experience in "the duties of civil administration," and his "incapacity as well as disinclination for the weighty and untried cares" facing him, he declared that "no event could have filled me with greater anxieties" than election to the presidency. Yet having been summoned by his country, whose voice he could "never hear but with veneration and love," he had no alternative but to follow duty over inclination. In doing so, however, he hoped that any errors he might make would be palliated by "the magnitude and difficulty of the trust" to which he had been called and by the high motives with which he was accepting it.

To some extent, Washington's opening sentiments can be accounted for by the highly ritualized rhetoric of office-taking during the eighteenth century. At the same time, they also expressed strong personal concerns. Washington was genuinely worried about the challenges facing him and about whether he could meet the lofty expectations of his fellow citizens. By accepting the presidency, he was putting at risk the glittering historical reputation he had earned during the Revolution. If the new government were to fail, much of the blame would inevitably fall on his shoulders. Moreover, when Washington had resigned his military commission at the end of the Revolution, he had pledged to return to private life. Now that he was reentering the public arena, he wanted to make sure no one would accuse him of duplicity or misconstrue his motives.

No less arresting than the personal comments with which Washington began his First Inaugural were the lengthy religious sentiments he expressed next. Tendering his "fervent supplications to that almighty being who rules over the universe, who presides in the council of nations, and whose providential aid can supply every human defect," Washington sought to cloak the Constitution and his presidency with the mantle of divine consecration. No people, he said, were indebted to "the invisible hand which conducts the affairs of men more than the people of the United States." Contrary to what some scholars have claimed, in expressing these thoughts Washington was not emulating the sermonic style of New England theocratic leaders. His invocation of divine support is best seen as a statement of his personal convictions and as a strategic response to the problem of developing confidence in the new government. The point he sought to drive home was that the blessings of "providential agency" would help ensure the success of America's fragile experiment in republicanism.

Washington devoted the remainder of his speech, excluding the peroration, to issues of congressional concern. First, under the guise of praising Congress, he admonished it to make sure that "no local prejudices or attachments, no separate views nor party animosities," would misdirect "the comprehensive and equal eye" that ought to control its proceedings. Second, he offered a carefully worded endorsement of amending the Constitution so as to settle "the degree of inquietude" aroused by the absence of a bill of rights. Third, he informed Congress that he would not accept a salary and requested that his remuneration "be limited to such actual expenditures" as he might confront in office. This was the same request he had made when taking command of the army during the Revolution. By repeating it upon his inauguration as President, he hoped to underscore the rectitude of his intentions in coming out of what he had characterized in 1783 as a permanent retirement from public life.

As with the rest of his major presidential speeches, Washington read his First Inaugural from manuscript. (Although he usually wore his spectacles while speaking so he could see the text clearly, he does not appear to have used them on this occasion.) He spoke rather slowly, probably at about one hundred words a minute, and his gestures seemed stiff and awkward in comparison to those of a practiced orator. But none of this mattered to most listeners. Washington was a charismatic leader, a towering figure whose hold on his contemporaries is almost impossible to recapture today. His lack of oratorical polish only seemed to reinforce his image as the embodiment of republican virtue. Fisher Ames, who was soon to make his reputation as the greatest orator in Congress, sat entranced during Washington's inaugural. "It was a very touching scene," he wrote afterward, "and quite of the solemn kind." The gravity of Washington's demeanor, his visible nervousness, his deep and slightly tremulous voice all "added to the series of objects presented to the mind and, overwhelming it, produced emotions of the most affecting kind. . . . It seemed to me an allegory in which virtue was personified, and addressing those whom she would make her votaries."

Although Washington's First Inaugural established a prototype followed by all subsequent presidents, his Second Inaugural did not. In that speech of 135 words, by far the briefest of presidential inaugurals, Washington perfunctorily acknowledged his reelection and signified his commitment to the oath of office he was about to take. Although the unusual nature of the Second Inaugural has puzzled many scholars, it is explained when we understand that Washington wanted a simple ceremony without the pomp and extravagance of his first inauguration. In Washington's view, the political situation of March 1793 did not require more than a few brief comments before being sworn into office for a second term, while that of April 1789 had demanded a major speech to help develop confidence in the new government. The prototype for second inaugurals was not established until Thomas Jefferson's speech of March 4, 1805.

Ceremonial Speeches: The Regional Tours

Throughout his presidency, Washington made effective use of ceremonial discourse to fortify his personal reputation and to cement the bonds of national union. Although he gave scores of such speeches during his years at the helm of government, none were more important than those presented during his three regional tours of the United States. The first tour was a twenty-nine-day journey through New England in October and November 1789. The second was a brief sojourn in Rhode Island during August 1790, after that state had finally ratified the Constitution. The third was a two-month visit to the southern states in the spring of 1791. Washington's aim in each tour was to assess how citizens felt about the new government and to strengthen their commitment to it.

As had been the case with Washington's official travels ever since the Revolution, during his tours as President he was greeted and feted by local dignitaries in town after town upon his route. As part of the festivities, which usually included a parade, a dinner, and illuminations, Washington was presented with a formal address of welcome and tribute. Sometimes the address was tendered as he rode into town on horseback. At other times, it was proffered in ceremonies at a town hall, church, college, Masonic lodge, or state legislature. Whenever possible, an advance copy of the address was given to one of Washington's aides, so the President could present a brief, formal speech in response. If Washington did not receive an advance copy of the address, he would say no more than a few words on the spot and send a formal written reply the next day. Usually both the address and Washington's reply were published in the local press. All told, Washington received and answered at least forty-three addresses during his three regional tours.

The addresses presented to Washington were highly formulaic and intensely laudatory. They typically opened by welcoming Washington, praising him for his service to his country during the Revolution, and congratulating him on his unanimous election as President. Many of the addresses apotheosized him in such terms as "the defender of liberty," "the guardian of his country," "the friend of mankind," and "the father of his country." Most affirmed the commitment to the new government of the group presenting the address, and almost all concluded by wishing Washington good health and a long life.

In keeping with eighteenth-century rhetorical conventions, Washington's replies were staunchly formal. Without exception he began by reciprocating the good wishes conveyed by the group addressing him. When responding to praise for his exploits in the Revolution or for his personal role in creating the Constitution, he deflected attention from himself by attributing both of those momentous achievements to the blessings of Divine Providence and the exertions of the American people. In keeping with Washington's customary practice, his speeches during the regional tours often praised his auditors for traits and actions he wanted them to adopt: industry, virtue, love of country, and, above all, attachment to the Constitution. Almost invariably he concluded by expressing his hope for the prosperity and happiness of the group addressing him.

The most memorable of Washington's speeches on his regional tours was his answer to an address from the Hebrew Congregation in Newport, Rhode Island, in August 1790. A strong supporter of religious freedom, Washington used this occasion to reaffirm the inviolability of liberty of conscience. The government of the United States, he said in an echo of the congregation's address, "gives to bigotry no sanction, to persecution no assistance." He then went well beyond the congregation's language by voicing his desire that "the children of the stock of Abraham who dwell in this land" would continue to enjoy "the good will of the other inhabitants, while everyone shall sit in safety under his own vine and fig tree, and there shall be none to make him afraid." There are few more eloquent statements of Washington's opposition to religious bigotry and intolerance than this passage with its powerful scriptural resonance.

By all signs, Washington's regional tours were highly successful. One newspaper reported that the President's presence in New England, "like the glorious luminary of heaven, appears to have totally dissipated the fog of Antifederalism." Certainly Washington was pleased with his journeys. After returning from the southern states, he recorded in his diary that he had learned "more accurately the disposition of the people than I could have done by any information." He was satisfied that "tranquillity reigns among the people, with that disposition towards the general government which is likely to preserve it." Although there is no way to gauge the exact impact of Washington's speeches during his regional tours, they were an important part of the ceremonies at every stop and no doubt contributed to the public's growing confidence in the new government.

Annual Messages to Congress

Typically circumspect in his public statements and exceedingly respectful of the prerogatives of Congress, Washington did not campaign for legislation as do modern presidents. His only major policy speeches were his eight annual messages to Congress. Modeled on the British monarch's speech from the throne at the beginning of each new session of Parliament and on its American analogue, the governor's speech to the colonial assembly, Washington's messages derived also from the constitutional provision that the President "shall from time to time give to the Congress information of the state of the Union, and recommend to their consideration such measures as he shall judge necessary and expedient."

Washington usually began work on his annual messages by soliciting ideas from members of his Cabinet about the topics to be discussed. Sometimes he would give those suggestions directly to the person responsible for drafting the speech. Or, working from the suggestions, he would draw up a list of main points, with notes on how they might be treated. From these materials one of his associates would prepare a draft. Washington would then review the draft, making suggestions and corrections as to the ideas and their manner of expression. At some stage, he would circulate the draft among his Cabinet. If further drafts were necessary, the process would continue until Washington had a text with which he was fully satisfied. At times he would write out his speaking copy in his own hand, all the while smoothing, refining, and amending. Consistent with Washington's thorough and cautious approach to decision making in general, it was a time-consuming operation designed, as he said of his eighth annual message, so that "the whole may be revised again and again before presentation."

Although presidents from Jefferson through Taft would send their annual messages to Congress in writing, Washington delivered his in person. He presented his first five messages in the Senate chamber and the last three in the House of Representatives, with the full Congress in attendance at all. A master of political ceremony, Washington staged the delivery of his messages with great care. On the day of his sixth message, for example, he rode to Philadelphia's Federal Hall in his magnificent white carriage, which was escorted by a procession of constables. Attired formally in black and wearing a dress sword, he entered the chamber of the House of Representatives at precisely twelve noon attended by Secretary of State Edmund Randolph, Secretary of War Henry Knox, and Attorney General William Bradford. The members of Congress rose upon his entrance and remained standing until he took his place between the Vice President and the Speaker of the House. After bowing to the audience, Washington reached into his coat pocket, removed his spectacles and a neatly folded text of his speech, which he proceeded to read in a clear and distinct voice. When he was finished speaking, Washington handed copies of his text to the Vice President and the Speaker. He then walked from the chamber as the entire audience stood at silent attention.

The most controversial of Washington's messages to Congress was that of November 17, 1794. Delivered three weeks after his return to Philadelphia from leading a force of 13,000 militiamen against the Whiskey Rebellion in western Pennsylvania, it was far and away the most strident speech of his presidency. Although he feared it might fan the embers of party spirit, he decided he had no choice but to be "more prolix in my speech to Congress on the commencement and progress of this insurrection than is usual in such an instrument." Concerned about the impact of the rebellion on domestic politics, as well as on international perceptions of American unity and stability, he believed it was better to discuss the matter in full rather than "to let it go naked into the world, to be dressed up according to the fancy or inclination of the readers, or the policy of our enemies."

Addressing a packed audience in the House chamber, Washington devoted almost his entire speech to the Whiskey Rebellion. Noting that the tax on whiskey had been accepted by most Americans, he blamed the troubles in Pennsylvania on a "prejudice, fostered and embittered by the artifice of men who labored for an ascendancy over the will of others by the guidance of their passions." After reviewing the history of the excise law, the attacks on federal officials who sought to enforce it, and efforts to quell the rebellion short of coercion, Washington explained that military measures had finally become necessary to "maintain the authority of the laws against licentious invasions." Turning to the Democratic Societies he held responsible for much of the tumult, he castigated "certain self-created societies" that, "careless of consequences and disregarding the unerring truth," had propagated "suspicions, jealousies, and accusations of the whole government." Yet there was also a positive side to the uprising, Washington explained, for despite the incendiaries' efforts to weaken the government and instill "a spirit inimical to all order," the American people had shown they were "now as ready to maintain the authority of the laws against licentious invasions, as they were to defend their rights against usurpation."

Reactions to the speech varied. A member of the gallery wrote that Washington "delivered one of the most animating, firm and manly addresses I ever heard from him or any other person. . . . I felt a strange mixture of passions that I cannot describe. Tears started into my eyes, and it was with difficulty I could suppress an involuntary effort to swear that I would support him." Washington's detractors were less impressed. In the House of Representatives, a fierce debate broke out over his inflammatory attack on "self-created societies." From Monticello, Thomas Jefferson raged that "an insurrection was announced and proclaimed and armed against, but could never be found." James Madison, who by now was firmly in the ranks of the opposition, deemed Washington's assault on the Democratic Societies his greatest political error. In the nation at large, however, the President's words carried the day. Resolutions endorsing his position came from every state and from every kind of meeting. Equally telling, within a year the number of Democratic Societies had declined precipitously. Notwithstanding Washington's growing body of critics, his hold on the minds and hearts of the people remained secure.

If Washington's speech on the Whiskey Rebellion was the most controversial of his annual messages, his address of December 8, 1795, was his most adroit. Delivered during the prolonged agitation over the Jay Treaty and at a time when Washington was under fierce attack in the Democratic-Republican press, it rose above the strife by focusing attention on America's "numerous and extraordinary blessings." After reviewing developments in foreign policy, the President found cause only for "consoling and gratifying reflections." He took the same approach to domestic affairs, in which he discovered "equal cause for contentment and satisfaction." While many of the nations of Europe were engulfed in foreign wars and domestic convulsions, the United States exhibited "a spectacle of national happiness never surpassed if ever before equalled." Even the region that had supported the Whiskey Rebellion now enjoyed "the blessings of quiet and order," and Washington had pardoned the convicted rebels in an effort to "mingle in the operations of government every degree of moderation and tenderness which the national justice, dignity and safety may permit." After making several specific recommendations, including the need to protect the Indians from "the violences of the lawless part of our frontier inhabitants," Washington concluded by stating that temperate discussion and mutual forbearance in the deliberations of Congress were "too obvious and necessary for the peace, happiness and welfare of our country to need any recommendation of mine."

A brilliant stroke, the speech left Washington's opponents gasping for air. By studiously avoiding any tone of strife, in contrast to his sharply worded message of the previous year, the President rose so far above the fray as to make his critics look pernicious and small-minded. Free and prosperous, growing rapidly in strength and population, the United States was indeed in an advantageous situation. In driving home this unassailable fact, Washington shifted attention from partisan discord to those elements that united Americans and made their future prospects so bright. By acting as if there were no cause for contention, he helped restore a measure of public harmony at a critical point in the life of the young republic.

Washington's last message to Congress, delivered December 7, 1796, two and a half months after publication of his Farewell Address, was witnessed by the "largest assemblage of citizens, ladies and gentlemen ever collected on a similar occasion." The thirty-minute speech touched on a multitude of topics, including progress in Indian affairs, the British evacuation of the Northwest posts, implementation of the Jay Treaty, creation of a navy, encouragement of manufactures, relations with the French, and the need for a national university. Exhibiting his sure touch in matters of ceremony, Washington concluded in valedictory terms by closing the circle on his presidency. Noting that he was meeting with Congress "for the last time," he looked back to "the period when the administration of the present form of government commenced." After congratulating Congress and the country on "the success of the experiment," he returned to the religious sentiments of his First Inaugural by again offering his "fervent supplications to the supreme ruler of the universe, and sovereign arbiter of nations, that his providential care may still be extended to the United States; that the virtue and happiness of the people may be preserved; and that the government which they have instituted for the protection of their liberties may be perpetual." When Washington ended, there were few dry eyes in the House chamber.

The Farewell Address

Although often treated as a speech, Washington's greatest paper, his Farewell Address, was not delivered orally. Released to the public through *Claypoole's Daily Advertiser* of September 19, 1796, it was quickly reprinted by other American newspapers, appeared in several European journals, and elicited almost universal praise as "the richest legacy of a father to his children." For the next century and a half it was revered as a sacred statement of American political principles, and it continued to be read in Congress each February 22 until the 1970s. Although no longer regarded as oracular, the Farewell Address ranks with the Declaration of Independence and the Gettysburg Address as the most honored of American political discourses.

The genesis of the Farewell Address can be traced to May 1792. Tired of the incessant bickering among members of his cabinet and dismayed at the growth of faction and party spirit, Washington told James Madison of his intention to step down from the presidency when his term of office expired the next year. Washington was eventually persuaded to serve again, but in the interim Madison acceded to his request to prepare a farewell message to the American people. Four years later, after Washington had made an irrevocable decision to retire, he penned his own draft of a valedictory, into which he incorporated all but one paragraph of Madison's 1792 text. Although Madison's words were, as always, decorous and restrained, Washington's, which made up two-thirds of the draft, betrayed his bitterness at the attacks on his character by Democratic-Republican propagandists throughout his second term.

Perhaps uneasy about the tone of his draft, on May 15, 1796, Washington sent a copy to Alexander Hamilton with a letter that left open to Hamilton the possibility of throwing "the *whole* into a different form." Washington's wish, he told Hamilton, was that the address "appear in a plain style and be handed to the public in an honest, unaffected, simple garb." A month and a half later, Hamilton returned two manuscripts to Washington, one a revision of Washington's draft, the other a completely new text that was considerably longer and more philosophical in tone. After careful consideration, Washington expressed his preference for Hamilton's new text, which he found "more dignified" and "more copious on material points." This text became the working draft of the Farewell Address.

After copying Hamilton's new text into his own hand, Washington edited it with an eye toward precision and economy. He also made several substantive changes, including the addition of a paragraph on the importance of education in a republican society. After showing the revised text to his Cabinet on September 15, Washington met the next day with David Claypoole, who readily agreed to print the Address in his newspaper. Once the Address was set in type, Washington corrected the proofs, changing little more than a few marks of punctuation. On Monday, September 19, it appeared, without comment or fanfare, on page two of the *Daily Advertiser.*

The reverence accorded Washington's Farewell Address as a personal legacy to his country helps explain the furor that arose in the nineteenth century when the public learned Hamilton had been its principal author. In fact, almost all of Washington's presidential discourse was composed with the assistance of ghostwriters. Burdened with a weighty load of official duties and insecure about his use of language in public documents, he relied heavily on the pens of Hamilton, Madison, David Humphreys, Tobias Lear, Edmund Randolph, William Jackson, and Timothy Pickering. But while Washington's aides and associates were responsible for much of his prose, he so thoroughly superintended the composition of his major addresses, including the Farewell, that they unquestionably bore his personal stamp.

The purpose and meaning of Washington's Farewell Address have been the objects of perennial debate. Hailed by some as an impartial statement of national principle, the Address has been debunked by others as nothing more than a partisan document designed to sustain Federalist political hegemony. In truth it is a complex and multifaceted document that resists simple interpretation. The first section of the text is a straightforward announcement of Washington's decision not to stand for reelection. Had Washington wanted to do no more than herald his retirement, he could have stopped here. But he also meant the Farewell Address to be his political testament, a valedictory enunciating the principles that should guide Americans in their relations with each other and with the rest of the world. And so he followed the announcement of his retirement by offering to the citizens of the United States "some sentiments . . . which appear to me all important to the permanency of your felicity as a people." In doing so, he duplicated the course he had taken in June 1783, in the last of his circular letters to the governors of the thirteen states during the Revolution. Widely celebrated throughout America as Washington's "Legacy," this letter had announced his retirement from the army and had offered his thoughts about the political principles the United States should follow to maintain its newly won status as an independent nation. Now, in 1796, Washington again shared his parting counsel with his country.

Washington's advice in the Farewell Address revolved around two broad themes. The first theme, which had also received attention in his 1783 circular letter, underscored the importance of maintaining political union. "The unity of government which constitutes you one people," he declared, is "the palladium of your political safety and prosperity" and must be guarded "with jealous anxiety." Of all the forces that could endanger the union, Washington expressed greatest concern about "the baneful effects of the spirit of party," the "worst enemy" of popular government. In Washington's view, this spirit placed the will of "a small but artful and enterprising minority of the community" above the "delegated will of the nation," thereby allowing "cunning, ambitious and unprincipled men to subvert the power of the people and to usurp for themselves the reins of government." Adopting much the same figure used almost a decade earlier by James Madison in the Tenth Federalist, Washington portrayed party spirit as "a fire not to be quenched" that required "uniform vigilance to prevent its bursting into a flame, lest instead of warming it should consume."

Washington's second theme, which had not appeared in his 1783 Legacy, dealt with the need for neutrality in foreign affairs. Just as Washington had cautioned Americans, earlier in the Farewell Address, to view with "jealous anxiety" the "baneful effects" of party spirit, here he portrayed "the insidious wiles of foreign influence" as "one of the most baneful foes of republican government" against which "the jealousy of a free people ought to be *constantly* awake." In his view, "permanent, inveterate antipathies against particular nations and passionate attachments for others" inevitably produced "sinister and pernicious motives" that prompted governments to act "contrary to the best calculations of policy" and to adopt "through passion what reason would reject."

From these general principles Washington deduced his "great rule of conduct" in regard to foreign nations, to extend commercial relations where feasible, but to have "as little *political* connection as possible." Drawing upon Enlightenment doctrines of statecraft, he held that Europe and America had separate spheres of interest. The United States, he declared in the most famous lines of the Address, had nothing to gain by entangling its "peace and prosperity in the toils of European ambition, rivalship, interest, humor or caprice. 'Tis our true policy to steer clear of permanent alliances with any portion of the foreign world." (Contrary to popular conception, Washington did not warn against "entangling alliances," a phrase from Jefferson's First Inaugural.) Temporary alliances, he allowed, were suitable for "extraordinary emergencies," but there could be "no greater error than to expect or calculate upon real favors from nation to nation." The true interest of the United States was to take advantage of its "detached and distant situation" and not to interweave its destiny with that of any part of Europe.

There can be little doubt that Washington was sincere when he characterized his thoughts about national union and foreign affairs as the unbiased counsel of "an old and affectionate friend." His private and public discourse alike had long evinced concern about the destructive force of party spirit. He had also stated on many occasions the importance of keeping free of European political conflicts, and much of his advice on foreign policy echoed language and ideas that had been prominent in American talk about affairs of state since the Revolution. Moreover, most of his directives in the Farewell Address were stated as maxims of national conduct, without explicit reference to particular controversies of his administrations. It was, in fact, this trait that gave the Farewell Address much of its testamentary power and helped transform it into an enduring guide to national policy.

And yet it would oversimplify the Farewell Address to see it solely as a disinterested statement of political principle. When viewed within the historical context of the 1790s, it emerges also as a masterful endorsement of Federalist political doctrines and an apologia for the country's first President. Although the Farewell seldom mentions by name the great controversies of Washington's years in office, they are all there, nestled between the lines of its seemingly ecumenical prose. Contemporary readers could not have helped but view Washington's warning against "all obstructions to the execution of the laws" as an oblique reference to the Whiskey Rebellion, and his condemnation of "all combinations and associations" that seek "to direct, control, counteract, or awe the regular deliberations and action of the constituted authorities" as an attack on the Democratic Societies he held accountable for the rebellion. Readers would also have seen his admonition against the unconstitutional "usurpation" of power by one branch of government against another as an implicit rebuke of Democratic-Republican leaders in the House of Representatives for their conduct in the battle over the Jay Treaty. The same was true of Washington's approval of commercial treaties in preference to political pacts and of his call for avoiding permanent alliances with European powers. Both were statements of principle, but both were simultaneously defenses of Federalist policy, the former of the Jay Treaty, the latter of Washington's Proclamation of Neutrality.

Not only did Washington's statements of principle carry double-edged meaning in the highly charged political climate in which they were issued, but he also tendered, just before his peroration, an explicit defense of his conduct of foreign policy as having been guided, "to the assurance of my own conscience," by the principles delineated earlier in the Address. Referring to the Proclamation of Neutrality as "the index to my plan," he claimed his predominant motive was to give the new nation time to "progress without interruption to that degree of strength and consistency which is necessary to give it, humanly speaking, command of its own fortunes." Whatever errors he might have made were unintentional; he wished his country would "never cease to view them with indulgence." It was a wish his country was more than happy to grant.

CONCLUSION

Although Washington died more than a century before Theodore Roosevelt ·lared the White House a bully pulpit and almost two centuries before scholars came enthralled with the rhetorical presidency, few presidents have managed the rhetorical resources of the office more adroitly than its first occupant. A master of political symbolism, Washington understood that politics is theater. As the chief actor in the drama of American politics, he played his role to perfection. Knowing that in a republican form of government the ability to wield power effectively depends ultimately upon popular opinion, he used his public addresses to shape and direct opinion through a series of crises that, with a lesser chief executive, might have imperiled the survival of the new nation.

In the process, he created precedents for presidential discourse that endure to this day. Because we take for granted the rhetorical conventions associated with the presidency, it is easy to overlook the fact that every step Washington took was on untrodden ground. Although many of his rhetorical practices were modeled on forms and customs derived from British tradition, he deftly adapted those forms and customs to a new system of government and a new set of political conditions. He was, lest we forget, the first President to deliver an inaugural speech. The first to go on tour among the American people. The first to present yearly messages to Congress. The first to leave a farewell address to his fellow citizens. Although presidential rhetoric today is manifestly different in numerous ways from presidential rhetoric in the young republic, there are also many deep and abiding continuities. In his rhetoric, as in other aspects of his presidency, Washington continues to cast a long shadow across the American political landscape.

RHETORICAL SOURCES

Archival Materials

The great bulk of Washington's surviving papers are in the Library of Congress, where they comprise 400 volumes of manuscripts. The standard published collection, Fitzpatrick's *Writings of Washington*, includes all of Washington's major presidential addresses, although it omits most of the ceremonial speeches he delivered on such occasions as his regional tours. This shortcoming will eventually be remedied by *The Papers of George Washington*, a comprehensive new edition begun under the general editorship of William Abbot. A CD-ROM version is also in preparation.

George Washington: A Collection. (*GWC*). Edited by W.B. Allen. Indianapolis, IN: Liberty Classics, 1988.

The Papers of George Washington: Presidential Series. (*PGW*). Edited by W. W. Abbot, et al. 4 Vols. to date. Charlottesville, VA: University Press of Virginia, 1987–.

The Writings of George Washington. (*GW*). Edited by John C. Fitzpatrick. 39 Vols. Washington, DC: Government Printing Office, 1931–1944.

Rhetorical Studies

Ferling, John E. *The First of Men: A Life of George Washington*. Knoxville, TN: University of Tennessee Press, 1988.

Flexner, James Thomas. *George Washington*. 4 Vols. Boston: Little, Brown, 1965–1972.

Freeman, Douglas Southall. *George Washington: A Biography*. 7 Vols. New York: Scribner's, 1948–1957. Volume 7 completed after Freeman's death by John Alexander Carroll and Mary Wells Ashworth.

Gilbert, Felix. *To the Farewell Address: Ideas of Early American Foreign Policy*. Princeton, NJ: Princeton University Press, 1961.

Morgan, Edmund S. *The Genius of George Washington*. New York: Norton, 1980.

Paltsits, Victor Hugo. *Washington's Farewell Address*. New York: New York Public Library, 1935.

Schwartz, Barry. *George Washington: The Making of an American Symbol*. New York: Free Press, 1987.

Smith, Richard Norton. *Patriarch: George Washington and the New American Nation*. Boston: Houghton Mifflin, 1993.

Wills, Gary. *Cincinnatus: George Washington and the Enlightenment*. New York: Doubleday, 1984.

Rhetorical Monographs

Asonevich, Walter J. "George Washington's Speeches and Addresses: Origins of an American Presidential Rhetoric." Ph.D. dissertation, University of Delaware, 1987.

Lucas, Stephen E. "Genre Criticism and Historical Context: The Case of George Washington's First Inaugural Address," *Southern Speech Communication Journal* 51 (1986): 354–70.

Chronology of Significant Presidential Persuasions

First Inaugural Address, New York, April 30, 1789. *GW*, 30: 291–96; *GWC*, 460–63; *PGW*, 2: 152–77.

First Annual Address Message to Congress, New York, January 8, 1790. *GW*, 30: 491–94; *GWC*, 467–70; *PGW*, 4: 543–49.

Address to the Hebrew Congregation in Newport, Rhode Island, August 1790. *GWC*, 547–48.

Second Annual Message to Congress, New York, December 8, 1790. *GW*, 31: 164–69; *GWC*, 467–70.

Third Annual Message to Congress, Philadelphia, October 24, 1791. *GW*, 31: 396–404; *GWC*, 470–74.

Fourth Annual Message to Congress, Philadelphia, November 6, 1792. *GW*, 32: 205–12; *GWC*, 480–86.

Second Inaugural Address, Philadelphia, March 4, 1793. *GW*, 32: 374–75; *GWC*, 486.

Fifth Annual Message to Congress, Philadelphia, December 3, 1793. *GW*, 33: 163–69; *GWC*, 486–91.

Sixth Annual Message to Congress, Philadelphia, November 19, 1794. *GW*, 34: 28–37; *GWC*, 492–99.

Seventh Annual Message to Congress, Philadelphia, December 8, 1795. *GW*, 34: 386–93; *GWC*, 499–504.

Eight Annual Message to Congress, Philadelphia, December 7, 1796. *GW*, 35: 310–20; *GWC*, 505–12.

Farewell Address, September 19, 1796. *GW*, 35: 214–38; *GWC*, 512–27.

James M. Farrell

John Adams
(1735–1826)

Can any thing essential, any thing more than mere ornament and decoration,
be added to this by robes and diamonds?

On July 2, 1826, a representative from the Independence Day committee of
Quincy, Massachusetts, visited the aged former president, John Adams, at his
home, inviting his participation in the planned celebration of the coming fiftieth
anniversary jubilee of the nation's independence. Unable to attend the celebration because of his failing health, the 90 year-old Adams instead suggested a
toast be offered in his name during the festivities. That toast, "Independence
Forever," was the last public utterance of John Adams. He died at six o'clock
in the evening on July 4, 1826.

Adam's final eloquent gesture enunciated the one essential principle that
guided his long and distinguished public career. Indeed, the compass of independence was never more important than when Adams steered America's course
during his presidency, from 1797–1801. Throughout his term in office, Adams
steadfastly resolved to allow neither domestic party passions, nor foreign intrigue to determine his executive direction of the nation. Ultimately, his independence from party cost him a second term. And, as Adams himself expected,
the slanders of his political enemies sullied his reputation and left a lasting, if
largely mistaken, historical impression.

But Adams was a great president. His administration was dominated by a
single foreign policy crisis—the danger of war with France—and his preservation of peace, his willingness to pursue every chance for an honorable settlement of hostilities, even when opposed by a disloyal cabinet, saved the republic
from what may have been, at that early age, a fatal national disaster. That he
managed with his policies to both incense the Republicans and alienate and

provoke many in his own Federal party, was of little concern to Adams. He considered his efforts to settle the French crisis as the greatest service he could have offered the nation. It was, he told James Lloyd in 1815, "the most splendid diamond in my crown; or if any one thinks this expression too monarchial, I will say the most brilliant feather in my cap."

Adams rose to the presidency after years of distinguished service to his country. He was born in Braintree (now Quincy), Massachusetts, on October 19, 1735 (Old Style). He was descended from Henry Adams, a Puritan settler from England. His father, also named John, and his mother, Susanna Boylston Adams, were modest farmers. Life in the small village of Braintree was punctuated by town meetings and regular services at the Congregational Church. At these sacred and political assemblies, central to life in colonial New England, John Adams no doubt formed his earliest views of eloquence and public deliberation.

In 1751, at age 15, Adams entered Harvard College. There he studied Latin and Greek and commenced his formal education in the subject of rhetoric. In the mid-eighteenth century, rhetoric was a central element of the Harvard curriculum, and Cicero's *De Oratore* was the principal work studied. Students read Cicero's speeches, probably read some Demosthenes as well, and met informally in debating societies and literary associations. Years later Adams recalled that his classmates determined he "had some faculty for public speaking."

After graduating in 1755, Adams taught school while he made up his mind about a career. Finally choosing law, he undertook his preparation for the bar under the guidance of James Putnam, of Worcester. Adams was sworn to the Boston bar in 1758, and there entered a fraternity of quick wits and eloquent pleaders. In 1764, after establishing his law practice in Braintree, Adams married Abigail Smith of Weymouth. In Abigail he gained not only a wife, but also a thoughtful partner and steady friend upon whom he would rely for both personal and intellectual companionship until her death in 1818.

As the dispute between Great Britain and her American colonies became increasingly warm, John Adams found himself drifting steadily into the uncertain currents of Anglo-American politics. In part as a response to the Stamp Act, Adams published the first of his important political works, *A Dissertation on the Canon and Feudal Law*, anonymously in 1765. Over the next several years, he remained engaged in the colonial cause, writing more to the newspapers, as he continued his law practice in Boston, where he had moved his family in 1768.

In 1770, Adams faced his first great political and rhetorical challenge, as he agreed to defend the British soldiers accused in the "Boston Massacre." His forensic effort, which he considered an unselfish and honorable service to his country, gained the acquittal of the soldiers. Although Adams was convinced that his defence of the soldiers would hurt his political standing in the community, he was later that year elected to the Massachusetts Legislature by a wide margin, and had improved his reputation as one of Boston's best lawyers.

A few years later, he was even asked by his cousin Samuel Adams to deliver the annual oration commemorating the "Massacre," an invitation he refused.

Adams remained at the center of Massachusetts politics and grew increasingly alarmed at the encroachments of the British ministry and the collusion and dissimulations of the royal executive in Massachusetts. He wrote numerous essays in the local newspapers arguing the colonial cause, the most effective and important being his "Novanglus" essays of 1775. Adams was also appointed to attend the Continental Congress, and there was able not only to display his own deliberative eloquence, but also to observe and admire the native political genius and public speaking of gentlemen from all over America. While in Philadelphia, Adams found time to write and publish anonymously *Thoughts on Government* (1776), a draft plan for American government, the influence of which can be observed in many of the original state constitutions.

In Congress, among many other speeches, Adams gave the 1775 oration nominating George Washington as General of the Continental Army. He was also appointed to the committee charged with drafting a Declaration of Independence and was the principal supporter of the completed Declaration in the debate of early July 1776. At that time Adams delivered what was perhaps his greatest speech. Although no text of the address remains (except that which sprang from the imagination of Daniel Webster), most witnesses agreed with Thomas Jefferson that Adams was the "Colossus of Independence."

In 1777 he was elected by Congress to replace Silas Deane on the American diplomatic commission in France, where he stayed for ten months. He returned to America briefly and took part in drafting the Constitution of Massachusetts in 1779. He then returned to Europe to serve, along with John Jay and Benjamin Franklin, as a minister in the negotiations for peace with Great Britain. For a time, Adams was also appointed minister to the Netherlands where, in 1782, he secured both diplomatic recognition and a substantial loan for the young republic from the Dutch government.

Following the conclusion of peace with Great Britain in 1783, Adams was appointed part of the commission, with Franklin and Jefferson, assigned to negotiate a commercial treaty with Britain. He later became the first American minister to the Court of St. James, for him a splendid honor and vindication of his dedicated service. In 1787, while stationed in London, Adams wrote *A Defence of the Constitutions of Government of the United States of America*. This dense three-volume work of history and political science was concerned primarily with revealing the genius of the state constitutions. It displayed Adams's unrivaled grasp of the intellectual elements of politics and may have had some impact on the debates in the Constitutional Convention assembled in Philadelphia.

Adams returned to the United States in 1788, after having served in Europe for the better part of ten years. The following year, Adams was elected as the first vice president of the United States. As vice president, Adams made every effort to remain impartial and independent as he presided over the new U.S.

Senate. In late 1790, as the French Revolution came to dominate European politics, Adams offered an academic investigation of that phenomena in his "Discourses on Davila." Published as a series of newspaper essays, this work was clearly the most conservative of Adams's political writings. Fearing that human nature was inevitably susceptible to the kind of wild enthusiasm and "democratical" corruption he was witnessing in France, Adams suggested that certain aristocratic safeguards, and some elements of hereditary rule, might eventually be necessary in his own country. But these views of Adams the philosopher were seized upon by his political enemies as evidence of Adams's anti-republicanism. It was a charge that Adams spent the rest of his life attempting to refute.

By the end of George Washington's second term in office, a clear party division had taken place in American politics. When Washington decided to retire, Adams and Jefferson became rivals for the presidency. In the first contested presidential election in 1796, John Adams defeated Thomas Jefferson by three electoral votes. Adams served one term as president 1797–1801. Jefferson was his vice president.

In 1800, after a bitter election season in which Adams was slandered by leading men in his own party, he was defeated by Jefferson. Adams retired to his farm in Quincy where he lived another twenty-five years. He often fretted about, and wrote in defense of, his own historical reputation. In particular, he aimed to answer that attack on his character published by Alexander Hamilton during the election of 1800. He also wrote his *Autobiography* in 1808. Eventually, Adams reconciled with Jefferson, and the two men engaged in a marvelous correspondence that lasted for the last thirteen years of their lives. Adams also participated as an elder statesmen in the Massachusetts Constitutional Convention of 1820. He gave his last public speech to the corps of cadets from West Point who stopped to pay tribute to him at his farm in Quincy during a summer expeditionary tour. Adams lived to see his son, John Quincy Adams, elected the sixth president of the United States in 1824. Adams died the same day as Jefferson—July 4, 1826.

RHETORICAL TRAINING AND PRACTICES

John Adams was familiar with a wide variety of rhetorical scholarship. He owned and read works by Quintilian, Hugh Blair, John Ward, Lord Kames, and his own son John Quincy Adams. The volumes of Charles Rollin's *Method of Teaching and Studying the Belles Lettres*, Adams at one time considered "worth their weight in gold." Adams was also a keen observer of eloquence, ever ready to remark on the skills or disabilities of a speaker in Congress or at a public ceremony. But unquestionably both Adams's rhetorical training, and his own perspective on the art of rhetoric, were decidedly Ciceronian.

Adams had read Cicero since his childhood and was intimately familiar with Cicero's orations, letters, philosophy, and rhetorical theory. Adams attended college at a time when classical rhetoric dominated the curriculum and when Cicero dominated classical rhetoric. Adams's own musings about eloquence in his diary show a distinct Ciceronian flavor and are interspersed with critical reflections on the best of Cicero's orations. Cicero's *De Officiis*, and especially his *De Oratore*, taught Adams that the virtue of eloquence was to always be used in the service of the community, in directing public policy or especially in aiding justice. It was this ideal that guided Adams in his early legal and political career.

As president, however, Adams had virtually no opportunity to engage in the sort of legal and political speaking that had earlier earned him a measure of rhetorical fame. The occasions for presidential oratory in the eighteenth century left little room for a Ciceronian display of eloquence. He made only six public speeches as president, each on a formal occasion, each addressed to both Houses of the Congress, each highly constrained by the dignity of his office and the circumstances that made the oration necessary, and most partly drafted by one or more cabinet secretaries.

But Adams had other outlets for his eloquence. Although he gave only six speeches, he spent countless hours writing proclamations, messages, and addresses. Most noteworthy among these other productions are the many replies Adams personally wrote to addresses he had received from communities and organizations all over the country. As the country faced a possible war with France, Adams used the opportunity of these replies to encourage feelings of unity, patriotism, and national honor. Typically both the original address and Adams's reply were printed in local newspapers, and then reprinted by other editors. In this way, as Abigail explained, the President had "the opportunity of diffusing his own sentiments, more extensively & probably where they will be more read and attended to than they would be through any other channel." In his public oratory, Adams spoke largely in the voice of his office. In these written replies, however, he gave a clearer view of his personal ethos, revealing much of the passion he felt about the French crisis. These brief retreats from his "official" voice are curiously emphasized by Adams's use of the third person to speak of the president, whom he often refers to as "the executive authority of the national government."

There are many ways to explain the oratory of Adams's presidency. As a body, his presidential speeches are marked by formality, precision, dignity, and constraint. To be sure, Adams was aware of the need to secure the establishment of official forms of address for the president and the government. He had only the example of Washington's addresses to guide and constrain his own oratory. The emphasis upon decorum and the effort to compose in a dignified style were necessary to bring the United States a measure of credibility and legitimacy as it assumed its station among the nations of the world. In addition, Adams, who lacked the public ethos of Washington, needed to maintain the confidence of the people and their representatives, and to demonstrate continually his own fitness to hold the office. He used the occasions of his public oratory as demonstrations not of his eloquence so much as of his character, temperament, and judgment. Adams was also conscious of the historical audience and the verdicts of posterity. He wished his official remarks to provide only the most prudent, clear, dignified, and reasoned examples of his political stewardship. His oratorical style was classical and conservative, without ornament, flourish, or metaphor. It often consisted of long periodic sentences, which had the advantage of adding precision to his discourse and ensured a more deliberate and careful delivery.

Adams returned to a number of common themes in much of his presidential oratory. He often opened his annual addresses with panegyrical reflections on the blessings of American liberty; the bounty of American agriculture, commerce, and industry; the genius of American political institutions; and the growth of American patriotism, education, and literature. Such remarks reminded the nation of the continued favor of, and their dependence upon, Providence. Moreover, these reflections were essential for cultivating a common American identity among the states, and for encouraging pride in distinctly American achievements and American independence.

Adams also showed an acute sensitivity to the boundaries of his executive office. His presidential oratory often explicitly marked out the constitutional separation of powers and showed his clear grasp of the limits upon and duties of the president. This effort by Adams answered the concern of some of his critics about his ''monarchial tendencies,'' but also helped to confirm the balance of power between branches of government and to secure the independence of the national executive.

JOHN ADAMS'S INAUGURAL ADDRESS

John Adams was inaugurated as the second president in Philadelphia on March 4, 1797. His speech has the odd distinction of containing perhaps the single longest sentence in all of American public address—an extended period with multiple conditional clauses, each expressing attributes of his character or experience, that continues for 724 words. Adams constructed the lengthy sentence as a way to communicate his readiness and qualifications to a somewhat uncertain official audience. This was the first occasion when there would be a transfer of the executive authority in the new republic. Although he was widely respected, Adams lacked the prestige of George Washington. His inauguration called for some gesture of assurance, some way to suggest that his talents and patriotism were equal to the office to which he had been only narrowly elected. The extended self-portrait provides not only a statement of principles upon which the Adams's administration would function, but also an icon of his public career. As the sentence itself was long, so was Adams's unselfish service to his country. The style of the remainder of the address also matched his consciousness of responsibility, and his need to depend upon and emphasize not his person, but the dignity of the office and the solemnity of the occasion. Adams's inaugural then, while largely epideictic, was also a less-than-subtle apologia.

Specifically, Adams was compelled to address the question that had been raised by his "Discourses on Davila" and not forgotten by his political opponents. Did Adams have faith in the American Constitution? Was he a monarchist? In response he rejected the "robes and diamonds" of royalty in favor of the simple dignity of a sovereign American people governing themselves. He also opened his inaugural with an extended historical narrative in which he traced the rise of the nation and the Constitution from its Revolutionary origins. In the narrative, Adams was not an agent but a spectator. He situated himself on the margins where he observed and approved the great experiment. The narrative was Adams's way of expressing his purchase in a constitution drafted without his participation while he was in Europe. The story also contributed to the cultivation of a national mythology, rehearsing historical events that would necessarily become the foundation for the American identity. Perhaps swept up in the inspiration of the occasion, even the opposition press generally approved the President's address.

JOHN ADAMS'S ADDRESS TO THE SPECIAL SESSION OF CONGRESS

On May 16, 1797, John Adams addressed a special joint session of Congress, called to deal with the crisis in relations with France. For some time, France, at war with Britain, had ignored American neutrality and plundered American shipping in the West Indies. Now, France had refused to receive American envoy Charles C. Pinkney, thereby suggesting that no grounds remained for negotiations. In his speech, perhaps the closest Adams came to a war message, he carefully explained the facts connected with the diplomatic developments and drew out the possible consequences. He insisted upon having America treated with the dignity and respect due a sovereign and independent nation. Citing the need to undertake actions in the national interest, he called for measures to improve America's naval defenses. But, he stopped short of asking for a declaration of war, still hopeful of finding some diplomatic solution.

In preparing the speech, Adams was assisted by both James McHenry, his Secretary of War, and Timothy Pickering, the Secretary of State. The address was carefully crafted. Adams began with epideictic themes, praising the genius of the American experiment. This was not a mere commonplace, but a necessary reminder and restatement of the principles that were to serve as a guide to American policy, principles that had not yet taken deep root in American soil. Adams was also cautious, anxious that Americans might lose sight of the basic tenets of the newly independent republic. The style of the address was solemn and precise, what one observer called "a masterly and dignified style." The speech contained no ultimatum or saber rattling, and was devoid of patriotic flourishes and unreserved passionate expressions. Indeed, the speech, like the solution Adams sought, was firmly diplomatic. The style itself enacted proof that the American government deserved French respect.

Republicans reacted to the speech with outrage, calling it Adams's "war whoop," while Federalists were thrilled by Adams's defense of American honor. But before long, Adams's preference for a diplomatic rather than a military solution to the French crisis would turn those same Federalists into his harshest critics.

JOHN ADAMS'S ANNUAL ADDRESSES

The remaining four speeches of Adams's presidency were the annual addresses he delivered to Congress. None of the speeches were remarkable except as exhibits of patience and moderation in a time of sensational party passion. The draft of each speech was prepared with the assistance of members of his cabinet. McHenry and Pickering, along with Oliver Wolcott, the Treasury Secretary, were all under the influence of Alexander Hamilton, and labored to add a Hamiltonian flavor to Adams's public statements. Late in his administration, Adams came to rely more on the loyal assistance of John Marshall who served briefly as Secretary of State.

The issue that dominated the four annual addresses was the French crisis. In each of the speeches, Adams tried to find a middle ground between war and dishonor. Even after the XYZ affair, another diplomatic insult, he continually sought a peaceful solution. Adams emphasized the need for strong defensive preparations, but resisted the Arch-Federalists who were hot for war. For a time, he refused to send a new envoy to France, but did not give up entirely on diplomacy. Although neither party was ever entirely happy with the president's speeches, what Theodore Sedgwick said after one address, could be said about them all: "he has exhibited a manly fortitude and dignified composure. His conduct has, indeed, increased the confidence of the friends of the government, and I am very much mistaken if it has not commanded the respect of his adversaries."

The moderation of Adam's policy was reflected in the moderation of his style. He refused the easy road of Franco-bashing, and instead used language as a policy instrument, a way to define and manage the crisis. His rhetoric was deliberate, cautious, and prudent; the style clear, firm, and formal. In many ways, the style of these addresses reflected both Adams's diplomatic experience and his basic understanding of the role of the executive in the government. Approaching these occasions as the political philosopher that he was, and sensible of his constitutional duty, he viewed the executive as above the fray, apart from the deliberations of the legislature. He would not engage in debate with those who opposed his policies and seldom gave them pretense to object on the grounds of his tone or rhetorical passion. At all times his rhetoric reflected his sense of decorum and a respect for the presidential office.

CONCLUSION

John Adams practiced the art of oratory as an essential element of republican government. He also believed that serving his country with patriotic eloquence would help him achieve historical fame. Yet Adams considered his most glorious rhetorical moments to have occurred during the Revolution. His presidency was not a time of heroic oratory. Rather, it was an occasion that tested his skills in diplomatic leadership and taxed his character of steady independence. At the same time, Adams's presidential speeches are monuments to the responsibility and dignity of presidential rhetoric. He clearly understood that to speak in the voice of his office was to speak for the nation, to reveal America's identity and express America's aspirations. Indeed, during the vital conflict with France, Adams's rhetoric, as much as the country's new navy, secured "the rights which belong to the United States as a free and independent nation," and "that weight and respect to which it is so justly entitled."

RHETORICAL SOURCES

Archival Materials

The 608-reel-microfilm collection of the Adams Papers, produced by the Massachusetts Historical Society, preserves the documentary history of four generations of the Adams family. That collection remains the single best source of primary material for the study of John Adams. Most of John Adams's library survives, including numerous books on rhetoric, and is kept at the Boston Public Library.

Adams Family Correspondence. 4 Vols. Edited by L. H. Butterfield. Cambridge, MA: Belknap Press, 1963.

Diary and Autobiography of John Adams. 4 Vols. Edited by L. H. Butterfield. Cambridge, MA: Belknap Press, 1961.

Legal Papers of John Adams. 3 Vols. Edited by L. Kinvin Wroth and Hiller B. Zobel. Cambridge, MA: Belknap Press, 1965.

Life and Works of John Adams. (*WJA*). 10 Vols. Edited by Charles Francis Adams. Boston: Little, Brown, 1850–1856.

Papers of John Adams. 8 Vols. to date. Edited by Robert J. Taylor, Mary-Jo Kline, and Gregg L. Lint. Cambridge, MA: Belknap Press, 1977–   .

Rhetorical Studies

Brown, Ralph Adams. *The Presidency of John Adams.* Lawrence, KS: University Press of Kansas, 1975.

Chinard, Gilbert. *Honest John Adams.* Boston: Little, Brown, 1933.

Dauer, Manning J. *The Adams Federalists.* Baltimore: Johns Hopkins Press, 1953.

DeConde, Alexander. *The Quasi-War: The Politics and Diplomacy of the Undeclared War with France 1797–1801.* New York: Charles Scribner's Sons, 1966.

Elkins, Stanley, and Eric McKitrick. *The Age of Federalism*. New York: Oxford, 1993.

Ferling, John. *John Adams: A Life*. Knoxville, TN: University of Tennessee Press, 1992.

Kurtz, Stephen G. *The Presidency of John Adams: The Collapse of Federalism 1795–1800*. Philadelphia: University of Pennsylvania Press, 1957.

Miller, John C. *The Federalist Era*. New York: Harper, 1960.

Shaw, Peter. *Character of John Adams*. Chapel Hill, NC: University of North Carolina Press, 1976.

Smith, Page. *John Adams*. 2 Vols. Garden City, NY: Doubleday, 1962.

Rhetorical Monographs

Bezayiff, David. "Legal Oratory of John Adams: An Early Instrument of Protest." *Western Journal of Speech Communication* 40 (1976): 63–71.

Chaly, Ingeborg. "John Adams and the Boston Massacre: A Rhetorical Reassessment." *Central States Speech Journal* 28 (1977): 36–46.

Dickson, Charles Ellis. "Jerimiads in the New American Republic: The Case of National Facts in the John Adams Administration." *New England Quarterly* 60 (1987): 187–207.

Farrell, James M. "John Adams's *Autobiography*: The Ciceronian Paradigm and the Quest for Fame." *New England Quarterly* 62 (1989): 505–28.

———. "New England's Cicero: John Adams and the Rhetoric of Conspiracy." Massachusetts Historical Society *Proceedings* 104 (1992): 55–72.

———. "*Pro Militibus Oratio*: John Adams's Imitation of Cicero in the Boston Massacre Trial." *Rhetorica* 9 (1991): 233–49.

———. " 'Syren Tully' and the Young John Adams." *Classical Journal* 87.4 (1992): 373–90.

Furtwangler, Albert. *American Silhouettes: Rhetorical Identities of the Founders*. New Haven, CT: Yale University Press, 1988, 40–63.

Huston, James M. "Letters from a Distinguished American: The American Revolution in Foreign Newspapers." *Quarterly Journal of the Library of Congress* 34 (1977): 292–305.

Reid, John Phillip. "A Lawyer Acquitted: John Adams and the Boston Massacre Trials." *American Journal of Legal History* 18 (1974): 189–207.

Rogers, Jimmie N. "John Adams' Summation Speech in Rex v. Wemms, Et Al.: A Delicate Act of Persuasion." *Southern Speech Communication Journal* 39 (1973): 134–44.

Saltmann, Helen Saltzberg. "John Adams's Earliest Essays: The Humphrey Ploughjogger Letters." *William and Mary Quarterly* 37 (1980): 125–35.

Chronology of Significant Presidential Persuasions

Inaugural Address. Philadelphia, March 4, 1797. *WJA*, 9:105–11.

Speech to Both Houses of Congress, Philadelphia, May 16, 1797. *WJA*, 9:111–19.

First Annual Message, Philadelphia, November 23, 1797. *WJA*, 9:121–26.

Second Annual Message, Philadelphia, December 8, 1798. *WJA*, 9:128–34.

Third Annual Message, Philadelphia, December 3, 1799. *WJA*, 9:136–41.

Fourth Annual Message, Washington, D.C., November 22, 1800. *WJA*, 9:143–47.

Daniel Ross Chandler

Thomas Jefferson
(1743–1826)

I have sworn upon the altar of God eternal hostility against every form of tyranny over the mind of men.

Above President Jefferson's grave at Monticello is the epitaph that he chose for inscription: "Here was buried Thomas Jefferson, author of the Declaration of American Independence, of the statute of Virginia for religious freedom, and father of the University of Virginia." The sage of Monticello died shortly before one o'clock on the afternoon of July 4, 1826, preceding President John Adams's death by a few hours. The man from Virginia and the man from Massachusetts both had wanted to live until the fiftieth anniversary of the signing of the Declaration of Independence.

Born at Shadwell, his father's estate in Albemarle County, Virginia, on April 13, 1743, Thomas was a son of a successful planter, surveyor, explorer, and map-maker. A man of legendary strength, Peter Jefferson served as a burgess and as a county lieutenant, positions that were occupied subsequently by young Thomas. Jane Randolph Jefferson represented one of Virginia's famous families. From his father, Thomas inherited a considerable landed estate; and he doubled his holdings when he inherited his father's-in-law possessions, although the Randolph inheritance initially imposed a burdensome indebtedness.

RHETORICAL TRAINING AND EDUCATION

Thomas Jefferson was especially well educated in small private schools and at the College of William and Mary, where he completed his course in 1762. While receiving an excellent classical education, he became a close friend of three prominent Williamsburg residents, whose companionship gave Thomas an urbane sophistication and introduced him to the pleasures of genteel society. William Small, a faculty member at William and Mary, introduced the youth to the natural sciences and the rational methods of scientific inquiry and investigation. George Wythe, a member of the Virginia bar and the greatest law teacher of his generation in Virginia, imparted invaluable instruction indicating that the legal profession provided not merely a confined vocational preparation but an approach for appreciating the history, institutions, and culture of the people. Small and Wythe instilled within the youth an impressive intellectual drive. Francis Fauquier, the lieutenant of the colony, provided practical guidance for a political career. Thomas Jefferson read law with Wythe between 1762 and 1767, was admitted to the Virginia bar in 1767 and practiced the law successfully until 1774. Jefferson's classical education and subsequent legal training illustrates Cicero's wisdom that a young speaker should study the liberal arts.

Jefferson's first major essay, "A Summary View of the Rights of British America," written in 1774, revealed the young man's impressive grasp of learning and command of logic; demonstrated Thomas' persistent passion and the rhetorical skills essential for effective communication; and indicated his intense inclination toward intellectual radicalism.

Beside these classical studies and legal practice, a second significant dimension pervading Jefferson's educational experience was foreign travel. In 1784 he ventured to France, and joined Benjamin Franklin and John Adams in negotiating treaties with European nations. Paris provided him with an intellectual and artistic culture that he experienced initially during his student days at William and Mary. Jefferson enjoyed the theatre and the opera, visited the museums and the university, pursued his incessant interest in science and inventions, and indulged his apparently endless passion for books. Jefferson was enriched by his association with the European intellectuals and scientists, and he exerted a mild influence upon the moderate political leaders. His excursions through France contributed enormously to the universality of spirit, versatility as a renaissance man, and outstanding achievement in which Jefferson, with the possible exception of Franklin, was unequalled.

Thomas Jefferson confirms that the finest education is ultimately self-education. He was an extraordinarily learned man and voracious reader, whose extensive knowledge and unending inquiry seemed almost infinite. Jefferson's reading evoked remembrances of Emerson's "man thinking." The Virginian knew Latin, Greek, French, Spanish, Italian, and Anglo-Saxon; languages equipped him to consider carefully the distinctions between the ancient and modern pronunciation of Greek and to instigate the first systematic collection of American Indian dialect. At the age of seventy-one, Jefferson commenced Plato's *Republic* in the original. The sage of Monticello abandoned newspapers, prefering the classics composed by Tacitus and Thucydides, feasting upon the finest continental literature, reading these authors in the original French, Spanish, and Italian.

THE ROAD TO THE WHITE HOUSE

Thomas Jefferson served as magistrate and county lieutenant of Albemarle County before at twenty-five, he was elected to the House of Burgesses, where he worked as an effective committeeman and skillful draftsman. Between 1769 and 1774, he was conscientious in completing committee assignments, a competent legal craftsman, and an outstanding scholar commanding extensive knowledge.

From the commencement of conflict with England for American independence, he advocated the political position assumed by the advanced patriots. In the spring of 1775, the Virginia legislature defied the royal governor and gathered as a revolutionary convention. Jefferson was appointed as a member of the Virginia delegation dispatched to the Second Continental Congress in Philadelphia. As an exceptionally skillful committeeman and effective rhetorical stylist, he was assigned to the committee charged with writing a statement expressing America's grievances. When Benjamin Franklin and John Adams recognized Jefferson's talents, the man from Monticello became the principal author of the Declaration of Independence. Within a single succinct paragraph, he summarized powerfully the prevailing revolutionary philosophy that current and subsequent generations cherished not merely as an American charter, but as a universal pronouncement. A timeless quality emanates from a specific section stating simply that all men possess certain rights regardless of birth, affluence, or social status.

Because Jefferson resided in Europe negotiating treaties, he never participated in framing or ratifying the Constitution. Indeed, the document aroused his fear that the rights of individuals were not guaranteed and an unlimited eligibility of the president for reelection might make an ambitious politician a virtual dictator. His apprehension was assuaged when he learned that a bill of rights would be included, and that a danger of monarchy was diminished by George Washington's election. Jefferson accepted Washington's invitation, became secretary of state, and served in that position between 1790 and 1793. Jefferson assisted Alexander Hamilton, the secretary of the treasury, to secure congressional consent for the assumption of state debts; a consequence emanating from this cooperation was the location of the federal capital on the Potomac River. In 1791, when the Bank of the United States was established, Jefferson and Hamilton submitted rival interpretations of the Constitution. Hamilton's doctrine of liberal construction, which asserted extensive national power, provoked Jefferson's distrust and doubt.

The Republicans supported Jefferson for the presidency in 1796. Running second to John Adams by three electoral votes, the Virginian became vice president. His eventual victory over Adams during the 1800 election was partly attributable to the dissension among the Federalists. Jefferson's victory remained uncertain when he tied with running mate Aaron Burr. When the election was being determined by the House of Representatives, the Federalists voted for

Burr; they later conformed to the evident will of the American people and selected Thomas Jefferson.

JEFFERSON'S RHETORICAL PRACTICE

The two auspicious occasions that particularly required the effective employment of Jefferson's rhetorical skills were the President's first and second inaugurations.

Jefferson's First Inaugural Address remains among the most memorable in American presidential history, was admirably adapted to the rhetorical situation, and contained qualities describable as timely and timeless. Although the specific statements contained in Jefferson's address concerned the immediate audience, the principles that he expressed are pertinent to posterity.

When the President-elect and his escorts arrived on March 4, 1801, at the entrance to the Senate chamber, the scene provided a dramatic contrast from his predecessors' inaugurations. Jefferson's reflected the simplicity that he professed and promised; these simple proceedings were consistent with the unpretentiousness that characterized the new, unfinished capital. The unpaved streets, scattered houses, and incomplete capitol building were sharply and strikingly different from the urban sophistication with which Philadelphia and New York had surrounded the previous presidential inaugurations. As Cunningham stated, Jefferson was appropriately the first president inaugurated in these environs. Symbolizing the change in administration, President Adams departed at four o'clock in the morning. The fifty-seven-year-old Jefferson delivered his carefully composed speech by reading from a text that he had compressed to fit on two sheets of paper written on both sides. Cunningham concluded that although Jefferson's voice was not audible throughout the Senate chamber, the First Inaugural Address was "one of the memorable inaugural addresses in American history."

Jefferson had approximately two weeks to prepare his address, which is less time than he had for writing the Declaration of Independence. He composed both statements without using secretarial assistance and possibly without consulting published books. Although he represented his fellow Republican-Democrats, the President inevitably spoke for himself. Although only a portion of those who gathered in the Senate chamber heard his almost inaudible voice, his immediate audience and citizens scattered across the country could read the published speech in the *National Intelligencer*, where the address was typeset preceding the inauguration. Malone stated that no precise estimate of the speech's immediate impact is possible.

Since the House delayed Jefferson's election until February 17, serious speculation suggested that the transition between administrations might be neither peaceful nor orderly. The election of the people's choice for the presidency followed the prescribed constitutional process and guaranteed popular sovereignty. Jefferson responded directly to this specific rhetorical situation by describing the necessary relationship between the majority and the minority, and the association among the states and the federal government. Jefferson sought rhetorically to place the most favorable and magnanimous interpretation upon the recent political controversy. Carefully he explained the "sacred" principle that "though the will of the majority is in all cases to prevail, that will, to be rightful, must be reasonable; that the minority possess their equal rights, which equal laws must protect, and to violate would be oppression." Although he neither denounced nor decried the possible "tyranny of the majority," he acknowledged the necessity for instituting safeguards. Jefferson attempted to promote unity without imposing ideological conformity among the citizenry. Emphasizing unity, he stated that nearly all Americans preferred a republic to a monarchy, accepted the federal government, and supported the Declaration of Independence and the American Revolution. He nurtured unity by recognizing the distinct difference between principles and opinions. He said: "But every difference of opinion is not a difference in principle. We have called by different names brethren of the same principle." In the intellectual tradition symbolized by John Milton's *Areopagitica*, he championed freedom of speech, contending that "error of opinion may be tolerated where reason is left free to combat it." Jefferson indicated the kind of government that he regarded as essential for the continuing happiness and prosperity enjoyed by the American people: "a wise and frugal government, which shall restrain men from injuring one another, shall leave them otherwise free to regulate their own pursuits of industry and improvement, and shall not take from the mouth of labor the bread it has earned." Supporting state rights as the surest bulwark resisting anti-republican tendencies, he simultaneously endorsed "the preservation of the general government in its whole constitutional vigor." Jefferson explained the principles of his political philosophy. "To the united nation," he specified, "belong our external and mutual relations; to each state severally the care of our persons, our property, our reputation, and religious freedom." Drawing upon his European experiences, he envisioned "a government too weak to aid the wolves, and yet strong enough to protect the sheep."

Shortly before noon on Monday, March 4, 1805, when Jefferson again arose in the Senate chamber and repeated his presidential oath, no appreciable anticipation surrounded the occasion. Malone reported that Jefferson's Second Inaugural Address attracted less attention than the first, that the second "has no such historical significance," and that Jefferson considered his speech simply as an account describing his presidential performance rather than a statement expressing a promise or profession of principles. The Capitol was buzzing with conversation concerning the impeachment trial of Justice Samuel Chase that ended on the previous Friday and the valedictory of Aaron Burr on Saturday. Jefferson subscribed to the oath administered by Chief Justice Marshall and delivered his second inaugural address in a crowded Senate chamber with no quorum representing either the Senate or the House. Congress adjourned *sine die* shortly before half past nine on the previous night, following the stormiest

and most unproductive session that had transpired during Jefferson's administration. Although Jefferson received an electoral majority unmatched by any
successor for almost a century, he continued his presidency under unpropitious
circumstances. The President never wished that his second inauguration should
be overshadowing; he preferred an unpretentious event rather than a triumphant
ceremonial occasion.

"There was no spectacle to miss and little to hear," Malone wrote, "for
Jefferson's second inaugural address, like his first, turned out to be only partly
audible." The President spoke with a low voice. Printed in advance as the first
address had been in the *National Intelligencer*, the text was readily available for
reading. From a rhetorical perspective, this speech is distinguished by what
Jefferson acknowledged as a disproportionate attention to the Native Americans
and their pathetic plight that inspired commiseration; a consequence emanating
from this compassion is what Malone described as "one of the most striking
condemnations of the ultra-conservative mind he ever penned." Recognizing
the prudence of silence above the dangers of speech, Jefferson modified his
statements about religion. The most eloquent statements were carefully crafted
sentences about the freedom of the press. During a presidential campaign when
some newspapers exhibited an irreverence and indecency unparalleled in American political history, Jefferson considered his re-election as demonstrable evidence that his administration could not be "written down by falsehood and
defamation." Acknowledging this journalistic irresponsibility and extreme political partisanship, he never attributed this demeaning criticism to his opponent's frustration. Instead, he lamented that "These abuses of an institution so
important to freedom and science, are deeply to be regretted, inasmuch as they
tend to lessen its usefulness, and to sap its safety." Repeating a sentiment expressed earlier by Milton, Jefferson stated that "since truth and reason have
maintained their ground against false opinions in league with false facts, the
press, confined to truth, needs no other legal restraint. . . . " Jefferson left unex-
pressed his intention or decision, whether his second term would be final.

Jefferson's biographers generally repeat the unfortunate and regrettable conclusion that a weak, almost inaudible voice made him an ineffective public
speaker. Scholars generally conclude that Jefferson was primarily a writer rather
than a speaker, and that the Virginian excelled at written instead of spoken
discourse. Brodie stated that Jefferson was never eloquent when presenting
speeches, but that sometimes when he was writing or casually conversing he
became eloquent. Chinard claimed that during the days when fluency characterized the legal profession, words came neither easily nor abundantly for Jefferson. Pleasant and modulated during conversation, his voice sank in his throat
when Jefferson spoke in public. Morse contended that a husky voice impaired
Jefferson's vocal delivery, that he was never able to speak well when addressing
a deliberative assembly, and that he instinctively prefered to remain silent when
confronted with wrangling and conflict. Most Jefferson biographers overesti-
mated vocal delivery and slighted a vastly more significant criterion, intellectual

content. In Weymouth's anthology, Kenneth Clark observed insightfully that Jefferson's honesty of mind as well as a weak voice prevented Jefferson from becoming an orator, that the Ciceronian arts of persuasion so carefully cultivated by the humanists would have been distasteful, and that all art contains artifice that was foreign to the constitution of his mind. With historical accuracy, Johnson recognized that Jefferson's First Inaugural Address was successful in content, if not in oration, and that the capacity to emotionally move an audience constitutes only one criterion. "Jefferson's brilliance as a writer," Johnson concluded correctly, "his charm and intelligence in small groups, and his admirable integrity as a public official make him nonetheless an American orator whose timeless texts and effectiveness over a long career cannot be dismissed." That extended career of distinguished public service included his contributions as Governor of Virginia, Congressman, Ambassador to France, Secretary of State, Vice-President, and President. Observing that perfected persuasion makes a president an effective, morally responsible advocate, Hellenbrand wrote that with his rhetoric, Jefferson was "the nation's mentor."

Besides these impressive and inspiring inaugural addresses, several significant speeches were evoked by specific situations that required Jefferson's rhetorical response. Illustrating the president's skillful leadership is the speech that recommended a Western exploring expedition delivered by Jefferson on January 18, 1803. Western and southern land provided an irresistable incentive for migration and scouting. During his first term, between 1801 and 1805, Jefferson envisioned the expedition exploring the Pacific successfully concluded by Lewis and Clark during his second term. Jefferson's consciousness of the country expanding across a complete continent was reflected in his transactions securing the Louisiana Purchase. This 1803 acquisition was enormously significant, justifying the judgment that this territorial expansion was the most important achievement during his presidency. Acquiring an entire imperial province rather than simply controlling the mouth of the mighty Mississippi River, Jefferson nearly doubled the size of the United States with the Louisiana Purchase. Jefferson's reputation as the presidential patron sponsoring exploration remains unequalled, with the possible exception of John F. Kennedy.

Two additional addresses that reflect Jefferson's rhetorical responses to specific situations were his speech on the occasion of the Burr conspiracy on January 22, 1807, and his address on gun boats on February 10, 1807. The conspiracy of former Vice President Burr was confirmed in Jefferson's thinking by Burr's expedition down the Mississippi River. Speculative historians question whether Burr intended to separate the western land from the Union or to invade Mexico, but Jefferson interpreted Burr's action as an unquestionable threat endangering national unity and domestic security. In the fall of 1806, Jefferson initiated an interception in which most of Burr's boats on the Ohio River were captured, and Burr was subsequently apprehended on the Mississippi. Special speeches provided the president with an appropriate opportunity for explaining this problematic situation. An inciting incident evoked the president's rhetorical response.

Other speeches indicated Jefferson's skillful responses to specific situations or particular problems. His departure from Albemarle County, Virginia, and his eventual return in 1809 furnished an appropriate occasion for speaking a few words. Jefferson's regular annual reports to the Congress were routine and perfunctory. Additional audience-centered or issue-oriented speeches that indicate the utility that rhetoric provided the president included Jefferson's address to Elias Shipman and a committee of merchants from New Haven, and another address to Nehemiah Dodge and a committee representing the Danbury Baptist Association. Jefferson employed public speaking not simply to proclaim philosophical principles but as an effective problem-solving technique. Several speeches suggest that he was exceptionally expert in communicating with Native Americans.

The event-filled, even epoch-making, rhetorical situations that ensued during Jefferson's vice presidency and presidency contained important imminent and eventually far-ranging consequences. A decisive speech might make a distinct difference. During Jefferson's strained confrontation with Alexander Hamilton during Washington's administration, the rhetorical exchange produced the precedent and pattern for a national two-party political system. The turbulent presidential election of 1800 happened during a crucial period in the new nation's history. These exceptional circumstances included the first party change of administration in the new government. Two significant principles that emerged are the right of political opposition against an incumbent administration and the enduring tradition of a peaceful transition between presidential administrations. During Jefferson's administration, the U.S. Supreme Court explicitly expressed the right of judicial review in *Marbury v. Madison*. Jefferson contested the authority asserted by the Supreme Court as the ultimate interpreter of the U.S. Constitution. In this situation, a speech might reflect or even possibly influence the country's historical development.

An invaluable resource for analyzing Jefferson's public addresses and in appreciating the rhetorical situations is his extensive correspondence. Jefferson explained that the only comprehensive and genuine journal detailing his life would be found in his letters. He expressed this conviction although he wrote an autobiography, an account describing the American Revolution, and a document entitled "Anas," which is a political memoir that continued the autobiography through the stormy years when he was intimately involved in the struggles between the Federalists and the Republicans. Approximately 18,000 letters are preserved. These private and sometimes especially personal letters reveal that he was a polymath who corresponded candidly with his prominent contemporaries. Among Jefferson's most frequent correspondents was Thomas Paine, whom some historians call America's godfather. These letters indicate that Jefferson shared many convictions that Paine expressed. These intellectual giants believed that formal government comprises a small segment of civilized life, that the contracts made by voluntary agreement among free people are infinitely more important than the best instituted government for assuring safety and prosperity of the individual and the nation, and that the more perfect society requires increasingly less government. Another frequent correspondent during Jefferson's later life was John Adams, who on various occasions was his colleague and his adversary. This lively correspondence reveals their continuing dialogue concerning the meaning of the American Revolution conducted through the turbulent fifty-year relationship between these two founding fathers. Another frequent correspondent was Jefferson's cherished colleague and collaborator, James Madison. One of their most important achievements is the monumental Virginia Statute for Religious Freedom drafted by Jefferson and defended by Madison before the Virginia legislature. Jefferson's religious convictions are expressed incisively in his correspondence; these letters suggest reasons that prompted President Jefferson to abandon the practice of issuing proclamations for public days of prayer and thanksgiving.

JEFFERSON'S RHETORICAL THEORY

Acknowledging and appreciating rhetoric as an essential academic discipline and necessary practical art, Jefferson was convinced that intellectual pursuits without effective communication were pedantic. The Virginian regarded rhetoric, belles-lettres, and the fine arts to be as necessary to the study of political philosophy as are languages, ethics, history, geography, and the sciences. He believed that rhetorical techniques and intellectual content should be categorized under a pedagogical pursuit described as ideology and that contained general grammar, ethics, rhetoric, belles-lettres, and the fine arts. Speculating about Jefferson's rhetorical theory, Berman stated that he embraced the Enlightenment practice of grouping rhetoric and oratory with belles-lettres, criticism, and ethics. Berman concluded that this "orchestration" of rhetoric with ethics, belles-lettres, the fine arts, and general grammar constitutes a Jeffersonian characteristic. Since he classified rhetoric with logic under oratory, assigned these disciplines to the faculty of reason, and placed them within the province of philosophy, he recognized rhetoric as a valuable educational discipline and scholarly endeavor.

Jefferson professed that speechmaking should be guided by a primary rhetorical purpose, promoting the freedom of the citizens. Sustaining liberty within a democratic society requires that speaking and writing be simple, flexible, lively, clear, and distinct. He discussed expressive discourse, especially literary composition written in prose; he considered the methods of employing language that produce a desired effect or calculated impression. Jefferson anticipated an American style in English, and he discerned a fundamental foundation supporting this style in Shakespeare, other English sources, a knowledge of Anglo-Saxon origins, and Greek and Roman history. What Jefferson cherished in the classics came the closest to his personal philosophy and practice of communication: logical form, clear and distinct conception, and compact statement.

Believing that communicative discourse should be composed carefully using an "honest heart" and a "knowing head," Jefferson maintained that no speaker or writer should be motivated by antipathies, provoked with paltry political passions, or seduced into substituting sentimental fancies for substantive facts. He denouuced the conventional eulogy, verbal inflation, unnecessary vagueness, hyperbole, inadequate amplification, elaborate philippics, and deliberate diatribe. Jefferson criticized passions that are vehement and viperous, denounced the incessant grasping for every gossip-filled story, decried supporting with suspicion allegations that can be sustained in no other manner, and repudiated arguments asserted with inadequate evidence. He professed that discourse should be brief, clear, distinct, diversified, forceful, and sympathetic. Jefferson encouraged speakers to study and imitate the finest models in the discipline of reasoning, present speeches frequently before competent critics, analyze an audience and carefully adapt the arguments, speak without using notes, employ new words that are appropriate, depreciate the pedantic adherence to rigid rules of grammar, and receive instruction from competent teachers. He criticized using contrived expressions and barbarisms, citing legal technicalities, straining for effect or originality, and employing philippics or vehemence. He abhorred overstatement, gossip, innuendo, intrigue, chicanery, and dissimulation. Essentially the Virginian encouraged a speaker or writer to develop an argument using exhaustive research and employing perfect knowledge, subjecting the discourse to strict logic and rigorous reason.

Thomas Jefferson expressed enduring principles of political philosophy and intellectual freedom in a dignified eloquence that became models for speechmaking. Further, he assisted in establishing the guidelines and procedures for congressional speaking. Jefferson's experiences in presiding over the U.S. Senate provided insight and information for his *Manual of Parliamentary Practice*, which was published when he assumed the presidency in 1801.

ACHIEVEMENTS AND ACCOMPLISHMENTS

The most distinguished champion defending political, intellectual, and spiritual freedom in American history, Jefferson served his commonwealth and country through forty eventful years and exercised an influence upon the Republican Party that was unequalled by any other nineteenth-century president. Using enduring, eloquent language, he expressed the highest idealism and finest aspirations of the American people.

Between 1781 and 1783, he compiled *Notes on the State of Virginia*, which was published during 1785. *Notes* reflects Jefferson's extensive knowledge and competent authority. Spanning an entire continent and containing comments concerning religion, slavery, and the Native Americans, this book is an outstanding natural history that describes not simply Virginia but North America. *Notes* emerged from comprehensive but routine questions addressed to Jefferson by the secretary of the French delegation who compiled information about America; Jefferson's *Notes* provided the literary foundation sustaining the author's rightful reputation as a scientist.

During the Continential Congress, from 1783–1784, Jefferson promoted the Ordinance of 1784, which foreshadowed the Ordinance of 1787 establishing the Northwest Territory. Jefferson proposed that slavery be abolished within the territories. While serving in the Virginia delegation to the Continental Congress, Jefferson drafted an ordinance for governing the lands that Virginia ceded to the national government located northwest of the Ohio River. He included a prohibition forbidding slavery after 1800 in this area and any other territory that the United States might secure. This provision was defeated by a single vote. Jefferson's proposal, had it been adopted and enforced, would have banished slavery throughout the territory of the Louisiana Purchase.

Although Jefferson's Virginia Statute for Religious Freedom evoked persistent controversy that delayed adoption until 1786, this statute required a separation between the church and state. This enduringly significant enactment prohibited the state from supporting any religion with public taxes, and forbade the civil disabilities and punishments that were imposed upon citizens because of their religious beliefs or unbeliefs.

Toward the conclusion of the warfare in 1812, Thomas Jefferson sold his outstanding collection of books to the government. Jefferson's extensive library provided the fundamental foundation upon which the Library of Congress developed. Jefferson became the recognized founder of this significant collection and depository.

Earlier in his career Jefferson commenced an important book that he completed during his retirement. Carefully and conscientiously excluding the stories that reported or described the miracles found in New Testament literature, Jefferson skillfully compiled extracts from the gospels written in Greek, Latin, French, and English. Entitled *The Life and Morals of Jesus of Nazareth*, Jefferson's edition was consistent with the early nineteenth-century religious philosophy that was expressed by William Ellery Channing. Jefferson's account would have pleased early Unitarians and Universalists who were sometimes described as liberal Christians. Jefferson's *The Life and Morals of Jesus Of Nazareth* remained unpublished until the twentieth century. The recent discovery of the Dead Sea scrolls does not undermine, but possible strengthens, Jefferson's interpretation.

On March 4, 1809, Thomas Jefferson relinquished the American presidency to successor James Madison, he then returned to Monticello, completing "the last of my mortal cares, and the last service I can render my country." The remaining official act that he contemplated completing was the establishment of the University of Virginia. As an architect, he designed the buildings and supervised their construction, giving careful consideration to each detail. Jefferson gathered the faculty, constructed the curriculum, and selected the readings that were assigned in some of the courses. With passing generations, the University of Virginia gained international recognition as a great university.

CONCLUSION

President Jefferson's speeches did not simply reflect his historic, transitional times, for they exerted a powerful influence upon these swiftly moving currents. His initial inaugural attested and affirmed America's ascendancy as "the world's best hope," anticipating Lincoln's description as "the last best hope on earth." Insightfully the Virginian recognized that the new nation was poised precariously in "the full tide of successful experiment." By speaking reasonably and responsibly about the relationship between the majority and the minority, and the balance of power between the state and federal governments, Jefferson emerged not primarily as an elected leader formenting political opposition but as a President guiding a united people. With unfeigned respect for popular sovereignty and public opinion, the man from Monticello complimented the competence of his American audience and concured with the constitutional guarantee that the government rests upon the will of the citizens. The promise provided by America was the unrealized possibility inherent within relatively unregimented, consenting individuals. Jefferson embodied the aspirations that he expressed. For all his graciousness, the gentleman from Virginia remained a champion of minimal government. He was a vibrant, multi-dimensional renaissance man who persistently demonstrated throughout his incessantly active and unceasingly useful career what a committed individual holding strong convictions can eventually accomplish when endowed with individual freedom.

When Jefferson as a distinguished elder statesman discussed "the revolution of 1800," he knew that this change was secured by the suffrage of the electorate rather than the power of the sword. He explained that 1800 marked a revolution in the principles of government as surely as the rebellion of 1776 signalled a change in the form of the government. By seeking incessantly to implement the principles proclaimed during the American Revolution, he thwarted the development of the counter-revolution sweeping unmercifully across the Continent. Aware that America invariably faced the early morning preceding a fresh dispensation, he stated during his first inaugural that this rising nation, stretching across a wide and fruitful land, was progressing beyond the reach of mortal eye. Jefferson was unyielding in his conviction that the earth belongs always to the living generation, steadfast in his conclusion that the new nation would witness unparalleled individual achievement, and undaunted in his confidence that a free people would subdue an entire continent. With this faith in free people, as Malone indicated, the herald of freedom wrote a notable chapter in the history of the American presidency, and, on the national scene, established his historic claim to the title of "father of American political democracy."

With words that were appropriate, dignified, and tasteful, Jefferson emphasized reason above tradition; but behind his rich rhetoric he remained a thinly concealed conservative pondering progressive social change. His enthusiasm for seeking social reform was tempered wisely with a realistic assessment calculating the difficulties discerned within a specific situation. Described by some critics as a visionary or an opportunist, he responded decisively to particular rhetorical situations with rare vision and extraordinary patience. A serious student familiar with ancient history, he knew that Rome, and much more the universe, was not created in a single day. Yet he communicated consistently a congenial optimism and unshaken confidence that the passing of time favored the causes and convictions that he championed. Schooling himself in a carefully moderated self-restraint and carefully controlling his exuberant imagination, he generally denied himself in public what Malone described as ''the extravagances of speech he not infrequently indulged in private.'' Like John Adams, he knew that the Revolution happened first in the minds of people, and he comprehended that the Revolution would be continuous. Jefferson's was a perpetual revolt, an enduring declaration of independence, against all powers and principalities that would diminish the unquenchable human spirit.

RHETORICAL SOURCES

Archival Materials

Jefferson's speeches have been gathered in several collections.

Jefferson, Thomas. *The Complete Jefferson.* (*CJ*). Assembled and arranged by Saul K. Padover. Freeport, NY: Books for Libraries Press, 1969.
———.*The Writings of Thomas Jefferson.* (*WTJ*). Vol. 8. Edited by H. A. Washington. New York: Riker, Thorne, and Company, 1854.
———.*Thomas Jefferson: Writings.* (*TJW*). Compiled by Merrill D. Peterson. New York: Literary Classics of the United States, 1984.

Rhetorical Studies

Adams, James Truslow. *The Living Jefferson.* New York: Charles Scribner's Sons, 1936.
Berman, Eleanor Davidson. *Thomas Jefferson Among the Arts.* New York: Philosophical Library, 1947.
Binger, Carl. *Thomas Jefferson: A Well-Tempered Mind.* New York: W. W. Norton, 1970.
Brodie, Fawn M. *Thomas Jefferson: An Intimate History.* New York: W. W. Norton, 1974.
Chinard, Gilbert. *Thomas Jefferson: Apostle of Americanism.* Boston: Little, Brown, 1944.
Cunningham, Noble E., Jr. *In Pursuit of Reason: The Life of Thomas Jefferson.* Baton Rouge, LA: Louisiana State University Press, 1987.
Fleming, Thomas. *The Man from Monticello: An Intimate Life of Thomas Jefferson.* New York: William Morrow, 1969.
Foote, Henry Wilder. *The Religion of Thomas Jefferson.* New York: Braziller, 1975.

Hellenbrand, Harold. *The Unfinished Revolution: Education and Politics in the Thought of Thomas Jefferson.* Newark, DE: University of Delaware Press, 1990.

Lehmann, Karl. *Thomas Jefferson: American Humanist.* Charlottesville, VA: University Press of Virginia, 1985.

Malone, Dumas. *Jefferson the President, First Term, 1801–1805.* Boston: Little, Brown and Company, 1970.

————.*Jefferson the President, Second Term, 1805–1809.* Boston: Little, Brown and Company, 1974.

Morse, John T. *Thomas Jefferson.* Boston: Houghton Mifflin Company, 1898.

Peterson, Merrill D. *The Jefferson Image in the American Mind.* New York: Oxford University Press, 1962.

————.*Thomas Jefferson and the Democratic Vision.* Chattanooga, TN: University of Tennessee at Chattanooga, 1975.

————.*Thomas Jefferson and the Enlightenment.* Great Neck, NY: Westminister, 1975.

Sanford, Charles B. *The Religious Life of Thomas Jefferson.* Charlottesville, VA: University Press of Virginia, 1984.

Smucker, Samuel M. *The Life and Times of Thomas Jefferson.* Philadelphia: J. W. Bradley, 1858.

Todd, Stephen J. "The Jeffersonian Synthesis: Civic Humanism and Classical Liberalism in the Political Thought of Thomas Jefferson." Ph.D. dissertation, St. Lawrence University, 1992.

Tucker, George. *The Life of Thomas Jefferson.* 2 Vols. Philadelphia: Carey, Lee and Blanchard, 1837.

Young, James Sterling. *The Washington Community, 1800–1828.* New York: Columbia University Press, 1987.

Rhetorical Monographs

Berman, Eleanor Davidson, and E. C. McClintock, Jr. "Thomas Jefferson and Rhetoric." *Quarterly Journal of Speech* 33 (1947): 1–8.

Hendrix, J. A. "Presidential Addresses to Congress: Woodrow Wilson and the Jeffersonian Tradition." *Southern Speech Journal* 31 (1966): 285–94.

Johnson, Loch K. "Thomas Jefferson." *American Orators Before 1900*, edited by Bernard K. Duffy and Halford Ross Ryan, 245–50. Westport, CT: Greenwood, 1987.

Oliver, Robert T. *History of Public Speaking in America.* Boston: Allyn and Bacon, 1965.

Webb, Royce. *The Rhetoric of Fawn M. Brodie in Thomas Jefferson: An Intimate History.* Henderson, TN: Fred-Hardeman College, 1987.

Weymouth, Lally, ed. *Thomas Jefferson: The Man, His World, His Influence.* New York: G. P. Putnam's, 1973.

Chronology of Significant Presidential Persuasions

Acceptance Speech as Governor, Williamsburg, Virginia, June 2, 1779. *CJ*, 1779: 381.

Response to the Citizens of Albemarle, Albemarle County, Virginia, February 12, 1790. *TJW*, 1790: 491.

First Inaugural Address, Washington, D.C., March 4, 1801. *CJ*, 1801: 384–87; *TJW*, 492–96; *WTJ*, 1–6.

To Elias Shipman and Others, a Committee of the Merchants of New Haven, Washington, D.C., July 12, 1801. *TJW*, 1801: 497–500.

First Annual Message, Washington, D.C., December 8, 1801. *CJ*, 1801: 387–93; *TJW*, 501–9; *WTJ*, 6–15.

To Messrs. Nehemiah Dodge and Others, a Committee of the Danbury Baptist Association, in the State of Connecticut, Washington, D.C., January 1, 1802. *TJW*, 1802: 510.

Confidential Message Recommending a Western Exploring Expedition, Washington, D.C., January 18, 1803. *CJ*, 1803: 398–401.

Third Annual Message, Washington, D.C., October 17, 1803. *CJ*, 1803: 401–5; *TJW*, 511–17; *WTJ*, 23–29.

Second Inaugural Address, Washington, D.C., March 4, 1805. *CJ*, 1805: 410–15; *TJW*, 518–23; *WTJ*, 40–45.

Sixth Annual Message, Washington, D.C., December 2, 1806. *CJ*, 1806: 421–26; *TJW*, 524–31; *WTJ*, 62–70.

Special Message on the Burr Conspiracy, Washington, D.C., January 22, 1807. *CJ*, 1807: 427–31; *TJW*, 532–38; *WTJ*, 71–78.

Special Message on Gun Boats, Washington, D.C., February 10, 1807. *CJ*, 1807: 432–34; *TJW*, 539–42; *WTJ*, 79–82.

Eighth Annual Message, Washington, D.C., November 8, 1808. *CJ*, 1808: 441–47; *TJW*, 543–49; *WTJ*, 103–11.

To the Inhabitants of Albemarle County, Virginia, Albemarle County, Virginia, April 3, 1809. *CJ*, 1809: 447; *TJW*, 550.

Lois J. Einhorn

James Madison
(1751–1836)

To prefer in all cases amicable discussion and reasonable accommodation
of differences to a decision of them by an appeal to arms.

James Madison's fame stems largely from the considerable influence he exerted
in his pre-presidential persuasions, especially in his speeches on the formation
and ratification of the Constitution. People today would honor and revere him
more had he never served as president. As "Father of the Constitution," he is
a hero, largely because his rhetoric convinced the American public of the worth
of his ideas. As president, he was unpopular, largely because his rhetoric failed
to convince the American public that although he preferred "amicable discussion and reasonable accommodation of differences to a decision of them by an
appeal to arms," the War of 1812 was necessary.

James Madison, Jr. was born in Port Conway, Virginia, on March 16, 1751.
He earned his B.A. degree in 1771 from the College of New Jersey, now Princeton University. Afterwards, he remained there for six months to study religion,
law, and Hebrew.

Madison held numerous pre-presidential offices: Member of the Orange
County Committee of Public Safety in 1774, Delegate to the Virginia Constitutional Convention in 1776, Member of the Virginia Legislature from 1776 to
1777, Member of the Virginia Executive Council from 1778 to 1779, Delegate
to the Continental Congress from 1780 to 1783 and 1787 to 1788, Member of
the Virginia House of Delegates from 1784 to 1786 and 1799 to 1800, Delegate
to the Annapolis Convention in 1786, Delegate to the Constitutional Convention
in 1787, Member of the Virginia Ratification Convention in 1788, Member of
the U.S. House of Representatives from 1789 to 1797, and Secretary of State
to Thomas Jefferson from 1801 to 1809. In addition, he coauthored *The Fed-*

eralist Papers, published in 1788, and served as ghostwriter for George Washington during Washington's presidency, from 1789 to 1797. Madison served two terms as the fourth president, from 1809–1817. After his presidency, he ministered to the University of Virginia as its rector from 1826 to 1836, and he served as a member of Virginia's constitutional convention in 1829. He died in his home in Montpellier, now spelled Montpelier, Virginia, on June 28, 1836.

RHETORICAL TRAINING

Madison's education, influenced by the Scottish Enlightenment, was thoroughly grounded in the liberal arts, including rhetoric, logic, moral philosophy, ethics, Greek, Latin, Hebrew, and political theory. While at Princeton University, he studied under the tutelage of the college's president, John Witherspoon, a Presbyterian minister and signer of the Declaration of Independence. Witherspoon required his students to read the works of Locke, Montesquieu, Kames, and other philosophers of the Age of Reason, and to declaim the works of Demosthenes, Cicero, and other orators. He stressed syllogistic logic, reasoned argument, and concise communication. A major maxim in his ideas on rhetoric was "Ne'er do ye speak unless ye ha' something to say, and when ye are done, be sure and leave off."

Madison accepted Witherspoon's rhetorical advice. In informal debates and discussions, young Madison argued logically and forcefully. But he was a shy, reluctant speaker who disliked the platform. He was the only member of his graduating class *not* to speak at commencement. Throughout his life he preferred writing to speaking.

MADISON'S PRE-PRESIDENTIAL PERSUASION

Madison's pre-presidential persuasion shows him to be a pragmatist who usually argued from the *topoi* or "stock issues" of deliberative debate. Need, desirability, workability, and practicality were frequent topics of his discourse. The Preamble to the Constitution exemplifies Madison's pragmatic view—"We the people of the United States, in order to form a *more perfect* Union . . . [emphasis added]." The use of the words "more perfect" shows that Madison took a nonabsolutist stance; he did not envision the Constitution as forming a *perfect* Union, only the best one possible.

Madison's assumptions about the nature of human beings were also nonabsolutist, and these assumptions affected his stands on concrete issues. He viewed people as neither totally depraved nor totally virtuous. Rather, he believed people were selfish and driven by passions in some respects, and virtuous and driven by reason in others. His balanced view of human nature blended Calvinistic pessimism with Enlightenment optimism. In Virginia's Ratification Debates on the Constitution, Madison mixed pessimism and optimism in unequal proportions, stressing the positive aspects of human nature. Throughout his speeches, he used words, such as "trust," "hope," "confidence," and "respect." He summed up his spirit of optimism when he said, "I choose rather to indulge my hopes than fears." Madison's optimism makes sense when considering the givens in the debates. Government would be unnecessary if people were completely virtuous and altruistic. Checks and balances in government would be unnecessary if people could trust leaders in government with unlimited power. Neither side debated these points. What was at issue was whether people possessed *enough* virtue to be trusted with *limited* power. Madison argued that civilized society implied this degree of trust.

In the ratification debates, Madison maintained that people's virtue would manifest itself in their choice of representatives. While the Antifederalists believed that representatives would serve as mere mouthpieces of the people, Madison and the other Federalists argued that representatives had the responsibility to exercise independent judgment. They would study all issues in the depth that all voters could if given the time. Since people would choose the best and most intelligent people to represent them, Madison reasoned aloud, the representatives probably would make wise decisions. Furthermore, he contended, since representatives held the same interests as their constituents, they had no reason to abuse their powers since they, too, had to live under the laws they made. Moreover, because representatives depended on the people for their political existence, they could not neglect the people's interests. Abuse of power might cost them re-election. In sum, Madison argued that people possessed *sufficient* virtue to make self-government possible, they retained *enough* checks over representatives, and representatives *probably* would act in the people's interests.

Before becoming president, the issue that most moved Madison to engage in persuasion was the separation of church and state. He deplored the intolerance, oppression, and persecution of the Anglican church toward dissenting religions. In Virginia's Declaration of Rights (1776), a document that served as a model for other states' documents, he wrote the provision stating that "all men are equally entitled to the full and free exercise of religion according to the dictates of Conscience." Madison championed the issue of freedom of conscience as a natural right through the passage of the Statute for Religious Freedom (1786) and the first amendment of the Bill of Rights (1791).

Madison argued that people's natural rights were in jeopardy by potential foreign invasions, not by potentially abusive representatives and other government leaders. In order to achieve security at home, he maintained, it was necessary to achieve dignity abroad. He claimed that the security of the people's natural rights depended on the image that the United States as a nation commanded in the eyes of foreign countries. If the United States was respected by other nations, she and her people would be free from external danger. And, without external danger, no challenges to personal rights would exist. Madison, then, emphasized the importance of a secure and stable government. He contended that a strong government would secure rather than threaten the sovereignty of the states and would protect rather than usurp the liberties of the people.

Madison usually structured his messages deductively, moving from the general to the specific. His mind seemed to function syllogistically. Whether deliberately or not, he followed Aristotle's contention that the two essential parts of a speech are the proposition and the proof of it. He was especially skilled at uncovering the heart of an issue, and at supporting his points and refuting the points of his opponents with an abundance of evidence.

Consistent with his rhetorical training, Madison's speaking style was matter-of-fact. He employed few metaphors and appealed almost exclusively to people's logic rather than to their emotions. His rhetoric was characterized primarily by reasoned arguments and incisive logic. Words, such as "reason," "syllogism," "deduction," "rationality," "proof," and "demonstration," permeated his discourse.

Madison delivered his pre-presidential messages in a calm voice. He spoke only when the topic concerned an issue that he could talk about with authority. Because his voice was weak and unexciting, his delivery did not add to the force of his arguments, but neither did it not detract appreciably.

MADISON'S MAJOR PRESIDENTIAL SPEECHES

Madison presented three major addresses during his presidency.

First Inaugural Address

Madison devoted much of his First Inaugural Address, March 4, 1809, to emphasizing principles he had supported throughout his life. These included his belief in the union as the foundation of the peace and happiness of the states, and the Constitution as "the cement of the Union." Madison also expressed his ongoing interest in respecting and preserving the natural rights of people, especially the "rights of conscience."

In the speech Madison discussed how the "present situation of the world is indeed without a parallel," because the United States wished to maintain peace while other nations were at war. Although he touched on the need for a strong military, he talked more about how the moral responsibilities of the United States would help to avert war:

Indulging no passions which trespass on the rights or the repose of other nations, it has been the true glory of the United States to cultivate peace by observing justice, and to entitle themselves to the respect of the nations at war by fulfilling their neutral obligations with the most scrupulous impartiality. If there be candor in the world, the truth of these assertions will not be questioned; posterity at least will do justice to them.

Good, Madison maintained, triumphs over evil; right is rooted in justice.

Madison's War Message

Madison, a peace-loving man, was reluctant to engage in another war against England. In June 1812, however, after England refused to repeal Orders-in-Council that prohibited American trade with France, Madison declared that war was the only possible remaining course of action to establish and maintain the commercial rights of the United States on the sea. In his Special Message to Congress, June 1, 1812, he requested a declaration of war. Madison was the first president to deliver a war message. Similar to war messages since, his speech presumed that Congress would declare war. Thus, rather than being a deliberative speech persuading Congress of the necessity of choosing to fight, the speech was really an epideictic speech blaming the actions of Great Britain and praising the actions of the United States. The speech was not one of assurance but of *re*assurance.

In the address Madison frequently used antithesis to contrast the wrongful behavior of Great Britain with the legitimate behavior of the United States. He called the British "lawless," "guilty," "inflexible," "unjust," and "illegal," while Americans were "responsible," "conciliatory," "just," "innocent," "virtuous," and "free." Great Britain was already at war while the United States was at peace: "We behold, in fine, on the side of Great Britain, a state of war, against the United States, and on the side of the United States a state of peace toward Great Britain."

Madison especially attacked British motives, speaking about "mock block-ades," "predatory measures," "commercial jealousies," "this flimsy veil," "forgeries and perjuries," "a false pride," "a predetermination," "a spirit of hostility," and "arbitrary edicts." He assigned malicious motives to the British when he said, "To the most insulting pretensions they have added the most lawless proceedings in our very harbors, and have wantonly spilt American blood within the sanctuary of our territorial jurisdiction." These vicious motives were contrasted with the virtuous motives of the United States. To describe the motives of his country, Madison used words with religious connotations, such as "sanctuary," "sacred," and "sacrifices."

Until now, Madison contended, the American government had responded to the crisis with "unexampled forbearance," "conciliatory efforts," and "friendly dispositions." But, declared Madison, "our moderation and conciliation have had no other effect than to encourage perseverance and to enlarge pretensions," so that the United States could no longer "continue passive under these progressive usurpations and these accumulating wrongs." Toward the end of the speech, Madison committed this "just cause into the hands of the Almighty Disposer of Events" and emphasized "a constant readiness to concur in an honorable re-establishment of peace and friendship."

Second Inaugural Address

Madison's Second Inaugural Address, March 4, 1813, was largely a repetition of his War Message. He reiterated that the United States engaged in war only after trying all other measures, to no avail:

It was not declared on the part of the United States until it had been long made on them, in reality though not in name; until arguments and expostulations had been exhausted; until a positive declaration had been received that the wrongs provoking it would not be discontinued; nor until this last appeal could no longer be delayed without breaking down the spirit of the nation, destroying all confidence in itself and in its graceful suffering or regaining by more costly sacrifices and more severe struggles our lost rank and respect among independent powers.

In the speech Madison explained how the war was "unavoidable" and "honorable." As in the War Message, he juxtaposed positive terms to refer to the actions of the United States with negative terms to describe the conduct of Great Britain. He defended the war by indicating that "the success of our arms now may long preserve our country from the necessity of another resort to them."

CHARACTERISTICS OF MADISON'S PRESIDENTIAL ORATORY

The weakness of Madison's delivery definitely and negatively affected his presidential rhetoric. He appeared diffident and bookish, and his voice was often difficult for listeners to hear. In fact, President Madison actually delivered very few speeches; from 1809 to 1812, for example, he presented only one speech— his First Inaugural Address. He preferred, instead, to send his speeches to the members of Congress to read. Historian Irving Brant suggests that Madison's reticence and often inaudible voice contributed to this decision: "Having too frail a voice for large audiences, Madison found it easy to follow Jefferson's example and send his message instead of reading it in person when the time came to address Congress . . . ." Contemporary reactions to the few speeches he did deliver were critical. For example, John Quincy Adams said that Madison's First Inaugural Address was "spoken in a tone of voice so low that scarcely any part of it was heard by three-fourths of the audience." Historian Henry Adams agreed, and further implied that Madison's delivery of the inaugural "suggested a doubt whether the new President wished to be understood."

Another major difficulty with Madison's presidential speeches was their extremely complex style. These speeches contained few personal pronouns, familiar words, or simple sentences. Madison seemed to talk essays, making it no surprise that he is remembered as a writer, not as a speaker. On the Flesch-Kincaid Index, a measure of readability that uses grade levels as its standard, Madison's First Inaugural Address, War Message, and Second Inaugural Address are each considered very difficult to read. The First Inaugural Address rates 25.4, the War Message scores 19.7, and the Second Inaugural Address rates 17.7. A score of 25.4 means that students who score in the fourth month of the 25th grade should be able to understand this speech! According to Robert Gunning's Fog Index, which is another yardstick of reading ease that is also based on grade levels, these speeches score as follows: First Inaugural Address, 29.6; War Message, 23.6; and Second Inaugural Address, 21.5. A mark over 14 crosses the "danger line" for readability. According to this scale, Madison's discourse is understandable only to people between grades 21 and 29!

Extremely long sentences, multiple levels of subordination, and a high level of abstraction contributed to Madison's very complex use of language. The following sentence from his War Message is typical:

When deprived of this flimsy veil for a prohibition of our trade with her enemy by the repeal of his prohibition of our trade with Great Britain, her cabinet, instead of a corresponding repeal or a practical discontinuance of its orders, formally avowed a determination to persist in them against the United States until the markets of her enemy should be laid open to British products, thus asserting an obligation on a neutral power to require one belligerent to encourage by its internal regulations the trade of another belligerent, contradicting her own practice toward all nations, in peace as well as in war, and betraying the insincerity of those professions which inculcated a belief that, having resorted to her orders with regret, she was anxious to find an occasion for putting an end to them.

To understand this paragraph, most readers must reread it. Madison's complex, formal, and impersonal style distanced him from his readers and listeners.

Madison organized his messages in a straightforward but unexciting manner. The body of his First Inaugural Address, for example, consisted of a list of principles that would guide his administration:

To cherish peace and friendly intercourse with all nations having correspondent dispositions; to maintain sincere neutrality toward belligerent nations; to prefer in all cases amicable discussion and reasonable accommodation of differences to a decision of them by an appeal to arms; to exclude foreign intrigues and foreign partialities, so degrading to all countries and so baneful to free ones; to foster a spirit of independence too just to invade the rights of others, too proud to surrender our own, too liberal to indulge unworthy prejudices ourselves and too elevated not to look down upon them in others; to hold the union of the States as the basis of their peace and happiness; to support the Constitution, which is the cement of the Union, as well in its limitations as in its authorities; to respect the rights and authorities reserved to the States and to the people as equally incorporated with and essential to the success of the general system; to avoid the slightest interference with the rights of conscience or the functions of religion, so wisely exempted from civil jurisdiction; to preserve in their full energy the other salutary provisions in behalf of private and personal rights, and of the freedom of the press; to observe economy in public expenditures; to liberate the public resources by an honorable discharge of the public debts; to keep within the requisite limits a standing military force;

always remembering that an armed and trained militia is the firmest bulwark of repub-
lics—that without standing armies their liberty can never be in danger, nor with large
ones safe; to promote by authorized means improvements friendly to agriculture, to
manufactures, and to external as well as internal commerce; to favor in like manner the
advancement of science and the diffusion of information as the best aliment to true
liberty; to carry on the benevolent plans which have been so meritoriously applied to the
conversion of our aboriginal neighbors from the degradation and wretchedness of savage
life to a participation of the improvements of which the human mind and manners are
susceptible in a civilized state—as far as sentiments and intentions such as these can aid
the fulfillment of my duty, they will be a resource which can not fail me.

By not elaborating on any of these principles, Madison did not indicate whether
he foresaw war, an issue debated by historians. His saying only at the end of
this 375-word sentence that these tenets would serve as "resources" to guide
him added to the complexity of the message.

Madison's presidential speeches in general lacked smooth transitions. Even
more obvious was his lack of attention-getting introductions and moving conclusions. For example, Madison began his First Inaugural Address in 1809 with
a direct but boring statement: "Unwilling to depart from examples of the most
revered authority, I avail myself of the occasion now presented to express the
profound impression made on me by the call of my country to the station to
the duties of which I am about to pledge myself by the most solemn of sanc-
tions." He ended his 1812 War Message with a brief discussion of relations
with France. The conclusion seems more like a footnote than a peroration. It
gives no sense of closure. Likewise, Madison concluded his Second Inaugural
Address in 1813 abruptly: "Already have the gallant exploits of our naval heroes
proved to the world our inherent capacity to maintain our rights on one element.
If the reputation of our arms has been thrown under clouds on the other, pre-
saging flashes of heroic enterprise assure us that nothing is wanting to correspondent triumphs there also, but the discipline and habits which are in daily
progress."

The brevity and the lack of uniqueness and excitement in Madison's introductions and conclusions probably relate to his overall preference for logical
rather than emotional appeals. As a group, his presidential speeches failed to
grip audiences or involve them emotionally. Rather than intimate and involving,
his speeches were impersonal and intangible. He used few sensory images, further lessening the speeches' interest. Intellectual or non-sensory images and
abstract concepts dominated, making it difficult for audiences to become emotionally involved.

Madison, then, appealed to his audience's rationality through his delivery,
style, organization, and overall choice of appeals. In addition, he frequently used
words, such as "calm," "neutral," "impartial," and "justice," emphasizing
his respect for reasoning. The following example from his First Inaugural Address is typical:

Indulging *no passions* which trespass on the rights or the repose of other nations, it has been the true glory of the United States to cultivate peace by observing *justice*, and to entitle themselves to the respect of the nations at war by fulfilling their *neutral* obligations with the most scrupulous *impartiality*. If there be *candor* in the world, the truth of these assertions will not be questioned; posterity at least will do *justice* to them. (emphasis added)

In short, Madison treated listeners as reasonable people, capable of making decisions rationally, calmly, and dispassionately. He failed to move his listeners and readers, in part, because of his extreme rationality and calmness.

CONCLUSION

"If Madison's fame as a statesman rested on what he wrote as President," Henry Adams wrote, "he would be thought not only among the weakest of Executives, but also among the dullest of men . . . no statesman suffered more than Madison from the constraints of official dress." Perhaps "the constraints of official dress" deal in part with differences in types of speaking. Perhaps Madison succeeded in controversy but failed in ceremony. Before assuming the presidency, most of Madison's speaking consisted of debates. By definition, debates are deliberative speeches where Madison's ability to advance astute arguments, extensive evidence, and powerful proofs were important. Debates are incomplete speeches, consisting only of a body; an eloquent introduction and conclusion was not expected from Madison and, in fact, would have been deemed inappropriate. Refuting arguments effectively is a major component of success in debates and, indeed, was an important part of Madison's rhetorical success. Organization is a given; Madison needed only to follow the debate's topics. By definition, logical reasoning is prized in debates. Audiences for most of these discussions consisted of a relatively small group of well-educated people, many of whom were influenced, like Madison, by the Age of Reason.

As president, most of Madison's speeches were epideictic or ceremonial in nature. Persuasion was more important than argumentation. The lack of eloquent introductions and passionate conclusions contributed to his failure as a presidential orator. So, too, did his complex style, weak delivery, and inability to arouse, excite, and move the American public, a large audience consisting of people from varying educational and economic backgrounds.

Despite his failure as a presidential persuader, Madison is rhetorically significant. As the first president to give a speech asking Congress to declare war, he set a standard for future presidential speeches justifying war. Subsequent presidents used his speech as a model of the genre of war messages. As one of the first presidents to veto Congressional legislation, he provided a framework for later presidential veto messages. Rhetorical critics Karlyn Kohrs Campbell and Kathleen Hall Jamieson noted the following examples: "The arguments Madison used to justify his veto of an act establishing a national bank on January

30, 1815, reappeared in Andrew Jackson's July 10, 1832, veto of a similar act, and the arguments he used in vetoing congressional legislation providing for internal improvements, on March 3, 1817, were adopted by a number of his successors.'' Madison, then, is rhetorically significant because he provided models for future presidents.

RHETORICAL SOURCES

Archival Materials

Manuscript Division, Library of Congress.
National Archives.
University of Virginia Library, Charlottesville, Virginia.
Virginia State Library, Richmond, Virginia.
Elliot, Jonathan. *The Debates in the Several State Conventions on the Adoption of the Federal Constitution as Recommended by the General Convention at Philadelphia.* 2d ed., Vol. 3. Philadelphia: J. B. Lippincott and Co., 1881.
Hunt, Gaillard, ed. *The Writings of James Madison.* (WJM). New York: G. P. Putnam's Sons, 1900–1910.
Hutchinson, William T., et al., eds. *The Papers of James Madison.* 15 Vols. Chicago and Charlottesville. University of Chicago Press and University Press of Virginia, 1962.
Veit, Helen E., Kenneth R. Bowling, and Charlene Bangs Bickford, eds. *Creating the Bill of Rights: The Documentary Record from the First Federal Congress.* Baltimore, MD: The Johns Hopkins University Press, 1991.

Rhetorical Studies

Brant, Irving. *James Madison: Father of the Constitution, 1787–1800.* New York: Bobbs-Merrill Co., 1950.
Burns, Edward M. *James Madison: Philosopher of the Constitution.* New York: Octagon Books, 1968.
Donovan, Frank R. *Mr. Madison's Constitution: The Story Behind the Constitutional Convention.* New York: Dodd, Mead, 1965.
Ketcham, Ralph L. *James Madison: A Biography.* New York: Macmillan, 1971.
Meyers, Marvin, ed. *The Mind of the Father: Sources of the Political Thought of James Madison.* New York: Bobbs-Merrill Co., Inc., 1973.
Riemer, Neal. *James Madison.* New York: Washington Square Press, 1968.
Smith, Craig R. *To Form a More Perfect Union: The Ratification of the Constitution and the Bill of Rights, 1787–1791.* New York: University Press of America, 1993.

Rhetorical Monographs

Andrews, James R. "They Chose the Sword: Appeals to War in Nineteenth-Century American Public Address." *Today's Speech* 17 (1969): 3–8.
Batty, Paul W. "An Examination and Evaluation of Selected Speeches of James Madison,

Father of the Constitution and Fourth President of the United States." Unpublished M.A. thesis, Northern Illinois University, 1966.

Campbell, Karlyn Kohrs, and Kathleen Hall Jamieson. *Deeds Done in Words: Presidential Rhetoric and the Genres of Governance.* Chicago: University of Chicago Press, 1990.

Einhorn, Lois J. "Basic Assumptions in the Virginia Ratification Debates: Patrick Henry vs. James Madison on the Nature of Man and Reason." *Southern Speech Communication Journal* 46 (1981): 327–40.

———. "A Twist of Principles: Presumption and Burden of Proof in the Virginia Ratification Debates on the Federal Constitution." *Southern States Communication Journal* 55 (1990): 144–61.

———. "The Virginia Ratification Convention: Determining the Political Fate of America." In *The Road to the Bill of Rights: The Constitutional Ratification Debates, 1787–1788,* edited by Craig R. Smith, 111–27. Long Beach, CA: The Freedom of Expression Foundation, 1988. Republished in *To Form a More Perfect Union,* by Craig R. Smith, 97–109. New York: University Press of America, 1993.

Ivie, Robert L. "Presidential Motives for War." *Quarterly Journal of Speech* 60 (1974): 337–45.

———. "The Metaphor of Force in Prowar Discourse: The Case of 1812." *Quarterly Journal of Speech* 68 (1982): 240–53.

———. "Vocabularies of Motive in Selected Presidential Justifications for War." Unpublished Ph.D. dissertation, Washington State University, 1972.

Ketcham, Ralph L. "James Madison: The Unimperial President." *Virginia Quarterly Review* 54 (1978): 116–36.

———. "James Madison and the Presidency." In *Inventing the American Presidency,* edited by T. E. Cronin. Lawrence, KS: University Press of Kansas, 1989.

Moore, Wilbur E. "An Analysis and Criticism of Madison as a Debater in the Virginia Federal Constitutional Convention." Unpublished M.A. thesis, State University of Iowa, 1932.

———. "James Madison the Speaker." *Quarterly Journal of Speech* 31 (1945): 155–62.

Phillips, Lois. "The Nature of Man and the Role of Reason as Reflected in the Rhetoric of Patrick Henry and James Madison in the Virginia Ratification Convention on the Federal Constitution." Unpublished M.A. thesis, The Pennsylvania State University, 1974.

Schaedler, Louis C. "James Madison, Literary Craftsman." *William and Mary Quarterly* (October 1946): 515–33.

Smith, Stephen A. "James Madison, Jr." In *American Orators Before 1900: Critical Studies and Sources,* edited by Bernard K. Duffy and Halford R. Ryan, 278–84. Westport, CT: Greenwood Press, 1987.

Synder, Adelaide Ruth. "A Rhetorical Study of James Madison." Unpublished M.A. thesis, Kent State University, 1950.

Chronology of Significant Presidential Persuasions

First Inaugural Address, Washington, D.C., March 4, 1809. *WJM,* 8: 47–50.
Special Message to Congress, Washington, D.C., June 1, 1812. *WJM,* 8: 192–200.
Second Inaugural Address, Washington, D.C., March 4, 1813. *WJM,* 8: 235–39.

Sean Patrick O'Rourke

John Quincy Adams
(1767–1848)

The great object of the institution of civil government is the improvement of the condition of those who are parties to the social compact.

John Quincy Adams achieved his greatest rhetorical successes before and after his presidency. Prior to serving as the sixth president, he helped to compose the Monroe doctrine, arguably the single most influential rhetorical instrument of American foreign policy in the nation's history. After his presidency he returned to Congress (and occasionally the courtroom) where, during the congressional debates and legal proceedings concerning slavery, he spoke frequently and well. In fact, his presidency may well mark the lowest ebb of his eloquence, certainly if eloquence is measured in part by effectiveness.

Nonetheless, Adams's presidential oratory is well worth studying. His presidency marks the crucial transition from classical republicanism to Jacksonian democracy, and his oratory is therefore important as evidence of a sort of rearguard action, classical eloquence in retreat. Adams may represent the end of a presidential line of statesmen/orators steeped in classical ideals. And, of course, Adams is the only president to have published a theory of rhetoric. But even more, Adams's presidential oratory embraced a theory of government that, despite its dismissal at the time, can now be seen as prophetic, for his vision of the active role of the federal government in the improvement of American society is now a working political assumption.

RHETORICAL TRAINING AND PRACTICES

Even at a time and in a social stratum that valued classical learning highly, Adams was regarded, however justifiably, as an exemplar of the Ciceronian ideal, the *orator perfectus*. As William Seward noted in his "Eulogy," the Ciceronian ideal animated all of Adams's public life, especially his rhetorical theory and oratorical practice. That ideal was ingrained in Adams's early education and deeply influenced his later views on rhetoric and oratory.

Adams's formal education included his early tutelage with his mother, preparation for Harvard under the guidance of his father and his uncle, the Reverend John Shaw, his years at Harvard, a law apprenticeship with Theophilus Parsons, and preparation for the Boylston Professorship. His informal education included his public service (which began at the age of fourteen), travel, and ongoing interaction with most of the leading statesmen and literary figures of the day. George Lipsky noted that Adams's education was "varied and comprehensive" and the "drive for education never ceased." He was a voracious reader, and by the time he became President Adams may well have had the finest classical education in the early republic, an education in which rhetoric and oratory figured prominently.

His reading provided the kind of broad liberal education Cicero recommended for the classical orator. The young Adams read widely in languages both classical and modern. His studies included grammar ("universal" as well as Greek, Latin, French, Russian, and German), music, ethics, logic, mental philosophy, mathematics, geography, history, law, politics, astronomy, theology, pneumatology, and the natural sciences, as well as the poetry, prose, drama, and oratory of several nations. Such reading formed a circle of moral studies, the goal of which was the cultivation of moral excellence or civic virtue. In this scheme rhetoric was central. Civic virtue in the early republic was inextricably bound up with public eloquence, for the stringent republican sense of civic duty demanded a high level of rhetorical competence. Not surprisingly, therefore, Adams complemented his wide reading by studying the precepts and practices of rhetoric.

Adams's diary reveals that his study of the preceptual tradition of rhetoric, as Jeffery Auer and Jerald Banninga have shown, included both ancient and modern writers. He translated Aristotle's *Rhetoric* from the Greek, read Cicero and Quintilian in French and English translations as well as the original Latin, and studied the works on rhetoric by Plato, Isocrates, Longinus, Tacitus, and the anonymous author of the *ad Herennium*. He appears also to have read many modern works on rhetoric, including those in English by Blair, Burke, Campbell, Gibbons, Kames, Lawson, Sheridan, and Walker, as well as those by Arleville, Batteau, Demarsais, Fenelon, Rapin, and Vossius.

Study of the great models of eloquence complemented his study of the preceptual tradition. Among the ancients, Adams read the orations of Demosthenes, Isaeus, Aeschines, Isocrates, Cicero, and those included in Homer, Thucydides, Sallust, and Livy, as well as the biographical and critical accounts of the orators in Suetonius and Plutarch. Modern exemplars included the speeches of Burke, Massillon, D'Aguesseau, Blair, Butler, Sterne, and Tillotson, supplemented by the essays in *The Idler*, *The Tatler*, and *The Spectator*. Throughout his life he remained a keen critic of public discourse, especially the political oratory of America and England.

The daily linguistic and rhetorical exercises that were a part of Adams's early education also shaped his presidential oratory. As a boy he read aloud to his mother nearly every night; in a now famous letter to his father, he reported that he was disappointed with his progress on Rollin's *L'histoire Romaine*—at age eleven. His practice of translating and abstracting the better works he read provided a facility with language and a strong memory for detail. As a student at Harvard he often participated in oral recitations, literary debates, classroom declamations, and, perhaps more often than the average student, occasional orations.

In 1804 Adams was nominated the first Boylston Chair of Rhetoric and Oratory at Harvard. The lectures he delivered between 1806 and 1809 were published in 1810. Far more than the mere restatement of Ciceronian precepts that some hold them to be, the lectures are in fact a careful declaration of the principles and protocol of public utterance in the oratorical culture of early republican society. The lectures provide unusually deep insight into the rhetorical assumptions that informed his presidential oratory.

Adams held that the faculty of speech was "the necessary adjunct and vehicle of reason." To the citizen in a free state, therefore, "eloquence was POWER," for it could "yield the guidance of a nation to the dominion of the voice." He recommended eloquence for both its rewards and its utility. Its rewards included positions of respect and leadership for its practitioners and, much more importantly, its utility was to be found in an improved society. Indeed, Adams wrote, the faculty of speech was "the source of all human improvements," for eloquence was an indispensable instrument of truly free deliberative assemblies. It was in this way "recommended by the most elevated usefulness." In his lectures he urged that, "Persuasion, or the influence of reason and of feeling, is the great if not the only instrument, whose operation can affect the acts of all our corporate bodies; of towns, cities, counties, states, and of the whole confederated empire." It is no surprise then that, as we shall see, Adams the presidential speaker used his oratory to advance his ambitious and far-sighted plan of "internal improvements."

To Adams, the early American republic was particularly well suited to the uses of eloquence. Rhetoric and oratory flourish, he told his students, among people of separate commonwealths, all founded on the principle of liberty, united in great national interests. The American republic was in these ways quite similar to the Greek city-states and the Roman republic, and oratory enjoyed the same conditions of freedom and usefulness. As he stated in the conclusion to his June 12, 1806 inaugural Boylston oration,

Under governments purely republican, where every citizen has a deep interest in the affairs of the nation, and, in some form of public assembly or other, has the means and opportunity of delivering his opinions, and of communicating his sentiments by speech; where government itself has no arms but persuasion; where prejudice has not acquired an uncontroled [sic] ascendency, and faction is yet confined within the barriers of peace; the voice of eloquence will not be heard in vain.

As the above suggests, Adams's belief that robust, unfettered debate was the essence of republican government led to his lifelong devotion to *public* discourse and his corresponding distrust of anything that undermined it. He was especially fearful of the ways in which party factionalism and private caucusing tainted public oratory and decision making by leaving them mere rhetorical facades. He therefore preferred a Ciceronian rhetoric, with its attention to the needs of the public orator, to the popular belletristic rhetoric of Blair and Kames, with its attention to private conversation and literary criticism.

Adams therefore crafted a theory of rhetoric and oratory founded on Ciceronian notions of the contingent realm of public affairs. He placed great emphasis on the intellectual and moral qualities of the speaker, especially the "qualities of the heart, the endowment of the understanding, and the dispositions of the temper." In Adams's view, the speaker in a republican society should be a man of "trust and honor," both willing and able to assume the responsibilities of leadership through persuasive discourse. He should be well educated and thoroughly acquainted with the controversies of his society. His mental agility, aided by a working knowledge of the classical system of topics, should allow him to move swiftly and cogently among the competing issues in a debate. His discourse should balance reason and passion, and his language should be elegant and dignified. And, especially in republican society, the orator must be able to speak against the threats of tyrants and at the same time "control the wayward dispositions of the people."

These precepts of rhetorical theory evidently were important to Adams's own development as an orator, for his contemporaries seemed to agree that he was not a naturally gifted speaker. Summarizing their views, Bennett Clark noted that Adams "possessed none of the graces of the orator," and Horace Rahskopf reported that Adam's "voice was not strong, but shrill and sometimes piercing." His delivery was usually characterized as "animated," "energetic," and "forceful." Nonverbal elements seemed to accentuate these characteristics: Contemporaries spoke of his "kindled eyes and tremulous frame," his "piercing looks," and "bald head kindled with excitement," all of which added to a forceful delivery. His presence was dignified and, later in his career, commanding, but lacked the "honey" and "charm" of those held to be more eloquent. And yet, to a generation that had known Daniel Webster, Henry Clay, John Calhoun, and others, Adams alone was known as "Old Man Eloquent."

The designation is probably the result of four features of his rhetorical practice: painstaking composition, lengthy rehearsal, a fine memory, and a moral force that, late in life, gave him a powerful presence. Justice David Brewer characterized Adams's speeches as standing for a "tradition of painstaking, scholastic finish hardly to be found elsewhere in American orations." Painstaking composition went hand in hand with constant, rigorous rehearsal for, as

Adams himself once said, "the power of unpremeditated speech is neither rare nor valuable." Before having his first annual message delivered to Congress, for example, Adams read drafts to various members of his cabinet on at least four separate occasions, incorporating some suggestions in several revisions. His diary attests to similar care in the preparation of his March 4, 1825 inaugural, the September 7, 1825 "Farewell to Lafayette," and the July 4, 1828 "Address on Breaking Ground for the Chesapeake and Ohio Canal." This process of speech composition, and even his occasional extemporaneous speaking, was greatly aided by what one biographer called his "remarkable memory of events" that "was supplemented by a remarkable diary." After his presidency, especially during his oratorical campaign against the gag rule in the House of Representatives, his delivery attained a strong moral force, which several contemporaries believed better enabled him to command an audience.

In short then, Adams's presidential oratory was informed by his Ciceronian notions of rhetoric and rigorous oratorical practice, notions that in turn assumed a republican society and an audience able and willing to respond in kind. Just how well *and* poorly this served him can be seen by a closer look at his presidential oratory.

ADAMS'S CAMPAIGN SPEAKING

Sympathetic biographers noted that Adams "refused to do anything to promote his own election," that he let his service speak for itself. This is not entirely true. Although he did not campaign in the modern sense, he did put forth his position on crucial questions, quite often in private correspondence with influential friends. Eventually his commitment to public discourse led him to seek a public platform to air his views. His oration in Washington on the Fourth of July, 1821, is surely the most notable. Despite his aversion to Fourth of July celebrations, the questionable propriety of a sitting Secretary of State delivering such an address, and the fact that he was the committee's third choice to speak, Adams accepted the invitation and spent three weeks preparing his address.

Responding to proposals made by the *Edinburgh Review* and Henry Clay, respectively, Adams argued against both an Anglo-American alliance and an inter-American alliance, holding that both policies sacrificed American independence for dubious and doubtful benefits. He urged instead a policy of isolationism and strict anti-colonialism.

The speech is most noteworthy for its vehement tone and stinging anti-British sarcasm, and these features received the bulk of contemporary criticism. The speech was widely condemned in diplomatic circles. The British ambassador was particularly appalled that a sitting member of the cabinet so lacked discretion. Several American statesmen found in the speech evidence of Adams's unfitness to serve in higher office.

Yet many leading American newspapers praised the speech and the immediate audience responded enthusiastically. Nine months after he delivered it, Adams was still responding to critics, evidence that the speech had served at least its campaign purpose of staking out identifiable positions on foreign policy. Despite the fact that, in Adams's own words, he failed to develop his ideas "according to rhetorical rule," he was able to denounce colonialism and advocate American isolationism in a manner that also allowed him to hint at what was to become a dominant theme of his presidency—his desire that the federal government devote its energies to "internal improvements" in the general welfare of the people.

As the election of 1824 drew near, he continued to develop his public commitment to internal improvements and a strong central government. In his June 1824 "Comment on Internal Improvements," a statement once again laced with invective, Adams urged that "the first object of human association is the improvement of the condition of the associated," by which he meant to suggest that the power to make internal improvements was inherent in the very idea of the federal government. States' rights advocates heard these words with some alarm and responded that Adams was usurping the exclusive prerogative of the states.

ADAMS'S INAUGURAL ADDRESS

In the election of 1824 none of the three leading candidates garnered adequate electoral votes for an outright victory, and the election was sent to the House of Representatives. Adams was elected President over Andrew Jackson, the leader in the popular and electoral votes, when Henry Clay threw his support to Adams. When Adams named Clay Secretary of State, charges of fraud and collusion were made by Jackson supporters.

Compared to the invective of the campaign, Adams's Inaugural Address is marked by a conciliatory tone and an attempt to extend the so-called era of good feelings into his own presidency. In part, of course, this can be explained by his desire to put the campaign's animosities, House election, and charges of fraud, which he called the "peculiar circumstances of the recent election," behind him, to smooth over the obvious fact that he was in truth a minority President. The tone can also be explained by Adams's desire to engender support for his ambitious program of internal improvements and his expansive interpretation of the constitutional powers of the federal government to provide such improvements.

Adams attempted to convey a sense of well-being by defining the current situation as one in which the fruits of an earlier generation were being reaped, and nearly "ten years of peace" had "blended into harmony the most discordant elements of public opinion." He also invoked the preceding administration, suggesting that his own could well be seen as a natural continuation of Monroe's.

Adams also knew that his presidency stood on unstable political ground unless and until he could dissolve or reduce the heat of party criticism and unite a majority behind him. He therefore attempted to isolate party rancor as the chief threat to national well-being. He urged those who "followed the standards of political party" to make "one effort of magnanimity, one sacrifice of prejudice and passion" by replacing party loyalty with trust in individual talent and virtue.

Once party rancor was eliminated, Adams suggested, the "whole action of the government" could then be devoted to preserving and extending the "precious inheritance" of the social compact formed by the generation before. That is, the federal government could embark on a policy of internal improvements. To support his plan Adams appealed to the language of the constitution's preamble which, he implied, envisioned broad federal powers to promote the social welfare. He also noted the precedent set by the federal government's building of the first national road and the "unquestioned" authority given the government to complete the project.

In one sense, then, the Inaugural Address can be seen as a sort of preamble to Adams's more detailed presentation of his administration's domestic policies in his first annual message to Congress. From the hindsight of history, however, the conciliatory language and upbeat tone of the Inaugural Address had no lasting effect for, as can be seen in the four annual messages, Adams became increasingly defensive as objections to his policies, both foreign and domestic, mounted.

ADAMS'S ANNUAL MESSAGES

First Annual Message

Adams's first annual message, delivered, in keeping with a tradition begun by Jefferson, by the Clerk of the House of Representatives, Matthew St. Clair Clarke, has been characterized by some as "high minded but naive." The criticism is not entirely unfair. The speech contains a rather glowing view of America's stake in international trade, an optimistic expectation of bankruptcy reform, a strong statement of his administration's commitment to neutrality in international affairs, a cursory review of recent treaties with "the aboriginal natives of this country," and an accurate but nonetheless effusive statement of "the flourishing state of our finances."

But this was preliminary to the real message. Adams spent the key portion of the speech outlining his broad plan of internal improvements and the expansive role he envisioned for the federal government. He held that "moral, political, and intellectual improvements" were duties assigned by God to "social no less than individual man." He suggested a national university, a permanent naval peace establishment, an expanded navy, the surveying of harbors, lighthouses, institutions of geographical and astronomical science (including an observatory), a uniform standard of weights and measures, roads, canals, and an expanded judicial system. And because the "spirit of improvement is abroad upon the earth,'' Adams argued that ''to refrain from exercising'' the powers granted by the people in the constitution to effect such improvements ''would be treachery to the most sacred of trusts.''

Given what we now know of the tide of events and the congressional opposition to such plans, Adams's speech may indeed seem naive. And though he buttressed the proposal with appeals to principle, God, national pride, and his audiences' sense of history, the proposal was simply out of touch with Adams's political reality. It was prophetic *and* doomed.

Second Annual Message

By 1826 Adams's Jacksonian opponents had begun to criticize his administration, especially its handling of the vexing problem of trade with the British colonies in North America. Adams spent a significant portion of his second message detailing his administration's efforts to negotiate an agreement with Great Britain. He implied that blame was to be placed on the British colonial principle of keeping an ''exclusive monopoly to herself.'' The defensive tone suggests that he was more than a little stung by the criticisms and found them unwarranted given the efforts his administration had made to secure a trade agreement.

The defensive tone crept into other subjects as well. For example, Adams explained, somewhat defensively, minor problems with the Army and, toward the end of the address, touched on the sensitive issue of unadjusted land titles in the Florida and Louisiana territories. More than anything else, his defensive tone was the common thread among his last three annual messages.

Third Annual Message

Despite the numerous steps taken pursuant to Adams's doctrine of internal improvements, very little of the brief third annual message was devoted to reporting them. The speech is colored by the defense of Adams's handling of the ongoing trade negotiations with the British. Because very little real progress had been made and the British continued to exclude vessels of the United States from her colonial ports, Adams could only detail the lengths to which his administration had gone to open those ports to American shipping and speculate on the reasons behind the British determination to keep them closed.

As a result, even the somewhat better news concerning internal improvements was overshadowed. Surveys had been conducted, roads had been extended, and harbor obstructions had been removed. But all these points seemed merely tagged on to the generally disappointing news of the trade with British colonies.

Fourth Annual Message

The tone of Adams's final annual message was perfunctory. He declared and dispatched topics quickly, often shading them with judgments of whether such news was to be expected, as with the revenue, or not, as with the "profits of agriculture" in the middle and western regions. The speech lacked the depth and enthusiasm of his first annual message and foreshadowed the end of his administration.

The speech was also marred by the lack of Adams's customarily strong sense of order. The criticism of his trade policies had by this time reached a peak. Adams's defensiveness, especially toward the haunting problem of British colonial trade, was evident throughout, for he raised the issue at three separate and largely disconnected points. Such uncharacteristic inattentiveness to the details of organization, coupled with the exasperated and almost plaintive tone throughout, made the speech decidedly forgettable.

ADAMS'S OCCASIONAL ADDRESSES

Over the course of his presidency Adams made several short speeches at ceremonial occasions. These may well be the best speeches of his presidency. Some argue that his temperament was given to strong judgments of praise and blame, the classical themes of epideictic, and ample evidence supports this view. Yet he knew from his study of classical rhetoric that, in his praise or reproach of a person or event, the demonstrative orator could align his own policies and ideals with those to be praised via amplification.

In his "Address to the Boston Schools," delivered August 23, 1826, for example, Adams took the opportunity to exalt the "moral and intellectual cultivation" of the "hundreds and thousands of the rising generation" in the course of praising the "blooming youth of Boston." Few present would have missed the obvious connection to his internal improvements doctrine. An even more extensive example is Adams's "Address on the Breaking of Ground for the Chesapeake and Ohio Canal," delivered outside Washington in 1828, very near the end of his term in office. The *Niles Register* reported that he approached his speech with "an animation of manner and countenance, which showed his whole heart was in the thing." Adams seized the opportunity to make the canal an example of "the adaptation of the powers, physical, moral, and intellectual, of this whole union, to the improvement of its own condition." In heightened language he invoked the "spirit of internal improvement" that was "catholic and liberal" and must be "extended to every individual." The attendant members of the cabinet, Congress, and military, as well as representatives of the municipal governments of the District of Columbia, responded, we are told, with great enthusiasm.

A nobility of language, as he would have called it, was a characteristic of his ceremonial addresses. In his highly regarded "Farewell to Lafayette," the new President spoke with great dignity of Lafayette's place in American culture and bade him a final farewell on behalf of a grateful nation. And in the "Canal" speech, he uncharacteristically conveyed deep personal emotion when he declared that, "I deem the duty [of breaking ground for the canal] one of the most fortunate incidents of my life." In moments such as these, Adams's speaking, shorn of invective and open rather than defensive, approached the level it was to attain far more frequently in later years.

CONCLUSION

In general, however, by the end of his term in office, Adams was an orator without an audience, a leader without his followers. His presidential oratory had grown increasingly defensive, and his stylized utterances failed to cajole a nation overwhelmingly ready for change. And yet, as his Chesapeake Address reveals, even in the end he remained true to his vision of a federal government with expansive powers for social improvement. Indeed, even as it failed to save his administration from the forces of Jacksonian democracy, Adams's Ciceronian rhetoric set forth a vision of American government that, nearly two hundred years later, has been fully realized. If the presidency of John Quincy Adams has a rhetorical legacy, internal improvements is it.

RHETORICAL SOURCES

Archival and Other Primary Materials

Adams, John Quincy. *The Diary of John Quincy Adams*. 2 Vols. Edited by David Grayson Allen, et al. Cambridge, MA: Belknap Press, 1981.

———. *Lectures on Rhetoric and Oratory*. 2 Vols. Cambridge, MA: Hilliard and Metcalf, 1810.

Adams Family Papers. Microfilm. Boston, MA: Massachusetts Historical Society.

A Compilation of the Messages and Papers of the Presidents, 1789–1902. (CMP). Edited by James D. Richardson. Vol. 2. New York: Bureau of National Literature and Art, 1904.

Rhetorical Studies

Parsons, Lynn H. *John Quincy Adams: A Bibliography*. Bibliographies of the Presidents of the United States 6. Westport, CT: Greenwood Press, 1993.

Rhetorical Monographs

Auer, J. Jeffery, and Jerald L. Banninga. "The Genesis of John Quincy Adams' Lectures on Rhetoric and Oratory." *Quarterly Journal of Speech* 49 (1963): 119–32.

Banninga, Jerald L. "John Quincy Adams: A Critic in the Golden Age of American Oratory." Ph.D. dissertation, Indiana University, 1963.

———."John Quincy Adams' Address of July 4, 1821." *Quarterly Journal of Speech* 53 (1967): 44–49.

———."John Quincy Adams' Doctrine of Internal Improvement." *Central States Speech Journal* 20 (1969): 286–93.

Bemis, Samuel Flagg. *John Quincy Adams and the Foundations of American Foreign Policy.* New York: Knopf, 1949.

———. *John Quincy Adams and the Union.* New York: Knopf, 1956.

Brewer, David J., ed. "John Quincy Adams." *The World's Best Orations.* Vol. 2, 57–58. Chicago: Ferd. P. Kaiser, 1923.

Clark, Bennett Champ. *John Quincy Adams: Old Man Eloquent.* Boston: Little, Brown, 1932.

Goodfellow, Donald M. "The First Boylston Professor of Rhetoric and Oratory." *New England Quarterly* 19 (1946): 372–89.

Hargreaves, Mary W. M. *The Presidency of John Quincy Adams.* Lawrence, KS: University Press of Kansas, 1985.

Hecht, Marie B. *John Quincy Adams.* New York: Macmillan, 1972.

Lipsky, George A. *John Quincy Adams: His Theory and Ideas.* New York: Thomas Y. Crowell, 1950.

Moran, Michael G. "John Quincy Adams (1767–1848), Sixth President of the United States." *American Orators before 1900: Critical Studies and Sources,* edited by Bernard K. Duffy and Halford R. Ryan, 7–13. Westport, CT: Greenwood Press, 1987.

Rahskopf, Horace G. "John Quincy Adams: Speaker and Rhetorician." *Quarterly Journal of Speech* 32 (1946): 435–41.

———. "John Quincy Adams' Theory and Practice of Public Speaking." *Archives of Speech* 1 (1936): 7–98.

Rousseau, Lousene G. "The Rhetorical Principles of Cicero and Adams." *Quarterly Journal of Public Speaking* 2 (1916): 397–410.

Seward, William H. "Eulogy." *The Life and Public Services of John Quincy Adams, Sixth President of the United States,* 357–404. Auburn, NY: Derby, Miller, and Co., 1849.

Chronology of Significant Presidential Persuasions

An Address, Delivered at the Request of a Committee of the Citizens of Washington; on the Occasion of Reading the Declaration of Independence, on the Fourth of July, 1821. Washington, DC: Davis and Force, 1821.

"Comment on Subject of Internal Improvements," c. June 1824. *Niles Register* 26 (1824): 251.

Inaugural Address, Washington D.C., March 4, 1825. *CMP,* 294–99.

"Farewell to Lafayette," Washington, D.C., September 7, 1825. *Niles' Register* 29 (1825): 41–42.

First Annual Message to Congress, Washington, D.C., December 6, 1825. *CMP,* 299–317.

"Address upon the Visitation of the Boston Public Schools," August 23, 1826. *Niles Register* 31 (1826): 18–19.

Second Annual Message to Congress, Washington, D.C., December 5, 1826. *CMP,* 350–64.

Third Annual Message to Congress, Washington, D.C., December 4, 1827. *CMP,* 378–92.

"Address on Breaking Ground for the Chesapeake and Ohio Canal," July 4, 1828. *Niles' Register* 34 (1828): 326–27.

Fourth Annual Message to Congress, Washington, D.C., December 2, 1828. *CMP,* 407–21.

Thomas M. Lessl

Andrew Jackson
(1767–1845)

Our Federal Union, it must be preserved.

Andrew Jackson the orator cannot possibly compete in our historical recollection with the hatchet-faced military hero who rode out of the frontier of western Tennessee to become this nation's seventh President. His speeches are eclipsed by other more pronounced and more colorful features of his presidency, the fiery political battles and the equally incendiary personality that made them possible. Jackson's persona dominates not only our recollection of his own life, but the life of his administration as well. It gives an identity to the entire period during which he and his appointed successors dominated the nation's political stage.

It would not be wise to lose sight of Jackson's character as we turn to look at his oratorical accomplishments. If we are to understand these messages as they were received in the two decades of Jackson's political dominance, we cannot fail to remember the giant figure that loomed over them. Jackson was, after all, the one who in the words of Herman Melville the "democratic God didst pick up . . . from the pebbles; who didst hurl him upon a warhorse; who didst thunder him higher than a throne!''

Jackson lived during the period of American history that is best known for its oratory, the generation that produced such cultivated speakers as John C. Calhoun, Henry Clay, and Daniel Webster. But Jackson's significance as a rhetorical figure is of a different order. Jackson did not own the sort of eloquence that arises from a classical education, nor did he practice a brand of politics that relies upon disputative powers to carry forth its policies. Jackson's greatness came from his ability to project his *ethos* into his speeches. The messages that survive from his political career enable us to glimpse this *ethos*, not in the various legends and anecdotes that float across the pages of history books, but in the living words of this popular and powerful president. We also are enabled to peer into the period that has become so closely identified with Jackson's personality, the adolescent years of the American Republic.

Jackson was also the first American president who owned a strong regional identification. His predecessors, of course, represented the political interests of the eastern and northern United States, but Jackson's identification with the South, where he was born, and the West, where he made his reputation, transcended politics. We might say, to employ a somewhat fanciful personification, that the East is the mind of America, the South its soul, and the West its spirit. Jackson, who was born in the South, who went West as a pioneer, and settled in the East as the nation's seventh President, united in his person the entire American identity. Thus he was, in a sense quite different from what the appellation means when applied to George Washington, the first American President.

RHETORICAL TRAINING AND PRACTICES

The few scattered details that are known of Jackson's early life show us a child who was precocious both in temperament and experience. Born in the Waxhaw settlement of South Carolina, Jackson came of age at the outset of the War for American Independence. As would be true much later in his life, the struggles of war reveal Jackson's remarkable courage and determination. A prisoner of war when he was only thirteen years old, Jackson refused to bow to the demand of a British officer that he clean his captor's boots. Jackson received a sabre blow for this defiance and consequently, through continued ill-treatment, was nearly lost to the world. This incident, which underlines the remarkable fearlessness that Jackson exhibited throughout his life, is also indicative of the willfulness for which his enemies so often vilified him.

Jackson's quite limited education would not have proceeded at all had his mother not recognized his gifts and determined to provide him with a tutor. Her ambition was for her son to occupy a pulpit, but from a very early age Jackson showed a greater proclivity for politics. Although not exceedingly learned, Jackson always exhibited strong rhetorical instincts. Despite being only nine years old, it was Jackson who was asked to give a public reading of the Declaration of Independence when a copy first reached his frontier town. Similarly, when the War for Independence was not going well, he took it upon himself, merely a boy of eleven, to compose and deliver before his South Carolinian classmates a rousing proclamation urging them to persevere in the bitter struggle.

After the war Jackson managed enough learning to gain admission to the bar and subsequently accepted an appointment as public prosecutor in western Tennessee, then a frontier of North Carolina. Jackson quickly connected himself with the political establishment of this developing region, and in 1796 he represented the new state of Tennessee both as a delegate to its constitutional convention and as one of the state's first representatives in the U.S. Congress. Two short stints as U.S. senator would follow latter, but altogether Jackson spent less than three years in federal politics before being elected president. His most enduring political post during this period of his life was a six-year term as a judge of the state superior court.

Jackson was in many respects a rustic. He was also an ambitious man whose iron determination could not be turned back once a course had been set for it. This last trait made him many enemies, and in fact Jackson was twice wounded in duels. But even his antagonists came to admire him. Thomas Hart Benton, whose brother was responsible for one of two bullets that Jackson still carried in his body when he came to Washington, became one of his staunchest allies. Daniel Webster experienced a similar conversion, although not a political one. Like many other representatives of the eastern political establishment, Webster feared the rise of this rough-hewn and unknown westerner, but he came to admire Jackson, whom he found to be "grave, mild and reserved," even "presidential."

This was, of course, a more developed speaker than the Senator from Tennessee that Thomas Jefferson encountered in 1797–1798. Jefferson observed an inexperienced political orator who exhibited a notable inability to restrain his passions. Perhaps it was this lack of emotional discipline that caused Jefferson to block the Tennessean's bid for a governorship in the newly acquired Louisiana Territory and later to question Jackson's viability as a presidential candidate. But as Jackson matured, and as his military reputation grew, these same attributes became the hallmarks of his greatness.

Despite his meager rhetorical training, Jackson's development as a political figure coincided with the maturation of his oratorical abilities. The younger Jackson appears to have been carried away by his own emotions, shaking a long forefinger as he spoke and, in moments of great excitement, spraying his startled listeners with saliva as he declaimed in a North Irish accent inherited from the immigrant settlement where he grew up. But observers of the elder Jackson describe a speaker whose self-control only increased as his anger mounted, enabling him to articulate cool political reprisals.

Jackson clearly had not gained much of this self-control by 1807, when he was called to Richmond as a witness in the trial of Aaron Burr, but he was able to impress many with the prodigious intensity of his speaking. As one sympathetic to Burr's plans for Westward expansion, Jackson believed that the former Vice President's prosecution was motivated by the Jefferson administration's need to draw attention away from its own weak response to mounting British aggression. Jackson did not hesitate to allege this in an hour-long speech he made from the steps of the state house, nor did he hesitate to aim his rhetorical darts at some rather powerful political personalities of the day. The venomous nature of this speech left some wondering whether Jackson would soon be fighting another of his duels. Others were merely impressed by the demonstration of Jackson's spirit.

From this extemporaneous speech given in June of 1807, only a few fragments reconstructed by listeners survive. One of these listeners was the newspaperman Thomas Ritchie, who saw in the oration unambiguous evidence of Jackson's prospects as a national leader. Ritchie also left behind his impressions of the general's oratory: "He spared none. His style of speaking was rude but strong. It was not the polished oratory Eastern audiences were accustomed to hear." This mode of public discourse is recognizable as an instance of what the ancients called the forceful style:

Mr. Jefferson has plenty of courage to seize peaceable Americans by military force and persecute them for political purposes. But he is too cowardly to resent foreign outrage upon the Republic. Here an English man-of war fires upon an American ship of inferior force, so near his Capital that he can almost hear the guns, and what does he do? Nothing more than . . . recommend to Congress a bill laying an embargo and shutting our commerce off from the seas. If a man kicks you downstairs you get revenge by standing out in the middle of the street and making faces at him! (1806)

The colloquial images that stand out in this attack on Jefferson would endure throughout his political career, but only as private utterances overheard in the press. Presidential decorum required that a more dignified style of speech go forth from the White House. Jackson developed a more formal style of oratory during his military career, through the composition of many addresses to his troops. But even as he became more refined than his frontier reputation might suggest, there remained in his presidential discourses some fire, some undercurrent of those same strong emotions that charged his earlier and less formal orations.

JACKSON'S NULLIFICATION PROCLAMATION

This is most evident in his proclamation on nullification given on December 10, 1832, a message that is arguably the most important of his first term of office. Disgruntlement over federal tariffs, already smoldering in South Carolina, was doused in the inflammatory doctrine of nullification and ignited by the oratory of Robert Hayne and John Calhoun. By the late fall of 1832, the conflagration threatened to spread into several states. Jackson himself had maintained a general silence on nullification, wishing not to alienate the Southern states that had given him strong political backing, but he was also a solid "Union man," who saw nullification as the death knell of the republic.

Jackson responded in two ways. He swore to use military intervention in South Carolina if the state continued to defy federal law, but he also prepared a statement designed, at least in part, to mollify his Southern constituents. Jackson had a reputation for meaning what he said, and thus the certainty of his threats enabled him to adopt a more conciliatory tone in the message that followed. Jackson did not back away from his conviction that nullification was an unconstitutional doctrine, "having for its object the destruction of the Union. . . . '' But he went to great lengths to lay out his reasons for this judgment and to adopt a paternal tone designed to quell sectional hostilities.

Like most of his political actions, the nullification message exudes the toughness for which Jackson was given the appellation "Old Hickory." But at certain moments in the proclamation we see a gentler side to Jackson's personality capable of adopting a paternal tone. "Fellow citizens of my native state!" Jackson pleaded, "let me not only admonish you as the first magistrate of our common country, not to incur the penalty of its laws, but to use the influence that a father would over his children whom he saw rushing to certain ruin." As we look at this passage, it is important to remember how thoroughly enraged Jackson was at the time that he and his Secretary of State, Edward Livingston, wrote the proclamation. Jackson had threatened to hang John Calhoun and any other nullificationists who would disobey the law, but the text of the speech shows an evident shrewdness that surmounted these passionate tendencies.

The proclamation was intended, in Jackson's own words, to "strike to the heart, and speak to the feelings" of his "deluded countrymen of South Carolina." In addressing himself thus to the people of South Carolina, rather than to the specific leaders who were directly responsible for the crisis, Jackson was effecting a political technique that has subsequently become commonplace. Jackson in fact employed this tactic quite often during his presidency, but in this instance it was likely calculated to drive a wedge between the people of South Carolina and John Calhoun. Jackson did this by constructing this issue as a conflict between "Every man of plain, unsophisticated understanding who hears the question," and the person of "Metaphysical subtlety, in pursuit of an impracticable theory," who sounds unmistakably like Calhoun himself. Jackson made it seem obvious that the plain understanding of the people of South Carolina "will give such an answer as will preserve the Union," while the philosophical subtlety of a Calhoun was "calculated to destroy it."

JACKSON'S BANK VETO

This pattern of bypassing more specific audiences for the sake of appealing directly to the general electorate is also evident in the messages produced by Jackson during his war against the Bank of the United States. Although Jackson had some popular support for his adamant opposition to the Bank, his iron determination to destroy the institution was not widely shared, even within his own cabinet. As this prolonged political chess game unfolded, Jackson's enemies were confident that he would fail. Webster and Clay in fact contrived to force Jackson's hand by bringing the Bank up for recharter fours years early. They did this in the hope that the economic suffering caused by a veto would undermine Jackson's popularity and thereby enhance Clay's chances of victory in the election of 1832.

At the time of his veto, July 10, 1832, Jackson's intention to destroy the Bank of the United States, was already evident. "Unless the corrupting monster should be shraven (sic) of its ill gotten power," Jackson told his trusted friend John Coffee, "my veto will meet it frankly & fearlessly." The only question that remained for his enemies was whether or not the old General could carry out his threats. When ultimately confronted with the bill to recharter the Bank, Jackson stood firm, responding with a veto message that may be one of the most important in American history.

It was his purpose in this address to solidify his position and, in keeping with his rhetorical style, to demonstrate to the larger American public the republican spirit of his decision. Still the historical importance of the message goes beyond its immediate effect of bringing the Bank of the United States to an end. It also articulates an expanded understanding of the veto power of the President. Rather than offering just constitutional justifications for denying the Bank its recharter, biographer Robert Remini notes that Jackson employed "political, social, economic and nationalistic" reasons for wanting to send the monster hydra to its grave. In each of the previous nine exercises of the presidential veto, Chief Executives had employed constitutional arguments exclusively. Jackson, however, worked with a significantly broader conception of presidential powers, a view of the executive office that very soon earned him the appellation "King Andrew the First."

This veto message resulted from a three-day marathon of writing and revision that was undertaken by Jackson in collaboration with various members of his cabinet. The message was formulated first by Jackson's trusted advisor, Amos Kendall, and then chiefly revised by Roger Taney, who would later be Jackson's appointee to the Supreme Court. The result of this endeavor was a forceful speech articulating an image of government free from laws that "undertake to add to these natural and just advantages artificial distinctions, to grant titles, gratuities and exclusive privileges, to make the rich richer, and the potent more powerful." Jackson's frequent use of words such as "privilege" "monopoly," and "special favor" reflect his view of the Bank conflict as a war between those who defended the founding principles of the American republic and a privileged few who sought to use its freedoms to enhance their own wealth.

Those partisan to the Old Hero saw it as a second Declaration of Independence. Jackson's political enemies regarded the message as an effort to incite class warfare. Worse yet, for these opponents, Jackson's treatment of the Bank's constitutionality indicated an expansion of the power assigned to the presidency. While he acknowledged that the Bank's constitutionality had been affirmed in *McCulloch v. Maryland*, Jackson diminished the importance of this decision by contending that some power to interpret the Constitution must be reserved for the legislative and executive branches of the government. By thus checking the power of the Supreme Court in this speech, Jackson tacitly expanded the power of his own office.

The message's peroration is a powerful summarization of Jackson's understanding of government as the protector of the people. In Jackson's view a just government would be strong in its preservation of equality under the law but weak in obtrusiveness lest it should violate the "rights and powers of the several States." Government cannot abolish "distinctions in society." "Equality of talents, of education, or of wealth can not be produced by human institutions." The responsibility of a government is to provide equal "protection by law." And since those who are less advantaged "have neither the time nor the means of securing like favors to themselves," it becomes the responsibility of the government to fight their battles. Jackson demonstrates here the Jeffersonian belief that in "attempting to make our general government strong we make it weak."

Its true strength consists in leaving individuals and States as much as possible to themselves—in making itself felt, not in its power, but in its beneficence; not in its control, but in its protection; not in binding the States more closely to the center, but leaving each to move unobstructed in its proper orbit.

As "heaven does its rain," a just government will "shower its favors alike on the high and low, the rich and the poor; it would be an unqualified blessing."

These statements are representative of the pattern of reasoning that governed much of Jackson's political judgment. Like other Southerners, Jackson was a strong advocate of state's rights, but he also believed that the power of the presidency could be extended if it was done to check abuses of governmental power lying outside the executive branch.

In the case of the Bank veto as elsewhere, this expansion of presidential powers aroused great passions in Congress. Webster declared that no one ever before brought forth such doctrines. No other president would have been tolerated in such a fashion. Webster was right, of course, but then again there had never been a president as popular as Andrew Jackson, nor one so readily inclined to see himself as an instrument of the public will.

Jackson's victory in his war against the Bank reflects his astute understanding of public sentiments and his willingness to use a variety of communication forms to prepare public opinion for his policies. Jackson did not presume that he could sustain popular support for his war against the Bank merely with one speech. To consolidate popular support in the aftermath of the veto and in preparation for the removal of the Bank's deposits, Jackson made sure that his views were broadcast through a number of partisan newspapers, most notably *The Washington Globe*. Jackson also undertook a tour of the New England states during the summer of 1832, despite his desperately poor health, in a deliberate effort to consolidate popular support in those states most friendly to the Bank.

JACKSON'S INAUGURAL ADDRESSES

Jackson's rhetorical legacy is also reflected in his two inaugural addresses. His First Inaugural Address, given in Washington, D.C., on March 4, 1829, lacked the visionary words and the militant vitality his followers had hoped to hear. The weakness of the speech reflected Jackson's poor heath and the grief brought on by the recent loss of his wife Rachel. Jackson was observed holding his inaugural text in quivering hands as he delivered a message that was barely audible.

But despite these disappointments, the speech also exhibited a conservative flavor that eased the fears of those most fearful of Jackson's promises of political reform. Parts of the speech have been attributed to John Calhoun, because of their strong states' rights theme, but the existence of a complete rough draft of the message written in Jackson's own hand indicates the Old Hero's close involvement with the writing of the speech. Despite his meager education, the rhetorical competence demonstrated in this text is considerable. The version of the speech that he ultimately presented was produced in collaboration with several of Jackson's advisors and was much less forceful than the draft penned by Jackson himself.

Jackson's Second Inaugural Address, delivered on March 4, 1833, was more generally popular than the First. Much like the first inaugural, the speech that Jackson actually read at the Inauguration ceremony was a version that had been toned down by a committee of his advisors. Jackson's handwritten draft, produced shortly after the nullification battle and Bank veto, delivers a rather wrathful expression of his nationalistic zeal. "If, in madness or delusion," Jackson wrote, "any one shall lift his paracidal (sic) hand against this blessed union . . . the arms of tens of thousands will be raised to save it, and the curse of millions will fall upon the head which may have plotted its destruction." While hardly appropriate for a Presidential Inauguration, this does demonstrate the mood in which this great President approached his second term. This draft went on to reiterate Jackson's strong commitment to the Union and to offer a remarkably personal meaning to the oath he was about to take. "I feel in the depths of my soul, that it is the highest, most sacred and most irreversible part of my obligation, to preserve the union of these states, although it may cost me my life." Jackson's feeling that he could make such a daring personal disclosure as this, reflects his firm conviction that he was bound up, heart and soul, with the will of the people. His astonishing popularity only confirmed this.

The theme of Jackson's Second Inaugural Address is the perpetuation of the Union, and it is a speech filled with forebodings of the schism that was to occur a few decades later. Jackson strove to redress the tensions threatening to lead to succession by insisting that the perpetuation of state's rights could only be assured under the protection of a strong union. Succession would only turn the states once again into the vassals of more powerful European nations.

In closing Jackson sought for a way to transcend the divisiveness of the nullification affair and Bank war by appealing to the electorate's sense of history.

The eyes of all nations are fixed on our Republic. The event of the existing crisis will be decisive in the opinion of mankind of the practicability of our federal system of government. Great is the stake placed in our hands; great is the responsibility which must rest upon the people of the United States. Let us realize the importance of the attitude in which we stand before the world. Let us exercise forbearance and firmness. Let us extricate our country from the dangers which surround it and learn wisdom from the lessons they inculcate.

In this passage Jackson expressed a profound sense of the historical responsibility that weighed upon the American Republic. This he felt was a responsibility that he was personally called upon to bear as one destined by Providence to act as the voice of the American people.

JACKSON'S FAREWELL ADDRESS

Jackson's Farewell Address of March 4, 1837, was like Washington's in three respects: it was ghostwritten by one of his chief advisors (Taney wrote Jackson's and Hamilton wrote Washington's), was never orally delivered, and, most importantly, it offered stern warnings about the future. Despite being composed by Chief Justice Roger Taney, there is little doubt of the message's fidelity to Jackson's beliefs. Quite explicitly it is an effort to view the future of the nation through Jacksonian eyes.

Jackson's message begins by reviewing the accomplishments of his own administration against the backdrop of the nation's first fifty years of constitutional government. But while celebrating the fact that the Constitution was "no longer a doubtful experiment," Jackson also followed the example of Washington in using this occasion to forewarn his people of dangers that lay ahead for the adolescent republic. This was no longer the danger of foreign entanglement but of internal corruption arising from the devices of sectionalism and monopolistic greed. These evils are obviously the same concerns against which Jackson fought in the nullification episode and Bank war, but they are treated in this final address as symptoms of what threatened to become a terminal illness for the republic.

Jackson was in earnest about the possibility of a divided Union. "If the Union is once severed," he prophesied, "the line of separation will grow wider and wider, and the controversies which are now debated and settled in the halls of legislation will then be tried in fields of battle and determined by the sword." The message also goes to considerable lengths to warn against the danger of the government passing "from the hands of the many to the hands of the few." In addressing this concern, Jackson reiterated his conviction that it is only the virtue of the people expressed in "a lofty spirit of patriotism," which can sustain a just government. "To you everyone placed in authority is ultimately responsible. It is always in your power to see that the wishes of the people are carried into faithful execution, and their will, when once made known, must sooner or later be obeyed.''

More than once in this speech, Jackson referred to himself as one of ''advanced age and failing health,'' who must soon ''pass beyond the reach of human events and cease to feel the vicissitudes of human affairs.'' One gains a strong sense, especially from the speech's peroration, of Jackson's belief that he was the anointed instrument of America's historical mission. This is evidenced in Jackson's emulation of St. Paul's identity in his closing words: ''My own race is nearly run. . . . I thank God that my life has been spent in a land of liberty and that He has given me a heart to love my country with the affection of a son. And filled with gratitude for your constant and unwavering kindness, I bid you a last and affectionate farewell.''

CONCLUSION

Andrew Jackson was as popular in life as Abraham Lincoln would become in death. The fact that the popularity of this nineteenth-century President has subsequently been overshadowed by the fame of Jefferson, Washington, and Lincoln may reflect the changing needs of American political culture. Jackson personified courage, toughness, and ardent nationalism at a time when these qualities of the American identity were most in doubt. It is notable in this regard that the chief cause of Jackson's fame was his victory at New Orleans. Jackson marched a rough band of frontiersmen armed mostly with hunting rifles against some of the best trained soldiers that Europe could put in the field of battle— veterans, many of them, of Waterloo. He did this at a time when the United States was suffering the insecurities of its adolescence, when it was being bullied by an elder European brother and needed a strong adult figure to assure it of its place in the family of nations.

Jackson clearly recognized the extent to which the electorate identified with him, and he never hesitated to draw on the rhetorical power of this bond. This enabled him to appeal directly to the American people and thereby to pressure an often obstinate Congress into compliance. The Jacksonian *ethos* thus showed itself more powerful than the rhetorical artistry of such eloquent opponents as Webster, Clay, and John Quincy Adams. Jackson brought to his public discourses a presence that countless observers have mentioned. Despite a frailty borne from chronic illnesses caused largely by a pair of bullets that Jackson carried in his body, observers consistently mention the remarkable strength exuded by the old warrior. One contemporary described him as ''the iron man of his age—the incarnation of American courage.''

To a notable extent Jackson presaged the hero of Western romance, a genre that was beginning to take shape during his lifetime. Jackson was in reality a genteel rustic. In the earliest biographies, written as much for their propaganda value as for historical purposes, Jackson was depicted as one who respected urban conventions of civility but never entirely identified with them. He is instead identified with the frontier, a near kinsman to its untamed inhabitants but also fiercely loyal to his country's most civilized ideals.

Jackson's rhetoric was energized by this persona, making him the first truly charismatic President that the nation had known. Intense popular feeling for Jackson was always matched by the zealous hatred of his detractors. Jackson, in fact, still evokes such polarized emotions. But even those who hated him were not immune to his rhetorical spell. During the summer of 1832 Jackson made an impromptu speech at the site where George Washington had taken command of his army sixty years earlier. Jackson spoke of the necessity for perseverance in defense of American liberties. John Quincy Adams, the aged professor of rhetoric who had once denounced Jackson as a "barbarian who could not write a sentence of grammar and hardly could spell his own name," watched from a distance and was moved to tears by the eloquence of the Hero of New Orleans.

RHETORICAL SOURCES

Archival Materials

There are two primary collections of Jackson manuscripts, one consisting of roughly 22,500 items, mostly correspondence, that is housed in the Library of Congress, and another in the care of the Tennessee Historical Society in Nashville consisting of over 10,000 pieces. Jackson's chief biographer, Robert Remini, has begun to collect these materials along with various other smaller collections in a series of volumes and also in a microfilm edition. Many drafts of Jackson's speeches, both in his own hand and in those of various of his advisors, can be found in the microfilm edition.

A Compilation of the Messages and Papers of the Presidents. (*CMPP*). Edited by James
    D. Richardson. Vols. 2 & 3. Washington, DC: U.S. Congress, 1899.
The Statesmanship of Andrew Jackson as Told in his Writings and Speeches. (*SAJ*).
    Edited by Francis Newton Thorpe. New York: Tandy-Thomas Co., 1909.

Rhetorical Studies

Meyers, Marvin. *The Jacksonian Persuasion: Politics and Belief.* Stanford, CA: Stanford
    University Press, 1957.
Remini, Robert V. *Andrew Jackson and the Course of American Democracy.* 3 Vols.
    New York: Harper and Row Publishers, 1978, 1981, 1984.
Ward, John William. *Andrew Jackson: Symbol for an Age.* New York: Oxford University
    Press, 1955.

Rhetorical Monographs

Lessl, Thomas M. "Andrew Jackson." In *American Orators Before 1900: Critical Studies and Sources*, edited by Bernard K. Duffy and Halford R. Ryan. Westport, CT: Greenwood Press, 1987.

Sullivan, John. *Politics and Personality: The Development of the Counter-Image of Andrew Jackson*. Unpublished Ph.D. dissertation, Indiana University, December, 1969.

Chronology of Significant Presidential Persuasions

First Inaugural Address, Washington, D.C., March 4, 1829. *CMPP*, II: 436–38; *SAJ*, 31–34.

Message on Indian Affairs, Washington, D.C., February 22, 1831. *SAJ*, 125–32.

"Bank of the United States Veto," Washington, D.C., July 10, 1832. *CMPP*, II: 576–91; *SAJ*, 154–76.

"Proclamation Against the Doctrine of Nullification," Washington, D.C., December 10, 1832. *CMPP*, II: 640–56; *SAJ*, 232–56.

Second Inaugural Address, Washington, D.C., March 4, 1833. *CMPP*, III: 3–5; *SAJ*, 257–60.

Farewell Address, Washington, D.C., March 4, 1837. *CMPP*, III: 292–308; *SAJ*, 493–515.

Lois J. Einhorn

Abraham Lincoln
(1809–1865)

The mystic chords of memory stretching from every battle-field and patriot grave to every living heart and hearthstone all over this broad land, will yet swell the chorus of the Union, when again touched, as surely they will be, by the better angels of our nature.

Ask Americans what presidents were concomitantly skilled speakers, and almost certainly they will name Abraham Lincoln and submit as proof Lincoln's appeals to the "better angels of our nature." Indeed, Lincoln's three most famous presidential addresses, the First Inaugural Address, March 4, 1861; the Gettysburg Address, November 19, 1863; and the Second Inaugural Address, March 4, 1865, are among the best presidential orations ever delivered.

Lincoln was born in Hodgenville, Kentucky, on February 12, 1809. He spent his youth as a poor boy in raucous, rustic, rural regions of Kentucky, Indiana, and later Illinois. He disliked the fierceness of frontier life that provided "absolutely nothing to excite ambition for education." When he "came of age," he claimed he "did not know much. Still somehow, I could read, write, and cipher to the Rule of Three." These skills were almost completely self-taught since he had little formal education. He once explained that as a boy he "went to A.B.C. schools by littles," a little here and a little there; the littles totaled less than a year. Lincoln is a consummate example of a self-educated man. He learned by observing, listening, discussing, and reading. As a boy he did not read many books, but he absorbed those he read. These included the *King James Bible, Aesop's Fables*, Mason Weem's *Life of Washington*, John Bunyan's *Pilgrim's Progress*, Daniel DeFoe's *Robinson Crusoe*, the *Revised Statutes of Indiana* that contained copies of the Declaration of Independence and the

Constitution, the plays of Shakespeare, and the humorous writings of Artemus Ward, Petroleum Nasby, and Orpheus Kerr.

Disliking farming, Lincoln tried several occupations including working as a rail-splitter, flatboatman, store clerk, store owner, ferry pilot, surveyor, postmaster, and blacksmith. He served as a volunteer and captain of his unit in the Black Hawk War of 1832.

Further educating himself, especially in law, logic, grammar, and mathematics, Lincoln decided to become a lawyer and legislator. He passed the bar examination in 1836 and then began to practice law. After initially being defeated as a candidate for the Illinois General Assembly, he was later repeatedly reelected, representing the Whig Party from 1834 to 1842. He served a single term, 1847–1849, as member of the U.S. House of Representatives, again affiliated with the Whig Party.

PRE-PRESIDENTIAL RHETORICAL PRACTICES

The place was Illinois, the time 1858, the players Lincoln and Stephen Douglas, the issue whether to permit slaveholding in new territories of the country, the situation the campaign for Douglas's seat in the U.S. Senate. Lincoln and Douglas held seven debates, each three hours long, in different cities in Illinois. These debates, and some significant speeches before, during, and after the direct verbal battles, helped launch Lincoln into the national spotlight. Historian Roy Basler noted, "It would be difficult to find in all history a precise instance in which rhetoric played a more important role than it did in Lincoln's speeches of 1858."

Lincoln declared that slavery was inherently a moral and social evil, and his rhetorical opposition to Douglas often focused on whether slavery was inherently wrong. In his last debate with Douglas, October 15, 1858, in Alton, Illinois, he charged, "The real issue in this controversy . . . is the sentiment on the part of one class that looks upon the institution of slavery *as a wrong*, and of another class that *does not* look upon it as a wrong." To Douglas's claims of not caring whether slavery "is voted up or down," Lincoln responded, "No man can logically say he don't care whether a wrong is voted up or voted down. He may say he don't care whether an indifferent thing is voted up or voted down, but he must logically have a choice between a right thing and a wrong thing."

Lincoln argued unceasingly that slavery was wrong because it defiled the nature of democracy, but he tried only to halt its spread—not to abolish it. In his pre-presidential rhetoric, he fought to protect slavery in the fifteen states where it then legally existed because to interfere with slavery here, he claimed, would be morally and legally wrong. He argued that Douglas's doctrine of popular sovereignty, a position allowing people in each state and territory to determine for themselves whether to permit slavery, would perpetuate slavery, whereas his proposal to prevent the spread of slavery into new territories would lead to the institution's ultimate extinction. Note the word "permanently" in the famous declaration of his "House Divided" speech of June 16, 1858, in Springfield, Illinois: " 'A house divided against itself cannot stand.' I believe this government cannot endure permanently half slave and half free."

Lincoln's Cooper Union Address, February 27, 1860, in New York City, represented the culmination of ideas he had expressed in his "House Divided" speech and his series of formal debates with Douglas. Among other points, Lincoln here reiterated that his ideas represented a moderate position, between the extremes of secession and abolition. He criticized Southerners and Democrats, respectively, for considering themselves conservative, claiming Republicans were the true conservatives:

But you say you are conservative—eminently conservative—while we are revolutionary, destructive, or something of the sort. What is conservatism? Is it not adherence to the old and tried, against the new and untried? We stick to, contend for, the identical old policy on the point in controversy [slavery] which was adopted by our fathers who framed the Government under which we live; while you with one accord reject, and scout, and spit upon that policy.... Not one of all your various plans can show a precedent or an advocate in the century within which our Government originated. Consider, then, whether your claim of conservatism for yourselves, and your charge of destructiveness against us, are based on the most clear and stable foundations.

Lincoln defined conservatism as adhering to policies that had historical precedent, especially to the beliefs of the Founding Fathers and the ideals of the Declaration of Independence. Much of his pre-presidential discourse concerned how his views on slavery were consistent with those of the Founding Fathers and with the ideals of the principal documents of the Fathers, the Declaration of Independence, and the Constitution.

Although Lincoln carefully prepared each word of his "House Divided" speech and his Cooper Union Address, much of his pre-presidential speaking was delivered extemporaneously. In the Lincoln-Douglas debates and in many speeches, the give-and-take of oral discourse was apparent with Lincoln responding immediately to audience feedback. Before becoming president, Lincoln usually gave long speeches. For example, the number of words contained in representative pre-presidential speeches are as follows: Lyceum Address, January 27, 1838, Springfield, Illinois, 3,584 words; Temperance Address, February 22, 1842, Springfield, Illinois, 3,912 words; "House Divided" speech, 3,177 words; and Cooper Union Address, 7,656 words.

RHETORICAL TRAINING AND PRACTICES

Lincoln believed that education was a lifelong process, and for him communication constituted an important part of education. As a boy he chose to read books specifically dealing with details of language, including William

Scott's *Lessons on Elocution*, Samuel Kirkham's *Grammar*, Thomas Dilworth's *Spelling Book* and *New Guide to the English Tongue*, and Noah Webster's *Spelling Book* and *The Kentucky Preceptor*. As a young man he read Blackstone's Commentaries, Chitty's Pleadings, and Euclid's six books on logic.

Throughout his life Lincoln purposefully experimented with words—how they work and how to adapt them to different kinds of audiences, subjects, and settings. He consciously experimented with various styles. As a boy he frequently heard itinerant preachers and went into the woods afterward to put what he had heard into his own words. Eager to practice speaking, he did so before neighborhood boys and even before cornfields and pumpkins. Later, he spoke on stumps and platforms, in store mills, and polling places, and at socials and barn raisings—wherever he could gain experience.

Lincoln experimented not only with using different styles but also with expressing points precisely. He frequently tried to phrase ideas in several different ways until he thought he had stated them as clearly as possible. Francis Carpenter, an artist who lived for six months at the White House, recorded Lincoln explaining how his childhood experiences related to his penchant for clarity:

I can remember going to my little bedroom, after hearing the neighbors talk of an evening with my father . . . and trying to make out what was the exact meaning of some of their, to me, dark sayings. I could not sleep . . . when I got on such a hunt after an idea, until I had repeated it over and over; until I had put it in language plain enough, as I thought, for any boy I knew to comprehend. This was a kind of passion with me, and it has stuck by me; for I am never easy now, when I am handling a thought, till I have bounded it north and bounded it south, and bounded it east and bounded it west.

William Herndon, Lincoln's law partner, also wrote of Lincoln's passion for finding the right word: "In the search for words Mr. Lincoln was often at a loss. He was often perplexed to give proper expression to his ideas . . . because there were, in the vast store of words, so few that contained the exact coloring, power, and shape of his ideas."

LINCOLN'S PRESIDENTIAL RHETORIC: A "YES, BUT" ANALYSIS

Historians and rhetoricians consistently have commended Lincoln's style for being clear, simple, brief, and unadorned. To a degree this is true, for Lincoln usually did speak in straightforward sentences consisting primarily of short, simple words. And for his time he usually was brief. In an age of long-winded orators, he tended to say what he had to say and stop when he was through. His use of stories and illustrations helped him to be epigrammatic. But his concern with being precise led to his conciseness more than his desire to be clear, simple, and unadorned. His penchant for precision had more to do with his style than any premise about style per se. His style was not derived from an aesthetic predilection; rather, his goal of precision frequently generated the qualities of style for which he has been commended.

Although Lincoln generally desired to be precise, sometimes he chose ambiguous words rather than concrete ones for practical reasons. Expressing his moderate positions sometimes required him to choose language that left maneuvering room for final, more specific choices. Moreover, exactness could divide or alienate audiences, whereas purposeful ambiguity often could help unite people around a general viewpoint. In her discussion of Lincoln's First Inaugural Address, rhetorical critic Marie Hochmuth gave the following explanation:

That Lincoln sought to control the behavior of his audience and the reader through the appropriately affective word is apparent throughout his address. There are times when even the level of specificity and concreteness, usually thought to be virtues of style, is altered in favor of the more general word or allusion. For instance, Lincoln had originally planned to say, "why may not South Carolina, a year or two hence, arbitrarily, secede from a new confederacy . . . ?" Finally, however, he avoided being specific, altering his remarks to read "why may not any portion of a new confederacy, a year or two hence, arbitrarily secede again?"

Most of Lincoln's Second Inaugural Address consisted of general, inclusive words that applied both to Northerners and Southerners. Lincoln's judicious use of ambiguity made his address precise but not completely clear.

Lincoln's style was also not always simple. For special effects and to make his thoughts more impressive, he sometimes reached beyond the elemental. "Fourscore and seven" was certainly not a simple way to say eighty-seven. The phrase encouraged some intellection and recognition of the spiritual undertone. Logically, even people deeply immersed in Biblical lore would need to calculate twenty times four, then add seven, and then subtract eighty-seven from 1863 to realize Lincoln was referring to 1776, the year of the Declaration of Independence. It is not likely that many listeners did this sort of calculation. More likely, listeners simply affirmed the dignity and importance of the Founding Fathers' actions. As this and like moments show, it is incorrect to generalize that Lincoln sought simplicity of expression at all times. Frequently, especially as chief executive, he sought to arouse special attitudes by recourse to terms and phrases that were not in common use but whose tone would not be missed.

Neither is it safe to accept without qualification the notion that Lincoln spoke briefly. Especially during his presidential years, he delivered short speeches, but before assuming the presidency, he often spoke for long periods of time. For example, his Peoria, Illinois Address, delivered October 16, 1854, was estimated to have taken over four hours. Lincoln also did not always express thoughts economically even in brief speeches. For instance, the following theological explanation for the Civil War from the Second Inaugural Address is neither brief nor simple:

If we shall suppose that American slavery is one of these offenses, which in the providence of God must needs come, but which having continued through His appointed time
He now wills to remove, and that He gives to both North and South this terrible war as
the woe due to those by whom the offense came, shall we discern therein any departure
from those Divine attributes which the believers in a living God always ascribe to Him?

Finally, Lincoln's speeches were not plain and unadorned but used various
figures of speech to bring abstract and complex ideas into the immediate ken of
varying audiences. His figures of speech were piquant, pungent, pithy, primitive,
and picturesque. Generally they were broad, sweeping, timeless, and inclusive
rather than narrow, folksy, or specific to particular situations or audiences. His
use of various forms of figuration infused his speeches with life, added vivacity
to his ideas, and helped him to state his points precisely. For example, on May
19, 1862, about his plan for emancipation with compensation, Lincoln explained
in his Proclamation Revoking General Hunter's Order of Military Emancipation,
"The change it contemplates would come gently as the dews of heaven, not
rending or wrecking anything."

With precision as a major goal, it was natural that Lincoln repeatedly refo-
cused, rephrased, and revised ideas and wordings. He especially prized writing
and meticulous planning of formal addresses. Throughout his life, he wrote
down memorable passages, relied on writing to express important ideas, prepared speeches carefully, and edited his speeches until the moment of delivery.

Unlike most presidents before and after him, Lincoln wrote his own speeches.
He did not employ ghostwriters. However, occasionally he asked colleagues and
friends for suggestions, which sometimes he accepted, ignored, or edited. Perhaps the most famous instance of ideas and words originating from someone
else occurred in Lincoln's First Inaugural Address. He initially planned to close
the speech as follows:

In *your* hands my dissatisfied fellow countrymen, and not in *mine*, is the momentous
issue of civil war. The government will not assail *you*, unless you *first* assail *it*. You
can have no conflict, without being yourselves the aggressors. *You* have no oath registered in Heaven to destroy the government, while *I* shall have the most solemn one to
"preserve, protect, and defend" it. *You* can forbear the *assault* upon it; *I* can *not* shrink
from the *defense* of it. With *you*, and not with *me*, is the solemn question of "Shall it
be peace, or a sword?"

William Seward, soon to be Lincoln's Secretary of State, advised Lincoln not
to conclude with a question because he might get the wrong answer. Suggesting
that Lincoln end on a more conciliatory note, Seward penned these words:

I close. We are not we must not be aliens or enemies but fellow countrymen and brethren.
Although passion has strained our bonds of affection too hardly they must not, I am sure
they will not be broken. The mystic chords which proceeding from so many battle fields
and so many patriot graves pass through all the hearts and all the hearths in this broad

continent of ours will yet again harmonize in their ancient music when breathed upon by the guardian angel of the nation.

Lincoln edited Seward's words and combined them with his original conclusion to produce his famous peroration:

In you hands, my dissatisfied fellow-countrymen, and not in mine, is the momentous issue of civil war. The Government will not assail you. You can have no conflict without being yourselves the aggressors. You have no oath registered in Heaven to destroy the Government, while I shall have the most solemn one to "preserve, protect, and defend" it. I am loth [sic] to close. We are not enemies, but friends. We must not be enemies. Though passion may have strained, it must not break our bonds of affection. The mystic chords of memory stretching from every battle-field and patriot grave to every living heart and hearthstone all over this broad land, will yet swell the chorus of the Union, when again touched, as surely they will be, by the better angels of our nature.

Lincoln's routine recasting and reshaping of ideas resulted in rhetoric characterized by logical argument, detailed documentation, and factual accuracy. Soundness of reasoning functioned for him as the *summum bonum* of intellectual pursuits. As Herndon explained:

He lived and acted from the standard of reason—that throne of logic, home of principle— the realm of Deity in man. . . . He reasoned from well-chosen principles with such clearness, force, and directness that the tallest intellects in the land bowed to him. He was the strongest man I ever saw, looking at him from the elevated standpoint of reason and logic. He came down from that height with irresistible and crashing force.

Contemporary reports of reactions to Lincoln's speeches supported Herndon's conclusions. Newspaper reporters and other ear-witnesses consistently described his speaking using terms such as "lucid logic," "accurate analysis," "thorough treatment," "convincing claims," and "unrefutable reasoning."

In delivering his speeches, Lincoln generally adopted an unassuming style. He spoke slowly, enunciated words clearly, and spoke in a deliberate, emphatic manner. His voice was high-pitched, clear, and powerful.

PRESIDENT LINCOLN'S RHETORIC: EVOLUTION OF HIS STYLE

When Lincoln assumed the presidency, his speaking changed in significant and noticeable ways. Before, he sought out opportunities to speak; as president he seemed keenly aware of the responsibilities and risks involved in the act of speaking and, hence, became a reluctant speaker. As president, he seemed to think the premium was not only on being understood, but on not being misunderstood. Most of his presidential rhetoric consisted of brief utterances, often discussing why it was inappropriate for him to speak. Below, for example, is a speech given in Frederick, Maryland, on October 4, 1862, printed in its entirety:

In my present position it is hardly proper for me to make speeches. Every word is so closely noted that it will not do to make trivial ones, and I cannot be expected to be prepared to make a matured one just now. If I were as I have been most of my life, I might perhaps, talk amusingly to you for half an hour, and it wouldn't hurt anybody; but as it is, I can only return my sincere thanks for the compliment paid our cause and our common country.

Lincoln's speaking also changed in other ways. Before becoming president, his speeches were generally spontaneous, long, and deliberative or forensic in nature. They often appealed to partisan concerns. Stylistically they were casual, colloquial, anecdotal, and full of sensory images. His pre-presidential speeches contained a generous amount of humor, including ridicule, and he generally presented these speeches extemporaneously. After becoming president, Lincoln's speeches were generally serious, short, and epideictic in nature. They appealed to national and universal concerns. The style was formal and employed primarily intellectual images. As president, Lincoln used ridicule and other types of humor sparingly in public speeches. He memorized most of his presidential speeches or read them from manuscript.

Three other qualities of Lincoln's speaking increased over time, especially when he assumed the presidency: his impersonal stance, his reliance on the Bible, and his use of stylistic devices usually associated with literature. Emotional detachment characterized his speeches in general, but the extent of this quality increased significantly when he became president. As president he sometimes projected a sense of isolation from himself, speaking as if he were talking aloud to himself, revealing his innermost thoughts. He often referred to himself in the third person. For instance, in his First Inaugural Address he referred to himself as "him who now addresses you," the "Chief-Magistrate," the "Executive," one of the government's "public servants," and the "Administration." He sometimes divorced himself from his message to such an extent that the resulting rhetoric sounded peculiar. For example, in one speech he called himself "my father's child." Throughout the Second Inaugural Address, Lincoln seemed deliberately to withdraw himself from the action, perhaps as a way to avoid culpability. In addition to referring to himself in the third person, he chose the passive voice and converted several verbs into nouns (e.g., appear/appearing, state/statement, declare/declaration, predict/prediction), another way of suggesting passivity. He used a first person singular pronoun only twice in the entire speech ("I," and "myself"). He went so far to avoid the active voice and personal constructions that his thoughts sometimes sounded awkward. Try, for example, to listen to the following:

"At this second appearing to take the oath of the Presidential office. . . . "

"Now at the expiration of four years . . . little that is new could be presented."

"With high hope for the future, no prediction in regard to it is ventured."

Rhetorical theorist Richard Weaver succinctly summarized Lincoln's practice of self-effacement: "It was as if he projected a view in which history was the duration, the world the stage, and himself a transitory actor upon it. Of all his utterances the Second Inaugural is in this way the most objective and remote, its tone even seems that of an actor about to quit the stage."

The Bible furnished frequent expressions for Lincoln's speeches throughout his public life, but his reliance on the Bible increased during his presidential years, contributing still further toward projecting a cosmic, detached perspective. The theme, language, tone, and rhythm of the Gettysburg Address echoed the Bible, and his Second Inaugural Address often has been called Lincoln's Sermon on the Mount. In discussing this speech, biographer Lord Charnwood wrote, "Probably no other speech of a modern statesman uses so unreservedly the language of intense religious feeling."

As the war progressed, Lincoln often referred to the New Testament. The Second Inaugural Address, for example, relied heavily on the Bible in general and the New Testament in particular, perhaps because the ideas of "laying aside malice" and being charitable are central themes of the New Testament. Although the concepts of malice and charity are present in the Old Testament, the words themselves appear only in the New Testament.

Lincoln's heavy reliance on the Bible was consistent with his increased use of stylistic devices generally associated with literature, such as grammatical parallelism, balancing ideas by putting them linguistically in a series; antithesis, contrasting ideas by directly opposing them linguistically; alliteration, repeating the initial sound of two or more words; and assonance, repeating the same vowel sound in two or more words. Throughout his public life, he made frequent use of these figures of speech, but he used them more extensively during his presidential years. These stylistic devices are especially prominent in the peroration of his First Inaugural Address and in his Gettysburg Address and Second Inaugural Address. Historian Roy Basler contended, "Repetition, grammatical parallelism, and antithesis may be considered the most obvious technical devices of Lincoln's general style. He uses these devices with such frequency and variety of effect that it seems to have been a consistent habit of his mind to seek repetitive sequences in both diction and sentence structure for the alignment of his thought." These observations are especially true of Lincoln's presidential speaking. He often combined parallelism and antithesis, creating in his speeches an overall tension between unity and division. The Gettysburg Address, for instance, was full of parallel and antithetical structures. Lincoln stressed that deeds were more important than words when he contrasted saying and doing: "The world will very little note nor long remember what we say here; but it can never forget what they did here."

Lincoln's parallel constructions sometimes took the form of tricolons, series of three harmonious parts, sometimes increasing in power. Two tricolons in the Gettysburg Address were "we cannot dedicate, we cannot consecrate, we cannot hallow, this ground" and "government of the people, by the people, for the people.'' Lincoln was fond of threes, especially in his presidential speeches. The clause ''of the people, by the people, for the people,'' for instance, contained three parallel phrases, each consisting of three words with ''people'' repeated three times. This phrase also used epistrophe, repeating the same word at the end of several consecutive phrases or sentences.

The Gettysburg Address also included anaphora, a linguistic form combining repetition and parallelism at the beginning of successive thoughts: ''that from these honored dead we take increased devotion to that cause for which they *here* gave the last full measure of devotion; that we here highly resolve that these dead shall not have died in vain; that the nation shall, under God, have a new birth of freedom, and that government of the people, by the people, for the people, shall not perish from the earth.''

Sometimes Lincoln's parallelism was subtle. For example, frequent use of parallel structure in the Second Inaugural Address indirectly argued that both North and South possessed parallel problems, fostering the impression that neither side was responsible for the war. His famous peroration to this speech contained three parallel clauses, each with six syllables: ''With malice toward none, with charity for all, with firmness in the right.'' Anaphora set the tone for a policy of reconstruction that would treat the North and South in a parallel fashion.

Alliteration and assonance appeared frequently in Lincoln's speeches, especially in his presidential ones. Usually they occurred as doublets (sets of two words) such as the following phrases from his Second Inaugural Address: ''point and phase,'' ''insurgent agents,'' ''high hope,'' and ''peculiar and powerful.'' He sometimes combined alliteration and assonance as when he said, ''Woe unto the world,'' and he sometimes combined alliteration and parallelism as when he said, ''Fondly do we hope, fervently do we pray.''

FROM AN ORATORICAL TO A LITERARY STYLE

Most scholars and lay people consider Lincoln's Gettysburg Address, Second Inaugural Address, and the peroration of the First Inaugural Address as among the best examples of oratorical excellence in recorded history. Significantly, most books and articles that discuss these *speeches* use words normally associated with *literature*, such as ''literary,'' ''prose,'' ''poetry,'' and ''writer.'' Carl Sandburg called the Gettysburg Address the ''Great American Poem.'' Some authors used literary terms in the titles of their books on Lincoln's *speaking*: Jacques Barzun, *Lincoln the Literary Genius*, and Herbert Joseph Edwards and John Erskine Hankins, *Lincoln the Writer: The Development of His Literary Style*. These writers seemed to sense that Lincoln composed his most famous speeches more on literary than oratorical principles.

Several factors may help to explain the evolution of Lincoln's style from oratorical to literary. First, these famous speeches used the structures and rhetorical techniques generally associated with literature: repetition, parallelism, antithesis, alliteration, tricolon, anaphora, and assonance. The pervasiveness of religious language and imagery, the intricate use of symbolism, the multiple levels of meaning, and the compelling rhythms helped to forge the subtle yet poignant messages of these famous speeches. By transcending immediate, particular, urgent situations, Lincoln addressed all people everywhere. He spoke with humanity, with "the better angels of our nature."

THE EFFECT OF LINCOLN'S FAMOUS SPEECHES:
A MAJOR PARADOX

The study of Lincoln's speaking reveals a major paradox: The addresses deemed his finest by later generations were not considered great speeches by immediate audiences. For example, most rhetorical and historical scholars today consider Lincoln's Gettysburg Address one of the greatest speeches in American history. Yet, most people who heard the address reacted to it with criticism or indifference. Press reaction to the speech varied greatly. Ronald F. Reid's examination of the responses of 260 newspapers revealed that a few praised Lincoln's remarks, several were critical, and still others made no comment. The political views of the newspaper editors were consistent with their evaluations of Lincoln's speech. In 1863, the Gettysburg Address was not considered a great speech by most people. Thus, we are faced with a speech, which is hailed today as one of the greatest, but which most people did not consider great when delivered.

Similarly, Lincoln's First Inaugural Address was received with mixed reactions. Although a generalization with some notable exceptions, most Northerners interpreted the speech as conciliatory and most Southerners as a declaration of war. The day after the speech, the *Albany Evening Journal* wrote, "No Message was ever received with greater favor. It is universally conceded to be alike clear, compact, and impressive—equally firm and conciliatory." On the same day the *Richmond Times Dispatch* reported, "The Inaugural Address of Abraham Lincoln inaugurates civil war, as we predicted it would. . . . The sword is drawn and the scabbard thrown away." These two quotations typify the varying reactions to Lincoln's first message as president.

Several factors may help to explain the mixed reactions to Lincoln's most famous addresses. First, Lincoln's balanced sentence structures did not have the building up qualities of his narratives. His metaphors, analogies, and fables, used primarily in pre-presidential speeches, usually took the form of rhetorical narratives or stories with a beginning, middle, and ending. Lincoln's balanced structures did not have this building up step. Thus, listeners did not have time to orient themselves to particular ideas. Moreover, the words and phrases in the Gettysburg Address and other literary speeches resonated and reverberated through multiple levels. Listeners did not have the time to contemplate complex meanings and savor subtle nuances.

The later, much admired excerpts of speeches were embedded in or preceded by pedestrian passages or events. Later generations read the peroration of Lincoln's First Inaugural Address without reading the entire speech and without having Northern or Southern biases. Similarly, scores read the Gettysburg Address without reading the long oration by Edward Everett that preceded it and without mourning a loved one.

Immediate hearers were also affected by the increased emotional detachment conveyed in Lincoln's rhetoric. To leisurely, reflective readers not engaged in the particular rhetorical situations, Lincoln's cosmic perspectives could seem impressive. His tendency to read a speech, which weakened his delivery, further distanced him from immediate audiences, but presented no problems for subsequent readers. Moreover, his habit of appearing hesitant and nervous during the first few minutes of a speech, until he warmed up, also helps explain why most listeners were not impressed by his delivery of the less than three-minute Gettysburg Address or his brief Second Inaugural Address.

Lincoln's Gettysburg Address, Second Inaugural Address, and peroration of the First Inaugural Address do not grip listeners instantly, but rather, render impressively certain ideas and attitudes. The deliberative elements of these speeches were not sharp, and the actions called for were not precise or immediately moving. Later readers were exonerated from *doing* anything and, hence, could contemplate and admire these addresses as epideictic texts.

Perhaps in his two inaugural addresses and in his Gettysburg Address, Lincoln chose to speak to posterity. Joshua F. Speed, one of Lincoln's few close friends and confidants, related a conversation in which Lincoln recalled a time in his life when he was deeply depressed because "he had 'done nothing to make any human being remember that he had lived,' and that to connect his name with the events transpiring in his day and generation, and so impress himself upon them as to link his name with something that would redound to the interest of his fellow man, was what he desired to live for."

CONCLUSION

Lincoln was an effective orator. His speaking brought him national prominence. Speeches, such as his Lyceum Address, considered "highly sophomoric" today, were greatly successful in their day. But Lincoln's most famous speeches today, his Gettysburg Address, Second Inaugural Address, and peroration of his First Inaugural Address, were not considered great by most people when he delivered them because these speeches were composed on literary more than on oratorical criteria. When delivered, the reactions to his pre-presidential speeches were generally more favorable than to his presidential orations. For example, the Lyceum Address was more effective than the Gettysburg Address as a speech to an immediate audience. As addresses to posterity and as records of the transcendent meanings of historic moments, Lincoln's famed presidential addresses continue to persevere as powerful, penetrating, poignant documents—a remarkable rhetorical achievement—but one not to be confused with discourse having qualities of immediacy and seizing the convictions and emotions of particular audiences in their unique rhetorical situations. Perhaps Lincoln found the best combination: successful speeches early in life that rocketed him to national power and more literary speeches later in life through which he speaks to the ages. As Basler wrote, "His prose may yet be recognized as his most permanent legacy to humanity."

RHETORICAL SOURCES

Archival Materials

Abraham Lincoln Association Papers (Lincoln reference file), Illinois State Historical Library.

Abraham Lincoln Papers, Library of Congress.

John G. Nicolay Papers, Library of Congress.

Louis A. Warren Lincoln Library and Museum, Fort Wayne, Indiana.

Papers of Lincoln's Cabinet Members, Lincoln National Life Foundation.

William Henry Seward Papers, University of Rochester.

Basler, Roy P., ed. *Abraham Lincoln: His Speeches and Writings*. Cleveland, OH: World Publishing Company, 1946.

———, Marion D. Pratt, and Lloyd A. Dunlap, eds. *The Collected Works of Abraham Lincoln*. (*CW*). 9 Vols. New Brunswick, NJ: Rutgers University Press, 1953.

Rhetorical Studies

Auer, J. Jeffery, ed. *Antislavery and Disunion, 1858–1861: Studies in the Rhetoric of Compromise and Conflict*. New York: Harper and Row, 1963.

Barton, William E. *Lincoln at Gettysburg: What He Intended to Say; What He Said; What He Was Reported to Have Said; What He Wished He Had Said*. Indianapolis, IN: Bobbs-Merrill, 1930.

Barzun, Jacques. *Lincoln the Literary Genius*. Evanston, IL: Evanston Publishing Company, 1960.

———. *On Writing, Editing, and Publishing*. 2d ed. 65–81. Chicago: University of Chicago Press, 1986.

Basler, Roy P., ed. *The Collected Works of Abraham Lincoln Supplement 1832–1865*. Westport, CT: Greenwood Press, 1974.

———, and Lloyd C. Dunlap, eds. *Long Remembered: Facsimiles of the Five Versions of the Gettysburg Address in the Handwriting of Abraham Lincoln*. Washington, DC: The Library of Congress, 1963.

Blegen, Theodore C. *Lincoln's Imagery: A Study in Word Power*. La Crosse, WI: Sumac Press, 1954.

Boritt, Gabor S. *The Historian's Lincoln: Pseudohistory, Psychohistory, and History*. Urbana, IL: University of Illinois Press, 1988.

Braden, Waldo W. *Abraham Lincoln, Public Speaker*. Baton Rouge, LA: Louisiana State University Press, 1988.

————. *Memorializing Abraham Lincoln: A Rhetorical Dimension*. Urbana, IL: University of Illinois Press, 1992.

Campbell, Karlyn Kohrs, and Kathleen Hall Jamieson. *Deeds Done in Words: Presidential Rhetoric and the Genres of Governance*. Chicago: University of Chicago Press, 1990.

DeAlvarez, Leo Paul S., ed. *Abraham Lincoln, The Gettysburg Address, and American Constitutionalism*. Irving, TX: University of Dallas, 1976.

Denton, Robert E., Jr. *The Symbolic Dimensions of the American Presidency: Description and Analysis*. Prospect Heights, IL: Waveland Press, 1982.

Dunlap, Leslie W., comp. "Materials on Display in the University of Illinois Library, February, 1959." In *The Enduring Lincoln*, edited by Norman A. Graebner, 95–121. Urbana IL: The Board of Trustees of the University of Illinois, 1959.

Edwards, Herbert Joseph, and John Erskine Hankins. *Lincoln, the Writer: The Development of His Literary Style*. Orono, ME: University of Maine, 1962.

Einhorn, Lois J. *Abraham Lincoln the Orator: Penetrating the Lincoln Legend*. Westport, CT: Greenwood Press, 1992.

Fehrenbacher, Don E. *Lincoln in Text and Context: Collected Essays*. Stanford, CA: Stanford University Press, 1987.

Index to the Abraham Lincoln Papers, Manuscript Division, Library of Congress. Washington, DC: U.S. Government Printing Office, 1960.

Nevins, Allan. *Lincoln and the Gettysburg Address: Commemorative Papers*. Urbana, IL: University of Illinois Press, 1964.

Sandburg, Carl. *Abraham Lincoln: The War Years*. 4 Vols. New York: Harcourt, Brace and World, 1939.

Stewart, Judd. *Lincoln's First Inaugural: Original Draft and Its Final Form*. Privately printed, 1920.

Thomas, Benjamin P. *Abraham Lincoln: A Biography*. New York: Alfred A. Knopf, 1952.

Tulis, Jeffrey K. *The Rhetorical Presidency*. Princeton, NJ: Princeton University Press, 1987.

Warren, Louis A. *Lincoln's Gettysburg Declaration: "A New Birth of Freedom."* Fort Wayne, IN: Lincoln National Life Foundation, 1964.

————. *Abraham Lincoln's Gettysburg Address: An Evaluation*. Columbus, OH: Charles E. Merrill, 1968.

Weaver, Richard. *The Ethics of Rhetoric*. Chicago, IL: Henry Regnery Company, 1953.

Wiley, Earl W. *Abraham Lincoln: Portrait of a Speaker*. New York: Vantage Press, 1970.

Wills, Garry. *Lincoln at Gettysburg: The Words that Remade America*. New York: Simon and Schuster, 1992.

Rhetorical Monographs

Angle, Paul M. "Lincoln's Power with Words." *Papers of the Abraham Lincoln Association*, 9–23. Springfield, IL: 1981.

Arnold, Carroll C. "The Senate Committee of Thirteen, December 6–31, 1860." In *Antislavery and Disunion, 1858–1861*, edited by J. Jeffery Auer, 310–30. NY: Harper and Row, 1963.

Aune, James Arnt. "Lincoln and the American Sublime." *Communication Reports* 1 (1988): 14–19.

Basler, Roy P. "Abraham Lincoln's Rhetoric." *American Literature* 11 (1939): 167–82.

Berry, Mildred Freburg. "Abraham Lincoln: His Development in the Skills of the Platform." In *A History and Criticism of American Public Address.* Vol 2. Edited by William Norwood Brigance, 828–58. New York: Russell and Russell, 1960.

———. "Lincoln—The Speaker (Part I)." *Quarterly Journal of Speech* 17 (1931): 25–40, 177–90.

———. "Lincoln—The Speaker (Part II)." *Quarterly Journal of Speech* 17 (1931): 177–90.

Bormann, Ernest G. "Fetching Good Out of Evil: A Rhetorical Use of Calamity." *Quarterly Journal of Speech* 63 (1977): 130–39.

Braden, Waldo W. "Abraham Lincoln." In *American Orators Before 1900: Critical Studies and Sources,* edited by Bernard K. Duffy and Halford R. Ryan, 259–70. Westport, CT: Greenwood Press, 1987.

Branham, Robert J., and W. Barnett Pearce. "Between Text and Context: Toward a Rhetoric of Contextual Reconstruction." *Quarterly Journal of Speech* 71 (1985): 19–36.

Emsley, Bert. "Phonetic Structure in Lincoln's Gettysburg Address." *Quarterly Journal of Speech* 24 (1938): 281–87.

Gunderson, Robert G. "Lincoln's Rhetorical Style." *Vital Speeches* 27 (15 February 1961): 273–75.

Hahn, Dan F., and Anne Morlando. "A Burkean Analysis of Lincoln's Second Inaugural Address." *Presidential Studies Quarterly* 9 (1979): 376–79.

Hochmuth, Marie. "Lincoln's First Inaugural." In *American Speeches,* edited by Wayland Maxfield Parrish and Marie Hochmuth, 21–71. New York: Longmans, Green and Company, 1954.

Hurt, James. "All the Living and the Dead: Lincoln's Imagery." *American Literature* 52 (1980): 351–80.

Leff, Michael. "Dimensions of Temporality in Lincoln's Second Inaugural." *Communication Reports* 1 (1988): 26–31.

McPherson, James M. "How Lincoln Won the War with Metaphors." The Eighth Annual R. Gerald McMurtry Lecture. Fort Wayne, IN: Louis A. Warren Lincoln Library and Museum, 1985.

Miller, William Lee. "Lincoln's Second Inaugural: The Zenith of Statecraft." *The Center Magazine* (July/August 1980) : 53–64.

Reid, Ronald F. "Newspaper Response to the Gettysburg Addresses." *Quarterly Journal of Speech* 53 (1967): 50–60.

Slagell, Amy R. "A Textual Analysis of Abraham Lincoln's Second Inaugural Address." Unpublished M.A. Thesis, University of Wisconsin-Madison, 1986.

Solomon, Martha. " ' With Firmness in the Right': The Creation of Moral Hegemony in Lincoln's Second Inaugural." *Communication Reports* 1 (1988): 32–37.

Somkin, Fred. "Scripture Notes to Lincoln's Second Inaugural." *Civil War History* 27 (1981): 172–73.

Warren, Louis A. "Biblical Influences in the Second Inaugural Address." *Lincoln Lore,* No. 1226 (October 6, 1952).

————. "Sources of the Second Inaugural Address." *Lincoln Lore*, No. 1352 (March 7, 1955).
Wiley, Earl W. "Abraham Lincoln: His Emergence as the Voice of the People." In *A History and Criticism of American Public Address*. Vol. 2. Edited by William Norwood Brigance, 859–77. New York: Russell and Russell, 1960.
————. "Buckeye Criticism of the Gettysburg Address." *Speech Monographs* 23 (1956): 1–8.
————. "Eloquence at Gettysburg and Daniel Webster." *Dartmouth Alumni Magazine* (April 1967): 11–12.
Williams, Joseph. "Lincoln's Second Inaugural: Benevolent Doublespeak." Paper presented at the Speech Communication Association Convention, Chicago, November 2, 1984.
Windt, Theodore. "Lincoln's Presidential Rhetoric." Address delivered at the Gettysburg Conference on Rhetorical Transactions in the Civil War Era, Gettysburg, PA, June 1983.
Zarefsky, David. "Approaching Lincoln's Second Inaugural Address." *Communication Reports* 1 (1988): 9–13.

Chronology of Significant Orations

"House Divided" Speech, Springfield, Illinois, June 16, 1858. *CW*, 2: 461–69.
Lincoln-Douglas Debates, Illinois, 1858. *CW*, 3: 1–325.
Address at Cooper Institute, New York City, February 27, 1860. *CW*, 3: 522–50.
First Inaugural Address, Washington, D.C., March 4, 1861. *CW*, 4: 249–71.
Address Delivered at the Dedication of the Cemetery at Gettysburg, Gettysburg, Pennsylvania, November 19, 1863. *CW*, 7: 17–23.
Second Inaugural Address, Washington, D.C., March 4, 1965. *CW*, 8: 332–33.

Robert V. Friedenberg

Theodore Roosevelt
(1858–1919)

The foundation-stone of national life is, and ever must be, the high individual character of the average citizen.

Ascending to the presidency in September of 1901 upon the assassination of President William McKinley, Theodore Roosevelt was essentially the first president of the twentieth century. Winning re-election in his own right in 1904, Roosevelt's almost two terms of office witnessed dramatic changes in the nation. Not the least among them was the beginning of what Jeffrey Tulis and others characterized as "the rhetorical presidency."

Ironically, in light of Roosevelt's deserved associations with the beginnings of the rhetorical presidency, the preponderance of his best remembered speeches were delivered either prior to his assumption of the presidency or after he left office. His most frequently anthologized speech, and perhaps the single address most associated with Roosevelt, "The Strenuous Life," was delivered in Chicago on April 10, 1899, two and a half years before he assumed the presidency. An enunciation of his values and beliefs, it helped the nation gain an understanding of the man who in the wake of leading his Rough Riders up San Juan Hill had become, as the contemporary press and historian Edmund Morris typified him, both "the most famous man in America" and the Governor of New York in a scant eighteen months.

His first nationally reported speech, "Washington's Forgotten Maxim," delivered to the Naval War College, Newport, Rhode Island, on June 2, 1897, was a remarkably clear, if unfortunately dramatic, expression of the basic foreign and military policy ideas that subsequently governed his conduct of American foreign affairs. The relentless preparedness speaking campaign he engaged in from 1914 to 1918 caused both contemporaries as well as subsequent historians, such as William H. Harbaugh, to admiringly call him "the bugle who woke America." Such speaking overshadowed his military and foreign policy speeches while in the White House, although not the military and foreign policy accomplishments of his White House years.

His call for "A New Nationalism," delivered in Osawatomie, Kansas, on August 31, 1910, reflected his growing progressive ideals on domestic policy and signaled his emerging leadership of the progressive wing of his party. That leadership eventually resulted in his 1912 nomination to head the Progressive Party ticket. Such speaking in his post–White House years endures and overshadows the "Square Deal" domestic policy addresses of his White House tenure.

Moreover, in his 1904 campaign Roosevelt was constrained by the nineteenth-century tradition that candidates, including incumbent presidents, did not campaign openly for the nation's highest office. Hence, he delivered his best remembered campaign speeches not as a successful Republican candidate in 1904, but in his unsuccessful Progressive Party campaign of 1912, when he actively spoke throughout the nation.

The preponderance of Theodore Roosevelt's rhetorical legacy was not delivered in successful campaigns for the presidency or during service as president. That fact may well distinguish him from virtually all of his twentieth-century presidential successors. Nevertheless, his rhetorical accomplishments while in the White House are striking. He delivered a variety of outstanding speeches while president, most notably "The Man With the Muck-Rake," which dealt with domestic economic issues. Nevertheless, his principal rhetorical accomplishment as president was his reconceptualization and use of the rhetorical potential inherent in the nation's highest office. For that, his White House successors owe him no small debt of gratitude.

EARLY RHETORICAL TRAINING

Although Theodore Roosevelt's development as a public speaker was a consequence of many early influences, four factors had an unusually strong influence upon his development as an individual and as a speaker: (1) the influence of his family; (2) his lifetime of diverse and eclectic reading, particularly that of his childhood; (3) his educational experiences at Harvard University; and (4) the speaking experience he had acquired in his twenties as the youngest member of the New York State Legislature.

Born on October 27, 1858, Roosevelt's asthma caused his family to utilize a series of tutors, most notably his Aunt Annie Bulloch, to provide for his early education. By the age of three he was memorizing hymns and psalms, and within a few years was listening to sermons and discussing them with his siblings and parents every Sunday evening. Those discussions focused not only upon the content but the manner of expression utilized by the sermonist.

The severity of Roosevelt's asthma made him a semi-invalid during much of his early childhood; hence young Roosevelt became a bookish child. As a boy Roosevelt favored stories of action and adventure. Novels of the sea, Ballantyne's novels, and the Leatherstocking tales of James Fenimore Cooper were among his favorites. Roosevelt's early readings, particularly his regular reading of *Our Young Folks* magazine, inspired him with examples of physical bravery and adventure, and reinforced the virtues of manliness, decency, good conduct, and the importance of character, which reinforced the values his parents instilled.

At Harvard, Roosevelt delivered his first few public speeches. His Harvard efforts were unpolished and he did little to improve upon his speaking while in college. However, he mastered both scientific and historical research methods that facilitated his later speech preparation. An exceedingly able student, Roosevelt graduated Phi Beta Kappa in the top tenth of his class, and wrote what eventually became the opening chapters of his still definitive naval history of the War of 1812.

Roosevelt won election to the New York State Legislature in 1880, at the age of twenty-two. He remembered his years in the legislature as ones in which he "had considerable difficulty in teaching myself to speak." But, with the same perseverance that characterized his struggle against asthma, Roosevelt overcame his difficulties. Two years of frequent speaking to the legislature produced a much more polished Theodore Roosevelt. His delivery improved greatly. His initial speeches were occasionally marked by some difficulties in enunciation as well as a lack of fluency. Those problems had completely disappeared by the end of his Albany years. His legislative addresses illustrated his efforts to make use of both balanced sentences and the graphic vigorous expressions that were so characteristic of his later speaking. He recognized the need to use evidence well, and, applying the research skills he had acquired at Harvard, he soon became known as a formidable adversary in legislative debates. He grew in his awareness of the need to adapt to an audience.

Roosevelt's legislative experience contributed importantly to his growing recognition of the importance not only of his immediate audience, but also of the wider audience that read his remarks in the press. His awareness of the press and its impact on public opinion soon made him a favorite of the Albany press corps. In his Albany experiences are the first examples of Roosevelt's awareness and exploitation of the rhetorical possibilities inherent in public office. As James Pollard, Nathan Miller, and others have observed, it was in Albany that Roosevelt first began to cultivate the press. Roosevelt's naturally outgoing personality, his propensity for turning a phrase, his conscious attempts to do what was right, and his willingness to accommodate the press, quickly made him a favorite of the journalists covering the legislature. Although the White House provided Roosevelt with the finest of "bully pulpits," he learned his first lessons about the rhetorical presidency in Albany. There, Roosevelt first clearly recognized that a sympathetic press could help him shape public opinion and hence move other decisionmakers in the legislature and Governor's mansion.

CAMPAIGN SPEAKING

In addition to races for lesser offices, Theodore Roosevelt ran for the vice presidency and presidency on three occasions. As William McKinley's vice presidential candidate in 1900, Roosevelt was the ticket's principal spokesman. But the campaign itself was a lackluster, one-sided race that in most respects failed to duplicate the excitement of the 1896 campaign between the same two presidential candidates, McKinley and William Jennings Bryan. McKinley, confident of victory and following tradition, did virtually no campaigning, scarcely even emulating his 1896 front porch campaign. As an incumbent whose "full dinner pail" programs seemed to be working and as a president who had presided over the successful prosecution of the Spanish American War, McKinley won handily.

Although in 1900 Bryan shifted the focus of his campaign from his 1896 emphasis on economics to argue primarily against growing American imperialism, he had little success. The hero of San Juan Hill vigorously defended the war and growing American imperialism. The question, claimed Roosevelt who traveled 21,000 miles delivering hundreds of speeches, was not whether America would expand, "for we have already expanded—but whether we shall contract."

Four years later, President Theodore Roosevelt headed the Republican ticket. Restrained by the tradition that had dominated presidential politics since Washington, that candidates should not seek the office but rather the office should seek the candidate, and following in the footsteps of his immediate predecessor, Roosevelt did not take to the stump, but rather let his "Square Deal" record speak for itself.

His three years of successfully battling the trusts, intervening in a national coal strike, securing veterans' legislation, and acquiring the Panama Canal Zone, as well as his enormous personal popularity, made Roosevelt a formidable opponent. The Democratic party nominated a relatively little-known New York judge, Alton B. Parker, whose principle virtue seemed to be that as a judge his position on most issues was unknown. Like Roosevelt, Parker also refrained from campaigning. The campaign was waged by surrogates until late October when Parker charged that George B. Cortelyou, Roosevelt's Secretary of Commerce, who also served as national Chairman of the Republican Party, had solicited major campaign contributions from corporations that his department was supposed to regulate. "Cortelyouism" was virtually the only controversy in a remarkably dull campaign. On November 8, 1904, the nation gave Roosevelt the greatest popular majority a presidential candidate had ever received, and an electoral majority of 336 to 140 against Parker, who failed to carry any state outside of the Democratic South.

Although Roosevelt's two successful national campaigns failed to produce any memorable addresses, his unsuccessful campaign for the Republican nomination against incumbent President William Howard Taft, and his subsequent general election race as the Progressive Party nominee against Taft and Democratic nominee Woodrow Wilson, gave rise to several of Roosevelt's most outstanding speeches.

"The New Nationalism" Opens the 1912 Campaign

As Roosevelt's presidency grew to a close and Taft succeeded him, the reform element of the Republican party grew stronger, and Theodore Roosevelt grew more sympathetic. Shortly after leaving office in 1909, Roosevelt read Herbert Croly's *The Promise of American Life*. Croly's book, and his subsequent discussions with Roosevelt, helped Roosevelt clarify his ideas about political and economic reform. As he did so, his estrangement from Taft grew. With insurgent Republicans looking to him for leadership, in the late summer of 1910 the ex-president set out on a major speaking tour. Accompanied initially by seventeen journalists, Roosevelt traveled 5,500 miles, delivering fourteen prepared speeches and hundreds of impromptu speeches to often tumultuous crowds. The original seventeen journalists soon swelled in number until it took three full railroad cars to carry all of the press that was reporting on Roosevelt's speaking.

On August 31, in Osawatomie, Kansas, at the dedication of the John Brown battlefield, with thousands of Civil War veterans in an audience estimated at 15,000, the governor of Kansas quieted an expectant audience: "Citizens of Kansas, be still for a minute and I will introduce the greatest man in the world." Roosevelt stepped to the podium and delivered "The New Nationalism" speech. This speech was quickly recognized as an explicit statement of his beliefs that widened the gap between Roosevelt and Taft's conservative wing of the Republican party. In effect it launched his unsuccessful bid for the 1912 Republican nomination and his subsequent campaign that year as the Progressive party nominee.

Roosevelt opened his address with a long acknowledgment of his audience of Civil War veterans and their contribution to the achievements of "the high purpose of Abraham Lincoln." This lengthy introduction culminated in Roosevelt's observation that Lincoln "forecast our present struggle and saw the way out." Then, like a minister quoting scripture, Roosevelt quoted Lincoln and expanded on Lincoln to present his thesis. Claiming that Lincoln "took substantially the attitude that we ought to take" toward the conflict between capital and labor, Roosevelt claimed that by 1910 this conflict appeared

as the struggle of freemen to gain and hold the right of self-government as against the special interests, who twist the methods of free government into machinery for defeating the popular will. At every stage, and under all circumstances, the essence of the struggle is to equalize opportunity, destroy privilege, and give to the life and citizenship of every individual the highest possible value both to himself and to the commonwealth.

In the body of this address Roosevelt presented six general goals for the United States. However, unlike many of his addresses, in this speech he generated specific policy recommendations for implementing most of his general goals. In so doing, Roosevelt presented his interpretation of progressivism and the platform upon which he would campaign throughout the next two years.

The first, and most extensively developed, goal that Roosevelt presented was the very essence of the Progressive movement and a logical consequence of Roosevelt's thesis. "The citizens of the United States," proclaimed Roosevelt, "must effectively control the mighty commercial forces which they have themselves called into being." To this end, Roosevelt presented a wide variety of proposals. Among them were: (1) prohibiting "the use of corporate funds directly or indirectly for political purposes"; (2) supervising "the capitalization of not only public-service corporations, including, particularly, railways, but of all corporations doing an interstate business"; (3) regulating in a "thorough-going and effective" manner businesses engaged in interstate commerce; (4) limiting the duration of grants to public-service corporation franchises, and "never without proper provision for compensation to the public"; (5) extending the concept of public-service corporation franchises "to combinations which control necessaries of life, such as meat, oil, and coal"; (6) holding the officers, especially the directors, "personally responsible when any corporation breaks the law"; and (7) establishing "an expert tariff commission, wholly removed from the possibility of political pressure or of improper business influence." Roosevelt's specific reforms to "control the mighty commercial forces" would forever change the face of the U.S. economy.

Roosevelt's second major goal was to put restraints on the acquisition and use of large fortunes. "The absence of effective state, and especially, national, restraint upon unfair money-getting," Roosevelt claimed, "has tended to create a small class of enormously wealthy and economically powerful men, whose chief object is to hold and increase their power." Roosevelt carefully pointed out that "we grudge no man a fortune in civil life," but only if it was gained fairly, "without doing damage to the community," and if it was used for the general welfare and benefit of the community.

Sensitive to the class from which he sprang and the conservative wing of his party, yet activated by deep concerns for social justice and deep fears of potential class war, Roosevelt offered two specific proposals to limit large fortunes. First, he advocated "a graduated income tax on big fortunes." Second, he advocated "another tax which is far more easily collected and far more effective—a graduated inheritance tax on big fortunes, properly safeguarded against evasion and increasing rapidly in amount with the size of the estate."

Roosevelt's penchant for inheritance taxes reflected his belief in the gospel of work. Inherited money is acquired largely without work. Yet, said Roosevelt in this address, "No man should receive a dollar unless that dollar has been fairly earned." Inheritance taxes, perhaps more than many types of taxes, may have been perceived by Roosevelt as fostering the work ethic.

Roosevelt presented his third, fourth, and fifth goals without recommending how to achieve them. "It is hardly necessary for me to repeat," he observed as he introduced his third goal, "that I believe in an efficient army and navy large enough to secure for us abroad that respect which is the surest guaranty of peace." Observing that he would speak about his fourth national goal, conservation, "at length elsewhere," in this speech Roosevelt treated the conservation issue briefly in several sentences. Roosevelt's fifth national goal was to enable farmers "to get for themselves and their wives and children not only the benefits of better farming, but also those of better business methods and better conditions of life on the farm."

Roosevelt introduced his sixth goal by claiming that "the right to regulate the use of wealth in the public interest is universally admitted. Let us admit also the right to regulate the terms and conditions of labor, which is the chief element of wealth, directly in the interest of the common good." Given these admissions, Roosevelt's sixth goal, improving the conditions of the American laborer, followed logically.

Roosevelt presented a variety of specific proposals to improve working conditions. They included a comprehensive workmen's compensation act, state and national laws to regulate child labor, regulation of work for women, increased vocational training in the public schools, better sanitary conditions for U.S. workers, and increasing the use of safety equipment in industry and commerce. Ever sensitive to the tightwire he was trying to walk between the conservative wing of his party and the insurgent progressive wing, Roosevelt tempered his advocacy of reforms on behalf of the workers by declaring that

in the interest of the working man himself we need to set our faces like flint against mob-violence, just as against corporate greed; against violence and injustice and lawlessness by wage-workers just as much as against lawlessness, cunning and greed and selfish arrogance of employers. If I could ask but one thing of my fellow countrymen, my request would be that, whenever they go in for reform, they remember the two sides, and that they always exact justice from one side as much as from the other.

Roosevelt's conclusion is notable for two reasons. First, he appropriated Herbert Croly's phrase and dubbed his program "The New Nationalism." Second, he used the conclusion to add one final idea that was familiar to those who frequently listened to Roosevelt. Roosevelt commented on the importance of individual character. "In the last analysis," Roosevelt claimed,

the most important elements in any man's career must be the sum of those qualities which, in the aggregate, we speak of as character. If he has not got it, then no law that the wit of man can devise, no administration of the law by the boldest and strongest executive, will avail to help him. You must have the right kind of character.

With a citizenry of character, and the progressive reforms of "The New Nationalism," the United States would overcome its current problems.

In addition to illustrating much of Roosevelt's thought, this speech also included many rhetorical techniques that he commonly employed. First, it was homiletic in nature. Roosevelt used this speech to preach a moralistic lesson to his congregants, the American people. Taking his text from Lincoln, Roosevelt preached that human rights must supercede property rights. He then amplified this text, applying it to contemporary problems. Hence, like much of Roosevelt's speaking, the homiletic nature of this speech was evident in both content and form.

Second, the supporting material Roosevelt used was limited. He relied primarily on his own assertions, although he did make limited use of historical examples. Third, as in many of his other addresses, Roosevelt used either/or and deductive reasoning. Finally, Roosevelt frequently used intense, highly connotative language and balanced sentences.

Roosevelt's use of balanced sentences in this speech seems designed to help contribute to his image as a just and impartial former president seeking the best for his nation. Roosevelt was aware that this speech would be controversial and was no doubt especially concerned about conservative reaction. Controversial it was. George Mowry, one of the foremost historians of the Progressive movement, claimed that ''when Roosevelt finished at Osawatomie he had probably delivered the most radical speech ever given by an ex-president.'' Even conservatives who were close to Roosevelt, such as Henry Cabot Lodge, had reservations about this address. In some of Roosevelt's speaking, his use of balanced sentences often seems almost platitudinous. However, in this speech Roosevelt's balanced sentences frequently attempted to satisfy not only the progressives but also the conservatives. Although delivered at the outset of what ultimately proved to be his only unsuccessful campaign for national office, ''The New Nationalism'' is among the finest examples of Roosevelt's campaign oratory, revealing Roosevelt's break from the conservative wing of his party and his willingness to assume leadership of the Progressive movement.

THEODORE ROOSEVELT AND THE BIRTH OF THE RHETORICAL PRESIDENCY

Today it is common for an American president to utilize the powers of his office to marshall public opinion behind his legislative proposals and thus to bring pressure on Congress to respond favorably to his proposals. Yet those actions were not commonplace for nineteenth-century presidents. As Jeffrey Tulis has noted, on those few occasions when earlier presidents took their cases directly to the people, e.g., Andrew Johnson, they were rarely successful. Rhetorical leadership gradually began to emerge as the essence of modern presidential leadership during the administration of Theodore Roosevelt.

Having won election in his own right, by 1905 Roosevelt found himself governing a country growing uneasy about large corporations. Press revelations about corporate abuses fueled the growing progressive spirit that Roosevelt, although more accepting of big business than many reformers, was nevertheless finding difficult to resist. Roosevelt's natural inclination toward reform and his activist perceptions of the presidency drove him closer to the reform movement. Yet this activist president, seeking reform, had entered office, as Richard Davis claims, "with the poorest relationship with his own political party of any president since the Civil War." Although it had improved during his first years in office, no doubt Roosevelt recognized that he would be less able to depend on working through the party machinery than many of his predecessors.

Ohio's wealthy political boss Mark Hanna had become virtually the dominant figure in the Republican party while mentoring his protege McKinley to the White House. He typified the feelings many traditionally conservative Republicans had of Roosevelt. Hanna claimed that it was a "mistake to nominate that wild man" when Roosevelt was nominated for the vice presidency and was subsequently bitter to find "that damned cowboy is President of the United States." Unable to rely confidently upon the support of his own party, Roosevelt's alternatives were limited. He would be dependent upon himself and favorable press coverage to mobilize support for reform. His would be a presidency whose accomplishments would be uniquely tied to his rhetorical successes.

By 1905 the railroad industry had become the target of many reform minded critics for what were perceived as a host of unfair business practices, most notably providing rebates to favored customers, often other large businesses. Critics claimed that such practices by a railroad, which often had monopoly-like control of routes in a given region, provided railroads unwarranted control of that region's economy. Such control could and was being abused. As railroads gave rebates and favored rates to larger shippers, they contributed appreciably to driving smaller firms out of business, unfairly reducing competition, creating unemployment, and raising consumer prices.

Throughout much of 1905, recognizing that regulatory legislation for the railroads would be exceedingly difficult to get through the Senate, and if passed would likely be tested by the railroads in the courts, Roosevelt nevertheless spoke favorably of such legislation. On January 30, he told a Philadelphia audience that "the great development of industrialism means that there must be an increase in the supervision exercised by the government over business enterprises." In April he told a Dallas audience that "I have advocated giving the Interstate Commerce Commission increased power," and went on to note specifically that he felt the ICC was the appropriate agency to deal with railroads. In May he told a Chicago audience that "I believe that the Federal Government must take an increasing control over corporations." Roosevelt met with sympathetic members of Congress to secure legislation. His meetings bore fruit in late 1905 when Senator Jonathan Dolliver and Representative William P. Hepburn, both Iowa Republicans, prepared legislation that Roosevelt could support. Their legislation placed maximum allowable rates on the railroads, prohibited railroad rebates to large shippers, and gave the Interstate Commerce Commission the authority to enforce these provisions.

As the legislation was being prepared, Roosevelt spoke about the need for railroad legislation when he toured the South during October. He laid out the case for it in his annual message of December 5, 1905. Utilizing other facets of the rhetorical potential of his office, six days after his annual message, Roosevelt had Attorney General William H. Moody direct federal prosecutors to institute proceedings against companies offering or receiving rebates. These cases were to be prosecuted under conspiracy statutes and generated yet another round of unfavorable publicity for the railroads. Additionally, behind the scenes, Roosevelt made the case against the railroads to cooperative journalists who reflected his ideas in many of the articles that began to appear in the nation's magazines.

The Dolliver-Hepburn bill was presented to Congress on January 24, 1906. Within weeks the bill was approved overwhelmingly in the House. Roosevelt's advocacy helped to make the House of Representatives receptive to railroad legislation. Moreover, the large Republican majority in the House knew that it had nothing to risk in voting with its president and the popular mood, for the real fight over what became known as the Hepburn Act was clearly going to be waged in the far more conservative Senate.

Debate in the Senate opened on February 28. By April it was clear that both South Carolina Democrat "Pitchfork" Ben Tillman, who had been intemperate in his criticism of Roosevelt for inviting Booker T. Washington to the White House, and the president, who found Tillman personally distasteful, had put aside their personal feelings to work for passage of the Hepburn Act. Tillman rallied most Democratic Senators behind the bill. Nelson Aldrich, Republican majority leader of the Senate, led the opposition and West Virginia Republican "Railroad Senators" Joe Foraker and Stephen Elkins, were Aldrich's principal aides in the floor fight. Many Senate Republicans, even strong Roosevelt supporters such as Philander Knox, once Roosevelt's attorney general, and Henry Cabot Lodge, perhaps Roosevelt's closest personal friend, added their voices in opposition.

But Roosevelt was not a passive observer to the Senate fight going on within his party. It was not a coincidence that the Bureau of Corporations released a report on Standard Oil during the debate that illustrated how Standard Oil had benefited by three-quarter of a million dollars from secret railroad rates and rebates in the preceding year. Moreover, Roosevelt eventually concluded that a major address was in order to rally public support and secure the support of Republican Senators torn between their president and their own Senate leadership. He chose to deliver that address at the ceremonies accompanying the laying of the cornerstone of the new three-million dollar House of Representatives office building. It would become the most memorable address of his presidency.

The Man with the Muck-Rake

Roosevelt had let it be known in advance that he anticipated using the cornerstone laying ceremonies for a major address with national implications. On

St. Patrick's Day, almost a month earlier, he had previously expressed some of his ideas in an off-the-record impromptu speech at the Washington Gridiron Club. Now, after thoroughly thinking through his ideas and devoting considerable time to preparing his speech, and with members of Congress, the Supreme Court, the diplomatic corps, and an expectant press corps listening, on a bright sunny Saturday morning, April 14, 1906, Roosevelt launched into one of the most remarkable speeches of his career.

After quickly acknowledging that Washington was the first American president to lay the cornerstone of a significant government building, Roosevelt observed that "under altered external form we war with the same tendencies toward evil that were evident in Washington's time, and are helped by the same tendencies for good. It is about these that I wish to say a word to-day." Having thus set the stage for a speech dealing with good and evil, Roosevelt took as his text a work of John Bunyan's:

In Bunyan's "Pilgrim's Progress" you may recall the description of the Man with the Muck-rake, the man who could look no way but downward, with the muck-rake in his hand; who was offered a celestial crown for his muck-rake, but who would neither look up nor regard the crown he was offered, but continued to rake to himself the filth of the floor.

With audience attention focused on the image of the man with the muck-rake, Roosevelt then expanded on that image by presenting his thesis.

Now, it is very necessary that we should not flinch from seeing what is vile and debasing. There is filth on the floor, and it must be scraped up with the muck-rake; and there are times and places where this service is the most needed of all the services that can be performed. But the man who never does anything else, who never thinks, or speaks or writes, save of his feats with the muck-rake, speedily becomes not a help to society, not an incitement to good, but one of the most potent forces for evil.

For Roosevelt, anything carried to excess, anything done without common sense and moderation, could create evil. Thus, journalists who spoke or wrote only of the negative aspects of society, whose work was marked by exaggeration and excess rather than accuracy and moderation, were not people of character contributing to the social good. Rather, they lacked character and hence were "potent forces for evil."

In the body of his speech Roosevelt argued four major points. The first two presented a carefully qualified amplification of the thesis. The muckrakers, Roosevelt suggested, created problems when their criticism was excessive. However, Roosevelt prudently observed that "to denounce mud-slinging does not mean the endorsement of whitewashing." Roosevelt well recognized that the muckrakers had exposed many fundamental problems with American life. He assiduously attempted to distinguish between legitimate criticism of the American political, economic, and social system, and excessive carping.

Roosevelt's focus on the excesses of the muckrakers was consistent with remarks he had made as early as 1901. Ultimately, as Roosevelt scholars William Harbaugh, John Semonche, and Nathan Miller have illustrated, Roosevelt's concern was that the muckrakers were stirring up class feelings. In so doing, he feared that they might well be laying the grounds for the disruption of American society by class warfare. Roosevelt expressed these thoughts in the second major point of his address.

So far as this movement of agitation throughout the country takes the form of a fierce discontent with evil, of a determination to punish the authors of evil, whether in industry or politics, the feeling is to be heartily welcomed as a sign of healthy life. If, on the other hand, it turns into a mere crusade of appetite against appetite, of a contest between the brutal greed of the ''have-nots'' and the brutal greed of the ''haves'' then it has no significance for good, but only for evil.

Thus, Roosevelt's second major point was that inherent in the exposures of the muckrakers was the potential to disrupt the very fabric of U.S. society by creating class conflict. Roosevelt consistently linked order to justice and equality. Without justice and equality, order was sure to perish. Hence, as the muckrakers illustrated the lack of justice and equality in the United States, Roosevelt grew to believe that responsible citizens and leaders should strive to implement reforms that would restore justice and equality to life in the United States. Failing to do so might well result in the disruption of the social order. Thus, as the Senate and public considered regulation of the railroads, Roosevelt preached that only through reform that redressed the legitimate evils exposed by the muckrakers could our social order be preserved.

Acknowledging the merit of much of the muckrakers criticism of American life, Roosevelt introduced his third and fourth major points by claiming that it was important for the United States ''to grapple with the problems connected with the amassing of enormous fortunes and the use of those fortunes, both corporate and individual, in business.'' He then presented two suggestions for better enabling the United States to grapple with these problems.

Roosevelt's third major point was that one way of treating enormous fortunes was to consider the adoption of a progressive inheritance tax. Roosevelt mentioned this idea but did not amplify it beyond noting that such a tax should be aimed ''merely at the inheritance or transmission in their entirety of those fortunes swollen beyond all healthy limits.'' A progressive inheritance tax was the most unappealing tax to conservative monied interests, such as those opposing the Hepburn Act. In the context of the ongoing Senate debate of regulatory legislation, Roosevelt's brief mention of harsh alternatives that he might unleash was his subtle method of reminding his audience that although thus far he had spoken softly, he could wield a big stick.

Having made that brief but pointed reminder, Roosevelt turned to his final point. He suggested that an additional way of treating the abuses of wealth would be for the national government to "in some form exercise supervision over corporations engaged in interstate business." Roosevelt observed that virtually all larger corporations were so engaged, and that his administration had already begun to take the first steps in this direction.

But Roosevelt did not stop by simply endorsing regulation. He attempted to comfort his foes by recognizing that regulation would require public servants of unquestioned integrity and character:

The eighth commandment reads: "Thou shall not steal." It does not read: "Thou shalt not steal from the rich man." It does not read: "Thou shalt not steal from the poor man." It reads simply and plainly: "Thou shalt not steal." No good whatever will come from that warped and mock morality which denounces the misdeeds of men of wealth and forgets the misdeeds practiced at their expense; which denounces bribery, but blinds itself to blackmail; which foams with rage if a corporation secures favors by improper methods, and merely leers with hideous mirth if the corporation is itself wronged. The only public servant who can be trusted honestly to protect the rights of the public against the misdeed of the corporation is that public man who will just as surely protect the corporation itself from wrongful aggression.

Few discussions of Roosevelt's "The Man with the Muck-rake" address place it in the context of the ongoing Senate debate over the Hepburn Act. Yet, it was a remarkable address in which Roosevelt chastised the excesses of his allies in the legislative battle, the muckraking press, while at the same time suggesting to his foes that fairly administered government regulation would be an appropriate means of managing the abuses of uncontrolled corporations, particularly in light of even harsher alternatives. This speech clearly illustrated many of the rhetorical strategies that Roosevelt used throughout his life. First, it is clearly homiletic in nature. Like a preacher, Roosevelt opened with a text, explained his text, and amplified it by applying it to contemporary problems. Like a preacher, Roosevelt spoke of good and evil throughout this address. Like a preacher, Roosevelt quoted Scripture.

Second, as in many of his other addresses, Roosevelt made relatively little use of evidence in this speech. He did draw on "Pilgrim's Progress," the work of an Elizabethan cleric, and Scripture. Nevertheless, the vast majority of the speech consisted of Roosevelt's assertions.

Third, while this speech made use of both analogy and causal reasoning, ultimately, like much of Roosevelt's speaking, its persuasive force rested on either/or reasoning. Either Americans followed his advice by recognizing that much of what the muckrakers had said is excessive and by acting prudently through government regulation to curb the legitimate evils that the muckrakers had exposed, or the United States would be faced with a conflict that "divides those who are well off from those who are less well off." Such a class conflict,

Roosevelt concluded, would be "fraught with immeasurable harm to the body politic."

Finally, more than most of his speeches, this speech revealed Roosevelt as a wordsmith. With this speech Roosevelt coined the term "muckraker" and made it a part of the language. He used highly connotative language throughout the speech. Roosevelt's characteristic invective was rarely more evident than in this address. The muckraker who abused his position was a "liar," "thief," "the despair of honest men," and "a wild preacher of unrest," who suffered from "moral color-blindness." His writing was "hysterical sensationalism," "lurid," and "untruthful." Moreover, wherever Roosevelt found muckrakers, he found evil lurking nearby. Muckrakers were "potent forces for evil," who produced, "tendencies toward evil," and "a sodden acquiescence in evil."

Reaction to the speech was predictable. Conservatives lauded Roosevelt's denunciation of the muckrakers, but they attacked his proposals for taxation and regulation. Liberals were disturbed by his denunciation of the muckrakers, although they lauded his proposals for taxation and regulation. In the Senate, Roosevelt's speech helped, but it was unable to break the deadlock. Four days after Roosevelt's address, in a caucus of all thirty-three Democratic Senators, Tillman was still unable to get more than the twenty-five or twenty-six votes he had secured early in the fight. The situation was even worse for Roosevelt within his own party where the bill was supported by less than half the Republican Senators, and Republican vote counters perceived no change on that side of the aisle.

Ultimately, Roosevelt accepted an amendment to the Hepburn proposal that had no impact on the specific provisions of the law but allowed conservatives to save face by providing the courts considerable latitude in ruling on cases that might arise from the law. With the amendment in place, the legislation sailed through the Senate with only three negative votes.

Tulis and others cite Roosevelt's campaign over the Hepburn Act as perhaps the first example of the rhetorical presidency, because Roosevelt attempted to exploit all the rhetorical options available to him to shift public opinion, and ultimately congressional opinion, to his own position. In the fight over the Hepburn Act, Roosevelt utilized the rhetorical potential of the office he so fondly called the nation's finest "bully pulpit" as it was rarely used in the past. The president helped create demand for the legislation by speaking of the need for regulation in the South and in the Midwest well before such legislation was fashioned. He worked closely with key members of both parties throughout the process. He directed the activities of several government agencies so that news stories would illustrate the need for the proposed legislation. He worked closely with the press to help build the need for the new legislation. In the midst of the legislative battle, he used a ceremonial occasion to deliver a major address illustrating the need for the new legislation. Thus, in one of the first examples of a President utilizing his office to its fullest rhetorical potential, Roosevelt helped create the need for this legislation, helped craft the legislation, worked to marshall the rhetorical potential of the government and the press to shape public opinion and influence the Congress on behalf of this legislation, and delivered a major address in the midst of the Senate debate. With this concerted effort, Roosevelt was among the first presidents to illustrate the rhetorical potentials of the presidency.

CONCLUSION

Although many of Theodore Roosevelt's most memorable public speeches were not made while he served as president, he nevertheless left an imposing rhetorical legacy for his successors in the White House. Years before assuming the presidency, Roosevelt recognized the importance of public opinion. Assuming the presidency upon McKinley's death, Roosevelt found himself more distanced from the Congressional leadership of his own party than most presidents. By exploiting the rhetorical potentials of the presidency, Roosevelt aroused public opinion behind his positions and hence exerted pressure on Congress. Prior presidents could work through the party structures and the congressional leadership to secure passage of their legislative agendas. Roosevelt was an "accidental president" whose growing progressive sympathies often antagonized the leaders of his own party. Hence, his exploitation of the rhetorical potentials of the presidency, especially evident in the fight to secure passage of the Hepburn Act, was the natural response of an activist president thwarted by the normal means of exerting leadership.

Roosevelt recognized and utilized the full rhetorical potential of the presidency better than most of his predecessors. During his stewardship, the presidency was a genuine "bully pulpit" as Roosevelt expanded the communicative potentialities of the presidency. Because he exploited the rhetorical power of the presidency to a greater extent than virtually any of his predecessors, Roosevelt is justifiably associated with the birth of the modern rhetorical presidency.

RHETORICAL SOURCES

Archival Materials

The principal Roosevelt collections are found at the Library of Congress and at Harvard University. The Library of Congress collection, which centers on Roosevelt's presidential years, is available on microfilm. That collection includes draft manuscripts that illustrate the evolution of some Roosevelt speeches.

The Roosevelt collection at Harvard is based upon the library of the Theodore Roosevelt Memorial Association, which was given to Harvard in the 1940s and has since been kept up to date. An exceptional collection, it is especially rich in contemporary periodical accounts of Roosevelt's speaking. It also includes speech manuscripts, Roosevelt diaries, and scrapbooks. The latter are especially helpful for newspaper accounts of Roosevelt's speaking.

The principal published primary sources for Roosevelt's speaking are:

Roosevelt, Theodore. *The Works of Theodore Roosevelt: The Memorial Edition.*
(*WTRME*). 24 Vols. New York: Charles Scribner's Sons, 1923–1926.
Roosevelt, Theodore. *The Works of Theodore Roosevelt: The National Edition.* (*WTRNE*).
22 Vols. New York: Charles Scribner's Sons, 1926.

The minor differences between these two editions are not critical for the
scholar interested in Roosevelt's speaking. Both editions contain Roosevelt's
best known speeches, well over a hundred of his lesser addresses and virtually
all of his major published works, including his biographies of Benton and Morris, his account of the Naval War of 1812, his study of western expansion, his
key works as a naturalist, and his own autobiography. Moreover, both editions
include all of the more popular collections of his speeches and essays, which
were published periodically throughout Roosevelt's career. They include *American Ideals, The Strenuous Life, Realizable Ideals, America and the World War,
Fear God and Take Your Own Part,* and *The Great Adventure.*
The only collection of Roosevelt materials that focuses on Roosevelt's perception of the relationships between government and business, the issue that
gave rise to his full exploitation of the rhetorical potentials of the presidency,
is:

Theodore Roosevelt, *The Roosevelt Policy.* (*TRP*). 2 Vols. Edited by William Griffin.
New York: The Current Literature Publishing Co., 1919.

The researcher interested in Roosevelt's speaking will find much valuable
material in the Roosevelt letters, including the reactions of many of his associates to Roosevelt's speeches, and Roosevelt's own explanations of the meaning
and intent of some of his speeches. The best readily available source of his
letters is:

Roosevelt, Theodore. *The Letters of Theodore Roosevelt.* (*LTR*). 8 Vols. Edited by Elting
E. Morison. Cambridge, MA: Harvard University Press. 1951–1954.

Rhetorical Studies

Blum, John M. *The Republican Roosevelt.* Cambridge, MA: Harvard University Press,
1954.
Davis, Richard. *The Press and American Politics: The New Mediator.* New York: Long-
man, 1992.
Friedenberg, Robert V. *Theodore Roosevelt and the Rhetoric of Militant Decency.* New
York: Greenwood Press, 1990.
Gould, Lewis L. *The Presidency of Theodore Roosevelt.* Lawrence, KS: University of
Kansas Press, 1991.
Harbaugh, William H. *The Life and Times of Theodore Roosevelt.* New York: Collier
Books, 1963.
Hart, Wilbert Bushnell, and Herbert Ferleger, eds. *Theodore Roosevelt Cyclopedia.* New
York: Theodore Roosevelt Association, 1941.
Marks, Frederick. *Velvet on Iron: The Diplomacy of Theodore Roosevelt.* Lincoln, NE:
University of Nebraska Press, 1979.

Miller, Nathan. *Theodore Roosevelt: A Life.* New York: William Morrow and Company, 1992.

Morris, Edmund. *The Rise of Theodore Roosevelt.* New York: Coward, McCann and Geoghegan Inc., 1979.

Perry, Ralph Barton. *The Plattsburgh Movement.* New York: E. P. Dutton and Company, 1921.

Pollard, James E. *The Presidents and the Press.* New York: Macmilliam Company, 1947.

Pringle, Henry F. *Theodore Roosevelt: A Biography.* New York: Harcourt Brace Janovich, 1956.

Putnam, Carleton. *Theodore Roosevelt: The Formative Years.* New York: Charles Scribner's Sons, 1958.

Tulis, Jeffrey K. *The Rhetorical Presidency.* Princeton, NJ: Princeton University Press, 1987.

Rhetorical Monographs

Behl, William B. "Theodore Roosevelt's Principles of Speech Preparation and Delivery." *Speech Monographs* (1945): 112–22.

———. "Theodore Roosevelt's Principles of Invention." *Speech Monographs* (1947): 93–110.

Beltz, Lynda. "Theodore Roosevelt's 'Man with the Muck-rake.' " *Central States Speech Journal* (Summer 1969): 97–103.

Braden, Waldo W. "Theodore Roosevelt." In *American Orators of the Twentieth Century,* edited by Bernard Duffy and Halford Ryan. Westport, CT: Greenwood Press, 1987.

Brigance, William Norwood. "In the Workshop of Great Speakers." *American Speech* (August 1926): 589–95.

Ceaser, James W., Glen E. Thurow, Jeffrey Tulis, and Joseph M. Bessette. "The Rise of the Rhetorical Presidency." *Presidential Studies Quarterly* (Spring 1981): 158–71.

Dalinger, Carl A. "Theodore Roosevelt: The Preacher Militant." In *American Public Address: Studies in Honor of Albert Craig Baird,* edited by Loren Reid. Colombia, MO: University of Missouri Press, 1961.

Friedenberg, Robert V. "Theodore Roosevelt's Inaugural Address of 1905." In *The Inaugural Addresses of Twentieth-Century American Presidents: Critical Rhetorical Studies,* edited by Halford R. Ryan. Westport, CT: Praeger Publishers, 1993.

Hale, William Baynard. "Friends and Fellow Citizens: Our Political Orators of All Parties and the Ways They Use to Win Us." *The World's Work* (April 1912): 673–83.

Karsten, Peter. "The Nature of 'Influence': Roosevelt, Mahan and the Concept of Sea Power." *American Quarterly* (October 1971): 585–600.

Lucas, Stephen E. "Theodore Roosevelt's 'The Man with the Muck-rake': A Reinterpretation." *Quarterly Journal of Speech* (December 1973): 452–62.

Moers, Ellen. "Teddy Roosevelt: Literary Feller." *Columbia University Forum* (Summer 1963): 10–16.

Morris, Edmund. "The Many Words and Works of Theodore Roosevelt." *Smithsonian* (November 1983): 86–97.

Murphy, Richard. "Theodore Roosevelt." In *A History and Criticism of American Public Address*, edited by Marie Hochmuth. New York: Russell and Russell, 1965.

Semonche, John E. "Theodore Roosevelt's 'Muck-rake' Speech: A Reassessment." *Mid-America* (April 1964): 114–25.

Silvestri, Vito N. "Theodore Roosevelt's Preparedness Oratory: The Minority Voice of an Ex-President." *Central States Speech Journal* (Fall 1969): 179–86.

Williams, Mark Wayne. "Preaching Presidents." *Homiletic Review* (August 1934): 90–96.

Zyskind, Harold. "A Case Study of Philosophical Rhetoric: Theodore Roosevelt." *Philosophy and Rhetoric* (Summer 1968): 228–54.

Chronology of Significant Presidential Persuasions

"Washington's Forgotten Maxim," Newport, Rhode Island, June 2, 1897. *WTRNE*, 13: 182–99.

"The Strenuous Life," Chicago, Illinois, April 10, 1899. *WTRNR*, 13: 319–31.

"Federal Regulation of the Interstate Railroads," Philadelphia, Pennsylvania, January 30, 1905. *TRP*, 1: 239–45.

"The Square Deal," Dallas, Texas, April 5, 1905. *TRP*, 1: 252–54.

"The Man With the Muck-rake," Washington, D.C., April 14, 1906. *WTRNE*, 16: 415–24.

"The New Nationalism" Address, Osawatomie, Kansas, August 31, 1910. *WTRNE*, 17: 5–22.

J. Michael Hogan and James R. Andrews

Woodrow Wilson
(1856–1924)

The world must be made safe for democracy.

Thomas Woodrow Wilson was born on December 28, 1856, in Staunton, Virginia, where his father, Joseph Wilson, was pastor of the Presbyterian church. In 1858, Joseph secured the pulpit of the First Presbyterian Church of Augusta, Georgia, where the family lived throughout the Civil War. Like so many families, the Wilsons were divided in their loyalties during the war. Joseph actively supported the Confederate war effort, while most of his relatives were Northerners; two of his brothers served as generals in the Union army.

Woodrow Wilson, "Tommy" as he was known to friends and family, was eight years old when the war ended and fourteen when his father became professor of pastoral theology at the Columbia, South Carolina seminary. In 1873, young Tommy entered Davidson College in North Carolina, a Presbyterian college favored by young men bound for the ministry. As an adolescent, he had been rather an indifferent student; now he excelled at English, rhetoric and composition, and Latin and Greek. In the summer of 1874, however, he left Davidson to join his family in Wilmington, North Carolina, where his father had moved after resigning from the Columbia seminary.

In Wilmington, Wilson prepared himself to enter the College of New Jersey (after 1896, Princeton University), cramming to bring himself up to par in a variety of subjects. He began college in the fall of 1875 and graduated in 1879. In October, he enrolled at the University of Virginia to study law. Although he found much to interest him at the University, the study of law proved tedious. Along with the lack of intellectual challenge, Wilson suffered from the bad food, poor lodgings, and generally unstable health. He left Charlottesville without completing the law course and went home to Wilmington where he stayed for almost a year before moving to Atlanta in 1881. It was at this time that he decided, at his mother's urging, to drop the use of "Tommy" and to style himself Woodrow Wilson.

Once in Atlanta, Wilson passed the bar examination and set up a law practice with an old friend. Law in the abstract fascinated Wilson; the practice of law, however, failed to enchant. After a year, Wilson decided that his call was teaching and scholarship. He entered the recently established John Hopkins University as a graduate student in history and political science, completing his Ph.D. in 1885. His thesis, *Congressional Government*, was published by Houghton Mifflin and established Wilson's scholarly reputation. He accepted a position at Bryn Mawr and taught history there for two years. In 1888 he moved to Wesleyan College in Middletown, Connecticut. During his short sojourn at Wesleyan, Wilson published his classic textbook on comparative government, *The State*. Then, in February 1890, the Board of Trustees of Princeton offered Woodrow Wilson the Chair of Jurisprudence and Political Economy at an annual salary of $3,000. In the fall of that year, Woodrow Wilson moved his family to New Jersey and began his twenty-year-long academic career at Princeton University.

Wilson was a very popular teacher at Princeton—and at Johns Hopkins where he annually taught a six-week course on administration, earning the admiration of a young graduate student, Frederick Jackson Turner. His reputation as a scholar grew as did his prestige and influence at Princeton. His writings in popular magazines, his biography of George Washington, and his lectures and addresses throughout the country extended his reputation in the academic community and beyond. He was tempted in 1898 by an offer of the presidency of the University of Virginia, but elected to stay on at Princeton. In June of 1902, reform-mined trustees, hoping to reinvigorate the University, succeeded in easing out President Patton and named Professor Woodrow Wilson as his successor.

During his eight years as president of Princeton, Wilson concentrated on curricular revision and the infusion of new blood into the faculty. He became best known, however, for his role in a bitter dispute over the location of the graduate school. Wilson wanted the school to be an integral part of the campus, while the Dean and the financial benefactor wanted it to exist in lordly isolation away from the undergraduates. Wilson's efforts failed, but he came to be seen outside the university as the defender of democratic values against a wealthy elite.

In the fall of 1910, Wilson's life took its most decisive turn. In an effort to thwart progressive elements in their own party, the old guard Democratic political bosses of New Jersey nominated Wilson for governor, secure in the belief that the political novice would be amenable to their control. Wilson resigned as President of Princeton, accepted the gubernatorial nomination, and launched an aggressively progressive campaign, denouncing the very bossism that had secured him the nomination. Garnering support from progressives of both parties, Wilson won the governorship by a substantial margin.

The progressive candidate attracted national attention; the reforming governor, whose efforts were in direct and public opposition to the politicians who origi- nally supported him, became a national figure. As Governor, Wilson lobbied the legislature for passage of electoral reforms, and he attacked the special in- terests of business. While these efforts earned him the everlasting enmity of the New Jersey political machine, they established Wilson as a strong contender for the Democratic presidential nomination.

Divided between conservatives and progressives, the Democratic National Convention, held in Baltimore in June 1912, nominated Wilson on the forty- sixth ballot. In the campaign of 1912, Wilson gave speech after speech focusing upon the progressive stands that later would be christened the "New Freedom." "The next four years," Wilson declared in a speech that virtually summed up his campaign, "will determine how we are to solve the question of the tariff, the question of trusts, the question of the reformation of our whole banking and currency systems, the conservation of our natural resources and of the health and vigor of our people. . . . " He pledged to his election eve audience that "the extension of the uses of government to . . . programs of uplift and betterment" would be the goal of his administration.

As expected, Wilson's opposition split the vote against him. Theodore Roo- sevelt, who had bolted the GOP and had run under the Progressive banner, won over four million votes, while the Republican Taft garnered almost three and a half million votes. Together they exceeded Wilson's six and a quarter million votes, but Wilson won what was, up to that time, the largest electoral majority in history: 435 electoral votes for Wilson, 88 for Roosevelt, 8 for Taft. Demo- crats also won majorities in both Houses of Congress. Wilson's powerful intel- lect, political skills, and progressive ideas had brought him to the nation's highest elective office. In no small measure, the new President's rhetorical abil- ities, nurtured and honed over many years, also contributed to that success.

RHETORICAL TRAINING AND PRACTICES

Woodrow Wilson, the son of a cleric known for his oratorical gifts, the son of a man who taught rhetoric early in his career, prized rhetorical ability and personally cultivated it. As a student at Davidson, Wilson not only joined the Euemean Society, a college debating club, but also read library books on ex- temporaneous speaking and the speeches of the great English orators. At Prince- ton, he began keeping his *Index Rerum*, in which he copied passages from the speeches of William Pitt, Lord Chatham, and Edmund Burke. He also helped form the Liberal Debating Club. The constitution of the new club, which made leadership dependent upon majority support, was clearly modeled along British lines. He further demonstrated his admiration for British orators by adding more contemporary British statesmen (John Bright and William Gladstone) to his reading list and by writing and later publishing an essay on Pitt. Wilson also espoused the study of public speaking as editor of the *Princetonian*; he entered oratorical contests; and he chaffed at the lack of weight given speaking and debate in the college curriculum.

At Virginia, Wilson turned to even more serious study of oratory and debate. Soon after arriving in Charlottesville, he won election to the debating club, the Jefferson Society, eventually becoming its president and principal author of a new constitution. He studied even more deeply the great English orators, and he delivered an address on Bright before the Jefferson Society that was later published in a university literary magazine. Wilson prized the parliamentarians' ability to speak extemporaneously and conversationally, in contrast to the more bombastic style that still had its adherents in the late nineteenth century. After a debate before the Jefferson Society against a brilliant young man who would one day earn a Pulitzer Prize and would represent Virginia in the U.S. Senate, William Cabell Bruce, Wilson was chagrined when Bruce won the prize as best debater while Wilson was named best orator. Although Wilson subsequently referred to "oratory" positively, his designation as an "orator" in this case came as a blow to his self-image as a practical, reasoned speaker. In contrast to debate, "oratory" suggested emotionalism and stylistic flourishes. Thereafter, Wilson made strenuous efforts to cultivate a simpler style.

Much of Wilson's skill as a speaker was developed through years of practice as a popular lecturer and fine tuned as President of Princeton, where Wilson's penchant for defining issues in terms of principles was most dramatically exhibited in the controversy over the graduate school. On April 17, 1910, Wilson addressed a group of Princeton alumni in Pittsburgh, placing the graduate school struggle in the wider context of democracy in America. In a passage that Judge Westcott saw fit to quote several years later as he nominated Wilson for President of the United States, the then President of Princeton said:

The great voice of America does not come from seats of learning. It comes in a murmur from the hills and woods and the farms and factories and the mills, rolling on and gaining volume until it comes to us from the homes of common men. Do these murmurs echo in the corridors of the universities? I have not heard them.

Wilson's passion for principle popularly defined him as an idealist. He also, however, was a rhetorical realist. In the New Jersey campaign for Governor, he at first was criticized for being too vague, too much the schoolmaster. On the advice of his progressive supporter, Joseph Tumulty, Wilson quickly adopted a harder-hitting political style: his campaign speeches sharpened the attacks on big business and political bossism. Wilson often got feedback from those close to him, but he wrote his own speeches. Many were given extemporaneously, especially the campaign speeches, and were penned in outline form by the candidate himself. Throughout his life, he wrote many speech drafts in shorthand, a skill he developed before entering Princeton, and he delivered his speeches extemporaneously in a clear, tenor voice that carried to the edges of crowds.

Following his election to the presidency, Woodrow Wilson began to put into practice a theory of leadership he had articulated in his academic writings, a theory that constitutes the intellectual foundation of the modern ''rhetorical presidency.'' As Jeffrey Tulis argues, Wilson the scholar perceived certain ''defects'' in the American constitutional order, most notably in the executive's role in the legislative process. Seeking to define a more energetic role for the president, Wilson wrote of the need for presidents not merely to react to Congress but to initiate change as the only public official elected by all of the people.

Wilson promoted a radically new view of the role of popular rhetoric in presidential leadership. Traditionally, presidents delivered public speeches largely upon ceremonial occasions, rarely delivering that staple of the modern presidency, the policy speech. Presidents advocated policies largely through written correspondence with Congress, not in popular oratory directed to the public at large. Theodore Roosevelt, of course, broke from this tradition, frequently going over the heads of Congress to build public support for his legislative initiatives. But as Tulis suggests, it was Wilson who first articulated the rationale for the rhetorical presidency. Reinterpreting the constitutional order, Wilson cast the president, not only as a public persuader and educator of the masses, but as the chief interpreter of those broad, enduring principles that defined ''true majority sentiment.''

Wilson's notion of leadership combined with faith in the power of the spoken word to define his rhetorical presidency. An intellectual and an idealist, he wrote his own speeches and saw in his policies the embodiment of great principles. As president, Wilson saw himself in a unique rhetorical role: more than a mere *representative* of the people, he served as a ''leader-interpreter.'' For Wilson, the true orator-leader needed that ''force of character, that readiness of resource, that clearness of vision, that grasp of intellect, that courage of conviction, that earnestness of purpose and that instinct and capacity for leadership which are the eight horses that draw the triumphal chariot of every leader and ruler of free men.'' During his first term in office, he largely lived up to this standard, effectively giving voice to the spirit of progressive reform. During his second term, however, the rhetorical presidency failed Woodrow Wilson, as his greatest popular crusade, his Western tour in support of the Treaty of Versailles, left him physically and spiritually broken.

WILSON'S PROGRESSIVE RHETORIC

During Woodrow Wilson's first administration, progressive reform was the order of the day. Wilson proved a highly successful political leader, able to use his majorities in Congress to effect legislative action. Wilson's request to Congress for a government controlled banking system was answered with the Federal Reserve System in 1913. In the same year the Underwood Tariff significantly lowered duties on imports and put some items on the free list. In 1914 the Federal Trade Commission was established to prevent unfair business practices, and the Clayton Anti-Trust Act further reduced the power of monopolies. The Clayton Act also included provisions favorable to union efforts to organize, even though these provisions were later emasculated by the courts. Legislation dealing with such matters as loan credits for farmers and charting the coasts of Alaska came before Congress at the instigation of the White House. This energetic enactment of "The New Freedom" was presaged in the President's address upon taking the oath of office on March 4, 1913.

First Inaugural Address

After sixteen years of Republican presidents, it must have given the new Democratic President great pleasure to begin his Inaugural Address with the simple pronouncement, "There has been a change in government." The change that Woodrow Wilson had in mind was sweeping but not revolutionary. In many ways, Wilson's "change" was but a change in style and tone, but he did bring to the office a firm conviction that the president must speak both for and to the people. Even before he began his Inaugural Address, Wilson took a symbolic step consistent with this conviction. Upon arriving at the platform, the President-elect ordered the cordon of troops holding back onlookers to give way, and thousands of whooping partisans surged to the very foot of the platform where they could better hear the new President speak.

The address itself embodied the themes of the 1912 campaign. After explaining in the opening paragraphs that the Democratic party would serve as the instrument to bring about change, Wilson asserted that American greatness had been achieved at a high price: its "exceeding bounty of nature" had not been conserved and "the human cost" not counted. Now, with his election, change indeed would come: the "scales of heedlessness have fallen from our eyes."

The specific changes Wilson proposed reflected the aims of the program he had enunciated in hundreds of campaign speeches. He would revise the tariff, reform the banking system, alter the industrial system, redirect agriculture, and conserve both natural and human resources.

Wilson assured his audience that the changes would not be radical, as "safeguarding of property and individual right" would still be a duty of government. At the same time, the government, which had "too often been debauched and made an instrument of evil," had to be made to serve the people. Wilson ended the address with a call to nonpartisanship, mustering on the people's behalf "not the forces of party, but the forces of humanity."

Wilson the idealist, the intellectual reformer, the progressive governor with strong moral convictions thus interpreted and articulated the principles he believed united all Americans. Antitheses formed the building blocks of Wilson's eloquence, both as a rhetorical device and as rhetorical form, with Wilson contrasting the principles shared by all Americans with prevailing political practice.

Throughout the Inaugural Address, Wilson contrasted what the nation had become with its founding principles. The new President recognized the country's greatness—"its material aspects . . . its body of wealth . . . energy . . . the industries that have been conceived and built," as well as the "moral force" of its "system of government." He could, nevertheless, point to antithetical characteristics of American life: that "evil has come with the good," riches had been obtained through "inexcusable waste," "industrial achievements" had come without regard to human cost, "great government" had been used for "private and selfish purposes."

Wilson's catalogue of evils stood in direct counterpoint to his assertion early in the address that "we see that in many things life is great." The things that needed altering were stated in negative terms, accentuating the contrast between the realities of life and the nation's potential. Tariffs had "cut us off" from world commerce; the industrial system had restricted "the liberties" and limited "the opportunities of labor"; watercourses were "undeveloped," forests "untended," waste heaps "unregarded" at the mines. Wilson reemphasized the contrast with yet another antithesis: "We have studied perhaps as no other nation has the most effective means of production, but we have not studied cost or economy as we should either as organizers of industry, as statesmen, or as individuals."

Wilson thus summarized the meaning of the change in government: "We see the bad with the good, the debased and decadent with the sound and vital." The exploitation of the people by the rising industrial power was captured in Wilson's mechanistic metaphor: America had created "giant machinery, which made it impossible that any but those who stood at the levers of control should have a chance to look out for themselves." Wilson envisioned government instead "at the service of humanity," shielding "men, women and children" from "the consequences of great industrial and social processes which they can not alter, control, or singly cope with." Otherwise, the "machine" would destroy itself: "society must see to it that it does not crush or weaken or damage its own constituent parts."

The American people, through a change in government, had made up their minds "to square every process of our national life again with the standards of justice and fair play we so proudly set up at the beginning and have always carried in our hearts." Wilson, their proxy at the levers of control, was the agent of change that would rise above all others, interpreting the people's will, voicing their values, serving as the articulate spokesman for the inarticulate masses.

Wilson concluded his Inaugural Address with a final set of antitheses. "This is not a day of triumph," he insisted, "it is a day of dedication." He urged his listeners to "muster, not the forces of party, but the forces of humanity." Thus the new President had infused into the meaning of the occasion his conception of change. The evils of the past, antithetical to the reform spirit of the nation, would be countered by the humane actions of his administration. This did not mean, however, that all traditional ideals would be abandoned. Rather, the "new freedom" rested upon an age-old principle, newly interpreted and fairly applied: "justice, and only justice, shall always be our motto."

Some Republican editorial writers grumbled that Wilson proposed to cure all social ills through legislative experimentation. Others suggested that Wilson's program owed its greatest debt to Roosevelt and the Progressives. Generally, however, reactions to the Wilson's Inaugural Address were favorable. However, the editorial writer for the Charleston, South Carolina *News and Courier* perhaps came nearest to describing Wilson as Wilson saw himself, as a president endowed with the ability to "divine the needs of the masses of his fellow-citizens," and who, as a consequence, had become "their spokesman and their champion."

That Wilson intended to interpret and champion the will of the people, especially in dealing with Congress, became abundantly clear a little more than a month after inauguration day. In a dramatic act that symbolized the change heralded in the Inaugural Address, President Wilson broke with tradition by appearing personally before Congress on April 8, 1913, to recommend tariff reform. By making such an appearance, Wilson affirmed much that had been implied by his writings before he became president, as well by the Inaugural Address: that he viewed the president not as the spokesman for a department of government but as the one person empowered to interpret and to give voice to the will of the people.

Address to Congress on Revision of the Tariff

The significance of Wilson's first speech to Congress lay not only in the precedent-shattering personal appearance of the president, but also in its demonstration of the rhetorical style and strategy that would come to define his rhetorical presidency. In arguing for revision of the Payne-Aldrich Tariff, one of the cardinal issues of his presidential campaign, Wilson stressed the larger principles that undergirded the mundane issue of tariff reform, and he claimed to appear before Congress at the request of the people. The speech was very short and direct. In about eleven minutes, Wilson entwined the practical arguments for tariff reform with the progressive principles that he now dubbed the mandate of the previous year's election.

In opening, Wilson acknowledged the unusual circumstance of the president delivering his message orally. He even interpreted the symbolism of the act for his listeners, explaining that "the President of the United States is a person, not a mere department of the Government hailing Congress from some isolated island of jealous power." By speaking "naturally and with his own voice," he hoped to join "with other human beings in a common service." Moving on to his arguments on the tariff, Wilson insisted that a "duty" had been "laid upon the party now in power at the recent elections": "It is clear to the whole country that the tariff duties must be altered." As in the Inaugural Address, Wilson elaborated by contrasting the original motivations for the tariff laws with the "radical alteration in the conditions of our economic life," the old principles governing tariff laws with the "new principles of action."

The concept of change, the same dynamic that drove his Inaugural Address, also moved this speech forward. While the "whole face and method of our industrial and commercial life" had changed, Wilson argued, the tariff laws "remained what they were before the change began." From the notion that import duties protected the country's industry, tariff legislation had wandered "very far afield." Looking "beneath the surface," the President discerned "the principles upon which recent tariff legislation had been based." From seeking protection, industries had moved to demanding government patronage. The tariff structure had been founded on principles clearly inimical to the progressive spirit that had swept the country. "Consciously or unconsciously," Wilson asserted, "we have built up a set of privileges and exemptions from competition behind which it was easy by any, even the crudest, forms of combination to organize monopoly . . . ." The result was that "nothing is obliged to stand the tests of efficiency and economy . . . everything thrives by concerted arrangement."

In contrasting the old and the new, Wilson forcefully assumed the persona of the leader articulating the public's demand that tariff reform be guided by certain principles. "It is plain what those principles must be," he contended. The most fundamental tenet directed that America "must abolish everything that bears even the semblance of privilege or of any kind of artificial advantage." Following from this was the principle that businessmen had to be "efficient, economical, and enterprising, masters of competitive supremacy, better workers and merchants than any in the world." This progression of principle led to the test to be applied to all future tariff legislation: "the object of the tariff duties henceforth laid must be effective competition, the whetting of American wits by contest with the wits of the rest of the world."

Moving to yet a higher order of principle, Wilson promised "freedom in the place of artificial stimulation," at least "so far as it will build, not pull down" business and provide "genuine remedies." If such principles animated tariff reform, Wilson assured Congress, then "our motives" would be "above just challenge."

Following in the wake of his Inaugural Address, Wilson's speech on the tariff began the president's efforts to translate progressive principles into concrete action. The theme of change and the momentum of a new and vigorous administration carried forward into this first policy statement. In this deliberative address, as in the Inaugural, principles still held sway as the spur to action. The new President had begun his speech by asserting that he came to Capitol Hill to speak "with his own voice," but within a few short minutes he cast himself as the voice of all the people.

Address to the Veterans of Gettysburg, July 4, 1913

The summer of 1913 was, as Washington summers are prone to be, hot and uncomfortable. The Wilsons had taken a summer house in Cornish, New Hampshire, but the President himself did not join his family there. He conceived it his duty to stay in Washington while the uncertain battle for tariff reform raged in Congress. Wilson did hope to leave Washington for the July 4th holiday; in this, however, he was to be disappointed. Instead, he found himself speaking, as the first president born in the South since the Civil War, to former enemies in that war, veterans of the battle of Gettysburg, now camped together on that hallowed ground to commemorate of the fiftieth anniversary of that most famous battle.

As a gesture of national reconciliation, the mere presence of the old soldiers defined the symbolism of the occasion. Moreover, President Lincoln's speech on the same ground, although shorter than Wilson's, had said all that needed to be said about the meaning of the war. For his part, Wilson praised the valor exhibited on both sides a half-century earlier, but he focused instead on challenges still to be met. The war became but a metaphor for the spirit of progressive reform.

Declining to recount the events of July 1–3, 1863 (to do so would have been an "impertinence," surrounded as he was by the men who actually fought there), Wilson instead questioned whether the nation had yet lived up to its ideals. Out of the war had grown a "great nation." From a "wholesome and healing" reunion had emerged the country "we love with undivided hearts." Still, Wilson wondered aloud: had the nation yet "squared itself with its own great standards set up at its birth, when it made that first, noble, naive appeal to the moral judgment of mankind to take notice that a government had now at last been established which was to serve men, not masters?" According to Wilson, the answer was clear: America still had a way to go to live on to its own "standards of righteousness and humanity." Much work remained to be done, "in another way but not in another spirit," if the sacrifices of the Civil War were to be redeemed.

"The days of sacrifice and cleansing are not closed," Wilson declared, and the future could prove even more difficult than those "heroic days of war." In peacetime, Wilson suggested, the right path was never so clear as in wartime. To see it required "more vision, more calm balance in judgment, a more candid searching of the very springs of right."

The necessary spirit, however, remained the same. Surveying the field of battle, Wilson recalled the "fierce heats and agony, . . . column hurled against column, battery bellowing to battery." Extolling the "self sacrifice" and the "high recklessness of exalted devotion which does not count the cost," he observed: "we are made to know by these tragic, epic things what it costs to make a nation . . . ." Then, making the connection between his martial imagery and his own political battles, Wilson asked his listeners to consider "how little except in form" a nation's "action in days of peace" he differs "from its action in days of war." Fighting "wickedness in high places" posed no less a challenge than war. "War fitted us for action," Wilson concluded, "and action never ceases."

Before volunteering to lead the charge, Wilson posed a rhetorical question:

"Are our forces disorganized, without constituted leaders?" His answer provided yet another clue to his conception of his own role as leader: "I have been chosen as the leader of this Nation. I cannot justify the choice by any qualities of my own, but so it has come about, and here I stand." The President thus placed his leadership beyond the person of Woodrow Wilson. No personal qualities or special qualifications had made him president. Rather, the people had chosen him and so, as Martin Luther proclaimed his faith at the Diet of Worms, "Here I stand." Whatever the merits of their choice, his duty was clear: to *act* on behalf of "the people themselves, the great and the small, without class or difference of kind or race or origin . . . ." Promising that "every day" he would "push the campaign forward," Wilson concluded by returning to the military metaphor undergirding the speech: "Do not put your uniforms by. . . . Come, let us be comrades and soldiers yet to serve our fellow men . . . ."

In yet another short speech, Wilson thus again revealed much about his conception of the presidency. Relying upon the setting to suggest the appropriate metaphor, he projected himself as a leader who, akin to a great military leader, directs and speaks for his troops, always mindful of their welfare, always urging them to action. The field of conflict may have been different from the bloody ground of Gettysburg, as the struggle now called for "quiet counsel" in places where "the blare of trumpets is neither heard nor heeded." If America were to realize its "great destiny," however, the same spirit, the same concerted action would be necessary—to amend the tariff, to restructure the banking system, to carry out the promises of progressive reform. In domestic affairs, of course, Wilson's call-to-arms remained just a metaphor. Before long, his wartime leadership would be put to the real test.

WILSON THE PEACEMAKER

When war broke out in Europe in 1914, Woodrow Wilson asked a lot of his fellow Americans: to put aside their "natural" and "inevitable" sympathies for one side or another and to embrace "the spirit of impartiality and fairness and friendliness to all concerned." "Every man who really loves America," Wilson averred in his "Neutrality Appeal" on August 19, 1914, "will act and speak in the true spirit of neutrality," whether in public meetings, in newspapers and magazines, in the pulpit, or "on the street." It would "be easy to excite passion" and "difficult to allay it," and "those responsible for exciting it" would "assume a heavy responsibility," the responsibility for dividing the nation into "camps of hostile opinion, hot against each other." This would involve the nation in the war itself, "in impulse and opinion if not in action."

The conduct of the war sorely tested the "spirit of neutrality." Outraged by violations of international law by both the British and the Germans, Americans could not help but take sides. Nevertheless, Wilson continued walking the thin line of neutrality, warning the Germans that they would be held to a "strict accountability" for American ships or lives lost to their submarines, while also urging the British to end their blockade of Germany. On May 7, 1915, however, events tested Wilson's resolve. Without warning, German U-boats sank the British passenger liner *Lusitania* off the coast of Ireland, killing 1,200 civilians, including 128 Americans. In a series of notes that prompted Secretary of State William Jennings Bryan to resign, Wilson warned the German government that the United States could not for long tolerate such violations of "the rights of humanity."

After a submarine sank yet another liner, the *Arabic*, Wilson's protests finally secured a German pledge not to sink unarmed passenger liners without warning. Tensions remained high, however, as German submarines continued to attack merchant vessels. The issue came to a head on March 24, 1916, when a submarine torpedoed an unarmed Channel packet, the *Sussex*, without warning and with the loss of eighty lives. Wilson finally issued an ultimatum, threatening to sever diplomatic relations with Germany. When the Germans promised to observe the rules of "visit and search" before sinking any more vessels, the crisis again passed for the moment.

On the domestic front, Wilson faced additional challenges to his neutrality doctrine. Aroused by new evidence of German intrigues within the United States, anti-German sentiment continued to grow. Meanwhile, a "preparedness" debate, which had been raging since the outbreak of fighting, polarized Congress, and Wilson found himself fighting against progressives within his own party. Caught between demands that he defend American rights yet keep the nation out of the war, Wilson approached the campaign of 1916 under heavy criticism from both sides.

The Republicans had their own problems articulating a solution to the dilemma. Torn between demands by Theodore Roosevelt and his followers for a strong policy against Germany and the pacifist views of western progressives, the Republican platform called for "a straight and honest neutrality" and only "adequate" preparedness. Nevertheless, Wilson managed to portray the Republicans as the party of war, campaigning on the slogan: "He kept us out of war." Also touting his record of progressive reform, Wilson won a narrow victory over his Republican challenger, Charles Evans Hughes.

Peace without Victory

Shortly after the election, Wilson made one last attempt to mediate the peace. Calling upon both sides to state their war aims, Wilson reported the results in a memorable speech to Congress on January 22, 1917: "Peace Without Victory." The Central Powers, Wilson reported, had "united in a reply which stated merely that they were ready to meet their antagonists in conference to discuss terms of peace." The "Entente Powers," on the other hand, "replied much more definitely," stating "in general terms" certain "arrangements, guarantees, and acts of reparation" which they deemed to be "the indispensable conditions of a satisfactory settlement." According to Wilson, the replies moved the two sides "much nearer a definite discussion of the peace which shall end the present war." Yet he said little further about the belligerents' responses, and for good reason. Despite Wilson's assurances, the two sides in fact remained far apart.

Wilson implicitly admitted as much by devoting most of "Peace Without Victory," not to the belligerents' demands, but to his own terms for peace. With strained optimism that neither side aspired "to crush their antagonists," Wilson *implied* that both sides would accept "peace without victory"—the only peace that, in Wilson's view, could guarantee a "tranquil" and "stable" Europe. "Victory," Wilson explained, "would mean peace forced upon the loser, a victor's terms imposed upon the vanquished." Such a peace would only "be accepted in humiliation, under duress, at an intolerable sacrifice, and would leave a sting, a resentment, a bitter memory upon which terms of peace would rest, not permanently, but only as upon quicksand."

In typical fashion, Wilson spoke of the principles upon which lasting peace must rest: the right of self-determination, equality among nations, limitations on arms, freedom of the seas, and the abandonment of secret alliances. Yet principles meant little without the means of enforcement, so Wilson emphasized the need for a League of Peace— "a force . . . so much greater than the force of any nation now engaged or any alliance hitherto formed or projected" that "no nation, no probable combination of nations could face or withstand it." If the peace were to endure, it had to be "a peace made secure by the organized major force of mankind." Wilson concluded by contrasting the old ways of the world with his proposed "new arrangement": "There must be, not a balance of power, but a community of power; not organized rivalries, but an organized common peace."

Consistent with his conception of presidential leadership, Wilson cast himself as interpreting and reporting the ""conditions"" under which the American people would add "their authority and their power to the authority and force of other nations to guarantee peace and justice throughout the world." "I am speaking as an individual," Wilson told Congress, "and yet I am speaking also, of course, as the responsible head of a great government, and I feel confident that I have said what the people of the United States would wish me to say." According to Wilson, the American people had directed him to champion the principles articulated in the speech. "These are American principles, American policies," Wilson concluded. "We could stand for no others."

Unfortunately, the Allies already had negotiated secret agreements at odds with those principles. More importantly, the Germans already had decided to resume unrestricted submarine warfare, and in February and March they sank several more liners and American merchant ships. On March 1, the Zimmerman note, the Germans' bizarre proposal to Mexico that they side with the Germans in exchange for the return of territory lost in the war of 1848, dashed any remaining hopes that America might stay neutral. Meanwhile, the Russian revolution gave advocates of war with the United States still more ammunition.

With the overthrow of the Russian Tsar, the war became a contest between the democracies and the despots.

Wilson's War Message

Convinced that he had no other choice, Woodrow Wilson called Congress into special session on April 2, 1917, to ask for a declaration of war. His "War Message," while in some ways a formality, clearly revealed the President's frustration over his failed peace initiatives. At the same time, it reflected his optimism that, by fighting "without rancor and without selfish object," the United States could play a major role in forging a lasting peace. For Wilson, the United States did not enter the war to fight *against* Germany but to fight *for* "the things which we have always carried nearest to our hearts"—democracy, "the rights and liberties of small nations," the "peace and safety" of "all nations," and a world "at last free."

Wilson began his "War Address" with a review of familiar events, now cast in the language of diabolical betrayal. Recalling the "extraordinary announcement" by the "Imperial German Government" that it would resume unrestricted submarine warfare, Wilson accused the Germans of casting aside "all restraints of law and humanity" and of warring against "all nations," against "mankind" itself.

America's only option was thus to "formally accept the status of belligerent," a status that had been "thrust upon" the nation by actions representing "nothing less than war against the government and people of the United States." Wilson followed with a list of measures needed to finance the war, build up the army and navy, and provide aid to the allies. But providing few specifics, he returned quickly to the larger principles behind his decision:

While we do these things, these deeply momentous things, let us be very clear, and make very clear to all the world what our motives and our objects are. . . . Our object . . . is to vindicate the principles of peace and justice in the life of the world as against selfish and autocratic power and to set up amongst the really free and self-governed peoples of the world such a concert of purpose and of action as will henceforth insure the observance of those principles.

What once had been a war Americans safely could ignore thus became a crusade to rid the world of "the menace" of "autocratic governments." "The world must be made safe for democracy," Wilson declared, "its peace must be planted upon the tested foundations of political liberty." By entering the war, America had "no selfish ends to serve. We desire no conquest, no dominion," Wilson assured the world. America would "freely make" the "sacrifices" of war, not for selfish gain, but to assure that "the rights of mankind" were "made as secure as the faith and the freedom of nations can make them."

Throughout his "War Address," Wilson carefully distinguished between the government and the people of Germany. "We have no quarrel with the German people," he averred midway through the address. "We have no feeling towards them but one of sympathy and friendship." It was not upon "their impulse that their government acted in this war," nor was it "with their previous knowledge or approval." Toward the end of the address, Wilson again professed no "enmity" toward the German people nor any "desire to bring any injury or disadvantage upon them." Describing America's entry into the war as "armed opposition to an irresponsible government," Wilson reiterated his heartfelt sympathies for the German people: "We are, let me say again, the sincere friends of the German people, and shall desire nothing so much as the early reestablishment of intimate relations of mutual advantage between us,—however hard it may be for them, for the time being, to believe that this is spoken from our hearts."

Like most calls-to-arms, Wilson's "War Address" painted a portrait of a diabolical foe, accusing the "Prussian autocracy" of filling "our unsuspecting communities and even our offices of government with spies" and of setting "criminal intrigues everywhere afoot." Recalling the Zimmerman note, Wilson deemed the German government a "natural foe to liberty," a predator "always lying in wait," and he declared that the United States could "never have a friend" in "such a Government, following such methods." Yet, again, Wilson stressed that the German people were in no way to blame. The "source" of the German conspiracies lay not "in any hostile feeling or purpose of the German people towards us," but only in "the selfish designs of a Government that did what it pleased and told its people nothing." Indeed, Wilson cast the war as a crusade, inpart, to liberate the German people themselves: "We are glad, now that we see the facts with no veil of false pretense about them, to fight thus for the ultimate peace of the world and for the liberation of its peoples, the German peoples included: for the rights of nations great and small and the privilege of men everywhere to choose their way of life and of obedience."

In distinguishing between the government and the people of Germany, Wilson hoped to guarantee both the loyalty and the fair treatment of "the millions of men of women of German birth and native sympathy" within the United States. "Most" German-Americans, he insisted, were "true and loyal Americans," and he predicted that they would be "prompt to stand with us in rebuking and restraining the few who may be of a different mind and purpose." Should a few prove disloyal, he warned, they would "be dealt with" by the "firm hand of stern repression." To those "in fact loyal to their neighbors and to the Government in the hour of test," however, the American people would "happily" prove their "friendship" in their "daily attitude and actions."

Wilson also had another, more important motive in driving a wedge between the government and the people of Germany: the need to reconcile the seemingly contradictory impulses of the "War Address." On the one hand, Wilson hoped to rally public passions with a call-to-arms, a purpose served well by his portrait of the German *government*. On the other hand, he hoped to restrain desires for vengeance, punishment, or national aggrandizement at the conclusion of the fighting. Calling upon his countrymen to "put excited feeling away," he declared that "our motive will not be revenge," but only "the vindication of right, of human right."

The "Fourteen Points"

Only nine months after America entered the war, Wilson appeared before a joint session of Congress to present his "program" for peace, the "only possible program" for peace, according to the President. Wilson's "Fourteen Points," delivered on January 8, 1918, represented more than a report to Congress on the administration's war aims. It became the opening shot of a massive propaganda campaign, both at home and abroad. Hundreds of thousands leaflets containing translations of the speech rained down from planes and balloons behind enemy lines, while George Creel's American Committee on Public Information distributed millions of additional copies around the world. The speech said little new: not only had Wilson articulated many of the same principles previously, but so too had Lloyd George of Great Britain and even Russia's new leaders. Indeed, the Russians had upstaged Wilson the month before by signing their own armistice with Germany and negotiating for a separate peace.

Hoping to recapture the peace-making initiative, Wilson began the "Fourteen Points" with praise for the "sincere" and "earnest" efforts of the Russians. Unfortunately, according to Wilson, they had secured from the Central Powers a proposed settlement that included "no concessions at all either to the sovereignty of Russia or to the preferences of the populations with whose fortunes it dealt." It would have allowed the Central Powers to keep "every foot" of their occupied territories.

Glossing over differences among the Allies, Wilson implied that the only thing still standing in the way of peace was the failure of the Central Powers to clarify their terms. Wilson spoke of "a voice" calling for "these definitions of principle and of purpose," a voice "more thrilling and more compelling than any of the many moving voices with which the troubled air of the world is filled": the "voice of the Russian people." They may be "prostrate" and "all but helpless . . . before the grim power of Germany," Wilson emoted, but their "soul" was "not subservient," and they would "not yield either in principle or in action." They had a "conception" of what was "right," of what it would be "humane and honorable for them to accept," and they had "refused to compound their ideals or desert others that they themselves may be safe."

Continuing to interpret Russian public opinion, Wilson further sensed the Russians' desire to know how, if at all, America's "purpose" and "spirit" differed from their own. Responding to the "wish" of "the people of the United States" that he respond "with utter simplicity and frankness," Wilson insisted that the United States indeed had the interests of the Russian people at heart: "Whether their present leaders believe it or not, it is our heartfelt desire and hope that . . . we may be privileged to assist the people of Russia to attain their utmost hope of liberty and ordered peace.'' These goals, Wilson continued, were "nothing peculiar to ourselves," and in language reminiscent of his "War Address" the President recalled America's purposes in entering the war:

What we demand in this war . . . is that the world be made fit and safe to live in; and particularly that it be made safe for every peace-loving nation which, like our own, wishes to live its own life, determine its own institutions, be assured of justice and fair dealing by the other peoples of the world as against force and selfish aggressions.

Wilson followed his assurances to the Russians with his "Fourteen Points." The first four points reiterated his idealistic principles of international conduct: (1) "open covenants of peace, openly arrived at"; (2) "absolute freedom of navigation upon the seas"; (3) removal of "economic barriers" and "the establishment of an equality of trade"; and (4) arms reductions. Points 5 through 13 contained Wilson's proposals for resolving the specific territorial questions of the war, all based upon the general principles of popular sovereignty and self-determination. Finally, of course, came Wilson's capstone proposal: a "general association of nations . . . formed under specific covenants for the purpose of affording mutual guarantees of political independence and territorial integrity to great and small states alike." Wilson presented his program, not as an American plan, but as the program of "all the governments and peoples associated together against the Imperialists." "We cannot be separated in interest or divided in purpose," he concluded. "We stand together until the end."

In closing the "Fourteen Points" speech, Wilson issued a subtle yet unmistakable warning to the German people. Professing no "grudge" against Germany nor any demand for "alteration or modification of her institutions," he nevertheless clearly implied that they would have to throw off the autocrats and the militarists who refused to embrace the principle behind his program, the "principle of justice to all peoples and nationalities, and their right to live on equal terms of liberty and safety with one another, whether they be strong or weak."

The German government answered Wilson with a string of spring offensives on the Western front. By July, however, the influx of fresh American troops had begun to turn the tide. By the end of September, the Germans realized that their military situation was hopeless. Fearing a bloody invasion of the Fatherland, the Kaiser finally abdicated and a new parliamentary government offered to make peace on the basis of the "Fourteen Points."

The Allies, however, remained reluctant to negotiate. Fearful of German treachery, they demanded more guarantees that Germany would be incapable of resuming the fighting, and they denied ever agreeing to the "Fourteen Points" as the basis for negotiations. Talks to resolve these differences proved difficult, but on November 11 the armistice was signed. The fighting had ended, but Wilson's crusade for a lasting peace had only just begun.

The Treaty Debate

On December 4, 1918, Wilson set sail as the head of a large American delegation to the Paris peace conference. Convinced that only his presence could guarantee the right kind of settlement, Wilson drew sharp criticism both for his unprecedented personal diplomacy and for the make-up of his delegation, which included but one Republican. In Europe, Wilson received a tumultuous welcome, with huge crowds cheering him in France, England, and Italy. At the talks themselves, however, Wilson faced serious Allied opposition to the "Fourteen Points," and he soon began compromising on his program for peace.

On the League of Nations, however, Wilson remained firm. Whatever the specific terms of settlement, Wilson demanded that the League be made integral to the treaty, and the conference rewarded his persistence by endorsing the League and naming him chair of the commission drafting its constitution. After considerable wrangling within the Commission, Wilson finally emerged with the League's twenty-two article Covenant. Presenting the Covenant to a plenary session of the conference on February 14, Wilson pronounced the proposed League an embodiment of "the moral force of the public opinion of the world."

Even as he conceded that the rest of the treaty was "far from ideal," Wilson left Paris proud of his achievement. Back home, however, congressional opponents found much to criticize in the Covenant. Concerned that the League might compromise U.S. sovereignty, more than a third of the senators and senators-elect signed a round-robin letter circulated by Senator Henry Cabot Lodge declaring that they would oppose the treaty without changes. Furious, Wilson issued what historians generally have considered an impetuous and ill-advised challenge. When the Senate received the treaty, Wilson declared, they would find the Covenant "not only in it" but tied by "so many threads" to the treaty itself that they could not "dissect the Covenant from the treaty without destroying the whole vital structure."

Wilson softened for a time following his presentation of the treaty to the Senate on July 10, 1918. Offering to meet with Lodge's Foreign Relations Committee, and eventually agreeing to accept what he called "interpretive" reservations, Wilson appeared headed for compromise on the chief sticking point of the Covenant: Article 10's guarantee that all member nations would come to the defense of any member threatened with "external aggression" against its "territorial integrity and existing political independence." Yet Wilson remained steadfastly opposed to substantive changes, and his stubbornness only strengthened his opponents' position. After the Foreign Relations Committee met with Wilson on August 19, Lodge left convinced that he could muster the votes to amend or even kill the treaty. For his part, Wilson sensed that his only hope lay in rallying public pressure on the Senate to ratify the treaty.

Warned by his doctor against such a campaign, Wilson nevertheless embarked on his famous Western tour on September 2, 1919. Planned to cover ten-thousand miles with thirty-three major appearances, the tour drew enthusiastic crowds as it proceeded from the Midwest to the West Coast, finally circling back to the Rocky Mountains. Yet Wilson's health deteriorated steadily during the tour, and by the time he reached California appearances had to be cancelled. Meanwhile, Lodge remained in Washington, parading witnesses hostile to the treaty before the Foreign Relations Committee and courting the "mild reservationists"—senators who supported the treaty with relatively minor changes. Wilson only helped Lodge's cause when he began attacking all who dared oppose him as "Bolshevistically inclined," "un-American," and even "pro-German."

When the Western tour reached the Mountain West, Wilson delivered the most famous, yet arguably most misguided, speech of the campaign: his address at the Fairgrounds Auditorium in Pueblo, Colorado, on September 25, 1919. Exhausted from twenty-two days of touring, Wilson could barely climb to the speaker's platform for what turned out to be the last speech of the tour, and in a hesitant, barely audible voice he began attacking those who had been "busy creating an absolutely false impression of what the treaty of peace and the Covenant of the League of Nations contain and mean." Wilson attributed this "organized propaganda" to "exactly the same sources" that had "threatened" the nation with "disloyalty" during the war: "certain bodies of foreign sympathies, certain bodies of sympathy with foreign nations." Before uttering a single word in defense of the treaty, Wilson thus accused all who opposed the treaty, not only of lying, but of betraying their country: "I want to say—and I cannot say too often—any man who carries a hyphen about with him carries a dagger that he is ready to plunge into the vitals of this Republic. If I can catch any man with a hyphen in this great contest I will know that I have got an enemy of the Republic."

In characteristic fashion, Wilson spoke of the treaty in terms of a broad moral principle, the principle that people had the right "to live under such governments as they chose themselves to erect." "That is the fundamental principle of this great settlement," Wilson declared, but it would mean nothing without the League of Nations: "Unless you get the united, concerted purpose and power of the great Governments of the world behind this settlement, it will fall down like a house of cards."

Reviewing specific criticisms of the treaty, Wilson not only discussed the territorial settlements but fears that the League Covenant would put the United States "at a disadvantage" in the voting, compromise the Monroe Doctrine, and threaten American sovereignty. Wilson did not so much answer his critics, however, as accuse them of "deliberately falsifying" the facts or of having "not read the Covenant," an accusation reinforced by his tone of disbelief. In responding to concerns about Article 10, for example, Wilson incredulously pointed out that the council could only "advise" member nations to come to the aid of a threatened member nation, and even then it required the approval of the U.S. representative. Similarly, Wilson reminded his audience that, after meeting with his congressional critics, he had returned to Paris to secure revisions that guaranteed America's right to withdraw from the League, safeguarded the Monroe Doctrine, and excluded all "domestic questions" from League action. Seemingly exasperated, Wilson asked: "What more could I have done? What more could have been obtained?"

In just the second sentence of his Pueblo speech, Wilson had portrayed his Western tour not as a sales job but as an effort "to express the public sentiment." Throughout the speech, he also insisted that the treaty itself, while perhaps misunderstood by the public, nevertheless "embodied the moral judgment of the citizens of the United States." Recalling the negotiations, Wilson declared that he would have "felt very lonely" at the peace table if he had been "expounding my own ideas." Claiming that he had "explicit instructions," Wilson talked of how he had "conscientiously . . . read the thought of the people of the United States" and had "proposed nothing whatever at the peace table at Paris" without "sufficiently certain knowledge" that it represented "the moral judgment of the United States and not my single judgment." In short, the whole treaty had been "written down and accepted beforehand" by the American people, with the delegates in Paris serving merely as "architects building on those specifications."

Nowhere in all of Wilson's speeches does one find a more explicit statement of his rhetorical theory of presidential leadership. Rather than attempt to impose his personal moral vision upon the rest of the world, as some critics complained, he simply had listened, and given voice to, the people themselves. At the same time, however, Wilson implicitly degraded the public he claimed to represent by presenting, as an expression of its sentiment, a speech that heaped invective on his political opponents, dismissed rather than refuted their arguments, and culminated in a combative refusal to compromise and maudlin emotionalism. America had to do "one or the other of two things—we have got to adopt it or reject it," Wilson insisted toward the end of the speech; there could be "no middle course." And should the treaty be rejected, Wilson suggested in a long peroration to the speech, opponents of the treaty would have blood on their hands.

Invoking "our pledges to the men that lie dead in France," Wilson began his impassioned conclusion recalling the "mothers" who "again and again" had come up to him and, taking his hand, had shed tears for sons killed in the war. Yet always they concluded: "God bless you, Mr. President!" Wilson feigned wonderment: "Why should they pray God to bless me? . . . I ordered their sons oversea. I consented to their sons being put in the most difficult parts of the battle line, where death was certain. . . . Why should they weep upon my hand and call down the blessings of God upon me?" The answer, of course, was that those mothers believed "their boys died for something that vastly transcends any of the immediate and palpable objects of the war." They believed, and "rightly" so, that "their sons saved the liberty of the world" and died for "the continuous protection of that liberty by the concerted powers of all civilized people." In other words, they died for the League of Nations, and if America now rejected the League, Wilson asked rhetorically, "would not something of the halo go away from the gun over the mantelpiece, or the sword? Would not the old uniform lose something of significance?"

Wilson continued to emote, suggesting that rejection or even qualification of the treaty would betray not only those mothers but "the serried ranks of those boys in khaki, not only those boys who came home, but those dear ghosts that still deploy upon the fields of France." Recalling his visit to a "beautiful hillside near Paris," to "the cemetery of Suresnes, a cemetery given over to the burial of the American dead," Wilson first described the scene:

Behind me on the slopes was rank upon rank of living American soldiers, and lying before me upon the levels of the plain was rank upon rank of departed American soldiers. Right by the side of the stand where I spoke there was a little group of French women who had adopted those graves, had made themselves mothers of those dear ghosts by putting flowers every day upon those graves, taking them as their own sons, their own beloved, because they had died in the same cause—France was free and the world was free because America had come!

Then, again suggesting that they died for the League of Nations, Wilson laid a heavy burden of guilt upon all who opposed the treaty:

I wish some men in public life who are now opposing the settlement for which these men died could visit such a spot as that. I wish that the thought that comes out of those graves could penetrate their consciousness. I wish that they could feel the moral obligation that rests upon us not to go back on those boys, but to see the thing through, to see it through to the end and make good their redemption of the world. For nothing less depends upon this decision, nothing less than the liberation and salvation of the world.

Of course, the Pueblo speech is best remembered not so much for what Wilson said as for what happened afterwards. On the train that night, Wilson broke down, portending the massive stroke he would suffer on October 2. The remaining five speeches were cancelled, and the train sped back to Washington, where Wilson remained virtually incapacitated for the next four months. On November 6, Senator Lodge introduced fourteen reservations to the treaty, which Wilson instructed his supporters to oppose. On November 19, the Senate defeated the treaty, both with and without the reservations. In effect, Wilson had sabotaged his own peacemaking efforts. Undertaking an ill-advised and ineffectual campaign rather than remaining in Washington to negotiate with the Senate, Wilson had mostly himself to blame for the tragic outcome.

CONCLUSION

On February 3, 1924, Woodrow Wilson died, his many accomplishments tarnished by the failure of his League of Nations campaign. Why did it fail?

Many factors conspired against the success of the campaign: partisanship, the insulation of the Senate from public opinion, and Wilson's own stubborn refusal to compromise, among others. Above all, however, Wilson probably failed because he tried to lead the public too far, too fast. In domestic affairs, Wilson harvested the fruits of a progressivist impulse planted long before he entered office and cultivated even by such political opponents as Theodore Roosevelt. In foreign affairs, by contrast, Wilson first urged a neutrality consistent with America's long isolationist tradition, only to urge, less than three years later, a crusade to make the world "safe for democracy." Then, going beyond even that, he asked Americans to commit to a permanent alliance to guarantee the peace.

Woodrow Wilson accomplished much in his life that can be attributed to his cultivation of oratorical skills and his conscious reflections upon rhetoric and leadership. When he followed his own rhetorical prescriptions, he generally tasted political success. He left a legacy of progressive reform, and he modeled the rhetorical presidency for all who came later. At the same time, however, Wilson's League of Nations campaign revealed that there are limits to what can be accomplished through popular persuasion. Actually alienating many senators, Wilson's passionate pleas for public support not only defined his tragic legacy but revealed the limits of the rhetorical presidency.

RHETORICAL SOURCES

Archival Material

Baker, Ray Stannard. *Woodrow Wilson, Life and Letters: Youth, 1856–1889; Princeton, 1890–1910; Governor, 1910–1913; President, 1913–1914; Neutrality, 1914–1915; Facing War, 1915–1917; War Leader, 1917–1918; Armistice.* Garden City, NY: Doubleday, Page, 1927–1939. (Baker's interview notes are available in the Library of Congress.)

Wilson, Woodrow. *The Public Papers of Woodrow Wilson. (PPWW),* 6 Vols. Edited by Ray Stannard Baker and William E. Dodd. New York: Harper, 1925–1927.

———. *The Papers of Woodrow Wilson. (PWW).* 68 Vols. Edited by Arthur Link, et al. Princeton, NJ: Princeton University Press, 1966–1993.

Rhetorical Studies and Biographies

Clements, Kendrick A. *The Presidency of Woodrow Wilson.* Lawrence, KS: University Press of Kansas, 1992.

Heckscher, August. *Woodrow Wilson.* New York: Charles Scribner's Sons, 1991.

Tulis, Jeffrey K. *The Rhetorical Presidency.* Princeton, NJ: Princeton University Press, 1987.

Rhetorical Monographs

Andrews, James R. "Wilson's First Inaugural." *The Inaugural Address of the Twentieth-Century American Presidents: Critical Rhetorical Studies,* edited by Halford Ross Ryan. Westport, CT: Praeger, 1993.

Balcer, Charles L. "Woodrow Wilson's Columbian Exposition Speech—'A Liberal Education.' " *Communication Education* 32 (1983): 330–38.

Carpenter, Ronald. "Woodrow Wilson as Speech Writer for George Creel: Presidential Style in Discourse as an Index of Personality." *Presidential Studies Quarterly* 19 (1989): 117–27.

Craig, Hardin. "Woodrow Wilson as an Orator." *Quarterly Journal of Speech* 38 (1952): 145–48.

Hendrix, J. A. "Presidential Addresses to Congress: Woodrow Wilson and the Jeffersonian Tradition." *Southern Speech Communication Journal* 31 (1966): 285–94.

Ivie, Robert L. "Presidential Motives for War." *Quarterly Journal of Speech* 60 (1974): 337–45.

McEdwards, Mary. "Woodrow Wilson: His Stylistic Progression." *Western Journal of Speech Communication* 26 (1962): 28–38.

Reid, Ronald. "The Young Wilson's Political Laboratories." *Southern Speech Communication Journal* 29 (1963): 227–35.

Chronology of Significant Presidential Persuasions

First Inaugural Address, Washington, D.C., March 4, 1913. *PPWW* 3: 1–6; *PWW* 27: 148–52.

Address on Tariff Revision to Joint Session of Congress, Washington, D.C., April 8, 1913. *PPWW* 3: 32–35; *PWW* 27: 269–72.

Address to the G.A.R. and Confederate Veterans, Gettysburg, Pennsylvania, July 4, 1913. *PPWW* 3: 41–44; *PWW* 28: 23–26.

"Peace Without Victory," Washington, D.C., January 22, 1917. *PPWW* 4: 407–14; *PWW* 40: 533–39.

"War Message," Washington, D.C., April 2, 1917. *PPWW* 5: 6–16; *PWW* 4: 519–27.

"The Fourteen Points," Washington, D.C., January 8, 1918. *PPWW* 5: 155–62; *PWW* 45: 534–39.

Address at Pueblo, Colorado, September 25, 1919. *PPWW* 6: 399–416; *PWW* 63: 500–13.

Carl R. Burgchardt

Herbert Clark Hoover
(1874–1964)

I have no fears for the future of our country.

Herbert Clark Hoover was born on August 10, 1874, in West Branch, Iowa. Thus, he was the first president born west of the Mississippi River. When his mother died in 1884, Hoover was left an orphan, but relatives cared for him in Iowa and later, after 1885, in Oregon, where his uncle was principal at the Quaker preparatory school Hoover attended in Newberg. Hoover's lifelong belief in self-reliance was probably rooted in his tragic childhood circumstances and his devout, Quaker upbringing.

In 1891 Hoover entered the first class of the newly created Stanford University. He graduated four years later with a geology degree. After leaving Stanford, Hoover worked as a mining engineer in California, Australia, and China. In 1901 he became a junior partner in a London mining company. Seven years later he created his own consulting business and built an international reputation by reviving inefficient or unprofitable mines. By 1914 he was a forty-year-old millionaire.

When World War I erupted in Europe, Hoover led the American Relief Committee, which helped over 100,000 of his fellow citizens return to the United States. He next directed an international commission that fed starving people in war-torn Belgium and France. As a result of Hoover's growing fame, in 1917 President Woodrow Wilson asked him to be the U.S. food administrator after America entered the war in 1917. Hoover worked to more efficiently manage the production and distribution of food for military and civilian needs. After the war, the Allies put Hoover in charge of relieving European food shortages. By 1920, Hoover's efforts had aided millions of people and earned him the sobriquet of the "Great Humanitarian."

Hoover returned to the United States in the fall of 1919 and was immediately considered a likely candidate for high public office. President Warren G. Harding, realizing Hoover's potential, appointed him Secretary of Commerce, 1921–1923. He continued in that office under President Calvin Coolidge, 1923–1928. Hoover, who was not tainted by political scandal, reorganized the commerce department, increased its responsibilities, and assisted businesses in avoiding waste and inefficiency. In 1922 he published *American Individualism,* which explained his political philosophy. Hoover bolstered his brilliant reputation by directing relief efforts in the 1927 Mississippi flood.

Hoover became the most prominent Republican candidate for president when Coolidge declared he would not seek another term. After easily receiving his party's nomination, Hoover delivered an acceptance speech and seven campaign addresses in various locations around the country. In all of his 1928 discourse, he stressed the optimistic view that America was entering a new era of moral achievement and economic development. As a progressive, Hoover advocated reform in the following areas: agricultural and labor policies, taxation, the judicial system, and the federal bureaucracy. Moreover, he favored federal regulation to maintain fair business competition. Hoover stood for continuation of prohibition, while his opponent, Al Smith, was for repeal. Although Hoover condemned religious bigotry, Smith's Catholicism and association with big-city, machine politics, undermined the Democrat's candidacy. In general, the Republican campaign stressed the winning themes of prosperity and peace. Furthermore, Republicans portrayed Hoover as a great humanitarian, a gifted engineer and businessman, and a new kind of politician who displayed unprecedented wisdom, probity, and competence. In the general election, Hoover defeated Smith in a landslide.

Hoover's administration started positively. In June of 1929 he obtained legislation designed to assist farmers who had not shared in the economic bonanza of the 1920s. Hoover's early success, however, was soon shattered by the stock market crash of October 29, 1929. At first Hoover organized conferences for leaders of labor, finance, business, and farming in order to avoid strife and support wages. By 1932 Hoover concluded reluctantly that voluntary efforts were not sufficient to offset the Great Depression. Congress established Hoover's major economic initiative in January of 1932: the Reconstruction Finance Corporation, which initially lent money to shore up financial institutions and businesses. He also supported federal conservation projects and construction of public works such as the Boulder Dam on the Colorado River. Hoover, was, however, opposed to direct, federal payments to the unemployed, which he thought would destroy the national character.

Despite Hoover's best efforts, the public perceived him as a distant, uncaring leader, and his popularity plunged. This image was exacerbated in the spring of 1932 when General Douglas MacArthur routed unemployed veterans from their makeshift camps in the nation's capital. A dispirited Republican party renominated Hoover for president in 1932, but Franklin D. Roosevelt crushed him at the polls in November.

After leaving public office, Hoover disputed President Roosevelt's New Deal doctrines through speeches and writings. Prior to the Japanese attack on Pearl Harbor, Hoover also opposed Roosevelt's foreign policy. After the war, President Harry Truman asked Hoover to study food distribution and to make recommendations about avoiding worldwide famine. In 1947 Truman appointed Hoover to chair the Commission on Organization of the Executive Branch of Government, later to be known as the Hoover Commission (1947–1949). This organization sought ways to make the government more efficient. After heading up a second efficiency commission under President Dwight D. Eisenhower (1953–1955), Hoover retired at the age of eighty.

Hoover devoted his final years to rationalizing his presidency and explicating his political philosophy. He published his three-volume memoirs from 1951–1952 and a well-received book on Woodrow Wilson in 1958, in addition to his four-volume *An American Epic* (1959–1964). His eight-volume *Addresses Upon the American Road* was published between 1936 and 1961. Over the years, Hoover's reputation gradually became that of respected, elder statesman, and today he is widely regarded as one of the most productive and successful ex-presidents in American history.

RHETORICAL TRAINING AND PRACTICES

Between 1919 and 1962, Hoover delivered over six hundred speeches. This number is especially impressive considering his lack of training or aptitude in rhetoric. Indeed, Hoover struggled with English as a young student and failed the composition portion of the entrance exam at Stanford. In addition, for most of his life, he was painfully shy and dreaded public speaking. In later years he became slightly more comfortable, but Hoover gave speeches out of duty or necessity, not because he enjoyed it.

Although Hoover was not a gifted orator, he labored diligently at the art of persuasion and wrote all of his major addresses. His method of speech preparation was methodical and dogged. After performing encyclopedic research, Hoover would dictate the first draft of a speech to a secretary or write it out in longhand. This draft would then be typed or printed and distributed to his political aides for criticism. The process of correcting and editing would continue through multiple versions. One of Hoover's 1931 speeches went through fourteen drafts before he was satisfied.

Despite Hoover's painstaking efforts, his speeches were generally not eloquent. Hoover habitually framed his wordy, awkward prose in the passive voice. As a consequence, he cluttered his discourse with unnecessary articles, prepositions, and conjunctions. Moreover, his long, complex sentences often contained erudite vocabulary or technical detail not well suited for ordinary audiences. His addresses featured few metaphors or rhythmic devices, although he occasionally penned a serviceable epigram. Hoover's engineering mentality, along with his austere, Quaker background, did not cultivate the proper temperament for soaring figures and stirring cadences. Indeed, Hoover disdained eloquence for its own sake, believing that plain language would speak for itself. He assumed that the nation wanted dispassionate analysis, not inspiration. Hoover apparently thought presidential discourse should sound ponderous and grave.

The arrangement of Hoover's oratory was exactly what one would expect from a pragmatic engineer: thorough and systematic. According to Theodore Joslin, a close political aide, Hoover "built his public utterances as he would drive a mine shaft or construct a bridge." Many of Hoover's political speeches followed variations of the "problem-solution" format, where he identified a problem, analyzed its causes, proposed a solution, answered possible objections, and, finally, urged immediate action. For the most part, Hoover used deductive logic. He first established general principles, then moved to specific conclusions. One of the weaknesses of Hoover's organization was the tendency to be redundant. In his zeal to consider comprehensively all of the relevant political, social, and economic dimensions of a topic, he often repeated excessively basic concepts or propositions. In sum, Hoover was more preoccupied with thoroughness than elegance.

Hoover's delivery skills were predictably weak, considering his shyness and fear of public speaking. Although he worked very hard on the content of orations, he rarely practiced them out loud, relying instead on a silent rehearsal. Moreover, Hoover read his manuscripts to audiences rather than performing them extemporaneously. This method resulted in weak eye contact, a fast rate, and little vocal variety or animation. Hoover was equally dull when reading a speech into a radio microphone. According to Joslin, on one occasion Hoover was asked if speaking over the radio gave him a "thrill." Hoover replied, "The same thrill I get when I rehearse an address to a door knob."

INAUGURAL ADDRESS

Ironically, the high point of Hoover's rhetorical presidency was his Inaugural Address, delivered on March 4, 1929, in Washington, D.C. The public expected Hoover, who was famous as an efficiency expert and pragmatic organizer, to make the federal government function more smoothly. Hoover did not disappoint this expectation, because his inaugural focused strongly on policy proposals. He argued that "disregard and disobedience of the law" was "the most malign" problem confronting the United States. In fact, Hoover devoted about one-fifth of his speech to an analysis of law enforcement. He first established that a serious problem existed concerning increasing crime. Next, he considered the causes for this expansion in criminal activity, concluding that inefficient organization was the explanation. To solve this problem, Hoover proposed a thorough reorganization of the structure of law enforcement to make it more productive. To correct evident problems with the enforcement of Prohibition,

Hoover pleaded with citizens to set a good example by not purchasing illegal alcohol. Moreover, he advocated the creation of a national commission to study legal procedures concerning the Eighteenth Amendment. In addition to judicial policies, Hoover reiterated some of his proposals from the 1928 campaign: tariff reform, agricultural relief, regulation of business to create a competitive environment, spending reductions, development of public works, and promotion of education.

Hoover's address also validated his public image as an advocate for world peace. The majority of the electorate, sickened by World War I, hoped to avoid future military conflict. In the emotional high point of the speech, Hoover reflected, "It is impossible, my countrymen, to speak of peace without profound emotion. In thousands of homes in America, millions of homes around the world, there are vacant chairs." Hoover pledged that, under his administration, there would be no armed aggression against neighbors in the western hemisphere. Moreover, Hoover supported armament reductions and American participation in the World Court. Hoover fervently proclaimed, "I covet for this administration a record of having further contributed to advance the cause of peace."

Hoover satisfied public expectations by projecting an optimistic tone throughout the speech. Indeed, he was so impressed by the advancement of the United States that he declared, "We are steadily building a new race—a new civilization great in its own attainments." The nation had made great progress under Republican leadership, Hoover maintained, and this progress was to be surpassed only by the future. Changes that Hoover proposed did not imply that there were national crises, simply that a good situation could be made better: "The questions before our country are problems of progress to higher standards; they are not the problems of degeneration." Hoover confidently concluded his address with the statement: "I have no fears for the future of our country. It is bright with hope."

Hoover's Inaugural Address was a success. The March 5th *New York Herald Tribune* exulted, "The President's inaugural address glowed with courage, confidence, and statesmanship." His position on Prohibition satisfied those who favored its continuation, yet, his proposal to investigate its enforcement pleased those who wished for repeal. Peace advocates and foreign audiences were encouraged to hear his international policies. Business owners liked his philosophy of encouraging fair competition, without unnecessary government intrusion. On the whole, the nation could relax with such a competent administrator in the White House. During such prosperous times, citizens did not desire an eloquent orator, but rather an engineer who could make the motor of economic progress run more smoothly. The *Washington Star Herald* captured this sentiment the next day: Mr. Hoover "is an engineer, and knows that work is done by machinery, not by words, loud or soft."

RADIO ADDRESSES

Hoover had little face-to-face interaction with Congress during his presidency, but he did deliver ninety-five addresses that were broadcast locally or nationally from 1929 to 1933. Unfortunately for him, most of these speeches were brief, ceremonial greetings to organizations such as the Red Cross, the 4-H Clubs, or the American Legion. Despite Hoover's belief in the power of radio to communicate with the electorate, he failed to use it effectively to motivate, inspire, or reassure a troubled nation. Nor did Hoover attempt to foster an empathetic, caring radio personality. When his staff advised him to make weekly, ten-minute radio speeches, Hoover declined on the grounds that such brief talks would inevitably be superficial and vague. His impulse was to delve into lengthy, comprehensive policy analyses. The contrast with his successor, Franklin Roosevelt, could not be more striking.

Memorial Day Address

One notable exception to Hoover's rhetorical diffidence was his 1931 Memorial Day Address, broadcast nationally and delivered to a crowd of approximately 20,000 people at Valley Forge Park, Pennsylvania. On May 30 Hoover sought to rally the people behind him in his fight against the depression. The occasion and setting for the speech led Hoover naturally to the topic of George Washington's heroic struggle during the American Revolution. Hoover praised "the transcendent fortitude and steadfastness of these men who in adversity and in suffering through the darkest hour of our history held faithful to an ideal." Using the obvious analogy, Hoover stated that "The American people are going through another Valley Forge at this time." The depression is "the same test of steadfastness of will, of clarity of thought, of resolution of character, of fixity of purpose, of loyalty to ideals and of unshaken conviction that they will prevail." Hoover argued that the American people should remain determined, preserve the great democratic traditions of the nation, and eschew radical new ideas or panaceas. The American revolution was fought to win independence, he averred, and "We are still fighting this war of independence. We must not be misled by the claim that the source of wisdom is in the Government. We know that the source of wisdom is in the people; that the people can win anew the victory." Hoover's speech was unusually emotional and sincere, but it had little effect on his flagging popularity. Many citizens were seeking new solutions for economic distress, not exhortations to stay the course.

ACCEPTANCE SPEECH

By the summer of 1932, it was obvious that the people of the United States wanted a change in the White House. Nonetheless, Hoover's party had little choice but to renominate him. In light of this, Hoover worked especially hard preparing his Acceptance Speech, to be presented on August 11, 1932, in Washington, D.C. Typically, he wanted this speech to outline clearly the political principles upon which he would conduct his campaign. He also wanted to express his ideas in his own way. Hoover delivered the speech at 9:30 P.M. to a crowd of about 4,000 in Constitution Hall, and it was also broadcast nationally.

Hoover's Acceptance Speech of 1932 stood in stark contrast to the optimism of 1928. Now, Hoover was forced to admit that "the last 3 years have been a time of unparalleled economic calamity. They have been years of greater suffering and hardship than any which have come to the American people since the aftermath of the Civil War." Hoover claimed that the depression unfolded in two stages: domestic and international. The first stage was the result of "reckless speculation" within the United States. This type of temporary, economic downturn "we have always passed safely after a relatively short period of losses, of hardship, and of adjustment." However, a second economic blow occurred when the "financial systems of foreign countries crashed one by one. . . . Thus beginning 18 months ago, the worldwide storm grew rapidly to hurricane force and the greatest economic emergency in all the history of the world." What had Hoover done in response to these two blows? "We might have done nothing," he answered. "That would have been utter ruin. Instead, we met the situation with proposals to private business and to the Congress of the most gigantic program of economic defense and counterattack ever evolved in the history of the Republic. We put that program into action." Hoover assiduously reviewed all of the emergency actions he had taken since the onset of the depression to prove that he had not stood idly by and done nothing. Hoover asserted, "Our measures have repelled these attacks of fear and panic. We have maintained the financial integrity of the Government."

In a long section, Hoover summarized his other leadership initiatives such as the protective tariff, immigration restrictions, conservation of national resources, spending reduction, sound currency, and foreign policies devoted to securing world peace. Hoover admitted that Prohibition was not working well, so he proposed that each state be permitted to regulate alcohol "as it may determine," but he wanted absolutely to avoid a return to the "saloon system."

Hoover conceded that, "As a government and as a people we still have much to do." He warned, though, that the nation should not overreact: "And in all these emergencies and crises, in all our future policies, we must also preserve the fundamental principles of our social and our economic system." The solution to the problems of the depression was "not to be found in haphazard experimentation or by revolution." Hoover opposed a "State-controlled or State-directed social or economic system in order to cure our troubles." The federal government should "use its powers to give leadership to the initiative, the courage, and the fortitude of the people themselves, but . . . it must insist upon individual, community, and State responsibility." Hoover concluded reasonably, "I rest the case of the Republican Party upon the intelligence and the just discernment of the American people."

Overall, Hoover called for "patience and perseverance," which was a continuation of his message at Valley Forge. But American citizens were not in a patient mood; they wanted fundamental change now. However, Hoover offered nothing new in the address, and the immediate audience gave him a tepid response. Nonetheless, he did receive a number of positive telegrams and letters from supporters who heard the speech on radio. Despite its shortcomings, the 1932 Acceptance Speech served as a blueprint for the remaining electoral contest.

1932 CAMPAIGN SPEECHES

Address at the Coliseum

Hoover made nine major campaign addresses in 1932, as well as dozens of "whistle-stop speeches" in between destinations. His strongest speech of the campaign is generally thought to be his first, delivered on October 4, 1932, in Des Moines, Iowa. Hoover selected Iowa to start his campaign so that he could talk to people like the ones with which he grew up in West Branch. He gave the speech in the Des Moines Coliseum to a packed house of carefully-screened Republicans who received him warmly. Overflow crowds of up to 10,000 heard the address over loudspeakers in the Shrine Auditorium and on the State House Plaza.

Hoover read his speech from a seventy-one-page manuscript, and it lasted ninety minutes. He opened this address with nostalgic musings concerning his boyhood in Iowa. For a moment, a charming, empathetic Herbert Hoover emerged, but as he replayed the major themes of the 1932 Acceptance Speech, he resumed his old persona. Hoover claimed that he had acted decisively in responding to the depression, and he used a military metaphor to express this idea, a technique that he employed frequently in his presidency: "Now, we have fought an unending war against the effect of these calamities upon our people in America. This is no time to recount the battles on a thousand fronts. We have fought the fight to protect our people in a thousand cities from hunger and cold."

Hoover stated that his efforts had prevented a much greater economic disaster than the current depression, a fact that the public did not realize. He then shared with these Iowans some of his bitterness and sense of martyrdom:

Many of these battles have had to be fought in silence, without the cheers of the limelight or the encouragement of public support, because the very disclosure of the forces opposed to us would have undermined the courage of the weak and induced panic in the timid and would have destroyed the very basis of success. Hideous misrepresentation and justified complaint have had to be accepted in silence for the national good.

Hoover portrayed himself as a sequestered president, doing lonely battle with hostile forces. Such a confession probably underscored the public's negative perception that Hoover was under siege in the White House.

Hoover assured his audience that he struggled to preserve the well-being of "the people in the homes and at the firesides of our country. I have had before me but one vision: that is, the vision of the millions of homes of the type which I knew as a boy in this State." However, his heartfelt expression of concern for the welfare of Iowans was soon lost in mind-numbing exposition. In attempting to itemize how he had defended the people's interests, Hoover said, "I know that it is the most involved of economics and the most complex of descriptions to attempt. But I shall try it if you will have patience." He then launched into a tedious explication "of gold and of currency, of credit and of banks and bonds and insurance policies and of loans. Do not think these things have no human interpretation." He followed this by outlining a twelve-point plan to revive American agriculture.

Hoover's dry, abstract policy discussions obscured his compassionate motives. He obviously realized that he needed to emphasize easily grasped human values and simple political principles, yet he seemed incapable of delivering. Despite his rhetorical errors, Hoover received over one hundred congratulatory messages from his radio audience. The reasonably favorable response to the Des Moines speech caused Hoover's advisors to plead for a more extensive speaking tour, but he refused.

In Wilton Eckley's analysis, Hoover's 1932 campaign orations rested on four major themes. First, Hoover claimed that he acted decisively in the past to establish innovative policies for ending the depression. Second, he proposed new legislative initiatives to restore the voter's faith in his ability to govern. Third, he blamed the severity of the depression on European circumstances rather than American policies. Finally, he attempted to create the fear that the depression would be much worse under a Democratic administration. In addition, throughout his speeches Hoover warned that the government should not undermine American character and precious democratic traditions by experimenting with radical social change. In the latter half of the campaign, Hoover was also preoccupied with answering Democratic party attacks on his leadership and character. Placed in such a defensive position, Hoover was never able to establish any positive momentum. As well, he was demoralized by a lack of campaign funds and by cruel or hostile demonstrations outside the meeting halls and along his travel routes. To make matters worse, hoarseness and fatigue plagued Hoover as the campaign ground on.

Overall, Hoover's 1932 campaign speeches were didactic, technical, and detailed. He thought of public speaking as an opportunity to instruct his fellow citizens rather than to motivate them. As he stated in his last campaign speech, delivered in Elko, Nevada, on November 7: "We have been through an arduous campaign. It has been almost unique as a campaign of education in the great domestic and international problems which have arisen out of the last 15 years."

VALEDICTORY

Address to the Gridiron Club

Although Hoover did not give an official farewell address, his last major speech as president, delivered on December 10, 1932, to the Gridiron Club, functioned as his valedictory. His audience, which was an organization of Washington newspaper people, gathered at the Willard Hotel. Hoover's comments were initially supposed to be off-the-record, but they were later published. After some pleasant ceremonial remarks about the history and purpose of the Gridiron Club, Hoover came to the point with typical bluntness: "You will expect me to discuss the late election. Well, as nearly as I can learn, we did not have enough votes on our side." He went on to express gratitude for the chance afforded to him by the United States: "I am indebted to my country beyond any human power to repay."

Hoover concluded by presenting his view of presidential responsibility. He conceived of the people of the United States as a river that needs to flow through clear channels, with dikes to prevent flooding: "The life stream of this Nation is the generations of millions of human particles acting under impulses of advancing ideas and national ideals gathered from a thousand springs." In Hoover's mind,

We are but transitory officials in Government whose duty is to keep these channels clear and to strengthen and extend their dikes. What counts toward the honor of public officials is that they sustain the national ideals upon which are patterned the design of these channels of progress and the construction of these dikes of safety. . . . God help the man or the group who breaks down these dikes, who diverts these channels to selfish ends. These waters will drown him or them in a tragedy that will spread over a thousand years.

This central metaphor, drawn from his experience as an engineer, reveals much about his presidency. The energy of a republic must be channeled properly to do useful work, but not allowed to overflow its banks. Hoover's ideal state was one of order and certainty, not the unpredictable world of floods—nor, indeed, economic depressions.

CONCLUSION

On March 4, 1929, a confident nation celebrated the inauguration of President Herbert Hoover. Eight months later, the United States plunged into economic and social disaster. While Hoover's political philosophy and rhetorical skills were more than sufficient to win the presidency in 1928, they were unequal to the task of restoring public confidence. Although presidential rhetoric has its limits in overcoming national crises, it also has unique potential to uplift the national psyche. Hoover failed to exploit this potential. For that mission, an orator was needed rather than an engineer. Indeed, in 1932 the nation gratefully embraced the energetic, eloquent Franklin D. Roosevelt.

Despite the generally negative judgment we must make of Hoover's rhetorical presidency, his career was full of irony. His inglorious defeat in 1932 obscured the striking popularity he enjoyed on his inauguration day. Hoover's confident predictions of unrivaled prosperity in 1928 were reduced to absurdity by the most severe depression in American history. Although the public criticized him for inaction, he was the first president of either party to harness the resources of the national government to combat economic collapse. He was widely thought to be an uncaring man, yet he worked tirelessly to help people within the constraints of his political philosophy.

Hoover believed that government should exist to permit each person the maximum amount of freedom to achieve. As a consequence, the nation must never stifle the responsibility, energy, and creative genius of individuals. Although Hoover realized that abuses could not be solved entirely through voluntary effort, nonetheless, the impetus for positive change must come from the people, not government. Considering Hoover's belief that the depression was temporary, his actions were really quite logical. He had faith that the system would soon right itself, that there was nothing fundamentally wrong with the United States of America. Those who question his decisions today can only do so with the certainty of historical hindsight.

RHETORICAL SOURCES

Archival Materials

Herbert Hoover's presidential papers are located at the Herbert Hoover Presidential Library, West Branch, Iowa. This collection contains correspondence, audio and film recordings, diaries, speech manuscripts, and files of newspaper clippings.

Hoover, Herbert Clark. *Public Papers of the Presidents of the United States: Herbert Hoover. (PPP)*. 4 Vols. Washington, DC: U.S. Government Printing Office, 1974–1977.

Rhetorical Studies

Eckley, Wilton. *Herbert Hoover*. Boston: Twayne Publishers, 1980.
Fausold, Martin L. *The Presidency of Herbert C. Hoover*. Lawrence, KS: University Press of Kansas, 1985.
Joslin, Theodore G. *Hoover Off the Record*. Garden City, NY: Doubleday, Doran & Company, Inc., 1934.
Lloyd, Craig. *Aggressive Introvert*. Columbus, OH: Ohio State University Press, 1972.
Wilson, Joan Hoff. *Herbert Hoover: Forgotten Progressive*. Boston: Little, Brown and Company, 1975.

Rhetorical Monographs

Burgchardt, Carl R. "President Herbert Hoover's Inaugural Address, 1929." In *The Inaugural Addresses of Twentieth-Century American Presidents*, edited by Halford Ryan, 81–92. Westport, CT: Praeger, 1993

Olson, James S. "Herbert Clark Hoover." In *American Orators of the Twentieth Century*, edited by Bernard K. Duffy and Halford R. Ryan, 203–8. Westport, CT: Greenwood Press, 1987.

Runkel, Howard W. "Hoover's Speeches During His Presidency." Ph.D. dissertation, Stanford University, 1950.

————."A President Prepares to Speak." *Western Journal of Speech Communication* 15 (1951): 5–9.

Short, Brant. "The Rhetoric of the Post-Presidency: Herbert Hoover's Campaign Against the New Deal, 1934–1936." *Presidential Studies Quarterly* 21 (1991): 333–50.

Chronology of Significant Presidential Persuasions

Inaugural Address, Washington, D.C., March 4, 1929. *PPP*, 1929: 1–12.

Memorial Day Address, Valley Forge, Pennsylvania, May 30, 1931. *PPP*, 1931: 272–77.

Address Accepting the Republican Presidential Nomination, Washington, D.C., August 11, 1932. *PPP*, 1932–1933: 357–76.

Address at the Coliseum, Des Moines, Iowa, October 4, 1932. *PPP*, 1932–1933: 459–86.

Address to the Gridiron Club, Washington, D.C., December 10, 1932. *PPP*, 1932–33: 891–95.

Franklin Delano Roosevelt (1882–1945)

The only thing we have to fear is fear itself.

Barring a resurgence of polished presidential rhetoric in 1996, one may venture that Franklin Roosevelt was the most successful presidential persuader in the twentieth century. Although the Kennedy crowd may quibble, Roosevelt was also the most eloquent.

Born January 30, 1882, in a patrician country estate in Hyde Park, New York, far from the plebeian people that he would come to champion during his presidency, Roosevelt was schooled as befitted his station in society. His elementary education was from his mother, private tutors, and travel in Europe. At age fourteen, FDR enrolled in Groton preparatory school, where he debated. At Groton, he also listened to strong readers, such as Endicott Peabody, the headmaster, who recited great literature.

In 1900, FDR enrolled at Harvard University, where he received predominantly the proverbial "Gentleman's C." He took a course in public speaking, debated, and continued listening to literature read aloud by Harvard's famous professors. FDR also attained the presidency of the Harvard student newspaper, the *Crimson.* Although an average student, by the time that FDR graduated from Harvard, he had a firm grounding in the skills that would serve him well in his political life. He mastered the structure and content of speeches, and he gained experience in effectively delivering oral communications.

After a desultory, short-lived career in law from 1907 to 1910, Roosevelt entered politics. He ran successfully as a Democrat for the New York State Senate in 1910 and again in 1912. Mirroring the political ascension of his distant cousin, Theodore Roosevelt, Franklin was appointed Assistant Secretary of the Navy by President Woodrow Wilson and served from 1913 to 1920. FDR ran in 1920 as the Democratic vice-presidential running mate with James Cox, who lost to Warren G. Harding and Calvin Coolidge.

In 1921, Roosevelt contracted polio at his summer home. Through the support of Eleanor, his wife, and Louis Howe, something of the man behind FDR, Franklin maintained contacts with prominent Democratic leaders. Roosevelt nominated Governor Alfred E. Smith, a fellow New Yorker, at the 1924 Democratic national convention with his famous "Happy Warrior" speech. Smith, a "wet" on Prohibition, lost the nomination to William McAdoo, a "dry." Smith, nominated again by FDR at the 1928 Democratic convention, campaigned unsuccessfully against Herbert Hoover. Smith persuaded FDR to run for his vacated governor's chair, which FDR won in 1928.

As the two-term governor of New York, FDR began rhetorical practices that he would carry with him to the White House. Of paramount importance, Roosevelt attracted Samuel Rosenman, who signed on for the 1928 campaign. Rosenman, a valued adviser and speechwriter, was the equal-among-equals on FDR's speech team for most of his presidency. FDR also used the radio to deliver talks directly to New Yorkers, which previewed his practice of using Fireside Chats to address the nation when president.

In 1932, FDR became the Democratic party's presidential candidate after a close nomination contest that was swung FDR's way by newspaperman William Randolph Hearst. John Garner, whom FDR had displaced, accepted the vice-presidential nomination. In November, Roosevelt beat President Herbert Hoover in a landslide. FDR then served four consecutive presidential terms; he died in Warm Springs, Georgia, on April 12, 1945.

FOUR CAMPAIGNS FOR THE PRESIDENCY

Roosevelt beat Hoover in 1932 by 22.8 million votes to 15.7; Alf Landon in 1936 by 27.5 million to 16.7; Wendell Willkie in 1940 by 27.2 million to 22.3; and Thomas Dewey in 1944 by 25.6 to 22 million votes. How he did it, follows.

The 1932 Campaign

This question always arises after a presidential election: "Did the candidate win because the people voted *for* him or *against* his opponent?" From a rhetorical standpoint, FDR usually gave the listener more reasons to vote against Hoover than to vote for himself. Thus, Roosevelt's strategy in the campaign was to attack rather than to defend, which wisely left Hoover saddled with the Depression, and to ignore Hoover's constant and bitter charges that Roosevelt's New Deal lacked specificity, which it did, and that his campaign rhetoric was contradictory, which it was.

Governor Roosevelt delivered five major orations in the campaign. He made two important speeches before the convention. The first speech was the "Forgotten Man" address, written largely by Raymond Moley, that FDR delivered to the nation over radio from Albany, New York, April 7, 1932; the second was his "Bold, Persistent Experimentation" speech, composed by Ernest Lindley, at Oglethorpe University in Atlanta, Georgia, on May 22, 1932. In his radio speech from Albany, the governor attacked Hoover's and the Republican's trickle-down economic theory of enhancing the rich so that the poor would eventually benefit. Although Hoover had established a two-billion-dollar fund to help railroads and corporations, Roosevelt reminded his audience that nothing was done for "the forgotten man at the bottom of the economic pyramid." Although the governor scolded the president for not addressing people's needs, Roosevelt was not at pains to reveal what he would do: He suggested a vague panacea for increasing purchasing power, he did not indicate how much it would cost to aid mortgage foreclosures, and he contradicted himself on tariff revisions. Never mind, for Roosevelt concluded his speech with a persuasive military metaphor, which was a precursor of his First Inaugural Address, "We are in the midst of an emergency at least equal to that of war. Let us mobilize to meet it." Presumably, the governor would remember forgotten voters and vanquish the Republican enemy.

Roosevelt continued his attack on Hoover in the Oglethorpe speech. He claimed that true leadership set goals and rallied public opinion to obtain the objectives. His technique coyly invited listeners to conclude that Hoover championed the wrong ends and hence was unable to persuade the nation to follow his lead. However, FDR touted solutions that were really nostrums. But one appeal certainly enticed the dispossessed: FDR promised to redistribute income. But he was still unclear how he would do it; indeed, the speech's famous line ended with a vague pronoun:

The country needs and, unless I mistake its temper, the country demands bold, persistent experimentation. It is common sense to take a method and try it: If it fails, admit it frankly and try another. But above all, try something.

(Those conversant with President Bill Clinton's Inaugural Address will recall that his "bold, persistent experimentation" phrase was borrowed from Roosevelt's Oglethorpe address.) As problem-solution speeches, the Albany and Atlanta addresses were platitudinous, which Hoover constantly reminded voters. But FDR would not move conservatives; rather, he tried to persuade the vast majority of the people who suffered from the Depression.

Having won the nomination, FDR delivered his famous New Deal acceptance speech at the Democratic convention in Chicago, July 2, 1932. FDR clearly understood the power of imagery, for he flew to Chicago, where he told the convention and the country that it was "symbolic that in so doing I broke traditions." Yet, the speech suffered from defects: It jibed Republicans, but lacked coherence; it was internally contradictory on the tariff issue; and "just one word more" was overused as a transitional device. But all of that did not really matter. Although most of the speech defined FDR by what he was not—

he was not Hoover—FDR delivered a line that has been associated forever with this speech and his presidency. He offered forgotten men and women a well-turned phrase: ''I pledge you, I pledge myself, to a new deal for the American people.'' The line, composed by Rosenman, was originally on the fourth page of a twenty-page draft, but it was moved to its rightful place in the speech's peroration.

Roosevelt canvassed the country in 1932, but one speech endures as one of Roosevelt's few coherent statements about the role of government. Delivered to San Francisco's Commonwealth Club on September 3, 1932, Roosevelt's so-called ''Progressive Government'' speech laid the philosophical groundwork for the New Deal. Written by Adolph Berle and revised by the Brain Trust, the speech posited a dichotomous choice for voters in 1932: Government could either benefit the rich, and Roosevelt subtly implied that Hoover and the Republicans used government for that end, or government could minister to the people, which FDR invited listeners to conclude was his and the Democratic party's aim. If the *raison d'etre* of Roosevelt's oratory throughout four terms could be stated in one sentence, then surely it is from his 1932 Commonwealth Club speech, for the innervation of Roosevelt's rhetorical presidency was stated eloquently: ''Government includes the art of formulating policy and using the political technique to attain so much of the policy as will receive general support; persuading, leading, sacrificing, teaching always, because the greatest duty of a statesman is to educate.''

In Pittsburgh, Pennsylvania, on October 19, 1932, the governor delivered an I-wish-I-never-gave-that-speech, for his words came back to haunt him in 1936. A tenet of Republicanism was a balanced budget, yet to combat the Depression, Hoover used deficit spending. But at Pittsburgh, FDR attacked Hoover for deficit spending, promised to balance the federal budget, but did not indicate how he would do that! Although an obvious attempt to appeal to conservatives, Roosevelt contradicted himself later in the speech by telling forgotten people that he would use deficit spending if necessary to fend off starvation.

In terms of delivery, Roosevelt was clearly Hoover's superior. Compared to FDR's inflected voice, reasonably good eye contact, and vigorous platform presence, Hoover's delivery was dour: He droned interminably without modulation, he read verbatim his speeches, and he rarely gestured for emphasis or variety. Whereas Hoover dryly defended the status quo, Roosevelt enthusiastically proffered smiles, gestures, and promises.

The 1936 Campaign

The 1936 campaign was perhaps FDR's greatest canvass from an oratorical perspective. He delivered some of his best fighting speeches. In 1936, FDR found himself in the position that Hoover held in 1932: FDR was now the defender of the status quo. Of course, Republicans Alfred Landon and William Knox attacked Roosevelt just as FDR savaged Hoover in 1932. But there was one critical difference: Roosevelt was not a Hoover. When the Republicans claimed the New Deal had not mastered the Depression, Roosevelt turned the charge to demonstrate more had to been done; when Republicans claimed they could solve the Depression better than FDR could, Roosevelt outflanked that posture with ridicule.

FDR's opening salvo was his acceptance speech at the Democratic national convention, Philadelphia, June 27, 1936. Roosevelt skewered the "economic royalists," which was Stanley High's phrase, and promised Americans they had a "rendezvous with destiny," which was Tommy Corcoran's contribution. FDR penned a line that showed his contempt for government-for-the-rich: "A small group had concentrated into their own hands an almost complete control over other people's property, other people's money, other people's labor—other people's lives." This demonstrates FDR's penchant for anaphora, asyndeton, and the periodic sentence. In the peroration of the speech, which FDR wrote, he declared war on the economic royalists: "We are fighting to save a great and precious form of government for ourselves. Re-enlist with me in the war. I accept the commission you have tendered me. I join with you. I am enlisted for the duration of the war."

War was, in fact, on voters minds in 1936, with the Spanish Civil War and the Neutrality Act of 1935. FDR was constrained by the isolationists, many of whom were Republicans. At Chautauqua, New York, August 14, 1936, Roosevelt delivered a well-known oral obfuscation, his "I Hate War" speech. He turned the tables on isolationists by claiming that only he, not the Republicans, could prevent war. He alleged a straw issue—that war profiteers or Republican economic royalists wanted war; but he assured Americans that the president would fight for peace: "If we face the choice of profits or peace, the Nation will answer—must answer—'We choose peace.' " In appealing to everyone by saying nothing, Roosevelt claimed: "We are not isolationists except in so far as we seek to isolate ourselves completely from war."

FDR opened his campaign at Syracuse, New York, on September 29, 1936. He took direct aim at the Republican stance of "me too, me better," which absurdly claimed that the Republicans could solve the Depression better than FDR could! In a memorable passage, the President skewered Republican hypocrisy:

Let me warn you and let me warn the Nation against the smooth evasion which says, "Of course we believe all these things; we believe in social security; we believe in work for the unemployed; we believe in saving homes. Cross our hearts and hope to die, we believe in all these things; but we do not like the way the present Administration is doing them. Just turn them over to us. We will do all of them—we will do more of them—we will do them better; and most of all, the doing of them will not cost anybody anything.

To appeal to all voters, FDR stated one of his ineffable maxims, which implied he embodied two contradictory philosophies: "I am that kind of conservative because I am that kind of liberal."

Many people's favorite campaign speech is Roosevelt's speech at Madison Square Garden, New York City, October 31, 1936, which is otherwise known as the "John Paul Jones" speech.

Contributed by Samuel Rosenman, Tommy Corcoran, Stanley High, and Donald Richberg, the speech was something for everyone. Religious allusions adorned the address. Anaphora, epistrophe, and antithesis abounded. FDR inveighed against the Republicans with the phrase, borrowed from John Paul Jones's famous reply during the Revolutionary War to the captain of the British warship *Serapis*, "we have only just begun to fight," which was Roosevelt's inclusion in the speech. He scorned Hooverism with the famous monkey metaphor: the "hear-nothing, see-nothing, do-nothing Government." He ended with a threat that worried thinking Americans, as it smacked of dictatorship: "I should like to have it said of my first Administration that in it the forces of selfishness and lust for power met their match. I should like to have it said of my second Administration that in it these forces met their master." Although re-elected, FDR would not master conservatives, as the Court fight and purge demonstrated.

The 1936 campaign was also characterized by FDR's utilization of the scapegoat device. He blamed Hooverism and Republicanism for the nation's ills in 1932 and warned that these economic royalists' evil practices—trickle-down theory, rugged individualism, and government for the rich—would return again in 1936 except for Roosevelt and the Democratic party. The American people evidently thought so, too, for FDR lost only two states, or as Jim Farley quipped, "As Maine goes, so goes Vermont."

The 1940 Campaign

From an oratorical standpoint, FDR's third campaign was pedestrian, because it was not noted for great speeches, as were earlier campaigns. The first part of the canvass, the non-campaign, lasted from the convention in mid-July to mid-October, when FDR gave so-called non-political speeches and made numerous tours of defense plants and military bases, which refuted Republican charges that he had neglected the country's defenses.

When campaign speeches became necessary, FDR had to walk a tightrope. Unable to forge a winning issue, Wendell Willkie, the Republican nominee, decided to attack Roosevelt as a warmonger, thus playing to isolationist sentiment. So, FDR had to appease the fear of war but assure Americans their national defenses were adequate. The first tactic Roosevelt used was turning-the-tables. He countercharged that Republicans had sabotaged national security by voting against naval appropriation bills, and specifically indicted three Republican legislators at Madison Square Garden, October 28, 1940, with this famous foray: "now wait, a perfectly beautiful rhythm—Congressmen Martin, Barton, and Fish." His second tactic was to admit candidly that he was arming the country, but for peace.

Roosevelt took substantial heat from his critics for his address at Boston, October 30, 1940. The Democratic platform promised peace, except for an armed-attack proviso.Willkie had charged in late October that Americans could expect war in 1941 if they elected FDR. Pressed to respond to Willkie's reckless charges, FDR promised at Boston, "I have said this before, but I shall it again and again and again: Your boys are not going to be sent to any foreign wars." Critics complained that FDR deleted the caveat to curry votes. He did, but there were rhetorical reasons: the Irish-Americans disliked the British, the Italian-Americans disliked FDR's hard line on Mussolini, and the Catholic vote was isolationist. Nonetheless, FDR advised the audience that he was requesting additional airplanes for the British, which he could have deleted as too antagonistic, and he attacked Congressman Joe Martin of the Bay State. The Boston audience joined FDR in the refrain against "Martin, Barton, and Fish."

The 1944 Campaign

In many respects, the 1944 campaign mirrored 1940. FDR was "drafted" by the convention, he gave nonpolitical speeches until goaded into defending his administration, and he beat Governor Thomas Dewey. Albeit, there were differences: Dewey was FDR's match over the radio, some were concerned about FDR's health, and many feared a low voter-turnout would harm Democrats.

The Teamsters' Union speech was what the doctor ordered. Delivered in Washington on September 23, 1944, the famous "Fala" speech invigorated the campaign. By scathing sarcasm against Republican distortions, Roosevelt proved his mastery in campaigning. And he took a new tack: He lifted the nation's spirits with humor. The following famous passage includes in brackets how FDR delivered the lines and the audience's response:

These Republican leaders have not been content with attacks on me, or my wife, or on my sons. No, not content with that, they now include my little dog Fala [FDR looked up from reading his manuscript and the audience laughed and applauded for twenty seconds]. Well, of course, I don't resent attacks, and my family don't resent attacks, *but Fala does resent them* [FDR punctuated every word, dropped his jaw in indignation, and the audience laughed for fifteen seconds]. You know, Fala is Scotch [laughter] and being a Scottie, as soon as he learned that the Republican fiction writers in Congress and out had concocted a story that I had left him behind on the Aleutian Islands and had sent a destroyer back to find him—at a cost to the taxpayers of two or three, or eight or twenty million dollars—*his Scotch soul was furious* [FDR again emphasized each word, dropped his jaw, and the audience laughed for ten seconds]. He has not been the same dog since [laughter].

The rest of the campaign revolved around three major themes: peace, the United Nations, and jobs after the war. With regard to peace, FDR easily demonstrated to the voters that he had successfully prepared the nation for war, and that he was best suited to determine the nature of the peace as the Commander-in-Chief. As for the United Nations (UN), he beat Dewey to the punch by announcing his support for the UN in an important speech at the Foreign Policy Association, New York City, October 21, 1944, thus leaving Dewey with too little, too late. As for jobs, FDR countered that Republicans never seriously wanted the working man to succeed, and that only the New Deal, which FDR would continue after the war, would help the average American voter.

FDR successfully ran four times for president, and some general tactics emerged from his canvasses. FDR excelled in attack. He ran against Hooverism four times, thus more defining himself by what he was not, than by what he was. FDR was a matchless defensive campaigner. He was much better at turning the tables on his opponents, thus demonstrating that Republicans were deceitful when they argued "me too, me better" with respect to the New Deal. Except for his advocating more of the same with regard to the New Deal, FDR generally did not champion new ground so that he would not have to defend it. Although FDR usually eschewed invective and sarcasm, these devices were especially evident in the 1940 and 1944 campaign, for he had to respond to reckless misrepresentations by Willkie and Dewey. But the bottom line was that FDR always did what it took to win the presidency.

FDR'S FOUR INAUGURAL ADDRESSES

First Inaugural Address, March 4, 1933

Roosevelt's First Inaugural was his best investiture speech. It ranks as a premier inaugural with Abraham Lincoln's second and John Kennedy's. It is one of his best addresses, in company with his Victory Dinner, "Teamsters' Union," and War Message speeches.

Raymond Moley composed major portions of the address, and Louis Howe probably contributed the famous fear statement. Nevertheless, FDR made numerous emendations on the drafts in order to make the speech his own address.

FDR's address was action-oriented. He sought legislation from the Congress and acquiescence from the people for his New Deal. The organization of the speech was problem-solution, the problem being the Depression. The solution was not *laissez-faire* economics, but governmental intervention in the nation's economy.

FDR's introduction set the tone. Using a periodic style, the thirty-first president spoke two of his memorable lines: "This is preeminently the time to speak the truth, the whole truth, frankly and boldly" and "So, first of all, let me assert my firm belief that the only thing we have to fear is fear itself.'' By orally stressing ''frankly and boldly,'' and by pausing just slightly: ''the only thing we have to fear is [slight pause] fear itself,'' FDR was able to communicate his periods.

The Depression, FDR told his listeners, was caused by the ''unscrupulous moneychangers,'' who were bankers and Wall Street brokers. This group was FDR's scapegoat: He blamed a vested interest for the Depression, and sought the nation's cooperation in constraining this powerful interest group. FDR would restore the country to its ''ancient truths'' by passing legislation that would manage banking and brokers in the United States. These laws were the core of the famous ''One Hundred Days'' New Deal.

Having vanquished Wall Street, FDR turned to gaining support from the people by employing military metaphors. Words, such as ''trained and loyal army,'' ''discipline,'' ''leadership,'' ''duty,'' and ''disciplined attack,'' laced the middle section of his speech wherein he figuratively enlisted Americans in his war on the Depression. The suasory efficacy of his military metaphors was to invite Americans to grant to the federal government (and many would say to FDR) some of their traditional freedoms, as one does in a time of war, in order to defeat the Depression.

Late in his speech, FDR squared off against Congress. He used the carrot-and-stick technique. The carrot was that he wanted to work with Congress in solving the crisis. But, in case Congress did not act, and here is the stick, FDR said that he would ''not evade the clear course of duty'' that would confront him. He would ask Congress for executive power, ''as great as the power that would be given to me if we were in fact invaded by a foreign foe,'' and the audience applauded FDR's rhetoric.

President Roosevelt's First Inaugural was persuasive. Ordinary Americans wrote of their support, which can be found in the public reaction files of the FDR Library (PPF 200-B). The news media generally supported FDR's gambit, and the newsreels showed clips of the more moving passages in the address.

Before moving on, some mention of the First Inaugural's *elocutio*, or verbal style, is in order. Here are other prime examples of periodicity:

> ''Restoration calls, however, not for changes in ethics alone. This nation is asking for action, and action now [applause].''

> ''Our greatest primary task is to put people to work [applause].''

> ''There are many ways in which it can be helped, but it can never be helped by merely talking about it [applause].''

Roosevelt also favored anaphora, or parallelism. When excoriating the bankers, he reiterated ''they have'' five times in order to impress on the audience Wall Street's betrayal of the public trust. Five times he indicated with the parallelism of ''It can be helped by'' how his administration would alleviate the Depression.

And three times he used anaphora, "There must be," to specify how he would check the "evils of the old order."

Second Inaugural Address, January 20, 1937

Although helped by writers Donald Richberg and Rosenman on this speech, FDR's Second was not as stellar as his First, perhaps owing to the fact that the nation was not in the depths of the Depression. Whereas the First was replete with an action-oriented agenda, the Second was philosophical and contemplative.

The speech had a three-fold time pattern. FDR first recounted the past four years that had demanded bold legislation, which his New Deal had given the American people. The second section demonstrated that his policies were working in the present, but he admitted that more had to be done. So, he drafted lines that made the Second Inaugural noteworthy (note FDR's penchant for anaphora):

> "I see millions of families trying to live on incomes so meager that the pall of family disaster hangs over them day by day."

> "I see millions whose daily lives in city and on farm continue under conditions labeled indecent by so-called polite society half a century ago."

> "I see millions denied education, recreation, and the opportunity to better their lot and the lot of their children."

> "I see millions lacking the means to buy the products of farm and factory and by their poverty denying work and productiveness to many other millions."

And then FDR wrote on the draft the line that best exemplifies the Second (note that he used parallelism and asyndeton): "I see one-third of a nation ill-housed, ill-clad, ill-nourished." In the last part of the speech, FDR looked to the future to solve the problem, for he told his audience "We will not listen to Comfort, Opportunism, and Timidity. We will carry on."

Unfortunately, FDR did not indicate how he would carry on. His problem was that the Supreme Court had ruled unconstitutional core legislation of the New Deal. Although observers expected something from the President on how he would deal with the Court, FDR disappointed. Perhaps he should have given some vague signal with regard to the Court. At any rate, the speech contained eloquent language, but it did not chart any course to solve the nation's problems in Roosevelt's second administration.

Third Inaugural Address, January 20, 1941

Although America was at peace, Europe was at war. Until Pearl Harbor, FDR was constrained by the isolationists, who checked the President's desire to help the Allies short-of-war with Germany. Hence, the speech is a rhetorical battle-field between belligerency, which FDR favored, and non-belligerency, which he gave the isolationists.

FDR penned the core thoughts for the address, and he was helped by Rosen-man. The speech was philosophical with a problem-solution structure. FDR used the metaphor of the nation-as-human to suggest that the New Deal had and would nurture mind, body, and soul at home and abroad. Yet, it was unclear from the address what Roosevelt would do on either front, which probably explains why the speech's effect was mediocre.

The one remarkable aspect of the address was Roosevelt's so-called misread-ing of the text. The reading copy of the speech stated: "we risk the real peril of inaction." When he delivered the speech, FDR did not misread but actually said: "we risk the real [slight pause and halt] peril of isolation [slight pause, but no halt] the real peril of inaction." FDR's uttering "isolation" was a ca-tharsis for his inability to act otherwise.

Fourth Inaugural Address, January 20, 1945

After George Washington's Second Inaugural Address, Roosevelt's Fourth is the shortest. Owing to the exigencies of World War II, the ceremony was as brief as the address and was held at the White House, rather than at the Capitol.

The speech evolved through a progression of drafts. FDR dictated four major ideas for the address: (1) from his school master Endicott Peabody, FDR wanted the thought that civilization always progresses upward; (2) he wrote "At a time like this most of us need the confidence which flows from conviction"; (3) he wanted a "fear" statement that resonated with the First Inaugural; and (4) he intimated that after the war he would try to perfect the Constitution: "The Constitution of 1787 was neither perfect nor complete. It was the best that could be obtained at that time." Roosevelt then gave copies of these thoughts to Archibald MacLeish, Samuel Rosenman, and Robert Sherwood, the speech writ-ers working on the Fourth, so that they could present the President with their individual drafts.

Roosevelt chose Sherwood's draft because it most closely followed FDR's thoughts, because it was the shortest of the contributed drafts, and because it contained the stylistic device of anaphora, which FDR appreciated. In conjunc-tion with Sherwood, Roosevelt went through three subsequent drafts before the final reading copy was done. FDR pared Sherwood's initial draft of 702 words down to 560 words as delivered.

The address was philosophical. Truly epideictic, Roosevelt praised communal values that energized American democracy at home and steeled soldiers on two battle fronts. He used anaphora, "We have learned," to detail lessons against isolationism that he would institutionalize in a strong United Nations organi-zation. He also hinted that Constitutional rights would be applied to all citizens, especially to "all races and colors and creeds." Some thought Roosevelt's fourth was a promise and a prayer.

FDR AND THE MEDIA

Roosevelt utilized the media to its fullest capacity. He communicated immediately with the people over radio, and the motion picture newsreels allowed Americans to see their president deliver a speech, albeit after the fact.

Radio and the Fireside Chats

Radio, by far, was FDR's most potent weapon. FDR's major speeches were broadcast to the nation, so he came into people's living rooms and spoke to them on a one-to-one basis; thus, he was unhampered by the printed page and by any negative editorial comments about his message. Roosevelt's expressive voice, his cadenced rate for vocal emphasis, and his warm, melodious tenor pitch combined to make a most persuasive presentation.

FDR's Fireside Chats were his greatest exploits, although the term "Fireside Chat" was dubbed by the press. Hard to define or enumerate precisely, FDR delivered approximately thirty chats during his four terms. Before Pearl Harbor, he gave eighteen chats on a variety of subjects, and the remaining twelve were given after December 7, 1941, on war topics.

FDR carefully calculated maximum media exposure for his chats. He gave many talks on Sunday—when most people would be home to listen—so that he could dominate the news on Monday. Interestingly, he never gave a chat on Saturday, for FDR believed that few people read the news section on Sunday! The following chart gives the incidence of chats on each day of the week:

Sun	Mon	Tue	Wed	Thu	Fri	Sat
12	6	6	2	2	2	0

Many of the Fireside Chats were economic or wartime pep talks. However, several of them merit special attention.

The first Fireside, "On the Banking Crisis," March 12, 1933, was arguably his most important. Following on the heels of his First Inaugural, this chat helped restore confidence in the banking system, for FDR humorously told his radio audience that it was safer to keep its "money in a reopened bank than under the mattress." Indeed, the 1930s Firesides usually concerned the New Deal, as, for instance, did the fifth, "On Economic Progress," June 28, 1934, wherein the President spiked complaints that the New Deal was not working. He asked a rhetorical question, and he knew how the audience would answer mentally to themselves: "Are you better off now than you were last year?"

Some of FDR's best Firesides were aggressive, spirited defenses of his policies. He took to the airwaves on September 30, 1934, for his sixth, "On the NRA," in order to gain support for the National Recovery Act, a backbone of the New Deal. The ninth, "On the Judiciary," March 9, 1937, was targeted to allay the nation's fears about his judicial reorganization bill. Some critics had successfully claimed that FDR was really trying to "pack" the Supreme Court, and Roosevelt tried to assure skeptical citizens that the charge was untrue. "On the Purge," June 24, 1938, the thirteenth, was a disingenuous attempt to fool the people, for Roosevelt claimed he would campaign, as *head* of the Democratic party, against opponents, when in reality most Americans plainly perceived that FDR, as *President*, was purging party politicians who did not support him. Despite eloquent Firesides on the court and the purge, FDR lost both battles.

Roosevelt used Firesides to prepare the nation for war. He assured his audience in his fourteenth, "On War in Europe," September 3, 1939, that the nation would remain neutral, and he pledged that there would be "no black-out of peace in the United States." Roosevelt began his sixteenth, "The Great Arsenal of Democracy," December 29, 1940, with "This is not a fireside chat on war," when in fact it was. This was FDR's opening salvo to get Lend-Lease through the Congress, and he sought the audience's acquiescence. The isolationists feared being dragged into war by giving help to the Allies, so FDR assured Americans that they could "nail any talk about sending armies to Europe as deliberate untruths." His eighteenth, "On Freedom of the Seas," September 11, 1941, was his last chat before Pearl Harbor. In that talk, FDR committed the United States to a *de facto* naval war with Hitler, on the pretext that a German submarine had torpedoed the destroyer *Greer* (FDR failed to reveal that the Nazi submarine had first been depth-charged by a British airplane, working with the *Greer*). During World War II, FDR delivered Firesides to steel morale and to encourage citizens to buy war bonds.

Newsreels

Americans could hear their president deliver a speech or Fireside on the radio, but the motion picture newsreels afforded them an opportunity to see him. The newsreels reinforced the idea of the rhetorical presidency, that speaking is governing, for movie patrons saw their president giving a speech, thus enacting the presidency. FDR did not disappoint. He gestured, although not as much as a Mussolini or a Hitler, in order to emphasize his rhetoric, but it was his face that was truly persuasive. He could scowl against economic royalists; he could optimistically uplift his chin to demonstrate mastery over the Depression; he could laugh at Republican campaign promises; and he could be deadly serious when discussing Nazi perfidy. In short, whereas Herbert Hoover had been dull and uninspiring on the newsreels, Franklin D. Roosevelt exuded confidence, and that image of hope became a reality for FDR's followers.

Press Conferences

As for news conferences, Roosevelt gave 999 in thirteen years of office. He used them to control the news, as best he could, by telling reporters his side of the story. Sometimes, FDR used the press conference to criticize the newspapers and their editors, especially when he needed a scapegoat to blame for his bad press. This was particularly so after the 1936 election. During that election, much of the "Tory press," FDR's pejorative term for conservative, Republican-leaning newspapers, supported Landon. When the Second New Deal turned sour in 1937–1938, he took to blaming the press. Nevertheless, he received a roasting from the press for his "Court packing" plan and for his "purge." But for his press conference on Lend-Lease, December 17, 1940, Roosevelt exhibited his mastery of oral obfuscation. Using a homey metaphor, he compared Lend-Lease to the neighbor's garden hose: after the neighbor (Great Britain) used the hose (U.S. destroyers and munitions), the lender merely wanted the hose back. Thus, FDR was able to skirt technical and legal problems that vexed the isolationists.

THE SUPREME COURT-PACKING SCHEME

Emboldened by his landslide victory in 1936, FDR determined in his second term to move against the Supreme Court. The conservative Court had ruled unconstitutional many of the central laws of the New Deal. With the Wagner Act, which allowed collective bargaining, and the Social Security Act on the Court's docket, FDR believed he should secure a Court that was responsive to his, the people's, and the Congress's expressed legislation. Therefore, in December 1936, after the election but before the inauguration, he secretly concocted a plan with Homer Cummings, Attorney General of the United States, to ensure a liberal Court.

President Roosevelt announced in a press conference on February 5, 1937, his ill-fated bill to reorganize the Federal judiciary. The conservative press quickly dubbed the legislation the Court-packing scheme, as it would add justices to the Court, presumably liberal ones, who would support the New Deal. FDR was unable to dislodge that negative connotation. The bill failed for a variety of reasons: the secrecy with which FDR originated the bill; the suddenness with which he sprang it on the Congress, Court, and country; the sudden death of Senator Joseph Robinson, who led FDR's battle in the Senate; and the plan itself, which was disingenuous. But FDR also made a serious rhetorical error. He affirmed a crafty reason for the bill. When that was exposed as fallacious, he finally presented the real reason; however, it was too late, for FDR validated his critics' charges by changing in midstream the bill's rationale.

Roosevelt made two interrelated mistakes in his press conference. Rather than candidly claiming that a conservative Court was thwarting the New Deal, a fact that was undisputable, FDR asserted that the Court was old and overburdened in its work, which was debatable. Hence, he called for a "constant infusion of new blood in the courts'' and, later, for an ''addition of younger blood.'' In a rare admission of failure, FDR acknowledged in his introduction to the 1937 volume of his public papers that ''I made one major mistake when I first presented the plan. I did not place enough emphasis on the real mischief—the kind of decisions, which, as a studied and continued policy, had been coming down from the Supreme Court. I soon corrected that mistake—in speeches which I later made about the plan.''

These addresses were two of FDR's best fighting speeches. They were also examples of the rhetorical presidency, for in them Roosevelt sought to go over the heads of the Senate to appeal to the American people to move their senators to support FDR's bill. The first speech was the Victory Dinner Address, delivered in the Mayflower Hotel in Washington, D.C., March 4, 1937. Changing tactics, FDR finally affirmed a bona fide exigence: a conservative Supreme Court had nullified advantageous New Deal legislation. The President appealed to Americans who benefitted from his New Deal programs—the farmers, wage earners, and conservationists—with a homey metaphor: ''For as yet there is no definite assurance that the three horse team of the American system of government will pull together. . . . If one horse lies down in the traces or plunges off in another direction, the field will not be ploughed.'' In the speech's peroration, FDR used seven lines of anaphora that began with ''Here are. . . . ''

Five days later, March 9, 1937, FDR delivered a Fireside Chat on the judiciary. Defensive in this speech, he sought to allay Americans that they need not worry about his vitiating the Court. ''You who know me,'' FDR assured Americans, ''will accept my solemn assurance that in a world in which democracy is under attack, I seek to make American democracy succeed.''

As eloquent as these speeches were, they did not succeed. Some critics hold that FDR waited too long to deliver them, which allowed for the Senatorial battle lines to harden. True, they moved public opinion from a pro/con ratio of 47 percent to 53 percent in February, to a 49 percent to 51 percent ratio in March. But the Senate did not budge. Part of the reason was Chief Justice Charles Evans Hughes's letter that he sent to the Senate Judiciary Committee, March 22, 1937. A devastating rebuttal to the President's reasons, Hughes's letter, more than any other rhetorical factor, contributed to FDR's failure. The Chief Justice refuted FDR's nine-old-men argument, which he accomplished by factually demonstrating that as the Court aged, it had heard more cases. He also claimed that more Supreme Court judges would clog the process, not streamline it. However, Hughes twice admitted that he did not wish to defend the Court's rulings. His reason was that he knew, but FDR, the Congress, and the public did not know, that the Court had reversed itself in December and would now cooperate with the New Deal.

FDR's defeat in the Court battle was a serious persuasive and political failure. It demonstrated the weakness of the rhetorical presidency, especially when a president affirms a tricky proposal. It showed conservatives that they could oppose Roosevelt, if the cause were just, and beat him. It did not take FDR long to give them another issue on which to do just that.

THE PURGE

Roosevelt's ill-fated Court-packing scheme had facilitated Democrats, of the closet conservative type, many of whom were Southerners, to jump ship. Finding a more comfortable berth with their Republican brethren, these conservatives joined ranks with Republicans to obstruct FDR's liberal agenda in 1937–1938. At issue was the Fair Labor Standards Act, which set wages and hours. In the spring of 1938, Roosevelt had some success in helping Senator Claude Pepper win an early primary race in Florida. With other liberal gains in the primaries, Representative John O'Connor, the chairman of the House Rules Committee, read the election returns and discharged the Fair Labor Act, which eventually passed Congress after a struggle. Thus, FDR faced no serious exigency, for his legislation had passed. Nevertheless, he concluded that he should move against the conservative elements in his own party.

On Tuesday, June 24, 1938, FDR announced his purge in his thirteenth Fireside Chat. He made two fatal mistakes in this radio talk. First, he did not specify the difference between two schools of thought, the liberal versus the conservative. Scoring Democrat's "general attitude," "inward desire," and a "yes, but" position on the New Deal, the President nevertheless failed to delineate policies on which the voters could judge a candidate's voting record. Thus, FDR's charge was vague. His second mistake was to underestimate the intelligence of the average American voter. FDR claimed that as *president*, he would not tell Americans how to vote. However, as *head* of the Democratic party, he would take part in some primaries. This distinction fooled few, for most perceived that Roosevelt, the head of the party, was also Roosevelt, the President of the United States. FDR frontally purged three men.

Purgee Senator Walter George

On August 11, 1938, before an audience of fifty thousand at Barnesville, Georgia, the President of the United States publicly attacked Walter George, Georgia's senior senator. George, FDR averred, did not believe in "his heart, deep down in his heart," the objectives the New Deal. Unfortunately, FDR did not indict George's voting record, so the attack seemed petty and personal.

George defended himself against the President with potent appeals. Since FDR had not specified a bill of particulars against George, the senator defended on his own grounds: He stocked his address with Southern speech staples—anti-Communism, allusions to carpetbaggers, Negro-baiting, and state's rights. For a variety of reasons, two of which were George's solid support from the business community and from the average Georgian voter, Senator George handily won his primary victory.

Purgee Representative John O'Connor

Whereas Roosevelt attacked George to his face, the President used a press conference for his second target. On August 16, FDR purged Representative O'Connor, who had finally released the Fair Labor bill from his House Rules Committee. FDR read an editorial against O'Connor in the *New York Post*. Thus, FDR made the newspaper's editorial, which claimed that the Congressman was one of the most effective obstructionists in the House, his own statement. O'Connor defended himself in a speech on August 19 by appealing heavily to the separation of powers doctrine. Of the lot, O'Connor was the only purgee rejected by the voters. But Richard Polenberg determined that O'Connor was defeated for many reasons, none of which had much to do with Roosevelt's purge.

Purgee Senator Millard Tydings

FDR purged Senator Tydings with Representative O'Connor in the same August 16 press conference. Again, on August 23, FDR complained that Republicans were crossing over in the Maryland primaries to vote for Tydings, which was proof enough that Tydings was not a New Deal Democrat! Tydings took to the airwaves on August 21 to defend himself. His speech sounded like George's, for it stressed anti-Communism and appealed to state sovereignty, but Tydings added new appeals: He raised the specter of Reconstructionism in Maryland, defended his vote against the Court-packing scheme, and charged that Roosevelt was the President no matter what titles he assumed. FDR delivered a parting shot at Tydings in a speech at Denton, Maryland, on September 15, 1938. But, FDR lost, as Tydings won re-election.

Roosevelt's defeat in the purge was his second, major rhetorical blunder. He failed to specify the urgency, and since there was none, he should not have embarked on the purge; he failed to mention specific policies, thus allowing the purgees wide latitude in responding to his charges because there was no liberal-conservative litmus test; and he failed to realize that although the President is the head of the party, one should not campaign against members of one's own party.

WAR RHETORIC

From 1937 to 1941, President Roosevelt delivered some of his most famous addresses, although not always his most successful ones, on preparation for war. Roosevelt was ahead of public opinion but was constrained by powerful isolationists. So, he used the rhetorical presidency to mold public opinion.

Reacting to war between Japan and China in 1937, FDR gave his famous "Quarantine" speech at Chicago on October 5. Beyond the metaphor of somehow quarantining the aggressors, the speech was vague. In truth, the address was an attitude more than a program, but it was FDR's first attempt to adjust Americans to war and war to Americans.

At the University of Virginia's commencement, June 10, 1940, FDR took a rhetorical stab at Mussolini, whose forces had invaded France in conjunction with the Nazis. As an impromptu insertion, FDR contemptuously castigated the Duce: "the hand that held the dagger has plunged it into the back of its neighbor."

For Lend-Lease, FDR delivered two memorable persuasions. He basically argued that by arming America and sending war materials to Great Britain, the United States best assured peace. On December 29, 1940, Roosevelt opened his rhetorical campaign with the "Arsenal of Democracy" Fireside Chat to the people. To assuage the isolationists, FDR asserted that Lend-Lease, rather than leading to war, would keep the country out of war. On January 6, 1941, FDR delivered to the Congress his "Four Freedoms" annual message, which urged aid for Britain short-of-war. In eloquent and patriotic language, the President pledged the nation to freedom of speech, freedom to worship God, freedom from want, and freedom from fear. The Congress passed Lend-Lease. As for his effect on public opinion, FDR moved people to support Great Britain short-of-war, but only a small percentage of Americans wanted the country actually to enter the war.

That all ended on December 7, 1941, "a date which will live in infamy." The next day, December 8, at 12:30 P.M., Roosevelt went before the Congress and delivered the best speech he ever composed. Unlike other addresses that ranged from substantially to almost totally the work of FDR's speech writers, his "War Message" was virtually his own work. He dictated a first draft to Grace Tully, his secretary, and made changes on a second draft in at least two sittings, for his handwriting was slightly different. As cables reached the White House, he added the anaphora of "Last night," which was followed by the latest target of the Japanese sneak attack.

"No matter how long it may take us to overcome this premeditated invasion, the American people in their righteous might will win through to absolute victory," arguably one of the most eloquent lines in the address, was inserted by FDR on the first draft. This thought illustrates FDR penchant for periodicity, which is constructing a sentence so that the listener must wait until its end to comprehend the sentence's full impact. Harry Hopkins contributed the speech's other memorable line. Noticing that FDR had failed to mention the deity in his address, Hopkins created an insert that did so. Notice the fine oral cadence of Hopkins's line, and also its potent periodicity with punchy, one syllable words: "With confidence in our armed forces—with the unbounding determination of our people—we will gain the inevitable triumph—so help us God." A letter in the FDR Library's public reaction files is an apt summary of Roosevelt's war rhetoric: "I have always been a Republican and have opposed many of your policies . . . but now I realize that you have been right in your analysis of the situation ever since Hitler began his overrunning of the various European states."

CONCLUSION

FDR was probably the nation's greatest presidential orator. He could energize thousands of live listeners as few presidents before or after him could, and he was a prototypical media president; he remains something of a benchmark on both accounts by which to judge successive presidents. He was a matchless campaigner, for he gave so many famous speeches and spoke so many memorable lines, which remain in the nation's collective memory. FDR's First Inaugural endures with Lincoln's First and Second and John Kennedy's. FDR used rhetoric to dominate, if not to destroy, laissez-faire government for the rich, which shows no signs of resuscitation sixty years after the New Deal. And consider this: FDR is still by common assent the *sine qua non* for the Democratic party—who is the other party's?

RHETORICAL SOURCES

Archival Materials

The Franklin D. Roosevelt Library, Hyde Park, New York, contains FDR's papers. Of particular interest are the President's Personal Files (PPF 1820) that contain drafts of speeches and the Final Reading Copy of most addresses. One can also locate drafts in the Papers of Samuel I. Rosenman, Adolph Berle, and Harry Hopkins. Letters and telegrams that Americans sent Roosevelt can be found in the public reaction file (PPF 200-B), indexed by speech. The Library has newspaper clippings that record reactions to the president's speeches.

The Library has newsreels and recordings for major speeches and Fireside Chats, a few home movies of FDR's speaking, and an extensive photographic file that is indexed by subject matter.

The best oral history is The Reminiscences of Samuel I. Rosenman (1959).

Roosevelt, Franklin D. *The Public Papers and Addresses of Franklin D. Roosevelt.* *(PPA).* 13 Vols. Edited by Samuel I. Rosenman. New York: Random House, 1938–1950.

Rhetorical Studies

Alsop, Joseph. *FDR 1882–1945.* New York: Viking Press, 1982.
———, and Turner Catledge. *The 168 Days.* Garden City, NY: Doubleday, Doran, and Co., 1938.
Burns, James MacGregor. *Roosevelt: The Lion and the Fox.* New York: Harcourt, Brace, and Co., 1956.

Davis, Kenneth S. *FDR: The Beckoning of Destiny 1882–1928.* New York: G. P. Putnam's Sons, 1971.

———. *FDR: The New York Years 1928–1933.* New York: Random House, 1985.

———. *FDR, The New Deal Years 1933–37: A History.* New York: Random House, 1986.

Farr, Finis. *FDR.* New Rochelle, NY: Arlington House, 1972.

Friedel, Frank. *Franklin D. Roosevelt Launching the New Deal.* Boston: Little, Brown, 1973.

Leuchtenburg, William E. *Franklin D. Roosevelt and the New Deal: 1932–1940.* New York: Harper and Row, 1963.

Moley, Raymond. *After Seven Years.* New York: Harper, 1939.

Pritchett, C. Herman. *The Roosevelt Court.* New York: Macmillan, 1948.

Pusey, Merlo J. *The Supreme Court Crisis.* New York: Macmillan, 1937.

Rauch, Basil. *The History of the New Deal: 1933–1938.* New York: Creative Age Press, 1944.

Robinson, Edgar Eugene. *The Roosevelt Leadership 1933–1945.* Philadelphia: J. B. Lippincott, 1955.

Rollins, Alfred B. *Roosevelt and Howe.* New York: Knopf, 1962.

Rosenman, Samuel I. *Working With Roosevelt.* New York: Harper and Brothers, 1952.

Ryan, Halford R. *Franklin D. Roosevelt's Rhetorical Presidency.* Westport, CT: Greenwood Press, 1988.

Sherwood, Robert E. *Roosevelt and Hopkins: An Intimate History.* New York: Harper and Brothers, 1948.

Tully, Grace. *F.D.R. My Boss.* New York: Charles Scribner's Sons, 1949.

Rhetorical Monographs

Benson, Thomas W. "Inaugurating Peace: Franklin D. Roosevelt's Last Speech." *Speech Monographs* 36 (1969): 138–47.

Borg, Dorothy. "Notes on Roosevelt's 'Quarantine' Speech." *Political Science Quarterly* 72 (1957): 405–33.

Braden, Waldo W., and Earnest Brandenburg. "Roosevelt's Fireside Chats." *Speech Monographs* 22 (1955): 290–302.

Brandenburg, Earnest, and Waldo W. Braden. "Franklin Delano Roosevelt." In *History and Criticism of American Public Address.* 3 Vols. Edited by Marie Hochmuth. New York: Russell and Russell, 1955.

Cowperthwaite, L. LeRoy. "Franklin D. Roosevelt at Harvard." *Quarterly Journal of Speech* 38 (1952): 37–41.

Crowell, Laura. "Roosevelt the Grotonian." *Quarterly Journal of Speech* 38 (1952): 31–36.

Daughton, Suzanne M. "Metaphoric Transcendence: Images of the Holy War in Franklin Roosevelt's First Inaugural." *Quarterly Journal of Speech* 79 (1993): 427–46.

Gravlee, G. Jack. "President Franklin D. Roosevelt and the 'Purge.' " In *Oratorical Encounters: Selected Studies and Sources of Twentieth-Century Political Accusations and Apologies,* edited by Halford Ross Ryan. Westport, CT: Greenwood Press, 1988.

———. "Franklin D. Roosevelt's Speech Preparation During His First National Campaign." *Speech Monographs* 31 (1964): 437–60.

Oliver, Robert T. "The Speech That Established Roosevelt's Reputation." *Quarterly Journal of Speech* 21 (1945): 274–82.

Polenberg, Richard. "Franklin Roosevelt and the Purge of John O'Connor: The Impact of Urban Change on Political Parties." *New York History* 49 (1968): 306–26.

Ryan, Halford R. "Franklin Delano Roosevelt." In *American Orators of the Twentieth Century: Critical Studies and Sources*, edited by Bernard K. Duffy and Halford R. Ryan. Westport, CT: Greenwood Press, 1987.

———. "Franklin D. Roosevelt's First Inaugural Address, 1933." In *The Inaugural Addresses of Twentieth-Century American Presidents*, edited by Halford Ryan. Westport, CT: Praeger Publishers, 1993.

———. "Roosevelt's First Inaugural: A Study of Technique." *Quarterly Journal of Speech* 65 (1979): 137–49.

———. "Roosevelt's Fourth Inaugural Address: A Study of Its Composition." *Quarterly Journal of Speech* 67 (1981): 157–66.

Sharon, John. "The Fireside Chat." *Franklin D. Roosevelt Collector* 2 (November 1949): 3–20.

Stelzner, Hermann G. " 'War Message,' December 8, 1941: An Approach to Language." *Speech Monographs* 33 (1966): 419–37.

Weiler, Michael. "President Franklin D. Roosevelt's Second Inaugural Address, 1937." In *The Inaugural Addresses of Twentieth-Century American Presidents*, edited by Halford Ryan. Westport, CT: Praeger Publishers, 1993.

———. "President Franklin D. Roosevelt's Third Inaugural Address, 1941." In *The Inaugural Addresses of Twentieth-Century American Presidents*, edited by Halford Ryan. Westport, CT: Praeger Publishers, 1993.

Zelko, Harold P. "Franklin D. Roosevelt's Rhythm in Rhetorical Style." *Quarterly Journal of Speech* 28 (1942): 138–41.

Chronology of Significant Presidential Persuasions

(Unless noted otherwise, all speeches and chats were delivered from the White House in Washington, D.C.)

"Forgotten Man" speech, Albany, New York, April 7, 1932. *PPA*, 1928–1932: 624–27.

"Bold, Persistent Experimentation," Oglethorpe University, Atlanta, Georgia, May 22, 1932. *PPA*, 1928–1932: 639–47.

Acceptance Address, Democratic National Convention, Chicago, Illinois, July 2, 1932. *PPA*, 1928–1932: 647–59.

"Progressive Government" at Commonwealth Club, San Francisco, California, September 3, 1932. *PPA*, 1928–1932: 742–46.

"Pittsburgh" speech, Pittsburgh, Pennsylvania, October 19, 1932. *PPA*, 1928–1932: 795–811.

First Inaugural Address, March 4, 1933. *PPA*, 1933: 11–16.

First Fireside Chat, "On the Banking Crisis," March 12, 1933. *PPA*, 1933: 61–65.

Fifth Fireside Chat, "Are you better off than you were last year," June 28, 1934. *PPA*, 1934: 312–18.

Sixth Fireside Chat, "On the NRA," September 30, 1934. *PPA*, 1934: 413–22.

Acceptance speech, Democratic National Convention, Philadelphia, Pennsylvania, June 27, 1936. *PPA*, 1936: 230–36.

"I Hate War," Chautauqua, New York, August 14, 1936. *PPA,* 1936: 285–92.

Campaign speech, Syracuse, New York, September 29, 1936. *PPA,* 1936: 383–90.

"We have only just begun to fight" speech, Madison Square Garden, New York City, October 31, 1936. *PPA,* 1936: 566–73.

Second Inaugural Address, January 20, 1937. *PPA,* 1937: 1–6.

Victory Dinner Address, March 4, 1937. *PPA,* 1937: 113–21.

Ninth Fireside Chat, "On the Judiciary," March 9, 1937. *PPA,* 1937: 122–33.

"Quarantine" speech, Chicago, Illinois, October 5, 1937. *PPA,* 1937: 406–11.

Thirteenth Fireside Chat, "On the Purge," June 24, 1938. *PPA,* 1938: 391–400.

Fourteenth Fireside Chat, "On War in Europe," September 3, 1939. *PPA,* 1939: 460–64.

"Dagger" speech, Charlottesville, Virginia, June 10, 1940. *PPA,* 1940: 259–64.

Campaign speech, Madison Square Garden, New York City, October 28, 1940. *PPA,* 1940: 499–514.

Campaign speech, Boston, Massachusetts, October 30, 1940. *PPA,* 1940: 514–24.

Lend-Lease, December 17, 1940. *PPA,* 1940: 604–15.

Sixteenth Fireside Chat, "The Great Arsenal of Democracy," December 29, 1940. *PPA,* 1940: 633–44.

"Four Freedoms," January 6, 1941. *PPA,* 1940: 633–72.

Third Inaugural Address, January 20, 1941. *PPA,* 1941: 3–6.

Eighteenth Fireside Chat, "On Freedom of the Seas," September 11, 1941. *PPA,* 1941: 384–92.

"War Message," December 7, 1941. *PPA,* 1941: 514–15.

Teamsters' Union, September 23, 1944. *PPA,* 1944–1945: 284–92.

Foreign Policy Association speech, New York City, October 21, 1944. *PPA,* 1944–1945: 342–47.

Fourth Inaugural Address, January 20, 1945. *PPA,* 1944–1945: 523–25.

Halford Ryan

Harry S. Truman
(1884–1972)

The country can't afford another Republican Congress.

He had a nasal, mid-Western voice; he tended to render his addresses with insufficient oral inflections; his vocal pacing was generally too fast; his eye contact was customarily poor; his gestures were hackneyed; and his speeches were habitually bereft of the well-turned, memorable phrase. Yet, for all of his apparent oratorical shortcomings, and some critics might even cavil at calling him an "orator," Harry S. Truman was a plain, yet persuasive, speaker.

Oratory did not come easily to Truman. Speech professors Eugene White and Clair Henderlider interviewed HST in 1953, and he told them that whatever he learned about oratory was mastered "the hard way," for he never had any formal training in speaking. Even his closest friends admitted that Truman's first political speech, delivered before the voters in Jackson County, Missouri, in 1922 was a disappointing effort. As a campaigner for the U.S. Senate in 1934 and 1940, Truman delivered numerous speeches, but being a New Deal Democrat, rather than a moving orator, secured his elections. Senator Truman was a workman, and he headed the so-called Truman committee, which investigated the seamy side of the military-industrial complex during World War II. When FDR jettisoned Henry Wallace as a vice presidential candidate in the 1944 election, he turned to Truman as a running mate because of Truman's popularity and not for his speaking prowess. And then, on April 12, 1945, Truman became the thirty-third president of the United States.

How, one might ask, did oratory empower Truman? The answer lies in what kind of speech he delivered. When he spoke scripted remarks, his delivery was characteristically poor, or a drone as the press dubbed his delivery. But when he spoke from limited notes, as he did for informal situations and especially in his whistle-stop campaign in 1948, a different Truman emerged. By all accounts, HST was more persuasive when he spoke extemporaneously, or as Truman liked to call it, "off-the-cuff." Freed from the constraints of a manuscript, HST would cadence his words in a more conversational and often bellicose manner, hence the sobriquet of "Give-em Hell Harry" from the 1948 canvass. In fact, Truman's acceptance address at the Democratic National Convention in 1948 was overwhelmingly successful, in part, because he spoke from a limited outline and extemporized at the actual moment of utterance. This *modus operandi* served him well in the 1948 campaign. Unfortunately, Truman used a manuscript to deliver his other presidential persuasions, and this made his formal speechmaking something to be endured.

RHETORICAL THEORY AND PRACTICE

President Truman had a rhetorical theory, of sorts, and his speech practices rested on settled ideas. As for the oratorical canon of *elocutio*, Truman preferred a plain style. Unlike Roosevelt, who spoke in a diction elevated from everyman, Truman believed, according to White and Hinderlider, that the American people wanted their president to speak plainly and simply:

People don't listen to a speaker just to admire his techniques or his manner; they go to learn. They want the meat of the speech—a direct statement of the facts and proof that the facts are correct—not oratorical trimmings. Of course, the political speaker must remember that the education of the average man is limited. Therefore, he must make his message as simple and clear as possible.

Whether an audience prefers diction that runs close to the ground versus elegant presidential discourse is debatable; rather, the point is that Truman thought so and thus instructed his writers to compose his speeches in unadorned language.

As for the canon of *dispositio*, how a speech is arranged, Truman paid some attention to the bare necessities of organizing an address. He preferred introductions that immediately broached the importance of his subject. Consider the unvarnished and taut introductions to three of HST's most important speeches: from his Truman Doctrine speech to a joint session of Congress, March 12, 1947: "The gravity of the situation which confronts the world today necessitates my appearance before a joint session of the Congress. The foreign policy and the national security of this country are involved"; from his acceptance speech, Democratic National Convention, Philadelphia, July 24, 1948: "Senator Barkley and I will win this election and make those Republicans like it—don't you forget that! We will do that because they are wrong and we are right, and I will prove it to you in just a few minutes;" and from his Far Eastern Policy address, by radio from the White House, April 11, 1951: "I want to talk to you tonight about what we are doing in Korea and about our policy in the Far East. In the simplest terms what we are doing in Korea is this: We are trying to prevent a third world war.''

In the body of his addresses, his major ones especially, Truman often delineated his points in a debater-like ''first,'' ''second,'' and so forth. Indeed, his September 6, 1945 Twenty-One Point Message, not a speech but a written message as it would have taken too long to deliver to the Congress, was known for its numerical nomenclature, as was Truman's Inaugural Address, January 20, 1949, which was tagged Point Four because it was organized around four foreign initiatives to fight Communism. Most of Truman's major speeches were also cast into the problem-solution pattern. After discussing the exigency, Truman proposed the means by which he would redress the issue.

Truman's conclusions were generally pedestrian. Eschewing the moving peroration, Truman preferred to summarize his points, for he thought the facts of an address should speak for themselves. ''Great responsibilities have been placed upon us by the swift movement of events. I am confident that the Congress will face these responsibilities squarely'' was Truman's ending for his most important and far-reaching Truman Doctrine speech, which initiated in earnest the Cold War.

HST's *actio*, the canon of delivering the speech, was his weakest link in the chain of presidential persuasions, and this was by choice. Truman disliked delivering speeches, so he tried to get through them quickly. HST's speaking rate before live audiences and over the radio was on average about 150 words-per-minute (wpm). By comparison, FDR's rate was about 95 wpm to live audiences and about 120 wpm on the radio; hence Truman raced along. Although aides tried to get him to slow down, they were unsuccessful. Moreover, Truman's delivery of speeches was awkward and stilted. By his own admission, Truman affirmed that he liked to read a speech aloud a time or two before delivering it, which frankly was not enough to master vocal emphasis and variety. Consequently, Truman often misspoke words, stressed unimportant thoughts, and sometimes even got lost when he turned the pages of his speech text. Clearly, Truman was not a gifted orator nor one who strove to overcome defects. When accounting for Truman's successful presidential persuasions, one must regard *what* he said as vastly more salient than *how* he said it.

TRUMAN'S SUPERNATION RHETORIC

The Truman Doctrine

On March 12, 1947, President Truman delivered to a joint session of Congress the most important speech of his presidency, and arguably one of the most consequential addresses of the post–war era. Originally entitled Aid to Greece and Turkey, but better known as the Truman Doctrine speech, HST's speech laid the rhetorical groundwork for the Cold War era that lasted from 1947 until the early 1990s collapse of the Soviet Union.

In this speech, as well as in subsequent major foreign policy addresses by succeeding presidents through George Bush, Truman utilized what has been termed by Dante Germino as supernation rhetoric. Truman committed the United States to an anti-Communistic crusade by helping countries that were, or claimed to be, democratic. The problem was that such a country was often defined as "democratic" merely because it was anti-Communistic; thus,Germino noted that "regimes formerly seen as unfree in terms of the American public philosophy (military dictatorships and feudal autocracies) now became bastions of 'liberty' if they appear to be threatened by Soviet expansion." Moreover, Germino determined that supernation rhetoric was communicated in a Manichaean mode, which divided the world into the forces of light and darkness. This competing duality found a congenial setting in the post–World War II era where the forces of good, the United States and its allies, battled the forces of evil, the Soviet Union and its allies.

The impetus for the Truman Doctrine was Great Britain's inability to give further aid to Greece and Turkey. With the Soviet Union attempting to expand in Europe, particularly in Greece and through Turkey to the Mideast oil fields, Truman seized the fortuitous moment. Truman appraised the Congressional leadership of the crisis; agreeing to support the President, they stipulated that Truman must present his case directly to the Congress and the American people.

The Manichaean dualities in the speech were conceived at the speech's inception. Joseph Jones wrote that two thematic criteria were established. One was to establish the facts for the American people, and the second was "to portray the world conflict between free and totalitarian or imposed forms of government." Jones, as well as speech writers George Elsey and Clark Clifford, produced the drafts, and Truman joined the process in its final stages. The speech that Truman delivered did a reasonably good job of being straightforward on Greece, less so on Turkey, and succeeded in painting the devil/angel polarities that would sell the program to the people.

The arrangement of the speech was problem-solution, which, baldly stated, was that Greece and Turkey needed U.S. aid, the Congress should give it, and the people should support the Congress. Truman relied on dichotomized, supernation language. HST stated that he did not believe "that the American people and the Congress wish to turn a deaf ear to the appeal of the Greek Government." The fear appeal of Greece's surviving as a free nation was based on the premise that the audience would supply to persuade itself: Communism threatened Greece, therefore the United States must fight Communism, therefore the United States must help Greece fight Communism: "Greece must have assistance if it is to become a self-supporting and self-respecting democracy. The United States must supply that assistance."

The second main head in Truman's problem-solution speech was Turkey. Frankly speaking, Turkey was not a momentous exigency. Yet Truman had to make Turkey's case compelling. To influence his audience, he argued the halo effect. The halo effect is a technique whereby the orator associates a weaker case (Turkey) with a stronger case (Greece) in the hopes that some of the halo's celestial dust would settle on the less needy example.

Truman alleged a persuasive parallelism between Greece and Turkey without strictly proving it. Whereas Greece had been depicted with heavily freighted fear appeals to tap the audience's emotions, a mere sentence sufficed: "[Turkey's] integrity is essential to the preservation of order in the Middle East." If one conjured Communists overrunning Greece, then it was a small mental step to behold them marching to Turkey. If amount of language is any indication of the drift of Truman's speech, one should recognize that Truman devoted about 433 percent more verbiage to Greece than to its neighbor. This imbalance suggests that Truman persuaded with supernation rhetoric on the issue of Greece and then, with the halo effect, invited the audience to shift that reasoning to Turkey.

The importance of the Truman Doctrine speech was that it moved the United States from a traditional public philosophy of the nation, which existed for the freedom and safety of the American people, to a new philosophy of the supernation, which implied that the United States now had a burden to make the world safe for democracy by fighting Communism. The solution part of Truman's speech was an aid package to Greece and Turkey, which, on closer examination, was actually military munitions.

HST's conclusion was a hard-hitting visceral appeal that reinforced the Manichaean, supernation rhetoric ubiquitous in his address. "The free peoples of the world," Truman preached, "look to us for support in maintaining their freedoms. If we falter in our leadership, we may endanger the peace of the world— and we shall surely endanger the welfare of our own nation. Great responsibilities have been placed upon us by the swift movement of events. I am confident that the Congress will face these responsibilities squarely." It did. The House passed the aid package 287 to 107, the Senate, 67 to 23, and on May 22, 1947, Truman signed the law.

The Koran War Rhetorics

The Korean War was sprung on Truman, the nation, and the world without warning on Saturday, June 24, 1950 (in U.S. time), the day when the North Korean Communists invaded South Korea.

The political motivations and rhetorical reasoning for the Korean War were stated in two top secret documents. These papers preceded the conflict, but served as rationales when the war came. The first paper was NSC-48, which was created by the National Security Council (NSC). Signed by Truman at the end of 1949 on the heels of the Soviet's exploding an atom bomb in September and Mao Tse-tung's Communist takeover of China in October from Chiang Kai-Shek, NSC-48 committed the United States to containing Communism in Asia and to reduce the spread of Communism generally. The second document, NSC-68, was created in April 1950. NSC-68 committed the United States to a military buildup to counter the Soviets. Thus, NSC-48 and NSC-68 gave the military and rhetorical warrants for the Korean War.

President Truman's persuasive communications to the Congress and the people escalated as the military vagaries worsened. His communications evolved from relatively simple, straightforward statements of facts to melodramatic morality plays replete with supernation appeals.

President Truman's first response to the Korean invasion was a concise and candid communication to the nation on June 26, 1950. Truman correctly defined the North Korean action as "unprovoked aggression," "invading forces," "serious breach of the peace," "lawless action," and "act of aggression." Most importantly, however, Truman framed the United Nation's rhetorical and political end: The invaders were to withdraw to "positions north of the 38th parallel." Hence, Truman publicly committed to the UN's war aim of a return to the *status quo ante bellum*. Victory was not defined as a traditional military triumph over North Korea but as a return to the status quo, which would then be proclaimed a victory.

Truman made his second, and somewhat longer, response one day later on June 27, 1950. What had started out on June 26 as an effort to contain Communism in North Korea was now transmuted into the United States-as-supernation to save the Far East. HST assured his audience that no more dominoes would fall. He ordered the Seventh Fleet "to prevent any attack on Formosa"; he "strengthened" the Philippines (would it be next?); and he furnished "military assistance" to "France and the Associated States of Indochina."

Truman ended his statement with supernation bluster. He rhetorically sideswiped the Soviet Union: "I know that all members of the United Nations will consider carefully the consequences of this latest aggression in Korea," for Truman said "The United States will continue to uphold the rule of law."

On June 29, 1950, Truman held a press conference in order to communicate with the American people. The definition of the Korean action evidently puzzled many Americans, for a reporter asked the President whether the country was at war, to which HST answered "We are not at war." Although it might appear absurd to claim that the United States was not at war, Truman was constrained to answer that way. Since HST had decided not to request a Congressional declaration of war, he could not call it a war, as he did not want to validate the charge that he had circumvented the Constitution by not requesting war.

The reporters pressed Truman to be more specific. Truman finally obliged by characterizing the assault on Korea as an unlawful attack "by a bunch of bandits" and stated that United Nations forces were "to suppress a bandit raid on the Republic of Korea." Another reporter asked whether it was a "police action," and Truman answered, "Yes. That is exactly what it amounts to."

Truman's leaving the definition to a reporter was probably a mistake. The "police action" metaphor highlighted the semantic difficulty in which the Truman administration found itself, for it underscored Truman's unwillingness to concede the obvious. "Bandits" are usually "suppressed" through capture and incarceration by the police. But Truman mixed the metaphor: The UN's resolution called only for the police to ensure that the "bandits" withdraw to their hideout in North Korea. Thus, the inherent contradictions in the "police action" metaphor festered until General Douglas MacArthur challenged the definition of Truman's limited war, "police action" theory in 1951.

Perhaps sensing a need to still troubled waters, the President finally delivered his first broadcast to the nation on July 19, 1950. The two speeches, one to Congress and one to the people in the evening, were similar in their bent and flavor, but Truman did adapt to his different audiences. For instance, to the Congress, Truman claimed that the Communist attack "was naked, deliberate, unprovoked aggression, without a shadow of justification"; but for the people, the language ran closer to the ground: "The attack came without provocation and without warning. It was an act of raw aggression, without a shadow of justification. I repeat that it was an act of raw aggression. It had no justification whatever"; and a bit later Truman colloquially called it a "sneak attack."

The preparation for the two speeches was similar. The address to the Congress was composed first and went through seven drafts; the speech to the people was finished in four drafts. Charles S. Murphy, who assumed leadership of Truman's speech staff as special counsel, composed both drafts with the aid of David Bell, an assistant speech writer.

President Truman gave this speech careful attention. He underlined thoughts on the reading copy that he wished to stress orally: "This challenge has been presented *squarely*. We *must meet* it *squarely*" (the stylistic device was epistrophe, which is defined as using the same word to end spoken thought groups); and "This attack came without *provocation* and without *warning*. It was an act of *raw aggression*, without a *shadow* of justification. I repeat—it was an act of *raw aggression*" (again, HST underscored the epistrophe). And he paid particular attention to his speech's peroration by rearranging for effect a paragraph that motivated the people to support the troops (the redeployment of the inserted paragraph is italicized):

We know that the cost of freedom is high. But we are determined to preserve our freedom—no matter what the cost.
I know that our people are willing to do their part to support our soldiers and sailors and airmen who are fighting in Korea. I know that they can count on each and every one of you.

The primary thrust of Truman's address, as a function of the rhetorical presidency, was to gain and maintain support from the American people for the Korean War. As may be expected, he touched on the major topics of supernation rhetoric.

Truman initiated the good guy/bad guy polarities in his introduction: "This attack has made it clear, beyond all doubt, that the international Communist movement is willing to use armed invasion to conquer independent nations. An act of aggression such as this creates a very real danger to the security of all free nations''; thus, Truman stressed the domino theory. Truman warmed to Manichaean, supernation rhetoric in his conclusion, where he sounded more ministerial than presidential: ''Our country stands before the world as an example of how free men, under God, can build a community of neighbors, working together for the good of all. That is the goal we seek not only for ourselves, but for all people. We believe that freedom and peace are essential if men are to live as our Creator intended us to live. It is this faith that has guided us in the past, and it is this faith that will fortify us in the stern days ahead.''

Truman alluded to the U.S. war aims. In a speech stressing peace, Truman did not define exactly what ''peace'' was. In the middle of the speech, one sentence sufficed: ''We know that it will take a hard, tough fight to halt the invasion, and to drive the Communists back.'' The aim seemed to be consistent with NSC-48 and NSC-68, as long as one assumed the preposition ''back'' meant back to the border between North and South Korea. Hence, the American people could gather that the United States was fighting in Korea to drive the invaders back. But Truman had done such an excellent job of reproaching the Soviets with Manichaean, supernation rhetoric that the argument begged to be extended: If the Soviet Union could not be disciplined directly, could not the United States punish North Korea and thereby indirectly teach the Soviets a lesson? (As we shall learn, it did not take long for this inexorable logic to seize the President, MacArthur, and even the liberal media.) HST received qualified support for his speech: Americans communicated about 5½ boxes of pro-mail, and 1½ boxes of con-mail.

By August 1950, the North Koreans had captured about seven-eighths of the South Korean peninsula. Truman again took to the airwaves to assure the American people. At last, he defined U.S. war aims at ten o'clock in the evening on September 1, 1950: ''Tonight I want to talk to you about Korea, about why we are there, and what our objectives are.'' True to form, the speech was organized around those three main heads.

The speech was a recapitulation of earlier themes. Manichaean rhetoric figured prominently: HST denounced Communism in artistic language that featured alliteration, ''Communist imperialism preaches peace but practices aggression.'' He again asserted his historical analogy, which he first used in his July 19 speech, for military action in Korea. ''If the history of the 1930's teaches us anything,'' and Truman assumed that it did, ''it is that appeasement of dictators is the sure road to world war. If aggression were allowed to succeed in Korea, it would be an open invitation to new acts of aggression elsewhere.''

But the speech also broke new ground. In the latter part of his address, Truman listed eight points, in what might be termed HST's penchant for government by enumeration. Truman's second point was a dramatic departure from the status quo, for he stated ''We believe the Koreans have a right to be free, independent, and united—as they want to be. Under the direction and guidance of the United

Nations, we, with others, will do our part to help them enjoy that right. The United States has no other aim in Korea." Truman's vision of a united Korea was obviously a pro-U.S. government that professed anti-Communism.

Truman's third point was a statement of U.S. war aims. "We do not want the fighting in Korea to expand into a general war," Truman pledged, but he warned "It will not spread unless Communist imperialism draws other armies and governments into the fight of the aggressors against the United Nations." HST kept his police action theory, but it was hard to reconcile his second point with the third point. If he dreaded a general war, then why tempt fate in redefining the war to reunite the two Koreas?

Donning the ministerial mantle of Manichaeanism in his speech's peroration, Truman waxed priestly: "The task which has fallen upon our beloved country is a great one. In carrying it out, we ask God to purge us of all selfishness and meanness, and to give us strength, and courage for the days ahead. We pray God to give us strength, ability, and wisdom for the great task we face." Assumedly, Americans would have affirmed an amen.

September 1950, was a watershed month in the Korean War. General MacArthur finally held the line at the Pusan Perimeter, and then on September 15, MacArthur invaded the port of Inchon, captured Seoul, and pushed the Communists to the border. The Security Council's resolution of the *status quo ante bellum* had been achieved. The Truman administration could have proclaimed a victory as North Korea had been expelled from the South.

At this juncture, the Truman administration took a fateful step that was previewed in his September 1 speech in which he pledged to reunite Korea. In late September 1950, Truman signed NSC-81, which committed the United States to roll back Communism in North Korea. General MacArthur championed such a program, and the United Nations finally, but reluctantly, endorsed the plan.

At Truman's behest, MacArthur ordered UN troops to advance toward China, and they reached the border at the Yalu River in late October, only to be pushed back by a combined Chinese-Korean army. MacArthur's launched another counteroffensive, which was supposed to be his final thrust, and UN troops advanced back to the Yalu River in late November. But, Communist forces struck back, hurled MacArthur's forces downward, recaptured the North Korean capital, and in early January 1951, retook Seoul.

However, in the interim, Truman had been beating the war tocsin. At San Francisco's War Memorial Opera House, October 17, 1950, Truman was full of bravado. Early in his speech, he stated: "I am confident that these [UN] forces will soon restore peace to the whole of Korea." It was not just South Korea anymore, but the entire Korean peninsula. Lest anyone miss the point, Truman later spelled it out. Name dropping MacArthur for persuasive purposes, Truman allowed that "we talked about plans for establishing a 'unified, independent, and democratic' government" in Korea. With such pledges from MacArthur, Truman assured Americans that his rhetoric would soon be reality: "We seek no territory or special privilege in Korea or anywhere else. We have no aggressive designs in Korea or in any other place in the Far East or elsewhere. And I want that to be perfectly clear to the whole world. . . . The only victory we seek is the victory of peace. . . . They [North Koreans] continue to put up stubborn, but futile resistance. . . . The power of the Korean Communists to resist effectively will soon come to an end.''

On the basis of an assumed military victory in Korea, Truman was emboldened to play semantic games. For all of his pious protestations to the contrary, it was the United States and the United Nations that now played the role of aggressor. Truman's definition of peace was in reality a war of aggression (NSC-81) to remove Communist North Koreans from power and to install an anti-Communist regime in Korea. Even the liberal media supported Truman's new war aims.

By February 1951, UN ground forces under the command of General Matthew Ridgway recaptured Seoul. At this juncture, China indicated that it was interested only in maintaining North Korea. The Truman administration decided to forego the rollback policy of NSC-81 in favor of a cease-fire that would maintain a divided Korea. The United States was back where it had been in September 1950, where Truman might have left well enough alone.

The persuasive problem that Harry Truman had with the Korean War was, according to Ray McKerrow, a ''juxtaposition of two incompatible realities: a rhetoric of limited war and one of victory,'' but McKerrow did not account for the two distinct stages, June to September 1950, and after September 1950, that characterized Truman's Korean War rhetorics. In the first stage, Truman's rhetoric ran to catch up with military actions; and then, in the second stage, HST's rhetoric ran ahead of military capabilities. In the first situation, the definition of limited war and victory were linguistically consistent. But in the second circumstance, HST was constrained from changing the definition of limited war to achieve a redefined victory.

Under the original UN Security Council's sanction, achieving the *status quo ante bellum* was the victory that Truman talked about in his early messages and speeches on the subject. When he achieved the announced end of driving the North Koreans from the South in September, Truman achieved his victory with a limited war (or police action), as he had consistently defined the U.N.'s aims. Truman uttered no incompatible realities with respect to victory via limited war from June to September 1950.

Truman created a new and altogether different persuasive problem when he decided to enact NSC-81. The National Security Council, the military, General MacArthur, the hawks in the Democratic and Republican party, the U.N. Security Council, and the media supported the transformation of a limited war (to achieve the *status quo ante bellum*) into an aggressive war (the destruction of the North Korean government). On an assumption of a quick military victory, however misguided it was, Truman miscalculated. Without changing the constraints and definition of a limited war, Truman escalated the definition of victory: Victory, redefined under NSC-81, was the capitulation of the Communists and the unification of Korea under a pro-U.S. government. All of this, as everyone hoped, could be achieved within the framework of the old definition of a limited war. When the military options were not escalated to match the increased rhetorical expectations, the incompatible realities ensued. Therefore, McKerrow was only correct in his assessment of the second stage of Truman's Korean War rhetorical strategy.

And once the second act of the Manichaean, supernation drama got under way in November 1950, there was little Harry Truman could do to disenthrall himself from a play he could no longer manage. Unfortunately, an increasing number of Americans became dissatisfied with the script, wanted it rewritten, and craved for their lead star, General Douglas MacArthur, to assume center stage. When Truman fired the prima donna, many Americans wanted to dismiss the director of America's most unsuccessful war.

THE PRESIDENT FIRES A GENERAL

In early March 1951, President Truman arranged a cease-fire with the Chinese on the basis of the *status quo ante bellum* of June 1950. MacArthur contented himself with issuing statements that countered Truman's policy, but on March 24, MacArthur cast aside all caution. He issued an unauthorized statement that called for the Chinese and Koreans to surrender or to face annihilation of their forces. Rather than fire the general then, Truman reminded MacArthur of the President's December 6, 1950, directive to clear all statements with Washington, and warned him not to make further unauthorized statements.

The straw that broke the general's back was his letter to Representative Joseph Martin (R-Massachusetts), the minority leader of the House. To Martin's request that the general state his views on the Far East, MacArthur obliged by urging various military actions, and he ended his letter with the now famous line: "There is no substitute for victory." Martin read the letter to the House on April 5, and HST decided to fire the general for insubordination.

At 10:30 P.M., April 11, 1951, President Truman took to the airwaves to deliver his Preventing a New World War speech, which was his response to the storm of protest that resulted from his dismissal of General MacArthur. Here are a few responses, which are collected in the Truman Library, that Truman received after he gave his speech:

Who are you trying to kid?

Your speeches stink and you stink.

I cannot help but feel you are 100% wrong.

From the perspective of the rhetorical presidency, HST delivered the address in order to gain and maintain support for his policy. But which policy? Since Truman was under attack for firing MacArthur, one would reasonably expect

Truman to defend the dismissal in his speech. As delivered, the speech basically defended Truman's Korean War policy and not his dismissal of the general. The firing demanded from Truman a direct defense for that action and not a general justification of the Korean War.

David Bell and Charles Murphy, speech writer and special counsel to the President, were the White House writers for the address. The reason for firing MacArthur was placed at the end of the address. However, by placing the dismissal justification at the end, the staff stressed the Korean War policy, and minimized, by burying it in the end of the speech, why MacArthur was fired. The speech implied that MacArthur was dismissed only because he differed with the administration's policy, which played to those who claimed that Truman's policy was wrong, and not because MacArthur was insubordinate.

Contemporary support for Truman's speech was weak. The White House mail showed some favorable movement from the initial pro-con ratio of 32 percent to 68 percent, but the final figures were not reassuring: pro, 45 percent, and con, 55 percent.

By now, the drone of supernation, Manichaean rhetoric that one encountered in Truman's Korean War speeches must have been deadening. So, suffice it to say, the speech was replete with good-guy, bad-guy polarities. However, the speech contained other noteworthy rhetorical techniques. As he had argued in his July 19 and September 1, 1950 speeches, Truman pressed the historical analogy to World War II as applicable to the Korean situation:

The best time to meet the threat is in the beginning.

It is easier to put out a fire in the beginning when it is small than after it has become a roaring blaze.

And the best way to meet the threat of aggression is for the peace-loving nations to act together. If they don't act together, they are likely to be picked off, one by one.

If they had followed the right policies in the 1930's—if the free countries had acted together, to crush the aggression of the dictators, and if they had acted in the beginning, when the aggression was small—there probably would have been no World War II.

Truman also used rhetorical repetition and restatement to inculcate his message. Lest confusion arise in Truman's Korean War policy, he stated his theme, with variations, at least ten times throughout the speech:

We are trying to prevent a third world war.

[B]efore they can result in a third world war.

[T]he best way of stopping it without a general war.

So far, we have prevented World War III.

We are trying to prevent a world war—not to start one.

[W]e would be running a very grave risk of starting a general war.

[A] full scale war with Red China.

[T]o avoid an all out war.

[T]o prevent a third world war.

The free nations have united in their strength in an effort to prevent a third world war.

The President also marshalled a refutation section in his speech to preempt attacks on his Korean War policy. Taking the objections from MacArthur's mouth, Truman paraphrased the general and the objections of MacArthur's supporters: "But you may ask why can't we take other steps to punish the aggressor? Why don't we bomb Manchuria and China itself? Why don't we assist the Chinese National troops to land on the mainland of China?" This was a master stroke in rhetorical refutation, because these were the very steps that MacArthur advocated. Truman twice answered that such activities would start a third world war, but he did not prove his claims. It just was the President's word against the general's, and many preferred MacArthur's.

However, in the final analysis, Truman prevailed. In Congressional hearings that were called to embarrass the President, it emerged that Truman's limited war policy, and not MacArthur's fight-to-win strategy, was best. This was warranted in Chairman of the Joint Chiefs of Staff General Omar Bradley's famous testimony: "Red China is not the powerful nation seeking to dominate the world. Frankly, in the opinion of the Joint Chiefs of Staff, this strategy would involve us in the wrong war, at the wrong place, at the wrong time, and with the wrong enemy."

THE 1948 CAMPAIGN

The right war and right place and right time and right enemy coalesced for Truman in the presidential campaign of 1948.

Democratic Convention Address

On July 15, 1948, Truman approached the rostrum in Philadelphia that had a bank of microphones attached to it. Reacting to shouts from the audience to move the microphones, Truman ad-libbed his memorable beginning. It was a harbinger of things to come, because Truman *was* able to see what he was doing:

I am sorry that the microphones are in the way, but I must leave them the way they are because I have got to be able to see what I am doing—[slight pause for effect] as I am always able to see what I am doing [applause].

The rhetorical efficacy of Truman's convention speech ensued from several factors. Truman stirred the Democratic audience's guilt by chastising those who might not vote Democratic. He then addressed their anger and frustration with the Republican party by identifying the Republican-controlled Congress as the scapegoat for the country's ills. Finally, he offered the convention audience salvation only if it supported and voted for the Democratic party and Harry S. Truman in the fall. The same persuasive method also worked for the radio audience and the American people: Only Harry S. Truman would battle the villains on behalf of the victimized people.

The guilt trip began early in the address. "Now is the time," Truman admonished the audience, "for us to get together and beat the common enemy. And that is up to you." A few lines later, the President laid guilt on two of the Democratic party's important constituencies, farmers and laborers:

Never in the world were the farmers of any republic or any kingdom or any other country as prosperous as the farmers of the United States; and if they don't do their duty by the Democratic Party, they are the most ungrateful people in the world!

And I say to labor what I have said to the farmers: they are the most ungrateful people in the world if they pass the Democratic Party by this year.

Having instilled some shame in Democrats who might not support the party, Truman wisely stirred their anger. He did this by ticking off the accomplishments of the Democratic party: turning away from isolationism, removing trade barriers, and starting foreign aid programs. Abruptly, Truman delineated the villain:

The Republican Party, as I said a while ago, favors the privileged few and not the common everyday man. Ever since its inception, that party has been under the control of special privilege; and they have completely proved it in the 80th Congress. They proved it by the things they did *to* the people, and not *for* them. They proved it by the thing they failed to do. [Emphasis in original.]

Truman then listed all of the legislation and programs that he had requested but the Republican Congress had failed to pass.

Calling the Republican's poker hand, Truman delivered his rhetorical coup de grace:

I am therefore calling this Congress back into session July 26th. . . . I am going to call Congress back and ask them to pass the laws to halt rising prices, to meet the housing crisis, which they say they are for in their platform. . . . Now, my friends, if there is any reality behind that Republican platform, we ought to get some action from a short session of the 80th Congress. They can do this job in 15 days if they want to do it. They will still have time to go out and run for office.

Having dispatched the duplicity of the Republican platform, Truman indicated how America could save itself. Truman made a direct appeal to the people, and it was vintage Truman:

Now my friends, with the help of God and the wholehearted push which you can put behind this campaign, we can save the country from a continuation of the 80th Congress, and from misrule from now on.

I must have your help. You must get in and push, and win this election. The country can't afford another Republican Congress.

After clinching the nomination, Truman went on whistle-stop tours of the United States in order to campaign against Governor Thomas Dewey of New York, the Republican candidate. The facts are impressive: Truman travelled nearly 20,000 miles by train, made 7 whistle-stop tours, delivered from 26 to 34 major addresses (depending on how one defines a major address), and delivered close to 250 impromptu remarks from his railroad car.

The whistle-stop talks were arduous. Rising early and retiring late, Truman usually spoke seven or eight times a day from the train. His two busiest whistle-stop days were: sixteen speeches in Oklahoma and Missouri on September 29, and sixteen speeches in Massachusetts, Rhode Island, Connecticut, and New York City (where he made six separate appearances) on October 28. Two days tied for second place: September 30 with thirteen stops in Illinois, Indiana, and Kentucky, and October 8 with thirteen stops in New York state, which was Dewey's bailiwick. One should realize that Truman also delivered a major address in the evening on each of these long days!

The whistle-stops had a format. Truman usually professed surprise that so many folks came out to see him, which also amazed pollsters because everyone knew that Dewey would win; thanked the people for attending; made some local color remarks; boosted regional Democratic candidates; and then lambasted the Republican good-for-nothing, do-nothing 80th Congress.

For the campaign, Truman repeated many themes from his convention address. For instance, he induced guilt at Burbank, California, September 23: "Now, if you stay at home this time you will get just what you deserve. I don't think you're going to do it—I don't think you are going to do it!"; at Yuma, Arizona, September 24, he preached self-interest: "I am not only asking you to vote for me, I am asking you to vote for yourselves in your own selfish interests"; and at Worchester, Massachusetts, October 27, 1948, he lectured on Republican economic theory: "The Republicans believe in what they call the 'trickle down' theory. They want the big, rich, and wealthy, privileged special interest groups to get the lion's share of the income and let the scraps fall down to the rest of us."

A major campaign address, perhaps Truman's best rhetorical effort, was his "Doctor Dewey and the Republican Record," Pittsburgh, Pennsylvania, October 23, 1948. The rhetorical situation was ripe for a ripping rebuttal against the Republican candidate and the 80th Congress because Dewey had delivered an address in Pittsburgh on October 11. Charles Murphy invented the famous "cracked record" metaphor:

It sounds to me like the same old phonograph record; but this year the record has a crack, and the needle gets stuck in that crack every once in a while.

Now the crack in the soothing syrup of that record was provided by the Republican 80th "do-nothing" Congress.

Now, in 1948, every time the Republican candidate says, "I can do it better," up comes an echo from the crack which says, "We're against it."

The broken record metaphor highlighted the hypocrisy in the Republican campaign. The audience loved it.

David Lloyd wrote the now-famous dialogue between Doctor Dewey and the American patient-voter. When HST played the role of Doctor Dewey, he lowered slightly the pitch of his voice in order to differentiate the Democratic patient from the Republican doctor. The following excerpt is from a recording of the speech, and audience reactions are included in brackets; moreover, Truman made a mistake in rendering one of the lines, which is not given in his public papers, and the ad-libbed remarks are italicized:

Now, let's imagine that we, the American people, are going to see this doctor. It's just our usual routine checkup which we have every four years.

Now, we go into this doctor's office. And "Doctor," we say, "we're feeling fine."

"Is that so?" says the doctor [laughter]. (Truman was supposed to say next, "You been bothered much by issues lately?" but he made a mistake and ad-libbed) *"I've been bothered much by issues lately."* (Then, sensing his mistake, he ad-libbed) *"Have you been bothered much by issues, lately, too?* [laughter])"

"Not bothered, exactly," we say. "Of course, we've had a few. We've had the issues of high prices, and housing, and education, and social security, and a few others."

"That's too bad," says the doctor [laughter]. "You shouldn't have so many issues [laughter]."

"Is that right?" we say. "We thought that issues were a sign of political health."

"Not at all," says the doctor [laughter]. "You shouldn't think about issues. What you need is my brand of soothing syrup [laughter]—I call it 'unity.' "

Then the doctor edges up a little closer.

And he says, "Say, you don't look so good [laughter]."

We say to him, "Well, that seems strange to me, Doc. I never felt stronger, never had more money, and never had a brighter future. What is wrong with me?"

Well, the doctor looks blank and he says [laughter], "I never discuss issues with a patient. But what you need is a major operation [laughter]."

"Will it be serious, Doc?" we say.

"Not so very serious," he says. "It will just mean taking out the complete works and putting in a Republican administration [prolonged laughter]."

The 1948 campaign was Truman's finest oratorical hour, for it proved conclusively that he could energize crowds with his appeals. Truman won the 1948 campaign on his own merit and against substantial odds. The popular vote was about 24,100,00 (49.5 percent) for Truman versus Dewey's 21,900,000 (45.1

percent), and the electoral vote was 303 against Dewey's 189 and Strom Thurmond's 39.

TRUMAN'S INAUGURAL ADDRESS, 1949: POINT FOUR

Although Truman ran against and beat Dewey on domestic issues, Truman's ability to work with a Republican-controlled Congress was necessarily limited. On the other hand, the President's forte had been in foreign policy. Truman had successfully committed the United States to the containment policy against Communism, which was passed by a bipartisan Congress. Thus, the political auguries of Truman's caretaker administration and of the 1948 campaign impinged on the Inaugural Address by anyone skilled enough to read them. Whereas it would be difficult for Truman on inaugural day, January 20, 1949, to speak as the *vox populi* on domestic issues that were divisive, Truman could address a fairly united country on foreign affairs, for anti-Communism sentiment was growing and containment was accepted as the Soviets expanded in Europe. Thus, Truman made a clean break with his 1948 campaign, which was devoted to lambasting Congress and the Republican party for not passing Truman's domestic agenda, and instead focused on foreign issues where he had some prior successes and would be less constrained by Congress.

Various writers contributed to the speech process. Benjamin Hardy, a junior officer in public affairs at the State Department, presented George Elsey with the outline of Point Four, and Elsey then conferred with Clark Clifford, who immediately seized upon the idea. Hardy's ideas are as follows:

1. Political institutions
      a. UN [United Nations]
      b. Respect for the rights of all peoples
2. Economic betterment
      a. ERP [European Recovery Program, or Marshall Plan]
      b. World trade
      c. Technological development
3. [Military Security*] Preservation of Law and Order
      1. Regional defense pacts
      2. Military aid and advice to other nations
      3. Our own military strength

Fourth, we will join with other nations in reducing barriers to international trade because world trade is one of the foundations of world peace.

These four points, with only slight modifications, innervated the speech, which went through five drafts.

*Military security was crossed out in the original, but it was changed to preservation of law and order.

Truman was the first president to deliver an inaugural after World War II, and his address is a prototype of Manichaean, supernation rhetoric. He made a clean break with historical inaugurals by focusing almost entirely on foreign issues.

President Truman sounded the leitmotif of supernation rhetoric in the second sentence of his Inaugural Address: "I accept it [the presidency] with a resolve to do all that I can for the welfare of this Nation and for the peace of the world." The rhetoric was for the people of the world and U.S. citizens, for Truman inextricably linked the welfare of the United States to world peace: "It is fitting, therefore, that we take this occasion to proclaim to the world the essential principles of the faith by which we live, and to declare our aims to all peoples."

Truman used the stylistic device of antithesis to juxtapose communism with democracy. Four pairs of antithetical units starkly communicated Manichaean divisions.

1. Communism believes "that man is so weak" that he "required the rule of strong masters," but democracy believes "that man has the moral and intellectual capacity . . . to govern himself."
2. Communism "subjects" individuals to invidious state controls whereas democracy protects "the rights of individuals."
3. Communism "maintains that social wrongs can be corrected only by violence" whereas democracy achieves "social justice . . . through peaceful change."
4. "Communism holds that the world is so widely divided into opposing classes that war is inevitable," but "Democracy holds that free nations can settle differences justly and maintain a lasting peace."

The anaphora of "Communism" and "Democracy," juxtaposing each of the four thought units, verbally reinforced the antithesis.

But he was not finished with his verbal portraiture of Communist perfidy. Continuing in the Manichaean vein, he warranted more evidence of the United States as hero versus the Soviet Union as villain. The audience easily supplied what nation was the antithesis of the United States. The listing had four paragraphs that began with the anaphora of "We have." First, "We have sought no territory." Americans and free peoples of the world would recall the Soviet Union's violating the Yalta agreements in Rumania, Bulgaria, and Poland, Russian pressures on Turkey and Iran, as well as the Berlin Blockade and the fall of Czechoslovakia in 1948. Second, "We have constantly and vigorously supported the United Nations." Americans would have remembered that the Soviet Union often used its veto power to stymie world peace. Third, "We have made every effort to secure agreement on effective international control of our most powerful weapon [the atom bomb]." The fact that the Soviet Union vetoed in 1946 a Security Council plan for international control of atomic energy warranted Truman's claim. Fourth, "We have encouraged . . . the expansion of world trade on a sound and fair basis." The 1947 Geneva agreement had produced the General Agreement on Tariffs and Trade [GATT].

As a U.S. solution to combat Soviet perfidy, Hardy's outline of Point Four remained remarkably intact. His first point was political institutions; Truman pledged: "First, we will continue to give unfaltering support to the United Nations." Hardy's second point, economic betterment, remained; Truman intoned: "Second, we will continue our programs for world economic recovery." Hardy's third point was preservation of law and order; Truman announced, "Third, we will strengthen freedom-loving nations against the dangers of aggression."

Hardy's fourth point was the reduction of trade barriers to international trade and peace. Of the four points, this one was redirected in the final address toward technological aid to developing countries. "Fourth," Truman proclaimed, "we must embark on a bold new program for making the benefits of our scientific advances and industrial progress available for the improvement and growth of underdeveloped areas."

The conclusion of Truman's Inaugural Address could be termed a classical peroration, an ending of unusual elegance and force. Truman constructed a series of five sentences that began with the anaphora of "We are aided by." Truman proclaimed "We are aided by all who wish to live in freedom from fear . . . who want relief from lies and propaganda . . . who desire self-government . . . who long for economic security . . . [and] who desire freedom of speech, freedom of religion, and freedom to live their own lives for useful ends." To bolster the Manichaean, supernation rhetoric that recurred throughout the speech, Truman waxed Biblically: "Our allies are the millions who hunger and thirst after righteousness." To motivate Americans to gird up their loins in the battle of good against evil, the President preached that it would "test our courage, our devotion to duty, and our concept of liberty." And, as if to verify the cliche that God is a being mentioned in the last sentence of a political speech, Truman intoned: "With God's help, the future of mankind will be assured in a world of justice, harmony, and peace."

CONCLUSION

President Truman's prototypical public persuasions from 1945 to 1952 inhered in the rhetoric of all presidents until the collapse of the Soviet Union in the early 1990s. He initiated Manichaean, supernation rhetoric, which invigorated the Cold War for almost half a century, in his Inaugural Address and in later speeches on the Korean War. His "containment policy," which was applied by subsequent presidents in dealings with Communism, was enunciated in his Truman Doctrine speech and applied to Korea. Even his ploy of running against the Congress in 1948 has been used by succeeding presidents with varying successes.

Perhaps not a Ciceronian orator, Truman was nevertheless an example of Quintilian's conception of a persuader as "The good man skilled in speaking." In his Valedictory, January 15, 1953, President Truman revealed his ethos as a president, which was a valid expression of his presidency then and is a fitting epitaph to his presidential oratory now: "I have a deep and abiding faith in the destiny of free men."

RHETORICAL SOURCES

Archival Materials

The most important sources for the study of Truman's presidential rhetoric are in the Harry S. Truman Library, Independence, Missouri. The papers of Harry S. Truman and speech files contain preliminary drafts as well as the final reading copy for all of his speeches. The President's secretary's files and speech files, also contain important drafts and memoranda for the process of inventing and editing the speeches. One may consult the papers of Truman's speech advisers: David Bell, Clark Clifford, George Elsey, Joseph Jones, David Lloyd, Charles Murphy, Richard Neustadt, and Samuel Rosenman.

The oral history interviews of David Bell, Clark Clifford, Matthew Connelly, George Elsey, Charles Murphy, Leonard Reinsch, and Samuel I. Rosenman concern Truman's rhetorical practices and his interactions with the speech staff.

The library collects audiovisual materials, including clips from newsreels, voice recordings, television tapes, and an extensive photographic collection.

The President's personal file, PPF-200, contains letters and telegrams that were sent with regard to his speeches.

The Public Papers of the Presidents: Harry S. Truman. (PPP). 8 Vols. Washington, DC: Government Printing Office, 1961–1966.

Rhetorical Studies

Burns, Richard Dean. *Harry S. Truman: A Bibliography of his Times and Presidency.* Wilmington, DE: Scholarly Resources, 1984.

Clifford, Clark. *Counsel to the President.* New York: Random House, 1991.

Donovan, Robert J. *Conflict and Crisis: The Presidency of Harry S. Truman, 1945–1948.* New York: W. W. Norton, 1977.

Germino, Dante. *The Inaugural Addresses of American Presidents.* Lanham, MD: University Press of America, 1984.

Gosnell, Harold F. *A Political Biography of Harry S. Truman.* Westport, CT: Greenwood Press, 1980.

Hinds, Lynn Boyd, and Theodore Otto Windt, Jr. *The Cold War as Rhetoric: The Beginnings, 1945–1950.* New York: Praeger, 1991.

Jones, Joseph. *The Fifteen Weeks.* New York: Viking Press, 1955.

Kirkendall, Richard S., ed. *The Truman Period as a Research Field.* Columbia, MO: University of Missouri Press, 1967.

———. *The Harry S. Truman Encyclopedia.* Boston: G. K. Hall, 1989.

McCoy, Donald R. *The Presidency of Harry S. Truman.* Lawrence, KS: University Press of Kansas, 1984.

McCullough, David. *Truman.* New York: Simon and Schuster, 1992.

Miller, Merle. *Plain Speaking: An Oral Biography of Harry S. Truman.* New York: G. P. Putnam's Sons, 1973.

Pemberton, William E. *Harry S. Truman: Fair Dealer and Cold Warrior.* Boston: Twayne, 1989.

Ryan, Halford R. *Harry S. Truman: Presidential Rhetoric.* Westport, CT: Greenwood Press, 1993.

Truman, Harry. *Memoirs.* 2 Vols. Garden City, NY: Doubleday, 1955–1956.

Truman, Margaret. *Harry S. Truman.* New York: William Morrow, 1973.

Underhill, Robert. *The Truman Persuasions.* Ames, IA: The Iowa State University Press, 1981.

Rhetorical Monographs

Brembeck, Cole. "Harry Truman at the Whistle Stops." *Quarterly Journal of Speech* 38 (1952): 42–50.

Duffy, Bernard K. "President Harry S. Truman and General Douglas MacArthur: A Study of Rhetorical Confrontation." In *Oratorical Encounters,* edited by Halford Ross Ryan. Westport, CT: Greenwood Press, 1988.

McKerrow, Ray E. "Truman and Korea: Rhetoric in the Pursuit of Victory." *Central States Speech Journal* 28 (1977): 1–12.

Ryan, Halford R. "Harry S. Truman: A Misdirected Defense for MacArthur's Dismissal." *Presidential Studies Quarterly* 11 (1981): 576–82.

———. "Harry Truman." In *American Orators of the Twentieth Century: Critical Studies and Sources,* edited by Bernard K. Duffy and Halford R. Ryan. Westport, CT: Greenwood Press, 1987.

Underhill, William R. "Harry S. Truman: Spokesman for Containment." *Quarterly Journal of Speech* 47 (1961): 268–74.

White, Eugene E., and Clair R. Henderlider. "What Harry S. Truman Told Us About His Speaking." *Quarterly Journal of Speech* 40 (1954): 37–42.

Chronology of Significant Presidential Persuasions.

[Unless otherwise stated, all speeches were delivered in Washington, D.C.]

The Truman Doctrine, joint session of Congress, March 12, 1947. *PPP,* 1947: 176–80

Acceptance speech, Democratic National Convention, Philadelphia, July 15, 1948. *PPP,* 1948: 406–10.

"Doctor Dewey and the Republican Record," Pittsburgh, Pennsylvania, October 23, 1948. *PPP,* 1948: 838–43.

Inaugural Address, January 20, 1949. *PPP,* 1949: 112–16.

Korean Speech I, June 26, 1950. *PPP,* 1950: 491–92.

Korean Speech II, June 27, 1950. *PPP,* 1950: 492

"Police-Action" press conference, June 29, 1950. *PPP,* 1950: 502–6.

Special Message to Congress on Korea, July 19, 1950. *PPP,* 1950: 527–37.

Address on Korea, July 19, 1950. *PPP,* 1950: 537–42.

The Situation in Korea, September 1, 1950. *PPP,* 1950: 609–14.

Address, War Memorial Opera House, San Francisco, California, October 17, 1950. *PPP,* 1950: 673–79.

Far Eastern Policy (''Preventing a Third World War'') radio address, April 11, 1951. *PPP,* 1951: 223–27.

Valedictory, January 15, 1953. *PPP,* 1952–1953: 1197–202.

Martin J. Medhurst

Dwight D. Eisenhower
(1890–1969)

> The plain truth is that security is planned, not blindly bought. It is the product of thought, and work, and our ability and readiness to bear our military burden for however long the threat to freedom persists.

Dwight D. Eisenhower was a strategic communicator, one who intentionally shaped thought and language to achieve specific ends. Neither stylistically eloquent nor particularly distinguished in delivery, Eisenhower nevertheless fashioned some of the most important and strategically effective speeches of the Cold War era. His First Inaugural Address, "The Chance for Peace," "Age of Peril," and "Atoms for Peace" speeches, all delivered during his first year as President, were masterpieces of rhetoric, discourse designed to achieve one or more specific ends with one or more audiences.

How did a man who had spent all but three years of his adult life in the military arrive at the presidency, at age sixty-three, with the ability to construct rhetoric that was not only clear and convincing, but strategically effective in implementing political, diplomatic, and economic policies? Such ability did not just happen, and it was not a gift of nature. Neither was it an accident nor the result of having employed a host of ghost writers. Although some of Eisenhower's effectiveness as a presidential communicator clearly came from his previously established ethos, the perception of his moral character held by the American electorate, even that resource cannot fully account for Eisenhower's success as a rhetorical strategist.

To understand Eisenhower's skills as a presidential communicator, one must search for the source of those skills in Ike's earlier life, primarily his military years, for in those years lay the key to the President's essentially strategic nature. His presidential speeches were an outworking of this nature. While Eisenhower probably developed an implicit theory of communication over the course of fifty years in public life, he did not start with a ready-made or well-formulated view of human persuasion. Indeed, it is doubtful that his studies at Abilene High School or the U.S. Military Academy at West Point ever provided any exposure to theoretical materials concerning rhetoric or public address, if by rhetoric one means the faculty of discovering in any case the available means of persuasion. Instead of theoretical instruction, Eisenhower relied upon practical experience and the emulation of models to mold himself into an effective public advocate.

IKE'S RHETORICAL TRAINING AND PRACTICES

Like most young people who attended high school or college in the early years of the twentieth century, Eisenhower's training in communication was limited to local dramatic productions, English grammar, and the study of great literature. In his senior year at Abilene High, Ike starred in the class play, an irreverent adaptation of Shakespeare's *The Merchant of Venice*. According to the local newspaper, "Dwight Eisenhower as Gobbo won plenty of applause and deserved it. He was the best amateur humorous character seen on the Abilene stage in this generation and gave an impression that many professionals fail to reach." That solitary performance in front of an audience of friends and parents appears to have been Eisenhower's only attempt to communicate with an audience prior to his enrollment at West Point in 1911.

By his own admission, Eisenhower was not bookish. Even so, two aspects stand out about Eisenhower as a high school student: 1) he was one of only nine boys to graduate from high school in Abilene, Kansas, during the 1909 school year; and 2) he seems to have learned his English grammar very well. When in 1910 Eisenhower took the examination to secure an appointment to one of the service academies, he scored a 99 percent in grammar, his highest score on a battery of tests in which he averaged 87.5 percent.

After winning an appointment to West Point (Annapolis had been his first choice), Eisenhower continued to do well in written expression. According to Stephen E. Ambrose, Ike could "produce a high-scoring essay a half hour before class." The composition course that Eisenhower took at West Point during the 1911–1912 academic year was taught under the auspices of the Department of English and History, and was the only formal instruction that members of Eisenhower's class would ever receive in anything remotely resembling communication skills. According to the Official Register of 1911: "In English, the course of instruction is planned to inculcate the essential principles of rhetoric, both by study of the text-book and by frequent practice in the various forms of composition (including practice in personal and official correspondence), to create an intelligent appreciation of the best in English literature by the study of selected literary master-pieces."

Eisenhower studied the textbook, Henry Canby's *English Composition in Theory and Practice*, well enough that nearly fifty years later one of his White

House speech writers, Arthur Larson, could testify that "no one I have ever known was more conscious about his writing, whether as to content, clarity, correctness, or style." Clearly Eisenhower must have had some natural ability and facility with the written word. Yet one year of a class that attempted to cover not only grammar and literature, but history as well, can hardly be credited with having produced a man who would go on to write a best-selling memoir, several other books, and literally scores of speeches between 1922 and 1942, virtually all of which were for other people.

Eisenhower's West Point training in oral communication was even less systematic, consisting entirely of extracurricular activities. Having had a promising football career cut short by injury, Eisenhower became a cheerleader. In this role one of his chief responsibilities was to deliver an extemporaneous and inspirational talk to the cadets on the night before a game. Giving a pep talk to excited cadets is probably not the best form of training in public speaking, but it was all that Eisenhower would have in four years at the Point. It was not until four years after he graduated that public speaking became a standard part of the English course.

As this brief survey illustrates, Eisenhower had little formal instruction in any form of communication. The theoretical materials to which he was exposed consisted of little more than the rules of grammar and sentence construction, along with the study of basic literary techniques as found in the works of Tennyson, Shakespeare, and other poets and playwrights. Therefore, to discover the sources of Eisenhower's communicative powers, one must turn from Abilene and West Point to the years following his graduation from the academy in 1915, for Ike's communicative abilities owed far more to the experiences he had and the role models he encountered between 1922 and 1945 than to any formal or theoretical instruction received during his formative years.

Three role models were crucial to Ike's rhetorical development: Fox Connor, Douglas MacArthur, and George C. Marshall. From Connor, Eisenhower learned the importance of broad reading and strategic analysis. Every day for three solid years Eisenhower wrote a field order for Connor. Connor insisted that the order be in the form of a five-paragraph statement in which everything essential for understanding and carrying out the order was covered, the mission, the terrain, the weather, detailed instructions, logistics, and communications. As a result of this instruction, Ike soon learned to express himself clearly, concisely, and with no extra verbiage or ornamental niceties. Communication, whether written or oral, was an instrumental art meant to accomplish a purpose.

From Douglas MacArthur, under whose command Eisenhower spent most of the 1930s, Ike learned how not to communicate. MacArthur was a political General, a talking General, and a General whose characteristic mode of interaction with juniors, and even at times with seniors, was arrogant and condescending. Eisenhower observed and rejected all three modes of interaction. To Ike, being a talking General was the worst fault of all. Not only did Ike find MacArthur's purple prose inappropriate to most situations, he also questioned

MacArthur's judgment concerning whether to speak, when to speak, and what to say when speech was necessary. For Eisenhower, silence was often the better part of wisdom; not so with MacArthur. Eisenhower's own practice would be to speak only when something needed to be said, usually to accomplish a specific goal. Ike believed that most leaders spoke far too often and accomplished far too little. He saw an inverse relationship between a man's wisdom and judgment and that man's interest in mounting the podium.

If MacArthur was the negative role model, then General George C. Marshall was the positive counterpart. Both Eisenhower and Marshall thought that words should be used sparingly and simply, and that deeds were the most eloquent form of expression. Both saw a person's communicative style as an important indication of character. Although Marshall was a clear and cogent speaker, he could never generate the human warmth or pleasing personality of Eisenhower. As Merle Miller put it: "Eisenhower made everyone feel at ease in his presence. Almost nobody felt at ease in Marshall's presence." But this was a matter of personality, not of trustworthiness, sincerity, or character, for along those dimensions Eisenhower and Marshall were equally effective. People could and did trust what they said, and that bond of trust became a powerful rhetorical resource that Eisenhower, in particular, used to his political advantage in the post–World War II era.

IKE'S PRE-PRESIDENTIAL RHETORIC

Between the end of World War II in 1945 and his inauguration as President in 1953, Eisenhower gave hundreds of formal speeches. Some were primarily ceremonial, such as his famous speech at Guildhall on June 12, 1945, in which he accepted the freedom of the City of London. But even his ceremonial speeches featured the themes that would come to characterize Ike's post–World War II speaking: teamwork, cooperation, unity, and partnership. At Guildhall, for example, Eisenhower said: "No one man could, alone, have brought about this result. Had I possessed the military skill of Marlborough, the wisdom of Solomon, the understanding of Lincoln, I still would have been helpless without the loyalty, the vision, the generosity of thousands upon thousands of British and Americans.... We were one great team." The notions of teamwork and cooperation pervaded Eisenhower's speaking and writing in the immediate aftermath of war.

After 1948, Eisenhower's speeches began to take on a more political tone. On September 5, 1949, for example, Ike addressed the annual meeting of the American Bar Association. In his speech, he articulated for the first time his emerging philosophy of "the middle way." Eisenhower warned the barristers that

When the center weakens piecemeal, disintegration and annihilation are only steps away, in a battle of arms or of political philosophies. The clearsighted and the courageous, fortunately, keep fighting in the middle of the war....

The middle of the road is derided by all of the right and of the left. They deliberately misrepresent the central position as a neutral, wishy-washy one. Yet here is the truly creative area in which we may obtain agreement for constructive social action compatible with basic American principles and with the just aspirations of every sincere American.

Eisenhower carried his "middle way" philosophy all the way to the White House where, as predicted, he was derided by both the left and the right. But it was precisely the strategy of staying in the middle of the political road and running to the right of the Democrats and to the left of the Republicans that allowed Eisenhower to win both the Republican nomination and the 1952 general election.

Between June 4 and November 4 of 1952, running against Adlai Stevenson, Eisenhower made scores of campaign speeches, a genre with which he was clearly not familiar. Even so, Eisenhower made some very important addresses, including his October 3, 1952 speech on "Communism and Freedom," and his October 8, 1952 speech on psychological warfare. Seven rhetorical strategies characterized his campaign speaking: 1) a focus on the theme of freedom; 2) articulation of the middle way philosophy of government; 3) juxtaposition of faith with fear; 4) repetition of World War II experiences and memories; 5) indictment of the incumbent Democratic administration for failing to keep the peace in Korea and losing China to the Communists; 6) defense of equality of opportunity before the law; and 7) identification of the Democrats with war and the Eisenhower agenda with peace. These strategies were used in different combinations throughout the summer and fall campaigns and proved to be extremely successful. When, in an October 24, 1952 speech in Detroit, Ike pledged "I shall go to Korea," most observers believed the election to have been won. On November 4, 1952, Eisenhower swept to victory, amassing some 27 million votes and carrying 39 out of the 48 states.

It is clear, therefore, that long before assuming the presidency, Eisenhower had gained valuable experience in impromptu, extemporaneous, and manuscript speaking. He had given after-dinner speeches, commencement addresses, lectures, oral reports and formal speeches to the Congress, made radio talks, and addressed numerous civic, professional, and political groups. He had conducted one of the toughest political campaigns of the twentieth century in 1952 and in the process learned that a politician often had to speak even when there was really nothing to say, a realization that continued to irk Eisenhower throughout his eight years in the White House.

While Eisenhower had the ability to come across to the American people as a person well-suited for civilian leadership, it is important to remember that he was first and last General Eisenhower. The formative influences on his life had been military men and his own training had been in high-level strategy and tactics. In many ways Eisenhower was the perfect choice for President during the height of the Cold War, for he approached his task as though it was, in fact, a war, although one fought primarily with words, images, perceptions, and attitudes rather than with guns or bullets. He saw his task as President as being both the prevention of World War III and the winning of the Cold War. Nowhere was this self-understanding more clearly articulated than in his initial speech as President of the United States.

EISENHOWER'S PRESIDENTIAL RHETORIC

In his First Inaugural Address, delivered on January 20, 1953, Eisenhower noted that the "forces of good and evil are massed and armed and opposed as rarely before in history." Even so, he proclaimed that "the future shall belong to the free." This, to Eisenhower, was the premier mission: to secure the future in such a way as to ensure that freedom would prevail. Much of Eisenhower's presidential speaking can be read as an effort to promote this goal. In the First Inaugural, Eisenhower intentionally divided the world into two camps, those who lived in freedom and those who labored under Communist slavery. Ike minced no words when he proclaimed:

The enemies of this faith know no god but force, no devotion but its use. They tutor men in treason. They feed upon the hunger of others. Whatever defies them, they torture, especially the truth.

Here, then, is joined no argument between slightly differing philosophies. This conflict strikes directly at the faith of our fathers and at the lives of our sons. . . .

Freedom is pitted against slavery; lightness against the dark.

Eisenhower then set forth nine "certain fixed principles" by which his administration would be guided. The first of these principles was a commitment "to develop the strength that will deter the forces of aggression and promote the conditions of peace." It was the first foreshadowing of what would come to be known as the New Look defense policy, a policy that placed heavy emphasis on the development and deployment of nuclear weapons.

In his first year in office, Eisenhower gave three more speeches that established both the themes and techniques that he would employ throughout his eight years in the presidency. "The Chance for Peace" was delivered on April 16, 1953, before the American Society of Newspaper Editors. "The Age of Peril" was a nationwide radio address given on May 19, 1953. And "Atoms for Peace" was delivered on December 8, 1953, before the General Assembly of the United Nations Organization. All three speeches expressed the hope for peace in a world that was fractured by ideology, values, and geography. "The Chance for Peace" is often described by scholars as being an eloquent plea on behalf of world peace, largely, it seems, on the basis of one paragraph in which Ike noted:

Every gun that is made, every warship launched, every rocket fired signifies, in the final sense, a theft from those who hunger and are not fed, those who are cold and are not clothed.

This world in arms is not spending money alone.

It is spending the sweat of its laborers, the genius of its scientists, the hopes of its children.

The cost of one heavy bomber is this: a modern brick school in more than 30 cities.

It is two electric power plants, each serving a town of 60,000 population.

It is two fine, fully equipped hospitals.

It is some fifty miles of concrete pavement.

We pay for a single fighter plane with a half million bushels of wheat.

We pay for a single destroyer with new homes that could have housed more than 8,000 people.

This is, I repeat, the best way of life to be found on the road the world has been taking.

This is not a way of life at all, in any true sense. Under the cloud of threatening war, it is humanity hanging from a cross of iron.

As noble as these sentiments are, they do not represent the actual thrust of the speech as a whole. "The Chance for Peace" was specifically designed to be a test of Soviet intentions. It was a probe used to determine whether the recent change in Soviet leadership, brought on by the death of Stalin, might prefigure a change in foreign policy. The heart of the speech actually came toward the end when Eisenhower said:

I know of only one question upon which progress waits. It is this: What is the Soviet Union ready to do?

Whatever the answer is, let it be plainly spoken.

Again we say: the hunger for peace is too great, the hour in history too late, for any government to mock men's hopes with mere words and promises and gestures.

Is the new leadership of the Soviet Union prepared to use its decisive influence in the Communist world, including control of the flow of arms, to bring not merely an expedient truce in Korea but genuine peace in Asia?

Is it prepared to allow other nations, including those in Eastern Europe, the free choice of their own form of government?

Is it prepared to act in concert with others upon serious disarmament proposals?

If not, where then is the Soviet Union's concern for peace?

This was one of the earliest in a series of "tests" that Eisenhower would issue to the Soviet leadership, using the medium of public speech. To pass the test, the Soviet Union would have to change its position on a host of issues, foremost among them Korea, a unified Germany, an Austrian peace treaty, the European Defense Community, and Indochina. Failure to change would be an admission that "peace" was not a Soviet goal.

Eisenhower clearly recognized that the Soviets were not likely to change their positions nor their global behaviors overnight. In fact, Ike believed that the United States was in for a long struggle in which economics, industrial capacity, and spiritual strength would be factors as important as military might. Thus, while holding out the olive branch of peace, Eisenhower simultaneously built the engines of war, engaging in the single largest nuclear weapons buildup in history between 1953 and 1957, while at the same time reducing the overall military budget through implementation of his New Look defense policy. That such a course was fraught with dangers, he well understood. Speaking to the American people on May 19, 1953, Ike warned that "our danger cannot be fixed or confined to one specific instant. We live in an age of peril." He then went on to say:

The course we must set for ourselves is a difficult one. It must avoid, on the one hand, the indefinite continuance of a needlessly high rate of Federal spending in excess of Federal income. It must avoid, on the other hand, any penny-wise, pound-foolish policy that could, through lack of needed strength, cripple the cause of freedom everywhere.

Life in a nuclear age entailed risks, and Ike was willing to risk nuclear war if that was the price for maintaining American freedoms. He was not, however, willing to scare the American people to death. His public pronouncements tended always to emphasize the hopes and aspirations of the nation for peace rather than the ongoing preparations for war. In what is regarded as one of his greatest speeches, Eisenhower held out the vision of world peace in his address of December 8, 1953, before the United Nations General Assembly. Speaking of "Atoms for Peace," Eisenhower said:

The United States would seek more than the mere reduction or elimination of atomic materials for military purposes.
It is not enough to take this weapon out of the hands of the soldiers. It must be put into the hands of those who will know how to strip its military casing and adapt it to the arts of peace.
The United States knows that if the fearful trend of atomic military buildup can be reversed, this greatest of destructive forces can be developed into a great boon, for the benefit of all mankind.

Eisenhower then proposed that all nations that were principally involved in disarmament talks agree to contribute a fixed amount of fissionable material to a new International Atomic Energy Agency, with the goal being the creation of a pool of fissionable materials dedicated to peaceful purposes. Even here, however, Ike had more than just peacetime applications of atomic energy in mind. He hoped once again to test the Soviet Union's sincerity, this time in a public forum with the whole world watching. Would the Soviets accept Ike's offer and agree to participate in a plan which, as outlined by the President, would be a boon to all mankind? Or, would the USSR refuse to participate, thus calling into question the sincerity of its overtures toward peace? Eisenhower made sure that a choice would have to be made by saying, "Of those 'principally involved' the Soviet Union must, of course, be one." Whether the Soviets chose to accept Ike's offer or reject his idea, it was believed that the United States would win a psychological victory by appearing to the world at large to be a champion of the peaceful atom. Efforts to ''test'' the sincerity of the Soviet protestations of peace characterized Eisenhower's first term in office, culminating with the 1955 Geneva Conference where Eisenhower proposed his Open Skies plan of mutual aerial reconnaissance. Speaking directly to the Soviet delegation, Eisenhower said:

Our two great countries admittedly possess new and terrible weapons in quantities which do give rise in other parts of the world, or reciprocally, to the fears and dangers of surprise attack.

I propose, therefore, that we take a practical step, that we begin an arrangement, very quickly, as between ourselves—immediately. These steps would include:

To give each other a complete blueprint of our military establishments, from beginning to end, from one end of our countries to the other; . . .

Next, to provide within our countries facilities for aerial photography to the other country.

Not surprisingly, the Soviets failed this and every test, thus blocking the road toward peace. With such an intransigent foe, the only recourse was to wage total Cold War. Eisenhower preferred to call his efforts ''waging peace,'' but in point of fact he was waging Cold War in an effort to, one day, reach a time of true peace. For the interim, however, ''peace'' consisted of nothing more than the absence of a shooting war. To maintain even this precarious sort of peace, Eisenhower resorted to a massive buildup of nuclear forces within both U.S. and NATO forces, expanded covert activities by the CIA, and signed mutual security pacts with nations around the globe.

One of the areas that was of special concern to Eisenhower was the Middle East. The United States had been the first nation to formally recognize the new State of Israel in 1948. Since that time the Israelis and their Arab neighbors had been in a constant state of warfare. That warfare intensified when in October of 1956 the Israelis, in concert with the British and French, undertook an invasion of the Suez Canal. The United States was not a party to the invasion, but the new U-2 spyplane had revealed to Eisenhower what was happening even before the invasion was launched. Ike was incensed that our British and French allies had undertaken an operation that was clearly in violation of the U.N. charter and that smacked of colonialism. He refused to cooperate with them and demanded that the Israelis withdraw to the preinvasion boundaries. On October 31, 1956, just one week before the presidential election in which Ike was again pitted against Adlai Stevenson, the President went on the air to explain America's stance in the face of an impending Middle East war. After explaining how events unfolded over a period of weeks, Ike said:

The United States was not consulted in any way about any phase of these actions. Nor were we informed of them in advance.

As it is the manifest right of any of these nations to take such decisions and actions, it is likewise our right—if our judgment so dictates—to dissent. We believe these actions to have been taken in error. For we do not accept the use of force as a wise or proper instrument for the settlement of international disputes. . . .

The action taken can scarcely be reconciled with the principles and purposes of the United Nations to which we have all subscribed. . . .

In all the recent troubles in the Middle East, there have indeed been injustices suffered by all nations involved. But I do not believe that another instrument of injustice—war—is the remedy for these wrongs.

There can be no peace without law. And there can be no law if we were to invoke one code of international conduct for those who oppose us and another for our friends.

From the outset, and without regard for how his actions might affect the presidential election, Eisenhower stood firm against the actions of our closest allies. On January 5, 1957, Eisenhower went before Congress to deliver what came to be known as the Eisenhower Doctrine speech. In his address, the President noted that "it is now essential that the United States should manifest through joint action of the President and the Congress our determination to assist those nations of the Mid East area, which desire that assistance." Eisenhower was concerned that the recent turmoil in the area would be used as a pretext for Communist exploitation. "In the situation now existing," said Ike, "the greatest risk, as is often the case, is that ambitious despots may miscalculate. If power-hungry Communists should either falsely or correctly estimate that the Middle East is inadequately defended, they might be tempted to use open measures of armed attack." To guard against this contingency, Eisenhower proposed that Congress

authorize the United States to cooperate with and assist any nation or group of nations in the general area of the Middle East in the development of economic strength dedicated to the maintenance of national independence.

It would, in the second place, authorize the Executive to undertake in the same region programs of military assistance and cooperation with any nation or group of nations which desires such aid.

It would, in the third place, authorize such assistance and cooperation to include the employment of the armed forces of the United States to secure and protect the territorial integrity and political independence of such nations, requesting such aid, against overt armed aggression from any nation controlled by International Communism.

The Eisenhower Doctrine put the Soviet Union on notice that the Middle East was not to be looked upon as an easy target for exploitation or infiltration. In 1958, Ike used the doctrine as a rationale for providing American troops to Lebanon to support the incumbent government of that nation. By virtue of the Suez crisis and the articulation of the Eisenhower Doctrine, the Middle East became a prime recipient of mutual security dollars.

Mutual security was, in fact, the central theme of Ike's Second Inaugural Address, delivered on January 21, 1957. In the Second Inaugural, Ike argued:

To counter the threat of those who seek to rule by force, we must pay the costs of our own needed military strength, and help to build the security of others.

We must use our skills and knowledge and, at times, our substance, to help others rise from misery, however far the scene of suffering may be from our shores. For wherever in the world a people knows desperate want, there must appear at least the spark of hope, the hope of progress—or there will surely rise at last the flames of conflict.

We recognize and accept our own deep involvement in the destiny of men everywhere.

Recognition of our "involvement" meant, for Eisenhower, massive infusions of foreign aid, particularly military, economic, and defense aid. Without such organizations as NATO, SEATO, and CENTO, the United States could not hope to contain the Soviet Union. Strength lay in numbers, and Eisenhower was committed to maintaining those numbers in ways that would prevent the bankrupting of the national economy.

While fighting Communism abroad, Eisenhower had to contend with numerous problems at home. Although much of his first administration had been devoted to dealing with the problems of internal Communist subversion and the equally great subversion caused by such unprincipled anti-Communists as Senator Joseph R. McCarthy, Ike's second term saw the problem of black civil rights rise to prominence. Prompted by the Supreme Court's 1954 decision in *Brown v. the Board of Education of Topeka*, black Americans began organized efforts to secure the rights guaranteed to them under the Constitution. The *Brown* decision had declared the principle of "separate but equal" school districts to be unconstitutional. In 1955, the Supreme Court ordered all school districts to move "with all deliberate speed" to end segregated educational facilities. By 1957, many school districts throughout the country were beginning to implement the new Supreme Court guidelines. One such district was in Little Rock, Arkansas.

The Little Rock school board had passed a plan to integrate Central High School, starting in the fall of 1957. It was a moderate plan that envisioned integration starting at the high school level and extending through the elementary schools over a six-year period, with complete integration not occurring until 1963. This plan had been approved by the courts and was proceeding apace when Arkansas Governor Orval Eugene Faubus decided to block the enrollment of nine black students at Central High School. He accomplished this by calling out the Arkansas National Guard and physically blocking the black students from entering the school grounds. This unprecedented action by Governor Faubus immediately led to a clash between state authorities and the federal government. For three weeks, the unfolding drama at Little Rock filled the newspapers. On September 24, 1957, the climax to the events occurred when President Eisenhower federalized the Arkansas National Guard and called up elite troops from the 101st Airborne Division to patrol the streets of Little Rock. On the evening of the 24th, Ike went on national television to explain his actions to the American people. Speaking from the Oval Office, Eisenhower said:

For a few minutes this evening I should like to speak to you about the serious situation that has arisen in Little Rock. . . .

In that city, under the leadership of demagogic extremists, disorderly mobs have deliberately prevented the carrying out of proper orders from a Federal Court. . . .

Whenever normal agencies prove inadequate to the task and it becomes necessary for the Executive Branch of the Federal Government to use its powers and authority to uphold Federal Courts, the President's responsibility is inescapable.

In accordance with that responsibility, I have today issued an Executive Order directing the use of troops under Federal authority to aid in the execution of Federal law at Little Rock, Arkansas.

Federal troops remained in Little Rock for a month after Ike's speech, and Arkansas National Guard units took up residence at Central High School for the rest of the school year. But the nation soon forgot about Little Rock when on October 4, 1957, the USSR launched Sputnik I into earth orbit.

Sputnik proved to be one of Eisenhower's greatest challenges. The launching of the satellite caught the general public by surprise and resulted in an outcry for more defense spending and greater efforts to "catch up" with the Soviet Union. Eisenhower resisted all such calls, at least for a while, and by virtue of his ethos and acknowledged military expertise was able to keep the military budget from ballooning out of all proportion to the threat. Although his speaking on the subject of Sputnik was not terribly effective, Ike was nonetheless able to head off the more hysterical responses to the Soviet launches. In a November 7, 1957 address to the American people, Ike reminded his listeners that even though "the Soviets are quite likely ahead in some missile and special areas, and are obviously ahead of us in satellite development, as of today the overall military strength of the free world is distinctly greater than that of the communist countries." Six days later, Ike was back on the air with a speech broadcast from Oklahoma City's Municipal Auditorium. This time, instead of reciting facts and figures, Eisenhower spoke of ideals and values. The President observed that

That real strength with which the self-governing democracies have met the tests of history is something denied dictatorships.

It is found in the quality of our life and the vigor of our ideals. It manifests itself in the ever-astonishing capacity of free men for voluntary heroism, sacrifice and accomplishment when the chips are down.

This is the weapon which has meant eventual downfall for every dictator who has made the familiar mistake of thinking all democracies "soft."

Now, once again, we hear an expansionist regime declaring "We will bury you."

In a bit of American vernacular, Oh, Yeah?

Eisenhower moved quickly to strengthen scientific education in America. He created within the Executive Office a new Special Assistant to the President for Science and Technology, and he moved forward with America's own space program. What Ike refused to do, however, was to depart from his basic strategy.

He would not infuse massive amounts of new money into defense nor would he pretend that the Soviet launch was of great strategic importance when he knew that it was not. What Ike failed to understand, however, was the great importance that the lay public placed on the Soviet achievement—and the willingness of his Democratic opponents to use the issue of Sputnik to call into question his stewardship of the national defenses. By 1960, the Democrats were using the supposed "missile gap" as a key component in their quest to retake the White House.

One of the reasons that Eisenhower was not terribly upset over the Sputnik launch was that he knew something the general public did not. Although the USSR had launched an earth satellite that with each orbit called attention to itself, the satellite had no military or strategic use. It was pure propaganda. What the President could not tell the public was that starting in 1956, the United States had been conducting high-altitude surveillance of the Soviet Union's most sensitive military installations using the supersecret U-2 spyplane. Unlike Sputnik, the U-2 was a real weapon in the ongoing Cold War, and one that gave a decided advantage to the United States. Indeed, the U-2 photos had revealed the pending Soviet launch of Sputnik some two weeks before it took place. The launch surprised the world; it did not come as a surprise to Eisenhower.

Throughout 1958, 1959, and 1960, while many worried about a "missile gap," the United States was gathering vital information about Soviet military capabilities. The U-2 was a weapon the Soviets could not match, and one which their air defense systems could not stop, at least not until May of 1960. In what was scheduled to be the final U-2 flight before the Paris Peace Summit, pilot Francis Gary Powers was shot down and captured by the Soviets. This proved to be an embarrassing situation for the United States inasmuch as Eisenhower first denied that there was a spyplane, then issued a patently false statement, and finally had to admit that we had indeed been spying on the Soviet Union. In the aftermath of this situation, the Paris Summit collapsed and Eisenhower's invitation to visit the Soviet Union was unceremoniously revoked. On May 25, 1960, Eisenhower sought to put the events of the preceding three weeks in context. This he did using a strategy of explanation as he addressed the American people:

Our safety, and that of the free world, demand, of course, effective systems for gathering information about the military capabilities of other powerful nations, especially those that make a fetish of secrecy. This involves many techniques and methods. In these times of vast military machines and nuclear-tipped missiles, the ferreting out of this information is indispensable to free world security. . . .

Now two questions have been raised about this particular flight; first, as to its timing, considering the imminence of the Summit meeting; second, our initial statements when we learned the flight had failed.

As to the timing, the question was really whether to halt the program and thus forego the gathering of important information that was essential and that was likely to be unavailable at a later date. The decision was that the program should not be halted.

The plain truth is this: when a nation needs intelligence activity, there is no time when vigilance can be relaxed. Incidentally, from Pearl Harbor we learned that even negotiation itself can be used to conceal preparations for a surprise attack.

Next, as to our government's initial statement about the flight, this was issued to protect the pilot, his mission, and our intelligence processes, at a time when the true facts were still undetermined.

Our first information about the failure of this mission did not disclose whether the pilot was still alive, was trying to escape, was avoiding interrogation, or whether both plane and pilot had been destroyed. Protection of our intelligence system and the pilot, and concealment of the plane's mission, seemed imperative.

Thus did Eisenhower seek to explain one of the most embarrassing failures of his eight year incumbency. Despite the failure of the mission and the collapse of the Summit, Eisenhower's public approval ratings actually increased, from 62 percent approval to 65 percent, during the course of the U-2 crisis.

The collapse of the Paris Summit dashed any hopes that Eisenhower might have had of ending his presidency with a treaty limiting the testing of nuclear weapons. The elections of November 1960 pitted Eisenhower's Vice-President, Richard M. Nixon, against Senator John F. Kennedy. In one of the closest elections ever, Senator Kennedy emerged the victor and eight years of Republican rule came to an end. Eisenhower was particularly distressed at the election outcome, believing that it was, at least in part, a repudiation of the governmental philosophy he had tried to instill during his presidency. Ike spent his last weeks in office thinking about the government and the man to whom he would soon be turning over the Oval Office. Eisenhower was leaving the presidency at the height of the Cold War, with no end in sight. To survive this prolonged struggle, the country would have to be strategically wary and fiscally prudent, as he told the American people in his Farewell Address of January 17, 1961.

Eisenhower's Farewell Address is rightly remembered for his warnings about the military-industrial complex and the scientific-technological elite. What is less well remembered is precisely what Ike said about those entities. Far from condemning the military-industrial complex—an interlocking set of communication networks, industries, defense contractors, and government officials that Eisenhower himself had helped to create—the President said that such a complex was an "imperative need." Nevertheless, he warned the citizens that

In the councils of government, we must guard against the acquisition of unwarranted influence, whether sought or unsought, by the military-industrial complex. The potential for the disastrous rise of misplaced power exists and will persist.

We must never let the weight of this combination endanger our liberties or democratic processes. We should take nothing for granted. Only an alert and knowledgeable citizenry can compel the proper meshing of the huge industrial and military machinery of defense with our peaceful methods and goals, so that security and liberty may prosper together.

Eisenhower's concern was twofold. First, he was concerned that the new president not succumb to the pressures sure to be brought on him by the munitions makers and defense contractors. Since Ike had spent his entire career in the military and had commanded more military might than any person in history, he had the public standing to be able to tell the military chieftains, in the words of his speech writer Bryce Harlow, to "go jam it." Ike was afraid that no other president, and certainly not John F. Kennedy, would have the self-confidence or public approval to stand up against the pressures of the military-industrial lobby. So Ike's first concern was that the office of the presidency might become hostage to outside influence. The second concern was directly related to the first. Without a professional military man in the White House, Ike feared that the Joint Chiefs, whom he had had to restrain throughout eight years of his presidency, would have a field day with a new, young, and inexperienced Chief Executive. Even before taking office, Kennedy was promising massive increases in the defense budget and setting up a structure that was sure to result in a budget deficit, something Ike found very disturbing, for he had always believed that it was economic weakness, not military weakness, that was America's greatest potential problem. For Eisenhower, the key was to keep everything in balance. If the economy became imbalanced in favor of military hardware and personnel, the nation could become a garrison state and thus undermine the very freedoms that the military was sworn to protect.

CONCLUSION

From his First Inaugural Address through his Farewell Address, Eisenhower waged Cold War. He used language purposefully and carefully to craft a strategic rhetoric that allowed him to pursue his goals of keeping the Soviets off balance, maintaining the diverse elements of the American economy in balance, avoiding World War III, containing Soviet expansionism through mutual security arrangements, competing for the loyalty of the third world countries, and building a nuclear arsenal that would be second to none. Many of Eisenhower's speeches were masterpieces of indirection, implication, and the strategic use of ambiguity. Always rhetoric served the larger goals of foreign and defense policy. Indeed, apart from understanding the policies that Ike was pursuing, it is virtually impossible to understand or appreciate the rhetoric he so carefully fashioned, for Eisenhower was the epitome of a strategic communicator.

RHETORICAL SOURCES

Archival Materials

The primary source for researching Eisenhower's rhetorical presidency is the Dwight D. Eisenhower Presidential Library in Abilene, Kansas. The *Dwight D. Eisenhower: Papers as President of the United States, 1953–1961* (Ann Whitman File) contains several series that are indispensable for rhetorical researchers. These include the Campaign Series, DDE Diary Series, Names Series, Press

Conference Series, and, most centrally, the Speech Series. Drafts of most major addresses can be found in the Speech Series as well as in the files of the individual speech writers, Kevin McCann, Bryce Harlow, Malcolm Moos, Arthur Larson, William Bragg Ewald, and Stephen Hess. Also of interest are the papers of C. D. Jackson and Nelson Rockefeller, Special Assistants for Cold War Strategy. Eisenhower's own views on speaking and writing are interspersed throughout his correspondence and can be found most readily by examining the DDE Diary Series and the Names Series.

The *Dwight D. Eisenhower: Records as President, White House Central Files, 1953–1961* contains other useful materials on presidential communication. Especially helpful are the Alphabetical File, the Confidential File, and the President's Personal File. The personal papers of Sherman Adams, John Bird, John Foster Dulles, Milton S. Eisenhower, William B. Ewald, Jr., James C. Hagerty, Bryce N. Harlow, Gabriel Hauge, Stephen Hess, C. D. Jackson, James M. Lambie, Jr., Arthur Larson, Kevin McCann, and Thomas E. Stephens are also available. More than five hundred oral history interviews with various administration officials are on file.

The Eisenhower Library also has an extensive audio-visual collection, including videotapes of many Eisenhower speeches and press conferences.

The papers of speech writer Emmet John Hughes are located in the Seeley Mudd Manuscript Library at Princeton University in Princeton, New Jersey. Drafts of the First Inaugural Address, "The Chance for Peace," and the Second Inaugural Address are in the Hughes papers. Also of interest is Hughes's private diary and his letters to Eisenhower. The Mudd Library has its own oral history collection that includes oral histories from Emmet John Hughes, James Hagerty, Bryce Harlow, and others intimately involved in the preparation of Eisenhower's speeches and messages.

The Public Papers of the Presidents of the United States: Dwight D. Eisenhower. (*PPP*). 8 Vol. Washington, DC: U.S. Government Printing Office, 1960–1961.

Rhetorical Studies

Allen, Craig. *Eisenhower and the Mass Media: Peace, Prosperity, and Prime-Time TV.* Chapel Hill, NC: University of North Carolina Press, 1993.

Ambrose, Stephen E. *Eisenhower: Soldier, General of the Army, President-Elect, 1890– 1952.* New York: Simon and Schuster, 1983.

———. *Eisenhower: The President.* New York: Simon and Schuster, 1984.

Brownell, Herbert and John P. Burke. *Advising Ike.* Lawrence, KS: University Press of Kansas, 1993.

Burk, Robert F. *Dwight D. Eisenhower: Hero and Politician.* Boston: Twayne Publishers, 1986.

Divine, Robert A. *Eisenhower and the Cold War.* New York: Oxford University Press, 1981.

Eisenhower, David. *Eisenhower at War 1943–1945.* New York: Random House, 1986.

Eisenhower, Dwight D. *Crusade in Europe.* New York: Doubleday, 1948.
———. *At Ease: Stories I Tell To Friends.* New York: Doubleday, 1967.
———. *The Eisenhower Diaries,* edited by Robert H. Ferrell. New York: W. W. Norton, 1981.
———. *Ike's Letters to a Friend 1941–1958,* edited by Robert Griffith. Lawrence, KS: University Press of Kansas, 1984.
———. *The Papers of Dwight David Eisenhower.* 13 Vol. Edited by Alfred E. Chandler, Jr. and Louis Galambos. Baltimore: Johns Hopkins University Press, 1970–1989.
Ewald, William Bragg, Jr. *Eisenhower the President: Crucial Days, 1951–1960.* Englewood Cliffs, NJ: Prentice-Hall, 1981.
Greenstein, Fred I. *The Hidden-Hand Presidency: Eisenhower as Leader.* New York: Basic Books, 1982.
Hughes, Emmet John. *The Ordeal of Power: A Political Memoir of the Eisenhower Years.* New York: Atheneum, 1963.
Kinnard, Douglas. *President Eisenhower and Strategy Management: A Study in Defense Politics.* Lexington, KY: University of Kentucky Press, 1977.
Kreig, Joann P., ed. *Dwight D. Eisenhower: Soldier, President, Statesman.* Westport, CT: Greenwood Press, 1987.
Larson, Arthur. *Eisenhower: The President Nobody Knew.* New York: Charles Scribner's Sons, 1968.
Lee, R. Alton. *Dwight D. Eisenhower: A Bibliography of His Times and Presidency.* Wilmington, DE: Scholarly Press, 1991.
Lyon, Peter. *Eisenhower: Portrait of the Hero.* Boston: Little, Brown, and Co., 1974.
Medhurst, Martin J. *Dwight D. Eisenhower: Strategic Communicator.* Westport, CT: Greenwood Press, 1993.
———, ed. *Eisenhower's War of Words: Rhetoric and Leadership.* East Lansing, MI: Michigan State University Press, 1994.
Medhurst, Martin J., Robert L. Ivie, Philip Wander, and Robert L. Scott. *Cold War Rhetoric: Strategy, Metaphor, and Ideology.* Westport, CT: Greenwood Press, 1990.
Miller, Merle. *Ike the Soldier: As They Knew Him.* New York: G. P. Putnam's Sons, 1987.
Parmet, Herbert S. *Eisenhower and the American Crusades.* New York: Macmillan, 1972.
Thompson, Kenneth W., ed. *The Eisenhower Presidency: Eleven Intimate Perspectives of Dwight D. Eisenhower.* Lanham, MD: University Press of America, 1984.
Treuenfels, Rudolph L., comp. *Eisenhower Speaks: Dwight D. Eisenhower in His Messages and Speeches.* New York: Farrar, Straus, & Co., 1948.

Rhetorical Monographs

Allen, Craig. "Our First 'Television' Candidate: Eisenhower Over Stevenson in 1956." *Journalism Quarterly* 65 (1988): 352–59.
———. "Robert Montgomery Presents: Hollywood Debut in the Eisenhower White House." *Journal of Broadcasting and Electronic Media* 35 (1991): 431–48.
Barkin, Steven M. "Eisenhower's Television Planning Board: An Unwritten Chapter in the History of Political Broadcasting." *Journal of Broadcasting* 27 (1983): 319–31.

————. "Eisenhower's Secret Strategy: Television Planning in the 1952 Campaign." *Journal of Advertising History* 9 (1986): 18–28.

Crable, Richard E. "Dwight David Eisenhower." In *American Orators of the Twentieth Century: Critical Studies and Sources*, edited by Bernard K. Duffy and Halford R. Ryan, 115–22. Westport, CT: Greenwood Press, 1987.

————. "Ike: Identification, Argument, and Paradoxical Appeal." *Quarterly Journal of Speech* 63 (1977): 188–95.

Freeley, Austin. "*Ethos*, Eisenhower, and the 1956 Campaign." *Central States Speech Journal* 9 (1958): 24–26.

Gilbert, Robert E. "The Eisenhower Campaign of 1952: War Hero as Television Candidate." *Political Communication and Persuasion* 3 (1985): 293–312.

Goldzwig, Steven R., and George N. Dionisopoulos. "Crisis at Little Rock: Eisenhower, History, and Mediated Political Realities." In *Eisenhower's War of Words*, edited by Martin J. Medhurst, 189–222. East Lansing, MI: Michigan State University Press, 1994.

Gregg, Richard B. "The Rhetoric of Distancing: Eisenhower's Suez Crisis Speech, 31 October 1956." In *Eisenhower's War of Words*, edited by Martin J. Medhurst, 157–87. East Lansing, MI: Michigan State University Press, 1994.

Griese, Noel L. "Rosser Reeves and the 1952 Eisenhower TV Spot Blitz." *Journal of Advertising* 4 (1975): 34–38.

Griffin, Charles J. G. "New Light on Eisenhower's Farewell Address." *Presidential Studies Quarterly* 22 (1992): 469–80.

Haapanen, Lawrence W. "Nikita S. Khrushchev vs. Dwight D. Eisenhower." In *Oratorical Encounters: Selected Studies and Sources of Twentieth-Century Political Accusations and Apologies*, edited by Halford Ross Ryan, 137–51. Westport, CT: Greenwood Press, 1988.

————. "The Missed Opportunity: The U-2 and Paris." In *Eisenhower's War of Words*, edited by Martin J. Medhurst, 251–72. East Lansing, MI: Michigan State University Press, 1994.

Henry, David. "Eisenhower and Sputnik: The Irony of Failed Leadership." In *Eisenhower's War of Words*, edited by Martin J. Medhurst, 223–50. East Lansing, MI: Michigan State University Press, 1994.

Hogan, J. Michael. "Eisenhower and Open Skies: A Case Study in 'Psychological Warfare.' " In *Eisenhower's War of Words*, edited by Martin J. Medhurst, 137–56. East Lansing, MI: Michigan State University Press, 1994.

Holloway, Rachel L. " 'Keeping the Faith': Eisenhower Introduces the Hydrogen Age." In *Eisenhower's War of Words*, edited by Martin J. Medhurst, 47–72. East Lansing, MI: Michigan State University Press, 1994.

Ivie, Robert L. "Eisenhower as Cold Warrior." In *Eisenhower's War of Words*, edited by Martin J. Medhurst, 7–26. East Lansing, MI: Michigan State University Press, 1994.

Kennedy, Theodore R. "Eisenhower as Extempore Speaker." *Journal of Communication* 8 (1958): 151–55.

Litfin, A. Duane. "Eisenhower on the Military-Industrial Complex: Critique of a Rhetorical Strategy." *Central States Speech Journal* 25 (1974): 198–209.

Medhurst, Martin J. "Dwight D. Eisenhower's First Inaugural Address, 1953." In *The Inaugural Addresses of Twentieth-Century American Presidents*, edited by Halford Ryan, 153–65. New York: Praeger, 1993.

————. "Dwight D. Eisenhower's Second Inaugural Address, 1957." In *The Inaugural Addresses of Twentieth-Century American Presidents*, edited by Halford Ryan, 166–79. New York: Praeger, 1993.

————. "Eisenhower, Little Rock, and the Rhetoric of Crisis." In *The Modern Presidency and Crisis Rhetoric*, edited by Amos Kiewe, 19–46. New York: Praeger, 1993.

————. "Eisenhower's Rhetorical Leadership: An Interpretation." In *Eisenhower's War of Words*, edited by Martin J. Medhurst, 285–97. East Lansing, MI: Michigan State University Press, 1994.

————. "Eisenhower's 'Atoms for Peace' Speech: A Case Study in the Strategic Use of Language." *Communication Monographs* 54 (1987): 204–20.

————. "Reconceptualizing Rhetorical History: Eisenhower's Farewell Address." *Quarterly Journal of Speech* 80 (1994): 195–218.

Olson, Gregory A. "Eisenhower and the Indochina Problem." In *Eisenhower's War of Words*, edited by Martin J. Medhurst, 97–136. East Lansing, MI: Michigan State University Press, 1994.

Rosteck, Thomas. "The Case of Eisenhower versus McCarthyism." In *Eisenhower's War of Words*, edited by Martin J. Medhurst, 73–96. East Lansing, MI: Michigan State University Press, 1994.

Schaefermeyer, Mark J. "Dulles and Eisenhower on 'Massive Retaliation.' " In *Eisenhower's War of Words*, edited by Martin J. Medhurst, 27–46. East Lansing, MI: Michigan State University Press, 1994.

Scheele, Henry Z. "The 1956 Nomination of Dwight D. Eisenhower: Maintaining the Hero Image." *Presidential Studies Quarterly* 17 (1987): 459–71.

Sillars, Malcolm O. "The Presidential Campaign of 1952." *Western Speech* 22 (1958): 94–99.

Wander, Philip. "The Rhetoric of American Foreign Policy." *Quarterly Journal of Speech* 70 (1984): 339–61.

Wood, Stephen C. "Television's First Political Spot Ad Campaign: Eisenhower Answers America." *Presidential Studies Quarterly* 20 (1990): 265–84.

Chronology of Significant Presidential Persuasions

Inaugural Address, Washington, D.C., January 20, 1953. *PPP*, 1953: 1–8.

Address on "The Chance for Peace" Delivered Before the American Society of Newspaper Editors, Washington, D.C., April 16, 1953. *PPP*, 1953: 179–88.

Radio Address to the American People on the National Security and Its Costs, Washington, D.C., May 19, 1953. *PPP*, 1953: 306–16.

Address Before the General Assembly of the United Nations on the Peaceful Uses of Atomic Energy, New York City, New York, December 8, 1953. *PPP*, 1953: 813–22.

Statement on Disarmament Presented at the Geneva Conference, Geneva, Switzerland, July 21, 1955. *PPP*, 1955: 713–23.

Radio and Television Report to the American People on the Developments in Eastern Europe and the Middle East, Washington, D.C., October 31, 1956. *PPP*, 1956: 1060–66.

Special Message to the Congress on the Situation in the Middle East, January 5, 1957. *PPP*, 1957: 6–16.

Second Inaugural Address, Washington, D.C., January 21, 1957. *PPP*, 1957: 60–65.

Radio and Television Address to the American People on the Situation in Little Rock, Washington, D.C., September 24, 1957. *PPP*, 1957: 689–94.

Radio and Television Address to the American People on Science in National Security, Washington, D.C., November 7, 1957. *PPP*, 1957: 789–99.

Radio and Television Address to the American People on "Our Future Security," Oklahoma City, Oklahoma, November 13, 1957. *PPP*, 1957: 807–16.

Radio and Television Report to the American People: Security in the Free World, Washington, D.C., March 16, 1959. *PPP*, 1959: 273–82.

Radio and Television Report to the American People on the Events in Paris, Washington, D.C., May 25, 1960. *PPP*, 1960: 437–45.

Farewell Radio and Television Address to the American People, Washington, D.C., January 17, 1961. *PPP*, 1960–61: 1035–40.

Vito N. Silvestri

John Fitzgerald Kennedy
(1917–1963)

> Ask not what your country can do for you; ask what you can do for your country.

Born May 29, 1917, in Brookline, Massachusetts, John Fitzgerald Kennedy was reared in a family that fostered physical and intellectual competition among the children. Because they were monetarily secure, Rose and Joe Kennedy, John's parents, encouraged the children to be active in public service in some way. The children lived with their father's expectation that their oldest brother Joe would become President.

In 1936, John Kennedy entered Harvard University. A political science major, he wrote an undergraduate thesis entitled, "Appeasement in Europe," a study of British apathy and lack of military preparedness before World War II. He graduated *cum laude* from Harvard. He subsequently revised his thesis and had it published as *Why England Slept*, which won him praise from reviewers and earned a place on the 1940 bestseller list.

During World War II, Kennedy served in the Navy. In 1943, he commanded a torpedo boat, PT-109, which was rammed by a Japanese destroyer in the South Pacific. He was awarded the Purple Heart and the Navy and Marine Corps Medal for his heroism in rescuing his crew. Honorably discharged in 1945, after hospitalization for malaria and a recurring back injury, Kennedy worked briefly as a reporter for the Hearst newspapers. In 1946, he successfully ran for Congressman from the Massachusetts Eleventh District and went on to serve three terms. He challenged Senator Henry Cabot Lodge, Jr., in 1953, and won a seat in the Senate.

Hospitalized in 1954 and 1955 for back operations, Kennedy wrote *Profiles in Courage,* a compilation of brief biographies of courageous American politicians. Published in 1956, the book was awarded a Pulitzer Prize for biography in 1957.

In 1956, when Adlai Stevenson opened the convention for vice-presidential nominees, Kennedy made a quick run for the position. He gained a substantial vote, but it was insufficient to match that of Senator Estes Kefauver. In 1958, Kennedy operated his senatorial campaign in Massachusetts as a rehearsal for presidential primaries that he planned to enter; he was reelected by nearly one million votes to a second term. In 1960, Kennedy entered the presidential primaries in New Hampshire, Wisconsin, West Virginia, Nebraska, Indiana, Maryland, and Oregon, gaining enough delegate strength to build a first ballot nomination at the convention.

THE 1960 PRESIDENTIAL CAMPAIGN

Kennedy was the second Roman Catholic to run for the presidency. Al Smith, Governor of New York and Democratic presidential candidate in 1928, had remained relatively silent on the Catholic issue. Kennedy had to confront the issue.

After his television appearances and vice-presidential campaign at the party convention, Kennedy emerged as the third most popular speaker in the party in 1956. His religion became equally well-known and was the subject of several magazine articles and discussions on television and radio. The press reified his religion as an issue at his speaking engagements, interviews, and press conferences. Kennedy dealt with the issue mainly through question and answer sessions. His answer became standardized. He noted that he had sworn to support the Constitution on six public occasions during his life; his record proved that he supported the Constitution, which maintained separation of church and state; and as president, he would be duty-bound to uphold this fundamental principle of the United States.

Kennedy's religion continued to influence his primary campaigns. Although he had won a majority in the Wisconsin primary, news analysts emphasized the strong Catholic vote in the election. When he campaigned in the West Virginia primary, a state with a ninety-five percent Protestant electorate, the religion issue emerged strongly. Kennedy directly confronted the issue, first with a speech, "I Am Not the Catholic Candidate for President," and subsequently in stump speaking throughout the state when he put West Virginians on the defensive: "Are you going to tell me that I lost this election the day I was baptized?" He asserted that there were more important issues than religion for West Virginians in the primary. Although the speech in Washington was considered as a calculated excuse in case he lost the primary and his presidential bid, Kennedy won a surprising victory in the Mountaineer State. He credited this primary as the one that gave impetus to his ultimate nomination victory at the convention.

During his presidential campaign, Norman Vincent Peale, a very popular Protestant minister, publicly questioned Kennedy's ability to withstand the pressures of the Roman Catholic Church. Some fundamentalist religious organizations spoke out against him because of his religion, and at the start of the presidential campaign the Fair Campaign Practices Committee indicated that unusually large mailings of anti-Catholic pamphlets, similar to those used against Al Smith, were sent to key states.

The Houston Speech

To reduce media attention and to defuse the issue, Kennedy appeared before a meeting of 300 ministers and an equal number of reporters in Houston, Texas. The speech was televised state-wide, and portions of it appeared on national television. Later, the film of the speech was used by each state's Democratic party for its own constituents.

Kennedy's Houston speech was the culmination of four years of responding to questions about his religion. It was also his opportunity to state unequivocally his allegiance to the United States. "There are far more critical issues in the 1960 election" such as poverty, hunger, the elderly, development of space frontiers, than the "so-called religious issue," Kennedy declared. Nevertheless, Kennedy countered in an elegant periodic statement, "it is apparently necessary for me to state once again—not what kind of church I believe in, for that would be important only to me, but what kind of America I believe in," and he earnestly defended his right to run for the presidency based on American principles.

He reversed positions with his audience by warning them, "Today, I may be the victim—but tomorrow it may be you." He used idealistic statements to outline the "kind of America I believe in" and spoke realistically about the America he fought for and his brother died for in World War II. No one, he emphasized, questioned them then about "divided loyalty." Using the more immediate surroundings of the historic Alamo in San Antonio, Kennedy cited the names of some of its heroes, "Fuentes and McCaffrey and Bailey and Bedillo . . . but no one knows whether they were Catholic or not. For there was no religious test there." Subtly, he questioned why there should be a test now.

Rather, Kennedy said, he was the "Democratic Party's candidate for President who happens to be a Catholic." In direct antithesis, Kennedy disassociated himself from his church: "I do not speak for the church on public matters—and the church does not speak for me." If, as President, he faced a choice between his conscience or the national interest, "then I would resign my office."

He closed the speech by arguing against religious bigotry. He declared that he would be satisfied if he lost the election on the basis of the issues, but if he lost because forty million Americans lost their chance to be President "on the day they were baptized," then the entire nation was the loser.

The religion issue made Kennedy a dramatic candidate. Immediately after the Houston speech the crowds he drew increased, more national politicians came forward to endorse his candidacy, the Democratic party received more contributions from its members, and public discussion of his religion diminished during the remaining nine weeks of the campaign. But a strong, silent drive by conservative Protestant and fundamentalist religious sects to saturate the nation with anti-Catholic literature emerged in the final weeks before the election, and anonymous hate literature had reached a record high according to the Fair Campaign Practices Committee.

The Televised Debates

A major event during the 1960 presidential campaign was the first use of television to present the candidates in four public debates that gained the largest audience ever gathered at one time in the history of the nation. The first debate gave the candidates eight-minute opening statements and three-to-five-minute closing ones with questions from reporters in the middle. The second and third debates were question and answer sessions, and the final debate used the same format as the original.

The first debate generally was conceded as the most critical in terms of impression making. By comparison, one candidate redefined another in the new media, and the familiar face of Richard Nixon seemed eclipsed by the more photographic and poised Kennedy. Nixon, who had gained much publicity from a "kitchen debate" in Moscow with Khrushchev, approached the new televised forum somewhat as a traditional debater by using argument, counterargument, and refutation, especially in the first debate. Those who heard the debates on radio thought Nixon made the more favorable impression, reflecting the difference of media effects and verbal skills.

In general, however, Kennedy seemed to gain the more favorable impression from the televised presentation. The Republicans and especially Nixon had emphasized that Kennedy was too inexperienced and young to handle the presidency and "stand up to the Russians." The visual evidence Kennedy presented effectively worked against this impression: he seldom smiled; he appeared poised, spoke resolutely and decisively; he listened seriously and took notes as if to refute Nixon; he maintained direct eye contact with the camera and, thus, with his national audience. Nixon, who was trying to communicate warmth by smiling and seeming affable to overcome criticism of being a cold personality, communicated a "shifty-eyed" stereotype as he frequently glanced at the studio clock. Poor makeup and an ill-fitting gray suit tended to distort and blur his image against a light studio background. Kennedy visually emerged more defined in a dark, well-fitted suit, and with a serious demeanor.

The national audience of an estimated seventy-seven million, at least sixty percent of the adult population, watched the first debate. The debate helped Kennedy to become known to the American public in a performance competition with the well-known Nixon. The nontraditional format for the debates presented the candidates to the greatest mass audience ever assembled in one viewing. Since the Kennedy-Nixon debates, all politicians have had to be concerned with their "image."

THE INAUGURAL ADDRESS

Kennedy's Inaugural Address stated the New Frontier philosophy for his administration. Faced with a stalemate in relations with the Soviet Union, aware of reduced cohesiveness among European NATO partners, and trying to vitalize the slow economy and apathy of the nation to "get it moving again," Kennedy's Inaugural Address vitally and stylistically presented the principles of the United States as he expected to translate them to the thermonuclear decade of the sixties.

To the Soviet Union he presented a clear message of willingness to negotiate and at the same time a determination to maintain the nation's military strength. To the allies he repledged the nation's fealty and support. To the United Nations he reaffirmed the U.S.' commitment to strengthen its effectiveness. To underdeveloped countries and to Latin America he offered support, new programs and approaches. To the American people, he asked them to rise to the challenge of the age, to sacrifice in a different way than before, bearing the burden of a "long twilight struggle" through a more active citizenship.

Using his generation, with himself as its most visible model, "born in this century, tempered by war, disciplined by a hard and bitter peace," Kennedy challenged them to commit anew to American and human rights principles; he committed the nation to support the cause of liberty throughout the world.

Kennedy's Inaugural Address, memorable for its elegant style, was also eloquent for its reexamination and reaffirmation of the principles of a democracy in a thermonuclear age: "We observe today, not a victory of a party but a celebration of freedom—symbolizing an end as well as a beginning—signifying renewal as well as change." Forty-two percent of the speech consisted of antithetical statements as Kennedy matched linguistic structure to political realities. All choices in 1961 were evaluated in terms of the "dark powers of destruction" of nuclear annihilation: "For man holds in his mortal hands the power to abolish all forms of human poverty and all forms of human life." For Kennedy, the choices were clear—continue nuclear stockpiling and the arms race and risk destruction, or negotiate: "Let us never negotiate out of fear, but let us never fear to negotiate." One could live freely or destroy the world. His Inaugural Address marked a public declaration of faith in the nation and in its democratic principles enlarged for the world. "Now the trumpet summons us again," Kennedy asserted, and he presented this antithetical challenge in a ringing peroration to the speech: "Ask not what your country can do for you; ask what you can do for your country." His Inaugural Address, anchored in a critical age of new beginnings for the nation, spoken at a time of great tension, served also as Kennedy's initial step toward peace.

PRESIDENTIAL CRISIS RHETORIC

When John Kennedy assumed the presidency, he inherited the international policies of massive deterrency and retaliation politics from nuclear stockpiling.

By 1957, the Soviet Union had achieved nuclear parity. Both nations had the capability to destroy each other's populations, so massive retaliation no longer served the nation as an inherent strength.

Eisenhower, drawing upon a period of cordiality with Premier Nikita Khrushchev, had tried to seek some accord between the two nuclear powers during his final years as president, and in 1959, this appeared to be a feasible possibility; but his hopes were destroyed when Khrushchev, just before a summit conference in 1960, announced the capture of an American U-2 spy plane performing a surveillance mission over Russia and refused to meet with the allied powers.

After the U-2 affair, Khrushchev began a series of challenges to the Western World and to the United States in particular. He disrupted a United Nations meeting by pounding his shoe on the table, dominating and demeaning the world assembly; he told American reporters, ''We will bury you''; and while Kennedy and Nixon were campaigning for the presidency, he began a series of stratagems in Laos, Cambodia, Vietnam, Berlin, and Cuba that came to dominate the Kennedy presidency.

Kennedy openly acknowledged in his Inaugural Address the threat of thermonuclear war. The choice was between maintaining the present course of nuclear stockpiling or seeking cooperative ventures toward peaceful solutions. Consistently, these choices influenced Kennedy's other speeches on nuclear age issues.

State of the Union

In his State of the Union speech, January 30, 1961, Kennedy described the state of the nation as in ''an hour of national peril and national opportunity'' and devoted at least fifty percent of the address to foreign policy concerns with a strong emphasis on Communist infiltration efforts in underdeveloped countries. He also underscored the need to improve relations with the Soviet Union. ''Our greatest challenge is still the world that lies beyond the cold war—but the first great obstacle is still our relations with the Soviet Union and Communist China. . . . our task is to convince them that aggression and subversion will not be profitable roots to pursue these ends.'' He invited the Soviet Union and other nations ''to invoke the wonders of science instead of its terrors'' and cited specific programs. *Pravda,* within a month of this speech, in an unusual departure from general policy, published Kennedy's Inaugural Address and his State of the Union speeches.

Critics felt that Kennedy was unusually grim about foreign policy in his State of the Union address. Events within his first six months in office, however, proved his views. The Soviets blocked progress on a test ban treaty; Khrushchev threatened to sign a separate treaty with East Germany, and thus, render ineffective all post–World War II agreements with western powers in Europe; and the USSR moved beyond its feat of sending a satellite into outer space by sending the first man into space. Kennedy's own Bay of Pigs defeat in Cuba after three months in office compounded the "grim" outlook.

Berlin Crisis

On July 25, 1961, Kennedy announced in a televised speech to the nation his major policy to deal with the Berlin crisis. In his most somber speech of his seven months' presidency, he declared that the "immediate threat to free men is in West Berlin," and stated that this was a worldwide threat. Kennedy explained the challenge about the borders and the test to western nations' resolve to maintain the freedom of Western Europe. He reaffirmed the right of the western nations to occupy West Berlin and restated the nation's commitment to the free people of West Berlin, and then detailed a series of preparations as part of a long-term build-up for the United States. Essentially, what he described in this speech became the largest increase in peacetime military forces in the history of the nation. To strengthen the nation further, he discussed executive orders he had issued to increase civilian defense, primarily nuclear fallout shelters to be used in case of an attack.

Asserting that the source of "tension is Moscow, not Berlin," that the "choice of peace or war is largely theirs, not ours," he again offered negotiations, and invited Khrushchev to "join in the community of peaceful men, in abandoning the use of force, and in respecting the sanctity of agreements." He added a personal note to the speech, written the night before, about the seriousness of the times and his responsibilities as President and Commander-in-Chief to avoid misjudgment and to assure there be no miscalculations of the nation's position or intentions or by its adversaries in a thermonuclear war. Three weeks later the Soviets built a wall dividing the eastern sector from the western part of Berlin. Kennedy dispatched 1,500 troops to West Berlin, without incident, and Khrushchev did not sign a separate treaty with East Germany.

The Cuban Missile Crisis

In October 1962, confronting a foreign power developing a nuclear presence in the Western Hemisphere, Kennedy delivered the most serious speech of his presidency. The speech was the result of two public warnings to the Soviets about deployment of missiles in Cuba, and the product of six days of intensive deliberation and examination of photographic and intelligence evidence. The next to final version of the speech emerged after Kennedy reviewed all options and developed a course of action that did not immediately lead to escalation of nuclear war. In this sense, the speech served as an instrument for a clear position of strength for Kennedy, but also as a bargaining position that allowed Khrushchev latitude to withdraw from the confrontation and still maintain political strength with his constituents in the Kremlin.

Kennedy edited the final drafts of the speech, choosing softer language, notably "quarantine" rather than "blockade" as an immediate course of action, and "false" rather than "a lie" about Russian deception. He avoided explaining that the specific megatonage of nuclear warheads in Cuba were so powerful that they could easily destroy entire cities, because he did not want to start a panic. Instead, he cited their striking capabilities. Kennedy also decided not to include Fidel Castro as part of the issue, but defined the controversy as a confrontation between the United States and the Soviet Union.

His televised address consisted of a statement of the findings of photographic and intelligence evidence, the nation's philosophical and political positions, and the courses of action he was taking. The speech was used as a briefing, translated into thirty-eight languages, sent to all capitols of the world, and broadcast on short and medium wave radio.

Speaking grimly, Kennedy began by citing the "hard evidence," telling the nation that the nuclear warheads ninety miles off the shore of the United States could strike cities in Southeastern United States, or in the case of the long range ones, cities in Canada and Peru. Pointing to violations of the Rio Pact, the UN Charter, and traditional positions of western hemispheric nations against foreign encroachment, Kennedy exposed several Soviet statements as "false." Emphasizing that the missiles were a "clear and present danger," he noted that the 1930s "taught us a lesson" about allowing "aggressive conduct . . . to go unchecked and unchallenged." He presented seven steps of implementation, including a quarantine of U.S. naval ships around Cuba to intercept any Soviet carriers with nuclear warheads for the missile sites, preparation of the military for any eventualities, and a "world wide alert to all U.S. personnel and military should the Soviets attempt a retaliation." He called for emergency meetings of the U.N. Security Council and the Organization of the American States.

He directly addressed Khrushchev by calling upon him "to abandon this course," to engage in a "historic effort to end the perilous arms race" and "to transform the history of man." Once again he presented his case for negotiating the elimination of arms and nuclear stockpiles, and reiterated the position of the United States that it had no wish for war with the Soviet Union. He reinforced his stand that the imposition of nuclear missile sites in the Western Hemisphere was intolerable and would impede any negotiation.

In a direct statement to the Cuban people, Kennedy asserted that he was speaking to them as a friend, and noted that he understood they were currently under foreign domination, no longer able to determine their own destiny, and that now, they were the first Latin American country to have nuclear warheads on their soil. These, he said, "contribute nothing to your peace and well-being." To the American people, he closed the speech by citing the need for sacrifice and discipline in the coming days and months of the crisis: "But the greatest danger of all would be to do nothing. . . . Our goal is not the victory of the might, but the vindication of the right—not peace at the expense of freedom, but both peace and freedom."

The crisis was diminished by private letters between Kennedy and Khrushchev. The missiles were removed, and the two leaders tried to move forward. A series of informal, off-the-record talks ensued between Russian and American representatives on a nuclear test ban treaty. Seven months later, a breakthrough came from Khrushchev in a private letter indicating his willingness to resume serious talks.

The American University Speech

Kennedy announced in a commencement address at American University, June 10, 1963, that high level talks on a test ban treaty were scheduled in Russia. He had wanted to make a speech about peace and the future of the nation in a thermonuclear age, rather than to center the speech on themes of the Cold War that had been typical of his earlier speeches. If his Inaugural Address was a blueprint for his New Frontier positions for reducing tensions through negotiation and military strength, his American University address was a statement of how the nation could move toward peace in a thermonuclear world.

Kennedy used the American University speech to initiate public discussion about changing the nation's attitude toward the Soviet Union if it truly wanted to strive toward peace in the world, and to announce the positive steps of negotiation for a test ban treaty in Moscow. He argued, in a syllogistic chain of reasoning, that if Americans wished to attain peace in a thermonuclear age, they needed to change their attitude toward the Soviet Union in order to gain it. To change their attitude, he stated, meant that they could not think of the Soviet Union only as an adversary, but also as a nation with whom they shared common interests. Americans could do this, he continued, by containing the nuclear arsenals and by moving toward a first step—a test ban treaty.

Toward that end, demonstrating good faith, Kennedy announced that the United States would refrain from atmospheric testing as long as other nations also refrained from nuclear tests. The national interests, he asserted, could still be maintained while pursuing human interests: ''And is not peace . . . basically a matter of human rights—the right to live out our lives without fear of devastation?''

World reaction to the speech was largely positive. Khrushchev announced that this was the best speech he had heard from an American president. *Izvestia* published the complete text of the speech. Moscow radio emphasized that Kennedy asked Americans to reconsider their attitudes toward the Cold War and the Soviet Union. During the ten days of negotiations in Moscow, the team produced a test ban treaty that both leaders could sign. But opposition to the treaty in Congress began shortly thereafter, and Kennedy, like Woodrow Wilson presenting his case to the American people on the Treaty of Versailles, toured the nation speaking to rally support for the treaty. From July to September 1963, Kennedy used every speaking occasion and press conference to promote ratification. In September, the Senate ratified the treaty, despite strong opposition from some nuclear experts, militarists, members of the Armed Services Committee, and those groups in the nation who could not believe the Soviets would honor the agreement.

"Ich bin ein Berliner"

The largest crowd Kennedy ever addressed was an estimated million and a half West Berliners in Rudolph Wilde Platz before the Berlin Wall, June 26, 1963. In late June 1963, Kennedy made a second trip to Europe to bolster the NATO alliance and to lend support to West Germany and, in particular, to West Berlin. News accounts and remembrances of his chief aides indicate that he was moved by the incredible size of the crowd chanting "Ken—ned—dy! Ken—ned—dy!" and, also, so angered by the brutal political reality of seeing the ugly wall, that he made two errors in his speech. One was humorous and a result of language translation problems in Kennedy's German statement, "Ich bin ein Berliner," and the other was Kennedy's zealous overstatement of his case against Communism leading to his repetition of "Lass' sie nach Berlin kommen."

Kennedy had written three statements on his speech text: "civis Romanus sum," "Ich bin ein Berliner" and "Lass' sie nach Berlin kommen." Observing to the crowd that the proudest boast two thousand years ago would have been "civis Romanus sum," he applied the notion to the current situation: "Today, in the world of freedom, the proudest boast is 'Ich bin ein Berliner.'" There was a pause and a stirring among the crowd response and then a delayed response of cheering, laughter, and applause. Kennedy noted this and said "I appreciate my interpreter translating my German!"

He intended to say "I am a Berliner," but, literally, to West Berliners, Kennedy was saying, "I am a jelly donut." The "Berliner" was peculiar to West Berliners as a special donut. Kennedy's German was constructed more from English syntax than from indigenous German language structure. Normal construction would dictate, "Ich bin Berliner"—"I am a Berliner."

In retrospect, Berliners and other Germans explain the error as a wonderful joke that helped Kennedy to connect even more with the West Berliners. Known for the sharpness of their humor, more so than in other parts of Germany, it was not unusual for them to use key food items as political objects of humor. His naivete about the language and unusual use of it in a serious way on such an occasion served to enhance his sense of bonding with West Berliners. When he earnestly used the phrase once again at the end of the speech, he did not know to correct it and repeated the error.

Of greater political importance, however, was Kennedy's overstatement about Communism. Two weeks earlier in his American University speech, Kennedy spoke about the need to rethink the harsh stances of the United States against Communism in order to build a peaceful world. In West Berlin, on such a momentous occasion Kennedy declared, "And there are some who say in Europe and elsewhere we can work with the Communists. Let them come to Berlin. . . . *Lass' sie nach Berlin kommen.''*

Looking forward to test ban treaty negotiations in the following month, and realizing, later, that such a statement could have negative ramifications in the detente he was hoping to develop with the Soviets, Kennedy added a statement in his next speech at Free University in West Berlin that he believed it necessary for all great powers in the world to work together to preserve peace.

The remark did not go unnoticed, however. It became a focal point of a speech Khrushchev delivered at City Hall in East Berlin a few days later. He condemned Kennedy's attacks on Communism in West Berlin, and ironically noted that two weeks before Kennedy had spoken of improving relations with the Soviet Union: ''one would think that the speeches were made by two different Presidents.''

KENNEDY ON CIVIL RIGHTS

Few domestic issues of Kennedy's presidency were as urgent as the Civil Rights issue. Kennedy had emerged from the 1950s believing that the most effective recourse minority people had was through the judicial branch of government. He was pessimistic about Congress fostering much progress after the 1957 debates in the House and Senate over Civil Rights. As he campaigned for the presidency, however, he become more optimistic about the possibilities of change coming about through the use of executive powers. During the convention he insisted on a strong Civil Rights plank in the party platform. Elected on a slim margin, an analysis of the African-American vote indicated that he could have lost the election if only whites had voted—the black vote was 68 to 78 percent in his favor.

Kennedy used his executive powers to appoint African-Americans to key positions in government, to desegregate housing in federal projects, and to enforce federal law when it was opposed. Two dramatic cases emerged during his presidency: James Meredith and the legal rulings he had gained in order to enter the University of Mississippi Law School in October 1962; and Vivian Malone and James Hood and their attempts to register for summer classes at the University of Alabama, in June 1963. Kennedy used these events to ''teach'' the nation about desegregation, to lend support to the Civil Rights movement, and to strengthen his position to initiate legislation.

In the Mississippi case, Kennedy, after several negotiations failed to get Governor Ross Barnett to comply with federal law, federalized the military reserves and occupied the campus in order to gain entrance for Meredith. He delivered a speech to the nation justifying the government's action on the basis of his responsibility to enforce federal law. In this instance, Kennedy argued from principle and used the federal requirements of his office to enforce the Constitution. He contrasted his position with Governor Barnett, who placed himself ''above and beyond the law,'' and Kennedy named southern judges who had mandated that Meredith be admitted.

In his second major speech to a televised audience, Kennedy scheduled the address after he had successfully coordinated the sequence of events with Robert Kennedy and Nicholas Katzenbach to gain admittance of the African-American students at the University of Alabama. He emphasized the moral principle of equality, noting that "the rights of every man are diminished when the rights of one are threatened." He cited the diversity of peoples who founded the nation and observed that "When Americans are sent to Vietnam or West Berlin, to risk their lives for yours and mine, we do not ask for whites only," a line of argument similar to one he used in his Houston speech in 1960. He appealed to Americans to understand that everyone should have the right of free access to public accommodations and the right to vote. Using guilt appeals, Kennedy asked, "If an American, because his skin is dark" cannot send his children to the "best public schools" and "cannot vote for public officials who represent him . . . then who among us would be content to be living in his skin and standing in his place?" Appealing to a sense of fairness and decency, he closed the speech by citing the Civil Rights Bill he was sending to Congress for enactment.

KENNEDY AND THE MEDIA

One of the communication innovations of Kennedy's presidency was the use of live television in covering his press conferences. Pierre Salinger made this proposal to Kennedy shortly after his election. Salinger argued that Kennedy had proven himself in his ability to handle the televised presidential debates; he would gain verbatim coverage of his ideas because few newspapers ever completely reported press coverage throughout the nation; and he could gain greater support for his programs by direct access to the nation if he encountered Congressional opposition.

Kennedy agreed to the new procedure after Salinger secured network concurrence, and the first telecast was held on January 25, 1961. Sixty-million people watched the live press conference that made news in and of itself and was deemed to be largely successful. By 1960–1961, a majority of the nation's households had a television set in the home. The press conferences enhanced the influence of network television as a major news source, reducing the position of newspapers as the immediate source of information for the public.

Kennedy reviewed his performances after each telecast, studying ways he could improve his presentations and identifying what was effective. Kennedy compared the telecasts to "preparing for a final exam twice a month." They also provided the administration with a regular opportunity to review issues and programs, and to report to the nation directly from the White House. Salinger, Sorensen, and other advisors regularly provided Kennedy with a large briefing book a few days before a scheduled telecast. Kennedy studied this information and then met with them, the Vice President, Bundy, and others at a breakfast meeting on the day of the telecast. They would present difficult questions to him. If he knew how to answer the question he would not answer it there, but he would answer questions he was uncertain about. Others amplified and supplied answers for him at the meetings. Afterward, Sorensen and Salinger would do additional research and then would meet again with him two hours before the press conference.

Kennedy's wide background of reading and his ability to digest large amounts of written material in a short time also helped to prepare him. His brief career as a reporter, his own level of comfort with the press, his extensive campaigning for the presidency, and the inevitable intensive question and answer sessions he encountered about his religion built a base of experience and confidence that allowed his wit, humor, information, and listening ability to flourish as well as his telegenic image.

Franklin Roosevelt, with his vigorous delivery and dramatic statements, connected with the public through radio. For Kennedy, television became his "Fireside Chats." Television was an active part of his presidential forum, as well as a means of access to the American people. In effect, he demonstrated his presidential performance with press conferences, reports, announcements to the nation, and in televised speeches representing important decisions of his presidency. He delivered nine major speeches and held sixty-three live press conferences on television. Television made his press conferences, according to Schlesinger, a "mass public affair." At the end of his second year, he held an unprecedented hour-long interview live from the White House with journalists of the three major networks, discussing the presidency and assessing his two years in office.

KENNEDY AS A SPEAKER

Kennedy had never attended a formal course work in public speaking. He learned to speak experientially and with advice and some coaching as he needed it—essentially as the expediency of the situation demanded special help. A year before his campaigns for the presidency, Kennedy, despite extensive speaking experience, was rated as a fair speaker, but not an orator. Other critics described Kennedy as an advocate who spoke almost in a monotone.

Kennedy had to conquer a fast rate of speaking. Facing labor audiences in the fall of 1959, Kennedy, who felt he was espousing positions favorable to labor groups, could not understand why his audiences were not responding. He learned from his advisors that he spoke too rapidly to be clearly understood. To overcome this problem, he shortened his speeches, committed them as much as he could to memory, and practiced speaking slower and waiting for audience response. Mrs. Kennedy and others would stay in the rear of the hall to provide feedback. Kennedy consciously learned to wait for audience response. Using humorous material at the beginning of a speech helped him to develop a rate of speaking that yielded audience validation; and this, in turn, encouraged him to pause after a sentence as well as to slow down in the main text. Although never a slow speaker, Kennedy did finally master a slower speaking rate.

Kennedy also learned to improve his delivery. Frequently hoarse during his primary campaigns, even though he often used a microphone, Kennedy had to learn how to use his voice after losing it entirely late in May 1960, in the West Virginia primary, and again in August 1960, a few weeks before he was to begin his presidential campaign. After medical treatment from an otolaryngologist, David Blair McClosky, Professor of Voice at Boston University, helped him gain a healthy voice unimpaired by hoarseness, inflamed vocal folds, or a tense approach to vocal production. McClosky taught Kennedy to relax the tension in his throat and to develop a richer and mellower tone through vocal relaxation and breathing exercises.

Kennedy worked with McClosky during the summer congressional sessions of 1960, when he tried unsuccessfully to promote his legislative programs. McClosky and Kennedy experimented with a set of hand signals in the Senate that seemed helpful. McClosky sat in the gallery when Kennedy spoke and signaled him when he spoke tensely, or needed to slow down, or breathe more fully. McClosky stated that Kennedy knew nothing about delivery until this time; for he had approached this aspect of speaking with little awareness of it.

JOHN F. KENNEDY'S STYLE

As a speaker, Kennedy relied on clear statement and researched information. Sorensen became his chief speechwriter in 1954, a key researcher on special issues, and coordinator of his public statements. Later, Richard Goodwin wrote speech drafts regularly. Others provided drafts occasionally: Arthur Schlesinger, Jr., Myer Feldman, Joseph Kraft, and John Galbraith. Sorensen observed that neither he nor Kennedy knew much about speaking. Their chief criterion was audience comprehension and comfort that translated into short speeches, short sentences when possible, a logical sequence of numbered points, and statements constructed to be clear. Although both approached speeches from a writing perspective, they tested the text of a speech for how it sounded rather than how it read.

Kennedy's own writing efforts since his first publication, *Why England Slept,* provided evidence of his respect for the simple and clear statement. His first book was written in a simple and clear expository style, devoid of the graceful statements that marked his presidential speaking. His style in *Profiles in Courage* was spare, but his sentences and his dramatic use of information seemed to emerge with narrative effectiveness. Kennedy used parallel construction of sentences in his prose, a technique that featured prominently in his stump speaking and presidential speaking from the late fifties throughout his presidency. From 1957 to 1959, much more in demand as a speaker, he spent much of his homework time editing drafts of speeches and reading background papers on issues as he made extensive tours across the nation.

One principle that he adhered to was to avoid clichéd statements and slang. On a reading copy of a speech to the Council of Economic Advisors, Kennedy eliminated the phrase, "carrying coals to New Castle." According to Sorensen, he disliked platitudes and excessive imagery because he detested the political stereotypes that accompanied such language. His attention to words was his way to communicate meanings so that the largest possible audience could comprehend what he was saying, a point he often made to his staff. When he wanted to avoid ambiguity and if it advantaged him politically, he would use the general statement rather than the specific. To reinforce the audience's recollection of his reasoning for a position, he often used alliteration.

Kennedy's style reflected his political personality and was honed by his speaking experience, especially during the two years before he won election to the presidency. He was comfortable presenting himself as a serious person, interested in the concerns of voters, willing to listen, and able to accept the heckling of Wisconsin farmers when he "asked" for their vote. He presented himself in a dignified way: "You kept your coat on and you wore cuff links," said Robert Healy, Political Editor of the *Boston Globe*, "even if the guy on the street didn't," or even when he entered miners' washrooms in West Virginia.

His style achieved its finest development in his Inaugural Address, matching language with political realities and American principles of democracy. He prepared the speech throughout December and most of January, testing it on others, asking for suggestions, and refining and editing it. As he spoke the words at the inauguration ceremony before a crowd of 20,000 people, Kennedy made 23 word changes, modified a statement from being too assertive to a politically relative one, avoided suggesting "cold war" on the written phrase "cold and bitter peace," and changed it to "hard and bitter peace." A careful scrutiny of his Inaugural Address indicates that Kennedy's use of antithesis, metaphor, and repetition clearly was designed to state his positions unequivocally, but also to maintain a semblance of an opening, not a hardening, of relations with the Soviets. The departures he made from text on that occasion seemed better political choices than the final written text.

CONCLUSION

President John F. Kennedy was a great orator. Not the first to use television, he nevertheless expanded the role and forum of television as a political influence. Other presidents, such as Lyndon Johnson and Richard Nixon, followed his example.

Kennedy's Inaugural Address was one of the nation's greatest inaugurals. It has resonated with subsequent generations since 1961, and it remains in publication in an average of twenty anthologies yearly. This and Martin Luther King's "I Have a Dream" speech have been the most frequently published addresses since 1950. His most quotable statement, "Ask not what your country can do for you; ask what you can do for your country," appears regularly in books of quotations. In more permanent form, Kennedy's commitment to the defense of freedom in his Inaugural Address is inscribed near the site of the signing of the

Magna Carta at Runnymede, England: "Let every nation know, whether it wishes us well or ill, that we shall pay any price, bear any burden, meet any-hardship, support any friend, oppose any foe to assure the survival and success of freedom."

Kennedy came to understand that speeches were instruments of persuasion to be used judiciously. He could use a speech as part of the broader strategy of response to the Civil Rights issue or to prepare the nation in the missile crisis. He could also decide, at the most critical moment, when not to deliver a speech. He decided against a formal speech declaring victory over the Soviets in Cuba, because he did not want to appear to be publicizing a "victory."

Kennedy also used speeches to educate the public. All of his crisis speaking, his speeches dealing with nuclear questions, and his speaking on Civil Rights indicate this. He was a transitional president attempting to move the nation and the world from hard-line Cold War positions to negotiating postures that ultimately could lead to securing peace. Kennedy even assumed a teaching role in his speech at the Dedication of the Robert Frost Library, for he wanted to emphasize that artistic endeavor is as important as political work in a society: "When power corrupts, poetry cleanses."

On November 22, 1963, in his undelivered speech for Dallas, Kennedy would have assumed a role of leader-teacher. Pragmatically, he planned to remind the audience of the progress his administration had made in strengthening its military resourcefulness, bolstering the economy, and regaining the initiative in outer space, which were basic themes of his presidency. But he was also pointing to the next frontier for the nation, toward the higher goal of realizing its ideology and thus developing its inner strength: "Only an America which practices what it preaches about equal rights and social justice will be respected by those whose choice affects our future."

RHETORICAL SOURCES

Archival Materials

The John F. Kennedy Library, Boston, Massachusetts, contains the Kennedy papers, including oral histories of associates, staff, cabinet, political figures, and family members, and Robert F. Kennedy's Files. Of particular interest are the President's Office Files, JFK's Personal Files, Theodore C. Sorensen's Files, and Robert F. Kennedy's Campaign Files. All of these sources contain speeches, drafts, final reading copies, background memoranda about preparation, and some response material. See Presidential Office Files, Speech Files Boxes 34–48; and Theodore Sorensen Papers, Speech Files, Boxes 60–77, 1961–63. The Library also has audio and visual material, movies, and videotapes available. Theodore C. Sorensen remains the most informed and organized source of Kennedy's speeches.

Kennedy, John F. *The Public Papers of the Presidents: John F. Kennedy. (PPP)*. 3 Vols. Edited by Bernard Boutin. Washington, DC: U.S. Government Printing Office, 1962–1964.

Rhetorical Studies

Burns, James MacGregor. *John F. Kennedy, A Political Profile*. New York: Harcourt Brace and Co., 1960.
Goodwin, Doris Kearns. *The Fitzgeralds and the Kennedys*. New York: Simon and Schuster, 1986.
Jamieson, Kathleen Hall, and David S. Birdsell. *Presidential Debates*. New York: Oxford University Press, 1988.
Kennedy, John F. *Profiles in Courage*. New York: Harper and Brothers, Inc., 1956.
Salinger, Pierre. *With Kennedy*. Garden City, NY: Doubleday and Co., 1978.
Schlesinger, Jr., Arthur. *A Thousand Days*. Boston: Houghton, Mifflin, 1965.
Sorensen, Theodore C. *Kennedy*. New York: Harper and Row, 1965.
White, Theodore H. *The Making of the President*. New York: Pocket Books, Inc., 1961.
——. *The Making of the President, 1960*. New York: Atheneum Publishers, 1960.

Rhetorical Monographs

Ernst, Harry W. *The Primary That Made A President: West Virginia, 1960*. Case 26, Eagleton Institute Publication. New York: McGraw-Hill, Inc. 1962.
Golden, James L. "John F. Kennedy and the 'Ghosts'." *Quarterly Journal of Speech* 52 (December 1966), 348–57.
Halberstam, David. "Introduction." In *The Kennedy Presidential Press Conferences*. New York: Earl Coleman Enterprises, Inc., 1978.
Henry, David. "Senator John F. Kennedy Encounters the Religious Question: I Am Not the Catholic Candidate for President." In *Oratorical Encounters*, edited by Halford Ross Ryan. Westport, CT: Greenwood Press, 1988.
Lang, Kurt, and Gladys Engel Lang. "Reaction of Viewers." In *The Great Debates, Background, Perspective, Effects*, edited by Sydney Kraus, 313–30. Bloomington, IN: Indiana University Press, 1962.
Lubell, Sam. "Personalities vs Issues." *The Great Debates, Background, Perspective, Effects*, edited by Sydney Kraus, 151–62. Bloomington, IN: Indiana University Press, 1962.
Silvestri, Vito. "Background Perspectives on John F. Kennedy's Inaugural Address." *Political Communication and Persuasion* 8 (1991): 1–15.
——. "John F. Kennedy: The Evolving Religion Issue in His Campaigns, 1956–1960." *In Search of Justice*, edited by Richard Jensen and John Hammerback, 205–28. Amsterdam: Rodolpi Press, 1987.
——. "John F. Kennedy: His Speaking in the Wisconsin and West Virginia Primaries, 1960." Unpublished Ph.D. dissertation, Indiana University, 1967.
Windt, Theodore O., Jr. "President John F. Kennedy's Inaugural Address, 1961." In *The Inaugural Addresses of Twentieth-Century American Presidents*, edited by Halford Ryan. Westport, CT: Praeger Publishers, 1993.
——. "The Kennedy-Nixon Presidential Debates." In *Rhetorical Studies of National*

Political Debates 1960–1988, edited by Robert V. Friedenberg. New York: Praeger, 1990.

Chronology of Significant Presidential Persuasions

"I Am Not the Catholic Candidate for President, April 12, 1960." American Society of Newspaper Editors, Washington D.C., *John F. Kennedy, Speeches, Statements and Remarks, Delivered during his Service in the Congress of the United States,* Senate Document 79, U.S. Government Printing Office, 1965.

"Speech to Greater Houston Ministerial Association, Houston, Texas, September 12, 1960." *The Speeches, Remarks, Press Conferences, and Statements of Senator John F. Kennedy, August 1, through November 7, 1960.* Report to U.S. Senate Committee on Commerce, Subcommittee on Freedom on Communications, 87 Congress, Report 994, 113.

Inaugural Address, January 20, 1961. *PPP,* 1962: 1–3.

State of Union Address, January 30, 1961. *PPP,* 1962: 19–28.

Special Message to Congress on Urgent National Needs, May 25, 1961. *PPP,* 1962: 396–406.

Radio-Television Address to American People on Berlin Crisis, July 25, 1961. *PPP,* 1962: 533–40.

Radio-Television Address to the American People: Nuclear Testing and Disarmament, March 2, 1962. *PPP,* 1963: 186–92.

Radio-Television Report to Nation on the Situation at the University of Mississippi, September 30, 1962. *PPP,* 1963: 726–28.

Radio-Television Report to the American People on the Soviet Arms Buildup in Cuba, October 22, 1962. *PPP,* 1963: 806–9.

Television and Radio Interview: "After Two Years—A conversation with the President, December 17, 1962." *PPP,* 1963: 889–904.

Radio-Television Remarks Following Removal of Racial Strife in Birmingham, May 12, 1963. *PPP,* 1964: 397–98.

Commencement Address at American University, Washington, D.C., June 16, 1963. *PPP,* 1964: 459–64.

Radio-Television Report to the American People on Civil Rights, June 11, 1963. *PPP,* 1964: 459–64.

Remarks in the Rudolph Wilde Platz, Berlin, June 26, 1963. *PPP,* 1964: 524.

Address at Free University of Berlin, June 26, 1963. *PPP,* 1964: 526–29.

Radio-Television Address to the American People on the Nuclear Test Ban Treaty, July 26, 1963. *PPP,* 601–6.

Radio-Television Address to the Nation on the Test Ban Treaty and the Tax Reduction Bill, September 18, 1963. *PPP,* 687–91.

Remarks Prepared for Delivery at the Trade Mart in Dallas, Texas, November 22, 1963. *PPP,* 1964: 890–93.

Kenneth S. Zagacki

Lyndon Baines Johnson
(1908–1973)

> Through all time to come, I think America will be a stronger nation, a more just society, and a land of greater opportunity and fulfillment because of what we have done together in three years of unparalleled achievement.

The political career of Lyndon Baines Johnson spanned the better part of the tumultuous twentieth century. As a congressman, a senator, and especially as president, Johnson struggled with many of the most critical issues of our time, compiling a record of achievement that has been both reviled and revered. Critics have pointed to Johnson's curious mixture of idealism and pragmatism, his failure to take a stand for Civil Rights during his early political career, and his disastrous Vietnam policy. Others have favorably noted Johnson's humble roots, his personal charm, his genuine concern for the downtrodden, and his mastery of political maneuvering.

Born on August 27, 1908, Johnson was reared in the hill country of central Texas. Johnson's early years were filled with insecurity and poverty. Living in such circumstance made for an unhappy childhood, something which dogged Johnson for the rest of his life. He graduated from Southwest Texas State Teachers College in 1930, paying his way with small loans and by working campus jobs. In 1931, at twenty-three years of age, Johnson's political education began when he managed the Washington office of a freshman congressman from South Texas. Here Johnson learned the political ropes and developed important relationships with powerful political officials.

As the depression took hold, Johnson endorsed Franklin Roosevelt's "New Deal," although he clearly was no liberal ideologue. He could talk conservatism with the best of the conservatives, a trait that served him well throughout his political career. During this period, Johnson became head of the Texas National

Youth Administration (NYA). He saw this post as a way of discharging his desire to help the poor and jobless; it was also a way of establishing statewide political contacts.

As the 1930s unfolded, Johnson's work with the NYA and his 1937 Congressional campaign drew notice from important political sources, including President Roosevelt. He went to Washington as a member of the House of Representatives, where accolades for his political performance were given by the likes of Harold Ickes, Tommy Corcoran, and President Roosevelt himself. By 1941, with backing from Roosevelt, Johnson sought a Senate seat from Texas. He lost a closely contested race where votes were apparently miscounted by Johnson's opponent. The fraudulent activity left Johnson embittered, but he learned valuable lessons about Texas politics.

These early campaigns reveal the foundational characteristics of Johnson's public speaking. The young politician, as William Gorden and Robert Bunker have noted, employed plenty of emotional appeals in his campaign speeches. Johnson bathed his Texas audiences in images of his patriotism and especially about his Texas roots. Robert N. Hall has shown how Johnson purposefully emphasized his associations with President Roosevelt and Roosevelt's New Deal in order to capture votes of the Texas New Dealers in Johnson's 1941 Senate campaign. Johnson made extensive use of the airplane as a means of political campaigning and appeared in various rallies that rivaled old-time vaudeville and medicine shows.

In 1945, after a brief stint as a naval officer in World War II, Johnson returned to political life. He decisively won his first Senate seat in 1946, where he continued his energetic support for relief of the needy and the federal development of health care. However, feeling the pressures of mounting conservatism in Texas, Johnson retreated from President Harry Truman's Civil Rights policy and voiced conventional southern views about race.

In 1948, Johnson won another term as senator after a close election. This time, Johnson allegedly reaped the profits of political skulduggery: correcting returns, stuffing ballot boxes, and buying off local political bosses. This tint of impropriety lingered into his next term.

Throughout the 1950s, Johnson worked hard to overcome the questionable reputation he had gained as a result of the 1948 campaign. His politics shifted to the right, although he never lost contact with his liberal associates. He avoided being labeled a southerner but developed important political alliances with influential southern leaders. He supported several New Deal policies of Truman but again diverged from the President's Civil Rights legislation.

In 1954, Johnson assumed the position of majority leader in the Senate. Drawing upon his leadership skills, his vast knowledge of political maneuvering, and his forceful style, which Doris Kearns has called "the treatment," Johnson became a very successful Senate majority leader. Robert Dallek called Johnson "the most effective Majority Leader in history." Marshalling his tremendous reserve of energy, Johnson was able to push 1,300 bills through the Senate, including his two greatest triumphs, his public housing legislation and a bipartisan vote in the Senate that ended the reign of Senator Joseph McCarthy.

In 1957, Johnson finally supported Civil Rights, driving a Civil Rights bill through the Senate. Although the legislation drew mixed reviews, it represented the first significant Civil Rights policy in eighty-two years.

By 1960, Johnson had gained so much influence that he believed himself capable of capturing the Democratic nomination for president. However, he did not wish to participate in the Democratic primaries directly. Instead, Johnson maintained his post as Majority Leader in the Senate, keeping his image as a statesman foremost in the public eye. Meanwhile, his old political ally, Sam Rayburn, opened campaign offices for him throughout the country. Harold Weiss and Haddon Robinson argue that Johnson waged a concerted, though low-key, effort for the nomination. Johnson travelled when he could to meet with delegates and usually delivered speeches that took middle-of-the-road positions. Once again, the majority leader proved himself an adaptive rhetor. When in the West, he did all he could to convince audiences he was really a westerner. In the Northeast, he talked about Civil Rights legislation. At home in Texas and in the South, he ignored his Civil Rights bill, choosing instead to emphasize "the need for vigor" and the race for outer space. By the time of the Democratic convention, however, John Kennedy had gained the momentum and won the presidential nomination. Kennedy turned to Johnson, and the Senate Majority Leader agreed to become Kennedy's vice-presidential running mate.

After Kennedy's assassination in November of 1963, Johnson took over as Commander-in-Chief becoming the 36th President of the United States. He was reelected in a landslide in 1964, although his campaign tactics have been called into question by F. Marlin Connelly, Jr., who characterized Johnson's presidential campaign rhetoric of 1964 about American involvement in Vietnam as inconsistent at best, willfully deceitful at worse.

Feeling the extreme pressures of a failed Vietnam policy and domestic strife, Johnson left office in January 1969. He retired to his ranch outside of Austin, shunning public appearances. His long political career came to an end on January 22, 1973, when Johnson died of a heart attack.

RHETORICAL TRAINING AND PRACTICES

Despite his success in Congress, Johnson seems not to have given much priority to public speaking, at least before he became president. The young Senator generally did not give public addresses, for he preferred instead to conduct his Congressional business on a more personal basis. Robert Hall, in his "Lyndon Johnson's Speech Preparation," noted that in his early political life Johnson eschewed rhetorical eloquence, deciding, as Johnson himself put it, to "tailor the procedure [for producing a speech] according to circumstances." As a senator, Johnson relied heavily upon manuscript speaking. With relatively unimportant speeches, he allotted the duty of speech development to his staff, although he gave final approval. In most instances, Johnson relied on his assistant, the former newspaperman George Reedy, who later became Johnson's presidential press secretary. Reedy made sure that Johnson's content and organization were correct. Typically, if Johnson and his staff believed a speech adequately satisfied a situation, then it was not revised. Perhaps this explains why many of Johnson's senatorial speeches were lacking in continuity, unity, and coherence.

On important speaking occasions, Senator Johnson sometimes conferred with his staff or personal acquaintances, such as Dean Acheson, Thomas Corcoran, Benjamin Cohen, James H. Rowe, and Clark Clifford. These important addresses often went through five or more revisions. On certain occasions, if drafts did not express exactly what Johnson wanted to say, he would attempt to write the speech himself. Thus, addresses Johnson considered more important were, by and large, coherent and unified.

Johnson's campaign speeches were prepared by combining his techniques for the preparation of minor and major addresses. Johnson was a tireless campaigner. At one point during his vice-presidential campaign, he made a five-day, 3,800 mile, fifty-seven speech, whistle-stop tour of the South. Throughout this campaign, Johnson utilized stock speeches that he delivered extemporaneously from the back of a train.

As vice president, Johnson employed senatorial techniques to develop major addresses. He depended on conferences, nongovernment personnel, and other authorities to help formulate and organize speeches. He spent a great deal of time and energy preparing these addresses. His speech writers remained basically the same, but they focused more on the mechanics of the speech text and also drew upon White House speech writers and other sources from the executive branch. Hence, Johnson's vice-presidential speeches were better organized, more stylistically refined, and better adapted to particular audiences.

As President, Johnson's rhetorical preparation reached its zenith. Initially, he utilized the writers he had inherited from Kennedy. His first major address, "The Forward Thrust of America," sometimes called the "Let Us Continue" speech, delivered to a joint session of Congress following President Kennedy's assassination, was prepared by Theodore Sorenson. Other drafts were constructed by John Kenneth Galbraith and Horace Busby. His second major address, a Thanksgiving Day message, was prepared by Busby, a veteran Johnson speech writer. A December 1963 speech to the United Nations was prepared by Dean Acheson. The U.N. speech marked something of a change in Johnson's preparation. Johnson shifted from the single ghost-writer approach of the first two major addresses of his administration to a ghost-written speech that was then reviewed and changed by a new brain trust and by the President. Johnson's first State of the Union message on January 8, 1964, underwent similar preparation. Sorenson and McGeorge Bundy began the speech, and then Johnson reviewed it with Senator Mike Mansfield, other Democratic leaders of Congress,

Cabinet members, and business and labor officials. Regardless of the process, Johnson's personal style was always imprinted into a given text.

Johnson's other speech writers included Douglass Cater, Harry McPherson, Harry Middleton, Robert Hardesty, and Richard Goodwin. Bill Moyers, Jack Valenti, Lee C. White, John Roche, and George Christian frequently assisted as speech editors.

Delivery

Occasionally, when Johnson abandoned his prepared remarks and spoke extemporaneously, he could be quite effective. Eric Goldman describes one such scenario during Johnson's 1964 campaign. Speaking in front of a mostly hostile Democratic audience in New Orleans on the topic of Civil Rights, the candidate broke from his text. He began a long monologue about how southerners had always felt themselves beleaguered by the moneyed and the prestigious, at home as well as in the North. He warned that politicians tried to keep Southerners down, often by using fear of blacks to divert voter's attention from economic concerns. Johnson told his audience that there were more important things for the average southern family to accomplish than holding the Negro down. As Goldman noted, the President emphasized his message with "two arms stretched high and he slashed the air with both of them as he hammered out" his speech. When Johnson finished, the audience gasped and then, slowly, he received a rousing ovation. "The nineteen hundred Louisiana Democrats," concluded Goldman, "knew they had heard truth, political skill and audacity combined in one electric moment."

Halford Ryan's description of President Johnson's 1965 "Voting Rights Address" is indicative of the way in which Johnson presented many of his more formal public speeches, including those that were televised. According to Ryan, Johnson relied heavily on a teleprompter for this address, although he looked directly at the camera to emphasize his points. Johnson often reinforced "salient arguments by tightening his lips and jaw." At other moments, he "stressed his language by leaning his head and whole body forward as if to menace the Congress." Johnson's speaking rate, reports Ryan, was generally slow, although it "did communicate a dignity and gravity that befitted the occasion."

Waldo Phelps and Andrea Beck examined the delivery of an early Johnson presidential speech on foreign affairs given at UCLA on February 21, 1964. According to these authors, Johnson faltered on several counts: his phrasing was too slow and encumbered by awkward pauses, thus making his phrases illogical and his rhythm abrupt; his volume varied from very loud to very soft, which distorted his ability to employ effective emphasis; and his stance was rigid, which hampered Johnson from being animated.

Style

Johnson's word choice has been the focus of several studies. Johnson the President, Roderick Hart argued, could never adapt to television. Stump speaking was more to Johnson's liking. Here, he could shake hands, and exchange jokes and stories, with the ordinary voters. The more informal the context, Hart observed, the more personal and moving Johnson became. When speaking on television, however, the President locked himself into his text. Indeed, Johnson's televised remarks decreased in self-reference and human interest statements, and his language became more complex.

Robert Ivie inspected the President's justifications for involvement in Vietnam. Ivie found that "peace" was the underlying motive behind Johnson's Vietnam rhetoric, and that the President described peace as dependent upon the survival of the nation and the freedom of its citizens. Warfare was therefore characterized by Johnson as a means of last resort, a necessary evil imposed upon a hesitant nation by the aggressive acts of an enemy determined to alienate humankind from their liberties. Ivie also determined that Johnson's speeches pictured the enemy as a "savage," an aggressor, motivated by irrational desires for conquest, who sought to tyrannize others by force of arms. Contrastingly, the United States was portrayed as a civilized and pacific society.

Press

Johnson's relationship with the press is worth noticing. Kathleen Turner argued that seeking the opinions of certain members of the press was a vital part of speech preparation for the Johnson administration. The President's April 7, 1965 "Johns Hopkins University" address on the Vietnam war, for example, was the product of presidential and press consultation. Early versions of this speech were shown to prominent members of the press for evaluation. Johnson apparently thought he could preempt criticism from the press by making members believe they had played an important part in the development of the President's policies.

Over the course of his Presidency, however, Johnson revealed serious limitations in his dealings with the press. Indeed, Turner linked Johnson's failings as a war rhetor to his inability to adapt to the personal, professional, and economic constraints of contemporary presidential-press relationships. Johnson poorly managed the members of the press: He disrupted their private lives by often disclosing last-minute news conferences and travel plans, and disregarded their professional needs by holding impromptu press conferences at inconvenient locations, thereby prohibiting the attendance of specialized reporters who might ask informed questions. Moreover, Johnson unnecessarily saddled profit-conscious newspapers with increased costs by scheduling Saturday morning briefings that produced unanticipated news and required costly changes in Sunday editions. As a result of these activities, the press came to believe the President was hostile to them. His version of the war, Turner concluded, was therefore treated with little sympathy by those upon whom a president relies most for access to the public.

Rhetorical Theory

Johnson operated with a definitive rhetorical theory in mind. Carroll Arnold provides critics with a useful way of thinking about this theory. Arnold argued that American public discourse has been distinguished by three rather discordant philosophical themes: idealism, doctrinalism, and pragmatism. Idealism refers to rhetorical themes based in intuitions about religion or ethical principles. Doctrinalism refers to political theories, traditions, and formulas inherited from past experiences that have provided formal and systematic grounds for many claims in American rhetoric. Pragmatism questions whether a policy will work, can it be afforded, and so forth. According to Arnold, when public problemsolving has failed, it has frequently done so because the relevant discourse was dominated by one or two but not all three of these themes. Arnold's analysis demonstrates weakness in Johnson's presidential speeches, which tend to be governed by idealism.

Johnson made a distinction between the thinkers and the doers, between the contemplative and activist life. He considered himself the consummate pragmatist. In domestic affairs, Kearns noted, "he was used to grasping practical realities first and then adapting his goals to those realities." Rhetorically, however, as President, Johnson did not stress pragmatic themes in his public speeches. He spoke as if rhetoric was not about systematic argument, not about explaining the particulars of policy proposals. Rather, rhetoric was concerned with pushing back the limits of human action by clarifying and articulating ideals, and its goal was to move people to action through the force of ideas. As a rhetor, Johnson operated on the assumption that if a policy could be thought of, if it could be dreamed and then talked about, it could therefore be done; thus, the audience would be moved to action through the dormant ideals that Johnson birthed in his speeches. Americans, Johnson believed, liked to be encouraged to dream first, then to have specific policies formulated later. Even in the absence of actual policy implementation, Johnson thought his rhetoric could fill the void. He believed the expression of an ideal vision was tantamount to the development of a practical program.

JOHNSON'S RHETORICAL PRESIDENCY

According to Theodore Windt, the Johnson Presidency can be divided into two major periods. The first extends from 1963 to 1966 and may accurately be referred to as a rhetoric of justification. This period, concerned mainly with justifying various social initiatives, included Johnson's Great Society and his call for voting rights. The second period, overlapping somewhat with the first, may be called a rhetoric of defense against the President's direction of the Vietnam War.

The Rhetoric of Justification

Johnson's first years as president were marked by considerable political successes. According to Windt, these achievements can be attributed to at least four sources: a mood of unity accompanying the assassination of Kennedy; Johnson's mastery over Congress; Johnson's overwhelming defeat of Barry Goldwater in the 1964 presidential campaign gave him a powerful mandate to lead; and this victory left his opposition in disarray. Johnson therefore performed as though he had a consensus authorized by the election. Although flawed in many respects, the Great Society was undoubtedly Johnson's greatest rhetorical accomplishment during this period. The Great Society involved passage of vast domestic programs, such as health care for the poor and the elderly, education reform, poverty relief, and urban renewal. David Zarefsky's *President Johnson's War on Poverty* catalogues all of Johnson's Great Society messages during 1964 and 1965. According to Zarefsky, these speeches highlighted three broad themes: to improve the quality of American life; to provide for all Americans, especially those who had not benefitted from the effects of macroeconomic policy; and to give government a more active role as a stimulator and guarantor in meeting the needs of the people. However, having people act on these themes depended on Johnson's ability to mobilize public and Congressional support for his legislation. Some of the legislation had been proposed before but had been stymied by various difficulties, whereas other's involved topics that had no pre-existing informed or aroused public. Zarefsky demonstrated that Johnson utilized three rhetorical tactics in his Great Society speeches to reach these ends: He stressed conservative themes, used moralistic rhetoric, including images of a war against poverty, and developed crucial distinctions in order to evade politically difficult choices.

In many ways, Johnson set the agenda for his Great Society in his very first major presidential address. His November 27, 1963 "The Forward Thrust of America" speech before the American people and a Joint Session of Congress was delivered immediately after the assassination of President Kennedy. Patricia Witherspoon noted that the purpose of the newly inducted President's speech was not only to eulogize Kennedy and to soothe peoples' fears, but to mobilize Congress and to cultivate a mandate from the divergent and disparate factions that were emerging in American society. Suggestions for the speech came from many illustrious Americans: President Dwight Eisenhower, Abe Fortas (then a Washington attorney), Hubert Humphrey, Mike Mansfield, John Kenneth Galbraith, Dean Rusk, Douglas Dillon, Adlai Stevenson, and Kermit Gordon (Director of the Bureau of the Budget). Sorensen, Galbraith, Bundy, Busby, and Moyers were all assigned to draft the speech.

The first section of Johnson's "The Forward Thrust of America" speech contained a rousing tribute to Kennedy. But only six sentences into the address, Johnson revealed the kind of idealism that would have rivaled that of his murdered presidential predecessor. Johnson spoke about the "dreams" he had for America, the dream "of conquering the vastness of space . . . of the Peace Corps . . . of education for all of our children . . . of jobs for all who seek them . . . of care for our elderly . . . of an all out attack on mental illness . . . of equal rights for all Americans." He presented the daunting, idealistic task of resolving great paradoxes, of preparing "at the same time for both the confrontation of power and the limitation of power. We must be ready to defend the national interest and to negotiate the common interest." These achievements, Johnson acknowledged, had to be "translated into effective action." Thus, at the end of the first section, Johnson challenged the nation, claiming that it "can and will act and act now." Still, while such calls to action were frequently employed in this speech and in many others, neither the general policy proposals nor the long-term policy ramifications were clearly "translated" into particular pragmatic terms.

In section two of his address, Johnson reaffirmed America's commitments at home and abroad in the most idealistic of terms. He told "all the world" that he was rededicating

this Government to the unswerving support of the United Nations, to the honorable and determined execution of our commitments to our allies, to the maintenance of military strength second to none, to the defense of the strength and the stability of the dollar, to the expansion of our foreign trade, to the reinforcement of our programs of mutual assistance and cooperation in Asia and Africa, and to our Alliance for Progress in this hemisphere.

To underscore the importance of this venture, the President again framed his agenda idealistically, by linking it to the great currents of history, for we must "fulfill the destiny that history has set for us."

In the final section, Johnson devoted considerable time discussing more specific policy proposals, although these, too, were framed idealistically. He spoke, for example, about his "civil right bill," which would "eliminate from this Nation every trace of discrimination and oppression." He advised "strong, forward-looking action on the pending education bills," while making it clear that "we are not forfeiting our responsibilities to this hemisphere or to the world." He also mentioned other plans, all of which revealed a mix of pragmatic and idealistic appeals, although the concentration was again on the latter.

In a sense, the painting of policy in bold, idealistic strokes was to be expected in such a transitional, dramatic situation. And perhaps this strongly idealistic slant helped make Johnson's first major presidential speech a successful one. As Witherspoon reported, the President received rave reviews from political sources, from the press, and from the general public after delivering his speech.

Kearns described the Congressional reaction to the address: "the audience was on its feet, fervently applauding the new President for the tradition he had summoned and so well embodied, and for the dead President whose programs he had taken as his own. And also because the formidable and elusive Majority Leader of the Senate sounded like a President."

The tendency toward idealism continued in Johnson's next major speech, his "War on Poverty" State of the Union, January 8, 1964, in which Johnson outlined issues later to become central to his Great Society. Theodore Windt thought this speech "was oriented to action, not thought," but that Johnson "promised more than he could possibly deliver." I offer a different assessment: Although the President set forth many broad proposals for action, this was primarily a speech about ideals, national purpose, and direction.

Early on in his address, Johnson delineated important goals for America's policymakers. He charged that everything from fighting poverty to health care reform to foreign aid had to be "done by this summer, and it could be done without any increase in spending." He then claimed that his budget would be "frugal," but nevertheless introduced his immense and expensive "unconditional war on poverty." This war involved many proposals for acting on Johnson's idealistic mandate, no less than thirteen in number and included programs for redistributing food in needy areas to creating housing for the poor and elderly. However, the source of rhetorical power here was not the policies themselves, but rather the idealistic way in which they were presented in terms of the war metaphor. Johnson's "war" was expansive and bold: He believed poverty could be aggressively conquered and defeated, just as an enemy was conquered and defeated in a mighty battle. For Johnson, not only could the symptoms of poverty be relieved—this would be the goal of a lesser president, a mere pragmatist—but poverty itself could be "cured" and "prevented."

The speech sounded another pragmatic chord when Johnson turned his attention to financing his war. He urged a new tax bill that, like the pragmatic proposals above, was short on specifics but nonetheless long on idealism. This bill would create a situation where "every American," "every American community," and "every individual tax payer," not just the poor and needy—would benefit from the prodigious struggle against poverty.

In the final part of this address, Johnson hoped his policies would result in "a world without war, a world made safe for diversity, in which all men, goods, and ideas can freely move across every border and every boundary." Such a noble goal could be facilitated through "military safety and superiority," arms control, exploration of space, and increasing the standard of living in foreign lands. Once again, the tax bill and this latter set of proposals were characterized in idealistic terms. Little pragmatic attention was given to them. Johnson concluded that the task for government was grand, for it had to resolve the most imposing of political paradoxes: "we must be constantly prepared for the worst, and constantly acting for the best. We must be strong enough to win any war, and we must be wise enough to prevent one." Johnson would have the nation do more than it had ever done before: It would solve every problem.

In these first two speeches, the President had introduced many themes that were put under a single heading of the "Great Society" in his "Commencement at the University of Michigan," May 22, 1964. Johnson devoted more effort in this address than in any prior message to advocating his Great Society, although the program was discussed in a commencement address the next week at the University of Texas and in important speeches the next year. References also were to be found in Johnson's 1965 State of the Union and in his Inaugural Address. In "The Great Society as a Rhetorical Proposition," Zarefsky notes that early drafts of this speech were written by Douglas Cater, Richard Goodwin, and Horace Busby. The final draft was prepared by Goodwin and Bill Moyers, who, in memoranda to the President, stressed the need for Johnson to define his own themes for the Presidency and to motivate America's youth to future action.

James Andrews and Zarefsky described the purpose of the speech at the University of Michigan as twofold. First, Johnson hoped to convince Americans to enact his Medicare and federal aid to education programs, both of which had been proposed earlier but had failed to resolve a particularly troublesome issue. Other issues, such as the war on poverty and aid to the cities, concerned topics that had no pre-existing base of public support, no special interest groups to speed their legislative passage. This speech was, as Windt noted, "simply written and spoken." But Johnson's plain speech did not conceal his idealism. In the first part of his address, for example, the President reviewed the nation's past commitments in grand terms; he claimed that "For a half a century we called upon unbounded invention and untiring industry to create an order of plenty for all of our people." The question, in Johnson's estimation, was whether Americans, particularly its youth, could draw upon their idealism to make America work: Americans had to use their "imagination . . . initiative . . . and indignation" to "build a society where progress is the servant of our needs, or a society where old values and new visions are buried under unbridled growth."

In the second part of his speech, the President defined his "Great Society" in an idealistic way: "The Great Society rests on abundance and liberty for all. It demands an end to poverty and racial injustice, to which we are totally committed in our time. But that is just the beginning." Indeed, Johnson then listed numerous goals for his Great Society, including rebuilding "the entire urban United States," creating a "countryside" of unprecedented beauty, and nourishing "excellence" in the classroom. Yet, for Johnson, the Great Society required that every dimension of intellect and idealism be engaged, that every "young mind is set free to scan the farthest reaches of thought and imagination."

In his ensuing comments, Johnson discussed some pragmatic themes. He promised, for instance, to "assemble the best thought and the broadest knowledge from all over the world to find . . . answers for America." He pledged "a series of White House conferences and meetings" to work on the nation's challenges. But this reprieve into the pragmatic quickly ended. For, as Johnson concluded, he again sounded an idealistic note, challenging his audience to move "beyond the bounds of our imagination," to "lead America toward a new age," to "join in the battle" to resolve all of our problems. "We have the power," Johnson boldly asserted, "to shape the civilization that we want."

Taken together, these Great Society speeches were immensely successful. At least initially, they were received favorably by most segments of American society. The President was able to pass eighty-nine major Administration bills in 1965 alone, with the only two major defeats being Congress' refusal to repeal right-to-work laws and to grant home rule to the District of Columbia. In light of the circumstances of divided or nonexistent constituencies, and hostile opposition in the South, Johnson's rhetorical success in building his Great Society program is quite impressive.

Idealism also permeated Johnson's rhetoric in his "The Right to Vote" address, delivered to the public and before a Joint Session of Congress, May 15, 1965. The major purpose of this speech was to link the right to vote with the right to register to vote. In some places in the nation, particularly in the South, blacks were being prevented from registering in substantial numbers. Johnson decided to advocate legislation, his "voting rights act," that he hoped would greatly reduce barriers to registration. Despite opposition from certain Congressional leaders, the President was determined to address a Joint Session of Congress in order to demonstrate the Congress' commitment to enacting Johnson's proposed legislation.

The speech itself was mostly composed by Richard Goodwin, although, as Ryan noted, the President "personalized the text with his own emendations." Horace Busby also assisted. In a memorandum, he had recommended that Johnson associate voting rights, something everyone in Congress agreed upon as a universal right, with the right to register, which in Busby's estimation was the real problem confronting the nation. Such an argumentative strategy allowed the President to adjust "the real need issue to Congress." At the same time, the members of Congress were adjusted to this association because no moral or logical argument could be raised against the right to vote, and therefore, the right to register.

This speech mixed idealism, pragmatism, and doctrine, although, as in earlier messages, its emphasis fell on the idealistic. The speech was divided into roughly two major sections, the first of which described American principles and ideals, and introduced Johnson's voting rights legislation: "Our mission is at once the oldest and the most basic of this country—to right wrong, to do justice, to serve man."

Johnson then turned to one of the most important American doctrinal principles, which was "equal rights for American negroes." With tremendous urgency, Johnson framed the issue idealistically: should "we defeat every enemy, and should we double our wealth and conquer the stars, and still be unequal to

this issue, then we will have failed as a people and as a nation.'' Johnson
continued to justify the right to vote on both idealistic and doctrinaire grounds:
''Those words are promised to every citizen that he shall share in the dignity
of man. . . . Our fathers believed that if this noble view of the rights of man was
to flourish it must be rooted in democracy. The most basic right of all was the
right to choose your own leaders. . . . Every American citizen must have an equal
right to vote.''

Johnson finally introduced his ''right to vote'' legislation, which he contended
would serve numerous pragmatic ends, the most important of which was to
reduce barriers to voting. It would ''strike down restrictions to voting,'' and
''eliminate tedious . . . lawsuits which delay the right to vote.'' But even that
short pragmatic excursion was surrounded by idealistic and doctrinal challenges
that served the central purpose of the speech, which was to link voting rights
with the right to register. Thus, Johnson called on Americans to ''Open your
polling places to all your people. Allow men and women to register and vote
whatever the color of their skins. Extend the rights of citizen to every citizen
of this land. . . . There must be no delay, or no hesitation, or no compromise
with our purpose. We cannot, we must not, refuse to protect the right of every
American to vote in every election that he may desire to participate in.''

In the second half of Johnson's speech, where he expanded his challenge to
Americans by linking voting rights to many other problems facing the nation,
he suggested that strengthening voting rights would also assist Americans in
overcoming ''bigotry,'' ''poverty, disease and ignorance''; it would help to educate ''all, black and white . . . North and South, sharecropper and city dweller'';
and it would ''root out injustice wherever it exists'' and ''rally [people] now
together in this cause to vindicate the freedom of all Americans.'' The association between doctrine, pragmatism, and idealism was once again made clear.
For Johnson, doctrine was not enough to preserve voting rights: ''I would like
to . . . remind you that to exercise these privileges takes much more than just a
legal right.'' It required certain pragmatic skills, such as ''a trained mind and a
healthy body. It required a decent home and the chance to find a job and the
opportunity to escape from the clutches of poverty''; and it required the realization of certain broad idealistic goals: ''All Americans must have the privileges
of citizenship, regardless of race, and they are going to have those privileges of
citizenship regardless of race.''

In the conclusion of his speech, Johnson cited his experiences as an educator
in the 1920s. These personal recollections seemingly associated voting rights
with another goal, educating the poor. He listed additional pragmatic initiatives,
all of which were cast idealistically. He wished to educate ''young children to
the wonders of their world,'' and to ''end war among the brothers of the earth.''
From Johnson's idealistic framework, securing the right to register to vote would
not only protect voting rights, but would also profoundly alter the course of
every single cultural and social problem in America and in the world.

However one understands this speech, Johnson's employment of doctrinal, pragmatic, and idealistic themes gained impressive results. The President's Voting Rights Act of 1965 was quickly passed and gained wide support from a variety of sources. In this instance, as Ryan concluded, Lyndon Baines Johnson was truly a successful persuader.

The Rhetoric of Defense: 1966–1968

By 1966, there were signs that the political tide was beginning to turn against Johnson. The sources of these changes were numerous. Many middle-class white Americans began to resent the President, for they believed he was ignoring their needs while improperly using government to give blacks too much.

Additional difficulties arose in the realm of foreign affairs. Confronted with a civil war in the Dominican Republic in April of 1965, the President rapidly escalated American military involvement until nearly 23,000 troops were sent to the small Caribbean nation. As Johnson's rationale for intervention shifted from merely protecting American citizens to saving democracy in the Republic, serious questions were raised by many Americans as to the efficacy of the President's policy.

Jeff Bass has shown how, in a series of speeches, Johnson adapted the archetypical "rescue/salvation" narrative to audiences during the Dominican crisis. According to Bass, Americans required that some sense of closure be brought to the Dominican situation. Johnson utilized narrative closure that made his military endeavors appear as though they were "efficient," a sense that did not exist prior to then. Thus, even though history has been critical of Johnson's handling of the Dominican affair, Bass finds that the President displayed a greater degree of rhetorical sophistication than most commentators are willing to allow.

The real foreign policy test, however, came in Vietnam. The war consumed and eventually destroyed the Johnson Presidency. During the last year and a half of his administration Johnson devoted nearly all of his attention to the American struggle in Southeast Asia. Conservatives attacked him for limiting the war and called for an all-out effort to win. Liberals charged he had embroiled Americans in an immoral war they had neither the desire nor ability to win, a war that was needlessly wasting American lives while domestic problems grew worse by the day. As a result of these attacks, Johnson neglected his Great Society to defend his policy in Vietnam.

Johnson's first major policy speech regarding Vietnam came in his April 7, 1965, address at Johns Hopkins University, often called "Seeking 'Peace Without Conquest' in Vietnam." Up to this period, the war had been going poorly for the South Vietnamese. To help, Johnson ordered the bombing of North Vietnam and sent American marines to protect air bases in the South. But the President had to justify his escalation of the war. Hence, to prepare for his address, Johnson consulted widely within his administration and among opinion leaders in American society.

Johnson opened with doctrine and pragmatism as he explained that Americans had to protect the rights of South Vietnam to "choose its own path to change," to "shape its own destiny." At least in the beginning of this speech, Johnson seemed cautious, more sober than in past addresses. He claimed that Americans had to remain realistic, acknowledging that victory would not be won by being overly idealistic: "we must deal with the world as it is, if it is ever to be as we wish."

However, Johnson then set forth America's mission in Southeast Asia in the boldest of terms. The nation had to stay in South Vietnam "to strengthen world order," to maintain our "continued responsibility for the defense of freedom." With that in mind, Johnson described a pragmatic plan for peace in Vietnam, what he named his "cooperative effort for development." This plan included various pragmatic goals, including "a billion dollar American investment," a "TVA" project for "the Mekong Delta," and dramatic improvements in health and education in Southeast Asia. With these accomplishments in place, Johnson believed the world would be closer to realizing its ultimate idealistic goal, what he called "the dream of world order." Unfortunately, Johnson did not define his plan for implementing this knowledge in the realm of foreign affairs, save for the few general proposals in his expansive "cooperative effort."

Johnson concluded idealistically, calling on Americans to do "everything" they could "to help unite the world, to try to bring peace and hope to all the peoples of the world." Americans, urged Johnson, "do all these things on a scale never dreamed of before. . . . In doing so we will prevail over the enemies within man, and over the natural enemies of all mankind."

Although Johnson was beamish about the prospects for Vietnam he outlined in this speech, his goals were never met. In Vietnam, the war became worse and North Vietnamese leaders turned a deaf ear on the President's bold initiatives. In Congress, reactions to Johnson's speech were not overly optimistic. As Andrews and Zarefsky pointed out, early positive responses proved fleeting, and criticism became more vocal as the size of the war grew.

Johnson's next serious Vietnam address was not delivered until May 17, 1966. Called "Nervous Nellies" by Windt, the May speech was given to a Democratic Party Dinner in Chicago. By 1966, anti-war sentiment was growing louder. Earlier, in February, Senator William Fulbright had opened the Senate Foreign Relations Committee Hearings into the war, much to Johnson's chagrin. The President used his speech in Chicago to criticize his opponents. Johnson made many idealistic references to his policy in Vietnam but was again short on specific policy proposals for concluding the conflict. The way in which his pragmatism was contained within his general idealistic demeanor is captured in these concluding remarks: "The men who fight for us out there tonight in Vietnam . . . are trying to find a way to peace. But they know . . . that we can't get peace just by wishing for it. We must get on with the job until these men can come marching home, someday, when peace is secure not only for the people of America, but peace is secure for peace-loving people everywhere in this world.''

By the fall of 1967, the war effort appeared to be improving. Americans and the South Vietnamese were making military advances, military leaders were predicting future success, and hawks outnumbered doves by nearly two to one. The TET offensive of February 1968, however, shattered these hopes and demonstrated the futility of American policy. The North Vietnamese and Viet Cong were able to penetrate Allied defenses within most of South Vietnam, including the capital city of Saigon. As Andrews and Zarefsky noted, in large numbers Americans came to doubt whether they were being told the truth about the war effort and more acutely questioned whether the purposes for which the war was being waged were really worth the tremendous cost. Politically, Johnson was in trouble. His own party was mobilizing against him, the economy was beginning to falter as a result of the taxing war effort, and polls showed that a majority of Americans opposed the President's war policy (albeit the opposition was split equally between hawks and doves).

Johnson was forced to reconsider his policy in Vietnam. On March 31, 1968, he set forth his conclusions in his famous "Johnson Steps Down" or "Renunciation" speech. Andrews and Zarefsky explained that before the address was given, it was the object of intense internal controversy. Johnson's informal speeches during March had been hawkish, but a collection of senior advisors from past administrations attempted to persuade Johnson that the war was not winnable and implored him to disengage and cut his losses. Johnson's speech was broken into two general parts, one explaining a new policy on Vietnam, the other announcing Johnson's decision to step down from office. According to Suzanne Condray, the first part had been the product of many months of intense discussions with advisors. Johnson's old Secretary of Defense, Robert McNamara, and McGeorge Bundy provided input. The new Secretary of Defense Clark Clifford, along with Walt Rostow, Secretary of State Dean Rusk, Assistant Secretary of State for East Asian and Pacific Affairs Bill Bundy, and White House assistant Harry McPherson, drafted the major first portion of the March 31 address. McPherson coordinated the drafting process and served as chief speechwriter for the final draft. Primarily four individuals contributed to the second part of the speech. These were Horace Busby, George Christian, Governor John Connally, and Mrs. Johnson. Busby wrote the actual text alone with the President.

Although the overall tone of this speech was conciliatory, the speech was not about peace per se. The President in fact addressed several issues. The first part reiterated the purposes of Johnson's Vietnam policy and discussed the aftermath of the TET offensive, which Johnson claimed did not destroy "the fighting power of South Vietnam and its allies.'' Then, after acknowledging the futility of continued struggle, Johnson conceded to anti-war protestors by announcing that he would end most of the bombing of North Vietnam, and that he would also seek a negotiated withdrawal of American forces. In a sense, these announcements were remarkably pragmatic: they reflected a concerted effort on the part of the President to develop a specific "unilateral" policy for disengaging from Vietnam. As Johnson put it, "Our purpose in this action is to bring about a reduction in the level of violence that now exists. It is to save the lives of brave men—and to save the lives of innocent women and children. It is to permit the contending forces to move closer to a political settlement."

Johnson then declared that American military efforts in Vietnam had been successful, which now allowed the nation to operate without an additional 206,000 troops requested earlier by General William Westmoreland. Albeit, Johnson made some strategically ambiguous comments about calling up additional military resources for Vietnam, should the situation have demanded such mobilization.

The President then turned to the economy at home, again displaying a certain amount of pragmatic prescience: "One thing is unmistakingly clear. . . . Our deficit just must be reduced. Failure to act could bring on conditions that would strike hardest at those people that all of us are trying so hard to help."

Johnson next delineated the possible effects of peace in Southeast Asia, which would be obtained because Americans acted on their idealism. To bolster his credibility, Johnson quoted John Kennedy in order to compel Americans to "pay any price, bear any burden, meet any hardship, support any friend, oppose any foe to assure the survival and the success of liberty." In short, Johnson's goals had been taxing but noble. The realization of these goals would make the world a remarkable place: "Through all time to come, I think America will be a stronger nation, a more just society, and a land of greater opportunity and fulfillment because of what we have done together in three years of unparalleled achievement."

In the final part of his address, Johnson made the startling announcement that he would not seek nor would he accept the Democratic nomination for reelection. The President, apparently, was going to step down so as not to permit "the Presidency to become involved in the partisan divisions that are developing in this political year." However, despite his absence, the nation would not be weakened as long as it maintained the ideals instilled by Johnson. As he concluded on a highly idealistic note, "But let men everywhere know . . . that a strong, a confident, and a vigilant America stands ready tonight to seek an honorable peace—and stands ready tonight to defend an honored cause—whatever the price, whatever the burden, whatever the sacrifice that duty may require."

The meaning of this dramatic speech, as Andrews and Zarefsky acknowledged, is still being debated. It seemingly had a significant impact upon the North Vietnamese, for within three days of Johnson's address, they agreed to open peace talks in Paris. Moreover, as Condray argues, the speech was important in that it manufactured a situation where Johnson could largely divorce the office of the president from a major political event during a campaign year.

CONCLUSION

Overall, despite Johnson's enormous legislative achievements, it is fair to conclude that scholars have been rather sober about the President's long-term impact. The problems with manipulation and deceit aside, the real source of difficulty for Johnson was the way in which idealism came to dominate his public speeches. Johnson's rhetorical endeavors, like his politics, were robust. On one hand, when meshed with pragmatic and doctrinal rhetoric, his idealism allowed him to actualize ambitious programs never before realized. He could persuade disparate audiences because he could strike to the fundamental ideals that linked them, and he could link these ideals to the disparate interests about which Americans were most concerned.

On the other hand, as Zarefsky argues, Johnson's moral exhortations and military metaphors used to justify the Great Society probably exaggerated expectations and led to frustration when these policies did not deliver all that Johnson had promised. The President's idealism often made liberals look like they lived in castles, not the real world. Hence, they became easy targets for conservatives wishing to demonstrate how liberals wasted tax dollars on overly ambitious social programs and overburdened government with social responsibility it could not realistically maintain. Johnson based policies in grand ideals he assumed that everyone, even those from other cultures, subscribed to. In this way, the President became blinded by his own principles. This was particularly true in Vietnam. Johnson's lack of specific knowledge about foreign policy and Vietnam led him to rely, instead, on his idealism. His idealistic goals, in turn, simply caused him to lose sight of his available means.

RHETORICAL SOURCES

Archival Materials

The most useful sources for materials on the Johnson presidency are found in the Lyndon Baines Johnson Library, Austin, Texas. This library includes the following research sources: the pre-presidential papers that cover Johnson's early life and political career; the presidential papers that contain the working documents of the Johnson administration; the White House Central Files that include memoranda to the President, memoranda among his staff members, letters to the administration members and their responses, and staff reports; the Statements of President Johnson that include ideas, drafts, and final copies for Johnson's speeches, remarks, and messages; the Daily Diary and Diary Backup that includes chronicles of the President's daily activities; and the National Security Files that contain the memoranda and reports from the National Security Council. Other supplementary sources in the library collection include donated papers, oral history interviews, and audiovisual archives. Many archivists and staff members, who worked for the administration, now tend to the presidential library.

Public Papers of the Presidents: Lyndon Baines Johnson. (PPP). 10 Vols. Washington, DC: U.S. Government Printing Office, 1965–1970.

Rhetorical Studies

Contemporary American Voices: Significant Speeches in American History, 1945–Present, edited by James R. Andrews and David Zarefsky. New York: Longman, 1992.

Dallek, Robert. *Lone Star Rising: Lyndon Johnson and His Times, 1908–1960.* New York: Oxford University Press, 1991.

Goldman, Eric F. *The Tragedy of Lyndon Johnson.* New York: Alfred A. Knopf, 1969.

Hart, Roderick P. *Verbal Style and the Presidency.* New York: Academic Press, 1984.

Kearns, Doris. *Lyndon Johnson and the American Dream.* New York: Harper & Row, 1966.

The Public Papers of the Presidents: Lyndon B. Johnson. Vols. 1 & 2. Washington, DC: United States Government Printing Office, 1965 (Volumes for years 1965–1969 appear similarly).

Turner, Kathleen J. *Lyndon Johnson's Dual War: Vietnam and the Press.* Chicago: University of Chicago Press, 1985.

White, Theodore H. *The Making of the President 1964.* New York: Atheneum, 1965.

Windt, Theodore, ed. *Presidential Rhetoric: 1961–to the Present.* Dubuque, IA: Kendall-Hunt Publishing Co., 1987.

Zarefsky, David. *President Johnson's War on Poverty.* Tuskaloosa, AL: University of Alabama Press, 1986.

Rhetorical Monographs

Andrews, James R. "The Rhetoric of Alliance." *Communication Quarterly* 16 (1968): 20–24.

Arnold, Carroll C. "Reflections on American Public Discourse." *Central States Speech Journal* 28 (1977): 73–85.

Bass, Jeff D. "The Appeal to Efficiency as Narrative Closure: Lyndon Johnson and the Dominican Crisis, 1965." *Southern Communication Journal* 50 (1985): 103–20.

Brooks, William D. "A Field Study of the Johnson and Goldwater Campaign Speeches in Pittsburgh." *Southern Communication Journal* 32 (1967): 273–81.

Cherwitz, Richard A. "Lyndon Johnson and the 'Crisis' of Tonkin Gulf: A President's Justification of War." *Western Journal of Speech Communication* 52 (1978): 93–104.

———. "Masking Inconsistency: The Tonkin Gulf Crisis." *Communication Quarterly* 28 (1980): 27–37.

———. "The Contributory Effect of Rhetorical Discourse: A Study of Language-in-use." *Quarterly Journal of Speech* 66 (1980): 33–50.

Condray, Suzanne C. "Speechwriting in Rhetorical Criticism: An Extension of Theory as Applied to the Johnson Administration.'' Ph.D. dissertation, Louisiana State University, 1980.

Connely, F. M. ''A Rhetorical Analysis of Selected Speeches of Lyndon Baines Johnson on the War in Vietnam.'' Ph.D. dissertation, Ohio State University, 1967.

———. ''Some Questions Concerning Lyndon Johnson's Rhetoric in the 1964 Presidential Campaign.'' *Southern Communication Journal* 37 (1971): 11–20.

Cornfield, M. ''Presidential Rhetoric and the Credibility Gap.'' *Communication Research* 14 (1987): 462–69.

Gorden, William, and Robert Bunker. ''The Sentimental Side of Mr. Johnson.'' *Southern Communication Journal* 32 (1966): 58–66.

Hahn, Dan F. ''Archetype and Signature in Johnson's 1965 State of the Union.'' *Communication Studies* 34 (1983): 236–46.

Hall, Robert N. ''Lyndon B. Johnson's Speaking in the Senate Campaign.'' *Southern Communication Journal* 30 (1964): 15–23.

———. ''Lyndon Johnson's Speech Preparation.'' *Quarterly Journal of Speech* 51 (1965): 168–76.

Harding, H. F. ''Democratic Nominee: Lyndon B. Johnson.'' *Quarterly Journal of Speech* 50 (1964): 409–14.

Ivie, Robert L. ''Presidential Motives For War.'' *Quarterly Journal of Speech* 60 (1974): 337–45.

———. ''Images of Savagery in American Justifications for War.'' *Communication Monographs* 47 (1980): 279–94.

Logue, Cal M., and John H. Patton. ''From Ambiguity to Dogma: The Rhetorical Symbols of Lyndon B. Johnson on Vietnam.'' *Southern Communication Journal* 47 (1982): 310–29.

McCroskey, James C., and Samuel V. O. Prichard. ''Selective-Exposure and Lyndon B. Johnson's 1966 'State of the Union' Address.'' *Journal of Broadcasting and Electronic Media* 11 (1967): 331–37.

Patton, John H. ''An End and a Beginning: Lyndon B. Johnson's Decisive Speech of March 31, 1968.'' *Communication Quarterly* 21 (1973): 33–41.

Phelps, Waldo, and Andrea Beck. ''Lyndon Johnson's Address at the U.C.L.A. Charter Day Ceremony.'' *Western Journal of Speech Communication* 29 (1965): 162–71.

Procter, David E. ''The Rescue Mission: Assigning Guilt to a Chaotic Scene.'' *Western Journal of Speech Communication* 51 (1987): 245–55.

Ryan, Halford R. ''LBJ's Voting Rights Address: Adjusting Civil Rights to the Congress and the Congress to Civil Rights.'' In *Contemporary American Public Discourse*, edited by Halford Ross Ryan. Prospects Heights, IL: Waveland Press, 1992.

Sigelman, Lee, and Lawrence Miller. ''Understanding Presidential Rhetoric: The Vietnam Statements of Lyndon Johnson.'' *Communication Research* 5 (1978): 25–56.

Smith, F. M. ''Rhetorical Implications of the 'Aggression' Thesis in the Johnson Administration's Vietnam Argumentation.'' *Communication Studies* 23 (1972): 217–24.

Smith, Robert W. ''The 'Second' Inaugural Address of Lyndon Baines Johnson: A Definitive Text.'' *Communication Monographs* 34 (1967): 102–8.

Turner, Kathleen J. ''Press Influence on Presidential Rhetoric: Lyndon Johnson at Johns Hopkins University, April 7, 1965.'' *Communication Studies* 33 (1982): 425–36.

———. ''The Presidential Libraries as Research Facilities: An Analysis of Resources for Rhetorical Scholarship.'' *Communication Education* 35 (1986): 243–53.

Weiss, Harold, and Haddon Robinson. "Lyndon B. Johnson." *Quarterly Journal of Speech* 46 (1960): 241.

Witherspoon, Patricia D. " 'Let Us Continue:' The Rhetorical Initiation of Lyndon Johnson's Presidency." *Presidential Studies Quarterly* 13 (1983): 613–22.

Zarefsky, David. "President Johnson's War on Poverty: The Rhetoric of Three 'Establishment' Movements." *Communication Monographs* 44 (1977): 352–73.

———. "The Great Society as a Rhetorical Proposition." *Quarterly Journal of Speech* 65 (1979): 364–78.

———. "Lyndon Johnson Redefines 'Equal Opportunity': The Beginnings of Affirmative Action." *Communication Studies* 31 (1980): 85–94.

———. "Subordinating the Civil Rights Issue: Lyndon Johnson in 1964." *Southern Communication Journal* 48 (1983): 103–18.

———. "Civil Rights and Civil Conflict: Presidential Communication in Crisis." *Communication Studies* 34 (1983): 59–66.

Chronology of Significant Presidential Persuasions

(Unless otherwise noted, all speeches were delivered from the White House, Washington, D.C.)

"The Forward Thrust of America," November 27, 1963. *PPP,* 1963–1964: 8–9.

"War on Poverty" State of the Union speech, January 8, 1964. *PPP,* 1963–1964: 112–18.

"The Great Society" Commencement speech, University of Michigan, May 22, 1964. *PPP,* 1963–1964: 704–77.

"War: Gulf of Tonkin," August 4, 1964. *PPP,* 1963–1964: 927–28.

"We Shall Overcome," March 15, 1965. *PPP,* 1965: 281–87.

"The Right to Vote," March 15, 1965. *PPP,* 1965: 287–91.

"Seeking 'Peace Without Conquest' in Vietnam," John Hopkins University, Baltimore, Maryland, April 7, 1965. *PPP,* 1965: 394–99.

"The Dominican Intervention I: American Lives are in Danger," April 28, 1965. *PPP,* 1965: 461–62.

"The Dominican Intervention II: Outsiders Are Seeking to Gain Control," April 30, 1965. *PPP,* 1965: 465–66.

"The Dominican Intervention III: The Revolutionary Movement Took A Tragic Turn," May 2, 1965. *PPP,* 1965: 469–74.

"The Vietnam War Becomes the American-Vietnamese War," televised news conference, White House, Washington, D.C., July 28, 1965. *PPP,* 1965: 794–803.

"Nervous Nellies" speech, Democratic Party Dinner, Chicago, Illinois, May 17, 1966. *PPP,* 1966: 513–20.

"The San Antonio Declaration," San Antonio, Texas, September 29, 1967. *PPP,* 1967: 876–81.

"Johnson Steps Down," March 31, 1968. *PPP,* 1968–1969: 469–76.

"The President and the Media," Chicago, Illinois, April 1, 1968. *PPP,* 1968–1969: 482–86.

Hal W. Bochin

Richard Milhous Nixon
(1913–1994)

And so tonight—to you, the great silent majority of my fellow Americans—
I ask for your support.

An emotional Richard Nixon described his own political career when he told a group of White House aides and staff gathered on August 9, 1974, to bid him farewell: "Only if you have been in the deepest valley can you ever know how magnificent it is to be on the highest mountain." No American political leader has known higher mountains or deeper valleys than Richard Nixon. After a meteoric rise from newly elected House member to vice president in six years, Nixon was within 120,000 votes of the top when he lost the 1960 presidential election to John Kennedy. When Pat Brown defeated him in the race for California governor in 1962, most commentators offered his political obituary. Nixon surprised them all with his election to the presidency in 1968. In 1972, he won re-election, capturing 60 percent of the popular vote as he defeated George McGovern. He had reached the summit; but two years later, he became the first president to resign his office. He left in disgrace, but he was not finished. Donning the mantle of elder statesman, Nixon wrote and spoke, most often about foreign policy, and eventually regained much of the respect he had lost. In 1990, sixteen years after his resignation, three U.S. presidents and thousands of cheering spectators attended the opening of the Nixon Library and Birthplace, a monument to his accomplishments.

Born on January 9, 1913, in Yorba Linda, California, to Francis "Frank" and Hannah Nixon, Richard was the second eldest of five sons. When Richard was nine, the family moved to Whittier where his father opened a gas station and later added a grocery store in which the entire family worked. An excellent student, Nixon had to refuse a scholarship to Harvard because of the high cost of transportation, housing, and other expenses at the Ivy League school. Instead he enrolled at Whittier College where he debated and served as student body president. Awarded a scholarship to Duke University Law School, Nixon ranked third in his class and, after graduation, he returned to California where he passed the bar exam and joined a small law firm in Whittier. While performing in a local little theater production, Nixon met Thelma "Pat" Ryan whom he married in June 1940. Shortly before the outbreak of World War II, Nixon accepted a job in Washington, D.C., working for the Office of Price Administration. In 1942 he received a naval commission and went into training at Quonset, Rhode Island. In 1943 he served in the South Pacific, and in 1944 was transferred to San Francisco and later to Washington where he served as a lieutenant commander on the Navy's legal staff.

Nixon's political career began in 1946 when Whittier Republicans selected him to campaign against a five-term incumbent, Jerry Voorhis. Outdebating Voorhis in a series of five joint appearances that drew large and enthusiastic audiences, Nixon won election to Congress at the age of 33. He rose swiftly in his new profession. As a member of the House Committee on Un-American Activities, he gained national headlines for his work in the investigation of alleged Communist spy, Alger Hiss. In 1950 he defeated Helen Gahagan Douglas and became the junior senator from California. In 1952 Dwight Eisenhower chose Nixon as his running mate and, by his fortieth birthday, Nixon was vice president of the United States. First, however, he had to survive the fight of his young political life. He also linked forever his own name with that of his dog.

The September 18, 1952 edition of the *New York Post* carried the headline "Secret Nixon Fund" and the accompanying story claimed, "Secret Rich Men's Trust Fund Keeps Nixon in Style Far Beyond His Salary." Since Republicans were arguing that they should be elected to clean up the "corruption in Washington," Democrats quickly pointed out that the Republican vice-presidential candidate's hands might not be clean and demanded that Eisenhower throw Nixon off the ticket.

Nixon decided to address the nation directly. A national hook-up of 64 NBC television stations, 194 CBS radio stations, and the entire 560 station Mutual Broadcasting System, was arranged. To capture the largest possible audience, the Republicans selected Tuesday night, September 23, following the "Milton Berle Show." Instead of telling the press what he was going to say, Nixon told them to watch the show. He later wrote in *Six Crises* that the speech had to fulfill three requirements, to meet the immediate attack by explaining the fund, to ward off future attacks along the same lines, and to rally the voters in support of Eisenhower.

The first requirement Nixon mentioned had to be met not only for the viewing audience that numbered about 58–60 million, but for Eisenhower as well. Nixon knew he had to show Eisenhower he was "clean as a hound's tooth" for Eisenhower and his top aides had been discussing Nixon's role on the Republican ticket for four days, and they were almost unanimously agreed that Nixon should offer to resign.

Nixon's instinct and background called for the attack to be met by a counterattack. His speech utilized arguments chosen for their proven ability to silence hecklers at campaign rallies in California and Oregon, following exposure of the fund, rather than for their logical soundness. Throughout the speech, instead of defending himself against the Democratic assault, Nixon launched his own offensive—on the Democratic vice-presidential nominee John Sparkman for putting his own wife on his payroll, on Adlai Stevenson for having secret funds of his own, and on the Truman administration for supposedly losing countries and men to Communism and for internal graft and corruption. The most often remembered section of Nixon's speech is when he mentioned Checkers, "a little cocker spaniel dog," a gift to his daughters from an admirer in Texas. With a tear in his eye and a quiver in his voice, Nixon declared that no matter what anyone said about it, he was not going to give the dog back.

Direct and conversational, Nixon used short sentences and a number of parenthetical remarks and rhetorical questions to bring himself closer to his audience. He enhanced the dramatic quality of his delivery by speaking from notes instead of a manuscript and he talked directly to the camera.

With both target audiences Nixon succeeded beyond his expectations. Before he had finished, many of those with Eisenhower, including Mrs. Eisenhower, were weeping and the crowd in the auditorium began chanting, "We want Dick! We want Dick!" Instead of addressing his supporters on the scheduled topic of inflation, Eisenhower talked to them about Nixon: "I have seen brave men in tough situations. I have never seen anyone come through in better fashion than Senator Nixon did tonight."

The reaction of the second audience to Nixon's speech was mixed but overwhelmingly favorable. More than three hundred thousand telegrams and letters, signed by more than one million people, poured into the national Republican headquarters to support Nixon by a margin of 350 to 1. A content analysis of the responses showed that writers tended to ignore issues and to comment instead on Nixon's personal qualities, such as honesty, courage, sincerity, patriotism, and devotion to family, exactly those qualities he attempted to enhance in his speech. Nixon learned the value of going directly to the public when he had an important message to deliver and the value of surprise in not revealing what he intended to say.

Because of his success on television and as a debater, Nixon agreed to meet the lesser known John F. Kennedy in 1960 in the first series of televised debates between presidential candidates in American history. This time, however, television proved less favorable to Nixon. Pale because of illness and injury, a nervous, perspiring Nixon did poorly in the first debate in front of sixty million viewers. A more aggressive Nixon more than held his own in the three subsequent debates, but many voters remembered only the first. Kennedy won the presidency, but Nixon learned an important lesson about appearance versus substance that strongly affected the way he would use television in the future.

His loss in the presidential election marked the first of Nixon's slides down the mountain. In 1962, he lost the race for governor of California to Pat Brown and in a news conference afterward, he angrily told reporters that they "wouldn't have Nixon to kick around anymore" because he was withdrawing from public life. Nevertheless he campaigned for Barry Goldwater in the presidential election of 1964 and for other Republican congressional candidates in 1966. The GOP rewarded his efforts by making him their presidential candidate in 1968, opposing Democrat Hubert Humphrey and Independent George Wallace. Nixon defeated his two opponents and 1972 found him once again at the top of the mountain, having won re-election with a landslide victory over George McGovern. Nixon's triumph, however, was short lived.

A "third-rate burglary" in the Watergate office building occurred during the election campaign, but at the time it had little impact on the electorate. When Nixon's role in the Watergate affair and other illegal activities became known, however, the House Judiciary Committee held impeachment hearings and indicted Nixon on three grounds—covering up the Watergate burglary and related crimes, violating the constitutional rights of citizens, and refusing to obey the committee's subpoenas to produce recordings of his conversations. Nixon prepared to fight the indictment on the floor of the House, but the revelation of yet another tape recording of Nixon's conversations with his staff undermined the President's defense. In it Nixon clearly called for a cover-up effort, and he lost any hope of maintaining enough political support to prevent impeachment by the full House and conviction by the Senate. Nixon resigned on August 8, 1974, in a nationally televised address. Following a nearly fatal illness, Nixon started the slow process of rebuilding his reputation; he began to climb the mountain again.

Between 1974 and 1990, Nixon wrote seven books and visited Russia and China a number of times, keeping the White House informed about what he had learned. On July 19, 1990, Nixon hosted the opening of the $25 million Nixon Library and Birthplace with Presidents Ford, Reagan, and Bush, together with hundreds of reporters and thousands of spectators, in attendance. The main exhibits showed Nixon's rise from the boy who grew up in the house built by his father to the man who negotiated with world leaders in the White House. According to biographer Stephen Ambrose, "What had seemed impossible in the summer of 1974 had happened by the summer of 1990. Nixon was respectable, even honored, certainly admired."

On March 11, 1992, a seventy-nine year old Nixon spoke at a Washington, D.C., foreign policy conference sponsored by the Nixon Library. In a number of respects the speech typified the kind of speaking Nixon had been doing since his resignation. He approached his specific topic, that the United States should aid the Russian government of Boris Yeltsin, as an elder statesman, offering advice to a younger generation. The audience consisted of two hundred scholars, diplomats, and government officials.

The delivery of the speech was vintage Nixon. He spoke for thirty minutes, without notes, without even a podium. A reporter for the *New York Times* felt his voice had become gravelly, but all the other hallmarks of his delivery remained, "the locked elbow gestures, the jowly visage, the hunched, high shouldered posture, and the heavily cadenced speech."

Nixon stressed the bipartisan nature of his proposal. "I recall vividly what Harry Truman did in 1947," he said. He compared the Russian situation today with Europe after World War II and noted that in spite of the fact that it was a "very tough vote" because of their constituents' misgivings, both he and John Kennedy had supported the economic aid to Turkey and Greece requested by Truman. The elder statesman was above partisan politics and revealed a little known admiration for Truman. Nixon concluded with a ringing call to action: "This is our moment of greatness. It is our moment of truth. We must seize this moment because we hold the future in our hands." The audience greeted Nixon's remarks with a standing ovation. He could never again reach the top; but, well past retirement age, Nixon continued his climb up the mountain.

RHETORICAL TRAINING AND PRACTICES

Richard Nixon's rhetorical training began in elementary school. Defending the affirmative side of the resolution, "It is more economical to rent a house than to own one," with the help of data supplied by his father, Nixon won the debate and took the first step in a public speaking career that would last more than fifty years. In high school, Nixon took classes in public speaking, participated in interscholastic debates, and entered public speaking contests. After graduation, he enrolled at a local Quaker institution, Whittier College, where he could commute to school and continue his debating career. Debate introduced Nixon to a number of important political questions and it left him with the belief that few complex issues were black or white. This attitude influenced his political life where he could champion ideas that he had previously spoken against.

It is not surprising that Nixon put to use what he had learned as soon as he entered the political arena. In fact Nixon probably wrote more of his own speeches than any of his contemporaries. As vice president, he wrote all his own material. As President, he had a number of speech writers, but he wrote his most important speeches himself or in collaboration with one other writer. During his first term Jim Keogh headed the writing staff. The senior writers were William Safire, Raymond K. Price, Jr., and Patrick J. Buchanan, assisted by Lee Huebner and John Andrews. During his second administration, Nixon put Price in charge of a speech writing staff that included Aram Bakshian, Huebner, Andrews, and Noel Koch. Price's assistant, David Gergen, edited drafts but usually did not initiate them.

Nixon did not want his writers to work together as a committee, but selected an individual writer to work with, depending on the tilt he wanted to give a particular speech. The conservative Buchanan provided hard-hitting answers for Nixon to use in his press conferences. Price attempted to put compassion and vision into Nixon's speeches. Safire, who considered himself ideologically between his two colleagues, worked with the President on economic matters, offered a touch of humor, and attempted to make complicated matters simpler. Because he believed that the "written word, no matter how eloquent, is different from the spoken word," Nixon would take a draft from his writers and dictate his own version into a tape recorder, working the language through aloud so that it would have the rhythm and punch he thought a speech needed.

In his autobiographical *In the Arena*, Nixon devoted a chapter to "Speaking," offering sage advice to a beginning speaker. Nixon favored an extemporaneous delivery. He experimented early in his political career with a manuscript but found that he got a much better response when he spoke without notes. He also learned it was easier to remember what he himself had written than what someone else had written for him. As president, he eschewed the use of a TelePrompTer, fearing that he would sound "leaden, lifeless, and insincere." He used a manuscript, however, for those important speeches in which he did not want to misstate anything.

Nixon warned novice speakers that they must make a speech writer's words their own, but he said little about one of the most distinguishing features of his own speechmaking, a simple style. Nixon's rhetoric seldom soared beyond the commonplace because he consciously strove for a simple style. He meant his words to be understood by an immediate audience not to be admired by future generations. Vice President Nixon reported, "I'm a great believer in making my speeches as simple as possible as far as vocabulary and sentence construction are concerned."

Based on a computer analysis of a number of Nixon's speeches in different time periods and before different types of audiences, Rod Hart discovered that although Nixon's language was simple and clear, his ideas can best be described as equivocal or ambivalent. What Hart called Nixon's "verbal absolutism" was generally quite low, except when he was addressing a highly favorable audience, such as a Republican National Convention. Hart claimed that Nixon mastered the best of both worlds, offering his listeners "forthright equivocality." Such a style allowed Nixon to reach outside Republican ranks to appeal to Democrats and Independents without losing his basic Republican support.

NIXON'S INAUGURAL ADDRESSES

First Inaugural Address

On January 15, 1969, Rosemary Woods and Ray Price joined Nixon at his vacation home in Key Biscayne, Florida, where Price and the president-elect spent the next few days collaborating on the last drafts of the speech. Woods,

Nixon's longtime personal secretary, took dictation as Nixon read from his long-hand drafts of the speech; she typed and returned them for further revision. As they began the final phase of writing the speech, Nixon told Price that his goal was to heal a divided country.

Nixon offered a fitting introduction. He asked the audience to share with him "the majesty of this moment," a moment "of beginning, in which courses are set that shape decades or centuries." The United States was close to its 200th anniversary as a nation and Nixon declared: "What kind of nation we will be—what kind of world we will live in . . . is ours to determine by our actions and our choices." This sentence served as a transition into the body of the speech where Nixon described his hopes for America's future, problems facing the country, their causes and solutions, and the relationship between the United States and the other nations of the world.

To unify the country, Nixon directed specific remarks at a number of groups that opposed him in the election. To African-Americans he said, "No man can be fully free while his neighbor is not. To go forward at all is to go forward together." Perhaps remembering how Lyndon Johnson had successful quoted from "We Shall Overcome," Nixon offered words from the second verse: "This means black and white together."

Nixon described the youth of America, many of whom opposed him because of the Vietnam war, as "better educated, more committed, more passionately driven by conscience than any generation in our history." To those protesting the war he said, "We cannot learn from one another until we stop shouting at one another—until we speak quietly enough so that our words can be heard as well as our voices."

Perhaps the best remembered section of the inaugural first appeared in one of Price's early drafts, in which he urged that we, as a nation, should "lower our voices." Nixon liked the idea and the final version contained these words: "The simple things are the ones most needed today. . . . To lower our voices would be a simple thing." Although some commentators ascribed the genesis of this passage to Nixon's Quaker background and this may have been what made it appealing to Nixon, Price suggested the idea.

Nixon's manuscript shows that he worked hard on his oral presentation. He underlined the most important two or three words in each sentence for vocal emphasis. Since the typescript is in outline form, it was easy for the President to give proper emphasis to various ideas. Nixon had little eye contact with his audience for he was tied to his manuscript.

Nixon's presidential demeanor, his attempt to unite the country (he used "we" sixty-six times in the speech), the abstract language that no one could disagree with, his quotations from and allusions to Democratic presidents, his emphasis on peace, and his special recognition of groups that had not supported him in the election combined to offer even the most skeptical listener the image of a concerned president.

Editorial writers of various political persuasions found the contemplative tone of Nixon's address appropriate. For instance, James Reston of the *New York Times* applauded Nixon's conversion from campaigner to President: "The hawkish, political, combative, anti-Democratic Nixon of the past was not the man on the platform today." He noted that Nixon had reached out to many who had opposed his election—"progressive Democrats, the young, the blacks, and the Soviets." Mary McGrory, never a fan of Nixon, spoke for many liberal columnists when she observed, "There's no dancing in the streets, but there's an acceptance that Richard Nixon has rarely known in his controversial career."

The speech drew much the same reaction from widely opposed political factions. A leading critic of the Vietnam conflict, J. William Fulbright called the address "a very superior speech and very hopeful for a more rational foreign policy," and in a statement issued from Walter Reed Army Medical Center, Dwight Eisenhower summarized the mood Nixon was trying to create in his Inaugural Address: "No longer are we partisans in a presidential campaign. Now we are Americans together."

Columnist Max Lerner may have offered the most perceptive analysis of the speech when he wrote, "While it was not, either in ideas or phrasing, a speech that will rank anywhere near the immortal ones, it was in its own way a good speech, projecting Nixon's self-image faithfully, prudent in not boxing Nixon in and thus reducing his options when he will have to act. It said little and said it passably well."

Second Inaugural Address

Nixon's Second Inaugural Address, however, must be considered a failure. As Nixon approached the podium on January 20, 1973, having won a landslide victory at the polls, having become only the thirteenth man in American history to be elected to the presidency twice, he was apparently in no mood to conciliate the minority who opposed him.

Nixon replaced the appeals to unity that had worked so well in the first speech with statements that tended to alienate rather than to conciliate. Instead of going forward together, African-Americans were told, "In trusting too much to government, we have ask of it more than it can deliver. This leads only to inflated expectations, to reduced individual effort, and to disappointment and frustration that erode confidence both in what government can do and in what people can do." Describing America's youth, the President complained, "Our children have been taught to be ashamed of their country, ashamed of their parents, ashamed of America's record at home and its role in the world." To anti-war protesters, some of whom could be heard as Nixon spoke, he responded, "At every turn we have been beset by those who find everything wrong with America and little that is right. But I am confident that this will not be the judgment of history on these remarkable times in which we are privileged to live."

Whereas in his First Inaugural Nixon showed bipartisanship by paraphrasing John Kennedy and quoting a number of his Democratic predecessors, in the

Second Inaugural Nixon explicitly contradicted two of Kennedy's most famous thoughts. In the area of foreign policy, where Kennedy announced that America would "bear any burden . . . ," Nixon rejoined, "The time has passed when America will make every other nation's conflict her own, or make every other nation's future our responsibility, or presume to tell the people of other nations how to manage their affairs." On the domestic front, Nixon reworded Kennedy's most famous quotation by saying, "let each of us ask—not just what will government do for me, but what can I do for myself?"

Nixon's delivery matched the mood and the weather. An editorial writer for the Toledo *Blade* complained: "Nixon's second inaugural address, delivered in an unimpassioned almost desultory manner, contained little of the inspirational rhetoric calculated to lift the nation's spirits." The *Nation* reported that the speech "was terse, arrogant and self-satisfied. Conciliation was not its theme." More ominously, editorial writers predicted that the speech would increase the growing rift between the White House and the Congress. Although Nixon asked that the nation "again learn to debate our differences with civility and decency," his actions immediately after the election—the pre-Christmas bombings of North Vietnam, the reorganization of the executive department, and the continued impounding of appropriated funds, all done without consultation with Congress or significant exposure to the press—spoke louder than his words, and a constitutional conflict with Congress seemed inevitable. Antagonism replaced conciliation. No wonder speech writer William Safire wrote that the First Inaugural was "infinitely better" than the second.

NIXON'S SPEECHES ON VIETNAM

The war in Vietnam overshadowed all other issues during the first four and a half years of the Nixon administration. Nixon delivered two major speeches on Vietnam, and like the inaugural addresses, the first was quite successful, the second was not.

"Silent Majority"

In the fall of 1969, Nixon prepared for a long promised address on the war by receiving recommendations from Henry Kissinger, Melvin Laird, William Rogers, Ellsworth Bunker, and Henry Cabot Lodge. The President, however, wrote the speech himself, working twelve to fourteen hours a day beginning at Camp David on the weekend of October 24, 1969. No one but Kissinger and Rose Mary Woods, who typed the final manuscript, knew exactly what he planned to say. Speculation in the media about the speech predicted some form of accelerated troop withdrawals or even a unilateral cease-fire, but remembering how his silence had built the audience for the "Checkers" speech, the President refused to reveal what he would say.

Nixon's plan worked. He had seventy-two million listeners the night of Monday, November 3, when he offered what has been called"the most effective speech of his presidency.'' Aiming directly at the large segment of the American populace who neither favored increased participation in the war nor immediate unconditional withdrawal, Nixon based his persuasive appeals on principles and values they would readily accept. He identified his position with truth, morality, dedication to duty, and patriotism. The most important was truth, especially in light of the "credibility gap'' that had plagued the last years of the Johnson administration. Nixon said: "The American people cannot and should not be asked to support a policy which involves the overriding issues of war and peace unless they know the truth about that policy.''

To further build his credibility, Nixon asserted that he would not take the politically easy way out of the Vietnam problem. He could have ordered the immediate withdrawal of American forces and blamed the defeat on Johnson; but Nixon claimed, "I had a greater obligation than to think only of the years of my administration and of the next election.'' Nixon repeated and implicitly supported the justification for the war offered by his predecessors, but he again distanced himself from the unpopular Johnson administration by adding: "Many others—I among them—have been strongly critical of the way the war has been conducted.''

Nixon hoped to negotiate an end to the war, but if that failed, he had a second plan, and this marked another difference between him and Johnson: "In the previous administration we Americanized the war in Vietnam. In this administration we are Vietnamizing the search for peace.'' America's mission would be "to enable the South Vietnamese forces to assume the responsibility for the security of South Vietnam.''

Nixon declared that he would not be influenced by "the minority'' who were trying to impose their views "on the Nation by mounting demonstrations in the street.'' Only elected officials should determine governmental policy. In attacking anti-war protesters, Nixon picked an easy target. Even among those who thought the war was a mistake, sixty-three percent viewed protesters negatively.

The most memorable phrase in the speech came in the conclusion when Nixon said, "And so tonight—to you, the great silent majority of my fellow Americans—I ask for your support.'' Although the term "silent majority'' had been used previously, by Vice President Spiro Agnew in May, it had attracted little notice. Within a few weeks of Nixon's use of the term, however, a number of groups within the United States eagerly identified themselves as members of the now not-so-silent majority.

When Nixon asked the "silent majority'' to speak out he did not know whether they would support his policies. They did. A Gallup telephone poll taken immediately after the broadcast indicated that 77 percent of those who listened to the speech supported Nixon's position, while fewer than 14 percent opposed it. More importantly, public reaction had the desired effect on Congress. Both the House and Senate passed resolutions expressing confidence in Nixon's handling of the war. Anti-war forces were shaken. They had hoped that Nixon's speech would offer something more in line with what they wanted, and they were terribly disappointed. Congressional doves made their displeasure with Nixon's policies known, but it was clear that they held a minority view.

Nixon's success was predictable. Throughout the speech the audience was asked to support a truthful man who portrayed himself as more competent than his predecessor, working hard to fulfill a moral commitment expressed by a long line of presidents, a lover of peace, a patriot who would not be swayed by demonstrators who wanted to impose their will on the nation. Much as he had done in the "Checkers" speech, Nixon appealed to his listeners' values of truth, morality, and patriotism and won their overwhelming support. This support, however, would not last forever. Six months later, military events in Southeast Asia forced Nixon to go again before the American people to talk about Vietnam. This second speech, described by William Safire as "harsh, self-pitying, and superpatriotic," succeeded with his friends but brought down on Nixon the wrath of his enemies. Polarization rather than support resulted.

"Cambodia"

Nixon recognized that the major result of his November 3 speech was "time," but by the spring of 1970 it was running out. The American people wanted action; and on April 20, Nixon announced that 150,000 American troops would be returning from Vietnam by the end of the year. An unexpected event in Cambodia, however, presented a new problem for the President. A pro-Western leader, Lon Nol, overthrew Prince Sihanouk, the cagey ruler of neutral Cambodia, and Lon Nol immediately asked for American military aid. Nixon responded by sending a South Vietnamese force against the North Vietnamese in that part of Cambodia known as the "Parrot's Beak," and a combined American and South Vietnamese force against the North Vietnamese in the area called the "Fishhook" where, it was thought, the central command of the North Vietnamese was headquartered. This second operation raised considerable opposition from Nixon's chief advisors, but Nixon decided that American forces were needed to make the operation successful. He would "go for broke."

Nixon selected Buchanan, his most conservative speech writer, to draft the justification for his decision, although the President himself took an active part in composing the speech that went through eight drafts. On the evening of April 30, 1970, Nixon went before a radio and television audience of 60 million to "describe the actions of the enemy, the actions I have ordered to deal with the situation, and the reasons for my decision."

Using a map of Southeast Asia to illustrate how close the North Vietnamese forces in the Parrot's Beak were to Saigon, Nixon argued that the protection of American forces demanded "cleaning out major North Vietnamese and Vietcong occupied territories—these sanctuaries which serve as bases for attacks on both Cambodia and American and South Vietnamese forces in South Vietnam." He promised that "once enemy forces are driven out of these sanctuaries and once their military supplies are destroyed, we will withdraw.'' He reviewed the course of Vietnamization and claimed that the actions he had taken in Cambodia were ''indispensable'' to the successful completion of the war.

Advisors had warned the President about the political reaction the incursion would have, but Nixon pointedly ignored the feelings of those who would see his move as an enlargement of the war. In fact, he seemed to go out of his way to attack his critics. He implied that anti-war protesters were destroying America's great universities, and that Americans were witnessing ''mindless attacks on all the great institutions which have been created by free civilizations in the last 500 years.'' Using the strongest language of the speech, he transcended the immediate Cambodian question to describe the global results of the situation: ''If, when the chips are down, the world's most powerful nation . . . acts like a pitiful, helpless giant, the forces of totalitarianism and anarchy will threaten free nations and free institutions throughout the world. It is not our power but our will and character that is being tested tonight.''

The effect of this speech was mixed but those Nixon antagonized had the louder voices. The *New York Times* noted that the speech ''appeared to harden previous convictions,'' and James Reston found more opposition in the Senate to Nixon's action than to ''any other Presidential action in the last ten years.'' But a CBS telephone survey taken immediately after the broadcast found the respondents two to one in favor of Nixon's position.

Anti-war sentiment filled the media because of two events that occurred immediately after the speech. Nixon was responsible for the first. Caught up the next day in a cheering crowd at the Pentagon, he compared the soldiers in Vietnam, ''the greatest,'' with ''these bums, you know, blowing up the campuses. . . . The boys that are on the college campuses today . . . are burning up the books, storming around about this issue.'' Within a few days it was widely believed, especially on college campuses, that Nixon had called all college protesters ''bums,'' and the estrangement between campus dissidents and the President increased tremendously.

The second event that flamed anti-war protest occurred on the campus of Kent State University. On May 4 two student demonstrators and two onlookers were killed by bullets fired by Ohio National Guardsmen. The grieving father of one of the dead students told the press, ''My child was not a bum.'' By the second week in May, almost 450 colleges and universities were on strike or closed. But on May 30 Nixon reported to the nation that the Cambodian incursion had met its objectives, and on June 30 he announced that the last American troops had left Cambodia. Safire concluded that the incursion was ''daring, surprising, successful in the short run and successful in the long run. But Nixon acting as a leader came across to all too many people as a belligerent con man.''

On November 3, 1969, President Nixon successfully persuaded a majority of Americans that his Vietnamization policy would work if only he had their support. Having built his ethos by demonstrating his competence and trustworthiness, Nixon identified his policy with morality and patriotism. He also attempted to find common ground in the search for peace with those with whom he disagreed. Nixon's speech was overwhelmingly successful. But when the war dragged on and Nixon decided that he should send American ground troops into Cambodia, he once again had to seek support for his Vietnam program. To a limited degree he succeeded, but his language and tone alienated rather than quieted his opposition, and the number and fervor of anti-war protests increased dramatically. The results included tragedy on college campuses and a country more divided than ever on the conduct of the war.

NIXON'S SPEECH ON WAGE-PRICE CONTROLS

President Nixon often used the tactic of surprise to gain an audience and to catch his opponents off guard. His speech of August 15, 1971, in which the champion of free markets announced a program of wage and price controls, provides an excellent example of this. With unemployment high, inflation increasing, and the British government demanding gold for $5 billion in currency, Nixon drew his principal advisors together at Camp David to discuss what should be done to protect the economy. "Circumstances change," he told them, "nobody is bound by past positions." Following a wide-ranging discussion, Nixon called on William Safire to write the speech announcing the program that had been decided upon. He selected Safire, who had never had an economics course, to write this speech because he wanted to avoid jargon and to put economic problems into a political and social context that an audience could understand.

Safire started to work on Friday night, August 13, hoping to have a draft ready for the President before breakfast on Saturday. When he went over at 7 A.M. to give the draft to Rosemary Woods for typing, he was surprised to find she was already at work. The President had arisen at 3 A.M. and started to write the speech himself. Safire combined what the President had written with his own draft, following Nixon's instructions: "On form the outline is right: the structure is jobs, prices, sound dollar, with two steps on the dollar—import tax and the gold window. Use gutsy rhetoric and keep the feeling—only correct it on the technical fronts."

On Sunday evening Nixon announced from the Oval Office: "The time has come for an new economic policy for the United States." The heart of the program was "a freeze on all prices and wages throughout the United States for a period of 90 days." Nixon's explanation of the effect of the devaluation of the dollar shows why he selected Safire: "If you want to buy a foreign car or take a trip abroad, market conditions may cause your dollar to buy slightly less. But if you are among the overwhelming majority of Americans who buy American-made products, in America, your dollar will be worth just as much tomorrow as it is today."

The immediate reaction to Nixon's speech was favorable. The stock market rose, the inflation rate fell during the year, and unemployment decreased from

6.1 percent to 5.1 percent. Ambrose described the effect of the speech on Nixon's image: "It surely made him look like the man in command, a bold and flexible leader willing to abandon a lifetime position when the reality demanded it." When all controls were finally lifted in the spring of 1974, however, the situation, in Nixon's own words, "was far from pleasant." In fact, Nixon admitted in his memoirs that the decision to impose economic controls was "wrong."

NIXON'S ADDRESS IN THE SOVIET UNION

Richard Nixon spoke on television from Moscow to the people of the Soviet Union on May 28, 1972. In "A World Free of Fear" he presented his views on international relations to the Soviet people without interruption or censorship. He also demonstrated the effective use of an emotional conclusion. According to Safire the speech was built upon "three images rooted in the Russian character. The first, the 'mushroom rain' that greeted him on his arrival in Moscow, a sunshower that makes the mushrooms grow, a good omen to Russians. . . . Second, a story of a traveler who wanted to know how far he was from town, and was only answered by a woodsman after he had established the length of his stride. Third, the reference to Tanya, a Leningrad heroine whose story moved the Russians the way Anne Frank's moves us." Each of these themes had a different genesis. Harriet Klosson, wife of the deputy chief of mission at the U.S. Embassy in Moscow, suggested the idea that a good omen had greeted Nixon upon his arrival. She told the story to Safire who relayed it to Price, who worked it into the speech. The woodsman tale had been told by Leonid Brezhnev to Henry Kissinger who passed it on to Price. A tour guide told Nixon about Tanya, the only member of her family to survive the Nazi siege of Leningrad, and he ended his speech by quoting from the twelve-year-old girl's diary: "All are dead. Only Tanya is left." He concluded: "As we work toward a more peaceful world, let us think of Tanya and of the other Tanyas and their brothers and sisters everywhere. Let us do all that we can to insure that no other children will have to endure what Tanya did and that your children and ours, all the children of the world, can live their lives together in friendship and in peace."

Ray Price reported that Nixon's insistence that Brezhnev's translator rather than his own be utilized during the broadcast added dramatic impact to the presentation. Viktor Sukhodrev, according to Price, "used his exceptionally expressive voice almost as a musical instrument, catching all the nuances of tone and inflection. . . . The fact that the voice that the Russian audience followed was Viktor's probably added substantially to its effectiveness." Brezhnev told Nixon that the mention of Tanya brought tears to his eyes. Other Americans living in Moscow reported the same tearful response from those Russians with whom they were viewing the speech. Clearly Nixon had analyzed his audience correctly.

NIXON'S SPEECHES ON WATERGATE

Three major radio and television addresses by President Nixon failed to convince the American people of his innocence in the Watergate matter. The televised investigation chaired by Senator Sam Ervin, the confessions resulting from the sentencing tactics of Judge John Sirica, the House Judiciary Committee's televised hearings, and Nixon's own words transcribed from tapes made in his offices proved to be far more persuasive than Nixon's rhetorical strategy of denial, and they ultimately forced his resignation. Throughout this period Nixon's supporters kept hoping for another "Checkers' speech, but that speech had come within a few days of the disclosure of Nixon's fund, and the facts of the case provided Nixon with a strong basis for his defense. This time Nixon did not offer a major address on Watergate until ten months after the burglary, and this time the facts were against him.

"Watergate Investigations"

During the week of April 9, 1973, Attorney General Richard Kleindienst reported to Nixon that John Ehrlichman, Bob Haldeman, and John Mitchell were indictable for various offenses before and after the Watergate burglary. Nixon had to act before further developments involved him personally in the affair. Regretfully he summoned Haldeman and Ehrlichman to Camp David and asked them to resign.

Nixon also invited Ray Price to Camp David that weekend to write a speech explaining to the public what had happened. Through Ron Zeigler, Nixon told Price what he wanted to say: that he had been given assurances that none of those close to him had been involved, that since March, when he had heard from John Dean that there was potential wrongdoing at a higher level, he had tried to investigate "this bizarre, senseless, wrong activity," and that the man at the top must assume responsibility for what happens in his organization. He wanted Price to point out that although it was important to investigate and punish the guilty, it was equally important to "get on with the nation's business."

Nixon felt so distraught that he considered resigning the presidency. Conferring with Price, Nixon's mind kept drifting away from the speech he did not want to give. Finally, his voice "flat, distant, defeated," he turned to Price and said, "If you think I should resign, just write it into the next draft, and I'll do it." Only by mentioning the unfinished business Nixon wanted to accomplish and the probable inability of Vice President Agnew to see it through, did Price encourage Nixon to remain in office.

William Benoit analyzed a number of rhetorical strategies used by Nixon in his Watergate speeches and press statements. Three important strategies he noted in this first address on Watergate were "emphasizing investigations," "shifting blame," and "refocusing attention." Nixon first portrayed himself as a tireless investigator, attempting to find out what really happened. He said that he was "determined that we should get to the bottom of the matter and that the truth should be fully brought out—no matter who was involved." By describing all that he had done to bring out the facts, Nixon implied that he personally had nothing to hide. He then attempted to shift the blame for the burglary and the cover-up to others. Although he protested that he wanted to avoid "any action that would appear to reflect on innocent people," he announced the resignations of Haldeman, Ehrlichman, Kleindienst, and Dean. The juxtaposition of the announcement of their resignations immediately following the statements that he had recently learned that facts had been concealed "from the public, from you, and from me," suggested that the perpetrators had been asked to resign. Finally, Nixon tried to focus public attention on other presidential activities and listed a number of goals that he hoped to accomplish. But his strategy did not work. Neither did his attempt to shift blame onto others. Nixon's reputation as the man in charge, most recently enhanced in the speech when he talked about how he was taking over the investigations, proved far stronger than his denials. Many listeners thought he might have directed the Watergate burglary himself. Fifty-four percent of the public polled by Harris did not believe that Nixon's own advisors lied to him to keep him from understanding the cover-up.

The basic problem with Nixon's speech was that he was not telling the truth. As he wrote later, he had known "some of the details" of the cover-up before March 21, and when he became aware of their implications, he "embarked upon an increasingly desperate search for ways to limit the damage to my friends, to my administration, and to myself." Nixon recognized that he had merely offered excuses: "They were not explanations of how a President of the United States could so incompetently allow himself to get in such a situation. That was what the people really wanted to know, and that was what my April 30 speech and all the other public statements I made about Watergate while I was President failed to tell them." By August 1973, Gallup reported that only 31 percent of the public thought the President was handling his job well.

"Watergate II"

Resolved to fight back, at 2 A.M., August 7, Nixon began a six-page outline of the main points he would cover in a second televised address designed to put Watergate behind him once and for all. The next day he asked Alexander Haig, who had taken Haldeman's position in the White House, to poll his staff on what he should say in his speech. Their suggestions ranged from "*mea culpas*" to a "two-fisted hard-line approach." On August 9, Nixon went to Camp David where he continued working on the speech with Ray Price and Patrick Buchanan. Not until August 14, when the speech had gone through eleven drafts, was Nixon satisfied.

Nixon attracted a large television audience on the evening of August 15, but he almost immediately disappointed his listeners by saying, "I shall not attempt to deal tonight with the various charges in detail." He provided instead a "perspective from the standpoint of the Presidency.'' Barry Brummett has pointed out the difficulty Nixon faced by approaching the topic as a problem of the presidency. The office of president was not in trouble; the holder of the office was. Nixon had to defend himself and he had to supply facts in support of his position. His word was not enough.

Nixon explained why he was unwilling to turn his taped conversations over to the Special Prosecutor or to the Senate Investigating Committee ''to help prove the truth of what I have said.'' Despite the strong case he made for confidentiality, many thought Nixon did not want to surrender the tapes because they would disprove what he had claimed. Thus the Scripps-Howard papers that usually supported Nixon editorialized: ''people with nothing to hide do not hide things.''

Since Nixon was guilty of many of the offenses he denied, he could not offer proof of innocence. He might have admitted what had happened, apologized, promised he would do better in the future, and ask the public's forgiveness. This was the route suggested by some supporters who, admittedly, did not know how much Nixon would have to confess. But Nixon's assertions of innocence, when compared to the hours of testimony the public had already heard, did little to exonerate him. The most common complaint about Nixon's speech was that he offered nothing new. Sixty-one percent of the audience were ''dissatisfied'' with his explanation.

On October 12, the Court of Appeals ruled that Nixon had to turn over to Judge Sirica nine tapes that Special Prosecutor Archibald Cox had requested. Attempting to preserve the principle of confidentiality, however, Nixon offered a compromise. He would release edited transcripts of the relevant materials to Cox and Senator John Stennis, a well respected Democrat. They could listen to the tapes to verify the accuracy of the material Nixon turned over. Cox rejected the offer and Nixon felt he had no option but to fire him. When Elliot Richardson and his deputy, William Ruckelshaus, resigned rather than carry out the order to fire Cox, Solicitor General Robert Bork accepted the responsibility and dismissed Cox.

''Presidential Tape Recordings''

The pressure on Nixon to release the tapes grew throughout the spring of 1974. On April 11, 1974, the House Judiciary Committee subpoenaed forty-two tapes relating to Nixon's role in Watergate. On April 16, Special Prosecutor Leon Jaworski asked a federal district court to subpoena sixty-three White House conversations to use as evidence against accused Watergate cover-up conspirators. By the end of April, five different subpoenas for tapes had been served on the President. Nixon searched for a dramatic way to end the requests for tapes and to dispose of the Watergate issue. The route he chose proved disastrous.

On April 29, 1974, Nixon offered his third televised address about Watergate, announcing that he was making public more than 1,200 pages of transcribed tape recordings of his personal conversations about Watergate. The transcripts included most of the conversations requested by the Judiciary Committee. Nixon claimed that "everything that is relevant is included—the rough as well as the smooth." To prepare the audience for what they would read in the transcripts, Nixon predicted that different readers would emphasize different things: "From the beginning, I have said that in many places on the tapes there were ambiguities—a statement and comments that different people with different perspectives might interpret in drastically different ways—but although the words may be ambiguous, though the discussions may have explored many alternatives, the record of my actions is totally clear now."

As the transcripts were read in their entirety, many of Nixon's supporters changed their minds. The *Chicago Tribune* declared: "The evidence against Mr. Nixon is in his own words, made public at his own direction. . . . It is saddening and hard to believe that for the first time in our history it is better that the President leave office than fight to keep it." Republicans in Congress quickly retreated from their previous statements of support. John Ashbrook spoke for many of his Congressional colleagues when he said, "I listened to him on television last Monday night and for the first time in a year I believed him. Then I read the March 21st transcript and it was incredible, unbelievable."

The House Judiciary Committee voted twenty-seven to eleven on July 27, 1974, to impeach Nixon for obstructing the Watergate investigation. On July 29, by vote of twenty-eight to ten, the committee declared that the President had abused the powers of the presidency, and on July 30, they charged that by defying the committee's requests for tapes and documents, Nixon had committed an impeachable offense.

NIXON'S RESIGNATION SPEECH

A unanimous Supreme Court ruled in *United States v. Nixon* that Nixon had to turn over to Special Prosecutor Leon Jaworski the sixty-four tapes he had subpoenaed. In preparing the tapes for submission to Jaworski. Fred Buzhardt, assistant to James St. Clair, who was handling Nixon's defense, heard a taped conversation between Nixon and Haldeman in which Haldeman told the President that John Mitchell had probably been aware of the Watergate operation from the beginning, and that the FBI was about to trace presidential campaign funds to the Watergate burglars. Nixon agreed with Haldeman that the CIA should be used to tell the FBI to drop their investigation and "don't go any further into this case period!" The tape showed Nixon guilty of obstructing justice and proved that he had lied about his efforts to get to the bottom of the affair. Buzhardt reported to St. Clair that the tape was the "smoking pistol" that Nixon supporters had dreaded and Nixon opponents had been searching for. St. Clair recognized the significance of the June 23 tape and told Nixon he would have to make it public immediately since it contained evidence of a crime. Nixon agreed reluctantly to release the tape on Monday, August 5, with a statement that the tape was "at variance" with certain of his previous statements. Nixon admitted that "those arguing my case, as well as those passing judgment on the case, did so with information that was incomplete and in some respects erroneous. This was a serious act of omission for which I take full responsibility and which I deeply regret."

Those few newspapers that had remained on Nixon's side throughout the revelations of the past two years immediately called for his resignation or impeachment in the light of the most recent disclosure. John Rhodes, the Republican minority leader in the House, announced that unless the President resigned, he would vote on the House floor for Article I of the Impeachment Articles, that Nixon had acted to obstruct justice. On Tuesday afternoon, Nixon decided that resignation was the only realistic course of action left to him and he told Haig to notify Ray Price to begin work on a statement: "Not a breast-beating *mea culpa*, not a speech proclaiming a guilt that he did not feel—but a healing speech, one that would help rally the country to his successor."

Nixon returned a draft to Price on Wednesday with the scribbled notation that he had met with Congressional leaders of both parties, and they had unanimously advised him that he did not have the support of Congress "for difficult decisions affecting peace abroad, and our fight against inflation at home." Nixon had written these words before the meeting had actually taken place, but he knew what he was going to be told. No more than a dozen representatives would support him in the House and, perhaps, a like number in the Senate.

In the margin of the Price draft Nixon wrote, "I have never been a quitter. To leave office is abhorrent to every instinct in my body," and Price added these words to the speech. Nixon also asked Price to look up a favorite quotation by Theodore Roosevelt that Nixon had given copies of to friends after his 1962 defeat for the governorship of California. In a speech delivered at the Sorbonne in 1910, Roosevelt said that it was not the critic who counts, but the man in the arena "whose face is marred by dust and sweat and blood; who strives valiantly . . . and who at the worst, if he fails, at least fails while daring greatly, so that his place shall never be with those cold and timid souls who know neither victory nor defeat." Price placed the emphasis of the quotation on the "man in the arena" and not on the "critic" or the "timid souls" and Nixon used it in his speech.

Throughout Wednesday evening and Thursday morning, Nixon called Price at his home to offer suggestions that Price incorporated into the speech. He wanted the speech to look to the future. He suggested words like: "We've started to limit nuclear arms between the US and the USSR. But our goal must be not just limitation of nuclear arms, but these terrible weapons that could destroy civilization as we know it must be destroyed." In his final telephone call on Thursday morning, Nixon instructed Price not to consult with his other advisers on the content of the speech because, "On this one, I just want to say the things that are in my heart. I want to make this *my* speech." By early afternoon, the speech was ready for delivery.

At 9 P.M. on August 8, 1974, Nixon went before an audience of 110 million to become the first President ever to resign his office. He spent little time on regret: "I regret deeply any injuries that may have been done in the course of the events that led to this decision. I would say only that if some of my judgments were wrong—and some were wrong—they were made in what I believed at the time to be the best interest of the Nation." Given that he faced criminal prosecution as he spoke, it is not surprising that Nixon never specified which of his judgments were wrong and never admitted that any of his deeds were unlawful.

Some critics have complained that Nixon failed to offer the real reason for his resignation. In Nixon's mind, he was leaving because he had lost his political base. If his supporters in Congress had remained steadfast in spite of the obstruction of justice heard in the Nixon-Haldeman tape, he would not have resigned. He was convinced that his predecessors had done the same or worse. His fault had been that he had taped himself talking about it. He was not resigning because he had committed a crime, but because he did not have enough support in Congress to continue.

Except for those who felt the President had not gone far enough in explaining his downfall, reaction to the speech and to the resignation was generally favorable. *Newsweek* reported that Nixon left office "with as much grace as he could muster and as much face as he could save." Gallup reported that 79 percent thought that Nixon had done the right thing by resigning; only 13 percent thought he should have remained in office. By a majority of 55 percent to 37 percent, the public thought he should not have to answer criminal charges.

CONCLUSION

In a radio address, "The Nature of the Presidency," delivered on September 19, 1968, during the presidential campaign, Nixon described how a president should act. Had he followed his own advice, he might never have had to resign. In the campaign speech he said, "The next president must unite America. He must calm its anger, ease its terrible frictions, and bring its people together once again in peace and mutual respect." In his First Inaugural Address and to a lesser extent in his first Vietnam speech, he attempted to bring people together and he succeeded. In his Second Inaugural Address and in his speech on Cambodia, he antagonized his enemies and he failed.

In that same 1968 campaign speech Nixon said: "The president has a responsibility . . . to lay out all the facts, and to explain not only why he chose as he did but also what it means for the future. Only through an open, candid dialogue with the people can a President maintain his trust and his leadership." On November 2, 1969, Nixon laid out the facts on Vietnam, just as he later presented the facts on wage and price controls. He gained the public's support for his policies. In December 1972, he did not talk to America about the massive bombing of North Vietnam, he failed to discuss his plans for reorganizing the executive branch, and he lost the confidence of the people and greatly increased the number of his enemies in Congress. His speeches on Watergate were anything but open and candid. Although he used many effective rhetorical strategies (extensive preparation, attention-getting introductions, emotional conclusions, a simple style and structure) that had proven successful on previous occasions, his Watergate speeches failed to save his presidency because he had squandered what he rightly called in his radio address "one of a President's greatest resources . . . the moral authority of his office." Twenty years later he was still trying to make up for his mistake. He died on April 22, 1994, and was buried next to his wife at the Nixon Library.

RHETORICAL SOURCES

Archival Materials

There are three main sources of Nixon materials: the Nixon Presidential Materials Project in Alexandria, Virginia, the pre-presidential papers at the Los Angeles branch of the National Archives in Laguna Nigel, California, and the Nixon Library and Birthplace in Yorba Linda, California. The Presidential Materials Project, operated by the National Archives, contains all the papers, documents, and correspondence from the 1969–1974 presidential terms. Of special interest are the President's Personal Files, the President's Office Files, the papers of his major staff members, and the Nixon White House tapes, some of which have been transcribed. Copies of important campaign and presidential speeches can be purchased. The western branch of the National Archives at Laguna Nigel houses more than 800 boxes of Nixon's pre-presidential papers, chronicling Nixon's early political career and years as vice president. The Nixon Library and Birthplace in Yorba Linda, which houses an archive containing drafts of his post-presidential books and speeches, opened in 1994. The library offers exhibits that feature taped speeches, and a large display traces the development of the "Silent Majority" speech from its origin in a rejected draft proposed by the National Security Council to the final version written solely by the President. For collections of Nixon's speeches, see:

Nixon, Richard M. *Public Papers of the Presidents: Richard Nixon.* (*PPP*). 6 Vols.
    Washington, DC: Government Printing Office, 1969–1974.
Vital Speeches of the Day. (*VS*). (Bimonthly).

Autobiographies

Nixon, Richard M. *Six Crises.* Garden City, NY: Doubleday, 1962.
————. *RN: The Memoirs of Richard Nixon.* New York: Grosset and Dunlap, 1978.
————. *In the Arena.* New York: Simon and Schuster, 1990.

Rhetorical Studies

Ambrose, Stephen E. *Nixon: The Education of a Politician, 1913–1962*. New York: Simon and Schuster, 1987.

———. *Nixon: The Triumph of a Politician, 1962–1972*. New York: Simon and Schuster, 1989.

———. *Nixon: Ruin and Recovery, 1973–1990*. New York: Simon and Schuster, 1991.

Anson, Robert S. *Exile: The Unquiet Oblivion of Richard M. Nixon*. New York: Simon and Schuster, 1984.

Barber, James D. *The Presidential Character: Predicting Performance in the White House*. Englewood Cliffs, NJ: Prentice-Hall, 1972.

Bochin, Hal W. *Richard Nixon: Rhetorical Strategist*. Westport CT: Greenwood Press, 1990.

Brodie, Fawn M. *Richard Nixon: The Shaping of His Character*. New York: Norton, 1981.

Casper, Dale E. *Richard M. Nixon: A Bibliographic Exploration*. New York: Garland, 1988.

Evans, Rowland, and Robert Novak. *Nixon in the White House: The Frustration of Power*. New York: Random House, 1971.

Hart, Roderick P. *Verbal Style and the Presidency: A Computer-Based Analysis*. Orlando, FL: Academic Press, 1984.

Keogh, James. *President Nixon and the Press*. New York: Funk and Wagnalls, 1972.

McGinniss, Joe. *The Selling of the President, 1968*. New York: Trident Press, 1969.

Mankiewicz, Frank. *Perfectly Clear: Nixon from Whittier to Watergate*. New York: Harper and Row, 1973.

Mazo, Earl, and Stephen Hess. *Nixon: A Political Portrait*. New York: Harper and Row, 1968.

Parmet, Herbert S. *Richard Nixon and His America*. Boston: Little, Brown, 1990.

Price, Raymond. *With Nixon*. New York: Viking Press, 1977.

Safire, William. *Before the Fall: An Insider's View of the Pre-Watergate White House*. New York: Doubleday, 1975.

Sulzberger, Cyrus L. *The World of Richard Nixon*. New York: Prentice-Hall, 1987.

White, Theodore. *Breach of Faith: The Fall of Richard Nixon*. New York: Atheneum, 1975.

Wicker, Tom. *One of Us: Richard Nixon and the American Dream*. New York: Random House, 1991.

Wills, Garry. *Nixon Agonistes*. Boston: Houghton-Mifflin, 1970.

Witcover, Jules. *The Resurrection of Richard Nixon*. New York: G. P. Putnam's Sons, 1970.

Rhetorical Monographs

Baudhuin, E. Scott. "From Campaign to Watergate: Nixon's Communication Image." *Western Speech* 38 (Summer 1974): 182–89.

Benoit, William L. "Richard M. Nixon's Rhetorical Strategies in his Public Statements on Watergate." *Southern Speech Communication Journal* 47 (Winter 1982): 192–211.

Bochin, Hal W. "President Richard Nixon's First Inaugural Address, 1969." In *The Inaugural Addresses of Twentieth-Century American Presidents*, edited by Halford Ryan, 209–22. Westport, CT: Praeger, 1993.

Brummett, Barry. "Presidential Substance: The Address of August 15, 1973." *Western Speech* 39 (Fall 1975): 249–59.

Campbell, Karlyn K. "An Exercise in the Rhetoric of Mythical America." In *Critiques of Contemporary Rhetoric*, edited by Karlyn K. Campbell, 50–57. Belmont, CA: Wadsworth, 1972.

Carpenter, Ronald H., and Robert V. Seltzer. "Nixon, *Patton*, and a Silent Majority Sentiment about the Viet Nam War." *Central States Speech Journal* 25 (Summer 1974): 105–10.

Chapel, Gage William. "Speechwriting in the Nixon Administration." *Journal of Communication* 26 (Spring 1976): 65–72.

Condit, Celeste Michelle. "Richard Milhous Nixon." In *American Orators of the Twentieth Century: Critical Studies and Sources*, edited by Bernard K. Duffy and Halford Ryan, 323–30. Westport, CT: Greenwood, 1987.

Fisher, Walter R. "Reaffirmation and Subversion of the American Dream." *Quarterly Journal of Speech* 59 (April 1973): 160–67.

Gibson, James W., and Patricia K. Felkins. "A Nixon Lexicon." *Western Speech* 38 (Summer 1974): 190–98.

Gonchar, Ruth M., and Dan F. Hahn. "The Rhetorical Predictability of Richard M. Nixon." *Today's Speech* 19 (Fall 1971): 3–13.

Gregg, Richard B., and Gerard Hauser. "Richard Nixon's April 30, 1970 Address on Cambodia: The 'Ceremony' of Confrontation." *Speech Monographs* 40 (April 1973): 167–81.

Hahn, Dan F., and Ruth Gonchar. "Richard Nixon and Presidential Mythology." *Journal of Applied Communication Research* 1 (Winter-Spring 1973): 25–48.

Harrell, Jackson, B. L. Ware, and Wil A. Linkugel. "Failure of Apology in American Politics: Nixon on Watergate." *Speech Monographs* 42 (November 1975): 245–61.

Harris, Barbara Ann. "The Inaugural of Richard Milhous Nixon: A Reply to Robert L. Scott." *Western Speech 34* (Summer 1970): 231–34.

Hart, Roderick P. "Absolutism and Situation: Prolegomena to a Rhetorical Biography of Richard M. Nixon." *Communication Monographs* 43 (August 1976): 204–28.

Hill, Forbes. "Conventional Wisdom—Traditional Form—The President's Message of November 3, 1969." *Quarterly Journal of Speech* 58 (December 1972): 373–86.

Hillbruner, Anthony. "Archetype and Signature: Nixon and the 1973 Inaugural." *Central States Speech Journal* 25 (Fall 1974): 169–81.

Hollihan, Thomas A. "President Richard Nixon's Second Inaugural Address, 1973." In *The Inaugural Addresses of Twentieth-Century American Presidents*, ed. Halford Ryan, 223–32. Westport CT: Praeger, 1993.

Jablonski, Carol J. "Richard Nixon's Irish Wake: A Case of Generic Transference." *Central States Speech Journal* 30 (Summer 1979): 164–73.

Katula, Richard A. "The Apology of Richard M. Nixon." *Today's Speech* 23 (Fall 1975): 1–5.

Kaufer, David S. "The Ironist and Hypocrite as Presidential Symbols: A Nixon-Kennedy Analog." *Communication Quarterly* 27 (Fall 1979): 20–26.

King, Andrew A., and Floyd Douglas Anderson. "Nixon, Agnew and the 'Silent Majority': A Case Study in the Rhetoric of Polarization.'' *Western Speech* 35 (Fall 1971): 243–55.

King, Robert L. ''Transforming Scandal into Tragedy: A Rhetoric of Political Apology.'' *Quarterly Journal of Speech* 71 (August 1985): 289–301.

Larson, Charles U., ed., ''A Pentadic Analysis of Richard Nixon and Watergate.'' *Speaker and Gavel* 15 (Fall 1977): 1–15.

Linkugel, Wil A., and Dixie Lee Cody. ''Nixon, McGovern, and the Female Electorate.'' *Today's Speech* 21 (Fall 1973): 25–32.

Newman, Robert P. ''Under the Veneer: Nixon's Vietnam Speech of November 3, 1969.'' *Quarterly Journal of Speech* 56 (April 1970): 169–78.

Rasmussen, Karen. ''Nixon and the Strategy of Avoidance.'' *Central States Speech Journal* 24 (Fall 1973): 193–202.

Rosenfield, Lawrence W. ''August 9, 1974: The Victimage of Richard Nixon.'' *Communication Quarterly* 24 (Fall 1976): 19–23.

Ryan, Halford Ross. ''Senator Richard M. Nixon's Apology for the ''Fund.' '' In *Oratorical Encounters*, edited by Halford Ross Ryan. Westport, CT: Greenwood Press, 1988.

Scott, Robert L. ''Rhetoric that Postures: An Intrinsic Reading of Richard M. Nixon's Inaugural Address.'' *Western Speech* 34 (Winter 1970): 46–52.

Smith, Craig Allen. ''President Richard M. Nixon and the Watergate Scandal.'' In *Oratorical Encounters*, edited by Halford Ryan, 201–26. Westport, CT: Greenwood, 1988.

Smith, Craig R. ''Richard Nixon's 1968 Acceptance Speech as a Model of Dual Audience Adaptation.'' *Today's Speech* 19 (Fall 1971): 15–22.

Stelzner, Herman G. ''The Quest Story and Nixon's November 3, 1969 Address.'' *Quarterly Journal of Speech* 57 (April 1971): 163–72.

Vartabedian, Robert A. ''Nixon's Vietnam Rhetoric: A Case Study of Apologia as Generic Paradox.'' *Southern Speech Communication Journal* 50 (Summer 1985): 366–81.

Wilson, Gerald L. ''A Strategy of Explanation: Richard M. Nixon's August 8, 1974, Resignation Speech.'' *Communication Quarterly* 24 (Summer 1976): 14–20.

Chronology of Significant Presidential Persuasions

''The Nature of the Presidency,'' New York City, September 19, 1968. *VS*, 19: 11–15.

First Inaugural Address, Washington, D.C., January 20, 1969. *PPP*, I: 1–4; *VS*, 35: 226–28.

Address to the Nation on Vietnam (''Silent Majority''), Washington, D.C., November 3, 1969. *PPP*, I: 901–9; *VS*, 36: 166–70.

''Cambodia,'' Washington, D.C., April 30, 1970. *PPP*, II: 405–10; *VS*, 36: 450–52.

''A New Economic Policy,'' Washington, D.C., August 15, 1971. *PPP*, III: 886–91; *VS*, 37: 674–76.

Address to the People of the Soviet Union,'' Moscow, USSR, May 28, 1972. *PPP*, IV: 629–32; *VS*, 38: 649–50.

Second Inaugural Address, Washington, D.C., January 20, 1973. *PPP*, V: 12–15; *VS*, 39: 266–68.

Address to the Nation about the Watergate Investigations, Washington, D.C. April 30, 1973. *PPP*, V: 328–33; *VS*, 39: 450–52.

Second Address to the Nation about the Watergate Investigations, Washington, D.C.,
     August 15, 1973. *PPP*, V: 691–98; *VS*, 39: 674–77.
"Presidential Tapes and Materials," Washington, D.C., April 29, 1974. *PPP*, VI: 389–
     97; *VS*, 40: 482–86.
"Resignation," Washington, D.C., August 8, 1974. *PPP*, VI: 626–30; *VS*, 40: 643–44.
"The Promise of Peace," Washington, D.C., March 11, 1992. *VS*, 58: 540–53.

Craig Allen Smith

Gerald R. Ford
(1913–   )

Just a little straight talk among friends.

"Orator Gerald Ford" is an oxymoron. Ford was no orator. He was a speaker or, perhaps more accurately, a talker. One colleague referred to him as the consummate Congressional committeeman. His words blended with those of thousands of other congressmen, before and since, and evaporated into the rhetorical cloud cover of American politics unheard and unnoticed as they helped to shape public dialogue. But when Richard Nixon selected Ford to replace the disgraced Spiro Agnew as vice president, and then later resigned the presidency, the consummate committeeman and forgettable talker assumed the bully pulpit of the American presidency, and his words suddenly commanded the attention of the entire world. But this book is not an Orators' Hall of Fame. It is based on the premise that twentieth-century presidential leadership hinges on the President's persuasive abilities. In that spirit, this chapter seeks neither to praise Ford nor to bury him, but to explain the character of his rhetoric and its contribution to the evolution of presidential leadership.

The future president was born in Omaha, Nebraska, on July 14, 1913, and christened Leslie L. King, Jr. His parents' stormy marriage ended in 1915, and he and his mother moved to Grand Rapids, Michigan, to be near her parents. There she met and married Gerald R. Ford, who later adopted Leslie L. King, Jr., as Gerald R. Ford, Jr. The boy was known, understandably, as Junior for many years. They moved into their first house, in a more prosperous part of town, when Junior was six. At about this time he developed a stuttering problem that Ford, himself, attributes to his parents' and teachers' efforts to curb his ambidexterity (he is left-handed when sitting and right-handed when standing up).

Very little in Ford's early childhood contributed to a rigid personality: He experienced two fathers, two names, lived in two towns, attended two schools, relied part of the time on each hand to do things, and false-started many of his words—all by the age of ten. Every child needs structure and stability, especially in the face of so many potentially traumatic changes. Gerald Ford found his personal foundation for life in four things. The first and most important was his parents' example: love, discipline, and community involvement. The second was his mother's decision to take him to the Grace Episcopal Church, rather than the Dutch Calvinist churches that dominated Grand Rapids. Whereas the Calvinists emphasized the Ten Commandments and punishment, the Episcopalians emphasized mercy, repentance, and forgiveness of sins. The third source of Ford's personal approach to life was the philosophy he developed around the time he was in seventh grade. He wrote in his memoirs that "several of my classmates hated each other. Because of this, I developed a philosophy that has sustained me ever since. Everyone, I decided, had more good qualities than bad. If I understood and tried to accentuate those good qualities in others, I could get along much better. Hating or even disliking people because of their bad qualities, it seemed to me, was a waste of time." This personal philosophy seemed to find expression in competitive athletics, in which the struggles between persons' good qualities and bad qualities is more game rather than war.

FORD'S PRE-PRESIDENTIAL YEARS

Indeed, football is a useful metaphor for Ford's approach to life. It is a disciplined, rule-governed struggle between teams of people with both good and bad qualities. Each team has fans and supporters that urge them on and stand by them, even when hard work results in defeat. After each game the players shake hands, forgive each other their grudges, learn from their mistakes, and prepare for the next game. Moreover, football influenced Ford much as Hollywood influenced Ronald Reagan.

Gerald Ford was neither quarterback nor running back, but the center who snapped the ball to his more glorified teammates. Today's football emphasizes spectacular offense, but that was not Gerald Ford's kind of football. He played a style of football at the University of Michigan, developed by former coach Fielding "Hurry-up" Yost, that emphasized defense. Ford's team always chose to kick-off, they would punt on second or third down when inside their forty yard line, and they would punt on first down when near their own goal line; all so that their defense could force the opposing offense into mistakes. This approach to football and life reflects the often overlooked power to put others in the hot seat. As congressman, Ford could turn to others for ideas and then help to shape them. But that experience may have undercut his capacity to develop and advocate original ideas. As President, Ford would be known more for vetoing bills than for the legislation he enacted; and his most serious problems occurred when he chose to take the offensive.

After graduating from Michigan Ford took a full-time job as an assistant coach at Yale, where he was eventually admitted to the Law School. He passed the Michigan bar and began a law practice with his friend Philip Buchen, who would later serve him as a key presidential advisor. Their firm folded while Ford was in the Navy during World War II, and when he returned to Grand Rapids he joined the same law firm as Buchen.

Republicans were the majority party in Grand Rapids, and Republican politics were dominated by one Frank McKay. Ford regarded McKay as a "powerful, arrogant and dictatorial" man reliant on patronage and intimidation who treated idealistic young Republicans like Ford with contempt. Perhaps it was inevitable that the young Turks would challenge McKay, but it was Gerald Ford who hiked the ball. In 1941 he helped form an organization to challenge McKay's county machine. They succeeded by 1946. But McKay's protégé, Bartel "Barney" Jonkman, was still the Fifth District Congressman, and he was a staunch isolationist who opposed the Marshall Plan. The war had changed Ford from an isolationist to an internationalist. When no one else would run, Ford, with the tacit support of Michigan Senator Arthur H. Vandenberg, announced his candidacy for the U.S. House of Representatives just prior to the deadline in June 1948. It was his first attempt for elective office, and he was a clear underdog.

Ford's 1948 persuasive strategy could have been devised by Coach Yost. Backed up to his own goal line by charges of ineffectiveness, President Harry Truman punted to incumbent Republicans by using his nomination acceptance address to challenge the Congress to enact the Republican platform in a special session. With Jonckman in Washington for this "Turnip Session," Ford had an open field to run all over the district: He turned up at plant gates, picnics, and county fairs; he shook hands and made speeches during the primary campaign. One of Ford's fans was the senior partner of his law firm, a Democrat, who wanted Jonckman defeated. Ford continually punted to Jonckman to force mistakes. Ford proposed a debate and the congressman declined (improved field position on the exchange of punts). Then Jonckman alienated the United Auto Workers Union's Leonard Woodcock, who endorsed Ford (fumble, recovered by Ford). When the Grand Rapids *Press* published an editorial critical of Jonckman's isolationism and his attacks on Senator Vandenberg, Jonckman attacked the newspaper with predictable consequences (penalty on Jonckman). Finally, Jonckman's frustration led him to make desperate charges that Ford easily handled (careless pass, intercepted for a touchdown). Ford won the primary by a two-to-one margin and the Fifth District seat with 61 percent of the vote. The inexperienced young lawyer-athlete had won an impossible election handily by punting and playing defense.

Ford recalled that early in his Congressional career, a senior member advised him to choose between two alternative legislative styles. He could spend his time attending to the problems of the district or he could spend his time on the floor listening to the debate, mastering procedures, and building interpersonal networks. He chose to spend time on the floor because he had a good staff to handle his constituents' problems. His explanation of this choice is quintessential Ford. Elected officials need both constituent approval (defense) and legislative skills (offense). Had Ford's district been more competitive he might have emphasized constituent service. But because he was the solid choice of a Republican district whose political machine he had already dismantled, he could delegate constituent services to his defensive coaching staff.

Gerald Ford aspired to become Speaker of the House. To achieve that ambition he needed to become the head Republican in the House and to make Republicans the majority party in the House. So he became a coalition builder in the House, guided by his philosophy of emphasizing his colleagues' good points, their areas of agreement, and forgiveness of differences. Critical passages in his memoirs are devoted to three men who tried to steer the Republican party toward rigid conservatism: Joseph McCarthy, Barry Goldwater, and Spiro Agnew. Congressman Ford was an idealistic man with a pragmatic and moderate legislative style, and he quickly earned the respect of his colleagues.

During Ford's Congressional tenure young upstarts twice sought to replace Republican leaders and, as in Grand Rapids, Ford anchored their line. Ford tried to persuade minority leader Joe Martin to step down after the 1958 election, but he refused. Ford then hiked the ball to Indiana Representative Charles Halleck who defeated Martin for the leadership post. Barely four years later Ford edged Charles Hoeven for the chairmanship of the basically dormant House Republican Conference, which he then energized.

By mid-1964 Republicans were plagued by the narrow appeal of the Goldwater campaign, the aura of the Kennedy-Johnson mystique, and the leadership of Charlie Halleck, whom the young Turks perceived to be lacking the progressive, affirmative image they wanted for their party. Halleck had defeated Martin in 1959 by only four votes, and the 1964 losses deprived Halleck of several valued supporters; and his support of the 1964 Civil Rights Act cost him the support of some southern members. Perhaps more than that, television was changing the face of politics. Henry Scheele noted that "Halleck was a product of the smoke-filled room genre. He was hard-hitting, aggressive and irascible; a power broker of an era vanishing from the American scene," whereas "Ford, a model in his youth and in college, provided Republicans with a newer, fresher face during a period when style often supplanted substance." In the end, Ford attributed his victory over Halleck to then-Representative Robert Dole, his vice presidential running mate in 1976, who delivered three of the Kansas delegation's five votes.

Richard Nixon first asked Ford if he would consider the vice presidency in 1968. Ford declined because he expected Republicans to win easily the 41 seats needed to take control of the House and make him Speaker. Ford suggested that Nixon pick New York mayor John V. Lindsay, and he was disturbed by the nomination of one term Maryland governor Spiro T. Agnew. In the election democrats Hubert Humphrey and Edmund Muskie closed the gap, with American Independent party candidate George C. Wallace carrying the Deep South states that Barry Goldwater had won for the Republicans in 1964. Republicans gained only five seats in the House, and Ford remained Minority Leader. In 1972 Nixon was re-elected in a landslide, but when Republicans gained only thirteen seats in the House, Ford was again denied his dream of becoming Speaker of the House. He and Betty agreed that he would run for one more term in 1974, possibly resigning his leadership role, and then return to private life in January of 1977.

But by late August 1973, the Nixon administration was embroiled in the Watergate controversy. Several of the President's aides had resigned, the Ervin Committee had completed its hearings, and Special Prosecutor Archibald Cox was engaged in litigation to obtain the audio tapes of the President's White House conversations. Then, Vice President Agnew was charged with accepting bribes while Governor of Maryland. He resigned his office and, on October 12, President Nixon asked Ford to be vice president. Ford believed himself to have been Nixon's fourth choice, after Nixon had concluded that Democratic convert John Connolly of Texas would be difficult to confirm, and that either Nelson Rockefeller or Ronald Reagan would divide Republicans along ideological lines.

Before Ford's confirmation hearings could begin in either the Senate Rules Committee or the House Judiciary Committee, President Nixon fired Special Prosecutor Cox, Attorney General Elliot Richardson, and Assistant Attorney General William Ruckleshouse in the "Saturday Night Massacre" of October 20, 1973. Reaction to the President's action was swift, and bills of impeachment were introduced in the House. It was in this climate of fear, anger, and suspicion that Gerald Ford's confirmation hearings began.

Ford was easily confirmed, and his confirmation raises an interesting question: Did the vice presidential change from Spiro Agnew to Gerald Ford make the impeachment of Richard Nixon more likely? The answer is, probably so. Agnew had little experience with national and international issues, and he was new to Washington. Gerald Ford had been working on national and international issues in Washington for twenty-five years. Furthermore, the House and Senate held the keys to impeachment, and both houses were controlled by Democrats. Agnew was a polarizing rhetor who was either loved or despised, and few Congressional Democrats loved him. Thus Agnew's continuation in the vice presidency would have complicated impeachment for Congressional Democrats: whom should they prefer for President, a disgraced Nixon or an unprepared, divisive conservative? Ford's confirmation made the choice less difficult because he was a known entity, a centrist, a man with whom members had worked for years, and a man of unquestioned integrity. And when Richard Nixon resigned on August 8, 1974, lest he be impeached, Gerald R. Ford became the first unelected President of the United States.

THE COALITIONLESS PRESIDENT

Gerald Ford is the only President never to have been part of a national electoral coalition. Worse, he could not use his vice presidency to plan his presidency without appearing to be ambitious and disloyal. When Nixon did resign, he attributed it not to his own misconduct or guilt, but to his conclusion that he "might not have the support of the Congress." Nixon could have bequeathed to Ford the right to claim a governing coalition by accepting personal responsibility for his resignation. But Nixon's decision to save face undermined Ford; therefore, it was crucial for Ford to establish immediately both his stature as President and the viability of his governing coalition. But he needed to forge that governing coalition from the ashes of the Nixon presidency with few resources. However, Ford began his presidency by dealing with the problems of legitimacy, preparation, and public disenchantment. The approach he took in dealing with these problems affected the success of his transition period.

Remarks on Taking the Oath of Office

Inaugural addresses are not required, but it is awkward to take an oath of investiture without addressing one's followers. Gerald Ford's investiture on August 9, 1974, was unusually awkward, and his inaugural came in two parts. First came these remarks that were, in his words, "Not in Inaugural Address, not a fireside chat, not a campaign speech—just a little straight talk among friends." He acknowledged that he had not been elected, but neither had he made secret promises. The speech made four appropriate main points. The first was that those who had nominated and confirmed Ford "were of *both parties*, elected by *all the people* and acting under the *Constitution* in their name" [emphases added]. Second, he warned that "there is no way we can go forward except together and no way anybody can win by serving the people's urgent needs." Third, he differentiated himself from Johnson and Nixon with his statement that, "I believe that truth is the glue that holds government together, not only our Government but civilization itself." Fourth, he announced that "our long national nightmare is over"—and this became the speech's most famous passage.

Despite Ford's claim that this was not an Inaugural Address, it functioned as one. Karlyn Kohrs Campbell and Kathleen Hall Jamieson write that, "his speech established that the office had been vacated, constituted the audience as the people, rehearsed basic constitutional principles, invited investiture, and previewed Ford's approach to the presidency." This speech was Ford's first attempt to create an "us," and he did so gradually. The first half of the speech contained fourteen references to others—"those," "them," "others," and "governments officials"—and no references to "America," "God," "togetherness," or "the family of man." But the second half of the speech changed that fourteen-to-zero ratio to three-to-twelve. The transition point was his warning that "We must go forward together." Thereafter, Ford used "our" rather than "your" and "God," "America," and "together" rather than "Congress," "them," and individual presidents or officials. This shift in nouns was consistent with the substance of his message.

But Ford's references to people, institutions, and documents were swamped by the waves of personal self-references. Ford referred to himself—"I," "me," or "my"—no fewer than fifty-one times in this brief address. "I" outnumbered "we" three-to-one, and there was no discernible difference between the halves of the speech. There was no "we" at the beginning of his speech, there was only Gerald Ford standing alone. By the end of the speech there was, at least linguistically, a unified nation; but Ford continued to stand apart. Ford closed by pledging himself to the country in a way that minimized his accountability to anyone but himself. Notice the thirteen self-references in his conclusion:

With all the strength and all the good sense *I* have gained from life, with all the confidence of *my* family, *my* friends, and *my* dedicated staff impart to *me*, and with the good will of countless Americans *I* have encountered in recent visits to 40 states, *I* now solemnly reaffirm *my* promise *I* made to you last December 6: to uphold the Constitution, to do what is right as God gives me to see the right, and to do the very best *I* can for America. God helping *me*, *I* will not let you down, [emphases added].

Ford's pledge suggested a trusteeship model of accountability as opposed to a delegate model. This was perhaps an effective means of establishing that he was *personally* in charge of the executive branch but, unnecessarily, it made the wisdom, the conscience, and the judgment of this unelected citizen the guiding star of the nation. Campbell and Jamieson judged the speech a success, as it was; but even a welcome breeze can carry the seeds of misfortune.

Ford's First Address to Congress

If the remarks on August 9 began Ford's Inaugural Address, then his address to Congress three days later was a combination of inaugural and state of the union. Ford reiterated a personal self-definition that had characterized his earlier remarks:

I am not asking for conformity. *I am dedicated* to the two-party system, and you know which party *I belong* to. *I do not want* a honeymoon, *I want* a good marriage. *I want* progress, and *I want* problemsolving . . . *I believe* in the very decency and fairness of America. *I believe* in the integrity and patriotism of the Congress. And while *I am aware* of the House rule that no one ever speaks to the galleries, *I believe* in the first amendment and the absolute necessity of a free press [emphases added].

This, again, was a man standing alone with his convictions and his principles. This was neither the discourse of a party standard bearer or of a national leader proclaiming unity with the people; rather, it was the discourse of a solitary man still needing to prove, and to position, himself for his citizens. But neither was it the discourse of an insecure leader who needed to prove himself to himself. Ford did not recount past triumphs, he merely reaffirmed past pledges and articulated his core principles. The circumstances invited such affirmation, but because of the unusual number of self-references, the essential "we" failed to jell.

President Ford then huddled his team, called the play, and assured them that they could win with the back-up player. "Now *I* ask *you* to join with *me* in getting *this country* revved up and moving." This was necessary because of the underlying national consensus that Ford discerned during his vice presidential travels: "Everywhere I have been as Vice President, some 118,000 miles in 40 states and some 55 press conferences, the unanimous concern of Americans is inflation. For once the polls seem to agree." But where many presidents would have presented a grocery list of legislative ideas, Ford punted on first down and prepared to play defense. He challenged voters to elect representatives committed to the restraint of federal spending. He announced a domestic summit on the economy at which others could devise an economic plan. He literally asked Congress for help on health care—"why don't we write a good health bill," without making any attempt to define "good." And lest Congress underestimate his defensive prowess, he provided a toothless threat: "Tonight, obviously, is no time to threaten you with vetoes. But I do have the last recourse, and I am a veteran of many a veto fight. . . . Can't we do a better job by reasonable compromise? I hope we can." Vetoes should prove unnecessary, Ford averred, because "As President, within the limits of basic principles, my motto toward the Congress is communication, conciliation, compromise, and cooperation." Ford evidently liked alliteration.

The speeches of August 9 and 12 functioned as a two-part Inaugural: the first informal, the latter more formal. The pair of speeches struck Bernard Brock as paradoxical. Ford called for action but advanced no plan of action; he sought continuity but made a new beginning; he chose the high road of statesmanship but spoke in a plain style. Nevertheless, they seemed to work. When the Gallup Organization took the first public pulse on the new Ford presidency, 71 percent approved and only 3 percent disapproved. President Ford was off to a flying start. But then he decided to play offense in a way that focused the attention of the unjelled "we" on his personal judgment.

FORD'S PRESIDENTIAL PARDON SPEECHES

In August 1974, better than 80 percent of the public agreed that inflation was the most important problem, but they were deeply divided over Vietnam and Watergate. Military involvement in Vietnam had ended, but people argued about those who had avoided the draft: Many regarded them as traitors, while others felt that they had been vindicated. Meanwhile, many people felt that President Nixon should be tried and punished for his misconduct, while others argued that he had suffered enough. Because presidents have the constitutional authority to pardon, Ford had the authority to pardon Nixon and/or the draft evaders. But because presidents who pardon indiscriminately soon dissipate their credibility, presidents have normally explained and justified their pardons.

President Ford faced policy choices, whether to punish, to ignore, or to pardon Nixon and/or the draft evaders, and therefore rhetorical choices as to how to justify his policy decisions. Campbell and Jamieson regard pardoning as a rhetorical genre in which "The impersonal tone, the archaic language, reliance on legalistic terminology, and the formality of the document overpower individual style and give these documents a quaint sameness." Pardoning rhetoric has three key generic elements: "(1) acting in the presidential role as symbolic head of state; (2) demonstrating that this is an opportune time for action; and (3) justifying the pardon as for the public good." Any decision to pardon would be especially dicey for Ford, given his tenuous legitimacy; and neither pardon would prove politically safe.

Ford needed the support of the Nixon loyalists, especially those who served in the White House. They had been selected by H. R. Haldermann and were loyal to Nixon and, therefore, the object of widespread public suspicion; but they were the only people acquainted with the routines, the personal networks, and the intimate details and operations of the executive office. Ford's people needed to learn from the Nixon holdovers so that they could, in time, create a Ford administration. But Ford's need for the Nixon holdovers, and their disloyalty to him, would be a continuing problem. Chief of Staff and speechwriter Robert Hartmann was especially sensitive to this cleavage, for he believed that the holdovers regarded Ford not as President but as someone in place of the President, and therefore someone to be changed into another Nixon. Things would have been different if Ford had removed them, wrote Hartmann. But Ford needed their expertise, and he sought it on the basis of their shared devotion to Nixon. He therefore needed persuasive arguments that would (1) keep the Nixon loyalists on board, (2) establish a positive relationship with Congress, (3) maintain his favorable relations with the press, (4) bolster Republican morale during the ninety days of midterm campaigning, and (5) translate his public approval into solid support for his policy leadership.

The Vietnam Pardons

Many of Ford's advisors encouraged him to deal with the draft evaders to unify the country. He decided to do so at a previously scheduled address to the annual Veterans of Foreign Wars convention in Chicago, August 19, 1974, his first presidential address outside of Washington. A long-standing VFW member, Ford could expect an enthusiastic reception. His address alluded to his membership in several veterans' organizations and promised an open office door. He articulated their frustrations about federal support programs, he urged the improvement of VA hospitals, and he vowed to "humanize the VA." The text called for Ford to move directly to his support for the VFW's new commander, educational programs, the employment of veterans, democracy, free enterprise, and faith in America, and later to come out against discrimination and inflation. The prepared text was music to the veterans' ears, and their cheers were the first public affirmation of Ford's presidency.

But Ford surprised everyone (except speechwriter Hartmann) by inserting a secret section justifying selective pardons for draft evaders. The surprise enabled the President to make the announcement without press leaks, and it precluded counterargument by Alexander Haig, formerly Nixon's Chief of Staff, who opposed the plan and who wielded considerable influence over the holdovers. It also enabled Ford to wrap the unpopular policy decision in his rhetorical identification with veterans. Finally, Ford's insertion enabled him to demonstrate that his presidency would not polarize the country as had his predecessors. Gerald Ford wanted to be president of "all the people" and the VFW address dramatized that point.

Ford's handling of the announcement reflected his coalitional dilemmas. He had to enact the role of president and to complete the presidency inaugurated in 1973 while distinguishing his administration from that of Nixon. He did this by grounding his announcement in the positions of Richard Nixon, the Pentagon, and previous presidents. The Pentagon had differentiated "amnesty" from "pardon" in Congressional testimony. Both are presidential actions that presume punishable misconduct and guilt, and release the offender from punishment. But whereas "amnesty" *forgives* the offense and removes the penalty, often contingent on the performance of certain conditions; a "pardon" *affirms the guilt* as it removes the punishment. This semantic distinction would later complicate Ford's program of pardons contingent upon performance of public service because, unlike the Pentagon, Ford differentiated between "*blanket* amnesty" and "pardons *in individual cases.*"

The speech insert used a variety of techniques to advantage. Ford reaffirmed his personal moral opposition to blanket amnesty: "As minority leader of the House and recently as Vice President, I stated my strong conviction that unconditional, blanket amnesty for anyone who illegally evaded or fled military service is wrong. It is wrong." This drew upon the common ground established in his introduction, affirmed his link to Nixon's policy, and laid the foundation for a treatise on semantic distinctions. Then he differentiated his personal beliefs from his presidential responsibility and emphasized Divine, rather than public, accountability. "Yet, in my first words as President of all the people," said Ford, "I acknowledged a Power, higher than the people, Who commands not only righteousness but love, not only justice but mercy." His position was to be understood neither as a change of heart nor as political expedience, but as a consequence of his ascension to higher, transcendent responsibilities. As his stunned audience listened, Ford quickly invoked Presidents Lincoln and Truman, the American system of justice, the all-volunteer army, and "the urgent problem of how to bind up the Nation's wounds"—a powerful metaphor for his audience of war veterans. But the Power higher than the people had not told Ford how to implement an "earned pardon" [sic] program. He explained that the Attorney General, the Secretary of Defense and other government officials would report "the full spectrum of American opinion . . . consolidating the known facts and legal precedents."

After this review Ford himself would decide "how best to deal with the different kinds of cases—and there are differences." This phrase was a gamble. Unlike Nixon, Ford and the Pentagon acknowledged differences among individual cases. Ford could have invoked that testimony, but by stating Pentagon reasoning as his own presidential judgment he enhanced his authority without fear of official contradiction. The theme of "differences" permitted Ford to avoid announcing a universal policy, and it invited Americans to differentiate Ford from advocates of unconditional amnesty as well as from Nixon. Because Nixon had said that amnesty was impossible until all Americans had returned from Vietnam, Ford noted that "the last combatant was withdrawn [from Vietnam] over a year ago by President Nixon. But all, in a sense, are casualties, still abroad or absent without leave from the real America." Thus Ford's willingness to pardon became an extension of Nixon's effort to end the war.

It remained for Ford to justify desertion and evasion to those whose loved ones had been killed in combat, and he did so masterfully. He recalled presenting fourteen Congressional Medals of Honor to parents, widows, and children and he emphasized their youthfulness: "I kept thinking how young they were. The few citizens of our country who, in my judgment, committed the supreme folly of shirking their duty at the expense of others, were also very young. All of us who served in one war or another know very well that all wars are the glory of the young. In my judgment, these young Americans should have a second chance to contribute their fair share to the rebuilding of peace among ourselves and with all nations."

This passage united Ford, the VFW membership, the Vietnam heroes, and the offenders in a recollection of youth. The conventioneers were there precisely because they shared memories from their younger days. Many had been seriously injured and all had either had, or dreamed of, second chances to rebuild their lives. Ford's remarks invited them, perhaps for the first time, to consider the offenders as fellow casualties of war: "I ask all Americans who ever asked for goodness and mercy in their lives, who ever sought forgiveness for their trespasses, to join in rehabilitating all the casualties of the tragic conflict of the past." Ford announced that he was "throwing the weight of my Presidency into the scales of justice on the side of leniency" and he emphasized that "As I reject [blanket] amnesty, so I reject [blanket] revenge."

The earned re-entry program was begun, and Ford suffered less damage than might have been expected. Bernard Brock noted that "Even though the response of his immediate audience was chilly, Americans generally were pleased." At his first press conference, nine days after the announcement and nineteen days before the actual program was proclaimed, Ford was not asked a single question about it. In the VFW address President Ford faced supporters who were ego-involved in the issue, then violated their legitimate expectations, but he escaped with a "chilly" reaction from the immediate audience, he received generalized public support, and he was not challenged by the press.

The Nixon Pardon Speech

President Ford had told the nation on August 9 that "our long national nightmare is over," but nightmares must be shaken off in the dawn's early light, and Americans needed his help to exorcise the nightmare of Watergate. He underestimated press interest in Nixon at the first press conference, despite warnings to the contrary because "it seemed to me that it would be inappropriate for the press to ask questions about a man whose fate was up to the Special Prosecutor and the courts." But questions about Nixon dominated the press conference, and Ford considered it a disastrous turn of events. The press conference forced him to face the issue squarely for the first time. "I had to get the monkey off my back," he wrote in his memoirs. But how?

President Ford unexpectedly took to the air at 11:05 on Sunday morning, September 8, 1974, to announce "a full, free and absolute pardon unto Richard Nixon for all offenses against the United States which he, Richard Nixon, has committed or may have committed or taken part in during the period [of his Presidency]." To be sure, it was the President's prerogative to pardon Nixon, but this was a unique case, which required an adroit rhetorical strategy to retain the support of the Nixon holdovers and Republicans without becoming part of the Watergate melodrama.

The speech contained the formal pardon and then Ford's justification for the pardon. Unfortunately, the reasons given for the pardon varied widely. The proclamation itself contained four reasons: "[1] a trial could not fairly begin until a year or more has elapsed, [2] In the meantime, the tranquillity to which this nation has been restored . . . could be irreparably lost, [3] by the prospects of bringing to trial a former President of the United States, thereby [4] exposing to further punishment and degradation a man who has already paid the unprecedented penalty of relinquishing the highest elective office of the United States." But Ford's remarks invoked four other justifications. These included (5) the absence of precedent, (6) the possibility that Nixon "would be cruelly and excessively penalized either in preserving the presumption of his innocence or in obtaining a speedy determination of his guilt," (7) the possibility that "the courts might well hold that [he] had been denied due process, and the verdict of history would be even more inconclusive," and (8) Ford's own belief that "My conscience tells me it is my duty, not merely to proclaim domestic tranquillity but to use every means that I have to insure it." Why did Ford's reasons vary?

Presidents can experiment with generic expectations, but Ford could not do so without undermining his, and the pardon's, credibility. The granting of the pardon was an enactment of the presidential role, but one that drew attention to Ford's tenuous grip on presidential legitimacy. He could not afford to invoke his personal morals, beliefs, conscience, or feelings lest he subject them to public challenge. Nor could he cite either the absence of precedent nor the potential dismissal of the case, lest he encourage Nixon to fight on. But neither could he afford to detail Nixon's misdeeds, lest Nixon and his people rebuke Ford and divide the Republican base. The proclamation therefore spoke only of "certain acts or omissions occurring before his resignation" and "offenses against the United States" by "a man who has already paid the unprecedented penalty of relinquishing the highest elective office." This was a characterization of Watergate that Nixon could accept. But Ford needed to contextualize the Nixon-oriented proclamation for his other audiences. He therefore provided the other reasons not given in the formal proclamation. Ford gave these reasons, not so that Nixon would acquiesce to the pardon, but so that Ford's audiences would acquiesce to his presidential pardon.

Response to the Nixon pardon was quick. Nixon accepted it, but the House of Representatives did not. Nixon loyalists did not defect, but Ford's press secretary denounced it and resigned. The reaction from the press and the public was such that two days later White House public relations advisor William J. Baroody, Jr. wrote that "the incident is likely to leave a reservoir of distrust and ill feeling toward the President." But Baroody referred to yet a ninth argument for the pardon: It precluded self-incrimination as a reason for Nixon not to testify in Watergate trials. Baroody's memorandum clearly regarded this reason as central to Ford's granting of the pardon. Ford's memoirs concur, describing as his most important precedent a 1915 case in which a U.S. Attorney produced a presidential pardon to prevent editor George Burdick from claiming the protection of the Fifth Amendment. Ford realized that the Supreme Court's Burdick decision had reaffirmed the President's power to pardon, even for a crime denied by the accused and of which the accused had yet to be convicted. Even more important to Ford, "the Justices found that a pardon 'carries an imputation of guilt, acceptance, a confession to it.' These opinions were clear and unambiguous and had remained the law of the land for nearly sixty years." Ford could have mollified Nixon's critics by articulating this ninth reason, but not without tipping his hand to Nixon, dividing Republicans, and alienating the Nixon people who were keeping his administration afloat.

Ford's proclamation used the impersonal, legalistic, archaic, and formal language of the pardon genre. But his *remarks* used sixty-four first person singular references to describe his personal decisionmaking. Note the sixteen italicized first person references in the following four pivotal sentences: "*I* have come to a decision which *I* felt *I* should tell you and all of *my* fellow American citizens, as soon as *I* was certain in *my* own mind and in *my* own conscience that it is the right thing to do. . . . *My* conscience tells *me* clearly and certainly that *I* cannot prolong the bad dreams that continue to reopen a chapter that is closed. *My* conscience tells *me* that only *I*, as President, have the constitutional power to firmly shut and seal this book. . . . *I* do believe that right makes might and that if *I* am wrong, 10 angels swearing *I* was right would make no difference" (emphases added).

The remarks enabled Ford to enact the power of the presidency and to contrast

his concern for principle with the amoral pragmatism of the previous administration. But he invested, unnecessarily and unwisely, his personal credibility in
the Nixon pardon without disclosing the legal reasons that warranted his decision. Ford could have mitigated the damage to his personal reputation caused
by this flood of personal pronouns, but instead he assumed personal responsibility.

The Nixon pardon remarks have been judged a failure by Brock, Campbell,
and Jamieson and by Klumpp and Lukehart. Ford wrote in his memoirs that ''I
have to confess that my televised talk failed to emphasize adequately that I
wanted to give my full attention to grave economic and policy matters. Nor did
I explain as fully as I should have the strong judicial underpinnings, in particular,
the Supreme Court's ruling that acceptance of a pardon means admission of
guilt.'' Perhaps the surest measure of the speech's failure is that Ford credited
Hartmann with its authorship, while Hartmann credited Ford. But most critiques
inadequately considered Ford's coalitionless presidency as the political situation
that invited and constrained his rhetoric. Ford could have provided less support
for the Nixon perspective in his address, but who would have served in his
administration? The only people in the White House familiar with the policy
apparatus were Nixon holdovers.

Ford lost the 1976 election when Jimmy Carter parlayed a 1.6 million plurality
into a 57 electoral vote advantage. Ford would have won had he drawn another
0.2 percent of the vote in Ohio and an extra 1.6 percent in Wisconsin. Voters
cited the Nixon pardon more frequently than any other reason for preferring
Carter. However, the problem was not the Nixon pardon, it was Ford's pardon
rhetoric.

ECONOMIC RHETORIC

President Ford issued the pardons, in part, to turn America's attention from
Vietnam and Watergate to festering policy problems, the most serious of which
was inflation. He convened the first session of his Conference on Inflation on
September 5, 1974, and in early October he declared war on inflation in a speech
to a joint session of Congress. As he waged his WIN campaign (''Whip Inflation
Now''), it became painfully obvious that the economy had entered a recession,
which necessitated a major shift in policy in January 1975.

Economic Address to Congress

The President used his October 8, 1974 address to declare war on inflation,
and the war motif was clever in several respects. The metaphor had the potential
to elevate the President's role as commander-in-chief, it required executive-
legislative cooperation, and it sought total public mobilization. Ford sprinkled
military expressions, such as ''marching orders,'' throughout the speech, and he
developed the war motif toward the end of his speech: ''I say to you with all

sincerity that our inflation, our public enemy number one, will, unless whipped, destroy our country, our homes, our liberties, our property, and finally our national pride, as surely as any well-armed wartime enemy. I concede there will be no sudden Pearl Harbor to shock us into unity and to sacrifice, but I think we have had enough early warnings. . . . Will you enlist now? Together with discipline and determination, we will win.'' Although the President spoke of war and used military language, he did not use generic war rhetoric.

American audiences have heard many presidents call them to war, and there is a generic sameness to such addresses. Campbell and Jamieson have observed that presidents typically use a detailed narrative to explain the causes of the problem and to eliminate alternatives other than war. The narrative embodies the evidence and arguments for Congressional authorization of extraordinary presidential actions and exhorts the nation to mobilize. Where Ford might have used such a narrative to advantage, he said instead, ''I will not take your time today with the discussion of the origins of inflation and its bad effect on the United States.'' This decision probably stemmed from the diversity of expert advice he had received and the fact that ''There is only one point on which all advisers have agreed: We must whip inflation right now.'' Unless his advisers agreed on the causes of inflation, he would be hard pressed to advance a coherent narrative.

The President's address identified ten fronts on which to attack inflation. He encouraged food production and the elimination of restraints on productivity. He encouraged energy conservation and development. He asked for an end to practices that restricted competition. He sought to generate more capital with an investment tax credit. He asked for changes in programs to help the ''casualties'' of inflation. He sought measures to stimulate the housing industry. He asked for reform of thrift institutions to facilitate mortgage credit. He sought cuts in federal spending and a one year 5 percent surtax on ''corporate and upper-level income'' to generate five billion dollars in revenue. Finally, he asked citizens to change their personal habits: ''Here is what we must do, what each and every one of you can do: To help increase food and lower prices, grow more and waste less; to help save scarce fuel in the energy crisis, drive less, heat less. Every housewife knows almost exactly how much she spent for food last week. If you cannot spare a penny from your food budget—and I know there are many—surely you can cut the food that you waste by 5 per cent.'' The President wore a WIN pin and encouraged his footsoldiers to wear them with pride.

Hermann G. Stelzner identified several problems with Ford's war on inflation. First, the drastic metaphor was inappropriate to Ford's cautious instincts and moderate policies, and his rhetoric seemed to require more dynamic policies than he was prepared to recommend. Second, the American people were tired of war and sacrifice after the long years of war in Vietnam. And third, the public eventually came to realize that they themselves were the enemy: It was their rate of consumption, their reluctance to pay taxes, their willingness to overextend their credit, their demand for expensive government services, and their willingness to waste that fueled inflation. "Politically," wrote Stelzner, "it was the wrong metaphor for the speaker, the audiences, and the time."

But President Ford's difficulties were not confined to the October 8th address. The next day he told a press conference that "I do not think the United States is in a recession." On October 29th, he said that "Whether it is a recession or not is immaterial. We have problems." By November 11th, Press Secretary Ron Nessen needed to dance around the recession question by saying that there was no recession according to the official data from September, although the data yet to be published would probably say that the economy had begun to enter a recession in October or November. By January 15th, when he delivered his first State of the Union Address, Ford had to say that the primary economic difficulty was not inflation but jobs. The situation had deteriorated to the point that the temporary 5 billion dollar tax increase had become a Presidential request for a 12 billion dollar tax rebate to stimulate the economy.

THE STATE OF THE UNION MESSAGES

President Ford delivered three State of the Union messages, and they make an interesting trilogy. He reported in 1975 that "the state of the Union is not good" and he presented a variety of proposals for action. By 1976, he said, "the state of our Union is better—in many ways a lot better—but still not good enough" and he preached a Bicentennial jeremiad of American renewal. And shortly before leaving office in 1977, he said that "Taken in sum, I can report that the state of the Union is good. There is room for improvement, as always, but today we have a more perfect Union than when my stewardship began."

The State of the Union, January 15, 1975

President Ford's first annual message was the culmination of his turbulent first six months in office. It contained a reprise of most of the familiar themes: the individual self-references, the call for cooperation, the people's need for action, and the serious economic problems, all in plain language. He combined these themes early in the speech as he concentrated on the economy: "Now, I want to speak very bluntly. I've got bad news, and I don't expect much, if any applause. The American people want action, and it will take both the Congress and the President to give them what they want. Progress and solutions *can* be achieved, and they *will* be achieved." This was a leader personally in command of the situation. But by this time, recession had replaced inflation as the economic crisis, and Ford used these themes to step adroitly across the embarrassing abyss:"The moment has come to move in a new direction. We can do this by fashioning a new partnership between the Congress on the one hand, the White House on the other, and the people we both represent. Let us mobilize the most powerful and most creative industrial nation that ever existed on this Earth to put all our people to work. *The emphasis on our economic efforts must now shift from inflation to jobs"* (emphasis added).

The President neither apologized for fighting inflation rather than recession nor blamed Congress. He simply took the offensive with a proposed $12 billion tax rebate instead of his earlier $5 billion tax surcharge. Ironically, the tax rebate was coupled with the news that the line would be held on Federal spending because "we have been self-indulgent . . . voting ever-increasing levels of Government benefits, and now the bill has come due." His critics could argue that increased Federal spending and no rebate could also stimulate the economy, but Ford's forthrightness and blunt language insured that they would be seen as undermining the partnership that was necessary to improve the state of the union.

This address also differed from his other major addresses because there was no mention of pardons or forgiveness, and he spoke at length about two new topics, energy and foreign policy. This was the prototypical Ford-Carter energy speech of the late 1970s: It warned of our dependence on foreign oil, it set energy goals, it encouraged conservation, and it proposed ways to increase our energy resources. But where he had called for a partnership, he now lapsed into the first-person singular, "I am proposing," "I am recommending," "I am requesting," "I plan to take," "I am prepared to use," and "I considered." His idea of partnership was reminiscent of the imperial presidency of his predecessors when the unelected president from Grand Rapids said that we could succeed, "If the Congress and the American people *will work with me"* (emphasis added).

The President moved from "I" to "we" when he turned to relations with Communist countries. Suddenly, the President spoke for a partnership: *"We must seek* to build a long-term basis for coexistence. *We will stand* by our principles. *We will stand* by our interests. *We will act* firmly when challenged. The kind of world *we want* depends on a broad policy of creating mutual incentives for restraint and for cooperation. As *we move forward* to meet our global challenges and opportunities, *we must have* the tools to do the job" (emphases added). This seemed normal enough, "we" being a country. But Ford soon made it clear that he thought the President should not be fettered by Congressional interference in foreign policy: "By the Constitution and tradition, the execution of foreign policy is the responsibility of the President. In recent years, under the stress of the Vietnam war, legislative restrictions on the President's ability to execute foreign policy and military decisions have proliferated. . . . As President, I welcome the advice and cooperation of the House and Senate. But if our foreign policy is to be successful, we cannot rigidly restrict in legislation the ability of the President to act." In short, Ford's approach to foreign policy and his language were in conflict.

The 1975 State of the Union address posed a difficult rhetorical problem for Gerald Ford. It was imperative that he turn the nation's attention to the recession, but he could not afford to compromise further his perceived competence. He handled that problem well enough by using straight, blunt talk to take the offensive. But the success of the speech was compromised by the President's paradoxical pronouns. He argued for a partnership in domestic affairs but disconnected his proposals from legislators and advisers by repeatedly speaking in the singular. But in foreign affairs he spoke for the national partnership as "we" while arguing that he alone was responsible for American foreign policy. In each case, his personal pronouns conflicted with the substance of his arguments and compromised his ability to win acceptance for both his philosophy of leadership and the substance of his leadership.

The State of the Union, January 19, 1976

What better way to report on the state of the union in the nation's bicentennial year than with a presidential jeremiad? Jeremiads evolved from Puritan political sermons and now abound in political rhetoric. The basic form casts the speaker in the role of preacher to a congregation of chosen people who are experiencing grave difficulties as divine punishments for straying from their sacred mission or covenant. The speaker emphasizes their "first principles," shows them how they have strayed from those principles, and admonishes them to return to the first principles so that they will be delivered from their hardships.

Jeremiads normally elevate the speaker relative to the audience. In this speech, there is a different Gerald Ford, for note the absence of the plain style, the simple language, the personal pronouns, and the references to everyday life in favor of cliches, hyperbole, transparent ornamentation, and emotional imagery:

As we begin our Bicentennial, America is still one of the youngest nations in recorded history. Long before our forefathers came to these shores, men and women had been struggling on this planet to forge a better life for themselves and their families. In man's long, upward march from savagery and slavery . . . there have been many deep, terrifying valleys, but also many bright and towering peaks. One peak stands highest in the range of human history. One example shines forth of a people uniting to produce abundance and to share the good life fairly and with freedom. One union holds out the promise of justice and opportunity for every citizen: That union is the United States of America.

Ford's Americans may have been the chosen people, but they were not perfect. "We sometimes forgot the sound principles that guided us through most of our history," said Ford. "We wanted to accomplish great things and solve age-old problems. And we became overconfident of our abilities. We tried to be a policeman abroad and the indulgent parent here at home. We thought we could transform the country through massive national programs, but often the programs did not work. Too often they only made things worse. In our rush to accomplish great deeds quickly, we trampled on sound principles of restraint and endangered the rights of individuals."

The answer to the difficulties of 1976 were therefore to be found in return to "the great principles upon which this Nation was founded." According to Ford,

"The genius of America has been its incredible ability to improve the lives of its citizens through a unique combination of governmental and free citizen activity." The phrase "new balance" became Ford's mantra in the prescriptive portion of his jeremiad: America needed a new balance in the economy, in federalism, between domestic and defense spending, and between promising and delivering.

The speech ended with the promise of jeremiadic salvation if the chosen people would return to basics. "Like our forefathers," he said, "we know that if we meet the challenges of our own time with a common sense of purpose and conviction, if we remain true to our Constitution and to our ideals, then we can know that the future will be better than the past." He closed with a peculiarly painful metaphor, asking Americans to engrave in their hearts the motto, "In God we trust."

Many reasons could have motivated Ford to employ a jeremiadic style in this address. The Bicentennial was an appropriate time to teach history lessons, he was running for election and could benefit from the ceremonial elevation that jeremiadic form provides; and Ritter and Henry note that Ford's primary rival, Ronald Reagan, frequently used the form himself. However, problems arose with the jeremiad. First, jeremiads rely on traumatic problems graphically portrayed to induce compliance, but Ford's message was that "The state of the union is better—in many ways a lot better—but still not good enough." Second, his recommendation was that the country "stick to that steady course," which is hardly the same as finding a new balance. Finally, the jeremiadic style sacrificed the familiar and popular "Good Old Gerry" style in favor of inflated, hyperbolic language. In short, the jeremiad was appropriate for the bicentennial state of the union, but it was inappropriate for the man and his message.

Moreover, Ford's jeremiad was poorly executed. The middle portion of the speech, which comprised most of it, was standard state of the union boilerplate about policies and directions that bore no apparent relation to either the theme of first principles or the new balance slogan. A speaker can use jeremiadic logic to advance policies, as Smith discussed the jeremiadic logic of Bill Clinton's 1992 campaign policy speeches, but this speech made no real effort to link the form and the policies. As a result, it rambled, and a speech that should have defined Ford's election year agenda failed to do so.

State of the Union, January 12, 1977

President Ford's last State of the Union address was delivered a week before he left office, and it functioned as his farewell address. It was a speech of vindication, if not of triumph. "When I became President," Ford recalled: "our Nation was deeply divided and tormented. . . . We were still struggling with the after effects of a long, bloody war in Southeast Asia. The economy was unstable and racing toward the worst recession in 40 years. People were losing jobs. The cost of living was soaring. The Congress and the Chief Executive were at loggerheads. The integrity of our constitutional process and other institutions were being questioned. . . . [and] our will to maintain our international leadership was in doubt." In that situation, "I asked for your prayers and went to work." "Now, after 30 months as your President," he reported that America had become "a more perfect Union than when my stewardship began."

A major theme of Ford's presidency from the beginning had been the need for cooperative action, and this speech was an appropriate final report. He expressed pride in the nation's accomplishments: restoration of confidence in the presidency, reduction of inflation from twelve percent to five percent, the creation of four million new jobs, the establishment of a strong national defense, and improving relations in Asia. He expressed his frustration with being unable to consolidate overlapping federal programs with the nation's continued dependence on foreign energy sources, but his list of disappointments included neither the Nixon pardon nor the disastrous swine flu inoculation program. The speech was unremarkable in most respects, but it provided a fitting eulogy for the Ford administration.

THE 1976 ELECTION CAMPAIGN

Gerald Ford had planned to retire from public life in 1977, but history rewrote the script. He accepted the vice presidency, in part, because it would not have altered his time table, and he and Richard Nixon both favored John Connolly for the 1976 Republican nomination. But once in office it became clear that he would need to run in 1976 if his leadership were to be taken seriously. The bicentennial festivities and the campaign combined to provide an unprecedented speaking schedule. His main challenge came from Ronald Reagan, who used the "giveaway" of the Panama Canal to win the North Carolina Republican primary. But Ford prevailed and won nomination at the convention in Kansas City.

Ford's Nomination Acceptance Address

Finally, Gerald Ford had won a national electoral coalition. He must have felt good on August 19th before the Republican convention in Kemper Arena, because this was his most confident and determined speech. "I am honored by your nomination," he began in his usual style, "and I accept it with pride, with gratitude, and with a total will to win a great victory for the American people." He portrayed himself as an activist president in the Truman mold, and like Truman, he went after the opposition party's Congress. He used a sequence of paragraphs that coupled "I called for" with "but their Congress won't act" to establish his claim that "Americans have made an incredible comeback since August 1974. Nobody can honestly say otherwise. And the plain truth is that the great progress we have made at home and abroad was in spite of the majority who run the Congress of the United States."

But the address was not mainly about the President or Congress, it was an attempt by Ford to reach out to "you the people." The people of America dominated the address, from his direct call to them: "You at home listening tonight, you are the people who pay the taxes and obey the laws. You are the people who make our system work. You are the people who make America what it is. It is from your ranks that I come and on your side that I stand," to his discussion of them:

As I try to use my imagination to look into the homes where families are watching the end of this great convention, I can't tell which faces are Republicans, which are Democrats, and which are Independents. I cannot see their color or their creed. I see only Americans. I see Americans who love their husbands, their wives, and their children. I see Americans who love their country for what it has been and what it must become. I see Americans who work hard, but who are willing to sacrifice all they have worked for to keep their children and their country free. I see Americans who in their own quiet way pray for peace among nations and peace among ourselves. We do love our neighbors, and we do forgive those who have trespassed against us.

These characterizations of the American people were appropriate to the Bicentennial convention, and they were long overdue in Ford's rhetoric. But he did not stop there.

Ford's address explicitly linked his ever-present "I" with "you the people" to forge an "US" more clearly than in any other speech. "For 2 years I have stood for all the people against a vote-hungry, free-spending congressional majority on Capitol Hill," he said. "Fifty-five times I vetoed extravagant and unwise legislation; 45 times I made those vetoes stick." This was a far cry from his inaugural hope that vetoes would be unnecessary, and it deflected attention from his inability to shape legislation that he could sign. "I come before you with a 2-year record of performance without your mandate. I offer you a 4-year pledge of greater performance with your mandate." He then laid out his plans for the next four years in an uncharacteristic list of "We will" statements in 23 of 26 consecutive sentences.

Ford's acceptance address was perhaps his peak performance. But it was not without problems. Most importantly, this approach came about thirty months too late, since he already trailed Jimmy Carter by 33 percentage points. Moreover, it suggests the extent to which Gerald Ford had been transformed. The man who had hoped to avoid vetoes was now proud of his 45 vetoes. The man who had promised a Congressional policy of "communication, conciliation, compromise, and cooperation" now blamed Congress for the nation's problems and claimed that America's successes had been achieved despite Congress. The unelected President from Grand Rapids who spoke in the first person singular was now his party's nominee, speaking in the first person plural. Perhaps these changes contributed to the fact that the man who had enjoyed 71 percent approval and 3 percent disapproval now had 45 percent approval, 40 percent disapproval, and trailed his opponent by 33 points. Nevertheless, the speech was reminiscent of Ford's old football strategy: He had Carter right where he wanted him. He just needed to force mistakes by the inexperienced Georgian. So he decided to debate Carter on national television.

The Ford-Carter Debates

President Ford's decision to debate is one of his lasting contributions because he became the first incumbent President to debate his challenger. They met September 23rd in Philadelphia, October 6th in San Francisco, and October 22nd in Williamsburg, Virginia. Lloyd Bitzer and Theodore Reuter observed that Ford was less skilled than Carter in face-to-face argument, that he made more errors, was prone to shallow arguments and weak analysis that failed to project a grasp of substantive issues, and that he had difficulty expressing feelings and principles. Fortunately for Ford, Carter seemed to exaggerate to compensate for poorly formulated positions, had an inflated view of presidential powers, and underestimated the importance of cooperation.

The only memorable moment occurred during the second debate, when Ford said that Eastern Europe was not under Soviet domination. Polls conducted right after the debate showed a dead heat: 44 percent for Ford, 43 percent for Carter. But the media's discussion of the Eastern Europe gaffe turned public opinion sharply toward Carter. Within 24 hours, 62 percent said that Carter had prevailed, while Ford's response had dropped all the way to 17 percent. This debate and attendant research established the importance of "spin" and post-debate commentary that still haunt such debates. In short, Ford failed to force Carter into serious mistakes and made some of his own. Carter seems to have benefited from the debates because each served to break a slide and to deflect Ford's catch-up offense.

CONCLUSION

This essay began with the observation that Gerald Ford was not an orator but a talker who was thrust into the bully pulpit of the American presidency. He had never been elected by voters beyond southwestern Michigan, he replaced a president who left him a government in shambles, he was surrounded by skeptical holdovers and aspiring candidates, the opposition party controlled the Congress, the 12 percent inflation was quickly turning into a hidden recession, and then there was the unpleasant aftermath of the Vietnam war. Nor was Ford a skilled speaker: He had stuttered as a child and regretted taking so few courses in writing and speaking. Despite all these constraints, Gerald Ford did a creditable job as president. He was a good man speaking plainly, if not always well.

Ford recognized that his primary job was to unite and heal America, and that theme pervaded his speeches. His main rhetorical problem in that regard was his tendency to express himself in the first person singular instead of the plural.

The founders expressed themselves as "We, the People" but Ford was "I, the President." This complicated his attempts at unification by dissociating him from the rest of the nation. The problem peaked when he used "we" to discuss foreign policy, where he objected to interference, and "I" in discussing domestic policy, for which he always stressed partnership. Ford's language and arguments sent mixed signals to his audiences. This problem changed in his acceptance speech when he spoke out forcefully, although belatedly, for what "we" would do in four-year term with a public mandate.

President Ford was most criticized for his controversial pardons. Both were grounded in his Episcopalian religion and its emphasis on forgiveness and mercy, and because he always looked for the good in people, he decided that people's mistakes should be weighed against their contributions. Richard Nixon had devoted his life to public service, and his career of accomplishments justified his pardon in Ford's eyes. Those who had deserted or evaded the draft had not yet compiled a record of public service sufficient to outweigh their transgressions, so Ford established a program that enabled them to earn pardons by doing so. Both pardons made perfect sense in Gerald Ford's philosophy of life. Unfortunately, he was never able to persuade quite enough Americans to his perspective. His VFW speech did a good job of inducing public quiescence over the earned pardons, but the case for the Nixon pardon was poorly made.

But if Gerald Ford was more talker than orator, he nevertheless significantly altered the nature of the rhetorical presidency. After ten years of the Johnson-Nixon deviousness, Gerald Ford restored presidential rhetoric to its rightful place in the process of representative government. More than they, Ford assumed public responsibility for his decisions, explained his reasons, and rarely resorted to blaming others. And by example he virtually insured that future incumbents would have to debate their challengers during the campaign or lose face. Gerald Ford was able to do all of this, perhaps, because of the lessons he had learned about forgiveness at the Episcopal church in Grand Rapids and on the football field at Michigan. Indeed, the themes of competition and forgiveness merge in a sentence near the end of his last State of the Union address. Speaking to the House, the Senate, his cabinet, the Supreme Court, the press, and the nation via television from the House chamber where he had served for so many years, Ford said, "It was here we waged many, many a lively battle—won some, lost some, but always remaining friends."

RHETORICAL SOURCES

Archival Materials

The Gerald R. Ford Library, on the campus of the University of Michigan in Ann Arbor, holds the archives from Ford's entire career. Because of the post-Watergate climate there are fewer informal memoranda and notations than in many of the other presidential libraries. Although a visitor to the Library can view Ford's reading drafts, these rarely differ from the texts available in the Public Papers. Most of the files of speech writers Robert Hartman, Paul Theis, and Robert Orben are open and useful.

Baroody, William J. "Responses to critics of the Nixon pardon." 1974.
Memorandum for Robert T. Hartmann, 9/10/74, folder "9-24-74 Nixon Pardon (2)," Box 1.
Files of Paul Miltich, Assistant Press Secretary, Gerald R. Ford Library.
Ford, Gerald R. *The Public Papers of the President: Gerald R. Ford.* (*PPP*). 6 Vols. Washington, DC: U.S. Government Printing Office, 1975–1979.

Rhetorical Studies

Barber, James David. *The Presidential Character: Predicting Performance in the White House.* Englewood Cliffs, NJ: Prentice-Hall, 1985.
Bitzer, Lloyd, and Theodore Reuter. *Carter vs. Ford: The Counterfeit Debates of 1976.* Madison, WI: University of Wisconsin Press, 1980.
Campbell, Karlyn Kohrs, and Kathleen Hall Jamieson. *Deeds Done in Words: Presidential Rhetoric and the Genres of Governance.* Chicago: University of Chicago Press, 1990.
Ford, Gerald R. *A Time to Heal: The Autobiography of Gerald R. Ford.* New York: Harper & Row, 1979.
Hartmann, Robert T. *Palace Politics: An Inside Account of the Ford Years.* New York: McGraw-Hill, 1980.
Kraus, Sidney, ed. *The Great Debates: Carter vs. Ford 1976.* Bloomington, IN: Indiana University Press, 1976.
Ritter, Kurt, and David Henry. *Ronald Reagan: The Great Communicator.* Westport, CT: Greenwood, 1992.
Smith, Craig Allen, and Kathy B. Smith, *The White House Speaks: Presidential Leadership as Persuasion.* Westport, CT: Praeger, 1994.

Rhetorical Monographs

Berquist, Goodwin. "The 1976 Carter-Ford Presidential Debates." In *Rhetorical Studies of National Political Debates*, 2d ed. Edited by Robert V. Friedenberg. Westport, CT: Praeger, 1994.
Brock, Bernard L. "Gerald R. Ford Encounters Richard Nixon's Legacy: On Amnesty and the Pardon." In *Oratorical Encounters: Selected Studies and Sources of Twentieth-Century Political Accusations and Apologia*, edited by Halford Ross Ryan. Westport, CT: Greenwood, 1988.
———. "President Gerald R. Ford's Inaugural Address, 1974." In *The Inaugural Addresses of Twentieth-Century American Presidents*, edited by Halford Ross Ryan. Westport, CT: Praeger, 1993.
Chapel, Gage William. "Humor in the White House: And [sic] Interview with Presidential Speechwriter Robert Orben." *Communication Quarterly* 26 (1978): 44–49.
Hahn, Dan F. "Corrupt Rhetoric: President Ford and the Mayaguez Affair." *Communication Quarterly* 28 (1980): 38–43.

Klumpp, James F., and Jeffrey K. Lukehart. "The Pardoning of Richard Nixon: A Failure in Motivational Strategy." *Western Journal of Speech Communication* 41 (1978): 116–23.

Scheele, Henry Z. "Prelude to the Presidency: An Examination of the Gerald R. Ford-Charles A. Halleck House Minority Leadership Contest." Paper presented at the Speech Communication Association national convention, 1993.

Smith, Craig Allen. "The Jeremiadic Logic of Clinton's Policy Speeches." In *Clinton on Stump, State, and Stage: The Rhetorical Road to the White House*, compiled by Stephen A. Smith. Fayetteville, AR: University of Arkansas Press, 1994.

Smith, Craig Allen, and Kathy B. Smith. "The Coalitional Crisis of the Ford Presidency." In *The Modern Presidency and Crisis Rhetoric*, edited by Amos Kiewe. Westport, CT: Praeger, 1994.

Smith, Craig R. "Addendum to 'Contemporary Political Speech Writing.' " *Southern Speech Communication Journal* 42 (1977): 191–94.

Stelzner, Hermann G. "Ford's War on Inflation: A Metaphor that Did Not Cross." *Communication Monographs* 44 (November 1977): 284–97.

———. "Gerald Rudolph Ford." In *American Orators of the Twentieth Century*, edited by Bernard K. Duffy and Halford R. Ryan. Westport, CT: Greenwood, 1987.

Stewart, Charles J., Craig Allen Smith, and Robert E. Denton. *Persuasion and Social Movements*, 3d ed. Prospect Heights, IL: Waveland, 1994.

Chronology of Significant Presidential Persuasions

Remarks on Taking the Oath of Office, Washington, D.C., August 9, 1974. *PPP*, 1974: 1–2.

Address to a Joint Session of Congress, Washington, D.C., August 12, 1974. *PPP*, 1974: 6–13.

Remarks to the Veterans of Foreign Wars annual convention, Chicago, Illinois, August 19, 1974. *PPP*, 1974: 22–28.

Proclamation 4311, Granting Pardon to Richard Nixon, Washington, D.C., September 8, 1974. *PPP*, 1974: 103–4.

Remarks on Signing a Proclamation Granting Pardon to Richard Nixon, Washington, D.C., September 8, 1974. *PPP*, 1974: 101–3.

Address to a Joint Session of the Congress on the Economy, Washington, D.C., October 8, 1974. *PPP*, 1974: 228–38.

Address Before a Joint Session of the Congress Reporting on the State of the Union, Washington, D.C., January 15, 1975. *PPP*, 1975: 36–46.

Address Before a Joint Session of the Congress Reporting on the State of the Union, Washington, D.C., January 19, 1976. *PPP*, 1976: 31–42.

Remarks Upon Accepting the 1976 Republican Presidential Nomination, Kansas City, Missouri, August 19, 1976. *PPP*, 1976: 2157–63.

Address Before a Joint Session of the Congress Reporting on the State of the Union, Washington, D.C., January 12, 1977. *PPP*, 1977: 2916–27.

Dan F. Hahn and Halford Ryan

Jimmy Carter
(1924–)

What doth the Lord require of thee, but to do justly, and to love mercy, and to walk humbly with God.

Born October 1, 1924, in Plains, Georgia, James Earl Carter was the eldest child of Earl Carter and Lillian Gordy. When he was twelve he came under the influence of a teacher named Julia Coleman, who introduced him to the delights of literature, and when he became president, he quoted this line of Julia Coleman's in his Inaugural Address: "We must adjust to changing times and still hold to unchanging principles."

In high school, Jimmy was a member of the debate team, but he did not care much for it. He was an able debater, but his delivery was relatively flat. In fact, he disdained public speaking, believing that only substance mattered, that all a speaker needed to do was to lay the facts before the audience, that delivery was irrelevant. This belief would later come to haunt his presidency.

After high school, Carter had hoped to attend the U.S. Naval Academy. He was finally accepted into the Naval Academy as a college junior. By the time he graduated from college, World War II was over, but he spent seven years in the navy, rising to the rank of lieutenant commander. During his years in the navy he came under the influence of Admiral Hyman Rickover. At one point he admitted to Rickover that he had not always done his best, to which Rickover responded "Why not?" That response gave Carter the title for his autobiography, *Why Not the Best?* and his slogan for the 1976 campaign.

PRE-PRESIDENTIAL RHETORIC

Jimmy Carter never evinced much interest in politics, yet friends were able to prevail upon him in the early 1960s to run for office. Narrowly winning a seat in the Georgia State Senate in 1962, he was re-elected in an uncontested race in 1964. In 1966 he declared his intention to run for the U.S. Congress against Howard ("Bo") Callaway. Four days before the deadline for filing, he changed his mind and ran for the governorship instead. That may have been a mistake, as he came in third in the Democratic primary. Yet he immediately initiated his plan for another try at the office, spent most of the next four years campaigning, and in 1970 won the governor's office.

Carter's gubernatorial inaugural address was an attack on racial discrimination, and it propelled him to the front page of the *New York Times* and the cover of *Time* magazine. Before long, he and his staff started angling to become the vice-presidential nominee in 1976. They then decided to run for president.

Moving slowly but inexorably, they positioned Carter to capitalize on the early 1976 events, the Iowa caucus, and the New Hampshire primary. He subsequently won both, propelling him to the nomination despite a coalition of his opponents dedicated to ABC, Anybody But Carter.

In 1976 Jimmy Carter surprised everybody by moving from the back of the pack to win the Democratic nomination, then going on to accomplish the nearly unprecedented task of unseating an incumbent president, especially when only several years before the common reaction to the name Jimmy Carter had been Jimmy Who?

The 1976 Campaign

Candidate Carter canvassed the country, but his debates with President Ford seemed to carry the greatest weight with the voters. Robert Denton concluded that in American elections, "the best image is one that is vague enough for the voters to complete. In the simplest terms, this means that 'conservatives' should be able to see the candidate as 'conservative' and, likewise, 'liberals' should be able to see the candidate as 'liberal.' Above all, this should be done without seeming contradictory or insincere." To accomplish his all-things-to-all-people political strategy, Carter utilized a number of rhetorical tactics in 1976.

Carter counterbalanced liberal and conservative positions. For instance, speaking in conservative Alabama in September of 1976, he called for an end to the "welfare mess" and support for a strong national defense. Then, to appeal to liberals, he recommended that welfare recipients who cannot work should be treated with dignity and respect, and he suggested that military budgets could be cut without endangering national security.

A second method he utilized was to give the policy to one side and the rhetoric to the other. His stand on abortion exemplifies this approach. Anti-abortionists wanted to amend the Constitution to make abortion illegal. Carter opposed such a measure, but in heavy Roman Catholic areas he prefaced the statement of his position with anti-abortion rhetoric, saying, "I think abortion is wrong. I don't think the government ought to do anything to encourage abortion."

Another tactic was to agree to study a proposal or a position that ran counter to his own. Thus, while Carter opposed federal aid to cities, he promised Mayor Beame of New York City that he would study the creation of a federal municipalities securities insurance corporation. The strength of this strategy was that Carter appeared to be open to rational persuasion without promising any substantive change at all.

Carter cleverly encouraged both sides to believe he was with them. He opposed socialized medicine but favored mandatory comprehensive federal health insurance. Carter's ambiguity usually was accomplished through some kind of verbal hedge. He made value statements that appealed to one sector of his audience and would then use oblique language that would satisfy another segment. Although such statements might be inconsistent or contradictory, many of the people listening would hear only the part that conformed to their views and would ignore or discount the other verbiage.

Carter used semantic distinctions to blur the liberal-conservative antipathy. Perhaps the best example of this approach was his position on amnesty for those who had resisted service in Vietnam. Carter opposed amnesty because it implied that what one did was right. But he added that, in his first week in office, he would issue a blanket pardon to defectors because a pardon says that you are forgiven for what you did, whether it was right or wrong. No one ever has located a dictionary that makes such a distinction, for ''amnesty'' is usually defined as ''a general pardon.''

No wonder, then, that Mr. Carter's fuzziness on the issues, fueled by his rhetorical tactics, led people from all points of the political spectrum to identify with him. That was the goal all along. As Betty Glad concluded, ''Mostly Carter skillfully fudged on the controversial issues. He did this by sending out complex messages that various listeners could interpret according to their own predispositions. From the multitude of signals—a word, a condition, a posture—Carter was able to send different people different signals about his positions.''

One of Carter's central positions in the campaign was his anti-Washington stance. To distance himself from the Capitol and to run as an outsider, he emphasized that he had not been a part of the group in Washington that had created the mess, and he was not even a lawyer. He further distanced symbolically: He dressed casually, carried his own suitcase, sometimes stayed in the homes of supporters rather than in hotels and, in general, pictured himself as an outsider. Thus he came to be seen not only as non-Washington but anti-Washington.

However, that was mostly facade. Substantively, Carter did not run against Washington at all. As Tom Bethel opined, ''Carter never said that government should be reduced or should do less. He said that the number of agencies should be reduced, but not that they should deliver fewer services or employ fewer people.'' At the same time, noted Bethel, both Carter's rhetoric and his symbolism were seen, and were meant to be perceived, ''as a cryptic way of saying that we need less government without actually having to alienate those who directly benefit from government.''

The 1976 Campaign Debates

Although last practiced in the famous Kennedy-Nixon encounters in 1960, both President Gerald Ford and Governor Jimmy Carter challenged one another to debate the issues on television before the public. Ford announced he would debate Carter in the President's party nomination acceptance speech, August 19, 1976, and Carter made his own offer a day later. Both men reasoned they would benefit from the debates. Carter would overcome his liability of "Jimmy, who?," and Ford would rest his case before the people as a public statesman. But only one candidate could win the debates, which in 1976 proved to be the critical factor in who won the election.

Carter debated three times. The first debate, held at Philadelphia on September 23rd, was given, if opinion polls are considered, to Ford by a slight edge. The second debate, San Francisco, October 6th, went to Carter by a large margin, as Ford made the infamous gaffe that the Soviet Union did not occupy Eastern European countries. This *faux pas* raised questions about Ford's competency in office. Carter carried with a slight edge the last debate at Williamsburg, Virginia, October 22nd.

Whereas many factors contributed to how one assessed the debates, they seem to revolve around why Ford lost and why Carter won. Lloyd Bitzer and Theodore Rueter studied the 1976 debates and determined the following reasons: Ford made more statements of error than Carter did, occasionally misanalyzed public issues, and had difficulty in communicating his personality. Goodwin Berquist noted that the debates created "the clear impression among the American public that Governor Carter was at least as qualified" as Ford.

CARTER'S PRESIDENTIAL RHETORIC

President Carter came to the office after two presidents who had been perceived as too strong. Lyndon Johnson and Richard Nixon had been condemned as "imperial," a charge that also descended upon Gerald Ford when he pardoned Nixon. So Carter was a beneficiary of the demand for a scaling back from that imperial legacy, and his early symbolic actions after taking the office, his walk to the White House after the inauguration, appearing on television in an open shirt and sweater, and attending town meetings, were calculated to demonstrate his non-imperial approach.

As the Carter presidency continued, that early humility came to be seen as a weakness. By mid-term, his presidency was in trouble, and by the end he was perceived as a poor communicator, whose *bete noire* was Ronald Reagan, the Great Communicator. At best, Carter was a pedestrian presidential speaker, and his stature as an orator suffered a diminution as his general reputation fell.

The Inaugural Address

"Carter attained the presidency," opined Craig Smith, "largely by seeming consistently the least objectionable available candidate, a difficult mandate from which to lead." His inaugural on January 20, 1977, was not a particularly auspicious introduction to his presidency.

In defining the world as two distinct parts, physical and spiritual, and then emphasizing the latter, President Carter set a religious mood for his Inaugural Address. In the very first sentence, when Carter thanked President Ford for "all he has done to heal our land," he implied that a presidential duty is to heal, a job that can be seen metaphorically as a divine responsibility.

Carter specifically referred to his faith by talking of the two Bibles before him and by quoting the prophet Micah. The speech was sprinkled with religious language. He declared that the inauguration attested to the "spiritual" strength of the nation, that there is "a new spirit among us all," and that "ours was the first society openly to define itself in terms of . . . spirituality." He used the word "spirit" seven times and other clearly religious words, such as "pray," "moral," "religious," an additional twenty-seven times.

At the end of the speech Carter listed six goals. Although they were stated in the past tense, the aphoristic form made them resemble the Ten Commandments. One statement followed another without explication, each with its own ideology, each pertaining to moral and spiritual issues. Each could be converted from aphorism to commandment by replacing "that we had" with "Thou Shalt." "That we had strengthened the American family" would thus become "Thou Shalt strengthen the American family."

Clearly, a religiosity ran through the speech. How was it undermined? By overkill. Americans do not like sermonizing. The description of somebody who does so is the pejorative term "preachy." Americans do expect a little religion to be interspersed in our political addresses, for "God" has been defined as a word in the final sentence of a political speech, but Americans cannot abide unbending fanaticism. Not only was religion over-emphasized in and of itself, it also interfered with his secular messages by casting them in a nonpolitical light. For instance, Carter undoubtedly was right in claiming that "our moral sense dictates a clear cut preference for those societies which share with us an abiding respect for individual human rights," but our international affinities are not exclusively morality-based, they also are political and economic. Carter's stressing religious/moral standpoints meant that his political topics seemed to float in limbo outside any point in political history. The resultant tone was that of a Southern preacher's eternal moralistic generalization rather than that of a presidential policymaker.

Carter's second subject, the American dream, inherently intertwined with the first. The religio-political analog draws one myth into the presence of the other. Both religion and the American dream function, amongst other ways, to provide hope to their audiences. But Carter's "dream" rhetoric seemed less hopeful than his religious, perhaps because he introduced it negatively: "the bold and brilliant dream which excited the founders of our nation still awaits consummation. I have no new dream to set forth today, but rather urge a fresh faith in the old dream." Carter implied an aura of stagnation. Further, he gave conflicting testimony to the state of the dream. First he said it "still awaits its consummation," then that it "endures," and finally that it is "undiminished" and "ever-expanding." For something to endure and expand while it still awaits consummation is disconcertingly confusing.

In sum, although Carter's Inaugural Address had its strengths, its weaknesses seemed to predominate its critical reception. Craig Smith isolated two strategic flaws that vitiated Carter's rhetoric: "the address accomplished few of the goals that most inaugurals need to do, and those few it did only moderately well," and "the inaugural choices set Carter's presidency back severely by undermining the public's, Washington's, and even his own grasp of the fact that he was indeed president."

First Fireside Chat

Two weeks after his inauguration, President Carter presented his first Fireside Chat, February 3, 1977, and again demonstrated rhetorically the weakness that eventually would destroy his presidency. In a word, he overstated problems and understated solutions.

Problem: "One of the most urgent projects is to develop a national energy policy."
Solution: [it] "started before this winter and will take much longer to solve."

Problem: "the worst economic slowdown of the last forty years."
Solution: "It will produce steady, balanced, sustainable growth."

Problem: "we must reform and reorganize the Federal Government."
Solution: the system "will take a long time to change."

Problem: the tax system is "a disgrace."
Solution: "The economic program . . . will . . . be just a first step."

Problem: "The welfare system also needs a complete overhaul."
Solution: "We have 'begun a review.' "

Finally, speaking generally about all of his proposals, Carter stated, "Many of them will take longer than I would like . . . ." How a listener reacted to all of these identifications of emergencies followed by a listing of slow and partial solutions depends on political orientation. A sympathizer might say that Carter was just being realistic about how long solutions take, whereas an opponent might contend that Carter tried to demonstrate a commitment to promises on which he had no intention, or chance, of delivering. The lesson is that any leader who oversells problems without a compensatory overselling of his solutions is bound to be perceived as incapable of coping with problems and, ultimately, with the presidency.

The Energy Problem

Delivered from the White House on April 18, 1977, and given the sobriquet of "The Moral Equivalent of War" speech, Carter's thesis was that the United States faced an energy shortage, and the people and Congress should rally around the President's plan. Carter began his speech on a serious, somber note: "Tonight I want to have an unpleasant talk with you about a problem that is unprecedented in our history. With the exception of preventing war, this is the greatest challenge that our country will face during our lifetime." Although the following quotation would have been at home in a presidential war crisis speech, Carter used that thematic evocation to heighten the exigency in the close of his introduction: "Our decision about energy will test the character of the American people and the ability of the President and the Congress to govern this Nation. This difficult effort will be the 'moral equivalent of war,' except that we will be united in our efforts to build and not to destroy."

The body of the speech followed a basic problem-solution organizational pattern, yet Carter employed some noteworthy classical rhetorical devices in his oration. He began his *narratio* of the problem with the transitional language of "Now, I know that some of you may doubt that we face real energy shortages." To confirm his claim, he listed copious statistical evidence. But then, with a hapless, self-inflicted wound, he undermined his credibility and position when he allowed that "I know that many of you have suspected that some supplies of oil and gas are being withheld from the market. You may be right . . . ." Nevertheless, as if it were immaterial whether people actually believed him, Carter blithely sallied forth with his solution.

To garner support for his energy plan, Carter used the classical method of residues or disjunctive syllogism [A, B, or C; not A, not B, therefore C]. The first disjunct was "to continue doing what we've been doing before. We can drift along for a few more years." To persuade Americans that this alternative was not viable, Carter adduced more statistics and reasoning to demonstrate the futility of drifting. Having dispatched the do-nothing disjunct, Carter turned to the do-something disjunct, which was his proposal: "But we still have another choice. We can begin to prepare right now. We can decide to act while there is still time.''

The solution was based on ''10 fundamental principles,'' which reinforced Carter's penchant for persuading-by-numbers. These principles, in turn, would fulfill certain goals by 1985. Although Carter eschewed numbering them—there were seven goals—he did at least introduce them with the anaphora, or parallelism, of the infinitive ''to'': ''to reduce,'' ''to establish,'' ''to insulate,'' etc.

Carter's conclusion also employed anaphora. In four instances, he began his entreaties with ''We've always been proud'' and once he said ''We've always wanted.'' These inclusive pronouns, linked to American patriotism, were stylistically and motivationally strong appeals to the American audience.

The Panama Canal Treaties Speech

On February 1, 1978, President Carter opened his campaign, as a part of the rhetorical presidency, to go to the people via radio and television to persuade them to urge their senators to pass Carter's Panama Canal treaties then before the U.S. Senate. Given that conservatives were aligned against Carter—they felt that he was giving away the Canal—and undecided citizens needed bolstering, Carter had to use a rhetorical one-two punch in his speech: to preempt conservative's reservations about the treaty and to move the undecided into his fold. To accomplish this task, he employed the classical organizational pattern.

His introduction was not an auspicious beginning. He played into the hands of his opponents by praising American prowess in building the Canal, which was exactly why opponents claimed the United States should not give it away.

His narration fared no better. Rather than recounting the sordid history of the underhanded manner in which the United States secured the Canal by gunboat diplomacy, Carter merely allowed that the original treaties were ''not so advantageous to Panama.'' To assume that the American people knew the real details of how President Teddy Roosevelt boasted in speeches that he took the Canal Zone and then let Congress debate it was a rhetorical mistake. Indeed, candidate Ronald Reagan scored heavily against Carter by claiming, erroneously, that we bought it, we paid for it, and it is ours. Carter missed an opportunity to set the record straight, which might have restrained conservatives in the range of their responses to his proposal.

Carter outlined in his *partitio* four contentions that he would prove. He claimed that the treaties would ensure U.S. security interests; the Canal would always be open to all and be neutral territory; U.S. warships could go to the head of the line; and U.S. forces could defend the Canal.

In the arguments section, the orator gives reasons for the proposal. Carter really did not adduce reasoning or evidence to sustain his four points, but rather explained how the treaty would work. He also used the bandwagon effect—he name-dropped important figures in previous administrations as well as five generals of the armed forces who approved the treaties—to imply to Americans that if important politicians and generals favored Carter's plan, then the average American listener should fall in line behind these national luminaries. Still, substantive proof was lacking.

Perhaps sensing that the onus of his speech was not so much in persuading the audience to be for his treaties as much as its problem was to assuage misgivings, Carter launched into his refutation section. He used this transitional device: "Tonight I want you to hear the facts. I want to answer the most serious questions and tell you why I feel the Panama Canal treaties should be approved." Why the treaties should be approved should have occurred in the arguments section. Carter evidently reasoned that if he overcame objections, that was warrant enough for people to support him. Carter counterargued eight issues that vexed Americans. Three are worth scrutinizing.

First, Carter alleged that the United States could defend the Canal. Quoting the treaties, Carter allayed fears; however, he acknowledged that the United States would take military actions to protect the Canal if necessary. This was an apparent contradiction, for Carter asserted on the one hand that the United States wanted "cooperation and not confrontation" with Panama, yet on the other hand, the United States would not hesitate to be confrontational if the military necessity arose. Little wonder that Ronald Sudol noted that this kind of argumentation aroused "suspicion and confusion."

Second, Carter successfully refuted the conservative's "We bought it, we paid for it, it's ours" campaign rhetoric. He demonstrated that the Panama Canal had always been under Panamanian sovereignty, which had always been acknowledged by the Supreme Court and by previous presidents. His one-liner was actually quite succinct and successful—"You do not pay rent on your own land."

Third, Carter tried to neutralize head-on a major, sentimental reason for keeping the Canal. He acknowledged that "when we talk of the canal . . . we are talking about very deep and elemental feelings about our own strength." Yet, Carter countered with a less-is-more refutation that raised more objections than it disproved. "This is not merely the surest way to protect and save the canal," Carter preached, "it's a strong, positive act of a people who are still confident, still creative, still great." Notwithstanding the stylistic devices of anaphora (the parallelism of "still") and asyndeton (leaving out the connective in the clause), the appeal raised a hypothetical question that invited the audience to infer just the opposite conclusion: If the United States is still confident and great, then why is it giving away the Canal?

Carter's conclusion or *peroratio* was also a persuasive paradox. Enticing Americans to mount the bandwagon once more, Carter asserted that President Theodore Roosevelt would support the treaties: "But if Theodore Roosevelt were to endorse the treaties, as I'm sure he would, it would be mainly because he could see the decision as one by which we are demonstrating the kind of great power we wish to be." Carter unsuccessfully ran the risk of claiming that a dead president would support his treaties, for surely the image of TR as the bully president who advocated the big stick in foreign policy was completely incongruous with Carter's image of a great power making concessions to a small power.

The two Panama Canal treaties passed the Senate in March and April of 1978. The link between the speech as a cause and the passage of the treaties as an effect is extremely tenuous, which is compounded by the lack of polling data. Rather, the vote was probably a reflection of Carter's political IOU's rather than one persuasive speech. Still, from a critical, rhetorical perspective, the speech was weak in adducing argumentation for the treaties, as well as in refuting objections against the treaties. The fault was not in the classical organizational pattern but in the lack of good reasons that were presented within its framework.

"A Crisis of Confidence"

Considering the background for Carter's speech, Robert Strong noted that "the national agenda in the late 1970s was full of complex problems with politically unpopular solutions." Indeed, Carter had determined to deliver a speech on energy to the nation in July of 1979, but on the Fourth of July he surprised almost everyone by canceling the address. Rather, he stayed at Camp David for ten days and consulted with American leaders from all walks of life. Carter then addressed citizens, July 15, 1979, on national goals and energy.

One way of analyzing the speech is to situate it as a sermon. Indeed, Dan Hahn believed that Carter delivered two speeches in one—"a sermon on the loss of American confidence and a presentation of his 'new' energy policy." And Theodore Windt believed the speech was sermonic in a Southern Baptist sense because Carter confessed his sins (in the first part of the speech wherein Carter criticized himself); reaffirmed his faith (the crisis of confidence section); and proved his faith by doing good works (the energy proposals). The speech could also be conceived of as a political jeremiad: the prophet/president called upon the chosen people/Americans to repent and then to return to the Biblical way by conserving energy. However one understands the address, it is certainly true, as Hahn remarked, that Carter "chose to flail the profligate."

From another perspective, one can appreciate why in the short run the speech had some initial success, but why its long-range impact was limited. At the macro-level, the speech was a problem-solution format. The problem was that the energy crisis was not being resolved, but the root cause was the crisis in confidence in the government. The solution was to regain national confidence by solving the energy problem, and to do that Carter listed six new points that would invigorate less reliance on foreign energy (Hint: How does solving the energy crisis address confidence in the government?).

At the micro-level, the speech had some logical dysfunctions. Although the speech was ostensibly about energy, Carter introduced other exigencies, in order to energize the problem, that unfortunately had little to do with energy per se. In a folksy attempt to connect with the people, Carter used nineteen quotations from visitors to Camp David. Unfortunately, they ran the gamut from "Mr. President, you are not leading this Nation—you're just managing the government" to "we are confronted with a moral and spiritual crisis" to "We can't go on consuming 40 percent more energy than we produce" to "When we enter the moral equivalent of war, Mr. president, don't issue us BB guns." The real problem was Carter and/or the government and/or the people (Hint: Do not blame Carter).

The solution was downright bizarre. Again using the method of residues, Carter first averred that the people (and Carter subsumed himself with the people) had turned to the federal government, which did not work, for "Often you see paralysis and stagnation and drift. You don't like it, and neither do I. What can we do?" Since the problem was with the Congress, one would reasonably assume Carter would stand up to the Congress (Hint: Do not expect that).

But, no, the solution was with the people or, as Carter again quoted a participant at Camp David: "The strength we need will not come from the White House, but from every house in America." If this logic is indeed true, it is unclear why the American people need a president or Congress to solve their problems (Hint: Are you totally confused?).

The last logical difficulty with the speech was Carter's inability to link the solving of the nation's energy needs with solving other non-related elements of the crisis of confidence. Even if the nation solved the energy problem, that does not necessarily imply that confidence in government, which Carter claimed did not function properly, would be restored. Indeed, Carter merely asserted the link, without actually proving it, in one longish sentence: "Just as the search for solutions to our energy shortages had now led us to a new awareness of our Nation's deeper problems, so our willingness to work for those solutions in energy can strengthen us to attack those deeper problems."

Perhaps Carter would have done better to stick with either energy or a crisis in confidence. By mixing the two, he compounded his persuasive problems, for the admixture was not necessarily related logically from a problem-solution perspective, and he ended up solving neither exigency.

State of the Union, 1980

The state of the nation in early 1980 was not propitious for President Carter. In 1979 the Soviet Union had invaded Afghanistan, and Iranian militants had stormed the American Embassy in Teheran and seized Americans as hostages. On January 23, 1980, Carter addressed a joint session of Congress to deliver his constitutionally mandated State of the Union Address, which came to be known as the Carter Doctrine speech. It was, according to Dan Hahn and Justin Gustainis, Carter's "chance to convert to toughness, to shed his 'Mr. Nice Guy' image and demonstrate that he was the right man for the job." For a variety of reasons, the speech did not succeed.

Carter enunciated the Carter Doctrine, his response to the importance of the

Persian Gulf, by asserting that any "assault on the vital interests of the United States of America . . . will be repelled by any means necessary, including military force" in the Gulf area. However, this tough talk was attenuated by a series of rhetorical mistakes. His tendency to use superlatives was scored by friend and foe alike when Carter claimed that the Soviet invasion of Afghanistan was "the most serious threat to the peace since the second world war," when clearly such was not the case. He also drew attention to the poor fit between his announcement that henceforth the United States would "face the world as it is" with his assertion that "the United States will remain the strongest of all nations" and "our nation has never been aroused and unified so greatly in peacetime."

In fact, Hahn and Gustainis noted that Carter even sabotaged his own superlatives and credibility. Carter characterized the Soviet invasion seventeen times in the speech. In the beginning, the Soviets were attempting "to subjugate" Afghanistan through "military aggression," but by the end of the address, the verbal portraiture was cropped to the Soviet Union's efforts "to consolidate a strategic position."

The address also suffered from a malaise of indirection, which exemplified James Fallows's claim that "Carter thinks in lists, not arguments." As if listing problems would somehow produce solutions (assuming, of course, that the so-called problems were *problems*), Hahn and Gustainis found that Carter "presented seven lists": he enumerated three contemporary challenges, five goals that he would continue pursuing, a four-part historical list of American-Soviet confrontations, six ways that America could work for world peace, five actions that Carter would undertake to improve the nation's economy, eight visions of America's future, and "a list of three things that all Americans could do together to make these visions realities." Little wonder, Hahn and Gustainis judged the speech a "failure."

The 1980 Presidential Debate

For a variety of reasons, which Kurt Ritter and David Henry carefully detailed, President Carter faced Ronald Reagan only once in the 1980 campaign. The debate was held at Cleveland, Ohio, on October 28th. Given that this would be the only face-to-face encounter, both candidates developed rhetorical tactics that would address their target audiences. Carter would portray Reagan as a risky, untried candidate who would be militaristic in the White House, as juxtaposed to Carter, who, his campaign team hoped, would be perceived as safe and experienced with the voters. On the other hand, Reagan wisely focused on Carter's record in the White House, which was not particularly sanguine in 1980.

Ritter and Henry determined that Carter, on the advice of his campaign advisors, adopted a three-fold strategy in the debate. Carter would attack, but not debate Reagan; Carter would list his accomplishments; and Carter would capitalize on Reagan's mistakes, which would demonstrate that Reagan was unfit for office. Unfortunately, Carter's strategy had some serious pitfalls. First, viewers expected a give-and-take debate: Reagan attacked and defended, whereas Carter only attacked, which helped to reinforce Reagan's portrayal of Carter as mean-spirited. Second, government-by-listing, which, as we have seen, was a favorite rhetorical device that had little persuasive efficacy in Carter's other speaking situations, did not work especially well in the debate. And third, Reagan did not make any serious mistakes, which enervated the third leg of Carter's strategy. In the end, as Ritter and Henry determined, Carter's oratorical performance did not find, whereas Reagan's did, the available means of persuasion: "Reagan won the debate because he executed an effective debating strategy that combined sustained argumentation with an appealing style of presentation. Carter lost the debate because his debate strategy was fatally flawed. It required Carter to attack without arguing, to list points without developing them fully, and to hope that Ronald Reagan would defeat himself."

CONCLUSION

Quintilian held that the exemplar of an orator is the good person speaking well. His ethics never really at issue, as it was with previous and later tenants of the White House, Carter was a good man, but one who spoke only reasonably well. From Quintilian's perspective, Carter fared rather well, as Quintilian stressed the goodness of the orator, at which Carter excelled, over speaking well, which characterizes the presidents immediately before and after Carter.

RHETORICAL SOURCES

Archival Materials

The Jimmy Carter Library, Atlanta, Georgia, contains the primary research materials for Carter's presidential oratory. The White House Central Files contain a category on Speeches, and the Staff Office Files has a category on Presidential Speechwriters, which are the primary places for drafts and texts of speeches. The Library has an indexing system that aids in locating specific documents. Audiovisual materials include photographs and videotapes of Carter's speeches and addresses. The Library holds oral histories of leading figures in Carter's administration, as well as additional oral history interviews conducted by the White Burkett Miller Center Jimmy Carter Project.

Public Papers of the Presidents of the United States. (*PPP*). 8 Vols. Washington, DC: U.S. Government Printing Office, 1977–1981.

Rhetorical Studies

Adams, William C., Ed. *Television Coverage of the 1980 Presidential Campaign.* Norwood, NJ: Ablex Publishing Corporation, 1983.

Baker, James Thomas. *A Southern Baptist in the White House*. Philadelphia: Westminster Press, 1977.

Barber, James David. *The Pulse of Politics: Ejecting Presidents in the Media Age*. New York: W. W. Norton and Company, 1980.

———, Ed. *Race for the Presidency*. Englewood Cliffs, NJ: Prentice-Hall, 1978.

Bitzer, Lloyd, and Theodore Rueter. *Carter vs. Ford: The Counterfeit Debates of 1976*. Madison, WI: University of Wisconsin Press, 1980.

Carter, Jimmy. *A Government as Good As Its People*. New York: Simon and Schuster, 1977.

———. *Keeping Faith: Memoirs of a President*. New York: Bantam Books, 1982.

Carter, Rosalynn. *First Lady from Plains*. Boston: Houghton Mifflin Co., 1984.

Collins, Tom. *The Search for Jimmy Carter*. Waco, TX: Word Books, 1976.

Denton, Robert E., Jr. *The Symbolic Dimensions of the American Presidency: Description and Analysis*. Prospect Heights, IL: Waveland Press, 1982.

Drew, Elizabeth. *American Journal: The Events of 1976*. New York: Random House, 1976.

Ferguson, Thomas, and Joel Rogers, Eds. *The Hidden Election: Politics and Economics in the 1980 Presidential Campaign*. New York: Pantheon Books, 1981.

Fink, Gary M. *Prelude to the Presidency: The Political Character and Legislative Leadership Style of Governor Jimmy Carter*. Westport, CT: Greenwood Press, 1980.

Germond, Jack W., and Jules Witcover. *Blue Smoke and Mirrors: How Reagan Won and Carter Lost the Election of 1980*. New York: The Viking Press, 1981.

Glad, Betty. *Jimmy Carter: In Search of the Great White House*. New York: W. W. Norton and Co., 1980.

Greenfield, Jeff. *The Real Campaign: How the Media Missed the Story of the 1980 Campaign*. New York: Summit Books, 1982.

Hyatt, Richard. *The Carters of Plains*. Huntsville, AL: Strode, 1977.

Jordan, Hamilton. *Crisis: The True Story of an Unforgettable Year in the White House*. New York: Berkley Books, 1982.

Kucharsky, David. *The Man from Plains: The Mind and Spirit of Jimmy Carter*. New York: Harper and Row, 1976.

Lankevich, George J., Ed. *James E. Carter, 1924– : Chronology-Documents-Bibliographical Aids*. Presidential Chronologies Series. Dobbs Ferry, NY: Oceana Publications, 1981.

Lasky, Victor. *Jimmy Carter: The Man and the Myth*. New York: Richard Marek Publishers, 1979.

Lynn, Laurence E., Jr., and David F. Whitman. *The President as Policymaker: Jimmy Carter and Welfare Reform*. Philadelphia: Temple University Press, 1981.

MacDougall, Malcolm D. *We Almost Made It*. New York: Crown Publishers, 1977.

Martel, Myles. *Political Campaign Debates: Images, Strategies, and Tactics*. New York: Longman, 1983.

Mazlish, Bruce, and Edwin Diamond. *Jimmy Carter: A Character Portrait*. New York: Simon and Schuster, 1979.

Miller, William Lee. *Yankee from Georgia: The Emergence of Jimmy Carter*. New York: New York Times Books, 1978.

Moore, Jonathan, Ed. *The Campaign for President: 1980 in Retrospect*. Cambridge, MA: Ballinger, 1981.

Moore, Jonathan, and Janet Fraser, Eds. *Campaign for President: The Managers Look at '76.* Cambridge, MA: Ballinger, 1977.

Nielson, Niels C., Jr. *The Religion of President Carter.* New York: Thomas Nelson, 1977.

Pomper, Gerald, et al. *The Election of 1976.* New York: David Mackay Co., 1977.

Schramm, Martin. *Running for President, 1976: The Carter Campaign.* New York: Stein and Day, 1977.

Shogan, Robert. *Promises to Keep: Carter's First Hundred Days.* New York: Thomas Y. Crowell Co., 1977.

Stroud, Kandy. *How Jimmy Won: The Victory Campaign from Plains to the White House.* New York: Morrow Publishing Co., 1977.

Thompson, Kenneth W., Ed. *The Carter Presidency: Fourteen Intimate Perspectives of Jimmy Carter.* Lanham, MD: University Press of America, 1990.

Turner, Robert W. *"I'll Never Lie to You": Jimmy Carter in His Own Words.* New York: Ballantine Books, 1976.

Underhill, Robert. *The Bully Pulpit: From Franklin Roosevelt to Ronald Reagan.* New York: Vantage Press, 1988.

Wheeler, Leslie. *Jimmy Who?* Woodbury, NY: Barron's, 1976.

Wooten, James. *Dasher: The Roots and Rising of Jimmy Carter.* New York: Summit Books, 1978.

Rhetorical Monographs

Altenberg, Les, and Robert Cathcart. "Jimmy Carter on Human Rights: A Thematic Analysis." *Central States Speech Journal* 33 (Fall 1982): 446–57.

Becker, Samuel L. "The Study of Campaign '76: An Overview." *Speech Monographs* 45 (November 1978): 265–67.

Berquist, Goodwin F., and James L. Golden. "Media Rhetoric, Criticism, and the Public Perception of the 1980 Presidential Debates." *Quarterly Journal of Speech* 67 (May 1981): 125–37.

Bethel, Tom. "The Need to Act." *Harper's* (November 1977): 34–40.

Bormann, Ernest G., Jolene Koester, and Janet Bennett. "Political Cartoons and Salient Rhetorical Fantasies: An Empirical Analysis of the '76 Presidential Campaign." *Speech Monographs* 45 (November 1978): 51–63.

Brennan, Ruth G. "Rhetorical Analysis of the Carter 1980 Nomination Acceptance Speech." *Exetasis* 6 (October 20, 1980): 17–20.

Burke, Ronald K., Robert Cathcart, and Les Altenberg. "Carter on Human Rights: An Exchange." *Central States Speech Journal* 35 (Summer 1984): 132–36.

"Campaign '76: Communication Studies of the Presidential Campaign." *Communication Monographs* 45 (1978): 265–388.

Campbell, J. Louis, III. "Jimmy Carter and the Rhetoric of Charisma." *Central States Speech Journal* 30 (Summer 1979): 174–86.

Chaffee, Steven H., and S.Y. Choe. "Time of Decision and Media Use During the Ford-Carter Campaign." *Public Opinion Quarterly* 44 (1980): 53–69.

Dennis, J., and S. H. Chaffee. "Legitimation in the 1976 U.S. Election Campaign." *Communication Research* 5 (1978): 371–94.

Devlin, L. Patrick. "Contrasts in Presidential Campaign Commercials of 1976." *Central States Speech Journal* 28 (Winter 1977): 238–49.

———. "Reagan's and Carter's Ad Men Review the 1980 Television Campaigns." *Communication Quarterly* 30 (Winter 1981): 3–12.

———. "Contrasts in Presidential Campaign Commercials of 1980." *Political Communications Review* 7 (1982): 1–38.

Erickson, Keith V. "Jimmy Carter: The Rhetoric of Private and Civic Piety." *Western Journal of Speech Communication* 44 (Summer 1980): 235–51.

Fallows, James. "A Passionless Presidency." *Atlantic Monthly* 243 (May 1979): 33–48.

Freshley, Dwight L. "Manipulating Public Expectations: Pre- and Post-primary Statements in the '76 Campaign." *Southern Speech Communication Journal* 45 (Spring 1980): 223–39.

Hahn, Don F. "One's Reborn Every Minute: Carter's Religious Appeal in 1976." *Communication Quarterly* 28 (Summer 1980): 56–62.

———. "Carter's First Fireside Chat." *Speaker and Gavel* 19 (Spring/Summer 1982): 64–69.

———. "Flailing the Profligate: Carter's Energy Sermon of 1979." *Presidential Studies Quarterly* 10 (Fall 1980): 583–87.

———. "The Rhetoric of Jimmy Carter, 1976–1980." *Presidential Studies Quarterly* 14 (Spring 1984): 265–88.

Hahn, Dan F., and J. Justin Gustainis. "Anatomy of an Enigma: Jimmy Carter's 1980 State of the Union Address." *Communication Quarterly* 33 (Winter 1985): 43–49.

Johnstone, Christopher Lyle. "Electing Ourselves in 1976: Jimmy Carter and the American Faith." *Western Journal of Speech Communication* 42 (Fall 1978): 241–49.

Jones, Charles O. "Keeping Faith and Losing Congress: The Carter Experience in Washington." *Presidential Studies Quarterly* 14 (Summer 1984): 437–45.

Kantowicz, Edward R. "Reminiscences of a Fated Presidency: Themes from the Carter Memoirs." *Presidential Studies Quarterly* 16 (Fall 1986): 651–65.

Krukones, Michael G. "The Campaign Promises of Jimmy Carter: Accomplishments and Failures." *Presidential Studies Quarterly* 15 (Winter 1985): 136–44.

Ladd, Everett Carl. "The Brittle Mandate: Electoral Dealignment and the 1980 Presidential Election." *Political Science Quarterly* 96 (Spring 1981): 1–26.

Locander, Robert. "Carter and the Press: The First Two Years." *Presidential Studies Quarterly* 10 (Winter 1980): 106–19.

Maloney, Gary D., and Terry F. Buss. "Information, Interest, and Attitude Change: Carter and the 1976 Post-Convention Campaign." *Central States Speech Journal* 31 (Spring 1980): 63–73.

Martin, Martha Anna. "Ideologues, Ideographs, and 'The Best Men': From Carter to Reagan." *Southern Speech Communication Journal* 49 (Fall 1983): 12–25.

Patton, John H. "A Government as Good as its People: Jimmy Carter and the Restoration of Transcendence to Politics." *Quarterly Journal of Speech* 63 (October 1977): 249–57.

Rarick, David L., Mary B. Duncan, David G. Lee, and Laurinda W. Porter. "The Carter Persona: An Empirical Analysis of the Rhetorical Visions of Campaign '76." *Quarterly Journal of Speech* 63 (October 1977): 258–73.

Roberts, Churchill L. "From Primary to the Presidency: A Panel Study of Images and Issues in the 1976 Election." *Western Journal of Speech Communication* 45 (Winter 1981): 60–70.

Ryan, Halford. "Jimmy Carter's 'The Panama Canal Treaties.'" In *Classical Commu-*

nication for the Contemporary Communicator, by Halford Ryan, 206–21. May-field, CA: Mayfield Publishing Co.

Smith, Craig Allen. "Leadership, Orientation, and Rhetorical Vision: Jimmy Carter, The 'New Right,' and the Panama Canal." *Presidential Studies Quarterly* 16 (Spring 1986): 317–28.

Smith, Raymond G. "The Carter-Ford Debates: Some Perceptions from Academe." *Central States Speech Journal* 28 (Winter 1977): 250–57.

Solomon, Martha. "Jimmy Carter and Playboy: A Sociolinguistic Perspective on Style." *Quarterly Journal of Speech* 64 (April 1978): 173–82.

Strong, Robert A. "Recapturing Leadership: The Carter Administration and the Crisis of Confidence." *Presidential Studies Quarterly* 16 (Fall 1986): 636–50.

Sudol, Ronald A. "The Rhetoric of Strategic Retreat: Carter and the Panama Canal Debate." *Quarterly Journal of Speech* 65 (December 1979): 379–91.

Swanson, David L. "And That's the Way It Was? Television Covers the 1976 Presidential Campaign." *Quarterly Journal of Speech* 63 (October 1977): 239–48.

Tiemens, Robert K. "Television's Portrayal of the 1976 Presidential Debates: An Analysis of Visual Content." *Speech Monographs* 45 (November 1978): 362–70.

Windt, Theodore. "Jimmy Carter, The Energy Problem: II." In *Presidential Rhetoric (1960–to the Present)*, 3d ed. Edited by Theodore Windt. Dubuque, IA: Kendall/ Hunt, 1983.

Wooten, James T. "The President as Orator: His Deliberative Style Appears to Run Counter to the Inspiration He Seeks to Instill." *New York Times*, January 26, 1978, p. A15.

Chronology of Significant Presidential Persuasions

[Unless otherwise indicated, all speeches were delivered from Washington, D.C.]

Inaugural Address, January 20, 1977. *PPP*, 1977, I: 1–4.

First Fireside Chat, February 3, 1977. *PPP*, 1977, I: 69–77.

The Energy Problem or "The Moral Equivalent of War," April 18, 1977. *PPP*, 1977, I: 656–62.

Panama Canal Treaties, February 1, 1978. *PPP*, 1978, I: 258–63.

Energy and National Goals or "A Crisis of Confidence," July 15, 1979. *PPP*, 1979, II: 1235–41.

State of the Union Address, January 23, 1980. *PPP*, 1980–1981, I: 194–200.

Kurt Ritter

Ronald Reagan
(1911–   )

Call it mysticism if you will, I have always believed there was some divine providence that placed this great land here between the two great oceans, to be found by a special kind of people from every corner of the world, who had a special love for freedom and a special courage that enabled them to leave their own land, leave their friends and their countrymen, and come to this new and strange land to build a new world of peace and freedom and hope.

When Ronald Reagan spoke at the Founder's Day convocation at his alma mater, tiny Eureka College near Peoria, Illinois, on his 73rd birthday, February 6, 1984, he was returning to the place where he had launched his career as "the Great Communicator" fifty-six years earlier. His speech at Eureka College came a little more than three years after his inauguration as president, and it gave him an opportunity to preview the rhetoric he would use in his 1984 re-election campaign. Closing his address with a historic sweep of the twentieth century, Reagan remarked: "In the past half century, America has had its flirtation with statism, but we're returning now to our roots: limited government, the defense of freedom, faith in the future and in our God." This restoration, Reagan asserted, would benefit not just Americans, but all mankind: "Believe me, there are great days ahead for you, for America, and for the cause of human freedom." As he had done many times before during the previous decade, Reagan reminded his audience that America had not sought world leadership, "it was thrust upon us. In the dark days after World War II when much of the civilized world lay in ruins, Pope Pius XII said, 'The American people have a genius for splendid

The research for this essay was supported, in part, by a research grant from the Center for Presidential Studies, Texas A&M University.

and unselfish action, and into the hands of America, God has placed the destinies of afflicted humanity.' ''

Reagan's speech at Eureka College summarized his optimistic vision of the American mission that would inform his presidential oratory throughout his eight years in the White House. Communication, he realized, would play a key role as he mobilized public support behind his efforts to restore what he saw as America's true principles. Indeed, Reagan's own career had always been tied to communication. As he observed: ''In 1932 . . . I graduated from Eureka and landed a job in radio. Though I didn't realize it at the time, I had become part of the communications revolution that was shrinking the dimensions of my world. . . . ''

As a student at Eureka College, Reagan prepared to take advantage of the communications revolution, for there he discovered that, ultimately, communication succeeds not because of technology, but because of a speaker's ability to establish an intimate relationship with an audience. In his pre-presidential autobiography, Reagan described his first major public speech, which he presented during a student strike in his freshman year at Eureka College. On November 28, 1928, Reagan was one of the students to address a midnight rally in the college chapel. His speech brought the audience ''to their feet with a roar. . . . It was heady wine.'' Looking back on the event, Reagan recalled: ''I discovered that night that an audience has a feel to it and, in the parlance of the theater, that audience and I were together.'' Reagan's considerable success as a presidential orator resulted in no small measure from the fact that he never forgot that lesson.

Although Eureka College was only Reagan's first step toward the White House, his enrollment as a college student represented a striking achievement for a person of his circumstances. Born in Tampico, Illinois, on February 6, 1911, Reagan was the younger of the two children of John Edward (Jack) and Nelle Wilson Reagan. The Reagans lived in a number of small Illinois towns (and for a time in Chicago) as Jack Reagan pursued his vocation as a shoe salesman. An alcoholic, who struggled to maintain a steady job, Jack Reagan finally took his family to Dixon, Illinois, in 1920. For the nine-year-old Ronald Reagan, Dixon became his hometown, where he completed grade school and high school, worked as a lifeguard at the city park along the Rock River, participated in the youth programs of the Christian Church (Disciples of Christ), excelled in school sports, and acted in high school drama productions.

At Eureka College he financed his education with a scholarship, loans, part-time jobs, and his summer earnings. Majoring in economics and sociology, Reagan continued to compete in football and swimming, participated in the college drama productions, and became a student leader (a cheerleader during basketball seasons, a writer on the student newspaper, a feature editor of the yearbook, and president of the student senate).

Upon graduating from Eureka College in the spring of 1932, Reagan pursued work in radio, eventually securing a position as an announcer and sportscaster first with WOC in Davenport, Iowa, and then WHO, an NBC affiliate in Des Moines, Iowa. His radio work took him to Hollywood in 1937 as a contract actor with Warner Brothers. He appeared in over fifty motion pictures between 1937 and 1964. During World War II Reagan served as a military officer with a unit based in the Los Angeles area that produced training films. Following the war, he became president of the Screen Actors Guild, a position he held into the 1950s. With the advent of television, Reagan's primary work shifted from films to television programs. He appeared in over fifty program episodes and became widely known for his work on "General Electric Theater," a Sunday evening drama program that he hosted from 1954 to 1962.

Long interested in politics, Reagan increasingly spoke on behalf of Republican and conservative candidates in the early 1960s, including presidential candidates Richard Nixon and Barry Goldwater. On October 27, 1964, Reagan presented his first nationally televised political address, as he called upon Americans to vote for Goldwater and presented a ringing endorsement of the emerging conservative movement. The speech could not rescue Goldwater's ill-fated campaign, but it did launch Reagan's political career. The speech was so well received by conservatives that during the last week of the presidential campaign it was rebroadcast twice nationally and hundreds of times in local television markets. By December 1964, conservatives were urging Reagan to run for president. In his anthology of speeches, Reagan simply observed: "The speech . . . changed my entire life."

In 1966, at the age of fifty-five, Reagan ran successfully for his first public office, Governor of California. He was re-elected to a second four-year term in 1970. Reagan left the Governor's office in January of 1975 when he was almost sixty-four years old. He promptly began to prepare for his 1976 campaign for the Republican presidential nomination through a daily radio commentary program, a weekly newspaper column, and extensive speaking activities. A serious, but unsuccessful contender for the nomination in 1976, Reagan was ultimately elected President in 1980.

After serving two full terms as President, Reagan retired from the White House in January 1989; he returned to California where he divided his time between his home in the Los Angeles suburb of Bel Air and his ranch in the Santa Ynez mountains above Santa Barbara. Although he was almost seventy-eight years old when he left office, Reagan occasionally presented public speeches. Perhaps his most notable post-presidential address was his stirring speech at the 1992 Republican National Convention in Houston, which he presented at the age of eight-one. That speech reflected the enduring themes of Reagan's career, including his uncanny ability to argue for conservative policies while maintaining an optimistic, forward-looking perspective: "I was born in 1911. . . . In my life's journey over these past eight decades, I have seen the human race through a period of unparalleled tumult and triumph. I have seen the birth of communism and the death of communism. . . . I have not only seen, but lived the marvel of what historians have called the 'American Century.' Yet, tonight is not a time to look backward. For while I take inspiration from the past, like most Americans, I live for the future. So this evening, . . . I hope you will let me talk about a country that is forever young.''

TRAINING FOR THE RHETORICAL PRESIDENCY

Reagan's own life paralleled the rise of the rhetorical presidency, and his careers in the mass media and in politics provided him with the skills and the personal disposition to excel in an office where speechmaking has become a central activity. He entered politics as an outsider; he was even an outsider to the Republican party. He had never been a city council member, the member of a county board, a state legislator, or a member of Congress. Reagan's first elective office was as governor of one of the largest states in the nation. Because Reagan's rise to power was built not on negotiation but on popular appeals, his first impulse as a political leader was to marshall public pressure to work his will on the legislative branch.

In California, when Reagan found his legislative initiatives blocked by the state Assembly and Senate, he went on television with ''Messages to the People.'' Only after gathering the political capital of public opinion was Reagan willing to negotiate with the state legislature on a specific issue. This constituted on-the-job training for the rhetorical presidency. As Reagan remarked in his post-presidential autobiography: ''In Sacramento, the most important lesson I learned was the value of making an end run around the legislature by going directly to the people; on television or radio, I'd lay out the problems we faced and asked their help to persuade the legislators to vote as *they* wanted, not the way special-interest groups did. As president, I intended to do the same thing. It had worked in Sacramento and I thought it would work in Washington.'' Indeed, Reagan's long-time speechwriter in the Governor's office, Jerry Martin, has revealed that even after Reagan's aides began to negotiate with representatives of the California legislature on a particular proposal, they found that they could induce concessions by observing that if a satisfactory compromise could not be reached, the Governor would have to go back on television with another speech to the public.

Of course, Reagan's career in radio, motion pictures, and television was also valuable training for the rhetorical presidency. During his acting career, Reagan did more than hone his skills of delivery: he gained an appreciation for the importance of a well-crafted script. He learned that a good script must be written for the ear rather than for the eye, and that the dialogue must portray a consistent character. During his Hollywood years, Reagan's constant efforts to rewrite the scripts of films and television programs brought him the reputation of being a ''script doctor,'' or less kindly, a pest to directors.

Reagan also mastered a kind a campaign speaking, which would later serve him well in the White House. Ever since his election as the president of the Screen Actors Guild in 1947, Reagan's primary means for influencing public policy had been to present public speeches. As a spokesperson for the motion picture industry, he addressed hundreds of community groups in the late 1940s and the 1950s arguing for freedom from government-imposed censorship on movies, for changes in tax policy, and for more favorable terms in foreign distribution of American films. During his eight years as host of "General Electric Theater" (1954–1962), he visited all of the corporation's 135 plants as part of his public relations duties. Those trips soon included formal addresses to community groups across the nation; by the end of his eight-year association with General Electric, Reagan had presented approximately 9,000 speeches. Those speeches initially concerned Hollywood, but they soon became vehicles for Reagan to warn of the threat of expanding Communism abroad and government infringements on free enterprise at home. Typical of Reagan's speeches during his years with General Electric was his commencement address at Eureka College on June 7, 1957, in which he spoke of Soviet Communism as "an evil force." In the early 1960s Reagan frequently spoke in support of the emerging conservative movement. When he finally ran for office, he used primary campaigns to defeat opponents from the Republican establishment.

REAGAN AS A RHETORICAL PRESIDENT

In analyzing Reagan's presidential rhetoric, the question is, what was the character of Reagan's oratory that served him so well as a rhetorical president? In the common categories of classical rhetoric, what distinguished his rhetorical invention, the arrangement of his speeches, his use of language, and his delivery?

Ideology as Rhetorical Invention

Reagan's rhetorical invention, the discovery and selection of the ideas, arguments and evidence used in his speeches, clearly reflected his political ideology. His presidential speeches articulated a set of political ideas he began to develop decades before. Garry Wills and Lou Cannon locate the origins of Reagan's political beliefs in his years as a public speaker on behalf of private enterprise while he was associated with General Electric. Stephen Vaughn traces Reagan's ideology to his Hollywood days, especially his years as the president of the Screen Actors Guild. In either case, Reagan both developed and expressed his ideology in thousands of speeches prior to entering politics. Upon becoming Governor of California, his staff distilled a philosophy of government from the corpus of his speeches, which they set forth as a series of propositions on a single sheet and distributed widely throughout Reagan's administration under the title of the "Governor's Philosophy." Gary G. Hamilton and Nicole Woolsey Biggart discovered, when interviewing hundreds of Reagan appointees in California government, that this statement of philosophy was routinely used to guide the appointees in their decisions.

The "Governor's Philosophy" was carried into the White House. The ideology that formed the substance of Reagan's presidential orations on domestic issues can be expressed in three propositions: 1) that the government that governs least, governs best; 2) that a society based upon individual freedom and private enterprise will prosper; and 3) that government regulations menace the freedom of Americans. To those domestic principles, Reagan added two foreign policy principles that had been featured in his public speeches since the 1950s: that Soviet Communism was the greatest threat to American freedom; and that America's military strength must be capable of confronting Communism everywhere in the world.

Amos Kiewe and Davis W. Houck argue that Reagan spoke from a fundamentally economic motive, that the ideology created and expressed in his orations focused on individual's economic freedom and prosperity. Even Reagan's strong opposition of Communism, they note, was rooted largely in its economic practices. Martin Medhurst's analysis of the subordinate position of Reagan's legislative agenda on social issues also indicates the centrality of the economic motive in Reagan's presidential rhetoric.

Certainly, Reagan's major orations applied his philosophy of limited government to the nation's economic policy. In his First Inaugural Address he focused on the nation's "economic ills"and argued that "in this present crisis, government is not the solution to our problem; government is the problem." Reagan was unambiguous about his goals: "It is my intention to curb the size and influence of the federal establishment." Kenneth Khachigian, the speechwriter who worked with Reagan on that Inaugural, described the speech as a "blueprint" of the president's economic policies. Reagan elaborated on that blueprint in his first "Address to the Nation" from the Oval Office on February 5, 1981. In that speech he rejected additional government intrusion into the private economy, and announced: "Our aim is to increase our national wealth so all will have more, not just redistribute what we already have which is just a sharing of scarcity." Two weeks later, on February 18th, Reagan presented his economic program in his first address to a joint session of Congress. In particular, he attacked the "mass of regulations" imposed on businesses, and he declared that "the taxing power of government . . . must not be used to regulate the economy or to bring about social change." The ideological consistency among the First Inaugural Address, the first address to the nation, and the first address to Congress was striking. That consistency resulted primarily from Reagan's longstanding views on the limited role of government, limited taxes, and limited government spending, but it also resulted from the circumstance that Khachigian drafted each speech.

The remarkable aspect of Reagan's economic rhetoric was that it extended not just across his first month in the White House, but across his entire presidency. Six years later in his 1987 State of the Union Address, for example, Reagan continued to stress his theme of limited government, when he noted that the essence of American government was that "the people are the masters and the government is their servant.'' A year later on January 25, 1988, in his last State of the Union address, Reagan returned to his favorite argument that individuals' economic freedom is only secure when their government is constrained. He affirmed "the individual's right to reach as far and as high as his or her talents will permit," and his faith in "the free market as an engine of economic progress." Those American values, Reagan argued, would be protected if the Congress recalled the words of an ancient Chinese philosopher: "Govern a great nation as you would cook a small fish; do not overdo it." Four months later Reagan carried his anti-government message to the heart of the "evil empire," as he told students at Moscow State University that "government planners, no matter how sophisticated," could never substitute "for millions of individuals working night and day to make their dreams come true."

Arguably, Reagan's most successful speeches were those that applied his ideology to foreign affairs, rather than to economic policy. In a series of major public addresses that spanned his presidency, Reagan confronted the Soviet Union and those who he saw as agents of Moscow. Those speeches included his address to the British Parliament in June 1982, the "Evil Empire" and "Star Wars" speeches in March 1983, the address in September 1983 denouncing the Soviets' shoot-down of Korean Airline Flight 007, the speech on Lebanon and Grenada in October 1983, his speech at the Berlin Wall in June 1987, and others. Peter Schweizer reports that such hard-line rhetoric was part of the Reagan administration's grand strategy to win the Cold War.

The address to Parliament, on June 8, 1982, was Reagan's most complete statement of his Cold War rhetoric. Like a number of Reagan's most effective foreign policy speeches, this address was initially drafted by Tony Dolan. In retrospect, the speech has an almost prophetic quality, for in it Reagan predicted the eventual collapse of Soviet Communism. He argued that the world was "at a turning point." Even in "the Communist world," Reagan noted, "man's instinctive desire for freedom and self-determination surfaces again and again . . . .How we conduct ourselves here in the Western democracies will determine whether this trend continues." Ultimately, Reagan argued, the failure of the Soviet Union and the Communist bloc of Eastern Europe could be foreseen in its totalitarian governments: "the regimes planted by totalitarianism have had more than thirty years to establish their legitimacy. But none—not one regime— has yet been able to risk free elections. Regimes planted by bayonets do not take root."

As Reagan reacted to (and precipitated) international events, he adapted the broad outlines of anti-Communist rhetoric to each particular situation. When the Soviets shot down a Korean airliner, Reagan characterized the tragedy in his address to the nation on September 5, 1983, as yet another instance of brutality by the evil empire of Communism. Eschewing the ambiguities of diplomatic language, Reagan spoke of the "Korean airline massacre, the attack by the Soviet Union against 269 innocent men, women, and children aboard an unarmed Korean passenger plane. This crime against humanity must never be forgotten, here or throughout the world.''

Reagan applied the same rhetoric to subsequent events in 1983 that were quite distant from Soviet soil: the U.S. invasion of Grenada and the bombing in Beirut, Lebanon, which killed over 200 U.S. Marines. Speaking to the nation from the Oval Office on October 27, 1983, Reagan not only combined two distinct military actions that had occurred half a world apart, but also connected them to Moscow. His first words were: ''My fellow Americans, some two months ago we were shocked by the brutal massacre of 269 men, women and children, more than 60 of them Americans, in the shooting down of a Korean airliner. Now in these past several days, violence has erupted again, in Lebanon and Grenada.'' The use of the passive voice (''violence has erupted again'') was a strategic choice consistent with Reagan's rhetorical posture of representing the free world as the innocent victims of the criminal acts of others, especially of the Soviets. Such a posture fit the Korean airline shoot-down and the Beirut bombing, but Reagan applied it with equal ease to Grenada, where U.S. troops had initiated military action.

The disparate nature of the events in Lebanon and Grenada made it difficult to discuss both in a single speech, yet the close connection in time between the two events made it necessary. Indeed, it would have been difficult to address one event without mentioning the other. Moreover, the Beirut bombing had been an unmitigated disaster for the U.S. forces. The impact of that incident on public opinion could be moderated by linking it with the Grenada invasion, which had been a success. One of the speechwriters working on this speech, retired U.S. Army Colonel Allan Myer, drafted an introduction that attempted to explain the geo-political connection of the Middle East with the Caribbean within the context of the Cold War. Myer struggled with the task and remained unsatisfied with his attempt. Reagan simply lined through those paragraphs and replaced them with a narrative of how the Beirut bombing took place. Within the framework of Reagan's anti-Communist rhetoric, it was not necessary to begin with an explanation (or even an assertion) that the Soviets were involved in both events. Such a connection was assumed.

A bit more than half way through his address, Reagan simply shifted from Lebanon to Grenada: ''Now, I know another part of the world is very much on our minds, a place much closer to our shores: Grenada.'' Reagan followed with an essentially separate speech on the political and military situation in Grenada, stressing the presence of troops from Communist Cuba. Only late in the speech did Reagan find it necessary to explicitly connect the two military events: ''The events in Lebanon and Grenada, though oceans apart, are closely related. Not only has Moscow assisted and encouraged the violence in both countries, but it provides direct support through a network of surrogates and terrorists.'' The key point about Reagan's speech on Grenada and Lebanon is not whether the Soviets were directly involved, but that Reagan's ideology (as expressed in his speeches) assumed such a connection. It required no more proof than a reference to another recent act of Communist savagery—the Korean airline massacre.

The consistency of Reagan's foreign policy rhetoric is illustrated by the fact that even as U.S. relations with the Soviet Union improved under Mikhail Gorbachev's policies of *perestroika* and *glasnost*, Reagan insisted on maintaining anti-Communist language in his speeches. When speechwriter Peter Robinson included a harsh denunciation of the Berlin Wall in a draft of a speech Reagan would deliver in West Berlin on June 12, 1987, the Department of State objected that the address was "too provocative." In his anthology of speeches, Reagan explained that he had no intentions of altering his ideological rhetoric: "Just because our relationship with the Soviet Union is improving doesn't mean we have to begin denying the truth. That is what got us into such a weak position with the Soviet Union in the first place." In his speech at the Brandenburg Gate, Reagan referred to the wall as "a gash" and a "scar." Speaking as if the Soviet leader were in his immediate audience, Reagan challenged: "There is one sign the Soviets can make that would be unmistakable, that would advance dramatically the cause of freedom and peace. General Secretary Gorbachev, if you seek peace, if you seek prosperity for the Soviet Union and Eastern Europe, if you seek liberalization: Come here to this gate! Mr. Gorbachev, open this gate! Mr. Gorbachev, tear down this wall!"

Reagan's belief in American exceptionalism united his free enterprise oratory with his anti-Communist rhetoric to create a cohesive whole that appealed to Americans' sense of their national identity and national destiny. Reagan's notion that Americans are a chosen people is fundamental to the nation's founding myth and finds its roots in the American Puritans. Craig Allen Smith observes that Reagan's use of the idea of a divinely ordained American destiny gave great power to his appeals in support of an American society based on a community of individuals (as opposed to a society controlled by government regulations): "Drawing upon familiar myths, symbols, values, and beliefs," Reagan's orations depicted "a community of extraordinary individuals who can accomplish anything because of their faith in a proud heritage of self-evident morality." Reagan interwove those themes "so skillfully that any criticism of the President or his policies is initially construed as an attack upon the very meaning of America."

Reagan had been speaking of America's mission since the 1950s; it was a theme that continued throughout his presidency. In his First Inaugural Address he declared that America must be worthy of the heritage of the American Revolution: "And as we renew ourselves here in our own land, . . . we will again be the exemplar of freedom and a beacon of hope for those who do not now have freedom." That mission, Reagan explained, came directly from God, for "we are a nation under God, and I believe God intended for us to be free." Eight years later as Reagan presented his farewell speech to the nation, he recalled his often repeated phrase that America was a "shining city on a hill." The phrase came from a speech by John Winthrop, Reagan explained. Ignoring the autocratic aspects early Puritan New England, Reagan preferred to think of Winthrop as "an early Pilgrim, an early freedom man. He journeyed here . . . like the other Pilgrims . . . looking for a home that would be free." Reagan called upon his audience to remember Winthrop, and a host of American heroes, because "as long as we remember our first principles and believe in ourselves, the future will always be ours."

The didactic nature of Reagan's speeches was not immediately apparent to those who heard him because Reagan self-consciously developed his principal ideas with a variety of supporting materials. Reagan is best remembered for his fondness for anecdotes—often a personal experience, sometimes an apocryphal story, and other times an actual example. In his post-presidential autobiography Reagan offered a general rule for speechmaking: "if you can, use an example. An example is better that a sermon." Reagan came to think of the anecdotes he used in his speeches as "parables," and as William F. Lewis reveals, those stories often cast Reagan as both the narrator and the hero. Five years before he was elected president, Reagan remarked in an interview with Sarah Ellen Cahill that "when I was talking against the government's interference with the agricultural economy, the government subsidies and the government land controls and planning controls and all that, you could go on for two pages saying this is wrong and the government shouldn't do it, or you could use one example, a parable."

When the occasion allowed, Reagan liked to cite a member of his audience as an example to illustrate his point. In his address at Omaha Beach on the 40th anniversary of D-Day, Reagan read from a letter that an adult daughter had written to her deceased father. The daughter, who sat weeping in the audience at the memorial where Reagan spoke, had gone to France for the commemoration in the place of her father. Reagan explained that the father had hoped to come himself: " 'Someday, Lis, I'll go back,' said Private First Class Peter Robert Zanatta, of the 37th Engineer Combat Battalion, and first assault wave to hit Omaha Beach. 'I'll go back, and I'll see it all again. I'll see the beach, the barricades, and the graves.' Those words of Private Zanatta come to us from his daughter, Lisa Zanatta Henn, in a heartrending story about the event her father spoke of so often." Reagan's entire, brief speech was built around the example of Private Zanatta (as related in his daughter's letter), who had faced the carnage of Omaha Beach as a twenty-year-old soldier. In reality, the Zanattas served as a double example for Reagan's speech: the father as an example of those whom the ceremony honored, and his daughter as an example of Reagan's promise that "we will always remember. We will always be proud. We will always be prepared, so we may always be free."

Whenever possible, Reagan would use humor in his addresses. In addition to the obvious appeal of such material to his immediate audience, Reagan found that humor could emphasize the substantive point of a speech; in his interview with Cahill, he commended: "the humor story punches it home." Reagan was especially skilled at employing self-deprecating humor, which promoted an unaffected image for a person whose entire adult life had been as a celebrity. When he addressed a joint session of Congress on April 28, 1981, Reagan was doing more than advocating his "Economic Recovery Program." Most fundamentally, he was reassuring the American people that its seventy-year-old president had recovered from the bullet wound he suffered a month earlier in an assassination attempt. Thanking the public for its expressions of concern, its prayers, and its get well cards, Reagan remarked: "The society we heard from is made up of millions of compassionate Americans and their children, from college age to kindergarten. As a matter of fact, as evidence of that I have a letter with me. The letter came from Peter Sweeney. He's in the second grade in the Riverside School in Rockville Centre, and he said, 'I hope you get well quick or you might have to make a speech in your pajamas.' And he added a postscript. 'P.S. If you have to make a speech in your pajamas, I warned you.' "

Reagan's humor also softened the hard edges of his conservative rhetoric, promoting the image of a concerned citizen of goodwill, rather than an idealogue of the far right. This was especially important in presidential debates, where his opponents hoped to portray Reagan as a dangerous extremist. In 1980 Reagan spent most of his presidential debate with Jimmy Carter replying to what he argued were mischaracterizations of his positions. Finally, Reagan brought the house down with an exasperated, but good natured comment to Carter: "There you go again." Four years later in his first presidential debate with Walter Mondale, Reagan appeared ill-informed and even confused, which raised questions about whether he was too old at age seventy-three for the demands of the presidency. In his second debate with Mondale, he used humor (as well as better debate preparation) to reassure the American public. When a panelist raised the "age issue" in a question, Reagan responded: "I will not make age an issue in this campaign. I am not going to exploit, for political purposes, my opponent's youth and inexperience." Once the sustained laughter and applause had receded, Reagan added: "I might add that it was Seneca or it was Cicero, I don't know which, that said, 'If it was not for the elders correcting the mistakes of the young, there would be no state."

The use of humor usually improved the coverage of a speech on television news programs. One of Reagan's White House speechwriters, C. Landon Parvin, has remarked: "It's to please the press that you do the sound-bites. . . . Their coverage of a story is so concise, that if you can somehow rap up your entire theme in one sentence or two sentences, they are much more likely to put it on [television news]. And I have also learned that if you can summarize your entire theme with a bit of humor, you're almost certain to get it on."

As much as Reagan enjoyed using humor, he also liked to cite quantitative data in his speeches. Lou Cannon has joked that Ronald Reagan never met a statistic that he did not like. In her White House memoir recounting two years as a full-time speechwriter for Ronald Reagan, Peggy Noonan commented that she found it odd that Reagan's own preliminary draft of his second inaugural address was "chock-full of facts and statistics and percentages." Her boss, the head of the speechwriting department, Bently Elliott, assured her: "no, this is the essential Reagan; everyone thinks he doesn't give a fig for facts but he loves his factoids, loves his numbers."

Bill Hogan reports that Reagan often culled speech material from conservative magazines and journals such as *Human Events*. He seized upon statistics and stories that illustrated what he regarded as enduring principles. Over his many decades as a public speaker, he had acquired the habit of accepting the accuracy of information simply because it conformed with his ideology. As Paul Erickson, Michael Rogin, and others have demonstrated, a number of Reagan's anecdotes and statistics were inaccurate; others could not be documented. But Reagan's most serious problem with accuracy in his public statements concerned the Iran-*Contra* affair, in which representatives of the U.S. government sold arms to the revolutionary regime in Iran (contrary to U.S. law) in an effort to gain the freedom of hostages (contrary to Reagan's publicly stated policy against bargaining with terrorists), and then diverted the profits from those sales to the *Contra* forces that were fighting a guerrilla war against the pro-Soviet *Sandinista* government of Nicaragua (again, contrary to U.S. law).

When Reagan could no longer ignore the press reports of an "arms for hostages" deal with Iran, he presented an address to the nation on November 13, 1986, in which he claimed such charges were "utterly false." After noting a variety of such reports, he asserted: "not one of them is true." Later events would show that Reagan's remarks were less than candid. Soon news reports had traced the arm sales profits to the *Contras*, which forced Reagan to again televise a brief address to the nation from the Oval Office on December 2, 1986. Reagan took the posture that illegal acts might have occurred: "If actions . . . were taken without my authorization, knowledge, or concurrence, this will be exposed and appropriate corrective steps will be implemented." Finally, with the release of an investigative report from the "Tower Commission" (which Reagan had appointed), he was obliged to address the nation yet again.

On March 4, 1987, Reagan admitted that his previous accounts of the Iran-*Contra* affair had been inaccurate: "A few months ago I told the American people I did not trade arms for hostages. My heart and my best intentions still tell me that's true, but the facts and the evidence tell me it is not." Still, Reagan could not bring himself to accept full responsibility, as he mentioned being "angry" over "activities undertaken without my knowledge." Reagan's *apologia* was not entirely successful, for in order to deny that he personally participated in illegal acts and that he had lied to the nation, Reagan presented himself as a president who was not in control of his administration. Years later the speechwriter who worked with Reagan in drafting the address, Landon Parvin, said that Reagan's real message in the speech was: "I didn't do it; and I promise I'll never do it again."

The Jeremiad as Speech Arrangement

In a technical sense, Reagan's speeches used a straightforward pattern of organization, usually discussing particular policy issues in terms of the President's basic ideology. Even Jeffrey K. Tulis, a political scientist who has despaired at the rise of the rhetorical presidency, has conceded that "a substantial number of those [Reagan's] speeches contain an ordered argument and relatively few, compared to the most recent [previous] presidents, are merely laundry lists of points." Kurt Ritter, in Ryan's *Contemporary American Public Discourse*, reports that Reagan's numerous speeches prior to entering politics so consistently advocated the same ideological principles, that Reagan himself believed that organizing a particular speech posed no difficulty. Reagan described the process as simply "taking an introduction from one [speech], the middle from another and the conclusion from a third."

On a broader level, the basic pattern used in Reagan's speeches often drew upon the rhetorical form of the jeremiad. Works by Perry Miller, Sacvan Bercovitch, and Kurt Ritter reveal that the jeremiad has been an important dimension of American public address since the colonial period. David Howard-Pitney provides the most concise summary of the three distinct parts of the American jeremiad:

1. *The promise*, which stresses America's special destiny as the promised land, literally, its covenant with God;
2. *The declension*, which cites America's failure to live up to its obligations as the chosen people, its neglect of its mission, its failure to progress sufficiently, its national sin of retrogression from the promise; and
3. *The prophecy*, which predicts that if Americans will repent and reform, the promise can still be fulfilled.

Much of the power of Reagan's presidential speeches derived from his skill at adapting this old Puritan sermon form to contemporary presidential speaking. His particular version of the jeremiad stressed the restoration motive, for he structured his speeches as a straightforward and hopeful argument: America had been blessed by God as the home of liberty. The constitutional concepts of individual freedom and limited governmental powers constituted America's covenant. Under it, America had flourished, ultimately becoming the most favored and most powerful nation in the world. But something had gone wrong. The people had been misguided by leaders who violated the covenant, and the nation was suffering. The solution was to restore the original covenant and recover its blessings before it was too late. Reagan's message was a secular version of the religious jeremiads from the Old Testament prophets, which are summarized by John Barton: "in every generation, sin leads to national disaster, but repentance to new life and salvation."

Reagan's jeremiad was particularly appealing because unlike the Old Testament prophets and the American Puritans, he blamed America's problems not on the people but upon their leaders. When accepting the Republican presidential nomination on July 17, 1980, Reagan blamed the nation's problems on his Democratic opposition: "The major issue of this campaign," Reagan claimed, was "the direct political, personal, and moral responsibility of Democratic Party leadership—in the White House and in Congress—for this unprecedented calamity which has befallen us." From such a perspective, electing Republicans represented an act of fidelity to America's historic mission. Toward the end of his speech Reagan urged his audience: "Tonight, let us dedicate ourselves to renewing the American Compact."

Within the basic pattern of the jeremiad, Reagan shifted his emphasis as he spoke throughout his presidency. Early in his presidency, he spoke from the perspective of "the declension," looking backward sadly to "the promise" and reminding his audience of America's divine covenant. His speeches consisted of a litany of the government's failure to live up to America's promise of individual liberty. As Reagan concluded his speeches, he would look forward to "the prophecy" and would reassure his audiences that they still had time to reform American government, to return America to her covenant.

By the time of his re-election campaign in 1984, Reagan spoke from the juncture between the "declension" and the "prophecy." In his view, America had begun to reform as the Congress had adopted some of his economic program and as America had confronted the "evil empire" of Soviet Communism. But the nation needed to complete its restoration in order to secure the "prophecy." In his nomination acceptance speech at the 1984 Republican National Convention, Reagan portrayed America as on the verge of achieving "the dream conceived by our Founding Fathers, . . . the ultimate in individual freedom consistent with an orderly society. . . . It's all coming together. . . . We're in the midst of a springtime of hope for America. Greatness lies ahead of us." After he secured his re-election, Reagan used his Second Inaugural Address to remind Americans that "the prophecy," while within reach, had not yet been fulfilled: "We are creating a nation once again vibrant, robust, and alive. But there are many mountains yet to climb. We will not rest until every American enjoys the fullness of freedom, dignity, and opportunity as our birthright." Still, Reagan could not resist using his address to predict ultimate success. "If we meet this challenge," he announced, "these will be years when Americans . . . turned the tide of history away from totalitarian darkness and into the warm sunlight of human freedom." Looking toward his next four years as president, Reagan proclaimed the immediate possibility of restoration: "Let history say of us: 'These were golden years—when the American Revolution was reborn, when freedom gained new life, and America reached for her best.' "

By the end of his presidency, Reagan spoke from the perspective of "the prophecy." The restoration had been achieved, but it needed to be preserved and institutionalized. In Reagan's address to the Republican National Convention on August 15, 1988, he invited his listeners to remember "the promise,"

to look back in shame at "the declension," but to celebrate with him the ongoing fulfillment of "the prophecy." With pride and joy he recalled how the
conservative movement had struggled to reform the nation: "You aren't quitters.
You walk not just precincts, but for causes. You stand for something—the finest
warriors for free government that I have known. Nancy and I thank you for
letting us be part of your tireless determination to leave a better world for our
children. That's why we're here, isn't it? A better world." As his conservative
loyalists wept in the convention hall, Reagan recounted: "We lit a prairie fire
a few years back. Those flames were fed by passionate ideas and convictions,
and we were determined to make them burn all across America. What times
we've had!" In short, Reagan had led a "crusade" to "rescue America" and
"to reclaim our government."

Reagan's purpose, of course, was not merely to celebrate "the prophecy,"
but to warn the nation against a future declension into big government, high
taxes, and other statist policies that would be reinstituted by the Democratic
candidate for president, Michael Dukakis. Looking out at his audience, Reagan
concluded: "Together we've fought for causes we love. But we can never let
the fire go out or quit the fight, because the battle is never over. Our freedom
must be defended over and over again. And then again."

Reagan's Style

In matters of style and presentation, Reagan believed in the dictum of television acting: less is more. He preferred clarity, directness, and simplicity.
Above all, he judged writing by how it would sound to the ear, not how it would
appear to the eye in print. In his post-presidential autobiography Reagan revealed
his view on language style by discussing how he tried to guide his White House
speechwriters: "Sometimes, speech writers write things that seem very eloquent
on paper, but sound convoluted or stilted when you say them to an audience.
'Use simple language,' I'd say. 'Remember, there are people out there sitting
and listening, they've got to be able to absorb what I'm saying."

Reagan's editorial changes on drafts of presidential speeches reflected his
desire for a direct, oral style. In editing his "Evil Empire" address on March
8, 1983, for example, Reagan revised the draft submitted by speechwriter Tony
Dolan to state more clearly his personal views. In his draft of the key passage
in that speech to the National Association of Evangelicals, Dolan had written:
"Surely, those historians will find in the councils of the Marxist-Leninists—
who preached the supremacy of the state, who declared its omnipotence over
individual man, who predicted its eventual domination of all peoples of the
Earth—surely historians will see there . . . [ellipses in the draft] the focus of evil
in the modern world." Reagan altered the passage in order to shorten it, and in
order present the indictment in his own voice instead of attributing it to future
historians. His revisions also made the indictment of Communism more compelling by placing it in the present tense rather than the past tense. In its edited

form, the final version of the passage expressed the hope that even the Soviet Communists would recant their ideology and "discover the joy of knowing God. But until they do, let us be aware that while they preach the supremacy of the state, declare its omnipotence over individual men, predict its eventual domination of all peoples of the Earth, they are the focus of evil in the modern world."

A similar movement toward a clearer, more simple style can be detected in Reagan's "Star Wars" address of March 23, 1983, in which he announced his Strategic Defense Initiative (SDI). The portion of the speech that announced the SDI was not known to the regular speechwriters. From his defense policy advisors, Reagan received an insert marked "sensitive." It is clear that this insert was drafted by individuals who had not been writing for him on a daily basis in the White House, for it included grandiloquent phrasing out of character with Reagan's style. Reagan took pen in hand and scaled back the language. One sentence originally stated: "And yet, as I have shouldered this awesome responsibility over the past two years, I have become more and more deeply convinced that the human spirit must be capable of rising above dealing with other nations and human beings by menacing their very existence." Reagan deleted the entire phrase with the self-aggrandizing language about his "awesome responsibility," and replaced "by menacing their very existence" with "by threatening their existence."

The draft of the "Star Wars" insert had also included an excessively elevated passage that would have had Reagan say: "I call upon the Nation—our men and women in uniform, our scientists and engineers, our entrepreneurs and industrial leaders, and all our citizens—to join with me in taking a bold new step forward in defense to ensure a more peaceful and stable world of the future." Reagan lined out every word and wrote instead: "I call upon the scientific community in our country, those who gave us nuclear weapons, to turn their great talents now to the cause of mankind and world peace, to give us the means of rendering these nuclear weapons impotent and obsolete."

Reagan's Delivery

When Reagan turned to the task of presenting his words to the American people, he consistently understated the visual dimension of his delivery. As Ritter and Henry have noted, "Reagan's trademark as a television speaker was a slow smile, a tilt of his head, followed by 'Well, . . . ' He presented himself as no more than a fellow citizen earnestly speaking his mind." Reagan's delivery proved to be a great asset in his presidential oratory. In fact, Ronald Carpenter argues that Reagan's remarkable success as a political speaker was primarily due to his delivery.

Reagan relied primarily on his vocal delivery to establish an intimate relationship with his audiences, especially his television audiences. As Kathleen Hall Jamieson notes, Reagan exemplified what is regarded as eloquence in an electronic age, because he understood that communicating to a mass audience through television was essentially a situation of interpersonal communication. He spoke personally and conversationally, not oratorically. He sounded comfortable and appeared natural as he expressed his personal reactions to the subjects of his speeches: pride as he spoke of America's heritage, concern over the economy, anger at the latest example of Soviet aggression, and sorrow over the deaths of American soldiers.

Reagan had developed his approach to vocal delivery long before television existed. In his post-presidential autobiography Reagan remarked: "When I was a sports announcer, I learned something about communicating with people I never forgot. I had a group of friends in Des Moines and we all happened to go to the same barber. My friends would sometimes sneak away from their . . . jobs when I was broadcasting a game and they'd get together at the barbershop to listen to it; . . . I began to picture these friends down at the shop when I was on the air and, knowing they were there, I'd try to imagine how my words sounded to them and how they were reacting, and I'd adjust accordingly and spoke as if I was speaking personally to them. There was a specific audience out there I could see in my mind, and I sort of aimed my words at them." In short, Reagan used his voice to invite his audience to be at one with him.

Reagan's address to the nation on January 28, 1986, following the explosion of the *Challenger* space shuttle illustrates his effective delivery. His short address opened with the camera showing a long shot of Reagan's head, shoulders, chest, and hands. Reagan was seated at his desk in the Oval Office, his hands resting on the table top, barely touching each other. He hardly moved his head or body during the speech, yet his voice riveted the audience. Speaking softly in a voice heavy with sadness, he announced "a day for mourning and remembering." He spoke as if in an extended conversation with people sitting in his office. Drawing on his technique from his days as a radio announcer, he spoke directly to different people in his audience. As the camera showed a tighter shot that no longer revealed Reagan's hands, he looked straight into the camera and told the families of the dead astronauts whose names he had just listed: "we cannot bear, as you do, the full impact of this tragedy. But we feel the loss, and we're thinking about you so very much."

As Reagan turned his voice to the children in his audience, the camera showed a tighter shot revealing only his head and shoulders so that Reagan's face filled much of the television screen. School children were especially aware of the disaster. Many had watched the shuttle launch from their classrooms across the nation, because one of the astronauts, Christa McAuliffe, was a school teacher. Reaching out to them, Reagan said: "I want to say something to the school-children of America. . . . I know it is hard to understand, but sometimes painful things like this happen. It's all part of the process of exploration and discovery. It's all part of taking a chance . . . ." Finally, Reagan spoke to "every man and woman who works for NASA or who worked on this mission: . . . we know of your anguish. We share it." Reagan's tone of voice left the impression that he spoke to each member of his audience individually, almost privately. But he allowed the rest of the nation to overhear his conversation. In the end, he turned his voice back to his entire audience and asked America to remember the astronauts as they were "the last time we saw them, this morning, as they prepared for their journey and waved good-bye and 'slipped the surly bonds of earth' to 'touch the face of God.' "

Reagan's Mnemonics

Although the canon of memory from classical rhetoric has become distinctly less important in an age of inexpensive paper, photocopying, and teleprompters, it has not entirely disappeared from contemporary rhetoric. Public speakers, especially presidents, do not attempt to memorize a speech when they can easily speak from notes or a manuscript. But Reagan wanted to speak as though he needed no manuscript. As the title of his anthology of speeches suggests, he wanted to be seen as simply "speaking my mind." For formal speeches, he accomplished this by learning to deliver a speech from a teleprompter with a quality of spontaneity that encouraged his audience to forget that they knew he was reading the speech. Oddly, as a Hollywood actor Reagan had never been comfortable or particularly effective reading from a written script. It was a skill he developed only after he entered politics.

Reagan's preferred method of delivery, however, was to transcribe the speech text on to 4" by 6" index cards, using an idiosyncratic form of short-hand. He had developed the technique while presenting speeches in the 1950s, because he had difficulty reading smoothly from a typed script, and because he wanted to maintain as much eye contact with his audience as possible. As he explained in his interview with Sarah Ellen Cahill, "I've always thought that [in] public speaking, number one, I don't read the speeches because I think that's death when someone reads it, so I've figured out my own way, which is a sort of cards in my own kind of shorthand. They [the shorthand notes] used to be briefer than they are now, but because of the variety of speeches I have to have more cues." Reagan advisors Martin Anderson and Peter Hannaford have each described Reagan's system of using his shorthand notes to recall the verbatim text of a speech as he presented it. It was a system he continued to use in the White House for briefer addresses and for less formal speeches, such as campaign stump speeches.

REAGAN'S PRESIDENTIAL SPEECHWRITERS

No analysis of Ronald Reagan's presidential oratory would be complete without a discussion of his staff of White House speechwriters. Political scientist John Maltese reports that the Speechwriting Department was a subunit of the Office of Communications, which was directed by such high-profile individuals as David Gergen and Patrick Buchanan. Their interest in the speechwriting operation, however, was episodic, at best. As a practical matter, the daily writing, revising, and final editing of speeches took place through the coordination of the head of the Speechwriting Department and the assistant to Reagan's Chief of Staff. From 1981 through 1984, Richard G. Darman was James Baker's assistant (staff secretary). In addition to providing a link between the speech-writers and the President, Darman decided which members of the administration should review a particular speech draft before it was sent to Reagan. By all accounts, Darman was quite successful in working with the Speechwriting De-partment. In Reagan's second term, Chief-of-Staff Donald Regan imposed much more rigid and intrusive controls on the Speechwriting Department through his top assistants. In general, the speechwriting operation suffered under Donald Regan, but returned to a degree of stability with his departure from the White House under the cloud of the Iran-*Contra* controversy in 1987.

In 1981 Reagan's Speechwriting Department was organized and directed by Kenneth Khachigian, and then was under the interim leadership of Tony Dolan. In late 1981 Aram Bakshian took over as department head; in 1983 he was followed by Bently Elliott. Elliott continued as the department head into Re-agan's second term, but as Peggy Noonan has reported, his conflicts with Donald Regan over the speechwriting process resulted in him leaving that post in 1986. Tony Dolan resumed the leadership role he had temporarily held in the first year of the administration, serving as head of the Speechwriting Department from 1986 until Reagan left office in January 1989.

The Speechwriting Department had six full-time writers (including the de-partment head), as well as researchers and secretaries. Because most writers stayed only a few years, a total of fourteen individuals worked as full-time speechwriters over the eight years of Reagan's presidency. Those who departed, however, were sometimes asked to return to work on an important speech. This was true of Kenneth Khachigian, Landon Parvin, and Peggy Noonan. Taken as a whole, the speechwriters reflected the different aspects of Ronald Reagan himself. Tony Dolan, a Pulitzer Prize-winning journalist, shared Reagan's fer-vent anti-Communism. Dana Rohrabacher was a libertarian; like Reagan, he harbored grave doubts about the wisdom of allowing government to have power over the lives of citizens. Bently Elliott was a born-again Christian who shared Reagan's views on economic policy; prior to joining the White House, he had been the chief writer at the U.S. Chamber of Commerce. Peggy Noonan shared a background in radio with Reagan, but more importantly, she shared his ap-preciation for the significance of ceremonial oratory. Landon Parvin, a skilled writer with a master's degree in industrial relations from Cornell University, excelled at writing humor. Allan Myer was a retired Army officer who had been a specialist on the Soviet military with the National Security Council. A Vietnam veteran, he embodied the patriotism that Reagan so often expressed in his speeches. No one speechwriter fully reflected Reagan's ideology and personality, but collectively, they became an extension of the President they served.

The speechwriters also provided Reagan with rhetorical links to other leaders in the Republican party and the conservative movement. Peter Robinson, Josh Gilder, and Clark Judge had each been speechwriters for Vice President George Bush before being promoted to Reagan's staff. Mari Maseng had worked for Senators Strom Thurmond (R-South Carolina) and Robert Dole (R-Kansas). Mark Klugman had worked on the staff of Senator Phil Gramm (R-Texas), and John Podhoretz's father was the editor of the neo-conservative journal, *Commentary*. Khachigian had worked as a writer in the Nixon White House; Bakshian had been a writer in both the Nixon and Ford administrations.

Following the trend of previous rhetorical presidencies, Reagan gave frequent addresses. This heavy workload placed a stress on the speechwriters, especially when it involved Reagan giving several speeches in response to the same general occasion. Peggy Noonan noted that she and Tony Dolan found themselves being goaded by White House aides to see who would write the better speech for the 40th anniversary of D-Day: Noonan's draft for the speech at Pointe du Hoc, or Dolan's draft for the speech at the Omaha Beach Memorial, which was presented later the same day. One year later Kenneth Khachigian and Josh Gilder confronted a parallel problem when drafting speeches for Reagan's controversial trip to Bitburg, Germany. As a gesture of reconciliation forty years after World War II, Reagan had promised West Germany's Chancellor Helmut Kohl that he would visit a cemetery that held some Germans who died in that war. After the trip was scheduled, it was learned that Nazi storm troopers (SS) were also buried in the cemetery at Bitburg. Unwilling to renege on his commitment, Reagan's speeches had the burden of justifying his visit. Khachigian drafted the speech that Reagan presented as he laid a wreath at the site of the Bergen-Belsen concentration camp. Reagan then proceeded to the Bitburg cemetery where he laid a wreath. Instead of speaking at the cemetery, he travelled to a nearby U.S. air base to present the remarks drafted by Gilder. Like the speeches on D-Day, these addresses had the potential of being redundant. To avoid that problem, the two speechwriters made the addresses so complementary, that they seemed to be two parts of one continuous address. This was possible, in part, because both speechwriters had assumed part of Reagan's persona; they had mastered the art of writing in Reagan's voice. When Reagan included the two discourses in his anthology of speeches, he presented them as a single entry, with the second speech text following uninterrupted after the first.

In general, the speechwriters wished they could have more time visiting with Reagan about his speeches, but they usually had to be satisfied with information passed on to them by the head of the Speechwriting Department. Yet, they deeply appreciated the detailed editorial suggestions that Reagan often wrote on the speech drafts they submitted. Although the press frequently criticized Reagan for his detached management of the White House, they acknowledged that he was deeply involved in the process of speechwriting. Reagan's former White House advisors provide conflicting testimony about the degree to which he was detached from policy-making, but they uniformly agree that Reagan was passionately involved with his speeches.

CONCLUSION

Ronald Reagan's oratory has become the bench mark for future presidents. Reagan's critics, including Sidney Blumenthal and Haynes Johnson, have argued that Reagan's presidency served the nation poorly. Yet, Reagan's speeches were enormously well suited to the rhetorical presidency. Subsequent presidents have had their leadership questioned, in part, because their speechmaking was less successful than Reagan's. Even President Bill Clinton, who was elected in 1992 based on a campaign that attacked Reagan's policies, attempted to emulate the style, if not the substance, of Reagan's oratory. Two examples from the Clinton presidency illustrate this point.

Clinton adopted Reagan's rhetorical formula for State of the Union addresses. During the Reagan years the annual State of the Union speech became a rhetorical hybrid of ceremony and policy proposals, a media drama in which Reagan's conservative agenda confronted a Congress largely controlled by the Democratic party. One of Reagan's rhetorical innovations to bridge the gap between the epideictic and deliberative dimensions of the occasion was to place "heroes in the balcony" at the House of Representatives, where the addresses were presented to joint sessions of Congress. The heroes sat with members of the Reagan family; during his speech, Reagan would explicitly acknowledge them. The heroes had accomplished deeds eminently worth of praise; yet, those deeds also embodied Reagan's political ideology: individual initiative rather than government initiative, patriotism, anti-Communism, and so forth.

Reagan created situations where the Congress rose to give a standing ovation to an everyday hero who dove into the icy waters of the Potomac River to rescue victims of an airplane crash (1982), to an Army medic who had saved lives during the invasion of Grenada (1984), to a West Point cadet who as a child had fled Communist Vietnam in a leaky boat (1985), to a 13-year-old volunteer worker who on his own initiative had distributed blankets to the homeless (1986), and so forth. The Congress was happy to oblige in the ceremony of honoring those heroes. Reagan knew that in doing so, the Congress implicitly, but publicly, acknowledged its approval of Reagan's political agenda. What appeared on the surface as merely a gimmick to create attractive television shots and a feeling of goodwill, was actually a strategy for using ceremonial rhetoric in support of the President's legislative program. Bill Clinton understood what Reagan had done; in Clinton's first State of the Union address, he brought his own heroes to the balcony.

One of the rhetorical highlights of Reagan's presidency was his commemoration of the 40th anniversary of D-Day. It was a powerful illustration that in the rhetorical presidency, the nation's leader must be able to employ some qualities of interpersonal communication in formal orations—the president must display emotion without betraying weakness. In recognizing the World War II veterans who had turned the tide of the war with their invasion of the Normandy coast of France on June 6, 1944, Reagan gave a series of emotional addresses in Europe. The centerpiece of the series was an address drafted by Peggy Noonan, which was presented at Pointe du Hoc, where in 1944 Colonel James Earl Rudder had led 225 American Army Rangers up 100-foot cliffs against withering enemy fire. As Reagan pointed out, when the Rangers reached the top of the cliffs only 90 could still bear arms. With a group of the survivors from that battle sitting in front of him atop those same cliffs, Reagan declared in a voice filled with admiration and gratitude: "These are the boys of Pointe du Hoc. These are the men who took the cliffs. These are the champions who helped free a continent. These are the heroes who helped end a war." A decade later, President Bill Clinton returned to Pointe du Hoc to present an address on the 50th anniversary of D-Day. Yet, Clinton had begun his preparations for his D-Day speeches months earlier, when his White House secured videotapes of Reagan's speeches at Normandy.

Reagan was often criticized for discussing complex issues in an oversimplified manner. Adopting an elitist perspective on public policy, scholars such as Jeffrey Tulis have charged that by simplifying public issues in order to persuade the public to support his policies, Reagan revealed that he himself was simple-minded: "He serves as a better illustration than any previous president of the possibility and danger that presidents might come themselves to think in the terms initially designed to persuade those not capable of fully understanding the policy itself. Having reconfigured the political landscape, the rhetorical presidency comes to reconstitute the president's political understanding." Martin Anderson (a senior fellow at the Hoover Institution of Stanford University) and other Reagan advisors vehemently reject Tulis' evaluation of Ronald Reagan. What is more important to the subject of this essay is that other scholars of the presidency, including James David Barber, cite Reagan's oratory as a model to be emulated.

This much is clear: while the merits of Reagan's presidential policies will continue to be debated, subsequent presidents (and those who aspire to be president) will use orations by Ronald Reagan along with those of Abraham Lincoln, Franklin D. Roosevelt, and John F. Kennedy as their rhetorical exemplars.

RHETORICAL SOURCES

Archival Materials

The *Public Affairs Video Archives*, (*C-SPAN*), Purdue University, holds videotapes and transcripts of many of Reagan's speeches as televised on the Cable-Satellite Public Affairs Network (C-SPAN) after 1986.

Public Papers of the Presidents of the United States: Ronald Reagan, 1981–1989. (*PPP*). 15 Vols. Washington, DC: U.S. Government Printing Office, 1982–1991.

The *Ronald Reagan Presidential Library*, (*RRPL*), Simi Valley, California, contains relevant speech sources. At the time this essay was written, the vast majority of Reagan's 1,700 presidential speech files remained unprocessed, although scholars may request that particular files be opened.

The *Vanderbilt Television News Archive, (VTNA)*, Vanderbilt University Library, Van-
    derbilt University, includes videotapes of selected television addresses and de-
    bates by Reagan from 1976 through 1992. This archive is the best source for
    network television news coverage of Reagan's orations.
Houck, Davis W., and Amos Kiewe, ed. *Actor, Ideologue, Politician: The Public
    Speeches of Ronald Reagan. (AIP)*. Westport, CT: Greenwood Press, 1993.
Reagan, Ronald. *Speaking My Mind: Selected Speeches. (SMM)*. New York: Simon and
    Schuster, 1989.
Ryan, Halford Ross, ed. *Contemporary American Public Discourse. (CAPD)*. Prospect
    Heights, IL: Waveland Press, 1992.

Rhetorical Studies

Anderson, Martin. *Revolution*. San Diego: Harcourt Brace Jovanovich, Publishers, 1988.
Bercovitch, Sacvan. *The American Jeremiad*. Madison, WI: University of Wisconsin
    Press, 1978.
Blumenthal, Sidney. *Our Long National Daydream: A Political Pageant of the Reagan
    Era*. New York: Harper & Row, 1988.
Cannon, Lou. *Reagan*. New York: Putnam Publishing Group, 1982.
————. *President Reagan: The Role of a Lifetime*. New York: Simon and Schuster,
    1991.
Dallek, Robert. *Ronald Reagan: The Politics of Symbolism*. Cambridge, MA: Harvard
    University Press, 1984.
Erickson, Paul D. *Reagan Speaks: The Making of an American Myth*. New York: New
    York University Press, 1985.
Hamilton, Gary G., and Nicole Woolsey Biggart. *Governor Reagan, Governor Brown:
    A Sociology of Executive Power*. New York: Columbia University Press, 1984.
Hannaford, Peter. *The Reagans: A Political Portrait*. New York: Coward-McCann, Inc.,
    1983.
Howard-Pitney, David. *The Afro-American Jeremiad: Appeals for Justice in America*.
    Philadelphia: Temple University Press, 1990.
Jamieson, Kathleen Hall. *Eloquence in an Electronic Age: The Transformation of Polit-
    ical Speechmaking*. New York: Oxford University Press, 1988.
Johnson, Haynes. *Sleepwalking Through History: America in the Reagan Years*. New
    York: W.W. Norton, 1991.
Kiewe, Amos, and David W. Houck. *A Shining City on a Hill: Ronald Reagan's Eco-
    nomic Rhetoric, 1951–1989*. New York: Praeger, 1991.
Maltese, John A. *Spin Control: The White House Office of Communications and the
    Management of Presidential News*. Chapel Hill, NC: University of North Carolina
    Press, 1992.
Miller, Perry. *The New England Mind: From Colony to Province*. Cambridge, MA: Har-
    vard University Press, 1953.
Muir, William Ker, Jr. *The Bully Pulpit: The Presidential Leadership of Ronald Reagan*.
    San Francisco: Institute for Contemporary Studies, 1992.
Noonan, Peggy. *What I Saw at the Revolution: A Political Life in the Reagan Era*. New
    York: Random House, 1990.
Reagan, Ronald. *An American Life*. New York: Simon and Schuster, 1990.

Reagan, Ronald, and Richard G. Hubler. *Where Is the Rest of Me?* New York: Duell, Sloan and Pearce, 1965.

Ritter, Kurt, and David Henry. *Ronald Reagan: The Great Communicator.* (*RRGC*). New York: Greenwood Press, 1992. Appendix includes texts of nine speeches.

Rogan, Michael Paul. *Ronald Reagan, the Movie and Other Episodes in Political Demonology.* Berkeley, CA: University of California Press, 1987.

Schweizer, Peter. *Victory: The Reagan Administration's Secret Strategy that Hastened the Collapse of the Soviet Union.* New York: Atlantic Monthly Press, 1994.

Stuckey, Mary E. *Playing the Game: The Presidential Rhetoric of Ronald Reagan.* New York: Praeger, 1990.

Tulis, Jeffrey K. *The Rhetorical Presidency.* Princeton, NJ: Princeton University Press, 1987.

Vaughn, Stephen. *Ronald Reagan in Hollywood: Movies and Politics.* New York: Cambridge University Press, 1994.

Weiler, Michael, and W. Barnett Pearce, ed. *Reagan and Pubic Discourse in America.* Tuscaloosa, AL: University of Alabama Press, 1992.

Wills, Garry. *Reagan's America: Innocents at Home.* Garden City, NY: Doubleday, 1987.

Rhetorical Monographs

Aden, Roger C. "Entrapment and Escape: Inventional Metaphors in Ronald Reagan's Economic Rhetoric." *Southern Communication Journal* 54 (1989): 384–400.

Barton, John. "History and Rhetoric in the Prophets." In *The Bible as Rhetoric: Studies in Biblical Persuasion and Credibility,* edited by Martin Warner. London: Routledge, 1990.

Birdsell, David S. "Ronald Reagan on Lebanon and Grenada: Flexibility and Interpretation in the Application of Kenneth Burke's Pentad." *Quarterly Journal of Speech* 73 (1987): 267–79.

Blankenship, Jane. "Toward a Developmental Model of Form: ABC's Treatment of the Reagan Inaugural and the Iranian Hostage Release as Oxymoron." In *Form, Genre, and the Study of Political Discourse,* edited by Herbert W. Simons and Aram A. Aghazarian. Columbia, SC: University of South Carolina Press, 1986.

Bormann, Ernest G. "A Fantasy Theme Analysis of the Television Coverage of the Hostage Release and the Reagan Inaugural." *Quarterly Journal of Speech* 68 (1982): 133–45.

Bradley, Bert E. "Jefferson and Reagan: The Rhetoric of Two Inaugurals." *Southern Speech Communication Journal* 48 (1983): 119–36.

Cahill, Sarah Ellen. "Ronald Reagan: A Rhetorical Study." M.A. Thesis, University of California, Santa Barbara, 1975.

Carpenter, Ronald H. "Ronald Reagan." In *American Orators of the Twentieth Century: Critical Studies and Sources,* edited by Bernard K. Duffy and Halford R. Ryan. New York: Greenwood Press, 1987.

Crable, Richard E., and Steven L. Vibbert. "Argumentative Stance and Political Faith Healing: 'The Dream Will Come True.' " *Quarterly Journal of Speech* 69 (1983): 290–301.

Dickinson, Greg. "Creating His Own Constraint: Ronald Reagan and the Iran-Contra Crisis." In *The Modern Presidency and Crisis Rhetoric,* edited by Amos Kiewe. Westport, CT: Praeger, 1994.

Dowling, Ralph E., and Gabrielle Marraro. "Grenada and the Great Communicator: A Study in Democratic Ethics." *Western Journal of Communication* 50 (1986): 350–67.

Fisher, Walter R. "Romantic Democracy, Ronald Reagan, and Presidential Heroes." *Western Journal of Communication* 46 (1982): 299–310.

Friedenberg, Robert V. "Elie Wiesel vs. President Ronald Reagan: The Visit to Bitburg." In *Oratorical Encounters: Selected Studies and Sources of Twentieth-Century Political Accusations and Apologies*, edited by Halford Ross Ryan. New York: Greenwood Press, 1988.

Gold, Ellen Reid. "Ronald Reagan and the Oral Tradition." *Central States Speech Journal* 39 (1988): 159–76.

Goodnight, G. Thomas. "Ronald Reagan's Re-formulation of the Rhetoric of War: Analysis of the 'Zero Option,' 'Evil Empire,' and 'Star Wars' Addresses." *Quarterly Journal of Speech* 72 (1986): 390–414.

Gronbeck, Bruce E. "Ronald Reagan's Enactment of the Presidency in his 1981 Inaugural Address." In *Form, Genre, and the Study of Political Discourse*, edited by Herbert W. Simons and Aram A. Aghazarian. Columbia, SC: University of South Carolina Press, 1986.

Hart, Roderick P. "Of Genre, Computers, and the Reagan Inaugural." In *Form, Genre, and the Study of Political Discourse*, edited by Herbert W. Simons and Aram A. Aghazarian. Columbia, SC: University of South Carolina Press, 1986.

Heisey, D. Ray. "President Ronald Reagan's Apologia on the Iran-*Contra* Affair." In *Oratorical Encounters: Selected Studies and Sources of Twentieth-Century Political Accusations and Apologies*, edited by Halford Ross Ryan. New York: Greenwood Press, 1988.

———. "Reagan and Mitterrand Respond to International Crisis: Creating Versus Transcending Appearances." *Western Journal of Communication* 50 (1986): 325–35.

Henry, David. "Ronald Reagan and Aid to the *Contras*: An Analysis of the Rhetorical Presidency." In *Rhetorical Dimensions in Media: A Critical Casebook*, 2d ed. Edited by Martin J. Medhurst and Thomas W. Benson. Dubuque, IA: Kendall/Hunt Publishers, 1991.

———. "President Ronald Reagan's First Inaugural Address, 1981." In *The Inaugural Addresses of Twentieth-Century American Presidents*, edited by Halford Ryan. Westport, CT: Praeger, 1993.

Hogan, Bill. "Reagan's Close Encounters with the Fourth Estate: What the President Really Thinks About the Press." *Washington Journalism Review* (March 1981): 32–35.

Ingold, Beth A. J., and Theodore Windt. "Trying to 'Stay the Course': President Reagan's Rhetoric During the 1982 Election." *Presidential Studies Quarterly* 14 (1984): 87–97.

Ivie, Robert L. "Speaking 'Common Sense' About the Soviet Threat: Reagan's Rhetorical Stance." *Western Journal of Communication* 48 (1984): 39–50.

Ivie, Robert L., and Kurt Ritter. "Whither the 'Evil Empire'? Reagan and the Presidential Candidates Debating Foreign Policy in the 1988 Campaign." *American Behavioral Scientist* 32 (1989): 436–50.

Johannesen, Richard L. "Ronald Reagan's Economic Jeremiad." *Central States Speech Journal* 37 (1986): 79–89.

Klope, David C. "Defusing a Foreign Policy Crisis: Myth and Victimage in Reagan's

1983 Lebanon/Grenada Address.'' *Western Journal of Communication* 50 (1986): 336–49.

Lewis, William F. ''Telling America's Story: Narrative Form and the Reagan Presidency.'' *Quarterly Journal of Speech* 73 (1987): 280–302

Medhurst, Martin J. ''Postponing the Social Agenda: Reagan's Strategy and Tactics.'' *Western Journal of Communication* 48 (1984): 262–76.

Meyer, John. ''Ronald Reagan and Humor: A Politician's Velvet Weapon.'' *Communication Studies* 41 (1990): 76–88.

Mister, Steven M. ''Reagan's *Challenger* Tribute: Combining Generic Constraints and Situational Demands.'' *Central States Speech Journal* 37 (1986): 158–65.

Moen, Mathew C. ''The Political Agenda of Ronald Reagan: A Content Analysis of the State of the Union Messages.'' *Presidential Studies Quarterly* 18 (1988): 775–85.

Moore, Mark P. ''Reagan's Quest for Freedom in the 1987 State of the Union Address.'' *Western Journal of Communication* 53 (1989): 52–65.

Olson, Kathryn M. ''The Controversy over President Reagan's Visit to Bitburg: Strategies of Definition and Redefinition.'' *Quarterly Journal of Speech* 75 (1989): 129–51.

Ritter, Kurt. ''Reagan's 1964 TV Speech for Goldwater: Millennial Themes in American Political Rhetoric.'' In *Rhetorical Dimensions in Media: A Critical Casebook.* 2d ed. Edited by Martin J. Medhurst and Thomas W. Benson. Dubuque, IA: Kendall/Hunt Publishers, 1991.

———. ''Ronald Reagan and 'The Speech': The Rhetoric of Public Relations Politics.'' In *Contemporary American Public Discourse*, edited by Halford Ross Ryan. Prospect Heights, IL: Waveland Press, 1992.

———. ''President Ronald Reagan's Second Inaugural Address, 1985.'' In *The Inaugural Addresses of Twentieth-Century American Presidents*, edited by Halford Ryan. Westport, CT: Praeger, 1993.

Ritter, Kurt, and David Henry. ''The 1980 Reagan-Carter Presidential Debate.'' In *Rhetorical Studies of National Political Debates, 1960–1988*, 2d ed. Edited by Robert V. Friedenberg. New York: Praeger, 1994.

Rowland, Robert C. ''The Substance of the 1980 Carter-Reagan Debate.'' *Southern Speech Communication Journal* 51 (1986): 142–65.

Rowland, Robert C., and Rodger A. Payne. ''The Effectiveness of Reagan's 'Star Wars' Address.'' *Political Communication and Persuasion* 4 (1987): 161–78.

Rushing, Janice Hocker. ''Ronald Reagan's 'Star Wars' Address: Mythic Containment of Technical Reasoning.'' *Quarterly Journal of Speech* 72 (1986): 415–33.

Scheele, Henry Z. ''Ronald Reagan's 1980 Acceptance Address: A Focus on American Values.'' *Western Journal of Communication* 48 (1984): 51–61.

Smith, Craig Allen. ''Mister Reagan's Neighborhood: Rhetoric and National Unity.'' *Southern Speech Communication Journal* 52 (1987): 219–39.

Smith, Craig Allen, and Kathy B. Smith. ''The 1984 Reagan-Mondale Presidential Debates.'' In *Rhetorical Studies of National Political Debates, 1960–1988.* 2d ed. Edited by Robert V. Friedenberg. New York: Praeger, 1994.

Zagacki, Kenneth S., and Andrew King. ''Reagan, Romance and Technology: A Critique of 'Star Wars.' '' *Communication Studies* 40 (1989): 1–12.

Zarefsky, David, Carol Miller-Tutzauer, and Frank E. Tutzauer. ''Reagan's Safety Net for the Truly Needy: The Rhetorical Uses of Definition.'' *Central States Speech Journal* 35 (1984): 113–19.

Chronology of Significant Presidential Persuasions

''Your America to Be Free,'' Eureka College, Eureka, IL, June 7, 1957. *RRGC*, 127–34.

''A Time for Choosing,'' Oct. 27, 1964. *RRGC*, 135–43; *SMM*, 22–36; *RRPL*.

Presidential Nomination Acceptance Address, Republican National Convention, Detroit, July 17, 1980. *AIP*, 158–66; *RRPL*; *VTNA*.

Debate with Jimmy Carter, Oct. 28, 1980. *PPP* (*Carter*), 1980–1981: 2476–502.

First Inaugural Address, Jan. 20, 1981. *PPP*, 1981: 1–4; *SMM*, 59–66; *RRPL*; *VTNA*.

Address to the Nation on the Economy, Feb. 5, 1981. *PPP*, 1981: 79–83; *SMM*, 74–83; *RRPL*; *VTNA*.

Address to Congress on the Program for Economic Recovery, Feb. 18, 1981. *PPP*, 1981: 108–15; *AIP*, 180–88; *RRPL*; *VTNA*.

Address to Congress on Economic Policy, April 28, 1981. *PPP*, 1981: 391–94; *RRGC*, 161–65; *RRPL*; *VTNA*.

State of the Union Address, Jan. 26, 1982. *PPP*, 1982: 72–79; *AIP*, 195–204; *RRPL*; *VTNA*.

Address to the British Parliament, London, June 8, 1982. *PPP*, 1982: 742–48; *SMM*, 107–20.

''Evil Empire'' Address to the National Association of Evangelicals, Orlando, FL, March 8, 1983. *PPP*, 1983: 359–64; *SMM*, 168–80; *RRPL*.

''Star Wars'' Address to the Nation, March 23, 1983. *PPP*, 1983: 437–43; *RRPL*; *VTNA*.

Address to the Nation on the Soviet Attack on a Korean Airliner (KAL 007), Sept. 5, 1983. *PPP*, 1983: 1227–30; *AIP*, 228–32; *RRGC*, 167–72; *RRPL*; *VTNA*.

Address to the Nation on Lebanon and Grenada, Oct. 27, 1983. *PPP*, 1983: 1517–22; *SMM*, 184–96; *AIP*, 233–40; *CAPD*, 345–53; *RRPL*; *VTNA*.

State of the Union Address, Jan. 25, 1984. *PPP*, 1984: 87–94; *AIP*, 246–55; *RRPL*; *VTNA*.

Address at Eureka College, Eureka, IL, Feb. 6, 1984. *PPP*, 1986: 172–77; *RRPL*.

Address at the U.S. Ranger Monument, 40th Anniversary of D-Day, Pointe du Hoc, France, June 6, 1984. *PPP*, 1984: 817–19; *SMM*, 217–22; *RRPL*; *VTNA*.

Address at the Omaha Beach Memorial, 40th Anniversary of D-Day, Omaha Beach, France, June 6 1984. *PPP*, 1984: 821–23; *SMM*, 223–26; *RRPL*; *VTNA*.

Presidential Nomination Acceptance Address, Republican National Convention, Dallas, Aug. 23, 1984. *PPP*, 1984: 1174–81; *SMM*, 199–216; *RRPL*; *VTNA*.

First Debate with Walter Mondale, Oct. 7, 1984. *PPP*, 1984: 1441–62; *RRPL*; *VTNA*.

Second Debate with Walter Mondale, Oct. 21, 1984. *PPP*, 1984: 1589–610; *RRPL*; *VTNA*.

Second Inaugural Address, Jan. 21, 1985. *PPP*, 1985: 55–58; *AIP*, 268–72; *RRPL*; *VTNA*.

State of the Union Address, Feb. 6, 1985. *PPP*, 1985: 130–36; *AIP*, 272–80; *RRPL*; *VTNA*.

Speech at the Bergen-Belsen Concentration Camp Memorial, Germany, May 5, 1985. *PPP*, 1985: 564–65; *SMM*, 258–61; *RRPL*; *VTNA*.

Speech at Bitburg Air Base, Germany, May 5, 1985. *PPP*, 1985: 565–68; *SMM*, 261–66; *RRPL*; *VTNA*.

Address to the Nation on the Explosion of the Space Shuttle *Challenger*, Jan. 28, 1986. *PPP*, 1986: 94–95; *SMM*, 289–92; *AIP*, 280–81; *RRGC*, 173–74; *RRPL*; *VTNA*.

State of the Union Address, Feb. 4, 1986. *PPP*, 1986: 125–30; *AIP*, 281–87; *RRPL*; *VTNA*.

Address at the Statue of Liberty, New York City, July 3, 1986. *PPP*, 1986: 918–19; *SMM*, 296–300; *RRPL*; *VTNA*.

Address to the Nation on the Iran-*Contra* Controversy, Nov. 13, 1986. *PPP*, 1986: 1546–48; *AIP*, 292–95; *CAPD*, 354–58; *RRPL*; *VTNA*.

Address to the Nation on the Investigation of the Iran-*Contra* Affair, Dec. 2, 1986. *PPP*, 1986: 1594–95; *AIP*, 295–96; *RRPL*.

State of the Union Address, Jan. 27, 1987. *PPP*, 1987: 56–61; *AIP*, 299–306; *RRPL*; *VTNA*.

Address to the Nation on the Iran-*Contra* Report, March 4, 1987. *PPP*, 1987: 208–11; *SMM*, 335–41; *RRGC*, 175–78; *RRPL*; *VTNA*.

Address at the Brandenburg Gate (Berlin Wall), Berlin, June 12, 1987. *PPP*, 1987: 634–37; *SMM*, 348–56; *RRPL*; *VTNA*.

State of the Union Address, Jan. 25, 1988. *PPP*, 1988: 84–90; *AIP*, 313–21; *RRPL*; *VTNA*; *C-SPAN*.

Address at Moscow State University, May 31, 1988. *PPP*, 1988: 683–92; *SMM*, 373–92; *RRPL*; *VTNA*.

Address to the Republican National Convention, New Orleans, Aug. 15, 1988. *PPP*, 1988–1989: 1080–86; *RRPL*; *VTNA*; *C-SPAN*.

Farewell Address to the Nation, Jan. 11, 1989. *PPP*, 1988–1989: 1718–23; *SMM*, 409–18; *AIP*, 322–27; *RRGC*, 179–85; *RRPL*; *VTNA*; *C-SPAN*.

Address to the Republican National Convention, Houston, Aug. 17, 1992. *AIP*, 330–35; *RRPL*; *VTNA*; *C-SPAN*.

Craig R. Smith

George Herbert Walker Bush
(1924–   )

I want a kinder, gentler nation.

Neither George Bush nor his father, Prescott, were born with silver spoons in their mouths. Prescott was raised in Ohio, graduated from Yale, served in an artillery unit in World War I, became a business manager in St. Louis, and was soon known for his troubleshooting abilities. When he was promoted to a senior position at U.S. Rubber, Prescott Bush settled his family of seven in Greenwich, Connecticut. In 1952, after his son was already established in Texas, Prescott won a special Congressional election and was re-elected in 1956 to a full term. George Bush was an heir to the progressive agenda within the Republican party, which is traceable to Teddy Roosevelt. In his autobiography, *Looking Forward*, he admits that his father had "a powerful impact on the way" he came to view the world. Prescott Bush retired from the Senate in 1962, the year his son George began his political life as Republican chairman of Harris County, Texas.

While George Bush was in his senior year at Phillips Academy in Andover, Pearl Harbor was bombed. The commencement speaker at the end of the year was Secretary of War Henry Stimson. Bush had just received his diploma when he joined the Navy. He became its youngest fighter pilot in World War II, distinguishing himself in battle and being rescued by a U.S. submarine after he was shot down by the Japanese. As in the case of John Kennedy, this war record would serve Bush well when it came to building credibility in the political world. After the war, Bush enrolled at Yale where he served as captain of the baseball team, graduating in three years, with a membership in Phi Beta Kappa. During his college days, he married Barbara and had a son, George, Jr.

Bush went to work for Dresser Industries, in Odessa, Texas, first as an equipment clerk in the summer of 1948, then as a salesman in California. In 1950

Dresser transferred him to Midland, Texas. Bush left Dresser, in 1951, to set up Bush-Overby Oil Development Company, which bought royalties on oil prospects with funds invested by his uncle Herbert Walker and Eugene Meyer, the owner of the *Washington Post*. At twenty-seven, Bush was an entrepreneur meeting a payroll, an experience he would not let audiences forget. By 1952, Bush was merged in a deal with Hugh Liedtke, who eventually ran Pennzoil. When their company, Zapata Petroleum, made a killing in the new enterprise of off-shore oil drilling, Bush moved to Houston where the operation was headquartered. There he entered Republican politics.

A decade later, in 1964, he won the U.S. Senate nomination. In the same year, as a delegate to the Republican National Convention, he supported Barry Goldwater, an indication that his Texas environment was overriding his natural progressive instincts. Bush's own opponent in November was incumbent Ralph Yarborough, a liberal Democrat who accused Bush of being the "darling of the John Birch Society." In the face of Lyndon Johnson's overwhelming victory, Bush did remarkably well just to keep the race close.

He was elected to Congress two years later and became the first freshman named to the House Ways and Means Committee since Thaddeus Stevens. But his first term also witnessed his first crisis—he decided to support the Open Housing bill of 1968. When he returned to Houston to explain his vote, he was roundly booed. In response, he paraphrased the sentiments of Edmund Burke expressed at Bristol: "Your representative owes you not only his industry, but his judgment and he betrays instead of serving you, if he sacrifices it to your opinion." Bush's speech converted many in the all white audience and was responsible in part for his unopposed re-election later that year. In 1970 when Bush decided to run for the Senate again, this district elected Barbara Jordan as his successor.

By 1970, Ralph Yarborough was an unpopular senator ripe for the picking. But the Democrats threw Bush a curve. Instead of Yarborough, they nominated a wealthy, moderately conservative business executive named Lloyd Bentsen. Bush lost a very close race. For his effort, Richard Nixon nominated Bush to be ambassador to the United Nations, a post that would provide invaluable foreign policy experience. Bush faced several Middle East crises, the expulsion of Taiwan from the United Nations, and the invasion of East Pakistan by India.

When Nixon won his 49 state landslide in 1972, he shook up his administration and asked Bush to chair the National Republican Party. The shift from international affairs to political affairs was intensified by the Watergate crisis that soon began its lengthy course. The crisis preoccupied Bush until he asked Nixon to resign in August of 1974. Gerald Ford, the new President, returned Bush to the world of foreign affairs, naming him ambassador to China.

When the Watergate crisis led to the William Colby's resignation as head of the Central Intelligence Agency, Ford nominated Bush to take the open position. Since he was a politician and not from the CIA, Senate Democrats complained that appointing Bush would further damage the Agency, which had been kept out of politics. During the hearings over his nomination, Bush promised not to seek or accept the vice presidential nomination should he be approached. Once at the CIA, Bush succeeded in improving morale and developing a loyal following that would serve him in subsequent political campaigns. At the time, however, Ford's loss of the presidency to Jimmy Carter meant the end of Bush's tenure at the CIA.

SPEECH PRACTICES

Out of public office for the first time in years, Bush began to assess his chances of winning the Republican nomination. He accepted speaking engagements at Republican fund-raisers across the country throughout 1977, 1978, and 1979. During this period Bush first employed the speechwriting and speech coaching process. In January of 1978, I met with Bush at his home in Houston and became one of his consulting speechwriters. The remainder of this study is supported by my personal experiences with Bush, for whom I continued to consult until his loss of the presidency in 1992. He also relied on Raymond Price who wrote Nixon's very effective acceptance in 1968, and Victor Gold, who had written for Agnew. Although each of us did entire speeches independent of the others, we had diverse strengths that were sometimes combined for major speeches. My charge was to take researched issue positions and craft them into the body of the speeches; Price worked on style; Gold worked on humor and political "zingers." During this run for the presidential nomination, Bush was also helped by his literate and witty Press Secretary Pete Teely. In a speech Bush delivered during the Pennsylvania primary that I had helped to write, Teely inserted a line that dubbed Reagan's budget proposals "voodoo economics." The joke would cost Bush later.

Throughout 1980 I fought for more organization in speeches, which Bush resisted. All of us argued that Bush should rehearse speeches more and stick to the text, but rehearsing bored him and he believed it to be unmanly. Furthermore, texts were not Bush's favorite format. He preferred speaking extemporaneously from notes as he had done when he campaigned for office in Texas. Ironically, the speeches for which Bush received plaudits were delivered from texts and heavily rehearsed.

Bush focused on the substance of his speeches. Prior to 1980, he and I often reworked speeches together as his Lear jet sped from one speaking event to another. The system seemed to be working well when Bush became known as the issue-candidate and won the Iowa caucuses. Bush's decision to abandon issues to talk about his momentum ("the big mo") in New Hampshire, hurt his candidacy, a judgment Bush acknowledges in *Looking Forward*. But a worse blow was delivered when, just before a one-on-one debate with Reagan, the aged movie star grabbed a microphone and upstaged Bush by arguing that all GOP candidates should participate in the debate. The move revived Reagan's flagging campaign.

The primary process eventually narrowed to the moderate Bush and the conservative Reagan. Bush supported the Equal Rights Amendment, but opposed a woman's right to an abortion except in the case of incest, rape, or the endangerment of the life of the mother. He favored a tax cut only if it was matched with a cut in spending. On May 20th, despite Bush's win in Michigan, Reagan cinched the nomination with a win in the Nebraska and Oregon primaries. Reagan selected Bush as his running mate after Ford was eliminated because of talk of a "co-presidency." Ironically, Bush's eloquent speech to the convention on Wednesday night when he was sure he would *not* be the nominee helped convince Reagan of Bush's potential.

Bush's role in the 1980 campaign was traditional and unremarkable. There was no vice presidential debate. When Reagan defeated Carter in their presidential debate, the undecided vote, along with some of independent candidate John Anderson's, shifted to Reagan, and Reagan-Bush won a landslide victory that included the first Republican Senate since 1954.

THE VICE PRESIDENCY

Bush was an active vice president. He was thrust to the fore when Reagan was shot on March 30, 1981. He worked behind the scenes as president of the Senate to help to pass the Reagan budget package and tax reform bills. He played a major role in developing foreign policy and eliminating government regulations. He headed major anti-drug efforts. He travelled to over seventy-five countries to represent the President in negotiations or at funerals. He spent a good deal of time at political fund-raisers for Republican candidates. In 1984 he performed better than the press expected in a "no win" vice presidential debate with Geraldine Ferraro.

But he assiduously avoided disagreement with or the taint of disloyalty to Reagan. This policy contributed to what became known as the "whimp" factor, which seriously hurt his credibility early in the 1988 presidential contest. Bush overcame this disability in several ways. First, Roger Ailes, a media consultant, taught Bush to "counterpunch." Ailes advised Bush to wait to be hit first and then to counterpunch in debates, interviews, and press conferences. The results of this policy were mainly effective, as in the Houston Republican nominees debates when Bush turned to former Governor DuPont and said, "Let me help you with that, Pierre." DuPont prefers to be called Pete. But in one significant instance the results were mixed. On the night of Reagan's last State of the Union Address, January 20, 1988, Dan Rather interviewed Bush live on the CBS Evening News. Bush had been led to believe the interview would cover many issues. Instead, Rather ran a prepared story on the Iran-Contra scandal that implicated Bush. Bush defended himself and asked that Rather move on. Rather refused. Bush then insulted Rather by bringing up an incident in which Rather had walked off the set. Rather abruptly cut off the interview, thus offending many viewers. Some critics believe that Bush's poor showing in the ensuing Iowa caucuses was due in part to his unpresidential performance in the Rather interview.

THE 1988 CAMPAIGN

Bush revived his presidential candidacy in New Hampshire by running negative advertising against the poll leader, Senator Bob Dole, and by appealing to voters in a more down to earth manner. The next primaries came in the South on "Super Tuesday," where campaign manager Lee Atwater put together the biggest single victory in terms of delegates that any nominee had ever achieved. Bush was effectively nominated on that night. Nonetheless, Bush's difficulties with the public continued into the summer of 1988. When Michael Dukakis finished his acceptance speech at the Democratic Convention in July, he led Bush by fifteen to seventeen percent in most opinion polls. Republican strategists believed that Bush's only hope for victory was to deliver "the speech of his life" in accepting the Republican nomination. Bush and his writers, who included Peggy Noonan for this one effort, did not disappoint them. After his acceptance speech, he led Dukakis by around 10 percent in most polls and never looked back.

The turn around in the polls indicates that Bush's acceptance was most effective in the short run. Its immediate success can be explained by several factors. First, Dukakis's more general speech left him open to redefinition by Bush. In one of the most effective passages in the acceptance, Bush compared himself to Dukakis on the issues in an effort to coalesce a majority of support. Notice Bush's rhetorical questions that ended with anaphora: "Should public school teachers be required to lead our children in the pledge of allegiance? My opponent says no—but I say yes. Should society be allowed to impose the death penalty on those who commit crimes of extraordinary cruelty and violence? My opponent says no—but I say yes." Identification also proved effective in personal terms as Bush for the first time spoke about himself and his approach to government with emotion: "I want a kinder, gentler nation." He then specifically identified with segments of his audience: "This is America: the Knights of Columbus, the Grange, Hadassah, the Disabled American Veterans, the Order of Ahepa, the Business and Professional Woman of America, the union hall, the Bible study group, LULAC, Holy Name—a brilliant diversity spread like stars, like a thousand points of light in a broad and peaceful sky." The press did not notice that Peggy Noonan had paraphrased her "thousand sparks of light" from Reagan's 1988 State of the Union Address.

Third, the speech contained humor that was both self-deprecating and effective in poking fun at the Democrats. Bush reinforced the humor by using Clint Eastwood-like phrasing, particularly when it came to domestic issues. "Read my lips, no new taxes," brought cheers from the audience, but would later compromise Bush's presidency.

Finally, the style of the speech was entertaining and often dazzling. It not only suited Bush, it demonstrated the importance of tropes and figures in modern rhetoric. Repetition, periodic structure, antithesis, alliteration, metaphor, and allegory provided subliminal support for the message.

None of Bush's presidential speeches proved as effective as this effort. In fact, Bush would be marked as a rhetorical failure by the end of his re-election campaign. He would also be rightly criticized for his indifferent performance in the three presidential debates of 1992. 1988 was a different story. In the two debates, Bush, unlike Dukakis, was warm and humorous. Although Dukakis was more specific, Bush was effective in listing the accomplishments of the Reagan/Bush administration and in labelling Dukakis a liberal. In fact, as Halford Ryan pointed out, "Bush would spend as much time in defining what he was not, which was Dukakis, as in defining what he was." On election night, Bush scored a sound victory.

PRESIDENTIAL RHETORIC

Bush had little training in public speaking. He seems to have learned to write prose well enough at Phillips Academy and Yale to have achieved high academic honors. Bush's ability in political speaking was learned on the hustings. When he took advantage of logographers and rehearsals, he could be formidable. When he spoke extemporaneously, he often mangled syntax and used incredibly cryptic phrases obviously assuming the audience could read his mind or that they possessed the same special knowledge he did.

Like presidents before him, Bush assembled a speechwriting staff at the White House that consisted of approximately five full-time writers and a dozen researchers. But more than most presidents, Bush was often dissatisfied with the results of in-house writing. Thus, outside consultants, such as Noonan, Gold, Price, Ailes, and I, were often consulted on major speeches. We made a conscious effort to make Bush sound Lincolnesque, particularly regarding rhetoric on the Gulf War. Ailes also worked with Bush on delivery, getting him to slow down and lower his pitch. The speechwriting office was a revolving door until the arrival of Tony Snow, a writer for the Washington *Times*. Snow's drafts impressed the President with their sound style and applause-getting lines.

The main problem with Bush's presidential rhetoric was Bush himself. He disdained rehearsal. His love of substance often caused him to neglect style, particularly in speeches he delivered from the Oval Office to television audiences. One of the most serious mistakes Bush made was to insist that his press conferences occur during the day. Bush was closer to the press than Reagan. He spoke easily with them. His press conferences were tremendous demonstrations of sagacity, wit, and humanity. But he did not want to appear to be imitating Reagan, so he refused to hold his press conferences at night when all of the nation could have seen them. When he agreed to a prime time press conference in June of 1992, the networks refused to cover it claiming it was a political event. This strategic error contributed to bringing down Bush's presidency.

Bush's Inaugural Address

On January 20, 1989, when George Bush finished the oath of office and began his Inaugural Address, he saluted George Washington, who had given the first inaugural 200 years earlier. Bush then uttered a prayer of his own composition. The tone was somber and the rest of the address was traditional.

It called for an end to the bitter divisions in Congress. And in its most original moment, claimed that "The final lesson of Vietnam is that no great nation can long afford to be sundered by a memory." There were also echoes of the 1988 acceptance speech, as when Bush stated his purpose: "It is to make kinder the face of the nation and gentler the face of the world," and he revisited the "thousand points of lights."

The style of the speech was appropriate and often moving. For example, early in the speech, Bush framed a unifying metaphor of a "new breeze"; at the end he said, "The new breeze blows, a page turns, the story unfolds. . . . " Alliteration was wisely used: "A president is neither prince nor pope." And some antitheses proved effective: "We need compromise; we have had dissension." But for the most part, the Inaugural Address was a simple speech that stated goals in clear, plain English.

The State of the Union Addresses

Like Ronald Reagan, Bush relished his State of the Union Addresses. He seemed to feel more at home in the House chamber than in the White House. His delivery was up to the standard of his 1988 acceptance in each of his State of the Union Addresses because he rehearsed them, because he knew how to use the teleprompters, and because he seemed genuinely buoyed by the cheering from the Congress and the galleries.

Only three weeks after his Inaugural, Bush appeared before a joint session of Congress to present his budget plan in a major address that was carried on national television. The speech, very like a State of the Union Address, purported to set out "a realistic plan for tackling" the deficit. Bush began the speech by renewing his inaugural pledge to work with Congress. He identified with his audience by recalling his time in "this historic chamber."

The President contextualized his plan by saying he did not intend to change direction from the Reagan administration. He then laid out "four broad features" including "attention to urgent priorities, investment in the future, an attack on the deficit, and no new taxes." The last phrase not only recalled his acceptance speech pledge but set off a wave of Republican cheering. Many other proposals in the speech were drawn from the Republican credo, including a call for a presidential line item veto, a balanced budget amendment, and reliance on the free enterprise system.

After an appeal to "family and faith," Bush turned to his specific agenda. He proposed increasing funds for scientific and technological research, creating enterprise zones and a council on competitiveness headed by the Vice President, and cutting the minimum tax on capital gains. Next, Bush targeted education by proposing "merit schools" for students and rewards for excellent teachers. He then called for a "war against drugs" led by a new drug czar. Later in the year, Bush would conduct a persuasive campaign on the issue.

The speech looked more and more like a traditional State of the Union Address as the President spelled out his agenda in other areas: more funds for AIDS research, more use of clean coal, protection for oceans, cleaning up environmental waste, welfare reform, honoring the nation's commitment to a sound Social Security system, and statehood for Puerto Rico. The address outlined principles to guide the budget process. Bush made a transition to foreign affairs by saying, "And frankly, don't take this wrong, we need less congressional micromanagement of our nation's military policy." Again, the Republican side of the aisle exploded with cheers, to which Bush ad libbed, "I detect a slight division on that question."

Once his foreign policy was set out, there could be little doubt that this was a State of the Union Address in the classic sense. The President defended the Strategic Defense Initiative, then called for a ban on chemical weapons, an end to nuclear proliferation, self-determination in Central America, and a strengthening of our European defensive ties.

In the conclusion of this lengthy address, Bush appealed to young Americans to "hold fast to your dreams" and quoted Churchill's famous lines "We shall not fail or falter. . . . Give us the tools and we will finish the job."

This speech effectively portrayed the President as the nation's leader by defining a blueprint for legislative action. Its references to Lincoln, Franklin Roosevelt, and Churchill helped identify Bush with recognized leaders. The speech was consistently interrupted by applause, albeit often partisan applause that undercut the bipartisan appeal of the opening. Its effectiveness was also limited because it was too long, because the use of parallel structure became monotonous, and because by agreeing to cooperate with Congress, the President appeared to be playing the budget game in the usual way. Rather than bold initiatives, the speech would produce a compromise that increased the deficit.

The State of the Union Address of January 31, 1990, was important because it began the process by which Bush became enmeshed in a plan to raise taxes thereby breaking his strongly worded acceptance speech pledge, "No new taxes." Bush signaled that he was in a mood to compromise at the beginning of the speech when reminded his audience that he had served in the House and had been president of the Senate.

Bush then reviewed the changes in the world and enhanced his credibility by associating with them: "Panama is free. . . . a free Poland. . . . [the Berlin] wall is history. . . . '' After a transition to the domestic scene, Bush set out his agenda, which differed little from that of the 1989 speech. One irony did occur when Bush discussed the education summit: "I'm very pleased that Governor Gardner and Governor Clinton, Governor Branstad, Governor Campbell, all of whom were very key in these discussions, these deliberations, are with us here tonight."

Bush then presented his plan for a balanced budget by 1993 "with no new taxes." A few paragraphs later, the first hint at compromise came in the lines, " . . . let me say again to all the members of Congress, the American people did not send us here to bicker. . . . In the spirit of cooperation, I offer my hand to all of you." As Amos Kiewe makes clear, Senator George Mitchell (D-Maine), the majority leader, would take that hand with dire consequences for Bush. In April 1990, on national television, first Bush, in a twelve-minute address, and then Mitchell, in a ten-minute speech, endorsed a budget plan that included new taxes. Bush was deserted by 126 members of his own party in the House when the measure came to a vote. The debacle severely damaged his chances of re-election.

But in his 1990 address, the President returned to foreign policy by quoting from a moving letter written by a private killed in action in Panama. Bush also quoted Harry Truman in the spirit of bi-partisanship. He announced new ties to the Soviet Union and a reduction of troops in Central Europe. In concluding Bush was more personal and emotional than usual. He spoke of standing at the gates of the Gdansk shipyard and seeing three crosses there with anchors on them, "an ancient symbol of hope." He spoke of his newly born "12th grandchild" and extended his sentiments "to the children and young people out there tonight" challenging them to "Fix your vision on a new century, your century. . . . ''

The State of the Union Address of January 29, 1991, began by building on Bush's credibility as a war leader. With the Gulf War underway "in the skies and on the seas and sands," as Bush noted with alliteration, the nation was more focused on what Bush said than at any other time in his presidency. He used the occasion to advance his notion of a "new world order, where diverse nations are drawn together in common cause, to achieve the universal aspiration of mankind: peace and security, freedom and the rule of law." Reinforcing the rationalization he had laid out earlier in his announcement of the start of the war, Bush accused Hussein of raping Kuwait and repeated that his action would not stand.

Next, Bush built on the credibility he had gained from the fall of Communism and the new found friendship he had developed with the Soviet Union. He concluded the foreign policy section of the speech with an encomium to the "American character." The passage worked as a neat transition to the domestic issues: "We are resolute and resourceful. If we can selflessly confront evil for the sake of good in a land so far away, then surely we can make this land all that it should be."

The remainder of the address was lengthy and rehearsed Bush's ideas for an American "renewal." But his claims of past success sounded like campaign rhetoric from 1988 and did not ring true in a troubled economic environment. He called for a capital gains tax, a reinforcement of the educational system, a new national highway system, research and development incentives, banking reform, approval for the Mexican Free Trade Agreement, ending drug abuse, elimination of political action committees, and turning $15 billion in federal programs over to the states. The litany won divided and often tepid applause from the Congress.

When the President returned to the topic of the war, however, he met with genuinely enthusiastic responses to his praise for our troops and his pledge that "we will prevail." He even stole a page from Ronald Reagan's book by introducing Mrs. Norman Schwarzkopf who was sitting with Barbara Bush in the gallery.

The President concluded strongly by discussing the burden of leadership: "[O]nly America has had both the moral standing and the means to back it up . . . .Our cause is just. Our cause is moral. Our cause is right." Anaphora, or parallel structure, and varying sentence length worked to provide an eloquent conclusion to the lengthy address.

The State of the Union Address of January 28, 1992, found Bush recovering from an embarrassing fainting spell in Japan that reminded the public not only of Bush's whimpy persona but of Dan Quayle's possible accession. Bush opened his speech by joking about the event and the popularity of his wife. For the next fifteen minutes, Bush reviewed foreign policy and once again reinforced his credibility as war leader. Throughout the speech he praised our armed forces, and then "The American taxpayer [who] bore the brunt of the burden, and deserves a hunk of the glory." The alliteration, homeoteuleton, and balance indicate some time was taken with the speech. Bush continued by proclaiming, "We liberated Kuwait . . . A world once divided into two armed camps now recognizes one sole and pre-eminent power: the United States of America." He emotionally reinforced the goodness of America's intentions by reading from a letter from the wife of the "first pilot killed in the Gulf." She wrote that she would tell her children "that their father went away to war because it was the right thing to do."

The President used this moment to appeal for bi-partisanship and showed good faith by announcing a series of major defense program cuts culminating with "an additional $50 billion over the next five years." With a neat antithesis, Bush once again demonstrated his prudent side: "To do less would be insensitive to progress—but to do more would be ignorant of history." A few paragraphs later, he paraphrased a Goldwater antithesis from 1964: "Strength in the pursuit of peace is no vice; isolationism in the pursuit of security is no virtue."

He immediately followed that line with one of his most inadequate transitions: "Now to our troubles at home." In an attempt to identify his war on unemployment with the Gulf effort he said, "I know we are in hard times, but I know something else: This will not stand." He went on to argue that if we could succeed on the international stage, we should certainly be able to solve our problems at home.

But what followed was the Republican litany that Americans had heard for the previous decade. These short-term proposals sounded to many like rearranging the deck chairs rather than taking a new course: reduce withholding from taxes; keep interest rates down; create a new investment tax credit; modify passive loss rules; cut the capital gains tax; extend unemployment benefits. Once again the President made a passionate plea for an end to partisan bickering and gave Congress a deadline of March 20th to pass his budget: "From the day after that, if it must be: the battle is joined."

The President's long-term proposals were also uninspired: education reform, less crime, free trade, health care reform, deficit reduction, a line item veto, tort reform, welfare reform. There were too many proposals to give any one of them serious development; many were not in the hands of the President but up to the Congress. The domestic sections of the speech lacked focus and raised partisan hackles. Instead of fresh vision, Bush concluded with a statement that reinforced the difficulty of his position while trying to link it to his success in the Gulf: "We are going to lift this nation out of hard times inch by inch and day by day, and those who would stop us had best step aside. Because I look at hard times and I make this vow: This will not stand."

The War Against Drugs

In his Inaugural Address Bush had pledged "This scourge will stop," a reference to drug abuse. The effort to stem the rising tide of drug abuse resulted in the appointment of William Bennet as "drug Czar" and a declaration of "war on drugs." The war included two notable speeches from the President in September 1989. The first, on September 5th, was directed to the American public and addressed the drug situation in the United States and in Latin America. The second, on September 12th from the White House library, was directed to junior high and high school students and carried a "front-line warfare" message encouraging children to fight drug use.

On September 14, 1989, following the President's speeches, polls revealed an incredible jump in the number of people who believed the drug crisis was the "most important problem facing America": sixty-three percent versus twenty-seven percent only months before. On October 1, 1989, the *Los Angeles Times* headlined that "Bush Wins First Battle in War on Drugs by Gaining Political Advantage." Bush's national address had "won resounding public approval, [according to polls], and enabled the President to put his Democratic opponents" at a disadvantage. A *Washington Post*-ABC News Poll taken just after the speeches showed that 75 percent of those interviewed approved of the way Bush was handling the drug problem, up from about 50 percent the month before. In short, perception of, and interest in, the factual condition of a drug problem seemed fairly congruent between the President and his adult audience.

There were several reasons for Bush's success with the adult audience. First, statistics such as those providing the number of drug users gave the audiences a description of the magnitude of the problem while enhancing the President's sagacity. "[A]lmost eight million people have used cocaine in the past year, almost one million of them used it frequently, once a week or more." Second, Bush stressed that "turf battles won't win this war. Teamwork will." He sought the cooperation of Congress and promised to help foreign governments. America's drug appetite helped cause "cocaine killers [to gun] down a leading statesman, [murder] almost 200 judges, and [murder] seven members of [Colombia's] Supreme Court." The United States has "a responsibility not to leave our brave friends in Colombia to fight alone." Bush pledged to find and prosecute those who initiated and funded drug production, "[a]nd for drug kingpins, the death penalty." In fact one cartel did begin negotiations with the Colombian government in exchange for amnesty.

Underlying these exigencies were the economic repercussions of drug use and the destructive nature of addiction on neighborhoods: drug traffic fostered gangs, murders, graffiti, and litter. Bush stressed this aspect of the problem by recounting a case of a neighborhood in which "children don't flinch at the sound of gunfire. And when they play, they pretend to sell to each other small white rocks they call crack."

Finally, the President carved out an audience composed of those opposed to drug abuse and urged them to take action: "If people you know are users, help them get off drugs. If you are a parent, talk to your children about drugs—tonight. Call your local drug prevention program. Be a big brother or sister to a child in need. . . . Whether you give your time or talent, everyone counts."

Bush's second speech addressed mainly school children and their teachers. For Bush, they represented the "future of America" and one target for drug sellers. They could change the situation, or, Bush warned, they could lose control of their futures: "For those who let drugs make their decision for them, you can almost hear the doors slamming shut. It isn't worth it. We know that now."

But where Bush led the adult audience to confront a serious problem in his first speech, the press argued that he was *perceived* to be behind the curve by some of the youngsters who heard the second. They already knew the factual condition existed and wanted more news from the President than he gave them. Trying to use the student's language often proved counterproductive because the President sounded condescending. For example, when dealing with their cynicism he said, "Now, I can imagine a few whispers out there." Later, he told the students that saying no to drugs "won't make you a nerd." Thus, Bush exacerbated an incongruity between himself and his young listeners.

On the other hand, Bush succeeded with upper-middle and high income students. They related to his real-life narrative about a policeman killed on duty:

"In the early hours of a cold February morning, sitting in a police cruiser, Eddie was blown away at point-blank range, killed on the order of a drug kingpin. Cold and calculated. . . . To me this badge is a constant reminder that Eddie Byrne's life was not given in vain." According to press reports, this narrative moved the students and when reported in the media served to reinforce with adults the image of a pro-active president, thereby strengthening his effort of September 5th.

Foreign Policy Speeches

On September 26, 1989, Bush returned to the United Nations where he had served as U.S. Representative in 1971 and 1972. Early in the speech, Bush praised U.N. peacekeeping forces, and singled out Lt. Col. William Higgins, who had been hanged by terrorists in the Middle East. Bush declared Marxism dead, identified democracy with individualism and capitalism, but resisted criticism of Soviet leader Mikhail Gorbachev. He surveyed the setbacks for totalitarianism around the world. In an awkward antithesis, he said, "Advocates of the totalitarian idea saw its triumph written in the laws of history. They failed to see the love of freedom that was written in the human heart."

Bush then called for the elimination of chemical weapons worldwide by proposing a three-part treaty that already had the tacit agreement of the Soviet Union. He praised the new "openness" or *glasnost* in the Soviet Union as a prelude to his call for replacing "conflict with consensus." Bush declared, "The new world of freedom is not a world where a few nations live in comfort while others live in want." But the generalities of the speech never gelled into a programmatic definition of what would become a call for a "new world order."

On December 20, 1989, the President announced a military incursion into Panama to capture its "dictator" Manuel Noriega. Bush justified the action on the grounds that Noriega was an "indicted drug trafficker" and a "thug." Coming in his first year as president, the action indicated that Bush was not afraid to use force to achieve his ends. It also revealed that Bush could rationalize his actions in a way that made them acceptable to the public. Despite the fact that Noriega had been an agent for the CIA and many innocent civilians were killed during the invasion, the public approved of Bush's action.

Panama was prelude to Bush's moves against the aggression of Iraq. On September 12, 1990, Bush addressed a joint session of Congress to assess the problem. On August 2nd, Iraq had invaded Kuwait threatening oil supplies from the region. In response Bush had organized a grand alliance of more than twenty nations to protect the Saudi frontier. In what would become two common places for speeches on the war, Bush read a letter from a soldier and then acknowledged the team work of Generals Colin Powell and Norman Schwartzkopf. Then the President presented his conditions to Iraq: "Kuwait's legitimate government must be restored. The security and stability of the Persian Gulf must be assured." As Thomas Kane pointed out, the rationale for the Gulf War evolved through a series of speeches. By January 16, 1991, when he asked for Congressional support, Bush declared that what Hussein had done "shall not stand." Finally, Bush rationalized American action by comparing Saddam Hussein to "Hitler" and Hussein's tanks to a "blitzkrieg." In this equation, "one small country" became Poland in 1939. Furthermore, Bush used the war to accomplish a goal he set out in his Inaugural Address, to put Vietnam behind us once and for all. Finally, by putting together a coalition of allies that included Arab as well as European nations, Bush demonstrated that world opinion was on America's side and that a "new world order" had been established.

When in March of 1991, the President appeared before a joint session of Congress to declare that the "war is over," he was greeted by effusive applause and chants from the Congress of "Bush, Bush, Bush." House Speaker Tom Foley departed from tradition by extending to the Commander-in-Chief his "warmest congratulations on a brilliant victory." Bush was humble in victory praising his team of advisors and "all who served in the field." He then extended the themes he had initiated in earlier speeches into vindication for his policy: "We went half way around the world to do what is moral and just and right. . . . We lifted the yoke of aggression. . . . " At the end of the speech, he was one of the most popular presidents in American history.

The 1992 Campaign

In *Looking Forward*, Bush told a prophetic story about a conversation with Jim Rhodes, Governor of Ohio. After Bush had listed everything he'd do if he became president, Rhodes pulled out his wallet and slapped it on the table. "That's it right there. . . . Who can put money in people's pockets. . . . That's what it's all about, George—jobs, jobs, jobs." The anecdote haunted Bush throughout 1992. From his State of the Union Address on, Bush prayed for an economic recovery but it never came. Thus, in the summer of 1992, he found himself where he had been four years earlier, behind his Democratic opponent. Again, Bush needed to give the speech of a lifetime.

The acceptance speech at the Republican Convention in Houston in August failed for a number of reasons. First, the public was concerned about the economy and foreign policy took a back seat in a world at peace. Second, Bush had failed to deliver on his promises and had clearly broken the one concerning "no new taxes." He failed to explain away that change of heart in believable terms. Third, Bush failed to contextualize America's economic difficulties in terms of the world picture. The fact of the matter was that the United States was doing well in a worldwide depression. Fourth, Bush's speech was framed by those who spoke earlier, including a rabidly right-wing Pat Buchanan who drowned out Reagan's marvelous swan song with a mean spirited attack of Hillary Clinton. A religiously intolerant Pat Robertson and a remarkably divisive Marilin Quayle identified the Republican party with a prudish social agenda. During these speeches, orchestrated chants from the floor rose up to a neo-classic imperial stage worthy of the worst fascist rallies.

Despite this environment, Bush's speech did have its strong points. He delivered it well and with uncharacteristic emotion. On foreign policy, he scored heavily with the delegates, the guests, and the national audience. The new world order was defined in a way the average American could understand. But the second half of the speech once again fell into partisan proposals that failed to come together in a unified way. One could begin to count the number of pens that had written paragraphs for the speech.

Much worse for Bush were the three presidential debates that followed in the fall. James Baker, who had reluctantly and tearfully resigned as Secretary of State to advise the Bush campaign, opposed Bush's entering the debates. His instinct was correct. Bush is not a natural debater: he speaks too elliptically for the public, he disdains the anecdotes that served Reagan so well, and attacking is not part of his personality. Furthermore, Bush believed that after winning the Gulf War he deserved re-election without having to go through the humiliating ordeal of a campaign, let alone debates. With the economy moribund, Bush would have to defend a failed domestic policy. Baker's worse nightmare came true when Ross Perot re-entered the campaign claiming he had been driven out earlier by dirty tricks on the part of the Bush campaign. In all three debates, Perot would aim most his verbal bullets at Bush, much to the delight of the smooth-talking Clinton. Bush's diffident performance was particularly evident in the second debate where he kept looking at his watch. In that debate, Bush's decision to attack Clinton's character was undercut by moderator Carol Simpson's representation of the audience's frustration with negative campaigns. He undermined his credibility on economic issues when he did not pay attention to a question from a black woman, and said, "He didn't get" what she meant. He undercut his defense of his administration by naively volunteering to answer questions first, which allowed Perot and Clinton to jump on his responses. Bush abandoned Ailes's strategy and it cost him dearly.

RHETORICAL SOURCES

Archival Materials

The Presidential Library for George Bush is being built at Texas A&M University in College Station, Texas. Bush's presidential papers and other biographical materials will be stored there.

Until the library is complete, scholars can use:

Weekly Compilation of Presidential Documents. (WCPD). Washington, DC: U.S. Government Printing Office, 1989–1993.

Vital Speeches of the Day. (VSD). Mount Pleasant, SC: City News Publishing Co., 1989–1993.

Videotapes of rhetorical events are available from C-SPAN, 444 North Capitol Street, NW, Washington, D.C. 20001. Videotapes of debates and major speeches are available at the Vanderbilt Television News Archive, Vanderbilt University Library, Vanderbilt University, Nashville, Tennessee 37240.

Rhetorical Studies

Bush, George. *Looking Forward.* New York: Bantam, 1988.

Drew, Elizabeth. *Election Journal: Political Events of 1987–1988.* New York: William Morrow, 1989.

Lemert, James B., William R. Elliott, James M. Bernstein, William L. Rosenberg, and Karl J. Nsetvold. *News Verdicts, the Debates, and Presidential Campaigns.* New York: Praeger, 1991.

Stuckey, Mary E. *The President as Interpreter-in-Chief.* Chatham, NJ: Chatham House Publishers, 1991.

Rhetorical Monographs

Clayman, Steven E. "Caveat Orator: Audience Disaffiliation in the 1988 Presidential Debates." *Quarterly Journal of Speech* 78 (1992): 33–60.

Downs, Valerie C., Lynda L. Kaid, and Sandra Ragan. "The Impact of Argumentativeness and Verbal Aggression on Communicator Image: The Exchange Between George Bush and Dan Rather." *Western Journal of Speech Communication* 54 (1990): 99–112.

Duffy, Bernard K. "President Bush's Inaugural Address, 1989." In *The Inaugural Address of Twentieth-Century American Presidents,* edited by Halford Ross Ryan. Westport CT: Praeger, 1993.

Hellweg, Susan A., and Steven L. Phillips. "A Verbal and Visual Analysis of the 1980 Houston Republican Presidential Primary Debate." *The Southern Speech Communication Journal* 47 (1981): 23–38.

Hogan, Michael J. "Media Nihilism and the Presidential Debates." *Journal of the American Forensic Association* 25 (1989): 220–25.

Kane, Thomas. "Foreign Policy Suppositions and Commanding Ideas." *Argumentation and Advocacy* 28 (1991): 80–90.

Kiewe, Amos. "From a Rhetorical Trap to Capitualion and Obviation: The Crisis Rhetoric of George Bush's 'Read My Lips; No New Taxes'." In *The Modern Presidency and Crisis Rhetoric,* edited by Amos Kiewe. Westport, CT: Praeger, 1994.

Olson, Kathryn M. "Constraining Open Deliberation in Times of War: Presidential War Justifications for Grenada and the Persian Gulf." *Argumentation and Advocacy* 28 (1991): 64–79.

Rosenberg, William L., and William R. Elliott. "Effect of Debate Exposure on Evaluation of 1984 Vice-Presidential Candidates." *Journalism Quarterly* 64 (1987): 55–64.

Ryan, Halford Ross. "The 1988 Bush-Dukakis Presidential Debates." In *Rhetorical Studies of National Political Debates,* edited by Robert Friedenberg. Westport, CT: Praeger, 1990.

Trent, Judith S. "The 1984 Bush-Ferraro Vice Presidential Debate." In *Rhetorical Stud-*

ies of National Political Debates, edited by Robert Friedenberg. Westport, CT: Praeger, 1990.

Chronology of Significant Presidential Persuasions

(Unless otherwise given, all speeches were delivered from the White House, Washington, D.C.)

"Acceptance Speech," Republican Convention, New Orleans, August 18, 1988. *VSD*, 55 (1988–1989): 3–5.

Inaugural Address: A New Breeze Is Blowing, Washington, D.C., January 20, 1989. *VSD*, 55 (1988–1989): 258–60.

"President's Budget Message," Washington, D.C., February 9, 1989. *VSD*, 55 (1988–1989): 290–94.

"War on Drugs," September 5, 1989. *VSD*, 55 (1988–1989): 738–40.

"Proclamation 6018—National Alcohol and Drug Treatment Month," September 12, 1989. *WCPD*, 25 (Part 3, July 3–September 25, 1989): 1357–58.

"New World Freedom," United Nations General Assembly, New York, September 26, 1989. *WCPD*, 25 (Part 4, October 2, 1989–January 1, 1990): 1435–40.

"Address to the Nation Announcing the United States Military Action in Panama," December 20, 1989. *VSD*, 56 (1989–1990): 194–95.

"State of the Union Address 1990," Washington, D.C., January 31, 1990. *VSD*, 56 (1989–1990): 258–61.

"Iraq's Invasion of Kuwait," Washington, D.C., September 11, 1990. *VSD*, 56 (1989–1990): 674–75.

"War with Iraq," January 16, 1991. *VSD*, 57 (1990–1991): 226–27.

"State of the Union Address 1991," Washington, D.C., January 29, 1991. *VSD*, 57 (1990–1991): 258–61.

"The War Is Over," Washington, D.C., March 6, 1991. *VSD*, 57 (1990–1991): 354–56.

"State of the Union Address 1992," Washington, D.C., January 28, 1992. *VSD*, 58 (1991–1992): 258–63.

"A New Crusade to Reap the Rewards of Our Global Victory," Republican Convention, Houston, Texas, August 20, 1992. *VSD*, 58 (1991–1992): 706–71.

Stephen C. Wood and Jean M. DeWitt

Bill Clinton
(1946–   )

A new season of American renewal has begun.

William Jefferson Clinton was born in Hope, Arkansas. He was named for his father who had died in an automobile accident before Clinton was born. He attended public schools in Hot Springs, Arkansas, where he graduated fourth in a class of 323. Clinton's bachelor degree is from Georgetown University (1964–1968); he was a Rhodes Scholar at Oxford University (1968–1970), and he earned a J.D. from Yale Law School (1970–1973). He practiced law in Fayetteville and was on the faculty of the University of Arkansas School of Law for one year before beginning his political career in 1974. Clinton narrowly lost his 1974 bid for Congress; however, he gained recognition and two years later was elected state attorney general. While serving in that office, he was elected governor (1978–1981), but was defeated in his first re-election campaign. In 1982 he successfully challenged the incumbent governor and won four consecutive terms. He is a founding member of the Democratic Leadership Council, a group of centrist party activists, organized in 1986. In 1992, Clinton's election ended the Democrat's twelve-year presidential losing streak. He married Hillary Rodham in 1975 and has one child, Chelsea.

CLINTON'S RHETORICAL PRACTICES

Clinton's rhetoric reveals some generalities, common themes, and forms of expression that could be considered rhetorical trademarks. For example, Clinton has a well known penchant for long speeches. Many of his major speeches have lasted close to or longer than an hour. His introduction to national politics was his 1988 nomination of Dukakis at the Democratic National Convention in a rambling hour plus speech that was notable only for its length. In his acceptance speech four years later, he jokingly referred to his opportunity to finish the Dukakis speech and spoke for close to another hour. Both his 1993 and 1994 State of the Union Addresses hit the hour mark. Clinton not only talks long, he talks often. As candidate and as President, Clinton has talked himself hoarse on issues he considers important. Americans are accustomed to presidential candidates ending their campaigns with strained voices, but Clinton is the first electronic media president to exhibit this level of voice strain several times during his first year in office.

In spite of occasional voice strain, Clinton's delivery is dynamic. He employs different styles of delivery for different types of audiences: casual and conversational in town meetings and interviews; powerful and hortatory from the political stump; and formal and somber in televised addresses. He exhibits a good command of vocal emphasis and variety. To punctuate points of emphasis, Clinton's physical gestures are characterized by a lightly clenched fist with his index finger bent, not quite pointing at the audience. On the stump, exemplified by Clinton's March 15, 1994 speech in Boston, the gesture that has caught the attention of the national media is his repeated striking of the speaker's platform with his fist, in the Boston speech as he characterized the Republicans as a party that just says, "no, no, no, no, no, no, no, no, no."

The Clinton presidency is still looking for its rhetorical slogan such as Roosevelt's New Deal, Kennedy's New Frontier, and Johnson's Great Society. One hopeful was the "New Covenant," which Clinton invoked consistently in his acceptance of the Democratic nomination. However, by the time his Inaugural Address was delivered, the "New Covenant" was gone. "American renewal" is probably as close to a rhetorical slogan as one will find to characterize the Clinton administration.

Clinton's rhetoric is heavily influenced by John and Robert Kennedy and Martin Luther King, Jr. Although echoing the rhetorical signatures of Kennedy and King is common among contemporary politicians, Clinton seems genuinely moved by the ideas and words of Kennedy and King. Echoes of Kennedy are heard when Clinton said, "And so, my fellow Americans, as we stand on the edge of the 21st century, let us begin anew." The rhetoric of King resonated in this passage from Clinton's Inaugural Address. "From this joyful mountaintop of celebration we hear a call to service in the valley." In King's "I Have a Dream" speech, the audience was taken from the valley to the mountaintop; and in Clinton's Inaugural, the audience was taken from the mountaintop to the valley.

Clinton also has a good sense of humor, both self-deprecating, "I wanted to come back to this convention and finish that speech I started four years ago," and directed, "But right now I know how President Lincoln felt when General McClellan wouldn't attack in the Civil War. He asked him, 'If you're not going to use your army, may I borrow it?' And so I say, George Bush, if you won't use your power to help America, step aside, I will."

Clinton perceives a speech as a part of a larger complex of events, which is amply illustrated in his inaugural and health care speeches. Certainly, any speech can be separated from its context, but given the "war-room" strategy sessions that precede and follow many of Clinton's major addresses, a contextual approach takes on increased viability.

CLINTON'S PRE-PRESIDENTIAL ADDRESSES

Clinton delivered five inaugural addresses as governor-elect of Arkansas in 1979, 1983, 1985, 1987, and 1991. In 1979, he was the youngest governor in the history of Arkansas, and his speech reflected that humble, thankful persona of a thirty-two-year-old Bill Clinton. With the zeal of youth, he promised to exercise the power well, but expressed concern that he may have to make unpopular decisions. He used the stylistic device of repetition heavily. The phrase, "For as long as I can remember," was used six times to introduce his values of equal opportunity, arbitrary exercise of power, waste in government, clean air, care for the elderly, and educational opportunities. He then outlined his platform: "There is much to be done." Reforms in education, energy, and health were the thrust of his address. He concluded with the watchwords pride and hope: "With these two emotions, we can go a long way. We can bring on a new era of achievement and excellence—we can fashion a life here that will be the envy of our nation."

In his second and shortest gubenatorial inaugural speech in 1983, Clinton preached hard times and the need to practice austerity. He held that the government must sustain cuts while delivering opportunities to the people. Clinton's priorities reflected the economic conditions, but continued to stress the importance of education as the key to economic revival. He admitted being criticized for an agenda full of promises but stated, "politics is about the promises of today and tomorrow." Although being defeated as a first-term incumbent governor and then being re-elected is somewhat unusual in American politics, Clinton's inaugural address failed to reflect that uniqueness.

Clinton's 1985 inaugural speech provides insight into his perception of speech making. Following his "I am humbled" rhetoric, he stated that he "thought hard" about his inaugural speech, and then made this observation: "I am well aware of the limitations of speech, especially in our time. The other night someone told me not to worry too much about my address because no one would pay attention no matter what was said and in the end all that would count is what appeared for a few seconds on the television news." He granted that possibility, but continued to deliver what may have been his longest Inaugural Address as governor. Clinton remained steadfast in his platform of educational reform and set his basic principles as belief in ourselves, economic growth, government for the people, and a decade of dedication to achieve these goals. During his third term, Arkansas would celebrate its 150th birthday. In honor of that event Clinton resolved to "move Arkansas from the economic backwaters to the crest of prosperity and opportunity in America."

A 1984 amendment to Arkansas's Constitution extended the length of the governor's term from two years to four years. Clinton outlined his plans for four years in his fourth inaugural address in 1987, which was comparable in length to his third inaugural. Clinton spoke of two goals: to modernize the economy and to give children educational opportunities. He self-consciously divided the speech into three main points: Good Beginnings, Good Schools, and Good Jobs. He explicated each one and proposed an agenda to satisfy the goals. His rhetoric expressed a more confident, self-assured politician who convincingly outlined his program and advised his fellow Arkansans to take responsibility for their own future. In the 1980s, Clinton was considered a rising star in Democratic politics.

In 1991, his fifth term and second four-year term, Clinton called for the biggest financial commitment to education since 1983. Throughout his service as governor he held steadfast to his pledge to improve the state's public education system. He stated four priorities for this term: education, medical care, roads and bridges, and the environment. Clinton's platform remained consistent throughout his gubernatorial years. Replacing promises with programs, his rhetoric matured and his focus intensified. Perhaps these were the building blocks of oratory for the heir apparent.

THE 1992 CAMPAIGN

Acceptance Speech, 1992 Democratic National Convention

On July 16, 1992, candidate Clinton spoke to the nation about his "hope for the future, my faith in the American people, and my vision of the kind of country we can build together." Politically, however, Clinton needed to establish his position in the political mythos and to counter the negative images of infidelity and draft dodging. The strategy was simple. He told the people about Bill Clinton through stories of his family: his father, who died before Clinton was born; his mother, "She taught me about family and hard work and sacrifice"; his grandfather, "He taught me more about equality in the eyes of the Lord than all my professors at Georgetown"; his wife, "She taught me that all children can learn, and that each of us has a duty to help them do it"; and his daughter, Chelsea, "As I stood in the delivery room, I was overcome with the thought that God had given me a blessing my own father never knew: the chance to hold my child in my arms." The family circle was completed with the linking of Chelsea and his father.

Humble beginnings is often a direct connection with American political mythos. Being part of the elite, the wealthy, and the well-educated is the norm for most candidates, yet these qualities often work against the humble-beginnings myth. Clinton, although not wealthy, was a part of the political elite and certainly was well-educated. To both counter and capitalize on these qualities, Clinton's speech blended his humble beginnings with the self-evident quality of the education he received at Georgetown, Oxford, and Yale Law School: "My grandfather just had a high-school education—a grade-school education. But in that country store he taught me more about equality in the eyes of the Lord than all my professors at Georgetown; more about the intrinsic worth of every individual than all the philosophers at Oxford, more about the need for justice under the law than all the jurists at Yale Law School."

The blue-collar work ethic is part of the American political mythos. Clinton said he was "raised to believe the American dream was built on rewarding hard work." Clinton's final link to the American political mythos was his Kennedy heritage. The delegates watched a short bio-film in which the clip of young Clinton, the apprentice, met Kennedy, Camelot's King. In the speech, Clinton said: "As a teen-ager I heard John Kennedy's summons to citizenship." The image of the torch of leadership being passed was neither accidental nor subtle.

Of course, the speech attacked George Bush and the eleven years of Republican rule, and included a broad-based agenda for his presidency. Clinton's attack on Bush was sharply focused in the later part of the speech and built to a climax which was broken with humor: "What is George Bush doing about America's economic problems? Well, he promised us 15 million new jobs by now. And he's over 14 million jobs short. . . . He has raised taxes on the people who drive pickup trucks and lowered taxes on people who ride in limousines. . . . He promised to balance the budget, but he didn't even try." Clinton's litany builds: Bush "won't take on the big insurance companies. . . . He won't streamline the Federal Government. . . . He never balanced a budget. . . . He won't break the stranglehold of special interests. . . . He doesn't have Al Gore. I do." Finding fault with the old order, however, was insufficient—Clinton sketched out his "new covenant." He envisioned "An America with millions of new jobs. . . . An America in which the doors of college are thrown open. . . . An America in which health care is a right, not a privilege. . . . An America in which middle-class families' incomes—not their taxes—are going up. . . . An America in which the wealthiest, those making over $200,000 a year, are asked to pay their fair share. . . . An America with the world's strongest defense. . . . [and] An America where we end welfare as we know it."

1992 Presidential Debates

In 1992, Clinton, Bush, and Perot participated in the fifth consecutive Presidential debates. There were three televised matches; Clinton "won" one while Perot was pronounced the victor in the other two.

In the first debate, 30% of the people felt that Clinton was the winner (47% Perot; 16% Bush). Clinton's strategy was to accentuate his strengths (and Bush's weaknesses) and to court Perot's supporters. Clinton used statistics to emphasize his points and elaborate upon his solutions. He described problems in layman's language thus aligned himself with the middle class. He attacked ''trickle-down'' economics and chose ''investment'' as his euphemism for tax. The word ''change'' resounded twelve times in this debate.

As expected, Bush stressed Clinton's anti-war activities. However, Clinton had carefully prepared his retort placing Bush in the Joe McCarthy camp: ''When Joe McCarthy went around this country attacking people's patriotism, he was wrong.'' Clinton continued with a slap to the other cheek when he intimated that Bush did not measure up to his father's values: ''And a Senator from Connecticut stood up to him named Prescott Bush. Your father was right to stand up to Joe McCarthy.''

Clinton's over reliance on statistics made him appear to be fact oriented, stiff, and formal. Although Clinton was judged second behind Perot, he won a clear victory over Bush and established himself as presidential material.

The second debate, held four days later, provided no room for major changes in image or tactics. However, Clinton made minor adjustments to his style and perhaps this refocus helped him. Fifty-eight percent of the people believed he won that debate, compared with (16% for Bush and 15% for Perot). He was clear and direct; he had analyzed the problems and took a stand. When asked about his position on term limits, he admitted, ''I know they're popular but I'm against them.''

His tenor changed from angry in the first debate to sad; he too was upset by the negative campaigning. Framing himself with compassion and warmth, he denounced the negative campaign strategy saying: ''I'm just as sick as you are by having to wake up and figure out how to defend myself everyday,'' and ''I never thought I'd be involved in anything like this.''

In the second debate Clinton clarified his position, not with statistics, but with examples and solutions. He softened the edges of an otherwise stiff image by speaking of his disappointment with the campaign rhetoric. By moving to the edge of the stage, closer to the audience, he appeared to be more comfortable, more accessible.

The voting on who won the third debate was more evenly distributed: 37% Perot; 28% Clinton; 28% Bush. Clinton continued to emphasize his strengths and to campaign for ''change.'' Bush's weaknesses, the faltering economy and dirty campaigning, were not overlooked. Clinton was cordial but firm in his opposition to Perot. He mollified disagreement by saying, ''I don't have any criticism of Mr. Perot,'' and ''I think Ross is right.'' However, Clinton intended to focus on his presidential bid in this final debate. He moved from campaigning to governing—his promises and inability to promise, e.g., ''no new taxes.'' And finally, as if in the formal transition of power, Clinton honored Bush for service to his country.

The American people had the opportunity to assess the strengths and weaknesses of each candidate. More than a forum for reiterating statistics and personal attacks, the debates shed light on person, policy, and presidential fitness.

Clinton adapted to his audience and made subtle stylistic changes to fashion himself in presidential garb.

INAUGURAL ADDRESS

The presidential Inaugural Address is part genre, part form and grammar, part rhetorical artifact to be studied in isolation or in comparison with other inaugurals, and most certainly is a complex of events that transcends and often overwhelms the inaugural speech. On January 20, 1993, President-elect Clinton faced a backdrop of domestic and international tensions. Pledged to give the middle class a tax cut, to remove strictures against gays in the military, and to reduce drastically the budget deficit by 1996, his campaign vision offered high hopes that were sometimes greeted with low expectations by a Congress acclimated to gridlock and a public wary of any politician's vision.

The fourteen-minute inaugural speech capped a five day calendar of inaugural activities. Some of the activities, however, hinted at a new kind of president. The message wall, a kind of democratic graffiti where citizens left thousands of messages for the new administration, and the 1–800–BELLS–93 toll-free number citizens could call to learn about inaugural events, symbolized that this presidency would be accessible to the people.

Clinton energized the Inaugural Address with four themes: convocation/invocation, renewal, foreign and domestic issues, and people before government. Historic imagery characterized the invocation theme. Clinton invoked images "From our Revolution to the Civil War, to the Great Depression, to the civil rights movement." Clinton directly quoted Washington, Jefferson, and FDR. Stylistically, Clinton's rhetoric reflected Churchill, "forgetting those people whose toil and sweat sends us here"; King, "From this joyful mountaintop of celebration we hear a call to service in the valley"; and Kennedy, "And so, my fellow Americans, as we stand on the edge of the 21st century, let us begin anew." Even the cadence and sound of Lincoln can be heard:

We rededicate ourselves to the very idea of America, an idea born in revolution and renewed through two centuries of challenge; an idea tempered by the knowledge that, but for fate, we, the fortunate, and the unfortunate, might have been each other; an idea ennobled by the faith that our nation can summon from its myriad diversity the deepest measure of unity; an idea infused with the conviction that America's long, heroic journey must go forever upward.

The renewal theme pervaded Clinton's Inaugural Address in the specific form of forcing the spring. The metaphor drives phrases such as "a new season of American renewal has begun," and "I challenge a new generation of young Americans to a season of service." Even gridlock was tied to the metaphor with Clinton's pledge to end "the era of deadlock and drift, and a new season of renewal has begun." Clinton literally positioned himself in the depth of winter with a vision toward spring, a spring forced by an "unmistakable chorus" of voices, "Yes, you, my fellow Americans have forced the spring." The new President was ready to "do the work the season demands." What the metaphor lacked, however, was completeness—Clinton's vision failed to include the work of summer and the harvest of fall.

Almost one-third of the Inaugural Address dealt with domestic concerns and about one-eighth dealt with foreign issues. What seems unique, though, was Clinton's overt linking of foreign and domestic matters. For example, "We earn our livelihood in America today in peaceful competition with people all across the Earth. To renew America we must meet challenges abroad as well as at home. There is no longer a clear division between what is foreign and what is domestic." Other contemporary inaugural speeches, such as Bush's, Reagan's, and Carter's, separated and compartmentalized foreign from domestic concerns. Clinton's inaugural fully assimilated the concept of the Global Village.

The last theme of Clinton's Inaugural Address stressed people before government. This theme is common to inaugurals, but Clinton reflected a new conservatism for his party, a stride away from what President Bush called in his 1989 inaugural "the old solution" of government as provider. Clinton declared that "It is time to break the bad habit of expecting something for nothing from our government or from each other . . . no President, no Congress, no government can undertake this mission [of renewal] alone." As part of the orderly transfer of power, as part of a complex of celebratory and symbolic events leading to the beginning of a new presidency, Clinton's Inaugural Address functioned effectively.

CLINTON'S PRESIDENTIAL RHETORIC

Economic Speeches

The first two major addresses following Clinton's Inaugural Address comprise one rhetorical strategy. The Oval Office address to the nation, February 15, 1993, and the nationally televised speech to a joint session of Congress, February 17, 1993, dealt with the unveiling of Clinton's economic plan.

The Oval Office speech was a sincere, simple, and direct appeal to the public. Two days later, a hard-hitting speech to Congress was followed by a flurry of administration officials, including the President, who canvassed the nation speaking to different groups. The President set his agenda for economic reforms. The coordinated rhetorical strategy, inspired by the Reagan administration, was refined and extended by the Clinton White House. The Clinton administration would mount similar rhetorical campaigns for NAFTA and Health Care.

Clinton's "Address to the Nation on the Economic Program," delivered from the Oval Office on February 15, 1993, was a ten-minute agenda setter, laying out Clinton's vision in broad, sweeping strokes. The President was intimately involved with the speechwriting process. He consulted many political and economic advisers, and he worked on it until moments before it was broadcast.

In ten minutes, Clinton laid out the problem, the solution, and the benefits. The problem was: "All during this last twelve-years the Federal deficit has roared out of control. Look at this: the big tax cuts for the wealthy, the growth in government spending, and soaring health care costs all caused the Federal deficit to explode." The solution was: "We just have to face the fact that to make the changes our country needs, more Americans must contribute today so that all Americans can do better tomorrow." Then, he portrayed the benefits of his solution: "millions of long-term, good-paying jobs . . . investments in education and training; a fairer tax system . . . welfare reform . . . and a system of affordable quality health care for all Americans." Thus, the stage was set for Clinton's address to a joint session of Congress.

On February 17, 1993, Clinton delivered a speech to a joint session of Congress that is sometimes referred to as a State of the Union address. Clinton hoped to create public sympathies for his program before delivering the speech. The President's speech preparation was intense. Clinton tinkered with the manuscript until the last minute. The White House did not have time to distribute copies of the speech before it was delivered. And still, Clinton ad-libbed substantially. David Kusnet, David Dreyer, and Michael Waldman, three of Clinton's speechwriters, worked through the night on Tuesday only to have the President rewrite it on Wednesday. Many in the Clinton administration, added a phrase, a thought, a sentence, or more to the speech. The results of so much intense editing was that the speech grew from about a half hour to over an hour.

Clinton emphasized that the Washington establishment could not continue business-as-usual. "After so many years of gridlock and indecision," the President insisted, "after so many hopeful beginnings and so few promising results, the American people are going to be harsh in their judgments of all of us if we fail to seize this moment." Cautious optimism was sparked by Clinton, for he focused his presidency by seizing on the major issue that worried many Americans—the economy. In the days following this speech, following through on the President's message, other administration officials spoke to groups of Americans from coast to coast.

The Health Care Speech

Clinton's health care speech was part of an orchestrated campaign of persuasion. The Clinton administration, under the leadership of first lady, Hillary, had spent months focusing intensely on the complex issues of health care. This address, delivered to a joint session of Congress on September 22, 1993, was televised nationally and was the formal unveiling of the blueprint for reform. As the President was ready to begin the speech, he turned to Vice President Al Gore and indicated that the wrong speech was on the teleprompter. Gore answered, "That's impossible." Clinton said, "You're not reading it. Read it."

Clinton began the speech using only his manuscript; it was seven minutes before the teleprompter was in sync with the President.

Clinton's thesis was clear: "This health care system of ours is badly broken and it is time to fix it." The President argued that any reform to the health system should meet six criteria: security, simplicity, savings, choice, quality, and responsibility. Before addressing each of the criteria, Clinton discussed some of the problems with the current system and praised the bipartisan commitment to respond to the "costliest and most wasteful system on the face of the Earth. . . . Both sides, I think, understand the literal ethical imperative of doing something about the system we have now."

The following excerpts indicate the kinds of appeals Clinton made for each of his criteria:

1. *Security*—"Means that those who do not now have health care coverage will have it; and for those who have it, it will never be taken away."

2. *Simplicity*—"Under our proposal there would be one standard insurance form—not hundreds of them. We will simplify . . . the government's rules and regulations, because they are a big part of this problem."

3. *Savings*—"Our competitiveness, our whole economy, the integrity of the way the government works and, ultimately, our living standards depend upon our ability to achieve savings without harming the quality of health care."

4. *Choice*—"Americans believe they ought to be able to choose their own health care plan and keep their own doctors. . . . But today, . . . in spite of the rhetoric of choice, the fact is that that power is slipping away for more and more Americans."

5. *Quality*—"If we reformed everything else in health care, but failed to preserve and enhance the high quality of our medical care, we will have taken a step backward, not forward. Quality is something that we simply can't leave to chance."

6. *Responsibility*—"In short, responsibility should apply to anybody who abuses this system and drives up the cost for honest, hard-working citizens and undermines confidence in the honest, gifted health care providers we have."

Clinton's peroration was a summons to facilitate the miracle of Congress's passing new, sweeping health care legislation. "This is our chance," Clinton concluded, "This is our journey. And when our work is done, we will know that we have answered the call of history and met the challenge of our time." Critics thought that the address was dignified and well-received, and several lawmakers thought the speech was Clinton's best, for he blended liberalism with hard-nosed economic policies.

Following such a major address, administration officials commonly are dispatched to key audiences carrying the rhetorical banner of the President. Clinton joined the fray. The day following the speech the President was on ABC's town meeting hosted by Ted Koppel. Clinton fielded questions for over two hours, thus giving the network plenty of material for the one-hour town meeting and another hour that was used on "Nightline." The President's televised town meeting was part of the administration's national blitz of rhetorical venues.

State of the Union Address, 1994

The State of the Union Address is an annual "agenda-setting" speech, and Clinton delivered his first one on January 25, 1994. Organizationally, Clinton began by complimenting Congress on the successes of the past year, then he laid out the problems yet to be addressed and previewed the legislative initiatives that would be forthcoming from the White House. This speech was an opportunity to continue the inaugural theme of renewal, which was absent from the first so-called State of the Union, as he talked about a "journey of renewal," of "renewal and reform," "let us resolve to continue the journey of renewal," and that "America will never be complete in its renewal until everyone shares in its bounty." With this metaphor driving his hour-long speech, Clinton discussed increasing taxes on the wealthy, eliminating one hundred domestic programs, supporting a global economy in order to create more jobs for Americans, increasing job training, establishing a technological super highway, and reforming education.

Clinton's three main themes were comprehensive welfare reform, national health care reform, and crime. He advocated welfare reform that would motivate people to get off the welfare roles. He wanted to reform child support provisions and activate a program to track down dead-beat dads to make them pay for child support. Echoing a theme repeated throughout his presidential campaign, he argued that those on welfare do not want to be on welfare, and that government's job is to facilitate their return to society as productive citizens.

Clinton's comments on health care represented the third nationally televised address in which he used the bully pulpit to press for health care reform. Clinton drew a line in the political sand: "If you send me legislation that does not guarantee every American private health insurance that can never be taken away, you will force me to take this pen [Clinton brandished a pen], veto the legislation, and we'll come right back here and start all over again."

Clinton also devoted attention to the topic of crime because "The national peace is shattered by crime." He urged further gun control by pleading with the gun lobby to help in banning assault weapons. In hopes of reclaiming our communities, Clinton outlined a legislative package that he would present to Congress.

A touch of Reagan-style pathos surfaced when Clinton used anecdotes, letters, and living visual symbols. The President told the touching story of a father visiting the White House with his critically ill daughter: "Don't you people up here ever think that what you do doesn't make a difference, it does." Clinton referred to a letter from Richard Anderson, who had to declare bankruptcy because shortly after he lost his job his wife suffered a major illness. Clinton concluded that "It was to help the Richard and Judy Andersons of America, that the first lady and so many others have worked so long and so hard on the health reform issue.'' Clinton invoked a living symbol from the Reagan administration. While referring to the Brady gun control bill passed by Congress, the President acknowledged Jim Brady sitting in the gallery. Clinton also introduced a New York City police officer, Kevin Jett, who walked one of the toughest neighborhoods in the city where ''Everyday he restores some sanity and safety and a sense of values and connection to the people whose lives he protects.'' On an emotional level, such concrete, specific examples were powerful bonding agents in the rhetorical cement.

Several unique features marked this speech. Clinton humorously opened with ''I'm not sure what speech is in the teleprompter tonight.'' Not only is the humor self-directed, but any presidential reference to the existence or use of a teleprompter is rare. Clinton also interacted with his Congressional audience directly at two points in the speech. When he said that he was talking about ''another issue where the people are way ahead of the politicians,'' the audience reacted more like a British Parliament than an American Congress. Although the audience did not boo, Congress's displeasure was obvious. Then Clinton ad-libbed, ''That may not be popular with either party, but it happens to be the truth.'' Congress expressed its skepticism audibly when Clinton said, ''This April 15th, the American people will learn the truth about taxes,'' to which the President ad-libbed a reminder that the tax increase already passed was limited to the wealthy.

FOREIGN POLICY SPEECHES

Not all presidential addresses are ceremonial or agenda-setting. Some articulate an administration's foreign policy. The major foreign policy addresses in Clinton's first year in office included the Address to the Nation on the Strike on Iraqi Intelligence Headquarters, June 26, 1993, and the speech on Somalia, October 7, 1993. The Somalia and Iraqi speeches were, for all intents and purposes, one-shot messages that were designed to explain and justify foreign policy decisions.

Address on the Strike on Iraqi Intelligence Headquarters

In response to a plot to assassinate former President Bush, the United States launched a missile attack against Iraq. Two hours later, President Clinton spoke to the nation to inform the public of the plot to kill the former U.S. President, to explain the steps taken to respond, and to justify the level of response.

Clinton began this speech by laying the blame squarely on Iraq: ''My fellow Americans, this evening I want to speak with you about an attack by the Government of Iraq against the United States and the actions just taken to respond.'' The President explained the long investigative process that began in April when the Kuwaiti government first exposed the plot to assassinate Bush. After an investigation was concluded by the Attorney General and the CIA Director, Clinton decided that there was "compelling evidence that there was in fact a plot to assassinate former President Bush."

The plot itself was probably enough to justify a limited U.S. military response. The Commander-in-Chief, however, wanted the American people to despise the enemy. Saddam Hussein's government, Clinton argued, "ruled by atrocity, slaughtered its own people, invaded two neighbors, attacked others and engaged in chemical and environmental warfare." He referred to Hussein as a tyrant who was "particularly loathsome and cowardly." All of that was true enough before the plot against Bush, but the new plot against Bush added an emotive charge to the U.S. response. Clinton further justified the missile attack by arguing that "The Iraqi attack against President Bush was an attack against our country and against all Americans." Clinton's final reason rested on an historical justification: "From the first days of our Revolution, America's security has depended on the clarity of this message: Don't tread on us." Therefore, Clinton concluded, "a firm and commensurate response was essential."

Clinton explained the nature of the cruise missile attack and how it was directed at crippling Iraq's ability to conduct terrorism. The President informed the nation that he had consulted with Congressional leadership and allies, and he announced his intention to present Iraq's crime before the U.N. Security Council.

"Somalia"

Clinton inherited the U.S. troop commitment to Somalia from George Bush. Troops were being withdrawn over time and much of the humanitarian assistance provided seemed to be having some positive effects. The threat of starvation was largely over, and U.S. troops working under the aegis of a United Nations peacekeeping force were concerned primarily with rebuilding the country and restoring political stability. On Sunday, October 3, 1993, twelve American soldiers were killed, seventy-five others wounded and one captured by Somalian gunmen. Clinton was faced with the need to respond quickly and appropriately.

On October 7, 1993, in a nationally televised address, Clinton reminded Americans that "This past weekend we all reacted with anger and horror as an armed Somali gang desecrated the bodies of our American soldiers and displayed a captured American pilot." His speech was an expression of national outrage and national sympathy for the families of the soldiers killed. But it was also a justification for beefing up our military presence in Somalia, while urging of a diplomatic solution to the problems plaguing that country.

First, Clinton justified the United States' commitment to Somalia: "Somalia children and their families lay dying by the tens of thousands—dying the slow, agonizing death of starvation. . . . In our nation's best tradition, we took action with bipartisan support." Clinton then argued that a continued U.S. presence was essential: "If we were to leave Somalia tomorrow, other nations would leave, too. Chaos would resume." The President discussed the continued commitment to withdraw our troops, "But we must also leave on our terms. We must do it right." To do it right, the President dispatched 1,700 additional troops to Somalia and stationed 3,600 combat Marines offshore. These forces would have four goals: "protect our troops and our bases, . . . keep open and secure the roads, the port and the lines of communication, . . . to keep the pressure on those who cut off relief supplies and attacked our people, . . . [and] through their pressure and their presence, our troops will help to make it possible for the Somali people . . . to reach agreements among themselves so that they can solve their problems and survive when we leave."

After Clinton, in stern sincerity, laid out the military response in Somalia, he concluded his remarks with an expression of "thanks and my gratitude and my profound sympathy to the families of the young Americans who were killed in Somalia." The Somalia and Iraq speeches were responses to short-term foreign policy threats. Neither incident festered and became worse. They represented Clinton's discreet, definable responses to specific acts of international terrorism.

CONCLUSION

Clinton is an accomplished speaker. Arguably, he fulfills the title of the great communicator more skillfully than the President for whom this phrase was coined. From televised talk shows to "Imus in the Morning" radio, from town halls to satellite hook-ups, from impromptu Q & A sessions with the press to a teleprompter that had the wrong speech on it for seven minutes, Clinton has demonstrated a command of the issues and an aplomb in speaking seldom seen in the history of the presidency. He faces critical issues of deficit reduction, health care, crime, welfare, and an often troubled international scene. A look at his first two years reveals a dynamic communicator struggling to mobilize a lethargic Congress and a skeptical public to "a new season of American renewal."

RHETORICAL RESOURCES

Weekly Compilation of Presidential Documents. (*WCPD*). WCPD is available in many libraries and is available directly from the Superintendent of Documents, Washington, DC.

Vital Speeches of the Day (*VS*).

Dreams of Power and the Power of Dreams: The Inaugural Addresses of the Governors of Arkansas. (*ARK*). Edited by Marvin E. Boer. Fayetteville, AR: University of Arkansas Press, 1988.

E-Mail Options

The Clinton presidency is the first administration to utilize e-mail. A variety of e-mail sources exist including, but not limited to, the White House, the National Technical Information Service (FedWorld), MIT, America On-Line, CompuServe, and MCI-Mail.

Now that the information superhighway has an on-ramp into the President's office, the problem quickly becomes one of quantity. For example, if one asks for an index via e-mail from the White House, the files that are sent back would choke most computers and consume hours of reading. Here are some e-mail addresses (confirmed accurate as of March 1994):

President@WhiteHouse.Gov (for sending messages to the President)

Publications@WhiteHouse.Gov (for requesting information from the White House)

FedWorld BBS—703-321-8020 (no parity, 8 bit, 1 stop)

Clinton—Info@Campaign92.Org (the MIT information service)

Chronology of Significant Presidential Persuasions

(Unless noted otherwise, all speeches were delivered from the White House in Washington, D.C.)

Inaugural Address, January 20, 1993. *WCPD*, 1993: 75–77.

Address to the Nation on the Economic Program, February 15, 1993. *WCPD*, 1993: 207–9.

Address Before a Joint Session of Congress on Administration Goals, February 17, 1993. *WCPD*, 1993: 215–24.

Address to the Nation on the Strike on Iraqi Intelligence Headquarters, June 26, 1993. *WCPD*, 1993: 1180–82.

"Health Care Reform," September 22, 1993. *WCPD*, 1993: 1836–46; *VS*, October 15, 1993: 2–8.

"Somalia," October 7, 1993. *WCPD*, 1993: 2022–25; *VS*, November 1, 1993: 34–36.

State of the Union Address, January 25, 1994. *VS*, February 15, 1994: 258–63.

Index

Each president has a subject listing, followed by a speech listing. Page numbers in bold indicate main entries.

Taft, William Howard, xiv, 96
Taney, Chief Justice Roger, 70, 73
Techne, ix
Teely, Pete, 346
Teleprompter, xi, 372
Televised debates, xiii. *See also under
names of specific presidents*
Thrasymachus of Chalcedonia, xv
Thurmond, Strom, 184
Tillman, "Pitchfork" Ben, 102
Tricolons, 85
Trivium, ix
Truman, Harry S., **168–89;** *actio*, 170;
anaphora, 185, 186; Attic orator, xi;
"cracked record" metaphor, 183; and
delivery, 168–69; *dispositio*, 169–70;
elocutio, 169, 185; epistrophe, 174;
halo effect, 171; Hoover Commission,
136; and Johnson, Lyndon Baines,
229; Korean war, 172–78; Library,
178, 187; and MacArthur, 174, 178–
80; Manichaeanism, 172, 176; National
Security Council, 172; NSC-48, 172,
175; NSC-68, 172, 175; "police-
action" metaphor, 173–74; pre-
presidential positions, 168; rhetorical
theory of, 169–79; speechwriters, 171,
174, 179, 184; *status quo ante bellum*,
173, 177; supernation rhetoric, 171,
174; "whistle-stop" tour, 182
Truman, Harry S., speeches of: acceptance address, 169, 180–82; address on
Korea, 175–76; campaign (1948), 180–
84; "Doctor Dewey and the Republican Record," 182–83; Far Eastern
Policy speech, 169–70, responses to,
178, 179; Inaugural Address, xii, 170,
184–86; Korea I, 173; Korea II, 173;
On Korea, 174; Truman Doctrine, 169,
170–72; Valedictory, 186–87; War Memorial Opera House, 176–77
Trumbull, John, 4
Tully, Grace, 163

U-2 incident, 202–3

Valenti, Jack, 232
Vandenberg, Arthur H., 276

Vietnam War. *See* Johnson, Lyndon Baines; Nixon, Richard Milhous
Vir bonus dicendi peritus, xiv

Wabash College, ix
Wallace, Henry, 168
Ward, John, 21
War messages. *See under names of specific presidents*
War rhetoric, xii, xiii
Washington, Booker T., 102
Washington, George, **3–17;** delivery of
First Inaugural, 6; "entangling alliances," 14; Farewell Address compared to Declaration of Independence
and Gettysburg Address, 11; meets
with Claypoole, 12; presidential rheto-
ric, 15; religious freedom, 8
Washington, George, speeches of: annual
messages, 8–11; Farewell Address, 11–
15; First Inaugural Address, 4–6; Hebrew Congregation, 7–8; pre-
presidential addresses, 3–4; regional
tours, 6–8; Second Inaugural Address,
6; speechwriters for Farewell Address,
12
Watergate 263–66
Weaver, Richard, 85
Webster, Daniel, xiv, 20, 67
Westmoreland, General William, 244
Whiskey Rebellion, 9
"Whistle-stop speeches," 141
Willkie, Wendell, 151
Wilson, Woodrow, **111–33;** antithesis,
117; armistice, 127; *Congressional
Government*, 112; education, 111; election of, 192, 113; League of Nations,
128–31; and Lodge, 128; "New
Freedom," 116; neutrality posture,
121–22; Payne-Aldrich Tariff, 118;
people of Germany v. German government, 125; peroration, 130; pre-
presidential positions, 112–13;
progressive rhetoric, 115–16; rhetorical
presidency, 115, 130; rhetorical question, 131; rhetorical training, 113–14;
Western tour, 128–29; writes own
speeches, 114; Zimmerman note, 123

About the Editor and Contributors

JAMES R. ANDREWS is Professor of Speech Communication at Indiana University. He has received the Winans-Wichelns Award and twice won the American Forensic Association's award for outstanding research. He authored or co-authored seven books, including *The Practice of Rhetorical Criticism*, *American Voices*, and *Contemporary American Voices*.

HAL W. BOCHIN is Professor of Speech Communication at California State University, Fresno. He co-authored *Hiram Johnson: A Bio-Bibliography* (Greenwood, 1988) and authored *Richard Nixon: Rhetorical Strategist* (Greenwood, 1990). He contributed essays to *American Orators Before 1900* (Greenwood, 1987) and *The Inaugural Addresses of Twentieth-Century American Presidents* (Praeger, 1993).

CARL R. BURGCHARDT is Associate Professor of Speech Communication at Colorado State University at Fort Collins. He wrote *Robert M. La Follette, Sr.: The Voice of Conscience* (Greenwood, 1992), and contributed essays to *Oratorical Encounters* (Greenwood, 1988) and *American Orators of the Twentieth Century* (Greenwood, 1987).

DANIEL ROSS CHANDLER is a post-doctoral research scholar at the Divinity School of the University of Chicago. He wrote *The Rev. Dr. Preston Bradley*, *The Rhetorical Tradition*, and *The History of Rhetoric*, and contributed essays to *American Orators Before 1900* (Greenwood, 1987), *American Orators of the Twentieth Century* (Greenwood, 1987), and *The Inaugural Addresses of Twentieth-Century American Presidents* (Praeger, 1993).

JEAN M. DeWITT is Associate Professor of Speech Communication at the University of Houston, Downtown. She has published in the *Quarterly Journal of Speech, Communication Education, Journal of Communication, Extasis,* and the *Journal of the National Forensic Association.* She was a Fulbright Lecturer in Mauritius.

LOIS J. EINHORN is Associate Professor of Rhetoric at Binghamton University. She is the co-author of *Effective Employment Interviewing,* author of *Abraham Lincoln the Orator: Penetrating the Lincoln Legend* (Greenwood, 1992), which won the Everett Lee Hunt Award, and is preparing *Helen Keller the Speaker: Visions of a Better Tomorrow.* She has received the Donald H. Ecroyd Award and Karl R. Wallace Memorial Award.

JAMES M. FARRELL is Assistant Professor of Communication at the University of New Hampshire. His essays have appeared in *New England Quarterly, Quarterly Journal of Speech, Rhetorica,* and *Classical Journal.* He has received the Karl R. Wallace Memorial Award.

ROBERT V. FRIEDENBERG is Professor of Communication at Miami (Ohio) University. The author of over seventy publications on political and religious rhetoric, he wrote *Theodore Roosevelt and the Rhetoric of Militant Decency* (Greenwood, 1991), as well as other articles, chapters, and papers on Roosevelt.

DAN F. HAHN is Chair and Professor of Communication at Florida Atlantic University. He has published over seventy articles in academic journals and co-authored two books: *Presidential Communication: Description and Analysis* (Praeger, 1986) and *Listening for a President: A Citizen's Campaign Methodology* (Praeger, 1990).

J. MICHAEL HOGAN is Associate Professor of Speech Communication and American studies at Indiana University. He has published numerous chapters and articles in speech and related disciplines. He is the author of *The Nuclear Freeze Campaign,* and his book, *The Panama Canal in American Politics,* won the Winans-Wichelns Award and the Speech Communication Associations Golden Anniversary Prize Book Award.

THOMAS M. LESSL is Associate Professor of Speech Communication at the University of Georgia. He has published articles in the *Quarterly Journal of Speech* and *Communication Theory,* and contributed to *American Orators Before 1900* (Greenwood, 1988).

STEPHEN E. LUCAS is Professor of Communication Arts at the University of Wisconsin, Madison. His *Portents of Rebellion: Rhetoric and Revolution in Philadelphia, 1765–1776* received the Speech Communication Association Golden Anniversary Award.

MARTIN J. MEDHURST is Professor of Speech Communication and Coordinator of the Program in Presidential Rhetoric at Texas A&M University. He is the author or editor of five books, including *Cold War Rhetoric: Strategy, Metaphor, and Ideology* (Greenwood, 1990) and *Dwight D. Eisenhower: Strategic Communicator* (Greenwood, 1993).

SEAN PATRICK O'ROURKE is Assistant Professor of Rhetoric at Vanderbilt University. He has published articles in *Southern Communication Journal* and *Communication Reports*.

KURT RITTER is Professor of Speech Communication at Texas A&M University. He is the co-author of *The American Idealogy: Reflections of the Revolution in American Rhetoric* and *Ronald Reagan: The Great Communicator* (Greenwood, 1992). He is presently preparing *The Making of the Great Communicator: Ronald Reagan, Speechwriting, and the Mass Media*.

HALFORD RYAN is Professor of English and Public Speaking at Washington and Lee University. He is the editor of three books, co-editor of two books, and author of six books, two of which are *Franklin D. Roosevelt's Rhetorical Presidency* (Greenwood, 1988) and *Harry S. Truman: Presidential Rhetoric* (Greenwood, 1993).

VITO N. SILVESTRI is Professor of Communication Studies at Emerson College. He has published essays on presidential rhetoric and is the author of *Interpersonal Communication: Principles and Applications*.

CRAIG ALLEN SMITH is Professor of Communication Studies at the University of North Carolina at Greensboro. He is the author, co-author, or editor of four books including *The White House Speaks: Presidential Leadership as Persuasion* (Praeger, 1994), *The President and the Public*, and *Persuasion and Social Movements*.

CRAIG R. SMITH is Professor and Chair of Speech Communication at California State University, Long Beach, where he also serves as director of the Center for First Amendment Studies. He is the author of *To Form a More Perfect Union, All Speech Is Created Equal, Partisan Politics and Freedom of Expression, Defender of the Union: An Oratorical Biography of Daniel Webster* (Greenwood, 1988), and *Orientations to Speech Criticism*.

STEPHEN C. WOOD is Associate Professor and Chair of Communication Studies at the University of Rhode Island. The editor of two books, he also contributed essays to *Presidential Studies Quarterly, Journal of the National Forensic Association, The Cross Examination Debate Association Yearbook*, and *Extasis*.

SUSAN ZAESKE is a doctoral student in the Department of Communication at the University of Wisconsin, Madison. She is writing her dissertation on the rhetoric of the petition campaign by American women against slavery during the 1830s and 1840s.

KENNETH S. ZAGACKI is Associate Professor of Communication at Louisiana State University. He has written articles on presidential rhetoric, foreign policy argument, and the philosophy of rhetoric, and contributed to *Postmodern Political Communication* (Praeger, 1992).

ISBN 0-313-29059-8

9 780313 290596

HARDCOVER BAR CODE